D0938005

Object-Oriented Software Development Using Java™

SECOND EDITION

Object-Oriented Software Development Using Java™

PRINCIPLES,

PATTERNS, AND

FRAMEWORKS

Xiaoping Jia
DePaul University

Addison
Wesley

Boston San Francisco New York
London Toronto Sydney Tokyo Singapore Madrid
Mexico City Munich Paris Cape Town Hong Kong Montreal

Senior Acquisitions Editor	Maite Suarez-Rivas
Project Editor	Katherine Harutunian
Senior Production Supervisor	Juliet Silveri
Production Services	P. M. Gordon Associates, Inc.
Composition and Text Illustration	Windfall Software, using ZzTEX
Cover Design Supervisor	Gina Hagen Kolenda
Cover Designer	Jean Wilcox
Executive Marketing Manager	Michael Hirsch
Print Buyer	Caroline Fell

Cover image © 2002 by PhotoDisc.

Access the latest information about Addison-Wesley titles from our World Wide Web site: www.aw.com/cs

Many of the designations used by manufacturers and sellers to distinguish their products are claimed as trademarks. Where those designations appear in this book, and Addison-Wesley was aware of a trademark claim, the designations have been printed in initial caps or all caps.

The programs and applications presented in this book have been included for their instructional value. They have been tested with care, but are not guaranteed for any particular purpose. The publisher does not offer any warranties or representations, nor does it accept any liabilities with respect to the programs or applications.

Credits: Figure 1.2: Kruchten, *Rational Unified Process* 2nd ed., Fig. 2.2 (p. 23), © 2000 Addison Wesley Longman Inc. Reprinted by permission of Pearson Education, Inc. Figure 3.1: Riggs et al, *Programming Wireless Devices w/Java 2 Platform, Micro Edition,* Fig. 2.1 (p. 8), © 2001 Sun Microsystems Inc. Reprinted by permission of Pearson Education, Inc.

Library of Congress Cataloging-in-Publication Data

Jia, Xiaoping.
    Object-oriented software development using Java : principles, patterns, and frameworks / Xiaoping Jia—2nd ed.
      p. cm.
    Includes bibliographical references and index.
    ISBN 0-201-73733-7
    1. Object-oriented programming (Computer science)   2. Computer software—Development.   3. Java (Computer program language)   I. Title.
QA76.64 J53 2003
005.13′3—dc21
2002032639

  2 3 4 5 6 7 8 9 10—HT—05 04 03

To Ai-Ling and Robin

CONTENTS

Preface   xv

CHAPTER 1   Object-Oriented Software Development   1

1.1   The Challenges of Software Development   2
1.2   An Engineering Perspective   4
    1.2.1   Software Development Activities   4
    1.2.2   Software Development Processes   5
    1.2.3   Desirable Qualities of Software Systems   6
    1.2.4   Is Software Development an Engineering Process?   8
1.3   Object Orientation   9
    1.3.1   Modeling the Real World   9
    1.3.2   Evolution of Programming Models   10
    1.3.3   A Brief History   10
1.4   Iterative Development Processes   11
    1.4.1   Object-Oriented Development Activities   12
    1.4.2   Rational Unified Process   13
    1.4.3   Extreme Programming   15
    Chapter Summary   16
    Further Readings   17
    Exercises   18

CHAPTER 2   Object-Oriented Modeling Using UML   19

2.1   Principles and Concepts   19
    2.1.1   Objects and Classes   20
    2.1.2   Principles   26
2.2   Modeling Relationships and Structures   29
    2.2.1   Inheritance   29
    2.2.2   Association   32
    2.2.3   Aggregation and Composition   34
    2.2.4   Dependency   35
2.3   Modeling Dynamic Behavior   36

2.3.1   Sequence Diagram   36
2.3.2   State Diagram   37
2.4   Modeling Requirements with Use Cases   41
2.4.1   Terms and Concepts   41
2.4.2   Use Case Diagrams   42
2.5   Case Study: An E-Bookstore   44
2.5.1   Conceptualization   44
2.5.2   Use Cases   44
2.5.3   Object Models   46
Chapter Summary   51
Further Readings   52
Exercises   52

CHAPTER 3   Introduction to Java   55
3.1   An Overview of the Java 2 Platform   56
3.2   The Java Run-Time Architecture   59
3.2.1   Program Execution Models   60
3.2.2   Java Virtual Machine   61
3.3   Getting Started with Java   65
3.3.1   A Simple Java Application   65
3.3.2   A Java Applet   67
Common Problems and Solutions   72
Chapter Summary   73
Further Readings   73
Exercises   74

CHAPTER 4   Elements of Java   75
4.1   Lexical Elements   76
4.1.1   Character Set   76
4.1.2   Identifiers   77
4.1.3   Primitive Types and Literals   77
4.1.4   Operators and Expressions   80
4.2   Variables and Types   87
4.2.1   Variable Declarations   88
4.2.2   Type Compatibility and Conversion   88
4.2.3   Reference Types   89
4.2.4   Arrays   91
4.3   Statements   93
4.3.1   Expression Statements   94
4.3.2   Statement Blocks   94
4.3.3   Local Variable Declarations   95
4.3.4   The return Statement   95
4.3.5   Selection Statements   96

4.3.6 Loop Statements 96
4.3.7 The **break** and **continue** Statements 99
4.4 Class Declarations 101
4.4.1 Syntax of Class Declarations 101
4.4.2 Creating and Initializing Objects 104
4.4.3 Accessing Fields and Methods 106
4.4.4 Method Invocation and Parameter Passing 107
4.4.5 Class (Static) Fields and Methods 110
4.4.6 Object Reference **this** 114
4.4.7 Interfaces and Abstract Classes 117
4.4.8 Strings 118
4.4.9 Wrapper Classes 128
4.5 Packages 134
4.5.1 Using Packages 135
4.5.2 Partitioning the Name Space 136
4.5.3 Packages and the Directory Structure 136
4.5.4 Organization of the Java Class Library 138
4.6 Exceptions 139
4.6.1 Sources of Exceptions 140
4.6.2 Hierarchy of Exceptions 140
4.6.3 Throwing Exceptions 143
4.6.4 Catching and Handling Exceptions 144
4.7 A Simple Animation Applet 148
Chapter Summary 155
Exercises 156
Project 157

CHAPTER 5   Classes and Inheritance   159
5.1 Overloading Methods and Constructors 159
5.2 Extending Classes 163
5.2.1 Constructors of Extended Classes 164
5.2.2 Subtypes and Polymorphism 165
5.2.3 Overriding Methods 171
5.3 Extending and Implementing Interfaces 176
5.3.1 Subtypes Revisited 177
5.3.2 Single Versus Multiple Inheritance 179
5.3.3 Name Collisions among Interfaces 183
5.3.4 Marker Interfaces 184
5.4 Hiding Fields and Class Methods 184
5.5 Applications—Animation Applets 186
5.5.1 Parameters of Applets 186
5.5.2 An Idiom for Animation Applets 188
5.5.3 Double-Buffered Animation 193
5.5.4 Reading Files in Applets 200

Common Problems and Solutions   202
Chapter Summary   202
Exercises   204
Projects   204

CHAPTER 6 **From Building Blocks to Projects**   **207**

6.1 Design and Implementation of Classes   207
    6.1.1   Public and Helper Classes   207
    6.1.2   Class Members   209
    6.1.3   Design Guidelines   209
    6.1.4   Documenting the Source Code   214
6.2 Contracts and Invariants   216
    6.2.1   Contracts of Methods   216
    6.2.2   Invaraints of Classes   222
    6.2.3   Assertions   224
    6.2.4   Design by Contract   226
6.3 The Canonical Form of Classes   227
    6.3.1   No-Argument Constructor   228
    6.3.2   Object Equality   228
    6.3.3   Hash Code of Objects   230
    6.3.4   Cloning Objects   231
    6.3.5   String Representation of Objects   234
    6.3.6   Serialization   234
6.4 Unit Testing   235
    6.4.1   Simple Unit Testing   235
    6.4.2   JUnit—A Unit-Testing Tool   239
    6.4.3   Testing Coverage Criteria   241
6.5 Project Build   243
    6.5.1   Ant—A Build Tool   243
    Chapter Summary   246
    Further Readings   247
    Exercises   247

CHAPTER 7 **Design by Abstraction**   **249**

7.1 Design Patterns   249
    7.1.1   Design Pattern: Singleton   251
7.2 Designing Generic Components   252
    7.2.1   Refactoring   252
    7.2.2   Design Pattern: Template Method   266
    7.2.3   Generalizing   271
    7.2.4   Design Pattern: Strategy   275
7.3 Abstract Coupling   276
    7.3.1   Enumerating Elements   278

       7.3.2   Design Pattern: Iterator   283

7.4   Design Case Study—Animation of Sorting Algorithms   284
       7.4.1   The Initial Implementation   285
       7.4.2   Separating Algorithms   290
       7.4.3   Design Pattern: Factory   296
       7.4.4   Separating Display Strategies   296
       Chapter Summary   302
       Further Readings   304
       Exercises   304
       Project   304

CHAPTER 8   Object-Oriented Application Frameworks   305
8.1   Application Frameworks   305
       8.1.1   Characteristics   306
       8.1.2   Design Requirements   307
       8.1.3   Specific Frameworks Considered   308
8.2   The Collections Framework   308
       8.2.1   Abstract Collections   309
       8.2.2   Interfaces of Collections   310
       8.2.3   Implementations of Collections   315
       8.2.4   Iterators of Collections   319
       8.2.5   Ordering and Sorting   324
8.3   The Graphical User Interface Framework—AWT and Swing   333
       8.3.1   The GUI Components   333
       8.3.2   Design Pattern: Composite   336
       8.3.3   Layout Managers   338
       8.3.4   Handling Events   348
       8.3.5   Frames and Dialogs   359
8.4   The Input/Output Framework   366
       8.4.1   Byte Streams   367
       8.4.2   Design Pattern: Decorator   380
       8.4.3   Character Streams   382
       8.4.4   Random Access Files   389
       Chapter Summary   392
       Further Reading   394
       Exercises   394
       Projects   395

CHAPTER 9   Design Case Study: A Drawing Pad   397
9.1   Planning   397
9.2   Iteration 1: A Simple Scribble Pad   398
       9.2.1   The Scribbling Canvas and Its Listener   399
       9.2.2   The Application   402

9.3 Iteration 2: Menus, Options, and Files   403
    9.3.1 Strokes   403
    9.3.2 The Scribble Canvas   405
    9.3.3 The Canvas Listener   408
    9.3.4 The Application   409
    9.3.5 Choosing Colors   416
9.4 Iteration 3: Refactoring   421
    9.4.1 The Shapes   421
    9.4.2 The Tools   424
    9.4.3 Extending Components   428
9.5 Iteration 4: Adding Shapes and Tools   432
    9.5.1 The Shapes   433
    9.5.2 The Toolkit   436
    9.5.3 Design Pattern: State   438
    9.5.4 A Concrete Tool—TwoEndsTool   439
    9.5.5 Extending Components   442
    9.5.6 Design Pattern: Factory Method   447
9.6 Iteration 5: More Drawing Tools   448
    9.6.1 Filled Shapes   448
    9.6.2 Drawing Filled Shapes   449
    9.6.3 The Application   452
9.7 Iteration 6: The Text Tool   453
    9.7.1 The Text Shape   454
    9.7.2 The Keyboard Input Tool   455
    9.7.3 The Font Option Menu   459
    Chapter Summary   462
    Further Readings   462
    Project   463

CHAPTER 10 More Design Patterns   **465**
10.1 Type-Safe Enumeration Types   465
    10.1.1 A Simple Maze Game   465
    10.1.2 Enumeration Types   466
    10.1.3 Unordered Type-Safe Enumeration Idiom   468
    10.1.4 Ordered Type-Safe Enumeration Idiom   469
10.2 Creational Design Patterns   470
    10.2.1 A Simple Design of the Maze Game   470
    10.2.2 Design Pattern: Abstract Factory   484
    10.2.3 Design Pattern: Factory Method   491
    10.2.4 Design Pattern: Prototype   495
    10.2.5 Design Pattern: Builder   502
10.3 Behavioral Patterns   507
    10.3.1 Design Pattern: Command   507

10.3.2 Supporting Undo   509
10.4 Structural Patterns   513
10.4.1 Design Pattern: Adapter   513
10.4.2 Design Pattern: Composite   531
Chapter Summary   544
Further Readings   545

CHAPTER 11   Concurrent Programming   547

11.1 Threads   547
11.1.1 Creation of Threads   548
11.1.2 Controlling Threads   553
11.2 Thread Safety and Liveness   556
11.2.1 Synchronization   557
11.2.2 Cooperation Among Threads   564
11.2.3 Liveness Failures   569
11.3 Design Case Study—Tic-Tac-Toe Game   571
11.3.1 The Game Board   572
11.3.2 The Game   577
11.3.3 The Players   579
11.3.4 Idiom: Taking Turns   582
Chapter Summary   583
Further Reading   584
Exercises   584
Projects   585

CHAPTER 12   Distributed Computing   587

12.1 Socket-Based Communication   588
12.1.1 Server and Client Sockets   588
12.1.2 Servers and Clients Using Sockets   590
12.1.3 Design Case Study—Stock Quotes I   600
12.2 Remote Method Invocation   614
12.2.1 The Architecture   614
12.2.2 Using RMI   616
12.2.3 Design Case Study—Stock Quotes II   620
12.3 Java Database Connectivity   628
12.4 Common Object Request Broker Architecture   640
Chapter Summary   641
Further Readings   642
Exercises   642
Projects   643

APPENDIX A Summary of the APPLET Tag   **645**

APPENDIX B Summary of Documentation Tags   **647**

APPENDIX C Summary of Java Naming Conventions   **649**

Glossary   653

References   663

Index   667

PREFACE

Object-oriented software development has been evolving for nearly 20 years and has matured significantly in recent years. Advances in the following areas have played crucial roles in the maturing of this technology:

- The convergence of object-oriented modeling techniques and notations resulted in the *Unified Modeling Language* (UML) as the de facto standard.
- The development of object-oriented frameworks and the widespread use of design patterns started with the milestone publication of the *Design Patterns* catalog by Gamma et al.
- The adoption of the object-oriented development paradigm by the software industry owes much to the emergence and popularity of *Java*.

Object-oriented technology in general—and Java in particular—enjoy unprecedented popularity today. However, the rapid pace of development presents educational challenges to computer science and software engineering students and software development professionals alike. This book is intended to provide reasonably broad and coherent coverage of object-oriented technology, including object-oriented modeling using UML, object-oriented design using design patterns, and object-oriented programming using Java. This book may be used for an introductory level graduate course or an advanced level undergraduate course in computer science and software engineering, as well as in professional development courses. It is not intended for an introductory course on programming in Java; students should have some previous experience in programming, preferably in C or C++.

In the object-oriented paradigm, programming and design are two distinct tasks; however, they are more tightly intertwined than in the conventional programming paradigm. Learning object-oriented software development using Java involves more than just learning Java's syntax and libraries. Object-oriented development is a dramatic departure from conventional programming, and to master it requires a new way of thinking. In this book I attempt to instill the object-oriented way of thinking in those who use it through the use of design patterns, exploration of the design of the Java class libraries, and illustration of iterative software development. I am both an educator and a practitioner in software engineering and object-oriented development. My intent is to provide a balanced view of object-oriented software development from different perspectives—academia and industry, theory and practice.

Complete coverage of the Java language and the Java class library is beyond the scope of this book. Therefore, my focus is on

- the most important and commonly used features of the language and the class libraries.
- the use of the Java class libraries to illustrate the applications of object-oriented design principles and design patterns.

This book can be adapted to fit the needs of courses on object-oriented software development with various objectives and for students with varied backgrounds.

- Chapter 1 provides a general overview of the challenges and solutions of object-oriented software development.
- Chapter 2 is an introduction to the object-oriented paradigm and the Unified Modeling Language (UML). For students who are familiar with UML, this chapter serves as a review. For students who are not familiar with UML, this chapter serves as a primer that covers the most important materials that are useful in the remainder of the book.
- Chapters 3–5 are intended for students who are not familiar with Java but have programming experience in a different programming language, such as C or C++. For students who are familiar with Java, these chapters serve as a review.
- Chapters 6 and 7 address some of the key issues in object-oriented programming and design. Several of the most commonly used design patterns are introduced in Chapter 7.
- Chapter 8 discusses three important frameworks in Java—collections, graphical user interfaces, and input/output—from the perspectives of using the frameworks as well as designing the framework using design patterns.
- Chapter 9 gives a complete case study illustrating an iterative development process, which involves using various design patterns and refactoring.
- Chapter 10 provides additional coverage on commonly used design patterns with concrete examples implemented in Java. This chapter is intended for courses focusing on object-oriented design and design patterns.
- Chapters 11 and 12 discuss concurrent and distributed computing in Java.

Throughout the book, Java applets are used in various examples to illustrate object-oriented programming and design concepts. With the recent developments in Java technology, the significance and usefulness of Java applets in practice has been reduced. However, I feel that Java applets still serve as a useful pedagogical tool to teach and learn object-oriented programming and design. Therefore, most of the examples using Java applets are retained in the second edition.

CHANGES TO THIS EDITION

The main changes to this edition include:

- Discussion of iterative software development processes in Section 1.4, including Rational Unified Process (RUP) and Extreme Programming (XP).
- Expanded coverage of Unified Modeling Language and object-oriented modeling in Chapter 2, including use case modeling and use case diagrams.
- Discussion of assertions, contracts, and invariants of classes in Section 6.2.
- Coverage of unit testing and project build in Sections 6.4 and 6.5.
- Expanded coverage of design patterns in Chapter 10.
- Revised and expanded design case study in Chapter 9 illustrating iterative development and refactoring.

NOTATIONS AND CONVENTIONS

The following fonts are used in presenting program code:

1. Code fragments that can be copied verbatim are set in `Monospace`. Code fragments in **`Boldface Monospace`** font are important or of particular interest.
2. Code fragments in upright Roman font are pseudocode, which are informal descriptions of program logic.
3. Entities in angle brackets, such as

   ⟨method `doSomething()` on page 108⟩

   represent placeholders. Code fragments that are defined elsewhere should be inserted here. The page numbers refer to the pages on which the code fragments to be inserted are defined.
4. Italicized names, such as *var*, may be replaced by any other specific and distinct names.

ONLINE SUPPLEMENTS

All programs in this book were developed using The Java 2 Software Development Kit (J2SDK) 1.4.[1] The J2SDK and the complete API documentation are available for downloading at

    http://java.sun.com/

---

1. Most of the programs only require JDK 1.1 or later.

The source code for all the examples in this book can be accessed by visiting www.aw.com/cssupport. Answers to the exercises are available online for qualified instructors. Please contact your Addison-Wesley representative for information.

ACKNOWLEDGMENTS

Writing this book has been a long journey. The rapid evolution of Java has made the journey both challenging and exciting. Throughout this journey, I was fortunate to have had the help and contributions of many people. I am deeply indebted to them. I'd like to thank my editor at Addison-Wesley, Maite Suarez-Rivas. This book would not have been possible without her continued encouragement, support, and guidance.

Thanks are extended to the staff at Addison-Wesley: Katherine Harutunian (Project Editor), Juliet Silveri (Senior Production Supervisor), Jean Wilcox (Cover Designer), Gina Hagen Kolenda (Cover Design Supervisor), Michael Hirsch (Executive Marketing Manager), and Lesly Hershman (Marketing Assistant). They have made this long journey a pleasant one. I'd also like to thank Peter Reinhart (copyeditor) for his thorough editing job. I appreciate the efforts of the reviewers: Charles Crowley (University of New Mexico), Anhtuan Q. Dinh (Mitre Corporation and George Mason University), Shyamal Mitra (University of Texas at Austin), Gleb Naumovich (Polytechnic University, Brooklyn), Juergen Rilling (Concordia University), Ken Slonneger (University of Iowa), Joe Wong (Worcester Polytechnic Institute), A. Yanushka (Christian Brothers University), and Huiming Yu (North Carolina A&T State University). Their comments and suggestions have greatly improved this book. Furthermore, I'd like to thank two of my wonderful colleagues at the School of CTI, James Riely and Chris Jones, who experimented with various draft versions of the second edition of the book in their classes. Their suggestions and feedback were invaluable. Also thanks go to Hongming Liu and Lizhang Qin for their many contributions in developing the supporting materials for the book.

I'd like to thank the School of Computer Science, Telecommunication, and Information Systems, DePaul University, for supporting me in bringing Java technology to the classroom in its early days. And to all my students in SE 450 during the past several years: Your enthusiasm for Java and my lectures convinced me to embark on this journey. Your feedback on my lectures and early drafts of the book were enormously helpful. I always considered you as my companions on this journey, and I truly enjoyed your company.

REQUEST FOR COMMENTS

I would appreciate any suggestions and feedback on any aspect of this book that may help me to improve it. Please send your comments via e-mail to

```
xjia@cti.depaul.edu
```

CHAPTER 1

Object-Oriented Software Development

CHAPTER OVERVIEW

In this chapter, we provide an overview of object-oriented software development. We start with a general discussion of software development processes and the desirable qualities of software products. Next, we discuss what makes software development difficult and the difference between software engineering and other more established engineering practices. Then we take a close look at iterative software development processes, including the Rational Unified Process (RUP) and Extreme Programming (XP).

Whether you are a novice or experienced computer user or programmer, you would agree that we are living in an exciting period of time with a constant flow of innovations in both computer hardware and software. The software industry was one of the most successful industries during the past two decades. Not only was its growth in market value exceptional, but it was also able to deliver technologically advanced and innovative products at an unrelenting pace. Today, computer software has become prevalent in every aspect of life. Societies are becoming more and more dependent on software systems, from autopilot systems of jetliners to computerized trading systems of stock markets to personal organizers on palm-top computers. However, software is

1

expensive. The cost of purchasing, developing, maintaining, and upgrading software systems has become the largest single expenditure for many businesses, and it continues to increase. This continuing increase in software costs contrasts sharply to the dramatic decrease in hardware costs and the equally dramatic increase in hardware performance and capabilities. The object-oriented software development methodology aims to significantly improve current software development practice. It has been well received and widely adopted by the software industry in recent years. It is the methodology of choice in today's software development practices.

1.1 THE CHALLENGES OF SOFTWARE DEVELOPMENT

During the past two decades, the software industry has produced many technologically advanced, innovative, and commercially successful products. However, the process of creating these successful products (i.e., software development) is a difficult, time-consuming, and costly endeavor. For example, the initial version of the Microsoft Windows NT operating system consisted of 6 million lines of code, cost $150 million to develop, and took 200 developers, testers, and technical writers 5 years to complete. The struggle to create Windows NT is vividly presented in *Show-Stopper* [Zachary, 1994]. Furthermore, software systems tend to be "buggy"; that is, they contain glitches that hamper or even disrupt their normal function or performance. Minor glitches can be merely annoying, but serious ones can be disastrous.

- On January 15, 1990, the AT&T long-distance telephone network broke down, interrupting nationwide long-distance telephone services in the United States for more than 8 hours. An ill-placed `break` statement in the switching software, written in the C language, was to blame for the breakdown.
- On June 4, 1996, the maiden flight of the new and improved Ariane 5 communication satellite launcher developed by the European Space Agency exploded 37 seconds after liftoff. An incorrectly handled software exception resulting from converting a 64-bit floating point to a 16-bit signed integer caused the disaster.
- On June 8, 2001, a software problem in the new trading software installed overnight for the New York Stock Exchange caused failures in trading on half of the floor of the exchange and forced the NYSE to shut down the entire trading floor for more than an hour.

Although such catastrophic failures are rare, minor glitches are common in almost all software. In other words, buggy software is the norm.

However, the state of software development practice is far from the "software crisis" many have proclaimed in the past. Advances in many aspects of software development methodologies and software engineering processes have made it possible to develop many large-scale software systems that perform as expected most of the time. We are not capable of delivering nor required to deliver 100% reliable software. The question is, How good is good enough?

Software development is labor intensive. A majority of software development projects are over budget and behind schedule. The reality of software development remains that software is very expensive and often unreliable. Despite the phenomenal success of the software industry in technological advance and innovation, it still faces challenges in delivering high-quality software on time and under budget. The object-oriented software development methodology is one of the solutions the software industry is embracing now, hoping to improve the reliability of software systems and the cost-effectiveness of software development.

In order to improve software development practice, let us first examine some of the underlying causes of the difficulties of software development: complexity, longevity and evolution, and high user expectations.

Complexity   The software systems being developed today are often very large and complex. Complexity is dictated by the problems the systems are intended to solve and the services they are intended to provide. From the engineering perspective, both requirements are often beyond the control of software developers. The complexity involved in a large-scale software system is so great that no individual can comprehend every detail of the system. To build such a complex system, it must be broken down into manageable parts and requires the cooperative efforts of a team of developers rather than the efforts of an individual. Methodologies, techniques, and tools that work well for small systems developed by individuals usually are not effective for large systems developed by teams.

Longevity and Evolution   Because of economic, political, and other constraints, software systems are often in service for very long periods of time. Today, some legacy systems have been operating for more than 20 years. During their lifetimes, software systems must constantly evolve to accommodate changes in users' needs and environments. However, making changes to software systems (i.e., maintenance) is a difficult task. Furthermore, maintenance not only is costly and time-consuming, but also usually degrades the quality of the systems being maintained. On average, the maintenance cost of a software system over its lifetime is far greater than its initial development cost.

High User Expectations   In the past, when computers were mainly used in universities, research institutions, and large corporations, the majority of software system users were scientists and engineers who had the technical skills to handle glitches they might encounter while using the systems. Today, computers are used in homes, schools, and businesses of all sizes, and are used for pleasure as well as for work. The majority of today's software users are nontechnical, ordinary people. Computer software products are considered more and more like consumer products and are expected to perform with the same dependability as household appliances. Occasional glitches that once were considered acceptable are now intolerable. Software systems are expected to be "bug-free," but such perfection is next to impossible.

The challenges faced by software development are to find effective solutions to control the complexities of software systems, to manage the longevity and evolution of software systems, and to deliver software systems with higher reliability and usability.

1.2 AN ENGINEERING PERSPECTIVE

The term *software engineering* was coined at a NATO workshop in 1968. It represented an aspiration to build the practice of software development on a solid scientific foundation and to attain the level of reliability and productivity associated with well-established engineering disciplines, such as civil and mechanical engineering.

Software engineering is an engineering discipline concerned with all aspects of developing and delivering high-quality and useful software in a cost-effective manner. Software engineering defines the various *activities* in the software development and the products, or deliverables, associated with these activities. Software engineering also defines the *software development processes*, which define the order for carrying out the development activities and the criteria for the deliverables of the activities.

1.2.1 Software Development Activities

The most important product of software development is obviously the software. Most people equate software to computer programs, or the source code. However, the source code is only a part of the products produced in software development. In software engineering, the term *software* is defined in a broader sense. It encompasses the source code as well as all the associated documentation produced during the various activities in the software development process. The documentation of software may include requirements specifications, architecture and design documents, configuration data, installation and user manuals, and so on. Software development usually involves the following activities:

Requirements Analysis The goal of requirements analysis is to establish the functions, services, and constraints of the software to be developed. For custom software, that is, software developed for one specific customer, this is usually accomplished by consultation with system users. For commercial ("shrink-wrapped") software, that is, software intended to be marketed and sold to any customers who are willing to buy it, this goal is usually accomplished by market analysis of perceived needs of potential customers and/or feedback from existing customers. There are two categories of requirements: *functional requirements*, which are concerned with functions and services to be performed by the software, and *nonfunctional requirements*, which are concerned with the constraints under which the software must operate, such as response time, memory consumption, and user friendliness. The main concern of requirements analysis is to define the problem to be solved. The requirements are documented in *requirements specifications* or *system specifications*.

Design The goal of design is to construct a solution to the problem by establishing an overall architecture of the software, by partitioning the software into components or subsystems, and by identifying the relationships and dependencies among them. These design activities can often be further divided into *system design*, which is primarily concerned with the decomposition of complex problems into manageable components, and *detail design*, which is primarily concerned with the solutions to each component. Software designs are often documented using various diagrams.

Implementation and Unit Testing   Implementation is the realization of the software design in programs, that is, source code. Each component is implemented separately. Unit testing is carried out to test each individual component, or unit, independently. The goal of unit testing is to ensure that each unit functions properly with respect to its specification before the units are integrated.

Integration and System Testing   The individual components or units are integrated and tested as a whole to ensure that the entire software system functions properly with respect to its specification.

Maintenance   Maintenance involves a variety of activities after the delivery of software systems. These activities include correcting bugs, improving performance, enhancing functions or services, and adapting to new environments. Software maintenance continues as long as the software is in service. It is usually the longest and most costly activity in the software life cycle.

1.2.2   Software Development Processes

The most well-known software development process is the "waterfall" model illustrated in Figure 1.1, which has been the de facto standard of the software development process. In the waterfall model, the development activities are carried out in successive phases linearly: requirements analysis, design, implementation and unit testing, integration and system testing, and maintenance. A *phase* is the span of time between two major milestones of the process in which a well-defined set of objectives are met, artifacts are completed, and decisions are made whether to move into the next phase. In principle, the deliverables of each phase must be approved ("signed off") before the

Figure 1.1

The waterfall model of software development.

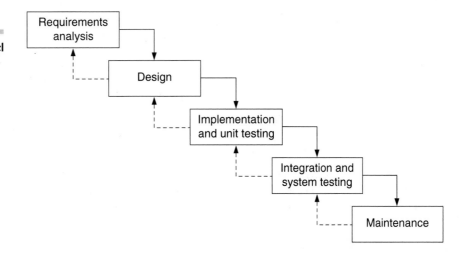

next phase can begin. The rationale is that changes to the requirements specification cost much less to implement in the requirements analysis than in the later phases. The later the phase in which a change to the requirements is introduced, the more it costs. So the goal is to minimize changes after the documents are delivered. This requires that the tasks of each phase be completed thoroughly, and that the deliverables of each phase be frozen once they are delivered and approved.

However, the waterfall model is not realistic. It is very common that changes occur during every phase of the development process. The changes may come from a number of sources: errors or faults of the specification and design may be discovered during implementation; assumptions made in design may be proven false during system testing; some features requested by the customers may be proven to be too slow, excessive in resource consumption, or infeasible during system testing; and user needs and requirements may have changed after the requirements analysis is completed. Therefore, in practice, it is often necessary to have several iterations of the phases in the waterfall model. However, one of the major shortcomings of the waterfall model is that it does not facilitate such iterations.

There are several alternative software development processes that are designed to carry out the software development activities in an iterative fashion. The iterative software development processes are becoming popular and gaining acceptance in practice, partly because of the wide acceptance of object-oriented development methodologies, which are especially suited to iterative development. We will discuss two of the common iterative development processes in Section 1.4.

1.2.3 Desirable Qualities of Software Systems

Let's now turn our attention to the products of software development—software systems. The following are the most desirable qualities of software systems:

Usefulness: Software systems should adequately address the needs of their intended users in solving problems and providing services.

Timeliness: Software systems should be completed and shipped in a timely manner. Otherwise, they may be less useful or even useless owing to changes in users' needs and operating environments. This factor is also important in the software vendor's ability to remain competitive.

Reliability: Software systems should perform as expected by users in terms of the correctness of the functions being performed, the availability of services, and an acceptable level of failures.

Maintainability: Software systems should be easily maintainable; that is, it should be possible to make corrections, adaptations, and extensions without undue costs.

Reusability: Components of software systems should not be designed as ad hoc solutions to specific problems in specific contexts; rather they should be designed as *general* solutions to a class of problems in different contexts. Such general components can be *adapted* and *reused* many times.

User friendliness: Software systems should provide user-friendly interfaces tailored to the capabilities and the background of the intended users to facilitate easy use and access to the full extent of the systems' capabilities.

Efficiency: Software systems should not make wasteful use of system resources, including processing time, memory, and disk space.

Not all of these desirable qualities are attainable at the same time, nor are they of equal importance. A crucial part of software development is dealing with the trade-offs among these different qualities to achieve a reasonable balance. Obviously, the object-oriented development approach cannot directly improve all these qualities. It focuses primarily on improving the maintainability and reusability of software systems. Maintainability should be the focus of the development process for three main reasons. First, for software systems with long lifetimes, maintenance costs will far exceed initial development costs. It is imprudent to compromise maintainability because any savings that may result initially will undoubtedly be dwarfed by maintenance cost penalties over the long run. Second, current development technology does not yield high reliability in the initial release of software systems. Reliability is usually attained through repeated corrections during the development phase and throughout the lifetimes of software systems. Software system reliability can be severely hampered by poor maintainability. Third, high maintainability requires flexibility in the design and implementation of software systems. Such flexibility facilitates the kind of incremental development that enhances reliability, usefulness, and user friendliness, as well as the ability to contain costs.

Several factors contribute to the maintainability of software systems:

Flexibility: Flexibility means that various aspects of software systems should be easily changeable. The impact of the changes can be confined to small regions, and the correctness of the changes can be verified locally, that is, by only examining the small affected regions rather than examining the entire software.

Simplicity: Human beings are fallible. It is impossible for people to avoid making mistakes. However, when things are simple, people are much less error-prone, and making sure that things are working properly is much easier. If there are errors, they become more obvious, and correcting them is easier. Complex software systems can be simplified by the effective use of the divide-and-conquer technique.

Readability: A prerequisite for maintainability is readability, or understandability, because software systems must be understood before they can be modified. Readability depends on the clarity and the simplicity of the design and the program code, the clarity and completeness of the accompanying documentation, and a simple and consistent style of design, implementation, and documentation.

These factors are the focus of our discussion of methods and techniques in later chapters.

1.2.4 Is Software Development an Engineering Process?

After more than 30 years since its inception, there is still little consensus on the precise definition of *software engineering*, and even the legitimacy of using *software engineer* as a professional title is still being debated. As Shaw and Garlan [1996] pointed out, software engineering is a label that

> refers to a collection of management processes, software tooling, and design activities for software development. The resulting practice, however, differs significantly from the practice of older forms of engineering.

A close examination of traditional, well-established engineering disciplines reveals that several essential characteristics of those practices are absent in today's software development practice.

Analysis of Designs

Over the centuries, craftsmanship clearly has proved capable of building magnificent structures, such as the Egyptian pyramids, Roman aqueducts, and Notre Dame Cathedral. However, modern engineering offers assurance, predictability, and efficiency that craftsmanship cannot match. One of the key differences between engineering and craftsmanship is that the success of engineering projects can be assured beforehand through scientific analysis of their designs, whereas the success of craftsmanship projects is attained through trial and error during current and prior construction.

Civil engineers depend on mechanics to help them predict with confidence before construction begins that a newly designed bridge or building will stand and function as it is supposed to. Aerospace engineers depend on aerodynamics and simulation to help them predict with confidence before it is built that a newly designed airplane will fly.

In contrast, software developers largely depend on testing and debugging (i.e., trial and error) to establish confidence in their products. Software development is like building modern skyscrapers with craftsmanship, with the success of software development projects rarely assured beforehand.

Nonrecurrence of Failures

Failures, sometimes catastrophic, also occur in well-established engineering fields. Perhaps one of the most spectacular failures in the history of engineering was the collapse of the Tacoma Narrows Bridge in 1940. Its design was unconventional and innovative, and the bridge was dramatic and elegant in appearance. Careful analysis was performed to ensure that the bridge would behave well under its own weight with anticipated traffic loads and winds as high as 45 miles per hour. However, the designer did not foresee that the slender bridge deck would act like an airplane wing in a moderate crosswind of less than 40 miles per hour, which twisted the bridge apart. As soon as the cause of the collapse was known, measures were developed to prevent such failures in the future. Hence, in well-established engineering fields, the same type of failure is rarely repeated.

In software development, the same types of failures recur all the time. Few practical measures can be taken to ensure the absence of certain types of faults in software systems. The sad truth about software development is that no one can ensure that the type of failure that occurred in Ariane 5 will never occur again.

Codification of Knowledge

The success of well-established engineering fields is due largely to the accumulation and codification of knowledge and the reuse of prior solutions. Design knowledge and solutions often are organized and presented in manuals and handbooks to make common and routine design not only easier and faster, but also more reliable, dependable, and manageable. Designers often find solutions in handbooks and then adapt and assemble the solutions to their specific design problems. Only rarely are original and innovative solutions needed. Usually, the codified knowledge includes what to avoid as well as what to do.

In software development, although a lot of design knowledge and experience has been accumulated, very little has been systematically codified. Without the benefit of prior design solutions, each design of a software system is treated as an original. Therefore, it is no surprise that software design is difficult, time-consuming, and unreliable.

Thus, software development is quite different from the traditional engineering disciplines. At best, it is an immature engineering discipline. For software development to become a true engineering discipline, software developers must have mechanisms to carry out the analysis of designs, ensure nonrecurrence of known failures, and codify design knowledge.

1.3 OBJECT ORIENTATION

1.3.1 Modeling the Real World

The main goal of software development is to build software systems that provide services to people and enhance their abilities to solve problems in the real world. A software system usually consists of two essential components: a *model*, which is a representation of a pertinent part of the real world, and an *algorithm*, which captures the computations involved in manipulating or processing the model.

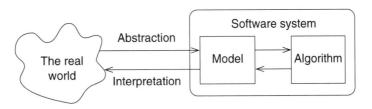

The real world is enormous and complex. Many of its aspects are fuzzy, unknown, or intangible. In contrast, the programming models used in software systems must be precise and relatively small. A model is necessarily an *abstraction* of the real world. It captures only the essential and relevant characteristics of the real world from a particular perspective and ignores others. Models are intended to be manipulated or processed, and their behaviors should mimic those of the real world to reflect the chosen perspectives reasonably accurately. The results of manipulations can be fed back to the real world through *interpretation* (i.e., the assignment of meanings to the entities in the models) and often represent solutions to real-world problems.

1.3.2   Evolution of Programming Models

Programming languages are the main tools used by software developers to describe computer models. The evolution of programming languages and programming methodologies is driven by the need to build more and more sophisticated and effective models. That need in turn is driven by the ever-increasing power of modern computers and the desire to utilize this power.

One of the fundamental problems in software development is, *How does someone model the real world?* The answer largely depends on the problems to be solved. One way to look at the evolution of software development methodologies is through the changing views of programming models.

In the 1950s and 1960s, the focus of software developers was on the algorithm. As a result, the main concerns at that time were solving computation problems, designing efficient algorithms, and controlling the complexity of *computation*. The models used were computation-oriented models, and the decomposition of complex systems was primarily based on *control flow*.

In the 1970s and 1980s, different types of models emerged to address the complexity of the *data* being processed. These systems were centered on data entities and data flows, with computation becoming a secondary concern. The models used were data-oriented models, and the decomposition of complex systems was primarily based on *data flow*.

Object-oriented models represent a balanced view of the data and computation aspects of software systems. Object-oriented models are composed of *objects*, which contain data and the associated computations. The decomposition of complex systems is based on the structure of objects, classes, and the relationships among them.

1.3.3   A Brief History

The origin of object-oriented software development dates back to the late 1960s. A computer simulation language called Simula was the first programming language that included some important features of object-oriented programming, such as class. The first full-blown and perhaps the best known object-oriented programming language was Smalltalk, developed by Xerox PARC in the 1970s. Object-oriented technology grew tremendously during the 1980s, with the emergence of several more sophisticated object-oriented programming languages, including C++, Objective-C, and Eiffel. It also evolved from a programming methodology to a software development methodology that addresses the analysis, design, testing, and evolution of software systems in addition to the implementation of software systems. Despite its long history of development, only recently has the object-oriented development approach matured and become widely accepted by the mainstream software industry. This acceptance is largely due to significant advances in several aspects of object-oriented development methodology in recent years:

- A number of object-oriented programming languages have become mature, practical, and widely accepted by the software industry, including C++ and later Java.
- A number of object-oriented analysis and modeling techniques and notations have been developed and eventually unified in the form of Unified Modeling Language. UML has been widely adopted in the industry.
- In 1995, the *Design Patterns* book was published. It represented the first systematic attempt at codifying object-oriented design knowledge.
- Iterative development processes have been gradually accepted in practice.

The object-oriented software development approach represents a dramatic departure from conventional software development approaches. It looks at the world from a rather different perspective.

1.4 ITERATIVE DEVELOPMENT PROCESSES

In contrast to the traditional waterfall software development model, Boehm [1988] proposed the first iterative software development process, known as the *spiral model*. Booch [1994] proposed an iterative software development process for object-oriented software development. Booch's iterative object-oriented development process consists of a number of successive iterations. Each iteration contains the following steps: identifying the classes, identifying the semantics (i.e., attributes and behaviors) of the classes, identifying the relationships among the classes, defining the class interface, and then implementing the classes. Each iteration deals with a relatively small increment of the system being developed. Thus the system is developed incrementally, not as a monolithic piece. The iterative process continues until the entire system is complete. This process is what Booch called the *micro* process. Booch also proposed a *macro* process to serve as the controlling framework of the micro process. The macro process consists of the following phases: analysis and modeling, design, implementation, and maintenance.

Booch's iterative development process became the foundation of the more complete and now widely adopted object-oriented development process, known as the *Rational Unified Process (RUP)*. It also inspired a number of lightweight object-oriented iterative development processes. The most well-known of these processes is the so-called *Extreme Programming (XP)*. In this section, we begin by taking a look at the activities of object-oriented development. We then discuss some of the common characteristics of iterative development processes. Next, we provide a brief overview of both RUP and XP. We will revisit and elaborate on many of the underlying principles and techniques of both RUP and XP throughout the remainder of the book.

1.4.1 Object-Oriented Development Activities

Object-oriented development processes consist of activities that are similar to those in the waterfall software development model discussed in Section 1.2.2. Compared to the activities in the waterfall software development model, the activities in object-oriented development processes have a rather different focus and adopt a rather different set of techniques, notations, tools, and criteria. Here are the common activities in object-oriented development processes:

Conceptualization: The goal of conceptualization is to establish the vision and the core requirements of the software system to be developed. Unlike the requirements analysis phase in the waterfall process model, the goal here does involve establishing the complete requirements of the system.

Object-oriented analysis and modeling: The goal of object-oriented analysis and modeling is to build models of the system's desired behavior, using notations such as the Unified Modeling Language (UML). A model intends to capture the essential relevant aspects of the real world and to define the services to be provided and/or the problems to be solved. A model is a simplification of reality, created to better understand the system to be developed. In contrast to the informal requirements analysis in the waterfall process, the emphasis here is to use notations such as UML, which includes use cases and class diagrams, and so on, to describe the models in a way that is semantically richer and more precise compared to informal paper documents.

Object-oriented design: The goal of object-oriented design is to create an architecture for implementation. Designs are represented in terms of objects and classes and the relationships among them. Key concerns of an object-oriented design include the following: (1) Does the design satisfy all the stated requirements and constraints and provide all the desired services adequately? (2) Is the design flexible enough to accommodate future changes and enhancements? (3) Is the design feasible for implementation, and, if so, can it be implemented efficiently?

Implementation: The goal of implementation is to implement the design by using an object-oriented programming language, such as Java. Implementation involves coding, unit testing, and debugging. Key concerns of implementation include these: (1) Is the implementation correct? (2) Is the implementation efficient and maintainable? (3) Is the implementation robust, that is, capable of tolerating faults and recovering from failures?

Maintenance: The goal of maintenance is to manage postdelivery evolution. The primary maintenance tasks include removing bugs, enhancing functionalities, and adapting the system to evolving needs and environments.

A key assumption in the iterative software development process is that changes occur throughout the life cycle of software development. Instead of trying to minimize or prevent changes, iterative software development processes try to facilitate and manage changes. In iterative development processes, software systems are developed in successive iterations. Each iteration represents a complete development cycle for a small piece, or increment, of the entire system, from analysis and design, to implementation and testing. The key characteristics of an iteration include the following:

- Each iteration is relatively small and can be completed in a relatively short period of time.
- Each iteration results in a release of an executable product or component, which is a part of the final product.

The final product is developed incrementally from iteration to iteration.

1.4.2   Rational Unified Process

The Rational Unified Process (RUP) is a complete software engineering process. It provides guidelines for carrying out every aspect of software development activities with the goal to "ensure the production of high-quality software that meets the needs of its end users within a predictable schedule and budget [Booch et al., 1999]." The RUP is not one process, but a process framework that can be adapted and extended to suit the needs of different organizations and different types of projects. The key practices of the RUP are to:

- develop software iteratively.
- systematically elicit, organize, and manage changing requirements.
- use component-based architecture.
- visually model software using UML.
- continuously verify software quality.
- control changes to software.

The emphasis of the RUP is on building *models* rather than paper documents. In the RUP, there are nine models that collectively cover all the important decisions that go into visualizing, specifying, constructing, and documenting a software-intensive system [Booch et al., 1999]:

1. *Business model:* Establishes an abstraction of the organization
2. *Domain model:* Establishes the context of the system
3. *Use case model:* Establishes the system's functional requirements
4. *Analysis model (optional):* Establishes an idea design

5. *Design model:* Establishes the vocabulary of the problem and its solution

6. *Process model (optional):* Establishes the system's concurrency and synchronization mechanisms

7. *Deployment model:* Establishes the hardware topology on which the system is executed

8. *Implementation model:* Establishes the parts used to assemble and release the physical system

9. *Test model:* Establishes the paths by which the system is validated and verified

The RUP is *use case driven*. Use cases defined for system requirements are the foundation for all other development activities, including design, implementation, and testing. The RUP is *architecture centric*. The main focus of early iteration of the development process is to produce and validate an executable architecture prototype, which gradually evolves to become the final system in later iterations.

The process structure of the RUP can be illustrated in a two-dimensional chart as shown in Figure 1.2. One dimension represents the time in terms of phases and iterations. The other dimension represents the process workflows. The chart shows roughly the amount of time or attention devoted to each process workflow during various phases and iterations.

A process *workflow* consists of a sequence of activities that produce a set of *artifacts*, or deliverables, which can be project plans, design models, source code, tests, and documentations. The RUP defines nine process workflows:

1. *Business modeling:* Describes the structure and dynamics of the organization

2. *Requirements:* Describes the use case–based method for eliciting requirements

3. *Analysis and design:* Describes the multiple architectural views

Figure 1.2

Rational Unified Process. (From Kruchten [2000] The Rational Unified Process, An Introduction. Addison-Wesley.)

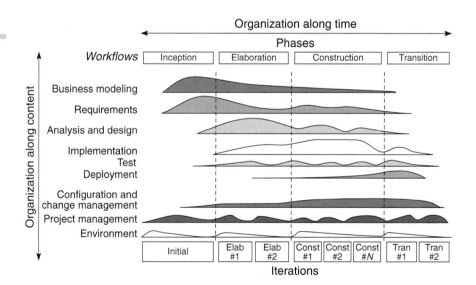

4. *Implementation:* Takes into account software development, unit test, and integration

5. *Test:* Describes test cases, procedures, and defect-tracking metrics

6. *Deployment:* Covers the deliverable system configuration

7. *Configuration management:* Controls changes to and maintains the integrity of a project's artifacts

8. *Project management:* Describes various strategies of working with an iterative process

9. *Environment:* Covers the necessary infrastructure required to develop a system

The RUP also defines four major *phases*:

1. *Inception:* Establishes the business case for the project

2. *Elaboration:* Establishes a project plan and a sound architecture

3. *Construction:* Grows the system

4. *Transition:* Supplies the system to its end users

Each phase is further broken down into one or more *iterations*. Each iteration goes through the various process workflows (described earlier) and is a complete development cycle that results in the release of an executable product. The phases serve as the controlling framework of the iterations. Iterations in different phases have different emphases on process workflows as illustrated in Figure 1.2. For example, iterations in the inception phase focus more on business modeling and requirements, while iterations in the construction phase focus more on implementation and configuration management.

1.4.3 Extreme Programming

Extreme Programming (XP) is a lightweight process with an emphasis on producing high-quality executable code throughout the development process. Since executable code is the most important part of the ultimate deliverables of the software development processes, the XP process focuses on executable code from the very beginning. Hence the name *Extreme Programming*. Extreme Programming is an iterative process with small iterations. Each iteration often lasts no more than a few days to a few weeks. The very first iteration will produce a minimum, skeletal, and executable implementation of the system to be developed. Each subsequent iteration should enhance or improve upon the deliverable of the preceding iteration and produce a new executable release of the system until the entire system is completed. Extreme Programming emphasizes maintaining high quality in the code delivered by each and every iteration, especially in terms of the extensibility and maintainability. The focus of each iteration can be either enhancement or refactoring. *Enhancements* introduce new functionalities or features. *Refactoring* restructures the code to improve the quality, including extensibility and maintainability, and the structure of the software system while maintaining its behavior. Extreme Programming depends heavily on refactoring to maintain and improve qualities and to facilitate changes and enhance-ments.

The core of XP consists of the following key practices:

Planning game: Start with a simple a plan for each iteration, and continually refine the plan as necessary.

Frequent and small releases: Make frequent and small releases starting as early as possible. Each iteration, that is, the duration for producing a release, should not be longer than a few weeks.

Metaphor: Use metaphors to start development and communicate with the customers.

Simple design: Make design as simple as possible. Refactor later if changes are necessary.

Test first: Write unit test before writing code.

Refactoring: Refactor to make the system simpler and clearer or to reduce duplication.

Pair programming: Write all production code in pairs.

Collective ownership: Anyone may change code anywhere in the system to improve it.

Continuous integration: Integrate as soon as a task is complete.

40-hour week: Teams are more productive if the members stay fresh and energetic than if they work overtime.

On-site customer: Have a customer available on-site and full time.

Coding standards: Adopt common standards and conventions for naming, source code formatting, documentation, and so on.

Undoubtedly, some of the practices are unique to XP, such as pair programming. Extreme programming and RUP share a lot in common. In some sense, XP can be viewed as a minimalistic form of the RUP. One of the key differences between the two is that the RUP emphasizes building object-oriented models using modeling notations defined in UML, while XP emphasizes producing executable code. However, building object-oriented models using UML is often done in XP as well. Several commonly used notations of UML will be discussed in Chapter 2. Unit testing and continued integration will be discussed in Chapter 6. Refactoring will be one of the main topics of Chapter 7.

CHAPTER SUMMARY

- Software development is difficult, time-consuming, and costly. The main causes of problems in software development include the complexity, longevity, evolu-tion, and high user expectations of software systems.

- The well-known waterfall model of software development consists of the following phases: requirements analysis, design, implementation and unit testing, integration and system testing, and maintenance.
- Software development lacks some key characteristics of well-established engineering disciplines, including analysis of designs, nonrecurrence of failures, and codification of knowledge. Software development is an immature field of engineering.
- The desirable qualities of software systems include usefulness, timeliness, reliability, maintainability, reusability, user friendliness, and efficiency. Of these qualities, maintainability is the most crucial and deserves the most attention during development. Factors contributing to maintainability include flexibility, simplicity, and readability. The object-oriented development approach focuses primarily on improving the maintainability and reusability of software systems.
- An iterative object-oriented development process consists of a number of successive iterations. Each iteration deals with a relatively small increment of the system being developed. The system is developed incrementally. The iterative process continues until the entire system is complete. Two of the common iterative development processes are the RUP and XP.
- The common activities in object-oriented development processes include conceptualization, object-oriented analysis and modeling, object-oriented design, implementation, and maintenance.

FURTHER READINGS

Beck, K. (2000). *Extreme Programming Explained*. Addison-Wesley.

Brooks, F. P. (1975). *The Mythical Man Month—Essays on Software Engineering*. Addison-Wesley.

Brooks, F. P. (1987). "No Silver Bullet—Essence and Accidents of Software Engineering," *IEEE Software* 20(4).

Jacobson, I., G. Booch, and J. Rumbaugh (1999). *The Unified Software Development Process*. Addison-Wesley.

Kruchten, P. (2000). *The Rational Unified Process, An Introduction*, 2nd ed. Addison-Wesley.

Pressman, R. S. (1997). *Software Engineering: A Practitioner's Approach*. McGraw-Hill.

Sommerville, I. (2001). *Software Engineering*, 6th ed. Addison-Wesley.

EXERCISES

1.1 Search the Web or libraries to find out details of some of the catastrophic failures of computer systems whose causes have been attributed to software failures, including the ones mentioned in this chapter.

1.2 Search the Web or libraries to find out details of some failed software development projects and the causes.

1.3 Search the Web or libraries to find out whether it is permissible to use *software engineer* as a professional title without certification in your country or state, and what the rationale is.

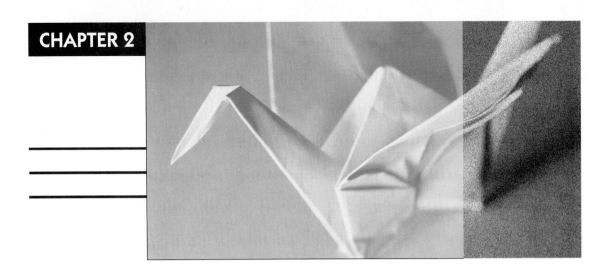

CHAPTER 2

Object-Oriented Modeling Using UML

CHAPTER OVERVIEW

In this chapter, we discuss the basic principles, concepts, and techniques of object-oriented modeling. We introduce a number of commonly used notations in the Unified Modeling Language (UML), including class diagrams, object diagrams, sequence diagrams, and use case diagrams. We conclude the chapter with a case study of object-oriented analysis and modeling.

2.1 PRINCIPLES AND CONCEPTS

In this section, we discuss the basic concepts and the principles of object-oriented development. We also introduce some simple graphical notations in the *Unified Modeling Language* (UML) [Booch et al., 1999][1] for describing object-oriented models. We use a subset of UML notations with minor adaptations in syntax for the sake of consistency with Java.

1. UML is a standard for object-oriented modeling notations endorsed by the Object Management Group (OMG), an industrial consortium on object technologies.

2.1.1 Objects and Classes

Terms and Concepts

Objects and *classes* are two of the fundamental concepts in object-oriented development. Both objects and classes can be viewed from two different perspectives: (1) their *representation* in the object-oriented models, and (2) their *interpretation* in the real world. The representation of objects and classes dealt with in the object-oriented models (including programs) is only an approximation of the interpretation of objects and classes in the real world. We can define objects and classes in terms of how they are interpreted in the real world, as well as how they are represented in the object-oriented models.

	Interpretation in the Real World	Representation in the Model
Object	An *object* represents anything in the real world that can be distinctly identified.	An *object* has an identity, a state, and a behavior.
Class	A *class* represents a set of objects with similar characteristics and behavior. These objects are called the *instances* of the class.	A *class* characterizes the structure of states and behaviors that are shared by all its instances.

Each object has a unique identity. The identity of an object distinguishes the object from all other objects. The state of an object is composed of a set of *fields*, or *attributes*. Each field has a name, a type, and a value. The behavior of an object is defined by a set of *methods* that may operate on the object. In other words, a method may access or manipulate the state of the object. Methods are sometimes called *operations*, and we consider these two terms to be synonymous. Each method also has a name, a type, and a value. The type of a method consists of the return type and the list of parameter types of the method. The return type can be void if the method does not return a value. The value of a method is the implementation of the method often expressed as a sequence of statements, in languages like Java or C++. The *features* of an object refer to the combination of the state and the behavior of the object.

Two objects are *equal* if their states are equal, that is, if the values of the corresponding fields of the two objects are equal. Two objects are *identical* if they are the same object, that is, if they have the same identity.

The values of the fields of an object are mutable. Those methods of an object that do not modify the state of the object are called *accessors*, and those methods of an object that could modify the state of the object are called *mutators*. A *mutable object* is an object whose state may be modified by some of its methods. A mutable object may have different states at different times. An *immutable object* is an object whose state may never be modified by any of its methods, that is, an object that has no mutators. The state of an immutable object remains constant. Objects are usually mutable. However, immutable objects are quite useful too.

A class defines a template for creating or instantiating its instances, that is, objects. The terms *object* and *instance* are often interchangeable. The class from which an object is created is referred to as the class of the object, and the object is referred to as an instance of the class. In most object-oriented languages, including Java and C++, instead of defining the features of individual objects, the features of objects are defined in the class that instantiates the objects. Specifically, a class defines (1) the names and types of all fields and (2) the names, types, and implementations of all methods. The values of the fields are not defined or fixed in the class definition. The values of the fields are mutable. Each instance of the class has its own state. Different instances of the class may have different states. The implementations of methods are defined in the class definition and are therefore fixed for a given object. In other words, the values of methods of an object are immutable.

Let's look at a simple class `Point` that represents points in a two-dimensional space. The Java code defining the class is shown on the right-hand side.

```
Class name   Point      class Point {
Fields       x, y           int x, y;
Method       move           public void move(int dx, int dy) {
                                 // implementation
                             }
                         }
```

The `Point` class defines two fields: x and y, and one method: `move()`. The type of both fields is `int`. The return type of `move()` is `void` and the list of the parameter types of `move()` is `(int, int)`, since it takes two parameters both of type `int`.

UML Notation for Classes

The UML notation for classes is a rectangular box with as many as three compartments.

```
ClassName      The top compartment shows the class name.
field₁
...            The middle compartment contains the declarations of the fields of
fieldₙ         the class.
method₁
...            The bottom compartment contains the declarations of the methods
methodₘ        of the class.
```

If, in some context, the detail of the fields and methods of the class is not important, one may omit both the middle and the bottom compartments.

The name of the field is required in a field declaration. Optionally, a field declaration may also include the visibility, the type, and/or the initial values of the field. In this book, the Java syntax is used for field declarations:[2]

[*Visibility*] [*Type*] *Name* [[*Multiplicity*]] [= *InitialValue*]

Alternatively, field declarations can also be in the following standard UML syntax:

[*Visibility*] *Name* [[*Multiplicity*]] [: *Type*] [= *InitialValue*]

The name of the method is required in a method declaration. Optionally, a method declaration may also include the visibility, the return type, and/or the list of parameters of the method. In this book, the Java syntax is used for method declarations:

[*Visibility*] [*Type*] *Name* ([*Parameter*, . . .])

Alternatively, method declarations can be also be in the following standard UML syntax:

[*Visibility*] *Name* ([*Parameter*, . . .]) [: *Type*]

The *visibility*, or accessibility, of fields and methods defines the scope in which features of classes are accessible. Visibility can be one of the following:

Public	The feature is accessible to any class.
Protected	The feature is accessible to the class itself, all the classes in the same package,[3] and all its subclasses.
Package	The feature is accessible to the class itself and all classes in the same package.
Private	The feature is only accessible within the class itself.

The accessibility of features will be discussed in more detail in Section 4.4.1. The Java and UML syntaxes for visibility are as follows:

Visibility	Java Syntax	UML Syntax
public	public	+
protected	protected	#
package		~
private	private	–

---

2. In this book, we use the following convention to define syntax: the notation *Foo* (e.g., *Type*) denotes a nonterminal symbol; terminal symbols are shown in boldface **Courier** font (e.g., **=**). The entities between square brackets [ ] (e.g., [*Type*]) are optional.

3. Packages are discussed later in this section [p. 25] and in Section 4.5 [p. 134].

The multiplicity specification of a field specifies whether an object may have multiple occurrences of the field. The multiplicity specification is defined in Section 2.2.2 [p. 33].

Each parameter of a method can be specified using the Java syntax as follows:

Type Name

Alternatively, a parameter can be specified using the UML syntax as follows:

Name : *Type*

The following are some examples of field and method declarations:

Field declarations

```
Date birthday                           (Java syntax)
birthday:Date                           (UML syntax)

public int duration = 100               (Java syntax)
+duration:int = 100                     (UML syntax)

private Student students[0..MAX_SIZE]   (Java syntax)
-students[0..MAX_SIZE]:Student          (UML syntax)
```

Method declarations

```
void move(int dx, int dy)    (Java syntax)
~move(dx:int, dy:int)        (UML syntax)

public int getSize()         (Java syntax)
+getSize():int               (UML syntax)
```

The Point class shown earlier can be represented in UML as follows, at different levels of detail.

Full details in Java syntax:

Point
private int x private int y
public void move(int dx, int dy)

Full details in UML syntax:

Point
-x:int -y:int
+move(dx:int, dy:int)

Abbreviated forms:

Point
x y
move()

Point

UML Notation for Objects

The UML notation for objects is a rectangular box with one or two compartments.

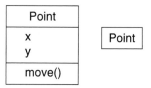

The top compartment shows the name of the object and its class. The object and class names are underlined to distinguish the object notation from the class notation.

The bottom compartment contains a list of the fields and their values.

There are a number of variations for the contents of the top compartment:

- objectName
  Omission of the colon and the class name denotes an object named objectName whose class is of no interest.
- : ClassName
  Omission of the object name denotes an anonymous object of class ClassName, which can be identified only through its relationship with other objects.

The fields and their values in the bottom compartment are described with the following syntax:

Field = Value

The bottom compartment may be omitted altogether if the attributes and values of an object are of no interest.

For example, instances of the `Point` class, with the states $(0, 0)$ and $(24, 40)$, can be represented graphically as follows:

p1:Point
x = 0
y = 0

p2:Point
x = 24
y = 40

```
Point p1 = new Point();
p1.x = 0;
p1.y = 0;
Point p2 = new Point();
p2.x = 24;
p2.y = 40;
```

The Java code segment, on the right, shows the creation of the instances and the assignment of the states.

Message Passing   Objects communicate with one another by means of *message passing*. A message represents a command sent to an object—known as the *recipient* (also known as the *receiving object* or the *receiver*) of the message—to perform a certain action by invoking one of the methods of the recipient. A *message* consists of the receiving object, the method to be invoked, and (optionally) the arguments to the method. Message passing is also known as *method invocation*. The following is a message to instruct the recipient, point p1, to move 10 units and 20 units in the x and y directions, respectively, by invoking the method `move()`.

	Recipient	p1
p1.move(10, 20)	Method	move()
	Arguments	(10, 20)

Packages

Style Convention   *Package Names*

Package names are all in lowercase letters, such as `java.awt.event`.
   Packages intended to be widely available should use the reverse of the Internet domain as the prefix of the package name so that it will be unique globally—for example, `edu.depaul.cs`.

Classes are often grouped into a *package*. Packages can be organized into a hierarchy. In other words, a package may contain classes and subpackages. It is important to point out that all classes in the same package must be closely related, since all features of a class, except those that are private, are accessible to all classes in the same package. Details for using packages in Java will be discussed in Section 4.5.1.

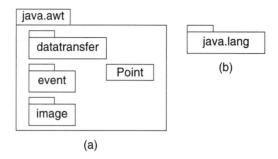

UML Notation of Packages

The UML notation of packages is shown in Figure 2.1. A package is represented by a
rectangular container with a tab at the upper left corner. The classes and subpackages
that belong to a package are sometimes depicted within the rectangular container. In
that case, the package name is placed in the tab, as in Figure 2.1(a). When the package
contents are not included, as in Figure 2.1(b), the package name can be placed inside
the rectangular container.

2.1.2   Principles

In this section, we discuss a number of important principles in the object-oriented
development approach.

Modularity

One of the fundamental principles of the object-oriented approach is the principle of
modularity. It is intended to control the complexity of large-scale systems through the
use of the divide-and-conquer technique.

Principle   *Modularity*

A complex software system should be decomposed into a set of highly cohesive but
loosely coupled *modules*.

Decomposition of complex software systems into modules is one of the most
intriguing tasks in software development and is more an art than a science. The reason
is that most of the entities in a software system are intricately interconnected like a
web and must be untangled. The basic criteria for decomposition are two of the best
known and most elusive concepts in software development—cohesion and coupling.

- *Cohesion* refers to the functional relatedness of the entities within a module.
- *Coupling* refers to the interdependency among different modules.

A system may be extremely complex in its totality, but a *modular decomposition* of the system aims to break it down into modules so that

- each module is relatively small and simple (that is, highly cohesive); and
- the interactions among modules are relatively simple (that is, loosely coupled), ensuring that—by examining the module *within*, not *without*—each module will be well-behaved and that, if all the modules are well-behaved, the entire system also will be well-behaved.

Typically, modular decompositions are hierarchical (that is, a module may contain other modules).

The concepts of modules, cohesion, and coupling all predate the object-oriented approach. The forms of modules have evolved over time. In the structured development approach, the modules take the form of routines and functions. In the object-oriented approach, modules take the form of classes and packages.

Abstraction

In its purest sense, *abstraction* means separating the essential from the nonessential characteristics of an entity. The result is a simpler but sufficiently accurate approximation of the original entity, obtained by removing or ignoring the nonessential characteristics. The abstraction principle in software development can be described as follows:

Principle *Abstraction*

The behaviors, or functionalities, of a module should be characterized in a succinct and precise description known as the *contractual interface* of the module. In other words, the contractual interface captures the essence of the behavior of the module. The contractual interface is an abstraction of the module.

We can view a module as a *service provider* and other modules that use the services provided by the module as *clients* of the module. We can view the contractual interface as the *service contract* between the service provider and its clients. A service contract need only describe *what* services can be provided, not *how* the services are to be provided. Therefore, despite the fact that the services to be provided are very complex, the service contract may be very simple. With a simple service contract and an assurance by the service provider of honoring the contract, the clients need only understand the simple contract in order to use the complex services. The contractual interface allows the clients to use the services and not be concerned with the complexity of the services. In other words, the complexity of the module is hidden within it.

Let us consider the example of the telephone. The mechanism for providing telephone service is a rather complex one. It involves routing and connecting calls, converting voice to electronic signals and back to voice, transmitting the signals in analog or digital mode, and possibly encrypting and decrypting the signals for security reasons. However, telephone users (that is, the clients of a telephone service) don't need to understand the mechanics of a phone system. All the users need to understand is the manual that comes with the telephone set, which includes instructions on dialing, speaking, and hanging up. The user's manual in this case is the contractual interface of the telephone service, and it serves as an abstraction of the telephone service from the user's perspective.

Encapsulation

A closely related and complementary principle is *encapsulation*, which stipulates that the clients need know nothing more than the service contract while using the service.

Principle *Encapsulation*

The implementation of a module should be separated from its contractual interface and hidden from the clients of the module.

Hence this principle is also known as *information hiding*. Encapsulation is intended to reduce coupling among modules. The less the clients know about the implementation of the module, the looser the coupling between the module and its clients can be. An important benefit of encapsulation is that, if the clients know nothing beyond the contractual interface, implementation can be modified without affecting the clients, so long as the contractual interface remains the same.

Telephone service is a good example of an application in which the contractual interface and implementation are separated. In the past, signals were transmitted in analog mode. Over time, telephone service has been upgraded until, nowadays, the signals can be transmitted in digital mode with encryption. Although the implementation of telephone service has changed, the contractual interface remains the same. The only effects on telephone users are that they enjoy better sound quality and greater security.

If a contractual interface is completely separated from implementation, the contractual interface can exist on its own. A contractual interface without any implementation associated with it is known as an *interface* in Java terminology. A module can be represented by two separate entities: an *interface* that describes the contractual interface of the module and a *class* that implements the contractual interface.

Polymorphism

Several different service providers can honor the same contractual interface. Moreover, these service providers can be interchanged without affecting the clients. The ability to interchange modules dynamically without affecting the clients is known as *polymorphism*.[4]

Let us take the telephone service example one step further and consider cellular telephone service. Digital cellular service uses more advanced technologies but has smaller service regions than does the more established analog cellular service. An analog/digital dual-mode cellular phone is an example of polymorphism. It provides a single contractual interface for using the phone but employs two different technologies to provide the service. Users need not be concerned with—and certainly are not affected by—which technology is used to provide the service at any given moment. The dual-mode cellular phone dynamically switches (a *soft switch*) between the digital and analog modes as the user crosses the boundary of the digital/analog service regions. We discuss polymorphism in more detail in Section 5.2.2 [p. 165].

2.2 MODELING RELATIONSHIPS AND STRUCTURES

In this section, we introduce the UML class diagram for modeling the static structures of object-oriented software systems and various types of relations among the classes. Class diagrams are the most common diagrams used in object-oriented modeling. A *class diagram* consists of

- a set of nodes that represent classes and interfaces; and
- a set of links that represent relationships among classes.

The following relationships among classes can be modeled in class diagrams:

- Inheritance, including extension and implementation
- Association, including aggregation and composition
- Dependency

The graphical notation for classes is discussed in Section 2.1.1. The graphical notations for various relationships are discussed in the next four subsections.

2.2.1 Inheritance

Inheritance is one of the most important relationships in object-oriented modeling. *Inheritance* defines a relationship among classes and interfaces. More specifically, there are several forms of inheritance relation:

- The *extension* relation between two classes. When class C2 *extends* class C1, class C2 is known as a *subclass* of class C1, and class C1 is known as a *superclass* of class C2.

---

4. The word *polymorphism* means an entity with multiple forms. In this particular context, it refers to a contractual interface with multiple interchangeable implementations.

- The *extension* relation between two interfaces. When interface I2 *extends* interface I1, interface I2 is known as a *subinterface* of interface I1, and interface I1 is known as a *superinterface* of interface I2.

- The *implementation* relation between a class and an interface. When class C2 *implements* interface I1, class C2 is known as an *implementation* of interface I1, and interface I1 is known as an *interface* of class C2.

UML uses a different terminology for inheritance relationships. The extension relation is also known as *specialization*, and the inverse relation is known as *generalization* in UML. The implementation relation is also know as *realization* in UML.

Graphically, the inheritance relation is represented by a link from the subclass/subinterface to the superclass/superinterface with a hollow triangle pointing toward the superclass. The extension relation is represented by a solid link, and the implementation relation is represented by a dashed link, as shown in Figure 2.2. In class diagrams, the regular class, field, and method names are shown in upright roman fonts, as in MyClass. The names of interfaces and its methods are shown in italic fonts, as in *MyInterface*.

Conceptually, inheritance models the *is-a(n)* relationship in the real world; that is, if C2 is a subclass/subinterface/implementation of C1, then every instance of C2 *is an* instance of C1, and everything that applies to instances of C1 also applies to instances of C2. The extension relation between two classes is commonly associated with the notion of *reusing* or *sharing* the implementation (that is, the fields and methods) of a superclass by its subclasses. The extension relation between two interfaces represents the expansion of the service contract. The implementation relation does not connote reuse of implementations, but rather the implementation of a contractual interface by a class.

As an example, let us consider the following set of classes that represent different groups of students in a university. The class diagram is shown in Figure 2.3.

Figure 2.2

UML notation for inheritance relationships.

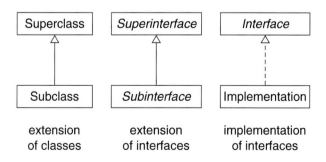

Figure 2.3

Class diagram: in-heritance relation among classes rep-resenting student groups.

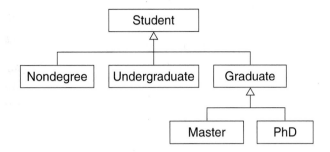

Class	Description
Student	Students in general
Graduate	Graduate students
Master	Graduate students pursuing a master's degree
PhD	Graduate students pursuing a PhD degree
Undergraduate	Undergraduate students
Nondegree	Nondegree students

It is easy to see in this example that inheritance can be interpreted as an is-a relation. For example, the `Graduate` class is a subclass of `Student`, as every graduate student *is a* student, and everything that applies to a student also applies to a graduate student. The set of students, that is, the set of the instances of the `Student` class, is a superset of the set of graduate students, that is, the set of the instances of the `Graduate` class.

A class may inherit from multiple superclasses. This capability is often referred to as *multiple inheritance*. However, many object-oriented programming languages, including Java, support only a restricted form of inheritance known as *single inheritance*, in which each class may inherit from only one superclass. Java supports a limited form of multiple inheritance by allowing classes to implement multiple interfaces. We discuss issues related to single and multiple inheritance in Section 5.3.2 [p. 179].

Levels of Abstraction

Classes and interfaces represent abstractions, and the inheritance relationship organizes the classes and interfaces into different levels of abstraction.

In other words, the superclasses represent more general abstractions and the subclasses represent more specialized abstractions. Consider again the example of students shown in Figure 2.3. The inheritance hierarchy shows different levels of abstraction of students in a university. The Student class represents the most general abstraction of students, whereas its subclasses represent various specialized abstractions of students. The leaf classes (that is, classes with no subclasses) represent the most specialized abstractions of students.

2.2.2   Association

Associations represent general binary relationships between classes. The association can be used to model a variety of relationships between classes, and the association relationship can also be implemented in a variety of different ways. It is common that either one or both classes in an association relation contain direct or indirect references to the other class. The graphical notation for association is a solid line between the two classes involved in the association with an optional label and optional adornments attached to either end, as shown in Figure 2.4. Figure 2.5 shows several associations among the Student, Faculty, and Course classes.

The graphical notation of an association may have an optional label that consists of a name and a direction drawn as a solid arrowhead with no tail. In Figure 2.5, *teach* and *enroll* are the names of the association between Faculty and Course, and between Student and Course, respectively. The direction arrows next to the names indicate the direction of association with respect to the name. For example, the arrow next to the *enroll* association means that "a student enrolls in a course," not that "a course enrolls in a student." By default, it is assumed that the direction of associations is from left to right and from top to bottom.

The graphical notation of an association also allows an optional *role name* and an optional *multiplicity specification* to be attached to either of the classes involved in the association. In Figure 2.5, *adviser* and *advisee* are the role names associated

Figure 2.4

UML notation for association relationship.

Figure 2.5

Class diagram: association relationships.

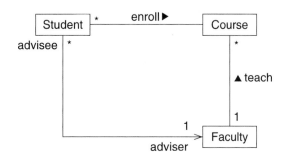

with `Faculty` and `Student`, respectively, in the association between `Faculty` and `Student`. The role name may also have an optional visibility designator, that is, +, #, ~, or -.

The multiplicity specification is a comma-separated sequence of integer intervals. An integer interval can be one of the following:

l..u　specifies a closed, that is, inclusive, range of integers from the lower bound *l* to the upper bound *u*. Both the lower and upper bound are integer literals. The upper bound may also be the asterisk character (*), which indicates an unlimited upper bound.

i　specifies a singleton range that contains integer *i*, which is an integer literal.

*　specifies the entire nonnegative integer range: 0, 1, 2, 3, . . .

Here are some examples of multiplicity specifications:

`0..*`	0 or more
`1..*`	1 or more
`2..5`	2 to 5
`2, 5, 7`	2, 5, and 7
`1, 3, 5..*`	1, 3, and 5 or more

In Figure 2.5, the *enroll* association is many-to-many; that is, a student may enroll in any number of courses, and a course may have any number of students enrolled in it. The *teach* association is one-to-many; that is, each course has only one faculty member to teach it, but a faculty member may teach any number of courses. The *adviser–advisee* association is also one-to-many; that is, each student has one adviser, but an adviser may have any number of advisees.

The graphical notation of an association may also indicate the *navigation* of the association. If there is a direct or indirect reference from class C1 to class C2, then it is navigable from C1 to C2. An association may be navigable in one or both directions. By default, an association is assumed to be navigable in both directions. If an association is only navigable in one direction, it must be explicitly shown with a navigation arrow at the end of the association link pointing in the direction that is navigable. The navigation arrows should not be confused with the name direction arrow. They are independent. In the class diagram shown in Figure 2.5, the *adviser–advisee* association is only navigable from an advisee to an adviser, not from an adviser to advisees.

2.2.3   Aggregation and Composition

Aggregation is a special form of association. It represents the *has-a* or *part-whole* relationship. Aggregation is simply a structural relationship that distinguishes the whole, that is, the aggregate class, from the parts, that is, the component class. Aggregation does not imply any relationship in the lifetime of the aggregate and the components. A stronger form of aggregation is called *composition*, which implies exclusive ownership of the component class by the aggregate class. Under composition, the lifetime of the components is entirely included in the lifetime of the aggregate. In class diagrams, aggregation is indicated by a hollow diamond at the end of the aggregate class. The composition relationship is indicated by a filled diamond; see Figure 2.6. It is obvious that the aggregation diamond may only appear at one end of the link. Since aggregation is a special form of association, the discussions on the names, multiplicity, and navigation of association also apply to aggregation.

Figure 2.7 shows an example of the aggregation relationships among the University, College, Department, Faculty, and Student classes. All relationships shown in the diagram are aggregation relationships, since

■   a student is a part of a department.
■   a faculty member is a part of a department.
■   a department is a part of a college.
■   a college is a part of a university.

However, the nature of the first two part-of relationships is somewhat different from the last two part-of relationships. A student or a faculty member may exist without being a part of a department. The lifetimes of the students and the faculty members are independent from the lifetime of the department to which they belong. On the other hand, a department exclusively belongs to a college, and a college exclusively belongs

Figure 2.6

UML notations for aggregation relationships.

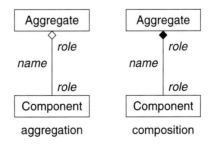

Figure 2.7

Class diagram: aggregation relationship.

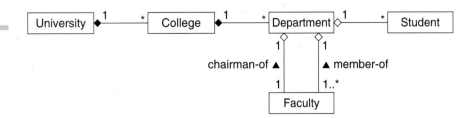

to a university. The lifetime of a department may not exceed the lifetime of the college it belongs to, and the lifetime of a college may not exceed the lifetime of the university it belongs to. The part-of relationships between a university and its colleges and departments are stronger than the part-of relationships between a department and its students and faculty members. The former are considered composition relationships.

The distinction between aggregation and composition is entirely conceptual. There is no distinction in how aggregation and composition relationships are implemented. The design models in this book will not distinguish aggregation and composition, and only the aggregation notation will be used.

2.2.4 Dependency

Dependency is a relationship between entities such that the proper operation of one entity depends on the presence of the other entity, and changes in one entity would affect the other entity. A common form of dependency is the *use* relation among classes. In other words, class C1 depends on class C2 if C1 uses C2 in places such as the parameters, local variables, or return types of its methods. The graphical notation for dependency relationships is a dashed line with an arrow pointing in the direction of dependency, as shown in Figure 2.8.

The class diagram shown in Figure 2.9 illustrates the dependency relationship. The Registrar class has a number of methods for adding and removing courses in the course schedules and enrolling and dropping students in courses. These methods take parameters that are instances of CourseSchedule, Course, and Student classes. Therefore, the Registrar class uses, that is, depends on, CourseSchedule, Course, and Student classes.

Figure 2.8

UML notations for dependency relationships.

Class1 depends on Class2.

Figure 2.9

Class diagram: dependency relationships.

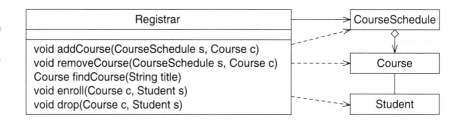

2.3 MODELING DYNAMIC BEHAVIOR

Class diagrams model the structure of software systems in terms of *static* relationships among classes. However, another important aspect of software systems—*dynamic behavior*—involves the interactions among objects and the ordering of events and actions related to the object. In this section, we discuss two of the commonly used graphical notations in UML for modeling the dynamic behavior of software systems: the *sequence diagram* and the *state diagram*.

2.3.1 Sequence Diagram

Sequence diagrams depict object interaction by highlighting the time ordering of method invocations. The notations for sequence diagrams are shown in Figure 2.10. The y-axis of a sequence diagram represents time in the downward direction. The objects that participate in the interaction are laid out on the *x*-axis represented by columns. The object that initiates the interaction is usually placed in the leftmost column, with increasingly subordinate objects shown on the right. The object represented by each column is shown at the top of the column, and a vertical dashed line shows the lifeline of the object. The rectangular bars over the lifeline indicate the focus of control of the object, that is, the duration in which one of the methods of the object is being executed. The solid horizontal links indicate the creation of new objects or invocation of methods. The dashed horizontal links indicate the return of method invocations. Method invocations are arranged in ascending order of time vertically downward.

Figure 2.10

UML notations for sequence diagrams.

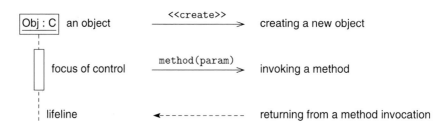

Figure 2.11

A sequence diagram: printing a document.

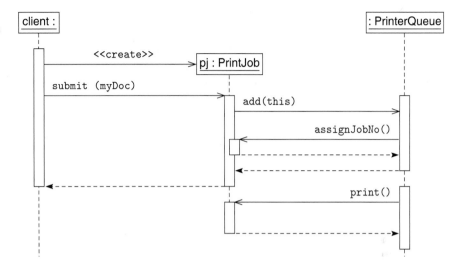

Figure 2.11 shows a sequence diagram that depicts the flow of execution when a client issues a request to print a document. It indicates the following sequence of method invocations:

1. An object client creates an instance of PrintJob.
2. The object client invokes the submit() method of PrintJob to print a documentation (myDoc).
3. The PrintJob object adds itself to a queue, which is an instance of Printer-Queue.
4. The PrinterQueue object invokes the assignJobNo() method of PrintJob to assign a number to the new print job being added to the queue.
5. The assignJobNo() method returns.
6. The add() method returns.
7. The submit() method returns.
8. Sometime later, when the print job becomes the first in the printer queue, the print() method of PrintJob is invoked to print to document.
9. The print() method returns.

2.3.2 State Diagram

State diagrams depict the flow of control using the concepts of *states* and *transitions*. State diagrams are generalizations of the traditional *finite state machines* (FSM). A *state* is a condition or situation in the life of an object during which it satisfies some condition, performs some actions, or waits for some events. A *transition* is a relationship between two states indicating that an object in the first state (the source state) will perform certain actions and enter the second state (the destination state) when a specified event occurs and certain conditions are satisfied. The graphical notations for the basic elements in state diagrams are shown in Figure 2.12. States are drawn as round-cornered rectangles. Each state has a name. Transitions are shown as links from the source states to the target states. The labels of transitions are in the following form:

[*Event-List*] [[*Guard*]] [/*Action*]

An *event* is an occurrence of a stimulus that can trigger a state transition. Each transition is labeled with a list of the names of the events that can trigger the transition. When there is more than one event name in the label of a transition, the event names are separated by vertical bars (|), for example, $e_1|e_2| \ldots |e_n$. When a transition has no triggering events, it is triggered without an event, and it is known as a *triggerless transition*. The label of a transition may also include a *guard* and an *action*. The guard in the label of a transition is a boolean condition that must evaluate to true for the transition to take place. The action in the label of a transition specifies the action to be carried out when the transition is made.

The life of an object begins in a designated *initial state*. It follows a series of transitions to reach various states. The life of the object ends when it reaches a *final state*. The following are the rules for state transitions:

1. If there is a triggerless transition originating from the current state, the transition is triggered and the object enters the destination state of the triggerless transition.
2. Otherwise, the object waits for some events to occur. When an event occurs,
   a. if there is a transition originating from the current state such that
      (1) the event that occurred matches one of the events specified in the label of the transition, and
      (2) all the guards specified in the label of the transition evaluate to true, then the transition is triggered, the action specified in the label of the transition, if any, is performed, and the object enters the destination state of the transition.
   b. Otherwise, the object remains in the current state.

Figure 2.12

UML notations for state diagram.

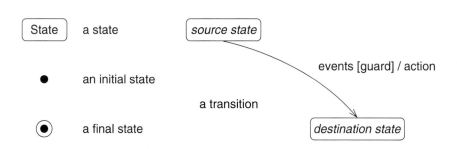

State — a state

● — an initial state

◉ — a final state

a transition

events [guard] / action

Each state may also have an *entry action* and an *exit action*, which can be specified as follows:

entry /*Action*$_1$

exit /*Action*$_2$

When an object enters a state, the entry action associated with the state, if any, is performed. When the object leaves a state, the exit action associated with the state, if any, is performed.

Nested State Diagram   In state diagrams, states can be nested, known as *composite states* or *superstates*. The notations for the nested states are shown in Figure 2.13. The nested states, or *substates*, can be either sequential or concurrent. A composite state with sequential substates contains a nested state diagram. When a transition enters such a composite state, it enters the initial state of the nested state diagram. At a given moment, an object is in exactly one of the substates. For example, in Figure 2.13(a), an object can be in either state S11 or S12. A composite state with concurrent substates is used to model concurrency. Each concurrent substate contains a state diagram. When a transition enters such a composite state, it simultaneously enters the initial states of the state diagrams in each concurrent substate. At a given moment, an object is simultaneously in one of the states of the nested state diagram in each concurrent substate. For example, in Figure 2.13(b), an object can simultaneously be in one of states S21a or S21b *and* one of states S22a or S22b. When a transition originates from a composite state, it means that the transition may originate from any of the states enclosed in the composite state.

Figure 2.14 is a state diagram describing the operation of a cellular phone. Operation starts in the initial state, which leads to the Off state. The *power-on* event triggers a transition that leads to the On state. As the On state is a composite state, the cellular phone enters the initial state of the state diagram nested in the On state, which leads to the Standby state. The transition labeled *power-off* originates from

Figure 2.13

UML notations for nested states in a state diagram.

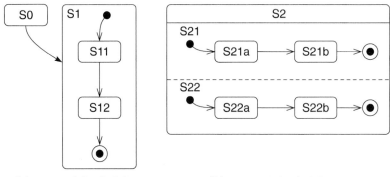

(a) sequential substates   (b) concurrent substates

Figure 2.14

A state diagram: operation of a cellular phone.

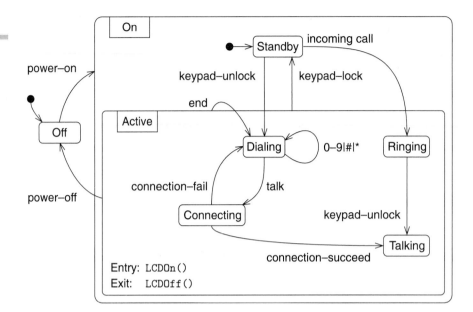

another composite Active state. Hence this transition may originate from any of the states inside the Active state. Note that the Active state has both entry and exit actions associated with it. Thus, whenever the cellular phone enters the Active state, the LCDOn() method (that is, the entry action) is invoked to turn on the LCD screen, and whenever the cellular phone leaves the Active state, the LCDOff() method (that is, the exit action) is invoked to turn off the LCD screen to conserve the battery. The state diagram nested inside the Active state depicts the flow of both making a call and receiving a call. To make a call requires the following sequence of events:

- From the Standby state, unlock the pad (the *keypad-unlock* event) to enter the Dialing state in Active.
- In the Dialing state, dial the phone number by using the number keys (0–9) or # or *, and the cellular phone remains in the Dialing state.
- From the Dialing state, push the `talk` key (the *talk* event) to enter the Connecting state.
- From the Connecting state, if the connection succeeds (the *connection-succeed* event), the cellular phone enters the Talking state. If the connection fails (the *connection-fail* event), the cellular phone returns to the Dialing state.

To receive a call requires the following sequence of events:

- From the Standby state, an incoming call (the *incoming-call* event) triggers a transition that leads to the Ringing state in Active.
- From the Ringing state, push the `talk` key (the *talk* event) to enter the Talking state.

Note that the transition labeled *end* originates from the composite state Active. Hence from any state in the Active state, pushing the end key (the *end* event) triggers this transition, and the cellular phone enters the Dialing state. Similarly, from any state in the Active state, locking the keypad (the *keypad-lock* event) triggers the transition labeled *keypad-lock*, which leads to the Standby state.

2.4 MODELING REQUIREMENTS WITH USE CASES

Use cases and use case diagrams are used for modeling the requirements of the systems to be developed and for deriving object-oriented models from the requirements. Although use cases are not essential in object-oriented software development, they provide important links between requirements and object-oriented models. Therefore, use cases and use case diagrams play an important role in the RUP and UML.

2.4.1 Terms and Concepts

Use cases describe the externally observable behavior of system functions, in the form of interactions between the system to be developed and the external entities, known as the *actors*, of the system. Each actor represents a role played by a set of external entities that interact with the system. Actors may represent roles played by human users of the system or by other systems. Use cases are intended to describe *what* the system does, not *how* the system does it.

Each use case has a name and a set of scenarios. One of the scenarios is the main scenario. Optionally, a use case may have any number of alternative and exceptional scenarios. Each scenario is a sequence of interactions between the actors and the system. The main scenario describes the normal flow of events and the outcome of the use case; that is, it describes what will happen when all the preconditions are met. Sometimes, there are a number of alternative flows of events and outcomes that are also considered to be normal. These alternative flows of events can be described as alternative scenarios that complement the main scenario. The exceptional scenarios describe the flows of events and the outcomes when certain preconditions of the normal scenarios are not met, or when errors or exceptions occur during the normal flow of events.

Scenarios of use cases are usually described informally. Following are some of the commonly used formats for describing a scenario:

- A paragraph that describes the flow of events in the scenario
- A two-column table with one column describing the input events generated by actors, and the other column describing the response produced by the system (see example shown in Figure 2.19).

2.4.2 Use Case Diagrams

A *use case diagram* consists of

- use cases,
- actors, and
- relationships among actors and use cases.

The graphical notation for use cases and actors is shown in Figure 2.15. Several types of relationships can be represented in use case diagrams:

- The extension, or generalization, relationship among actors.
- The association relationship between actors and use cases.
- The dependency relationship among use cases. Furthermore, there are two types of dependencies among use cases: *include* and *extend*.

The extension relationship among actors is similar to the extension relationship among classes. An actor representing a general group of users can be extended, or specialized, by another actor representing a more specialized group of users. For actors a_1 and a_2, a_1 extends a_2 means that the set of external entities represented by a_1 is a subset of the set of external entities represented by a_2. Let us consider the example in Figure 2.16, in which the actor User represents the set of all users of the system to be developed, while the actors Student, Faculty, and Administrator each represent a more specific set of the users of the system, that is, the set of students, faculty, and administrators, respectively. The sets of students, faculty, and administrators are all subsets of the set of all users, hence, the extension relationship among the actors shown in Figure 2.16.

Actors are related to use cases via the association relationship. An actor is associated with a use case if the actor is a participant in the interactions described in one of the scenarios of the use case.

There are two types of dependencies among use cases: *include* and *extend*. For use cases c_1 and c_2,

- c_1 includes c_2 means that use case c_2 is part of use case c_1, and
- c_2 extends c_1 means that use case c_2 is a special case of use case c_1.

Figure 2.15

UML notations for actors and use cases.

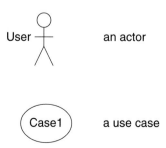

User — an actor

Case1 — a use case

Figure 2.16

Extension relation-
ships among ac-
tors.

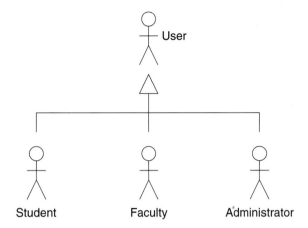

Let us consider the use case diagram shown in Figure 2.17. Association relationships between the actors and the use cases indicate that

- a student may participate in use case Check grades.
- a faculty member may participate in use cases Get Roster and Enter Grades.
- an administrator may participate in use case Verify grades.
- any user may participate in use case Validate User.

Furthermore, the include relationship indicates that use case Validate User is part of
all the other use cases shown in the diagram. The extension relationship indicates that
use case Enter Grades is a special case of use case Get Roster, since entering grades
requires getting the roster with an editable grade field.

Figure 2.17

Dependency rela-
tionships among
use cases.

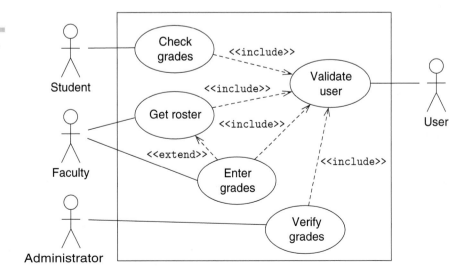

2.5   CASE STUDY: AN E-BOOKSTORE

In this case study, we develop an object-oriented model for an *online bookstore* to illustrate some of the activities in the object-oriented development approach.

2.5.1   Conceptualization

The conceptualization phase is not intended to establish *complete* system requirements. Rather it is to establish the *vision* and *core* requirements of the system. A prototype could be developed as a proof-of-concept demonstration and to validate important assumptions.

The core requirements of the e-bookstore are to allow its customers to browse and order books, music CDs, and computer software through the Internet. The main functionalities of the system are to provide information about the titles it carries to help customers make purchasing decisions; handle customer registration, order processing, and shipping; and support management of the system, such as adding, deleting, and updating titles, updating customer information, and the like.

This core requirements statement allows us to start the analysis phase. Many aspects of the requirements need further elaboration and refinement, which can be done in later iterations.

2.5.2   Use Cases

Based on the core requirements of the system, we can start to identify the main actors and the key use cases. In an iterative development process, the initial set of actors and use cases rarely needs to be complete or exhaustive. It is common that more actors and use cases will emerge in later iterations when the requirements are further elaborated and become more complete. It is also common that the actors and use cases will be extended in later iterations. The initial set of actors and use cases should focus on the main functions to be provided by the system and deal with the most common scenarios. The goals of the initial use case analysis should be as follows:

1. To define the key functions and main scenarios, so that these key function scenarios can be implemented in early iterations and secondary functions and exceptional scenarios can be deferred to later iterations.
2. To identify the actors and use cases to be elaborated or extended in later iterations.

The initial use case analysis of the e-bookstore results in the use case diagram shown in Figure 2.18. Clearly one of the key actors of the system is the Customer, and one of the key use cases is Shop, which we will elaborate later. A related use case also involving the customers is Registration, which is a necessary step before customers can start shopping. From the core requirements of the system, it is also easy to see that another important aspect of the e-bookstore is the management of the

Figure 2.18

Use case diagram of e-bookstore.

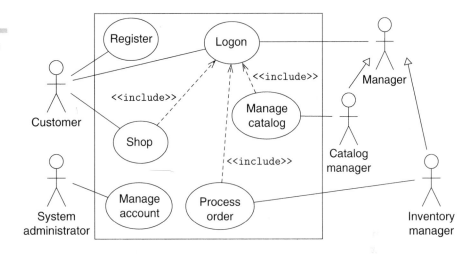

e-bookstore. Although we decide to focus on the customer side of the system first, it is also important to identify most of the important actors and use cases in the system early on. The elaboration and implementation of these use cases can be deferred to later iterations. The main actor for the management side is identified as Manager. However, it also appears that there are two categories of distinct management tasks: one deals with the management of the catalog of the merchandise offered by the e-bookstore, and the other deals with the management of the inventories and the processing of the orders. Therefore, we further identify two extended actors of Manager: Catalog Manager and Inventory Manager, which are associated with use cases corresponding to their main tasks: Manage Catalog and Process Order, respectively. A common function for both customers and managers is to log on to the system. So it is reasonable to define Logon as a separate use case that is included by other use cases involving customers or managers. The logon function also leads us to a function that is not explicitly specified but implied in the requirements, that is, the management of the accounts for both the customers and managers. Therefore, a new use case Manage Account is identified. Since the tasks of managing the accounts are distinct from all the other tasks, it is also reasonable to introduce a new actor, System Administrator, to be associated with the new use case.

The use case Shop will be the focus of the early iteration. Use case Shop is described in Figure 2.19. A use case usually has a precondition, which specifies the condition under which the use case is applicable. The main scenario of use case Shop is described using a two-column table, in which the left-hand column describes the input events generated by actors and the right-hand column describes the response produced by the system.

Figure 2.19

The scenarios of use case Shop.

<u>**Use Case: Shop**</u>

Actor: Customer

Precondition: The customer is already registered.

Main scenario:

Input Events from Actor Customer	System Events and Responses
Log on	Display a welcome message and request customer ID and password
Enter customer ID and password	Authenticate customer Customer authentication succeeds

Repeat the following until done:
    Search and browse titles
    Select a title to buy
	
	Show information about the titles
	Add the title to the shopping cart

Done with shopping and check out	Display shopping cart contents and shipping/billing addresses
Confirm order and payment method	Validate payment method
	Payment validation succeeds
	Process order, issue an electronic receipt, and notify warehouse for shipping
Log off	

Alternative scenario:
   The customer saves the shopping cart without checking out.

Exceptional scenario:
   Customer authentication fails; repeat the logon procedure.

Exceptional scenario:
   Payment validation fails; prompt the customer for new payment information.

2.5.3   Object Models

Identifying Classes

The first step in building an object model of the system is to identify the classes involved in the use cases. This step is perhaps one of the more perplexing tasks in object-oriented modeling. The questions are *What can be a class?* and *What features (that is, fields and methods) should a class have?*

The answers largely depend on the domain and the problem to be solved. The following are some simple guidelines. Classes represent entities, not actions, and can represent many different types of entities, including

- physical objects, such as equipment, devices, and products;
- people, such as students, faculty, and customers, and the roles they play;
- organizations, such as universities, companies, and departments;
- places, such as buildings, rooms, and seats;
- events, such as mouse clicks, service requests, and purchase orders; and
- concepts, such as multidimensional spaces, transactions, and weather maps.

Actions should be modeled as the methods of classes. A simple rule is that class names should be noun phrases and that method names should be verb phrases.

Only the classes and features of classes that are relevant to the problem to be solved need be included in the model. One of the most straightforward methods of identifying classes is the following:

- Underline the verbs and nouns in the description of the requirements and use cases.
- The nouns are the candidates for classes or attributes, and the verbs are the candidates for methods.

By identifying the nouns in the core requirements of the e-bookstore, we can at least identify the following classes:

Class	Description
EBookstore	The entire system
Customer	The customers of the e-bookstore
Book	Books, a type of merchandise offered by the e-bookstore
MusicCD	Music CDs, a type of merchandise offered by the e-bookstore
Software	Computer software, a type of merchandise offered by the e-bookstore

Furthermore, by analyzing the description of the use case Shop, we can identify the following additional classes:

Class	Description
ShoppingCart	A temporary list of titles that a customer intends to buy
Order	An order placed by a customer
Address	Customer's address

Identifying the Features of Classes

In this phase, we try to identify all the relevant fields and methods for each class that we have identified from the use case analysis. For example, for the e-bookstore, let's start with the Customer classes. We identify the fields by analyzing the requirements and the use cases to find the relevant fields associated with customers.

Customer
name customerID password shippingAddress billingAddress

The list of fields may still be incomplete, but it is a start. As we go through more iterations, additional fields that belong to the Customer class should become clear. At this stage, it isn't necessary to completely specify the type or visibility of each field. The key issue here is what fields a class should have.

The fields shippingAddress and billingAddress in Customer represent addresses. This observation naturally leads to a new class Address. The shipping-Address and billingAddress fields are both instances of the Address class. To identify the fields of the Address class, we simply rely on common sense and knowledge of actual forms of addresses.

Address
street city state country postalCode

Now, let us move on to classes representing merchandise items, including books, music CDs, and computer software.

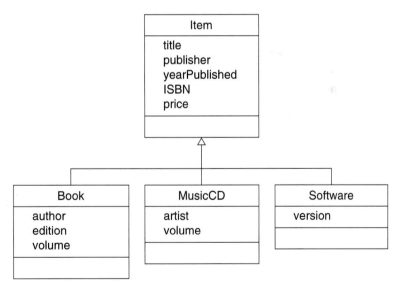

Obviously, some fields are common to all three classes. The commonalities are not coincidental because when calculating the total price of a mixed order of books, CDs, and software, each item should be treated the same way. The three classes then should be subclasses of a common superclass, and the common fields of the three classes should belong to their common superclass. Thus, another way of identifying classes is by identifying the commonalities among existing classes and extracting the commonalities to a common superclass. This process is known as *generalization*. The following are the revised classes after extracting the common fields to the Item superclass:

Identifying Relationships among Classes

Now, let us consider the ShoppingCart class, which seems simply to contain a set of items. However, some customers might want to order multiple copies of the same item. A shopping cart therefore should be able to represent the quantity of each item ordered. Thus, an auxiliary class OrderItem is needed. Each instance of OrderItem contains the item and the quantity ordered. An instance of ShoppingCart contains a set of instances of OrderItem.

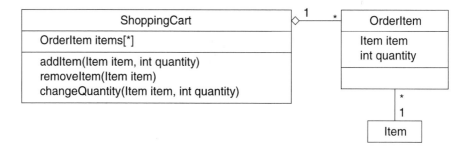

The Order class represents orders placed by customers. Each order contains the set of items that have been ordered, which are stored in the shopping cart, along with the information about the customer, various fees, the total amount of the order, and the payment method information. The Payment class represents information on methods of payment, such as credit card type, card number, expiration date, and so on.

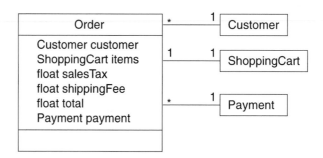

Now, let us consider the main class EBookstore, which represents the entire system. Obviously, the system has to keep records of a variety of things, including all the items on sale, all the customers, and all the orders that have been placed. The relationships among the classes identified so far are shown in the following diagram.

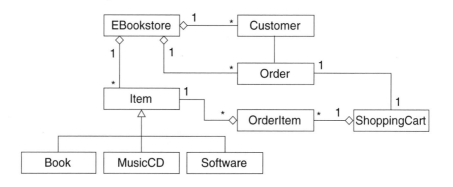

This step completes the *initial* version of the object model of the e-bookstore. An initial object model captures the most important and obvious aspects of the system but is often incomplete. Several iterations are usually necessary to derive a complete object model. A useful technique for deriving complete analysis models is through the analysis of responsibilities of classes and collaboration among classes. The idea is to enumerate and analyze all the use case scenarios, assign responsibilities to classes, and identify the collaborators of each class. This usually leads to identifying new responsibilities for existing classes or identifying new classes. The process continues until all the responsibilities have been assigned and all the collaborators have been identified.

In the e-bookstore example, additional responsibilities and classes can be identified by analyzing additional use cases and scenarios, such as new customer registration, and by elaborating the requirements for inventory management, order processing, and so on. The derivation of a more complete object model of the e-bookstore is left as an exercise.

CHAPTER SUMMARY

- Object-oriented modeling involves describing the essential and relevant aspects of the problem domain and the problems to be solved in terms of objects, classes, and relationships among them.
- An *object* represents anything in the real world that can be distinctly identified. An *object* has an identity, a state, and a behavior. A *class* represents a set of objects with similar characteristics and behavior. These objects are called the *instances* of the class. A *class* characterizes the structure of states and behaviors that are shared by all its instances.
- The fundamental principles of object-oriented development are modularity, abstraction, encapsulation, and levels of abstraction. Their purpose is to reduce complexity and enhance flexibility.
- The basic criteria for decomposition are two well-known but elusive concepts in software development: cohesion and coupling. Cohesion refers to the functional relatedness of the entities within a module. Coupling indicates the interdependency among different modules.
- Class diagrams are the most common diagrams for modeling the static structures of object-oriented software systems and various types of relations among the classes. The relationships among classes and interfaces depicted in class diagrams include inheritance (which includes extension and implementation), association (which includes aggregation and composition), and dependency.
- The dynamic behaviors of software systems can be modeled by sequence diagrams and state diagrams. The sequence diagrams depict object interaction by highlighting the time ordering of method invocations. The state diagrams depict the flow of control using the concepts of states and transitions.

- Use cases and use case diagrams are used for modeling the requirements of the systems to be developed and for deriving object-oriented models from the requirements. They provide important links between requirements and object-oriented models. Use cases describe the externally observable behavior of a system function, in the form of interactions between the system to be developed and the external entities, known as the actors of the system. Use cases are intended to describe what the system does, not how the system does it.

FURTHER READINGS

Booch, G. (1994). *Object-Oriented Analysis and Design with Applications*. Addison-Wesley.

Booch, G., J. Rumbaugh, and I. Jacobson (1999). *The Unified Modeling Language User Guide*. Addison-Wesley.

Fowler, M., and K. Scott (1997). *UML Distilled: Applying the Standard Object Modelling Language*. Addison-Wesley.

Larman, C. (2002). *Applying UML and Patterns*, 2nd ed. Prentice Hall.

OMG (2001). *OMG–Unified Modeling Language*, vol. 4, http://www.omg.org /uml

Rumbaugh, J., I. Jacobson, and G. Booch (1999). *The Unified Modeling Language Reference Manual*. Addison-Wesley.

EXERCISES

2.1 Based on your experience of using bank ATM machines, precisely model the behavior of an ATM machine using state diagrams. The state diagrams should describe at least the following scenarios:

- Cash deposit
- Cash withdrawal
- Checking account balance

2.2 Based on your experience of using portable music CD players, precisely model the behavior of a portable music CD player using state diagrams.

Develop an object-oriented model for each of the following systems described in Exercises 2.3–2.5.

a. Determine the actors and use cases of the system, and describe the relationships among them using use case diagrams.

b. Elaborate each of the use cases. Describe the scenarios in each of the use cases.

c. Identify the classes of the system, and describe the responsibilities and the features of each class.

d. Determine the relationships among the classes, and use class diagrams to depict these relationships.

2.3 An airline ticket reservation system. The system should allow a customer to specify the origin and destination of travel, preference on the departing and returning dates, the time of the day for departure, and the airline carriers. The system will display the availability and information of the flights matching the customer's requirements. The customer may then proceed to choose the flights, select the seats, and purchase the tickets.

2.4 A university online system. The system should allow students to browse courses offered by the university and the schedule. The students will be able to add and drop classes. The instructors will be able to get the roster of a class and enter grades for each student in the class.

2.5 An online discussion group similar to Yahoo! groups. Each discussion group consists of an owner or moderator and a number of members. Each member of the group may post messages, which may be sent to all the members in the group, and read messages posted by other members in the group. Users may create new groups or join existing groups.

CHAPTER 3

Introduction to Java

CHAPTER OVERVIEW

In this chapter, we discuss the key characteristics of Java and examine its run-time architecture. We use two very simple programs, an application and an applet, to illustrate the basic structure of Java programs and use of the Java development tools and environment.

Java is an object-oriented programming language that was developed by a research team led by James Gosling at Sun Microsystems. Java is suitable for developing a wide range of applications, including graphical user interfaces (GUIs) and multimedia, network and distributed applications, database and enterprise applications, and numerical computations. Java's popularity is due partly to the fact that it is largely based on proven technologies. Its key characteristics are that the language is

- *Object-oriented.* Java is one of the most recent in a family of object-oriented programming languages. It not only supports object-oriented programming in the strongest sense, as do Smalltalk and Objective-C, but it also prohibits many "bad" programming styles and practices.

- *Distributed.* Java is designed for developing distributed applications, which consist of multiple autonomous programs residing on different computers, or hosts, in a computer network and cooperating with one another. It provides a variety of mechanisms to support communication and interoperability for both server and client applications.

- *Platform independent.* The most unique characteristic of Java is that compiled Java programs can run on almost all platforms with functionally identical behavior. This capability makes Java an ideal choice for operating in heterogeneous networks, such as the Internet, and eliminates the need for porting programs to different platforms.

- *Secure.* The Java run-time environment can execute Java programs in a so-called *sandbox*, which consists of a limited set of resources on the host computer. Java programs can be strictly confined within the sandbox, so that a potentially malicious program cannot penetrate, compromise, or otherwise cause harm to the host computer. This capability is essential to distributed or Web-based applications, on both the client and server side.

From the software development perspective, Java is a superior programming language because it supports many features that facilitate the development of large-scale and reliable software systems. These include strong type checking, packages, exception handling, and automatic memory management (i.e., garbage collection). These features make software development using Java much more effective and manageable than using many other languages.

3.1 AN OVERVIEW OF THE JAVA 2 PLATFORM

The first official release of Java, JDK 1.0, took place in January 1996. Since then, there have been a number of major releases of Java, each of which offered significant enhancements and improvements to the preceding release. JDK 1.1 was released in February 1997. It introduced many significant changes from JDK 1.0, some of which are not backward compatible with JDK 1.0. Today, JDK 1.0 is obsolete, while JDK 1.1 remains at the core of the subsequent releases and is compatible with subsequent releases. A number of key technologies were introduced in JDK 1.1, including security and authentication, object serialization, remote method invocation (RMI), and Java beans. These technologies have become the foundation of many other technologies introduced in later releases. In many ways, JDK 1.1 was the coming of age for Java. One of the most significant milestones of Java was the release of the Java 2 Platform, that is, JDK 1.2, in December 1998 (Figure 3.1). The Java 2 Platform introduced three separate editions of Java: *Standard Edition (J2SE)*, *Enterprise Edition (J2EE)*, and *Micro Edition (J2ME)*.[1] Each Java platform edition defines a set of technologies

---

1. J2EE and J2ME were announced in December 1998 but were not released until June 1999 at the *JavaOne Developer Conference.*

Figure 3.1

The Java 2 Platform. (From Riggd et al. [2001]. Programming Wireless Devices with the Java 2 Platform, Micro Edition. Addison-Wesley.)

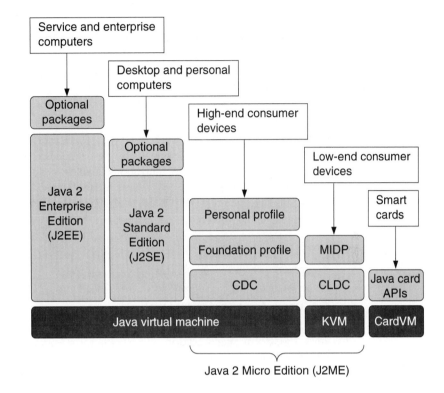

Java 2 Micro Edition (J2ME)

that aim at a particular category of computing devices: Java virtual machines that fit the type of computing device, libraries and Application Program Interfaces (APIs) specialized for the type of computing device, and tools for deployment and device configuration.

Java 2 Platform Standard Edition   The Java 2 Platform Standard Edition (J2SE) is for developing applications that run on desktop computers. Such computers usually have reasonably powerful processors with an adequate amount of memory and disk space and serve a single user.

J2SE includes the following components:

- Java virtual machine to execute Java programs.
- Development tools, including compiler, debugger, profiler, and documentation generator.
- The core APIs, including core language support, utilities, input and output, networking, preferences, collections, security, locale support, logging, Java beans, XML processing, and native interface.
- Graphical user interface (GUI) APIs, including AWT, Swing, two-dimensional graphics, and sound support.

- Integration APIs, including remote method invocation (RMI), database connectivity (JDBC), naming and directory services (JNDI), and common object request broker architecture (CORBA).
- Deployment tools: Java Web start, and Java plug-in.

This book primarily focuses on technologies in J2SE.

Java 2 Platform Enterprise Edition Java 2 Platform Enterprise Edition (J2EE) is for developing server applications that serve the needs of customers, suppliers, and employees of enterprises and organizations of all sizes. Such applications usually run on powerful servers and can serve a large number of users simultaneously.

J2EE is built on top of J2SE and is a superset of J2SE. It includes the following components in addition to the components in J2SE:

- Java servlets and Java server pages (JSP).
- Enterprise Java beans (EJB).
- E-mail and messaging services.
- Transaction management.

Java 2 Platform Micro Edition Java 2 Platform Micro Edition (J2ME) is for developing applications that run on small, resource-constrained devices, such as palmtop computers, cellular phones, and television set-top boxes. Compared to desktop computers, such devices usually have much less powerful processors, very limited memory space, and small screens.

J2ME defines two *configurations* to target two broad categories of devices:

- Connected Device Configuration (CDC) for high-end consumer electronic devices such as TV set-top boxes and automobile entertainment/navigation systems. Such devices usually have several megabytes of available memory with high-bandwidth network connections.
- Connected, Limited Device Configuration (CLDC) for low-end information devices such as PDAs and cellular phones. Such devices may have only a few hundred kilobytes of available memory with low-bandwidth, intermittent network connections.

Each configuration also defines a number of *profiles* to address the special needs of specific families of devices. One of the profiles in CDC is the Personal Profile, also known as Personal Java, which supports a subset of the class libraries supported by J2SE. One of the profiles in CLDC is the Mobile Information Device Profile (MIDP) for cellular phones.

A number of Java virtual machines are available on different types of devices including the KVM, the K-Virtual Machine, which runs on a number of PDAs and cell phones.

3.2 THE JAVA RUN-TIME ARCHITECTURE

Java is designed for distributed computing in a heterogeneous network environment, such as the Internet and the World Wide Web. The primary goals of Java's run-time architecture design are platform independence, security, and efficiency.

Platforms

The Internet is a heterogeneous, open, and self-organizing anarchy. It consists of a vast number of computers with different CPUs running different operating systems. The combination of the CPU and operating system of a computer is referred to as the *platform* of the computer,[2] which defines the key characteristics of the operating environment of that machine. Popular platforms include the Sun Sparc CPU with the Sun Solaris operating system (Sparc/Solaris); the Intel Pentium CPU with Linux operating system (Intel/Linux); the Intel Pentium CPU with the Microsoft Windows operating system (Intel/Windows); and the PowerPC CPU with the MacIntosh operating system (PowerPC/MacOS).

Programs usually are *platform specific;* that is, a program developed and compiled for one platform will not automatically run on a different platform, unless the two platforms are *compatible* or one platform can emulate the other.[3] Most of the time, when a program needs to run on different platforms, special versions of the program must be developed and compiled for each environment. Converting a program to run on a different platform is called *porting*. In general, porting is a nontrivial task. One of Java's advantages is that it is platform independent; Java programs are designed to run on different platforms without porting.

Security

Owing to the open nature of the Internet, computers connected to the Internet are all susceptible to attacks from malicious programs in a wide variety of forms. An attacker who manages to break into a computer could access or modify data, eavesdrop on messages including e-mails and online transactions using credit cards, or even cause irrecoverable damage to the software and hardware on the computer.

A completely secure but open environment is unattainable. However, some effective methods in network technology and cryptography have been developed to reduce significantly the risk of security breaches. The Java run-time environment is designed to prevent potential security breaches while running Java programs on both the client and server machines.

---

2. Sometimes, the phrases *hardware platform* and *software platform* are used to refer to the CPU and the operating system of the computer, respectively.
3. There are a number of DOS/Windows emulators for MacOS and Solaris.

3.2.1   Program Execution Models

There are two conventional models for executing programs: compilation and interpretation.

Compilation

In compilation, a *compiler* translates, or compiles, the source code of a program into machine code, allowing the program to be executed directly by the operating systems and the hardware. The compilation approach is invariably used in programming languages intended for developing large-scale, efficient, and reliable systems, such as C, C++, Ada, and Eiffel. The compilation approach has several important advantages:

- Modern compilers perform extensive static analysis, such as *strong type checking* and *dataflow analysis*, to detect many potential errors in programs at compile time.
- Modern compilers apply sophisticated optimization techniques, such as *common expression extraction* and *loop strength reduction*, before generating machine code. Optimization produces efficient code and eliminates the need for hand optimization, so programmers can focus on the functionality and maintainability of the programs, not their efficiency.
- Executing machine code generated by compilers is far more efficient than interpreting source code directly.
- For commercial software vendors, software can be delivered to customers in binary executable form, thus protecting the source code as a trade secret.

The main deficiency of the compilation approach is that the executables are platform dependent. Two options are available for allowing a program to run on different platforms, but neither one is appealing. The first option is to port and compile the source code for each platform. However, porting source code to different platforms is tedious, time-consuming, and error-prone. In addition, the number of different platforms is potentially large, and porting to all of them may not be economically feasible. This approach is adopted for the widely available Netscape browser, which is mostly written in C and ported to every major platform.

The second option is to provide source code and porting instructions to allow customers to port programs themselves to the platforms they use. This approach shifts the burden to the customers and causes the original developer to lose control over software quality and compatibility. This approach also exposes the source code to outsiders. However, it is often adopted for noncommercial or open-source software products, such as the Linux operating system. There are large-scale and industrial-strength software systems that have been ported to different platforms in this fashion.

Interpretation

In interpretation, an *interpreter* directly parses and executes the source code of a program without generating machine code. The main advantage of the interpretation approach is its quick turnaround of edit–run cycles while developing the code.

Figure 3.2

**Execution of Java
programs.**

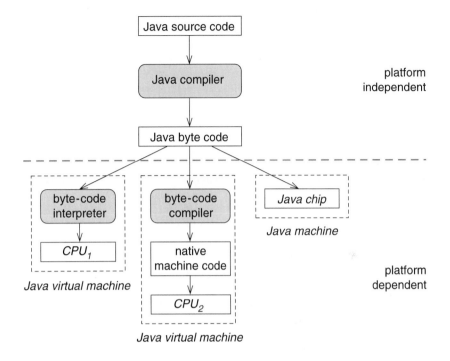

Thus the interpretation approach is often adopted for programming languages used for prototyping, or *rapid application development* (RAD), such as BASIC, LISP, and Smalltalk.[4] This technique requires no compilation, and errors can be discovered only at run time. The interpretation approach is platform independent because programs exist only in their source form. However, software products developed with interpretive languages must be delivered as source code. The main disadvantages of the interpretation approach are the loss of static analysis and code optimization and the much slower execution speeds than those generally achieved with compiled executables.

3.2.2   Java Virtual Machine

Neither of the conventional approaches to program execution can accomplish platform independence and efficiency. Java adopts a different approach to executing programs, which is a compromise between the conventional compilation and interpretation approaches, as illustrated in Figure 3.2. Java programs are executed in two stages.

---

4. Some of these languages also have compilers. For example, Microsoft Visual BASIC includes both an interpreter and a compiler.

Stage 1—Compilation of the Source Code to Byte-Code

Java is a compiled language. However, unlike the conventional compilers, the Java compiler compiles the source code to the machine code of the *Java virtual machine* (JVM) [Lindholm and Yellin 1996]. The JVM is an abstraction of the CPU of a real computer. It shares many common characteristics of a real CPU and thus can be implemented on a real CPU in a relatively straightforward way. The machine code of the JVM is known as *byte-code*.

Stage 2—Execution of Byte-Code

Byte-code is platform independent and can be executed on different platforms. There are three ways of executing Java byte-code:

1. *Interpretation.* On a given platform, an interpreter of the Java virtual machine interprets the JVM instructions and executes them.[5] This approach is adopted in original JVM from Sun, known as the classic JVM.
2. *JIT compilation.* On a given platform, a *Just-in-Time* (JIT) *compiler* compiles the Java byte-code to the native machine code on the fly and then executes the native machine code. Most modern JVMs support JIT compilation.
3. *Direct execution.* Special platforms can be built by using *Java chips*, which use Java byte-code as their native machine code. On such platforms, Java byte-code can be executed directly without a compiler or interpreter. Java chips are most commonly used in embedded electronic devices, such as TV set-top boxes, personal digital assistants (PDA), mobile information devices (MID), and cellular phones.

The Java execution model essentially maintains all the advantages of the compilation approach and accomplishes platform independence. The execution of byte-code is far more efficient than the direct interpretation of source code, but it still is not as efficient as the direct execution of native machine code.[6] With further improvements in byte-code optimization and compilation, as well as improvements in the JVM, the efficiency of Java will approach that of compilation languages targeting native machine code, such as C++.

Java Byte-Code

Java byte-code refers to the instructions of the Java virtual machine. A JVM instruction consists of a 1-byte *opcode*, short for operation code (hence the name byte-code), and zero or more *operands*, which are the parameters of the instruction. Operands

---

5. Sometimes, we simply use the term *Java virtual machine* to refer to the interpreter of the Java virtual machine.

6. Java wasn't the first to be based on this approach. P-code for PASCAL developed at the University of California at San Diego in the late 1970s was the first platform-independent, or *portable*, intermediate code for high-level languages. A few other languages, such as Emacs LISP, also compile source code to byte-code.

vary in length, and the number and lengths of the operands are determined by the opcode.

opcode(1-byte)
operand₁
operand₂
...

The core of the JVM involves a loop that can be described roughly as follows:

```
do {
    fetch the opcode byte of the current instruction;
    fetch the operands, depending on the value of the opcode byte;
    execute the instruction;
} while ( not done );
```

The JVM executes byte-code much as a simple reduced-instruction-set computer (RISC) CPU does, using several 32-bit registers.

- The pc (program counter) register contains the address of the next instruction to be executed.
- The optop register points to the top of the operand stack.
- The vars register points to a set of local variables of the current method.
- The frame register points to the execution environment structure.

The JVM also uses a garbage-collected heap to store all objects at run time.

The JVM instructions take operands from the operand stack, operate on them, and return the results to the stack. The operand stack is 32 bits wide. The JVM instructions perform the following functions:

- Stack manipulation
- Array management
- Arithmetic and logical operations
- Method invocation and return
- Exception handling
- Synchronization of multiple threads

A detailed specification of the JVM and the format of the .class file are presented in Lindholm and Yellin [1996].

Applications and Applets

We will first deal with two types of Java programs: *applications* (app for short) and *applets*. An application is a full-fledged program with full access to system resources. An applet is a program embedded in a Web page with restricted access to system resources to prevent security breaches to the host that runs the applet.

A Java application must be explicitly invoked, like any other program, by issuing a command on the command line or selecting a command from a menu. Therefore, an app can be invoked only by an authorized user of a host, unless the security of the host has already been compromised. Java imposes no restrictions on the behavior of apps and their access to the host environment. Presumably, authorized users are responsible for the consequences of executing applications.

Applets are embedded in Web pages and are invoked automatically when the Web pages containing the applets are loaded by Java-enabled browsers. Most of the time, a user is unaware of the contents and behavior of the applets embedded in a Web page before it is loaded in a browser. Thus, ensuring that executing applets will not compromise the security of the host on which the browser and the applet are running is imperative.

Security of JVM

Java virtual machine provides several layers of defense against potential security attacks through applets.

Shielded memory addresses: The Java language does not allow direct manipulation of memory addresses. There is no way for someone to access a specific memory cell or forge a pointer to an address. Memory allocation and deallocation are handled automatically and transparently by the JVM at run time.

Verification of byte-code: The JVM enforces *verification* of the byte-code before it is executed. Verification involves looking for any improper structures and control flows in the byte-code, any violation of access restrictions, and any violation of the type system. The purpose of the verification is to ensure that the byte-code is the output of a legitimate Java compiler, is generated from a consistent version of the source code, and has not been tampered with.

Run-time security manager: While executing an applet, the JVM consults a *security manager* whenever a potentially insecure operation is about to be performed. The security manager decides whether to allow the operation. The security manager is customizable to allow implementation of different security policies. In fact, browsers from different vendors implement slightly different security policies.

The security policies enforced by the security manager are configurable. Commonly implemented security policies include the following restrictions on applets:

- An applet usually is not allowed to read or write files on the host that is executing it. Some browsers allow certain exceptions.
- An applet is not allowed to communicate with hosts other than the one that it comes from.
- An applet is not allowed to start other programs, execute operating system commands, or inquire about certain system properties of the host.

These Java security measures form the so-called *sandbox*, within which all applets are confined. McGraw and Felton [1997] discuss the security issues involving Java applets in detail. Schneier [1996] gives an excellent general introduction to cryptography and computer security.

3.3 GETTING STARTED WITH JAVA

In this section, we present two simple Java programs—an app and an applet—to illustrate the basic structures of Java programs and the fundamentals of compiling and running Java programs.

3.3.1 A Simple Java Application

As the Internet has reached almost everywhere on Earth, the next logical step would be an interplanetary Internet. NASA is planning to have the first Internet host beyond planet Earth online early in the twenty-first century. Imagine how exciting it would be to receive a greeting from a close neighbor—Venus.

EXAMPLE 3.1   The "Hello from Venus!" Application.

PURPOSE

To illustrate the basic structure of Java programs.

DESCRIPTION

This application displays a greeting message: *Hello from Venus!* The message is in plain text and is written to the standard output (that is, the command console from which the application is invoked).

SOLUTION

Assuming that you have installed the Java Development Kit on your system, here are the steps to build and run the Java application.

1. Type in and save the following Java source code in a file named `Hello.java`.

"Hello from Venus!" application: `Hello.java`

```java
// Filename: Hello.java
/**
 * A Java app that prints the message: "Hello from Venus!"
 */
public class Hello {
  public static void main (String[] args) {
    System.out.println ("Hello from Venus!");
    /* System.out refers to the standard output */
  }
}
```

2. Compile the Java source code, using the Java compiler `javac`:[7]

```
venus% javac Hello.java
```

If the compilation is successful, a file named `Hello.class` will be generated. This is the Java byte-code file.

3. Execute the application by invoking the Java virtual machine `java`:

```
venus% java Hello
Hello from Venus!
```

Note that the argument of `java` is the class name, not the file name, that is, without the extension `.java` or `.class`. ▪

Basic Structure of Programs

The "Hello from Venus!" app illustrates two essential elements of Java programs:

1. A program—application or applet—comprises one or more classes. In this case, the program comprises a single class named `Hello`.

2. An application must contain a class that includes the `main()` method. Similar to the `main()` function of C and C++ programs, the `main()` method is the entry point of a Java application. The `main()` method must be declared as shown in Example 3.1.

```
public static void main (String[] args) {
    ⟨body of the main() method⟩
}
```

In this case, class `Hello` has only one method—the `main()` method. (See Section 4.4.5 [p. 113] for discussion of the `main()` method.)

The `main()` method of the `Hello` class simply prints out the following message to the console, or the standard output:

```
Hello from Venus!
```

`System.out` refers to the standard output. The `println()` method prints out its argument as a string with a new-line character appended to the end.

Source Files

Java programs are stored in *files*. Unlike many other languages, Java enforces certain rules about how classes should be placed in files and how files should be named. A simplified version of the rules is as follows:

▪ All Java source files must have the extension `.java`.

---

7. Throughout this book, `venus%` is used to stand for the command prompt in a console or shell window.

- Usually, each file should contain a single class. However, Java allows a single file to contain multiple classes, but with certain restrictions. (See Sections 4.5.1 and 6.1 [p. 134] for details.)
- The file name should match the class name, including the capitalization. Java is case sensitive.

These rules make it easy to locate the source code of a class by simply listing or searching the file names.

Comments

There are three types of comments allowed in Java programs:

> *C-style comments:* C-style comments are delimited by /* and */. C-style comments can span multiple lines. All characters between the delimiters, including the delimiters, are ignored by the Java compiler.
>
> *C++-style comments:* C++-style comments begin with // and extend to the end of the line. C++-style comments are short one-liners. All characters from // to the end of the line are ignored by the Java compiler.
>
> *Java documentation comments:* Documentation comments are delimited by /** and */. Documentation comments serve a special purpose. They are used by a documentation generation utility called javadoc to generate HTML-style documentation automatically by extracting information from the source code. All characters between /** and */, including the delimiters, are ignored by the Java compiler. (We discuss the use of documentation comments and the javadoc tool in Section 4.5 [p. 134].)

Example 3.1 illustrates the use of all three types of comments.

3.3.2 A Java Applet

Java applications must be invoked from command consoles. Java applets can be embedded in Web pages. They are downloaded via the World Wide Web and invoked by Java-enabled browsers.

EXAMPLE 3.2   The "Hello from Venus!" Applet

PURPOSE

To illustrate the basic structure of Java applets and the basic graphics capability of displaying text and choosing font, size, style, and color.

DESCRIPTION

This applet displays the greeting message *Hello from Venus!* graphically. It consists of a text message and an image of the planet Venus.

SOLUTION

Here are the steps to build and run the Java applet:

1. Type in and save the following Java source code in a file named
   `HelloFromVenus.java`.

   > **Hello from Venus! applet: `HelloFromVenus.java`**

   ```java
   import java.awt.*;
   import java.applet.Applet;
   public class HelloFromVenus extends Applet {
       public void paint(Graphics g) {
           Dimension d = getSize( );
           g.setColor(Color.black);
           g.fillRect(0,0,d.width,d.height);
           g.setFont(new Font("Sans-serif", Font.BOLD, 24));
           g.setColor(new Color(255, 215, 0)); // gold color
           g.drawString("Hello from Venus!", 40, 25);
           g.drawImage(getImage(getCodeBase( ), "Venus.gif"),
                       20, 60, this);
       }
   }
   ```

2. Compile the Java source, using the Java compiler to generate the byte-code file
   `HelloFromVenus.class`.

   ```
   venus% javac HelloFromVenus.java
   ```

3. Type in and save the following HTML source in a file named `HelloDemo.html`.
   We may name the HTML file anything we want to.

   > **HTML source: `HelloDemo.html`**

   ```html
   <html>
     <head>
       <title> Hello from Venus Applet </title>
     </head>
     <body bgcolor=black text=white>
       <center>
         <applet code="HelloFromVenus.class"
           width=300 height=350>
         </applet>
       </center>
       <hr>
       <a href="HelloFromVenus.java">The source.</a>
     </body>
   </html>
   ```

Be sure that the HTML file, the Java source file, and the byte-code file are in the
same directory. The image of planet Venus is stored in a separate file named
`Venus.gif`. Be sure to place the image file in the same directory with the other
files.

Figure 3.3

The Hello from
Venus! applet.

4. One way to view the applet is to use the applet viewer in JDK:

   ```
   venus% appletviewer HelloDemo.html
   ```

   Note that the argument of `appletviewer` is the HTML file name.

5. Another way to view the applet is to use a Java-enabled browser, such as the
   Netscape Communicator:

   ```
   venus% netscape HelloDemo.html
   ```

   The result of the applet is shown in Figure 3.3.

Basic Structure of Applets

The "Hello from Venus!" applet illustrates several essential elements of Java applets.
In general, an applet must extend the `Applet` class (either directly or indirectly),
does not need a `main()` method, and should have the `paint()` method. An applet is
quite different from an application. It is indirectly invoked through the applet viewer
or, more commonly, a Java-enabled browser. An applet is not a stand-alone program.
Therefore the `main()` method is not needed. An applet is invoked in an *applet context*,

Figure 3.4

Viewing area of
applets and the
Java coordinate
system.

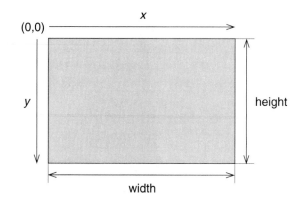

usually a browser. An applet must interact with its applet context according to a set of prescribed conventions (that is, *contracts*).

The contract regarding the paint() method of an applet includes the following:[8]

■ Each applet is assigned a rectangular region on the Web page in which it is embedded. The dimension of this rectangular region is set in the <applet> tag in the HTML file.

■ An applet implements the paint() method to *paint* the appearance of the applet in the rectangular region. The origin $(0, 0)$ is located at the upper left corner of the rectangular region, as shown in Figure 3.4.

■ The paint() method is invoked by the applet context whenever the applet is active and the rectangular region designated to the applet becomes visible. This statement implies that the paint() method will be invoked when the applet is initially loaded in a browser.

Later, we discuss in detail most of the language features and classes involved in this applet. A cursory understanding of what is going on in the paint() method of the HelloFromVenus applet is sufficient at this point. Line by line, each statement in the paint() method

1. gets the dimension of the rectangular region designated to the applet;
2. sets the pen color to black;
3. fills the entire rectangular region with black color, which paints the background;
4. sets the font to sans serif, boldface style, and 24-point size;
5. sets the pen color to gold;
6. draws the text message at the top in gold color; and
7. draws the image of the planet Venus below the message. The image is stored in a file named Venus.gif.

---

8. The paint() method is declared in the Component class, which is a superclass of Applet. See Section 5.5 for details about the paint() method.

Embedding Applets in Web Pages

Applets are embedded in Web pages by using the applet tag, which is included in the official specification of HTML.[9] The simplest form of the <applet> tag is

```
<applet code = bytecode-filename
        width = pixels
        height = pixels>
</applet>
```

consisting of three required *attributes*, which are key-value pairs.

Attribute	Description
code	Specify the name of the byte-code file containing the applet
width	Specify the width of the applet in pixels
height	Specify the height of the applet in pixels

The <applet> tag for the HelloFromVenus applet is highlighted in the HelloDemo.html file in step 3 of Example 3.2. For a complete description of the <applet> tag, see "Summary of the Applet Tag" [p. 645].

Placing Applets on the World Wide Web

To make your applets accessible on the World Wide Web, you simply put Web pages, the applet class files, and other related files (e.g., image or audio files) on a host that is connected to the Internet and has a *Web server* (that is, an *HTTP server*).

An applet may involve several files. For example, an applet might have several class files, as well as image and audio files. To run an applet that resides on a remote server requires that all the related files be downloaded to the host that is running the applet. By default, a single connection to a remote HTTP server will download only one file. Therefore, an applet that involves multiple files requires several connections to the same server in order to download all the files needed to run the applet. Multiple connections to the remote server involve significant overhead and may cause substantial delays in downloading the files. An archive and compression utility, called jar, is provided in the JDK. Using jar, we can pack all the files involved in an applet into a single compressed archive file. Hence, the files needed to run an applet can be downloaded with a single connection to the remote server, reducing download time and network load.

The Hello from Venus! applet contains two files: the class file HelloFromVenus .class and the image file Venus.gif. To take advantage of the jar utility, we first pack these two files,

```
venus% jar cf Hello.jar HelloFromVenus.class Venus.gif
```

---

9. Raggett et al. (2000) gives a complete and definitive description of HTML 4.0, the current standard. The most up-to-date information about HTML can be obtained from the W^3 Consortium at *www.w3.org*.

which creates a *Java archive* (JAR) file named `Hello.jar`.[10] In order to use the JAR file, we must specify the JAR file name in the `<applet>` tag, using the `archive` attribute:

```
<applet code="HelloFromVenus.class
        archive="Hello.jar"
        width=300 height=350>
</applet>
```

A browser that supports the `archive` feature will download the JAR file instead of the class file. The class and image files will be extracted from the JAR file.

COMMON PROBLEMS AND SOLUTIONS

Symptoms	Possible Causes and/or Fixes
You are unable to invoke JDK tools such as `javac`, `java`, or `appletviewer`.	Be sure that the `PATH` environment variable includes the JDK `bin` directory.
You get deprecation messages while compiling programs.	The programs contain features that are deprecated. The programs were developed for an older version of Java compiler than the one you are using. As of version 1.4, deprecation is only a warning, so programs using deprecated features should still run without problems. However, you should remove deprecated features from programs because they may not be supported in future JDK releases.
Your applets run fine when you use the applet viewer but do not run in a browser.	Be sure that the version of JVM in your browser is equal to or higher than the version of JDK you used to compile your programs. When transferring files to a Web host via FTP, be sure that you transfer the class files in binary mode and that the file names are intact, not truncated or converted to all uppercase.

---

10. Use of command-line utility `jar` is similar to use of the UNIX `tar` utility. Its syntax is

   `jar [options] destination input-files`

See JDK tools documentation for details.

CHAPTER SUMMARY

- Java is object-oriented, distributed, platform independent, and secure.

- The Java 2 Platform consists of the Standard Edition (J2SE) for desktop client applications, the Enterprise Edition (J2EE) for server applications, and the Micro Edition (J2ME) for applications on mobile, handheld, and embedded devices.

- The primary design goals of the Java run-time architecture are platform independence, efficiency, and security.

- The Java run-time architecture is a compromise between the conventional approaches of executing programs through compilation or interpretation. Java source code is compiled to byte-code and executed by the Java virtual machine (JVM).

- The JVM is an abstract computing machine that executes Java byte-code. It can be implemented as interpreters, just-in-time (JIT) compilers, or Java chips—hardware implementations of the JVM. The instructions of the Java virtual machine are called byte-code. The Java compiler compiles Java source code to Java byte-code and stores the resulting code in files with the extension `.class`.

- The two common types of Java programs are applications and applets. Applications (apps) are full-fledged Java programs with full access to system resources. Applets are programs that are embedded in Web pages with restricted access to system resources to prevent break-ins to the hosts that run the applets.

FURTHER READINGS

Arnold, K., and J. Gosling (2001). *The Java Programming Language*, 3rd ed. Addison-Wesley.

Kassem, N., and Enterprise Team (2000). *Designing Enterprise Applications with Java 2 Platform, Enterprise Edition*. Addison-Wesley.

Lindholm, T., and F. Yellin (1996). *The Java Virtual Machine*. Addison-Wesley.

McGraw, G., and E. W. Felten (1997). *Java Security—Hostile Applets, Holes, and Antidotes*. John Wiley & Sons.

Riggd, R., A. Taivalsaari, and M. Vandenbrink (2001). *Programming Wireless Devices with the Java 2 Platform, Micro Edition*. Addison-Wesley.

EXERCISES

3.1 Write a Java application similar to the Hello.Java application in Example 3.1. This new program should contain a class named MyFavoritePoem. It should call System.out .println() to display a poem that you like. (*Hint:* Look ahead to the next chapter for information on the Java printing features that can be used to display this poem neatly and elegantly.)

3.2 Develop an applet similar to the HelloFrom-Venus applet in Example 3.2. Your new applet should display an image of your choice. Change the color, size, and textual display of the image as necessary.

CHAPTER 4

Elements of Java

CHAPTER OVERVIEW

In this chapter, we discuss the basic elements of Java, including operators and expressions, data types, garbage collection, control structures, class declaration, parameter passing, packages, and exceptions. We also discuss some of the more commonly used classes in the Java class library. We present several simple programs to demonstrate string manipulation and basic input and output operations. Finally, we develop a simple animation applet.

Java is a recent entry in the evolution of object-oriented programming languages. It has benefited tremendously from the lessons learned from its predecessors, most notably C++ [Ellis and Stroustrup 1990; Stroustrup 1994; Stroustrup 1997], Smalltalk [Goldberg 1985; Goldberg and Robson 1983], Objective C [Pinson and Wiener 1991], Modula3 [Harbison 1992], Eiffel [Meyer 1992; Meyer 1997], and Ada [Booch 1987]. Java is a well-designed language comprising constructs that have been proven effective in other languages. Java bears some resemblance to its direct ancestor—C++. However, their similarities are largely syntactical and superficial, whereas their differences are more fundamental. One of the most striking differences between Java and C++ is in their design philosophies. C++ is designed to be a rather comprehensive, expressive, and permissive language. A high priority for C++ is to allow *very efficient* implementation. Many of its features were developed with good intentions and sound justifications but are often subject to misuse and bad programming practices, partly because of backward compatibility with C. In contrast, Java is designed to be (1) more selective and restrictive—to prevent bad programming practices, even at the cost of sacrificing expressiveness and convenience in some cases; (2) easy to use, and versatile; and (3) suitable for a variety of tasks, including object-oriented programming, numeric computation, and system programming.

Java differs from other object-oriented programming languages in several important respects:

- Unlike C++, Java is purely object-oriented. All nonstatic methods in Java are polymorphic (i.e., virtual in C++ terminology). It does not allow global variables and stand-alone functions, as C++ does.

- Unlike Smalltalk, in which everything is an object, including values of primitive types, such as `int` and `char`, in Java, values of primitive types are not objects.

- Unlike C++, Java does not support multiple inheritance in general. Like Objective-C, only a limited form of multiple inheritance, accomplished by the use of *interfaces*, is supported in Java.

- Unlike most other procedural and object-oriented programming languages, in Java, the `goto` statement was eliminated.

- Unlike most other programming languages, Java utilizes 16-bit characters instead of 8-bit characters to support internationalization.

- Java supports exception handling, automatic memory management (i.e., garbage collection), and multithreaded programming. These mechanisms are considered to be essential in object-oriented programming.

Perhaps the most notable feature of Java is its support for *distributed computing*. Unlike most other programming languages that depend on platform-dependent add-on utilities to support distributed computing, Java provides built-in language constructs and standard libraries for distributed computing.

4.1   LEXICAL ELEMENTS

Lexical elements are the basic building blocks of programming languages. We begin with a look at Java's characters, identifiers, and literals. Then we discuss the operators and expressions used in Java.

4.1.1   Character Set

Java programs are written in *Unicode*,[1] an international standard of 16-bit character sets that contain encodings of characters of most languages used in the world today.

---

1. *The Unicode Standard 2.0* is defined in [The Unicode Consortium 1996]. Unicode related information, including various tables and programs, can be obtained from the Unicode Consortium at http://www.unicode.org.

The commonly used 7-bit ASCII character set is equivalent to the first 128 characters of Unicode, known as the ISO Latin-1[2] character set, also known as ISO-8859-1. The Java development environment can be localized to accommodate many different locales. A *locale* is a country or region with distinct characteristics in culture and language. The most widely distributed version of the Java Development Kit (JDK) is localized to U.S. English. It performs the conversion between ASCII and Unicode characters on the fly; that is, the U.S. English version of JDK reads and writes ASCII files by default.

4.1.2 Identifiers

Identifiers are used in Java programs to denote the name of classes, methods, variables, and so on. A Java identifier can begin with a letter, followed by letters or digits. In Java, *letters* include the characters in the alphabets of all languages in Unicode, the underscore (_), and the dollar sign ($). Examples of Java identifiers are

```
MyClass    value1   _aField    A$B
```

Because Java programs are written in Unicode, you may use the following as identifiers in Java:[3]

多语言   πολυγωσσικο

4.1.3 Primitive Types and Literals

The following primitive types are defined in Java:

- Boolean type: `boolean`
- Integer types: `byte`, `short`, `int`, and `long`
- Character type: `char`
- Floating-point types: `float` and `double`

The constant values of each primitive type are expressed as *literals*.

Boolean Type

The `boolean` type consists of two boolean literals: `true` and `false`. In Java, the `boolean` type is not compatible with integer types. The results of comparisons are of type `boolean`, not integer as in C and C++. The conditions of control statements, such as `if` and `while` statements (see Sections 4.3.5 [p. 96] and 4.3.6 [p. 96]), are expected to be of type `boolean`, not integer types.

---

2. ISO stands for International Standardization Organization.
3. These are the word "multilingual" in Chinese and Greek, respectively.

Integer Types

Java provides several integer types of different sizes.

Type	Size	Minimum Value	Maximum Value
byte	8-bit	−128	127
short	16-bit	−32768	32767
int	32-bit	−2147483648	2147483647
long	64-bit	−9223372036854775808	9223372036854775807

However, Java provides no unsigned integer types. Integer literals can be written in decimals, octals, and hexadecimals.

- A *decimal integer literal* begins with a nonzero decimal digit, followed by decimal digits (e.g., 30).
- An *octal integer literal* begins with a leading zero (0), followed by octal digits (e.g., 036).
- A *hexadecimal integer literal* begins with a leading 0x or 0X, followed by hexadecimal digits (e.g., 0x1E and 0X1e).

The default type of integer literals are int. An integer literal may be followed by an *integer type suffix*, l or L, to indicate that it is of type long (e.g., 0x1L). The uppercase letter L is preferred, since the lowercase letter l could be easily mistaken as digit 1 (one).

Floating-Point Types

Java provides two floating-point types.

Type	Size	Description
float	32-bit	Single precision IEEE-754 floating-point
double	64-bit	Double precision IEEE-754 floating-point

Floating-point literals are written as a decimal number with an optional exponent part.

Digits. [*Digits*] [(e|E) *SignedInteger*]

Some examples of floating-point literals are

```
23.f    .5    0.0    3.1415    1e-9    1e+9    1E12
```

The default type of floating-point literals is double. A floating-point literal may be followed by a floating-point type suffix to indicate its type:

- Letter f or F indicates that the type of the floating-point literal is float.
- Letter d or D indicates that the type of the floating-point literal is double. (This is optional.)

Some examples of floating-point literals with floating-point type suffix are

```
1e-9f    1e+9f    1E12F    1e-9d    1e+9d    1E12D
```

Character Type

Most programming languages provide a single-byte (8-bit) character type that is capable of encoding up to 256 printable characters and control characters. Although it is adequate for Western languages, which all have small alphabets, it is quite inadequate for some Oriental languages, such as Chinese and Japanese. Modern Chinese consists of more than 15,000 characters, of which some 6,000 are in common daily use. For languages with large alphabets, a double-byte character type capable of encoding as many as 65,536 printable characters and control characters is needed.

In the past, the vast majority of commercial software was developed and available only in English. As nations' economies become more and more global, the huge market potentials of non–English-speaking countries, such as the People's Republic of China, have prompted commercial software vendors to port their software to other languages. Microsoft, for example, released its Windows operating system in several different languages simultaneously. Owing to the different size requirements of characters, however, porting the English version of software (where 8-bit characters were used) to Oriental languages (where 16-bit characters are necessary) has proved to be extremely tedious and costly.

To support the internationalization of software, Java provides a single character type char that is 16-bit unsigned and uses the Unicode character encoding.

Character Literals

ASCII characters can be written directly (e.g., a or C). Non-ASCII characters can be written in their hexadecimal or octal codes.

- In hexadecimal code, \u is followed by four hexadecimal digits, as in \u00E6 (æ in French), and \u5496 \u5561 (咖啡, "coffee" in Chinese).
- In octal code, \ is followed by one to three octal digits, as in \040. Octal character code may not exceed \377 (\u00FF).

The following special characters can be written by using *escape sequences*.

Escape Sequence	Unicode	Description
\n	\u000A	New line
\t	\u0009	Tab
\b	\u0008	Backspace
\r	\u000D	Carriage return
\f	\u000C	Form feed
\\	\u005C	Backslash
\'	\u0027	Single quote
\"	\u0022	Double quote

Character literals such as the following appear between single quotes:

```
'a'    'C'
'\u00E6'    '\u5496'    '\u5561'
'\040'
'\n'    '\t'    '\\'    '\''    '\"'
```

String Literals

The `String` type is not a primitive type in Java. It is a class. However, string constants can be written as literals. A string literal consists of a sequence of characters, including escape sequences, enclosed by a pair of double quotes, as in the following examples.

String literal	Value
"A string literal"	A string literal
"\u5469 \u5561"	咖啡
"\"A quote\" "	"A quote"

See also "String Concatenation" in Section 4.1.4 [p. 84] and Section 4.4.8 [p. 118] for operations on strings.

4.1.4   Operators and Expressions

Java provides operators that are very similar to those in C and C++. These operators and expressions are summarized in Table 4.1. The leftmost column indicates the precedence of the operators, with 1 as the highest precedence and 14 the lowest. A *numeric* type is either an integer or a floating-point type. All operators that can be applied to integer types can also be applied to type char. All the binary operators, except the assignment operators, are left-associative. The assignment operators are right-associative. Note the following examples:

Expression	Interpreted As	Reason
u + v * w	u + (v * w)	* has higher precedence than +.
x - y + z	(x - y) + z	+ and - have the same precedence and are left-associative.
a = b = c	a = (b = c)	Assignment operators are right-associative.

Arithmetic Operators

The following arithmetic operators can be applied to all integer and floating-point types.

Infix Binary		Prefix Unary	
+	Addition	+	Positive sign
-	Subtraction	-	Negative sign
*	Multiplication		
/	Division		
%	Remainder		

Integer addition, subtraction, and multiplication follow the customary rules. Integer division truncates the result toward zero. The integer remainder is defined as

x % y == x - (x / y) * y

The following examples show integer division and remainder and their relationship:

Expression	Result	Relationship
7 / 3	2	$7 == 3 * 2 + 1$
7 % 3	1	
(-7) / 3	-2	$(-7) == 3 * (-2) + (-1)$
(-7) % 3	-1	

TABLE 4.1

Operators and Expressions

	Expression	Operand Types	Description
1.	exp++	Numeric	Postfix increment; result is the value before
	exp--	Numeric	Postfix decrement; result is the value before
2.	++exp	Numeric	Prefix increment; result is the value after
	--exp	Numeric	Prefix decrement; result is the value after
	+exp	Numeric	Unary positive
	-exp	Numeric	Unary negative
	~exp	Integer, boolean	Bitwise complement
	!exp	Boolean	Logical negation
3.	exp_1 * exp_2	Numeric	Multiplication
	exp_1 / exp_2	Numeric	Division
	exp_1 % exp_2	Numeric	Remainder, modulus
4.	exp_1 + exp_2	Numeric	Addition
		String	String concatenation
	exp_1 - exp_2	Numeric	Subtraction
5.	exp_1 << exp_2	Integer	Left shift, filling with 0s
	exp_1 >> exp_2	Integer	Signed right shift, filling with the highest bit
	exp_1 >>> exp_2	Integer	Unsigned right shift, filling with 0s
6.	exp_1 < exp_2	Numeric	Less than
	exp_1 > exp_2	Numeric	Greater than
	exp_1 <= exp_2	Numeric	Less than or equal to
	exp_1 >= exp_2	Numeric	Greater than or equal to
7.	exp_1 == exp_2	Any	Equality
	exp_1 != exp_2	Any	Inequality
8.	exp_1 & exp_2	Integer, boolean	Bitwise and
9.	exp_1 ^ exp_2	Integer, boolean	Bitwise exclusive or (xor)
10.	exp_1 | exp_2	Integer, boolean	Bitwise inclusive or
11.	exp_1 && exp_2	Boolean	Conditional and
12.	exp_1 || exp_2	Boolean	Conditional or
13.	exp_1 ? exp_2 : exp_3	exp_1: boolean exp_2, exp_3: any	Conditional expression

TABLE 4.1

Operators and Expressions (continued)

Expression	Operand Types	Description
14. *var = exp*	Any	Assignment
var += exp	Numeric, string	
var −= exp	Numeric	*var op= exp*
var *= exp	Numeric	is equivalent to
var /= exp	Numeric	*var = (var) op (exp)* except that
var %= exp	Numeric	*var* is evaluated only once
var <<= exp	Integer	
var >>= exp	Integer	
var >>>= exp	Integer	
var &= exp	Integer, boolean	
var ^= exp	Integer, boolean	
var |= exp	Integer, boolean	

Java integer arithmetic never overflows or underflows. If a value exceeds the range of its type, it will be wrapped modulo the range.

For expressions x / y and x % y, an `ArithmeticException` is thrown when y is 0 (see Section 4.6 [p. 139] for a discussion of exceptions).

Java floating-point arithmetic conforms to the IEEE-754-1985 standard [IEEE 1985]. One advantage of this type of arithmetic is that an exception will not be generated under any circumstance. In other words, your program will not crash, even when you divide a floating-point number by zero. The IEEE-754 standard defines two magic numbers: infinity and NaN (representing *not a number*). Floating-point arithmetic is closed with the addition of infinity and NaN. Two rules govern floating-point multiplication and division:

1. If neither operand is NaN, then the results are as follows:

x	y	x / y	x * y
Finite	±0.0	±∞	±0.0
Finite	±∞	±0.0	±∞
±0.0	±0.0	NaN	±0.0
±∞	Finite	±∞	±∞
±∞	±∞	NaN	±∞
±0.0	±∞	±0.0	NaN

2. If either operand is NaN, then the result is NaN.

The floating-point remainder is defined much the same as the integer remainder, or

```
x % y == x - (x / y) * y
```

See "The Float and Double Classes" [p. 130] and "Mathematical Constants and Functions" [p. 131] for floating-point constants and commonly used mathematical functions.

String Concatenation

The + operator can also be used to concatenate two strings. If one of the operands is a string and the other is of some other type, the nonstring operand will be converted to a string representation of its value and concatenated to the string operand, as in the following examples:

Expression	Result
"object" + "-" + "oriented"	Object-oriented
"object" + '-' + "oriented"	Object-oriented
"Mail Stop" + 205	Mail Stop 205
123 + ' ' + "Oak Street"	123 Oak Street

The conversion of primitive type values to their string representations follows customary conventions. The conversion of objects to their string representation is carried out by the toString() method, which we discuss in Section 4.4.8 [p. 122].

Increment and Decrement Operators

The increment operator ++ and the decrement operator -- can be applied to all integer and floating-point types. Both operators can be either prefix or postfix. For example, i++ and ++i increment the value of i by 1; i-- and --i decrement the value of i by 1. The result of the postfix increment or decrement expression is the value of i *before* the increment or decrement, respectively. The result of the prefix increment or decrement expression is the value of i *after* the increment or decrement, respectively. For example, if we let the initial value of i be 8, the effects of the postfix/prefix and increment/decrement expressions are as shown in the following table. (These expressions are evaluated independently, not consecutively.)

Expression	Result of the Expression	Value of i Afterward
i++	8	9
++i	9	9
i--	8	7
--i	7	7

Relational Operators

The equality operator == and the inequality operator != can be applied to any type. The comparison operators < (less than), <= (less than or equal to), > (greater than), and >= (greater than or equal to) can be applied only to numeric types. All relational expressions yield boolean results. The meaning of relational expressions on primitive types follows customary conventions. We discuss the meaning of equality and inequality of reference types in Section 4.2.3 [p. 91].

Logical Operators

The logical operators ! (negation), && (and), and || (or) can be applied to operands of type boolean. The binary logical operators are *conditional*. That is, in expression exp_1 && exp_2, exp_2 is evaluated only when exp_1 evaluates to true. Similarly, in expression exp_1 || exp_2, exp_2 is evaluated only when exp_1 evaluates to false.

Bitwise and Shift Operators

Bitwise operators can be applied to both integer and boolean types. The following bitwise operators are supported in Java:

Bitwise Expression	Description
~x	Bitwise complement of x
x & y	Bitwise and of x and y
x | y	Bitwise inclusive or of x and y
x ^ y	Bitwise exclusive or of x and y

Unlike the conditional logical operators, when the bitwise operators &, |, and ^ are applied to operands of type boolean, both operands are always evaluated.

The shift operators can be applied only to integer types. The following shift operators are supported in Java:

Shift Expression	Description
x << k	Shift the bits in x k places to the left, filling in with 0 bits on the right-hand side.
x >> k	Shift the bits in x k places to the right, filling in with the highest bit (i.e., the sign bit) on the left-hand side.
x >>> k	Shift the bits in x k places to the right, filling in with 0 bits on the left-hand side.

The following examples illustrate use of the bitwise and shift operators:

Expression	Description
~0x0	All bits are set to 1.
0x1 << k	All except the kth bit are set to 0.
~(0x1 << k)	All except the kth bit are set to 1.
x << k	The result is $x * 2^k$.
x >> k	The result is $x / 2^k$.

Conditional Operators

A conditional expression takes the form

$$exp_1 \ ? \ exp_2 \ : \ exp_3$$

where exp_1 must be of type boolean, and exp_2 and exp_3 can be of any type. The value of this conditional expression is exp_2, if exp_1 evaluates to true, and exp_3, if exp_1 evaluates to false. Examples of conditional expressions include the following:

Expression	Description
(x < y) ? x : y	The minimum of x and y
(x >= 0) ? x : -x	The absolute value of x

Assignment Operators

An assignment operator is either the simple = or one of these:

+=   -=   *=   /=   %=   <<=   >>=   >>>=   &=   ^= |=

These operators are formed by concatenating a binary operator with =. The assignment expression

var op= exp

is equivalent to

var = (var) op (exp)

except that *var* is evaluated only once in the original expression. When *var* is a simple variable, these two expressions are always equivalent. However, they may yield different results when *var* has side effects. These typically occur when array indexes are involved. Let us assume that a is an integer array and that the initial value of i is 2. The assignment expressions a[i++] += i and a[i++] = a[i++] + i will have different effects:

Expression	Effect
a[i++] += i	a[2] = a[2] + 3
a[i++] = a[i++] + i	a[2] = a[3] + 4

The following are examples of assignment expressions:

Expression	Description
b |= (0x1 << k)	Set the *k*th bit of *b* to 1.
b &= ~(0x1 << k)	Set the *k*th bit of *b* to 0.

4.2   VARIABLES AND TYPES

A *type* denotes the set of all the legal values of that type. A *variable* refers to a location in memory where a value can be stored. Each variable is associated with a type. The variable type restricts the values that the variable may hold. Variables and their types are declared in variable declarations.

4.2.1 Variable Declarations

The basic syntax of *variable declarations* is

> *Type VarName$_1$* [=*InitialValue$_1$*], *VarName$_2$* [=*InitialValue$_2$*] . . . ;

It declares one or more variables, *VarName$_1$*, *VarName$_2$*, . . . , to be of type *Type*. When a declaration contains more than one variable, the variables are separated by commas (,). Optionally, each variable can be assigned an initial value. A variable declaration determines the type and the scope of the variables in the declaration at compile time. We discuss the scope of variables in more detail later (see Sections 4.3.3 [p. 95] and 4.4.6 [p. 116]).

Java supports two kinds of types: *primitive types* and *reference types*. We discussed all the primitive types in Section 4.1.3 [p. 77]. A primitive type variable holds a value of the type, whereas a reference type variable holds a reference to an object or array.

Default Initial Values

Each type has a *default initial value*. These values are used in initializing objects and arrays. The default initial values of various types are summarized as follows:

Type	Default Initial Value
Integer	0
Floating-point	0.0
char	\u0000
boolean	false
Reference	null

4.2.2 Type Compatibility and Conversion

Type compatibility is an important relationship between types.

Definition 4.1 *Type Compatibility*

Type T_1 is *compatible* with type T_2 if a value of type T_1 can appear wherever a value of type T_2 is expected, and vice versa.

Type conversion is the conversion of values of one type to values of another type. We discuss the conversion of primitive types here and the conversion of reference types in Section 5.2.2. Conversions between different numeric types are allowed. There are two different forms of conversion.

Definition 4.2 *Widening and Narrowing (of Numeric Types)*

Converting a numeric type of a smaller range to a numeric type of a larger range is called *widening*. Converting a numeric type of a larger range to a numeric type of a smaller range is called *narrowing*.

The sizes of ranges of numeric types are ordered from small to large:

```
byte    short    int    long    float    double
```

Examples of widening include converting `int` to `long` or `int` to `double`. Examples of narrowing include converting `long` to `int` or `float` to `long`. On the one hand, widening is carried out implicitly whenever necessary. On the other hand, narrowing may result in overflow or loss of precision. Therefore, explicit casts are necessary for narrowing.

```
int i = 10;
long m = 10000L;
double d = Math.PI;  // the value 3.1415926...
i = (int) m;         // narrowing, cast necessary
m = i;               // widening, no cast necessary
m = (long) d;        // narrowing, cast necessary
d = m;               // widening, no cast necessary
```

4.2.3 Reference Types

A reference type is a *class* type, an *interface* type, or an *array* type. A reference variable (i.e., a variable of a reference type) may hold references to objects or arrays.[4] A reference variable may also hold a special value, `null`, which indicates that no object or array is being referenced.

References in Java are implemented as 32-bit pointers. Reference variables do not directly hold values, as variables of primitive types do. Instead, reference variables hold *indirect references* to object or array instances, as illustrated in Figure 4.1. Java references are very different from pointers in C and C++ in two respects. First, in C and C++, pointers can be cast to any type, modified through pointer arithmetics, and assigned arbitrary values. In Java, none of that is allowed: Java prohibits the direct manipulation of reference variables. Second, in C and C++, pointers usually reference chunks of memory that are dynamically allocated from a heap. Programmers assume full responsibility for managing allocation and deallocation of memory. In

---

4. Arrays are actually objects too; see Section 5.2.2 [p. 170].

Figure 4.1

Primitive and reference types.

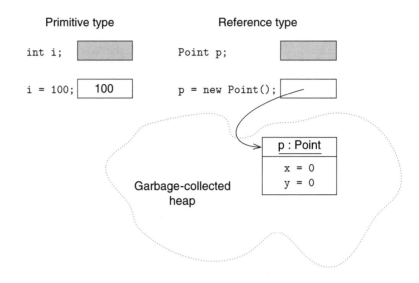

Java, reference variables point to memory space that is dynamically allocated from a garbage-collected heap. Programmers are thus freed from the responsibility of managing the deallocation of memory.

Garbage Collection

Garbage collection refers to a mechanism that automatically deallocates unreferenced or unreachable objects (i.e., garbage). It is one of the most important features of Java. Garbage collection not only simplifies the programming task, but it also eliminates one of the major sources of faults in programs involving memory leaks and dereferencing invalid pointers, which are common and notoriously difficult to trace and remove. Garbage collection significantly reduces the amount of effort and time associated with programming, testing, and debugging.

Whether to use garbage collection is perhaps one of the most hotly debated issues in programming language design. Despite its obvious and significant advantages, garbage collection imposes rather severe penalties on the performance of programs of which it is a part.

Most garbage collection techniques involve exhaustive examination of the *entire* memory space, either all at once or rotating through segments of the memory space one at a time. Even with various improvements, such as *generational* garbage collection, garbage collection techniques are inherently time-consuming. Those that do not involve exhaustive examination of memory space, such as *reference counting*, often incur per-use penalties (i.e., a small penalty every time a variable is referenced), which can become a significant cumulative penalty. Techniques such as reference counting also suffer from various limitations, such as circular references. In addition, the garbage collection process could start at any moment, the timing of which is unpredictable and usually beyond the control of the programmer. Therefore, programming languages containing garbage collection are not suitable for developing hard real-time systems that require the assurance of completing certain tasks within a specified period of time.

To summarize, Java does not require the programmer to keep track of objects created and destroy these objects when no longer needed. Java uses garbage collection to manage automatically the deallocation of objects. Garbage collection does impose some additional demands on hardware components. But, with the continuing increase of CPU speed and drop in CPU and memory costs, the penalty on performance becomes at least acceptable, if not negligible, for the vast majority of software systems. The benefits of garbage collection far outweigh any penalty on performance imposed by this mechanism.

Creating Objects and Arrays

Declaring a variable of a primitive type creates a storage location for its values. However, declaring a variable of a reference type does *not* create a storage location for an object or an array. Only a storage location for the *reference* is created. The object or array to which the reference variable refers must be created, or allocated, using the new operator or an *initializer*.

```
Point p;          // declare a reference variable of type Point
p = new Point();  // create a new instance of Point
int[] ia;         // declare a reference variable of an array of integers
ia = new int[3];  // create an integer array of size 3
```

See Sections 4.2.4 [p. 91] and 4.4.2 [p. 104] for the details of creating objects and arrays.

Equality of References

For two reference variables r1 and r2, the expression r1 == r2 tests to the equality of the two *references*, not the equality of the *states* of the objects or arrays referred to by them. In other words, r1 == r2 tests the identity of two objects or arrays. To test the equality (of the states) of two objects or arrays, the equals() method should be used, such as r1.equals(r2). See the discussion of the equals() method in Section 6.3.2 [p. 228].

4.2.4   Arrays

An array variable holds a reference to an array. An array is a fixed-size sequential collection of elements of identical types. Arrays are created with either the new operator or array initializers. The storage space for arrays is allocated from the garbage-collected heap.

One-Dimensional Arrays

The elements in a one-dimensional array are indexed by the integers 0 to $n - 1$, where n is the size of the array. A one-dimensional array of size n can be created and initialized with either of the following methods:

1. Using the `new` operator:

> new *Type* [*n*]

In this case the size of the array must be specified, and all the elements in the array are initialized to the default initial values (see Section 4.2.1 [p. 88]) based on the type of the elements.

2. Using the one-dimensional array initializer:

> { $v_0, v_1, \ldots, v_{n-1}$ }

The values $v_0, v_1, \ldots, v_{n-1}$ are the initial values of the elements in the array. The size of the array is determined by the number of initial values provided in the array initializer.

The following are some examples of creating and initializing one-dimensional arrays:

`int ia1[] = new int[3];`	Create an integer array of size 3; all elements are initialized to 0.
`int ia2[] = {1, 2, 3};`	Create an integer array of size 3; elements are initialized to 1, 2, and 3, respectively.
`Point pa[] = new Point[10];`	Create an array of points of size 10; all elements are initialized to `null`.

Let a be a one-dimensional array; the common operations on arrays are as follows:

Operation	Description
`a.length`	The length of array a
`a[i]`	The ith element of array a

Examples 4.1 [p. 97], 4.2 [p. 98], and 4.9 [p. 133] illustrate the use of one-dimensional arrays.

One of the main differences between the arrays in Java and those in C and C++ is that Java arrays are always bound-checked at run time. Array bound-checking will automatically detect a major source of faults in programs, that is, exceeding the bounds of arrays while accessing or manipulating their elements. An `IndexOutOfBounds-Exception` will be thrown at run time when a program attempts to access an array with an out-of-bound index (see Section 4.6 [p. 139] for a discussion of exceptions).

Multidimensional Arrays

A multidimensional array is treated simply as an array of arrays. Let a be a k-dimensional array; the elements of a can be accessed using the following syntax:

$$a\,[\,i_1\,]\,[\,i_2\,]\,\ldots\,[\,i_k\,]$$

where $n_1, n_2, \ldots, n_k$ are the indices.

A k-dimensional array can be created with either of the following methods:

1. Using the `new` operator:

    new *Type* $[\,n_1\,]\,[\,n_2\,]\,\ldots\,[\,n_k\,]$

    The size of each dimension is $n_1, n_2, \ldots, n_k$, respectively. All the elements in the array are initialized to the default initial values (see Section 4.2.1 [p. 88]) based on the type of the elements.

2. Using the k-dimensional array initializer:

    $\{\,I_1,\,I_2,\,\ldots,\,I_k\,\}$

    where each $I_1, I_2, \ldots, I_k$ is a $(k-1)$-dimensional array initializer.

    The following are examples of creating and initializing two-dimensional arrays:

    ```
    double mat1[][] = new double[4][5];
    ```

    Create a 4×5 two-dimensional array. All elements are initialized to 0.0.

    ```
    int mat2[][] = {{1, 2, 3} , {4, 5, 6}};
    ```

    Create a 2×3 two-dimensional array. The elements are initialized as

    ```
    mat2[0][0] = 1, mat2[0][1] = 2, mat2[0][2] = 3
    mat2[1][0] = 4, mat2[1][1] = 5, mat2[1][2] = 6
    ```

    Example 4.10 [p. 133] illustrates the use of a two-dimensional array.

4.3 STATEMENTS

The syntax and semantics of statements in Java are nearly identical to those of C and C++. There is one exception: The `goto` statement was eliminated. As early as 1966, Böhm and Jacopini [1966] pointed out that the `goto` statement is unnecessary. That is, any program containing `goto` statements can be converted to a functionally equivalent program without `goto` statements. In 1968, Dijkstra made perhaps the best known assertion about the `goto` statement, considering it to be harmful [Dijkstra 1968]. More than 30 years later, the `goto` statement remains in almost every programming language in use because occasionally it is useful. However, the designer of Java eliminated the `goto` statement[5] by providing some sensible alternatives: multilevel break and continue (see Section 4.3.7 [p. 99]) and exception handling (see Section 4.6 [p. 139]).

There are two major categories of statement in Java: the *simple statement* and the *compound statement*. Simple statements are the basic building blocks of statements. Compound statements are statements that are composed of other statements. Simple statements include *expression* statements, *local variable declarations*, *break* statements, *continue* statements, and *return* statements. Compound statements include *statement blocks*, *selection* statements, *loop* statements, and *try-catch* statements.

4.3.1 Expression Statements

Assignment expressions and increment/decrement expressions can be made into statements by appending a terminating semicolon. For example, the following are expression statements:

```
x = 5;
m <<= k;
i++;
--j;
```

Expressions for object creation and method invocation can also be made into statements by appending a semicolon to the expressions, as in

```
point1 = new Point();
point1.move(10, 10);
ia = new int[3];
```

We discuss object creation and method invocation in Sections 4.4.2 [p. 104] and 4.4.4 [p. 107].

4.3.2 Statement Blocks

A *statement block* simply consists of a sequence of statements or local variable declarations (which are also considered statements) enclosed by a pair of braces, { }. The statements in a statement block can be either simple or compound and are executed sequentially:

```
{
    Statement₁
    Statement₂
    . . .
    Statementₙ
}
```

---

5. The word `goto` remains a reserved word in Java, although it is unused.

For example,

```
{
    int i = 0;
    prime[i++] = 2;
    prime[i++] = 3;
    prime[i++] = 5;
}
```

4.3.3 Local Variable Declarations

Local variable declarations are also simple statements. They must be terminated by a semicolon (;). Local variable declarations can occur anywhere in a statement block and can be intermixed with other statements. The variables declared are called *local variables*. Each variable declaration has a *scope*, which is the extent of the code in which the variable is visible, that is, accessible. The scope of a local variable begins at its declaration and extends to the end of the immediate enclosing statement block. For example,

```
{
    . . .
    int i;        // i's scope begins here
    i = 10;
    int j = 10;   // j's scope begins here
    i += j;
    . . .
}                 // both i's scope and j's scope end here
```

Local variables are not automatically initialized. They must be assigned values explicitly. It is a compilation error if a local variable is used before it has been assigned a value.

4.3.4 The return Statement

The return statement terminates the execution of a method and returns control to its caller. The syntax of the return statement is

return [*Expression*] ;

The type of the expression must match the return type of the method that contains the return statement. The return statement may not have an expression if the return type of the method that contains the return statement is void. (See Section 4.4.4 [p. 107] for a discussion of methods.)

4.3.5 Selection Statements

Java has two types of selection statements: the `if` statement,

```
if ( Condition )        if ( Condition )
    Statement               Statement₁
                        else
                            Statement₂
```

and the `switch` statement,

```
switch ( Expression ) {
case CaseLabel₁ :
    Statement₁
        . . .
case CaseLabelₙ :
    Statementₙ
default:
    Statementₙ₊₁
}
```

The expression following the `switch` keyword must be an integer expression. The *case labels* in `switch` statements are different from statement labels. Case labels must be *constant* integer expressions. Each branch in a `switch` statement may have one or more labels. Although the `default` branch is optional, you should include the `default` branch at the end.

The execution of a `switch` statement begins with evaluation of the integer expression and comparison of the result with each case label sequentially. The first branch with a matching case label will be executed. If none of the case labels match the result of the expression, the default branch will be executed. If the default branch is absent, the entire `switch` statement is skipped. Each branch is usually terminated by a `break` statement, in which case execution continues with the statement following the `switch` statement. If a branch is not terminated by a `break` statement, execution will fall through and continue with the next branch of the `switch` statement. This *fall-through* feature allows several branches to share common code.

4.3.6 Loop Statements

There are three types of loop statements:

The `while` *loop*

```
while ( Condition ) Statement
```

The `do-while` *loop*

```
do
    Statement
while ( Condition ) ;
```

The **for** *loop*

      for (*InitExpr* ; *Condition* ; *IncrExpr*)
         Statement

The **do-while** loop shown is equivalent to the following:

```
Statement
while ( Condition )
    Statement
```

wherein the two occurrences of *Statement* refer to the same statement.
The **for** loop shown is equivalent to the following:

```
InitExpr;
while ( Condition ) {
    Statement
    IncrExpr;
}
```

The following are two simple examples using the loop statements to manipulate one-dimensional arrays.

EXAMPLE 4.1   The Sum of an Array of Integers

PURPOSE

To illustrate the for loop statement and one-dimensional arrays.

DESCRIPTION

The following program calculates the sum of the values in the array.

SOLUTION

The sum of an array of integers: Sum.java

```java
public class Sum {

    public static void main(String[]args) {
        int a[] = 1, 2, 3, 4, 5, 6, 7, 8, 9, 10;
        int sum = 0;
        for (int i = 0; i < a.length; i++) {
            sum += a[i];
        }
        System.out.println("The sum is: " + sum);
    }
}
```

Running the program produces the following results:

```
venus% java Sum
The sum is: 55
```

EXAMPLE 4.2   Sorting a One-Dimensional Array Using Bubble Sort

PURPOSE

To illustrate nested loop statements and one-dimensional arrays.

DESCRIPTION

The following program—using the *bubble sort* algorithm—sorts the array in ascending order and prints the sorted array to the standard output.

SOLUTION

Sorting a one-dimensional array: BubbleSort.java

```java
public class BubbleSort {

    public static void main(String[]args) {
        int a[] = { 21, 9, 45, 17, 33, 72, 50, 12, 41, 39 };

        for (int i = a.length; --i >= 0; ) {
            for (int j = 0; j < i; j++) {
                if (a[j] > a[j+1]) {
                    int temp = a[j];
                    a[j] = a[j + 1];
                    a[j + 1] = temp;
                }
            }
        }

        // print the sorted array
        for (int k = 0; k < a.length; k++) {
            System.out.println("a[" + k + "]: " + a[k]);
        }
    }
}
```

Running the program produces the following results:

```
venus% java BubbleSort
a[0]: 9
a[1]: 12
a[2]: 17
a[3]: 21
a[4]: 33
a[5]: 39
a[6]: 41
a[7]: 45
a[8]: 50
a[9]: 72
```

4.3.7 The break and continue Statements

Statement Labels

Each statement can have an optional label, which is simply an identifier. A labeled statement has the syntax

[StatementLabel :] *Statement*

Labels can be used in break and continue statements. In Java, although it is legal to attach a label to any statement, it is only meaningful to attach a label to a statement block, a switch statement, or a loop statement. In the following program segment, Loop1 and Loop2 are labels:

```
Loop1: while (i-- > 0) {
   Loop2: while (j++ < 100) {
      // . . .
   }
}
```

Breaking and Continuing Loops

A break statement abruptly terminates an enclosing compound statement. A continue statement completes the current iteration of one of the enclosing loop statements. The syntax of the break and continue statements is

break *[StatementLabel]* ;
continue *[StatementLabel]* ;

An unlabeled break statement must be enclosed in a loop statement or a switch statement. It terminates the immediate enclosing loop or switch statement. An unlabeled continue statement completes the current iteration of the immediate enclosing loop statement and starts a new iteration.

A labeled break statement must occur within a labeled compound statement, which can be a loop statement, switch statement, or a statement block. The labeled break statement will transfer control to the statement immediately following the labeled statement. A labeled continue statement must occur within a labeled loop statement. The labeled continue statement completes the current iteration of the labeled loop statement and starts a new iteration.

Labeled break and continue statements can be used to break out of a loop that is not the immediate enclosing loop statement, as for example in

```
outer: while (cond1) {
   inner: while (cond2) {
      // . . .
      break;
      // . . .
   }
}
```

With the preceding pair of nested loops, the `break` statement will break out of the inner loop but not the outer loop. Using a `break` statement to break out of an inner loop and outer loop simultaneously also is known as multilevel breaking. Sometimes, multilevel breaking is desirable. Let us consider the two-dimensional array

```
double matrix[][];
```

We try to determine whether all the values are nonnegative. The following is a solution in C and C++, which uses a `goto` statement to break out of the nested loop.

```
boolean nonNegative = true;
for (int i = 0; i < matrix.length; i++) {
   for (int j = 0; j < matrix[i].length; j++) {
      if (matrix[i][j] < 0.0) {
         nonNegative = false;
         goto Done;
      }
   }
}
Done: // ...
```

One way of eliminating the `goto` statement requires a new boolean variable, `isDone`, and a more complicated loop condition for the outer loop.

```
boolean nonNegative = true;
boolean isDone = false;
for (int i = 0; !isDone && i < matrix.length; i++) {
   for (int j = 0; j < matrix[i].length; j++) {
      if (matrix[i][j] < 0.0) {
         nonNegative = false;
         isDone = true;
         break; // breaks out of the inner loop
      }
   }
}
```

In Java, however, the labeled `break` statement can be used to break out of the outer loop.

```
boolean nonNegative = true;
OuterLoop:
   for (int i = 0; i < matrix.length; i++) {
      for (int j = 0; j < matrix[i].length; j++) {
         if (matrix[i][j] < 0.0) {
            nonNegative = false;
            break OuterLoop; // breaks out of the outer loop
         }
      }
   }
```

Using the labeled `break` statement, we can accomplish the same task without introducing unnecessary boolean variables.

4.4 CLASS DECLARATIONS

Classes are the basic compilation units, that is, units that can be compiled individually, of Java programs. A Java program consists of one or more class declarations. A *class declaration* defines a *class*, which also defines a reference type.

4.4.1 Syntax of Class Declarations

A class declaration consists of the *class name* and a sequence of fields, methods, and nested class declarations. The fields of a class are also known as the *variables* or *attributes* of the class. The syntax of class, field, and method declarations is summarized as follows:

[*ClassModifiers*] `class` *ClassName*
    [`extends` *SuperClass*]
    [`implements` *Interface*$_1$, *Interface*$_2$ ...] `{`
  ClassMemberDeclarations
`}`

A class declaration may begin with a list of *class modifiers*, which are summarized as follows:

<none>	When no modifier is present, by default, the class is accessible by all the classes within the same package (see Section 4.5.1 [p. 135]).
`public`	A public class is accessible by any class.
`abstract`	An abstract class contains abstract methods (see Section 7.2.1 [p. 252]).
`final`	A final class may not be extended, that is, have subclasses.

Each file can contain only one class that is declared public. The name of the file and the name of the public class it contains must coincide, and the file must have the extension `.java`. For example, the class declaration of public class `Point` must be stored in a file named `Point.java`. Each file may also contain any number of nonpublic classes.

The `extends` clause specifies the superclass of this class. The `implements` clause specifies the interfaces being implemented by this class. We discuss extending classes in Section 5.2 [p. 163], and implementing interfaces in Section 5.3 [p. 176].

The body of a class declaration consists of a list of member declarations. Member declarations can be declarations of *fields*, *methods*, and *nested classes*. The field, method, and nested class declarations can be intermixed. The order of declarations is immaterial to the compiler. Thus, they should be ordered in a way that is most logical and comprehensible.

A method declaration takes the form

[MethodModifiers] ReturnType MethodName ([ParameterList]) {
    Statements
}

A field declaration takes the form

[FieldModifiers] Type FieldName$_1$ [= Initializer$_1$] , FieldName$_2$ [= Initializer$_2$] . . . ;

A nested class declaration has the same syntax as the top-level class declaration. Each class member declaration begins with an optional list of modifiers. Modifiers that can be applied to method, field, and inner class declarations include

<none>	When no modifier is present, by default, a member is accessible by all the classes within the same package (see Section 4.5.1 [p. 135]).
public	A public member is accessible by any class.
protected	A protected member is accessible by the class itself, all its subclasses (see Section 5.2 [p. 163]), and all the classes within the same package.
private	A private member is accessible only by the class itself.
static	A static field is shared by all instances of the class. A static method accesses only static fields (see Section 4.4.5 [p. 110]). A static nested class does not have an implicit reference to the enclosing class (see Section 4.4.6 [p. 114]).
final	A final method may not be overridden in subclasses (see Section 5.2.3 [p. 174]). A final field has a constant value, which may not be changed (see Section 4.4.5 [p. 112]).

Modifiers that can be applied only to method declarations include

abstract	An abstract method defers implementation to its subclasses (see Section 7.2.1 [p. 252]).
synchronized	A synchronized method is atomic in a multithread environment (see Section 11.2.1 [p. 557]).
native	A native method is implemented in C and C++.

Modifiers that can be applied only to field declarations include

volatile	A volatile field may be modified by nonsynchronized methods in a multithread environment (see Section 11.2.1 [p. 557]).
transient	A transient field is not part of the persistent state of the instances (see Section 8.4.1 [p. 377]).

Only one public, protected, or private modifier may appear in the modifiers list for each member. Member accessibility is summarized in Table 4.2.

TABLE 4.2

Accessibility of Class Members

	Public	Protected	Package	Private
The class itself	Yes*	Yes	Yes	Yes
Classes in the same package	Yes	Yes	Yes	No†
Subclasses in a different package	Yes	Yes	No	No
Nonsubclasses in a different package	Yes	No	No	No

* Yes: Accessible.
† No: Not accessible.

Method Declarations

The return type of a method is required. If a method does not return a value, the return type should be specified as `void`. A method may take a list of parameter declarations separated by commas (the list could be empty). Parameters are declared in the form

[**final**] *Type ParameterName*

A final parameter is one that cannot be assigned a value inside the method (see "Pitfall: Final Parameters" in Section 4.4.4 [p. 109]).

The following class declaration declares a simple `Point` class, which represents points in a two-dimensional space.

```
public class Point {
   public double x, y;

   public void move(double dx, double dy) {
      x += dx; y += dy;
   }
}
```

Style Convention   *Class and Object Names*

Class and interface names should begin with uppercase letters, as in `Point`. Field and method names should begin with lowercase letters, as in `point`.

If a name consists of multiple words, it is formed by concatenating the words and capitalizing each word except the first, as in

- a long class name, `CheckBoxMenuItem`.
- a long object name, `printOptionMenu`.

4.4.2 Creating and Initializing Objects

There are four ways of initializing the fields of a class: an explicit initializer in a declaration, default initial values, constructors, or an initialization block.

Explicit Initializer

A field can be assigned an initial value in the declaration with an *explicit initializer*. For example, the x and y in the Point class can be explicitly initialized as

```
public double x = 0.0, y = 0.0;
```

Default Initial Values

If the fields are not explicitly initialized, they are implicitly initialized to their default initial values (see Section 4.2.1 [p. 88]).

Constructors

Another way to initialize fields is to use constructors. *Constructors* are special methods that have the same name as the class; their return type must be omitted. A class may have multiple constructors, provided that they take different numbers of arguments or arguments of different types.[6] The following is an enhanced Point class declaration with two constructors.

```
public class Point {
    public double x, y;

    public Point() { // no-arg constructor
        x = 0.0; y = 0.0;
    }

    public Point(double init_x, double init_y) {
        x = init_x; y = init_y;
    }

    public void move(double dx, double dy) {
        x += dx; y += dy;
    }
}
```

A constructor that takes no parameters is known as a *no-arg constructor* (shorthand for a no-arguments constructor). Instances of a class can be created with the new operator followed by an invocation of one of the constructors of the class. For example,

```
Point p1 = new Point();          // using the no-arg constructor
Point p2 = new Point(20.0, 20.0); // using the other constructor
```

If no constructor is provided for a class, a default no-arg constructor with an empty body is provided implicitly. In other words, even if none of the constructors

---

6. Constructors can be *overloaded*; see Section 5.1 [p. 159].

of the Point class in the preceding example were provided, creating instances of the Point class with the no-arg constructor would still be legal, as in

```
Point p3 = new Point();
```

The instance p3 would be initialized to (0, 0) by virtue of the default initial values. When constructors are provided explicitly, the default no-arg constructor is no longer provided implicitly. It must be provided explicitly if it is desired. In other words, if the no-arg constructor of Point class were removed but the other constructor remained, new Point() would be illegal. Hence, in general, the no-arg constructor should be provided for all classes.

Initialization Block

Fields can be also initialized by means of an *initialization block*, which is a statement block directly enclosed in the class declaration. The initialization block is executed before the body of any constructor is executed. The initialization block can be used to avoid duplicating identical statements for initializing fields in several constructors. These identical statements can be factored to the initialization block. This block is needed only when the initializations are too complicated for initializers, such as those that require loops. For example, the following Card and Deck classes model the cards and decks used in card games such as bridge:

```
public class Card {
   // the following are symbolic constants
   public static final byte CLUBSUIT    = 0;
   public static final byte DIAMONDSUIT = 1;
   public static final byte HEARTSUIT   = 2;
   public static final byte SPADESUIT   = 3;

   public byte suit; // range: CLUBSUIT -- SPADESUIT
   public byte rank; // range: 2 -- 14
                     //    11=Jack, 12=Queen, 13=King, 14=Ace
}

public class Deck {
   public Card[] cards = new Card[52];

   { // initialization block
      int i = 0;
      for (byte suit = Card.CLUBSUIT; suit <= Card.SPADESUIT; suit++) {
         for (byte rank = 2; rank <= 14; rank++) {
            cards[i] = new Card();
            cards[i].suit = suit;
            cards[i].rank = rank;
            i++;
         }
      }
   }
   // constructors and methods . . .
}
```

The initialization of `cards` is more suited to the use of loops than enumerating all 52 cards in an array initializer. The `Deck` class may have several constructors. Placing the initialization of `cards` in the initialization block avoids duplication of code in several constructors.

4.4.3 Accessing Fields and Methods

After an instance has been created, the fields and methods of the instance can be accessed as follows:

objectReference.*method* (*Parameters*)

objectReference.*field*

For example,

```
Point p1 = new Point();
double x1 = p1.x;      // the value is 0.0
double y1 = p1.y;      // the value is 0.0
p1.move(10.0, 20.0);
double x2 = p1.x;      // the value is 10.0
double y2 = p1.y;      // the value is 20.0
```

Comparison with C++

In C++, variables of a class type can be declared in three different ways.

```
Point p1;      // an object
Point *p2;     // a pointer to an object
Point &p3;     // a reference to an object

p1.x           // access a field of an object directly
p2->x          // access a field of an object through a pointer
p3.x           // access a field of an object through a reference
```

Memory space for object variables is automatically allocated and deallocated on the stack. No explicit allocation using the `new` operator is necessary. Memory space for pointer variables is also allocated on the stack. The memory space for objects referenced by the pointer variable must be explicitly allocated on the heap, using the `new` operator, and explicitly deallocated, using the `delete` operator. Reference variables serve as aliases for objects either on the stack or on the heap.

In Java, a variable of a class type can be declared in only one way.

```
Point p1;   // a reference to an object
p1.x;       // access a field of an object through a reference
```

In terms of Java reference variables, memory space for objects must always be explicitly allocated on the garbage-collected heap by the `new` operator. Java reference variables are analogous to C++ pointer variables but use the syntax of C++ object variables for accessing members. In Java, deallocation of memory space is automatically handled through garbage collection. No explicit deallocation is necessary. Hence there is no Java counterpart of the C++ destructor, whose main responsibility is to deallocate memory space.[7]

4.4.4 Method Invocation and Parameter Passing

Implementing Methods

The body of a method is simply a block statement. If the return type of a method is void, the return statements in the method body may not return values. If the return type of a method is not void, *all* the paths of the method body must be terminated by a return statement with an expression that matches the return type. The following calculateItemTotal() method will cause a compilation error because the path of quantity < 0 is not terminated by a return statement.

```
public class PurchaseOrder {
  // ...
  public double calculateItemTotal(double unitPrice, int quantity) {
    if (quantity >= 0) {
      return unitPrice * quantity;
    }
  }
}
```

To correct this error, we must add a return statement to return a value when the quantity is negative, or an exception must be thrown (see Section 4.6 [p. 139]).

The local variables declared in method bodies are not automatically initialized to their default initial values. Local variables must be explicitly initialized on all paths that lead to their uses. For example, the following calculateItemTotal method will cause a compilation error because the local variable total is not initialized on the path of quantity < 0.

```
public class PurchaseOrder {
  // ...
  public double calculateItemTotal(double unitPrice, int quantity) {
    double total;
    if (quantity >= 0) {
      total = unitPrice * quantity;
    }
    return total;
  }
}
```

7. When some cleanup must to be done before an object is deallocated, such as closing files or flushing changes to files, the finalize() method in the Object class can be used.

This error can be corrected in one of two ways:

```
public class PurchaseOrder {
    // ...
    public double calculateItemTotal(double unitPrice, int quantity) {
        double total = 0.0;
        if (quantity >= 0) {
            total = unitPrice * quantity;
        }
        return total;
    }
}
```

or

```
public class PurchaseOrder {
    // ...
    public double calculateItemTotal(double unitPrice, int quantity) {
        double total;
        if (quantity >= 0) {
            total = unitPrice * quantity;
        } else {
            total = 0.0;
        }
        return total;
    }
}
```

Parameter Passing

In Java, all parameters of methods are passed *by value*. In other words, modifications to parameters of primitive types inside a method will be made on copies of the actual parameters and will have no effect on the actual parameters themselves. Consider the example of class C1,

```
public class C1 {
    public void inc(int i) { i++; }
}
```

and an invocation of the inc method,

```
C1 c1 = new C1();
int k = 1;
c1.inc(k);  // k is still 1 afterward
```

For parameters of reference types, the fields of the actual parameters can indeed be affected inside a method. Consider the example of class C2,

```
public class C2 {
    public void pointInc(Point p) { p.x++; p.y++; }
}
```

and an invocation of the `pointInc` method,

```
C2 c2 = new C2();
Point p = new Point(10.0, 10.0);
c2.pointInc(p); // now p is (11.0, 11.0)
```

Hence parameters of reference types can serve as in–out parameters. In order for a parameter of primitive type to do so, it must be wrapped inside a class. Consider the example of an integer wrapped in the `IntRef` class so that it may act as an in–out parameter,

```
class IntRef {
    public int val;
    public IntRef(int i) { val = i; }
}
public class C3 {
    public void inc(IntRef i) { i.val++; }
}
```

and an invocation of the `inc` method,

```
C3 c3 = new C3();
IntRef k = new IntRef(1);
c3.inc(k); // now k.val is 2
```

Usually, a method passes values back to its caller via the return value of the method. In–out parameters are necessary only when the method needs to pass multiple values back to the caller.

Pitfall: Final Parameters

The notion of final parameters in Java is rather weak. A final parameter of a method may not be assigned a new value in the body of the method. However, if the parameter is of reference type, it is allowed to modify the object or array referenced by the final parameter. Let us consider the following method:

```
void aMethod(final IntRef i) {
    // . . .
    i = new IntRef(2); // not allowed
}
```

This code segment will cause a compilation error because it is not allowed to assign a new value to a final parameter. However, the following method is allowed:

```
void aMethod(final IntRef i) {
    // . . .
    i.val++; // ok.
}
```

Java `final` parameters are not the same as `const` parameters in C++. Furthermore, there is no Java counterpart of C++ `const` methods, which do not modify the state of the receiving object.

4.4.5   Class (Static) Fields and Methods

By default the fields declared in a class are *instance fields*, which means that each instance of the class carries its own copy of these fields, and modifications to the fields of one instance will not affect any other instances. In contrast, *class fields* are shared by all the instances of the same class. There is only one copy of each class field for the class. Modifications to class fields will affect all the instances of the class. By default the methods of a class are also called *instance methods*, which means that they operate on a specific instance of the class when they are invoked. If a method accesses only class fields, then it is called a *class method*. Class fields and class methods are declared using the `static` modifier. Thus they are also often called *static fields* and *static methods*.[8]

Instance fields and methods can be accessed only through an object reference. Class fields and methods may be accessed through either an object reference or the class name.

> *objectReference.classMethod (Parameters)*
> *objectReference.classField*
>
> *ClassName.classMethod (Parameters)*
> *ClassName.classField*

Class and instance fields and methods are subject to the same accessibility controls. Class fields and methods should be accessed through class names, not object references. Then instance fields and methods can easily be distinguished from class fields and methods by the way they are accessed.

The following is a simple class `Robot` representing the position of robots. It contains an instance field `instanceMoveCount`, which counts the number of moves made by each instance of the `Robot` class. Its value can be retrieved by an instance method `getInstanceMoveCount()`. The `Robot` class also contains a class field `classMoveCount`, which counts the total number of moves made by *all* instances of the `Robot` class. Its value can be retrieved by a class method `getInstanceMove-Count()`. The method `getClassMoveCount()` is a class method because it accesses only a class field.

```
public class Robot {
   public int x, y;
   private int instanceMoveCount;
   static private int classMoveCount;

   public Robot(int x, int y) {
      this.x = x; this.y = y;
   }
```

---

8. The term *static* refers to the way class fields and methods are implemented. *Class fields* and *methods* are more appropriate terms, since they connote their behavior as being per-class versus per-instance. Although the terms are interchangeable, we will use the term *class fields and methods* throughout this book.

```
    public void move(int dx, int dy) {
        x += dx; y += dy;
        instanceMoveCount++;
        classMoveCount++;
    }
    public int getInstanceMoveCount() {
        return instanceMoveCount;
    }
    static public int getClassMoveCount() {
        return classMoveCount;
    }
}
```

The following code segment illustrates the invocation of static methods.

```
Robot r1 = new Robot(0, 0);
Robot r2 = new Robot(0, 0);
r1.move(20, 10);
r1.move(10, 20);
r2.move(10, 10);
int count1 = r1.getInstanceMoveCount();  // count1 is 2
int count2 = r2.getInstanceMoveCount();  // count2 is 1
// The next three statements will get the same result.
int count3 = r1.getClassMoveCount();     // count3 is 3
int count4 = r2.getClassMoveCount();     // count4 is 3
int count5 = Robot.getClassMoveCount();  // count5 is 3
```

Initialization of Class Fields

Class fields can exist without any instances of the class being created. In fact, class fields are initialized before any of the instances of the class are created and before any of the class fields or methods are accessed. The lifetime of class fields extends until the program terminates. With respect to lifetime, class fields are similar to the global variables of C and C++.

Class fields can be initialized in the following ways:

1. With default initial values. This is how `classMoveCount` is initialized in the preceding example. It is initialized to the default initial value 0.

2. With an explicit initializer in its declaration. The `classMoveCount` field in the preceding example can also be initialized with an explicit initializer.

   ```
   public class Robot {
       // ...
       static private int classMoveCount = 0;
       // ...
   }
   ```

3. By the static initialization block. The static initialization block is similar to the instance fields initialization block, except that it begins with the keyword

static. The classMoveCount field in the preceding example can also be initialized with a static initialization block.

```
public class Robot {
    // ...
    static private int classMoveCount;
    static {
        classMoveCount = 0;
    }
    // ...
}
```

Class fields should not be initialized in constructors, as constructors are executed only when instances are created. Therefore, constructors are used for initializing instance fields only.

Constants

In Java, constants can be declared as final class fields. For example, several integer constants for specifying font styles are defined in the Font class.

```
public class Font {
public final static int PLAIN  = 0;
public final static int BOLD   = 1;
public final static int ITALIC = 2;
    // ...
}
```

We may also define constant objects. In the Color class, some commonly used colors are declared as follows.

```
public class Color {
    public final static Color BLACK  = new Color(0, 0, 0);
    public final static Color BLUE   = new Color(0, 0, 255);
    public final static Color GRAY   = new Color(128, 128, 128);
    public final static Color WHITE  = new Color(255, 255, 255);
    public final static Color YELLOW = new Color(255, 255, 0);
    // ...
}
```

Style Convention *Constant Names*

Name of constants should be in all uppercase letters (e.g., the constants in the Font and Color class).

When there are multiple words in the names, separate the words with underscores (_) (e.g., STANDARD_RATE, MAXIMUM_CLASS_SIZE).

The main() Method

Each class can have a special class method main(), which must be declared as

```
public static void main(String[] args) { . . . }
```

The main() method serves as the entry point of a Java application. Java applications are invoked as

venus% java *ClassName* [*arguments* . . .]

ClassName.main() is invoked to start an application. When the application starts, no instance of *ClassName* has been created, so only a static method can be invoked. Thus, the start-up method main() must be static.

Optionally, a number of arguments can be specified on the command line and passed to the application when it is invoked. The command-line arguments, not including java or the class name, are passed to the main() method through the args parameter as an array of strings.

EXAMPLE 4.3   Command-Line Arguments

PURPOSE

To illustrate retrieving command-line arguments passed to the main() method of a Java application.

DESCRIPTION

The following program prints the command-line arguments to the standard output.

SOLUTION

Print command line arguments: Arguments.java

```java
public class Arguments {

    public static void main(String[] args) {
        if (args.length > 0) {
            for (int i = 0; i < args.length; i++) {
                System.out.println("args[" + i + "]: " + args[i]);
            }
        } else {
            System.out.println("No arguments.");
        }
    }
}
```

If the program is invoked as

```
venus% java Arguments foo bar
```

the result is

```
args[0]: foo
args[1]: bar
```

Singleton Classes

Some classes are not supposed to have more than one instance at a time. Examples are the top-level window of an application and the timer of an entire system. Classes that can have no more than one instance at a time are called *singleton classes*. Using class fields and methods, we can ensure that no more than one instance of a singleton class exits at any given moment. The following is a schematic implementation of a singleton class:

```
public class Singleton {
    static public Singleton getInstance() {
        return theInstance;
    }

    protected Singleton() {
        // initializing instance fields
    }

    // other fields and methods

    private static Singleton theInstance = new Singleton();
}
```

The unique instance of the `Singleton` class is stored in a class field, `theInstance`. Note that the constructor of the `Singleton` class is *protected*. Therefore, clients are prohibited from creating an instance of the `Singleton` class by doing

```
myInstance = new Singleton();
```

The only way for clients to obtain an instance of the `Singleton` class is to use the class method `getInstance()`:

```
myInstance = Singleton.getInstance();
```

The `getInstance()` ensures that a new instance of the class will be created only when it is invoked the very first time. Hence, just one instance of the `Singleton` class can be created!

4.4.6 Object Reference this

Instance methods operate on a specific instance of a class. This object instance is often referred to as the *receiving instance* (also known as the *receiver* or the *recipient*) of the instance method, that is, the object instance through which the instance method is invoked. Inside instance methods, a special object reference `this` is used to denote the receiving instance. Since class methods operate on class fields only, the object reference `this` may not be used in class methods.

The two common uses of `this` are (1) to pass the receiving object instance as a parameter to other methods and (2) to access instance fields that are shadowed, or hidden, by local variables.

Passing `this` as a Parameter

Let us consider the composition relationship between `Faculty` and `Department`, as shown previously in Figure 2.7. The relationship can be implemented as follows:

```
public class Faculty {
   protected Department dept;
   protected String name;

   public Faculty(String n, Department d) {
      name = n; dept = d;
   }

   public Department getDepartment() {
      return dept;
   }
   // . . . other methods
}
```

Each faculty member has a name and a reference to the department to which the faculty member belongs.

```
public class Department {
   protected String name;
   protected Faculty facultyList[] = new Faculty[100];
   protected int numOfFaculty = 0;

   public Department(String n) {
      name = n;
   }
   public void newFaculty(String name) {
      facultyList[numOfFaculty++] =
         new Faculty(name, this);
   }
   // . . . other methods
}
```

Each department has a name and a list of faculty members who belong to the department. For consistency, it is important to maintain the following requirement among the instances of these two classes:

> If a faculty member a occurs in the `facultyList` of department d, then a.dept should refer to d.

This requirement is maintained in the `newFaculty()` method by passing the `this` reference—the department to which the new faculty member belongs—as the parameter to the constructor of the `Faculty` class.

Accessing Shadowed Fields

A field declared in a class can be *shadowed*, or *hidden*, inside a method by a parameter or a local variable of the same name, as in the following code segment:

```java
public class MyClass {
    int var; // an instance field

    void method1() {
        float var; // the local variable var shadows the instance field
        // ...
    }
    void method2(int var) {
        // the parameter var also shadows the instance field
        // ...
    }
}
```

Java adopts the usual scope rule: When a name in an outer scope is shadowed by a name in an inner scope, the name in the outer scope is hidden. In the case of a shadowed instance field of a class, the shadowed field `var` can be accessed via the receiving object reference `this` as `this.var`. In general, the shadowing of variable names in outer scopes is a bad programming practice and should be avoided, as it is a common source of program bugs. In contrast, the shadowing of instance fields of a class from within its methods is an acceptable and common practice, if the local variables are indeed copies of the fields of the same class. The purpose is to avoid the confusion of introducing a new set of variable names to mirror the fields of the class. The following program segment is another version of the `Point` class.

```java
public class Point {
    public double x, y;
    public Point() { }

    public Point(double x, double y) {
        // the parameters x and y are simply the initial values of
        // fields x and y of class Point
        this.x = x; this.y = y;
    }
    public void adjustPosition(. . . ) {
        double x = this.x, y = this.y;
        // do calculation using the local x and y
        // commit the changes when done
        this.x = x; this.y = y;
    }

    // ... other methods
}
```

In the preceding constructor, parameters x and y represent the initial values of the corresponding instance fields of class `Point`. The expressions `this.x` and `this.y` refer to the instance fields. In method `adjustPosition()`, the instance fields are copied to the local variables with the same names. Calculations are performed on these local copies. Only when the calculations have been completed will the results be committed to the instance fields of class `Point`. Therefore, no intermediate values are ever stored in the instance fields. The advantages of this approach are to avoid leaving intermediate results in the instance fields in case an exception is encountered (see Section 4.6 [p. 139]) and to avoid synchronizing an entire method of a multithreaded program. Only the reading and writing of instance fields should be synchronized. The calculation portion can be unsynchronized (see Section 11.2.1 [p. 557]).

Guideline *Shadowing Variables*

Avoid shadowing variables. Shadow only the instance fields with local variables that serve as temporary copies of the instance fields in an instance method or constructor. Upon successul completion of the method, copy the local variables back to the instance fields before leaving the method.

4.4.7   Interfaces and Abstract Classes

Interfaces can be thought of as a special form of class, which declares only the features to be supported by the class. Java interfaces provide no implementation. Implementation is deferred to the classes that implement the interface. The syntax of an interface declaration is

> [*ClassModifiers*] `interface` *InterfaceName*
>   [`extends` *Interface₁*, *Interface₂* ...] {
>   *InterfaceMemberDeclarations*
> }

Interface members can be either *abstract methods* or constants (that is, static and final fields). Implementation of abstract methods is deferred to subclasses. Abstract methods are declared as

> *MethodModifiers ReturnType MethodName* ([*ParameterList*]) ;

All interfaces are public, and all methods and constants declared in interfaces are public. The `public` modifier can be omitted in interface declarations. Class (static) methods are not allowed in interfaces. Interfaces have no constructors, and no instances of interfaces are allowed.

Here are two commonly used interfaces in Java: the `Runnable` interface,

```
public interface Runnable {
    public void run();
}
```

and the `Iterator` interface,

```
public interface Iterator {
   public boolean hasNext();
   public Object next();
   public Object remove();
}
```

Classes can implement an interface by overriding the methods declared in the interface. Classes may also declare abstract methods by using the modifier `abstract`:

abstract *MethodModifiers ReturnType MethodName* (*[ParameterList]*) ;

An *abstract class* is a class that includes or inherits at least one abstract method. In other words, an abstract class is a class with partial implementation. Although the presence of an abstract method in a class implies that the class is abstract, the class must still be declared abstract explicitly; that is, the class modifier `abstract` must be present for the sake of readability. Like interfaces, an abstract class may not have instances. We discuss the implementation, extension, and use of interfaces in detail in Chapters 5 and 7.

4.4.8 Strings

A *string* is a sequence of characters. The `String` type is not a primitive type in Java; it is a class type. Java provides two classes to support strings: (1) the `String` class, whose instances are immutable (that is, constant strings), and (2) the `StringBuffer` class, whose instances are mutable strings. The rationale for distinguishing mutable from immutable strings is that in a typical program most strings are immutable. Immutable strings allow simpler implementation and a more compact representation than do mutable strings.

The `String` class is special in the sense that it enjoys some unique privileges not shared by ordinary classes.

- A string, that is, an instance of the `String` class, can be created using *string literals* (see "String Literals" in Section 4.1.3 [p. 80]).
- Operators + and += can be applied to strings (see "String Concatenation" in Section 4.1.4 [p. 84]).

The characters in a string are indexed by integers 0 to $n - 1$, where n is the length of the string. The common operations on strings are summarized in Table 4.3.

The `StringBuffer` class provides an overloaded `append()` method that appends the text representation of its arguments to the string buffer.

String Comparison

For two string variables s1 and s2, s1 == s2 tests the equality of the two references, not the equality of the strings referenced by them. Thus s1 == s2 is true if and

TABLE 4.3

Methods of String Class

Method	Description
s.length()	Returns the length of string s.
s.charAt(i)	Returns the ith character of string s.
s.indexOf(c)	Returns the index of the first occurrence of character c; returns −1 if c does not occur in s.
s.indexOf(c, i)	Returns the index of the first occurrence of character c after (including) index i; returns −1 if c does not occur in s after index i.
s.indexOf(s1)	Returns the index of the first occurrence of string s1; returns −1 if s1 does not occur in s.
s.indexOf(s1, i)	Returns the index of the first occurrence of string s1 after (including) index i; returns −1 if s1 does not occur in s after index i.
s.substring(i)	Returns the substring of s from i to the end.
s.substring(i, j)	Returns the substring of s from i to $j - 1$, inclusive.
s.toLowerCase()	Returns a string with all the characters in s converted to lowercase.
s.toUpperCase()	Returns a string with all the characters in s converted to uppercase.
s.trim()	Returns a string with all the leading and trailing white space of s removed.
s.endsWith(s1)	Returns true if string s1 is a suffix of s.
s.startsWith(s1)	Returns true if string s1 is a prefix of s.

only if both s1 and s2 reference the same string (that is, point to the same memory location). The equivalence of two strings can be tested in several ways:

```
s1.equals(s2)
```

returns a boolean value,

true   if s1 and s2 are identical in content (case-sensitive).

false   otherwise.

```
s1.equalsIgnoreCase(s2)
```

is the same as `equals()`, except that the comparison is case-insensitive.

```
s1.compareTo(s2)
```

compares the two strings lexicographically, according to the Unicode; the comparison is case-sensitive and returns an integer value of

- < 0 if s1 is lexicographically less than s2.
- 0 if s1 and s2 are equal.
- > 0 if s2 is lexicographically less than s1.

The following code segment illustrates the differences between comparing string references and string contents. Three strings str1, str2, and str3 are initialized in different ways as follows:

```
String str1 = "FooBar";
String str2 = str1;
String str3 = new String("FooBar");
```

The first two strings str1 and str2 reference the same string object, while str3 is a different string object with the same contents.

The following table shows different ways of comparing the strings and their results:

Expression	Result
str1 == str2	true
str1 == str3	false
str1.equals(str2)	true
str1.equals(str3)	true
str1.compareTo(str2)	0
str1.compareTo(str3)	0

Note that comparisons of the identity and equality of strings do not always yield the same results. String comparison is a very common operation in many programs. Comparing the identity of two strings takes far less time than comparing the equality of two strings. The `String` class supports a canonical representation of string objects. It maintains an internal pool of unique string objects. A string object can be *interned* by calling the `intern()` method of the `String` class, which returns a string that has the same contents as the original string, but is guaranteed to be from the internal pool of unique strings. For interned strings, comparison of the identity and equality of the strings *always* yield the same results.

The following example expands the preceding example to illustrate the difference between comparisons of the identity and equality of strings, and the effect of interning:

```
public class StringComparison {

  public static void main(String[] args) {
    String str1 = "FooBar";
    String str2 = str1;
    String str3 = new String("FooBar");
    String str4 = "FooBar";
    String str5 = "Foo" + "Bar";
    String str6 = new String("Foo") + new String("Bar");

    System.out.println("str1 == str2: " + (str1 == str2));
    System.out.println("str1 == str3: " + (str1 == str3));
    System.out.println("str1 == str4: " + (str1 == str4));
    System.out.println("str1 == str5: " + (str1 == str5));
    System.out.println("str1 == str6: " + (str1 == str6));
    System.out.println("str1.equals(str2): " + str1.equals(str2));
    System.out.println("str1.equals(str3): " + str1.equals(str3));
    System.out.println("str1.equals(str4): " + str1.equals(str4));
    System.out.println("str1.equals(str5): " + str1.equals(str5));
    System.out.println("str1.equals(str6): " + str1.equals(str6));
    System.out.println("str1.compareTo(str2): " + str1.compareTo(str2));
    System.out.println("str1.compareTo(str3): " + str1.compareTo(str3));
    System.out.println("str1.compareTo(str4): " + str1.compareTo(str4));
    System.out.println("str1.compareTo(str5): " + str1.compareTo(str5));
    System.out.println("str1.compareTo(str6): " + str1.compareTo(str6));

    str2 = str2.intern();
    str3 = str3.intern();
    str4 = str4.intern();
    str5 = str5.intern();
    str6 = str6.intern();
    System.out.println("After interning");
    System.out.println("str1 == str2: " + (str1 == str2));
    System.out.println("str1 == str3: " + (str1 == str3));
    System.out.println("str1 == str4: " + (str1 == str4));
    System.out.println("str1 == str5: " + (str1 == str5));
    System.out.println("str1 == str6: " + (str1 == str6));
  }
}
```

The results are

```
str1 == str2: true
str1 == str3: false
str1 == str4: true
str1 == str5: true
str1 == str6: false
str1.equals(str2): true
str1.equals(str3): true
str1.equals(str4): true
str1.equals(str5): true
str1.equals(str6): true
str1.compareTo(str2): 0
str1.compareTo(str3): 0
str1.compareTo(str4): 0
str1.compareTo(str5): 0
str1.compareTo(str6): 0
After interning
str1 == str2: true
str1 == str3: true
str1 == str4: true
str1 == str5: true
str1 == str6: true
```

Note that all string literals are automatically interned (compare the results concerning `str1`, `str4`, and `str5`). In most cases, interning strings will significantly improve the performance of programs.

The `toString()` Method

The `toString()` method of a class allows it to define a string representation of the instances of the class. For example, we can add the following `toString()` method to the `Point` class.

```java
public class Point {
   public double x, y;

   // other methods . . .

   public String toString() {
      return "(" + x + ", " + y + ")";
   }
}
```

If we assume that `str` is a string variable and that `obj` is a variable of class type, the expression

```java
str + obj
```

is interpreted as

```java
str + obj.toString()
```

Now, having added the `toString()` method to the `Point` class, we may do the following.

```
Point p = new Point(10.0, 20.0);
System.out.println("A point at" + p);
```

The output will be

```
A point at (10.0, 20.0)
```

String and Character Array

Unlike those in C and C++, strings in Java are not arrays of characters, that is, `char []`. However, strings can be converted to character arrays and vice versa.

```
char data[] = { 'F', 'o', 'o'} ;
String str = new String(data);
```

is equivalent to

```
String str = "Foo";
```

and

```
String str = "Bar";
char data[] = str.toCharArray();
```

is equivalent to

```
char data[] = { 'B', 'a', 'r'} ;
```

More sophisticated methods for string–`char` array conversions are available also.

Reading and Writing Strings

We begin with an example of how strings can be read from and written to the standard input and output streams. The standard input and output refer to the character-based input and output associated with a command console or terminal window. The standard input and output streams are declared as class fields in the `System` class, which also contains declarations of other systemwide resources.

```
public class System {
    public static final InputStream in;   // the standard input
    public static final PrintStream out; // the standard output
    public static final PrintStream err; // the standard error output
    // . . .
}
```

The Java input and output mechanism is both versatile and nontrivial (we discuss it in detail in Section 8.4 [p. 366]). We begin with some simple use of the input and output mechanism to read and write strings.

EXAMPLE 4.4   Copying from Standard Input to Standard Output

PURPOSE

To illustrate reading and writing strings.

DESCRIPTION

The following program reads the characters read from the standard input line by line and writes each line to the standard output.

SOLUTION

Copy from standard input to standard output: `Copy.java`

```java
import java.io.*;

public class Copy {

    public static void main(String[] args) {
        try {
            BufferedReader in = new BufferedReader(
                                    new InputStreamReader(System.in));
            String line;
            while ((line = in.readLine()) != null) {
                System.out.println(line);
            }
        } catch (IOException e) {}
    }
}
```

We discuss the `BufferedReader` and `InputStreamReader` classes in Section 8.4 [p. 366]. The `readLine()` method simply reads a line of characters from the input stream. It returns `null` when the end of the stream is reached. We invoke the program as follows:

```
venus% java Copy < infile.txt > outfile.txt
```

Here, the standard input and output are redirected to two files named infile.txt to outfile.txt, respectively. The preceding invocation of Copy copies infile.txt to outfile.txt.

EXAMPLE 4.5   Copying Text Files

PURPOSE

To illustrate reading and writing text files.

DESCRIPTION

The following program simply copies the contents of one text file to another text file, line by line.

SOLUTION

> **Copy a text file: `CopyTextFile.java`**

```java
import java.io.*;
public class CopyTextFile {

    public static void main(String[] args) {
        if (args.length >= 2) {
            try {
                BufferedReader in = new BufferedReader(
                                new FileReader(args[0]));

                PrintWriter out = new PrintWriter(
                                new BufferedWriter(
                                new FileWriter(args[1])));
                String line;
                while ((line = in.readLine()) != null) {
                    out.println(line);
                }
                out.flush();
                out.close();
            } catch (IOException e) { }
        }
    }
}
```

Again, we discuss the `FileReader`, `FileWriter`, `PrintWriter`, and `BufferedWriter` classes in Section 8.4 [p. 366]. This program takes two arguments: the first argument is the name of the input file, and the second argument is the name of the output file. The following invocation copies a text file named `infile.txt` to `outfile.txt`:

```
venus% java CopyTextFile infile.txt outfile.txt
```

Working with Strings

We often need to divide strings into smaller pieces, known as *tokens*, that are separated by *separators* or *delimiters*. For example, it may be useful to break strings that represent sentences or paragraphs into words that are separated by spaces or some type of punctuation. The colon-delimited record format is a common format for storing a variety of tabular text data, in which each record is a single line of text that consists of fields delimited by colons (`:`). The following example contains two colon-delimited records in an address book:

```
Michael:Owen:123 Oak Street:Chicago:IL:60606
James:Gosling:456 Sun Blvd.:Mountain View:CA:45454
```

To extract the information stored in the colon-delimited record format, each record needs to be divided into fields. One way to break strings into tokens is to use the `indexOf()` and `substring()` methods of the `String` class.

EXAMPLE 4.6   Breaking Colon-Delimited Records

PURPOSE
To illustrate string manipulation.

DESCRIPTION
The following program reads colon-delimited records from the standard input and breaks each record into fields.

SOLUTION

Break colon-delimited records: `BreakRecords.java`

```java
import java.io.*;

public class BreakRecords {
  public static void main(String[] args) {
    BufferedReader in = new BufferedReader(
                        new InputStreamReader(System.in));
    try {
      String record, field;
      char delim =':';  // the delimiter

      for (int n = 1; (record = in.readLine()) != null; n++) {
        System.out.println("Record " + n);
        int begin, end, i;
        begin = 0;
        for (i = 0; (end = record.indexOf(delim, begin)) >= 0; i++) {
          field = record.substring(begin, end);
          begin = end + 1; // skip the delimiter
          System.out.println("\tField " + i + ": " + field);
        }
        field = record.substring(begin); // the last field
        System.out.println("\tField " + i + ": " + field);
      }
    } catch (IOException e) {  }
  }
}
```

The following output of the program is obtained when the two name and address records shown previously are used as input:

```
Record 1
        Field 0: Michael
        Field 1: Owen
        Field 2: 123 Oak Street
        Field 3: Chicago
        Field 4: IL
        Field 5: 60606
```

```
Record 2
        Field 0: James
        Field 1: Gosling
        Field 2: 456 Sun Blvd.
        Field 3: Mountain View
        Field 4: CA
        Field 5: 45454
```

The second approach breaks strings into tokens with the help of the `StringTo-kenizer` class.

EXAMPLE 4.7   Breaking Text into Words

PURPOSE

To illustrate the use of `StringTokenizer`.

DESCRIPTION

The following program reads text from standard input and breaks the text into words.

SOLUTION

Break text into words: `Words.java`

```java
import java.io.*;
import java.util.*;

public class Words {
    public static void main(String[] args) {
        BufferedReader in =
            new BufferedReader(new InputStreamReader(System.in));
        try {
            String line, word;
            String delim = "\t\n.,:;?!-/()[]\"\'"; // spaces and punctuations
            while ((line = in.readLine()) != null) {
                StringTokenizer st = new StringTokenizer(line, delim);
                while (st.hasMoreTokens()) {
                    System.out.println(st.nextToken());
                }
            }
        } catch (IOException e) {}
    }
}
```

The constructor call in Example 4.7 creates an instance of the `StringTo-kenizer` class that discards the delimiters indicated by the string `delim`. The `StringTokenizer` class has two other constructors. All three `StringTokenizer` constructors are summarized in the following table. Parameter *str* is the string to be tokenized, *delim* is a string of delimiters, and *keep* is a boolean value indicating whether the delimiters should be returned as tokens.

Constructor	Description
`StringTokenizer`(*str*)	Tokens are delimited by one or more white spaces, and the delimiters are discarded.
`StringTokenizer`(*str*, *delim*)	Tokens are delimited by any character in *delim*, and the delimiters are discarded.
`StringTokenizer`(*str*, *delim*, *keep*)	Tokens are delimited by any character in *delim*. The delimiters are returned as tokens if *keep* is `true`. Otherwise, the delimiters are discarded.

The methods of the `StringTokenizer` class are summarized as follows.

Method	Description
`hasMoreTokens()`	Returns `true` if there are remaining tokens.
`nextToken()`	Returns the next token and advance.
`countTokens()`	Returns the number of remaining tokens.

4.4.9 Wrapper Classes

Because in Java values of primitive types are not objects, a *wrapper* class is provided to "wrap" the values of primitive types into objects when needed. Each primitive type has a corresponding wrapper class as shown in the following table:

Primitive Type	Wrapper Class
`boolean`	`Boolean`
`byte`	`Byte`
`char`	`Character`
`double`	`Double`
`float`	`Float`
`int`	`Integer`
`long`	`Long`
`short`	`Short`

Wrapper classes allow values of primitive types to be used in places where objects are expected, as in the elements of collection classes such as List or Hashtable (we discuss collections in Section 8.2 [p. 308]). Wrapper classes also provide useful methods and constants for manipulating the values of primitive types.

Seemingly, instances of wrapper classes could also be used for in–out parameters for primitive types. Unfortunately, however, they may not. The reason is that instances of wrapper classes are immutable; that is, they provide no way to modify the state of their instances.

If we let *Type* be a wrapper class of primitive type named *type*, for each wrapper class *Type* at least two constructors are provided. One takes a value of *type*, and the other takes a string representation of a literal of *type*. For example, the Integer class has the constructors

```
Integer(int value)
Integer(String value)
```

Instances of wrapper classes can also be created by using the class method valueOf(). The valueOf() method of wrapper class *Type* takes a string representation of a literal of *type* and returns an instance of *Type*. Each wrapper class also provides methods for retrieving its value as a primitive type.

Wrapper Class	Method of Retrieving Values
Boolean	booleanValue()
Character	charValue()
Byte	byteValue()
Double	doubleValue()
Float	floatValue()
Integer	intValue()
Long	longValue()
Short	shortValue()

For a string representation of a literal of primitive type *type*, the value represented by the literal can be obtained as

Type.valueOf(*literal*).*type*Value()

For example, the following expressions give the results shown:

Expression	Result
Integer.valueOf("100").intValue()	100
Double.valueOf("1E3").doubleValue()	1000.0

The class method `parseInt()` of the `Integer` class can also be used to parse integers. It parses a string representation of an integer literal and returns an `int` value. For example, the expression `Integer.parseInt("100")` produces the result 100.

A common use of the parsing method is to parse the input values to a program, which are often provided as strings.

EXAMPLE 4.8   The Maximum of Two Integers

PURPOSE

To illustrate the use of the `parseInt()` method to parse command-line arguments.

DESCRIPTION

The following program takes two integers as command-line arguments. It converts the string arguments into integers using the `parseInt()` method and finds the maximum of the two integers.

SOLUTION

The maximum of two integer arguments: `Maximum.java`

```java
public class Maximum {

    public static void main(String[] args) {
        if (args.length >= 2) {
            int i1 = Integer.parseInt(args[0]);
            int i2 = Integer.parseInt(args[1]);
            System.out.println("The maximum of " + i1 + " and " + i2 +
                               " is: " + ((i1 >= i2) ? i1 : i2));
        } else {
            System.out.println("Usage: java Maximum integer1 integer2");
        }
    }
}
```

Running the program produces the following results:

```
venus% java Maximum 12 11
The maximum of 12 and 11 is: 12
```

The `Float` and `Double` Classes

Classes `Float` and `Double` provide some useful constants and methods for floating-point arithmetic. The constants that follow are declared in both classes.

In Double	In Float	Description
double POSITIVE_INFINITY	float POSITIVE_INFINITY	$+\infty$
double NEGATIVE_INFINITY	float NEGATIVE_INFINITY	$-\infty$
double NaN	float NaN	NaN

The following instance methods are declared in both classes. These methods can be used to test whether the value wrapped in the instance is NaN or infinity.

In Double	In Float
boolean isNaN()	boolean isNaN()
boolean isInfinite()	boolean isInfinite()

And the following class methods are also declared in both classes. These methods can be used to test whether a parameter is NaN or infinity, such as

In Double	In Float
boolean isNaN(double v)	boolean isNaN(float v)
boolean isInfinite(double v)	boolean isInfinite(float v)

Mathematical Constants and Functions

Table 4.4 shows the commonly used mathematical constants and functions defined in class Math. All the methods are class methods. The following are some simple examples of the use of these functions:

```
Point p1, p2;
double dx = (p2.x - p1.x);
double dy = (p2.y - p1.y);
// the distance between p1 and p2
double distance = Math.sqrt(dx * dx + dy * dy);
// the angle between the line connecting p1 and p2 and the X axis
double angle = Math.atan2(dy, dx);
```

TABLE 4.4

Mathematical Constants and Functions

Constant/Method	Description
double E	$e = 2.7182818284590452345$
double PI	$\pi = 3.14159265358979323846$
double sin(double a)	$\sin(a)$, a an angle in radians
double cos(double a)	$\cos(a)$, a an angle in radians
double tan(double a)	$\tan(a)$, a an angle in radians
double asin(double a)	$\arcsin(a)$, result in $[-\pi/2, \pi/2]$
double acos(double a)	$\arccos(a)$, result in $[0, \pi]$
double atan(double a)	$\arctan(a)$, result in $[-\pi/2, \pi/2]$
double atan2(double a, double b)	$\arctan(b/a)$, result in $[-\pi, \pi]$
double exp(double a)	e^a
double pow(double a, double b)	a^b
double log(double a)	$\ln(a)$, the natural logarithm of a
double sqrt(double a)	$\sqrt{a}$, the square root of a
double rint(double a)	truncated integer value of a
double random()	a pseudorandom number in $[0.0, 1.0)$
double ceil(double a)	$\lceil a \rceil$, the ceiling of a
double floor(double a)	$\lfloor a \rfloor$, the floor of a
int round(float a)	$\lfloor a + 0.5 \rfloor$, the rounding of a
int round(double a)	
int abs(int a)	$|a|$, the absolute value of a
long abs(long a)	
float abs(float a)	
double abs(double a)	
int max(int a, int b)	$\max(a, b)$, the maximum of a and b
long max(long a, long b)	
float max(float a, float b)	
double max(double a, double b)	
int min(int a, int b)	$\min(a, b)$, the minimum of a and b
long min(long a, long b)	
float min(float a, float b)	
double min(double a, double b)	

EXAMPLE 4.9   The Minimum of an Array of Integers

PURPOSE

To illustrate the use of mathematical functions in `Math` class.

DESCRIPTION

The following program finds the minimum value of an array.

SOLUTION

The minimum of an array of integers: `Minimum.java`

```java
public class Minimum {

    public static void main(String[]args) {
        int a[] = { 75, 34, 80, 11, 95, 34, 53, 81, 33, 13 };

        int min = a[0];
        for (int i = 1; i < a.length; i++) {
            min = Math.min(min, a[i]);
        }
        System.out.println("The minimum value is: " + min);
    }
}
```

Running the program produces the following results:

```
venus% java Minimum
The minimum value is: 11
```

EXAMPLE 4.10   The Max–Min Value of a Two-Dimensional Array

PURPOSE

To illustrate the use of mathematical functions in `Math` class and handling of two-dimensional arrays.

DESCRIPTION

Assume the following declaration of a matrix of `doubles`:

```java
double mat[][];
```

The following program segment finds the max–min value of a two-dimensional array, that is, the maximum of the minimums of each column, or

$$\max_{0 \le j \le m} \min_{0 \le i \le n} \mathrm{mat}[i][j]$$

where n and m are the number of rows and columns, respectively.

SOLUTION

The max–min value of a two-dimensional array: `MaxMin.java`

```java
public class MaxMin {

    public static void main(String[]args) {
        double mat[][] = { { 2.3, 5.1, 9.9 },
                           { 8.3, 4.5, 7.7 },
                           { 5.2, 6.1, 2.8 } };

        int n = mat.length;
        int m = mat[0].length;
        double maxmin = 0.0;

        for (int j = 0; j < m; j++) {
            double min = mat[j][0];
            for (int i = 1; i < n; i++) {
                min = Math.min(min, mat[i][j]);
            }
            if (j == 0) {
                maxmin = min;
            } else {
                maxmin = Math.max(maxmin, min);
            }
        }
        System.out.println("The max-min value is " + maxmin);
    }
}
```

Running the program produces the following results:

```
venus% java MaxMin
The max-min value is 4.5
```

4.5   PACKAGES

Classes are the basic building blocks of Java programs, and a Java program consists of one or more classes. Classes should be relatively small and comprise highly cohesive functionalities. Because a large program may consist of thousands of classes, providing a mechanism for logically organizing large programs is necessary. Java provides two such mechanisms:

1. *Files*, which may contain a main public class and possibly a few nonpublic helper classes.

2. *Packages*, which comprise many related classes, interfaces, or other packages.

Files are the *compilation units* of Java; that is, each file can be compiled separately. Packages support hierarchical organization and are used to organize large programs into logical and manageable units.

4.5.1 Using Packages

In Java each class belongs to a package. Package declaration is file based; that is, all classes in the same source file belong to the same package. Each source file may contain an optional *package declaration* in the following form:

```
package PackageName ;
```

Let us consider the source file `Point.java`, for example.

```
package geometry;
public class Point {
    public double x, y;
    // ...
}
```

The package declaration at the top of the source file declares that the `Point` class belongs to the package named `geometry`. When the package declaration is absent from a file, all the classes contained in the file belong to an *unnamed* package.

Packages serve as a useful mechanism for grouping closely related classes and interfaces. The classes that belong to a package should be closely related because a class may access not only the public fields and methods of other classes belonging to the same package, but also all except the private fields and methods of these classes.

A class in a named package can be referred to in two different ways:

1. Using the fully qualified name,

   PackageName.ClassName

   we can refer to the `Point` class in package `geometry` as

   ```
   geometry.Point
   ```

2. Importing the class and using the simple class name. We can import a class in the designated package using

   ```
   import PackageName.ClassName ;
   ```

   or, we can import all the classes in the designated package using

   ```
   import PackageName.* ;
   ```

The `Point` class in package `geometry` can simply be referred to as `Point` when either of the following `import` clauses occurs at the top of the source file:

```
import geometry.Point;
import geometry.*;
```

Some of most fundamental and most commonly used classes are defined in the `java.lang` package. The `java.lang` package is implicitly imported by all Java programs. So it is unnecessary to explicitly import the `java.lang` package.

4.5.2 Partitioning the Name Space

Packages serve as a useful mechanism for partitioning name space and preventing name collisions. When they belong to different packages, classes with the same name can be used by the same class without causing name collision. The Java Class Library, for example, contains another `Point` class, whose fields x and y are declared as type `int` instead of type `double`. This other version of the `Point` class is defined in package `java.awt`. However, both classes can be used by the same class by using their fully qualified names.

```
geometry.Point = new geometry.Point(10.0, 20.0);
java.awt.Point = new java.awt.Point(10, 20);
```

Alternatively, we can use the `import` clause to import one of the classes so that it can be directly referenced using only its class name.

```
import geometry;
...
Point = new Point(10.0, 20.0); // this refers to geometry.Point
java.awt.Point = new java.awt.Point(10, 20);
```

In practice, all classes are placed in packages for all applications. The basic rule for placing classes in packages is stated in the following guideline:

4.5.3 Packages and the Directory Structure

When packages are used, source and class files must be placed in directories whose structures match the structures of the packages. Several directory paths are important to the Java compiler, `javac`, as described in Table 4.5.

TABLE 4.5

Directory Paths

Path	Description
The source directory root	This is where the compiler looks for the source files. The default is the current working directory.
The destination directory root	This is where the compiler places the class files (that is, the files that the compiler generates). The default is the current working directory. It can be specified on the command line by using the -d option.
The CLASSPATH	A list of directories and/or jar files. The compiler will look in these directories for any precompiled class files it needs. The CLASSPATH can be set as an environment variable or specified on the command line by using the -classpath option. The CLASSPATH is also used by the Java Virtual Machine to load classes. *

* Consult the JDK/JRE installation guide for instructions on setting the CLASSPATH environment variable on specific platforms.

For example, let *srcdir* be the source directory root and *classdir* be the destination directory root. Let us assume that we have a class Foo in package package1.package2. In this case, the source file Foo.java must be located at

srcdir/package1/package2/Foo.java

After compilation, the class file will be located at

classdir/package1/package2/Foo.class

To compile the program, we must change the working directory to the *source* directory root (that is, *srcdir*) and issue the following command for compilation:

```
venus% javac package1/package2/Foo.java
```

To run the program, we change the working directory to the *destination* directory root (that is, *classdir*) and do the following:

```
venus% java package1.package2.Foo
```

If we want a different program to use the precompiled class package1.package2.Foo.class, we must include the *classdir* in the CLASSPATH for that program.

The following is the same program Maximum as in Example 4.8, except it is placed in a package named xj.num:

```
package xj.num;
public class Maximum {

    public static void main(String[] args) {
        if (args.length >= 2) {
            int i1 = Integer.parseInt(args[0]);
            int i2 = Integer.parseInt(args[1]);
            System.out.println("The maximum of " + i1 + " and " + i2 +
                               " is: " + ((i1 >= i2) ? i1 : i2));
        } else {
            System.out.println("Usage: java Maximum integer1 integer2");
        }
    }
}
```

Assuming *srcdir* is the source directory, the source file Maximum.java must be placed in the subdirectory *classdir*/xj/num. To compile the program, change the current directory to *srcdir* and do

```
venus% java xj/num/Maximum.java
```

In this case, the *srcdir* directory is also the destination directory. The Java compiler generates the byte-code file Maximum.class in the same directory as the source code file, that is, *classdir*/xj/num. To run the program, remain at the *srcdir* directory and do

```
venus% java xj.num.Maximum 11 12
The maximum of 11 and 12 is: 12
```

You may choose to use a destination directory, say *destdir*, that is different from the source directory. To compile the program, change the current directory to the source directory *srcdir* and do

```
venus% java -d destdir xj/num/Maximum.java
```

The Java compiler generates the byte-code file Maximum.class in *destdir*/xj/num. To run the program, change the current directory to the destination directory *destdir* and do

```
venus% java xj.num.Maximum 11 12
The maximum of 11 and 12 is: 12
```

4.5.4 Organization of the Java Class Library

An integral part of Java is the *Java Class Library*, which in Java 2 comprises more than 1,900 classes. The Java Class Library consists of the *core packages*, or those whose names begin with the prefix java, and the *extension packages*, or those whose names begin with the prefix javax. These classes are organized as a hierarchy of packages according to their functionalities. Table 4.6 gives a brief summary of some of the packages in Java 2.

TABLE 4.6

Selected Packages in J2SE

Package	Description
java.applet	Support for applets
java.awt	*AWT (Abstract Window Toolkit)* for graphical user interfaces
java.beans	Support for pluggable components
java.io	Support for input and output
java.lang	Basic language and run-time support, including manipulation of simple data types, common mathematical functions, threads, security, and system resource management
java.math	Support for large numbers
java.net	Support for network communication
java.rmi	Support for *remote method invocation*
java.security	Support for data encryption and digital signature
java.sql	Support for Java database connectivity (JDBC)
java.text	Support for text processing and formatting
java.util	Support for common utilities, including collections, time management, and data compression
java.vecmath	Support for tuples and matrices
javax.activation	Support for the JavaBean Activation Framework
javax.mail	Support for electronic mail
javax.media	Support for a variety of formats of multimedia data, including streaming and stored audio and video
javax.naming	Support for Java naming and directory services (JNDI)
org.omg.CORBA	Support for common object request broker architecture (CORBA)

4.6   EXCEPTIONS

Exceptions are *unexpected* conditions in programs. The Java exception-handling mechanism facilitates recovery from unexpected conditions or failures. There are at least three reasons for having a special mechanism to handle exceptions instead of using the regular control statements. First, the location at which an exception usually occurs is not where it can be reasonably dealt with. Therefore, handling exceptions disrupts the normal flow of execution and provides a legitimate excuse for using `goto` statements. Second, mixing the logic of error handling with the logic of regular tasks makes a program unnecessarily large and complex and thus more difficult to read and maintain. Finally, ad hoc methods for error handling, such as `longjmp` (a common way of handling exceptions in C), are often platform specific and nonportable.

Moreover, when systems require high reliability and fail-safe processing, an effective exception-handling mechanism is essential in the effort to deliver such assurance. An exception-handling mechanism should be an integral part of a programming language if that language is to support effectively the development of large-scale, complex, and reliable software systems.

4.6.1 Sources of Exceptions

When an exception occurs in a Java program, the normal flow of execution is interrupted, and we say that an exception has been *thrown*. Exceptions originate from two sources:

1. The run-time environment (that is, the JVM). Performing an illegal operation, such as dereferencing a null pointer or accessing an array with an out-of-bound index, causes a *run-time exception* to be thrown.
2. Java programs, including the Java Class Library. When a unexpected condition is encountered in a program, an exception can be explicitly thrown with the `throw` statement.

A variety of exceptions are defined in the Java Class Library. Programmers may also introduce their own exceptions.

It is important to point out that most of the run-time exceptions represent logical errors in programs that should be fixed. Exception handling is only a mechanism to allow recovery at run-time in the event such an error is encountered. It is not a replacement for debugging.

4.6.2 Hierarchy of Exceptions

Exceptions are modeled as objects of exception classes. Different types of exceptions are characterized by different exception classes, which are organized into a hierarchy as shown in Figure 4.2.[9]

The `Throwable` class is the superclass of all errors and exceptions. Only instances of the `Throwable` class, or one of its subclasses, are thrown by the Java Virtual Machine or can be thrown by Java programs. The different categories of throwables

---

9. This diagram only shows some of the most common error and exception classes. For a complete list of the error and exception classes, see the API documentation of the `java.lang` package.

Figure 4.2

Class hierarchy of errors and exceptions.

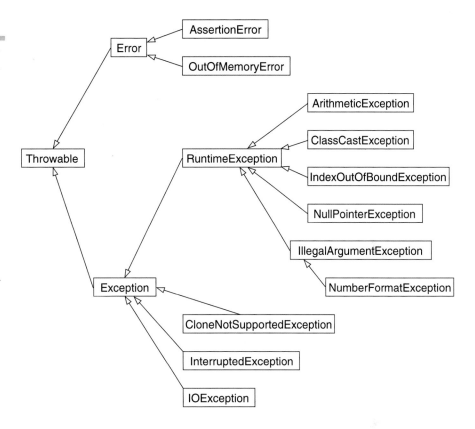

are represented by various subclasses. The major categories are errors, exceptions, and run-time exceptions, which are summarized in the following table:

Category	Description
Error	A subclass of Throwable. Errors are serious and fatal problems in programs. Errors are thrown by the JVM and are typically not handled by regular programs.
Exception	A subclass of Throwable. Exceptions can be thrown by any program. All user-defined exceptions should be a subclass of Exception.
RuntimeException	A subclass of Exception. Run-time exceptions are caused by illegal operations and thrown by the JVM.

Errors and run-time exceptions are called *unchecked exceptions*. All others are called *checked exceptions*. Checked exceptions must be caught or declared in the `throws` clause (see Sections 4.6.3 and 4.6.4). The following are the most common run-time exceptions:

Run-Time Exceptions	Common Causes
`ArithmeticException`	Dividing an integer by zero
`ClassCastException`	Casting an object to a wrong class (see Section 5.2.2 [p. 168])
`IndexOutOfBoundException`	Accessing an array with an out-of-bound index, that is, an index that is negative, greater than or equal to the length of the array
`IllegalArgumentException`	Passing an illegal or inappropriate argument to a method
`NullPointerException`	Deferencing a reference variable that is `null`
`NumberFormatException`	Attempting to convert a string to one of the numeric types, but the string does not have the appropriate format

The following are some of the most common checked exceptions:

Exceptions	Common Causes
`CloneNotSupportedException`	Attempting to clone an object whose class does not implement the `Cloneable` interface (see Section 6.3.4 [p. 231])
`InterruptedException`	Interrupting a thread that is not running (see Section 11.1.2 [p. 553])
`IOException`	Encountering problems while performing input/output operations (see Section 8.4 [p. 366])

The following are some of the most common errors:

Errors	Common Causes
`AssertionError`	An assertion has failed (see Section 6.2.3 [p. 224])
`OutOfMemoryError`	JVM cannot allocate an object because it is out of memory, and no more memory could be made available by the garbage collector

Programmers may introduce additional user-defined exception classes. All user-defined exception classes should extend the `Exception` class, directly or indirectly. User-defined exception classes should not extend the `RuntimeException` class.

4.6.3 Throwing Exceptions

Most of the exceptions are thrown by the Java Virtual Machine. However, exceptions can also be thrown anywhere in a program to signify that an unexpected or abnormal condition has occurred and it is impossible to continue the normal flow of control. Exceptions can be thrown using `throw` statements. The syntax of the `throw` statement is

> **throw** *Exception* ;

where *Exception* is an instance of `Throwable` or one of its subclasses.

A method *must* declare the checked exceptions that it *may* throw, using the `throws` clause, as follows:

> [*MethodModifiers*] *ReturnType MethodName* ([*ParameterList*])
>   [**throws** *Exception*₁, *Exception*₂ ...]
> {
>   *Statements*
> }

Statements that may throw a checked exception must be placed in either of the following two contexts:

1. In a try-catch statement with a matching catch block for the exception, such as

```
try {
    // . . .
    throw new MyException();
    // . . .
} catch (MyException e) {
    // handle MyException
}
```

2. In a method that declares the exception in its throws clause, such as

```
void aMethod() throws MyException {
    // ...
    throw new MyException();
    // ...
}
```

4.6.4 Catching and Handling Exceptions

The main purpose of the Java exception-handling mechanism is to allow an exception to be caught and handled by a code segment located elsewhere, perhaps a good distance from the origin of the source. When an exception is thrown, the exception-handling mechanism will attempt to locate and transfer control to a matching *exception handler*. The exception handler determines whether the exception can be handled and if so, how. Statements that may throw exceptions can be enclosed in a try-catch statement.

```
try {
    ⟨statements that may throw exceptions⟩
} catch (Exception1 e1) {
    ⟨exception handler 1⟩
} catch (Exception2 e2) {
    ⟨exception handler 2⟩
} finally {
    ⟨finish up (optional)⟩
}
```

A try-catch statement begins with a `try` block, which consists of the normal flow of control. Some of the statements in the `try` block may throw exceptions. A try-catch statement can have one or more `catch` blocks (that is, exception handlers) and an optional `finally` block. Each catch block takes a single parameter, whose type must be `Throwable` or one of its subclasses. When an exception is thrown, the catch blocks of the immediate enclosing try-catch statement are searched *sequentially* for a match. A catch block matches the exception thrown if the class of the exception thrown matches the parameter type of the catch block or one of its subclasses. If a match is found, the flow of control is transfered to the matching catch block. If a `finally` block is present, it will be executed just before the flow of control leaves the try-catch statement, whether or not another exception is thrown.

Suppose that there are two catch blocks for exception classes `Exception1` and `Exception2`, respectively, and `Exception1` extends `Exception2`. In other words, `Exception1` represents a more specific type of exceptions than `Exception2`, and `Exception2` represents a more general type of exceptions than `Exception1`. Since the catch blocks are searched sequentially, it is imporatnt to place the catch block for `Exception1` before the catch block for `Exception2`, or the catch block for `Exception1` will never be reached. The catch blocks for very general types of exceptions, such as

```
catch (Throwable e)  or  catch (Exception e)
```

should be avoided, since they catch almost all types of exceptions. If such indiscriminatory catch blocks are needed, they should appear as the last catch block.

There are several options in handling exceptions: (1) Recover from the exception and resume execution with the statement immediately following the try-catch statement; (2) throw another exception, and pass the responsibility to another exception handler; or (3) terminate the program gracefully when unable to recover from the exception. In any case, the `finally` block, if present, will be executed before leaving the try-catch statement.

Printing out the execution stack trace at the point where the exception occurred in the catch block, as in the following code segment, is useful for debugging.

```
catch (AnException e) {
    e.printStackTrace();
}
```

It is usually a bad practice to catch an exception, then ignore it, that is, to do nothing in the exception handler, as in this code segment:

```
catch (AnException e) {}
```

Using Exception Handling

Let us consider the following `PurchaseOrder` class, which contains a method `calculateItemTotal()` that attempts to calculate the total amount of an order based on the unit price of the item and the quantity ordered. A precondition of the method is that the quantity must be greater than or equal to zero. If the quantity is negative, it is an exception; an error must have occurred somewhere. The `calculateItemTotal()` method cannot proceed after a negative quantity is detected. The only reasonable thing to do is to notify the caller that an exception has occurred. We compare two solutions to this problem: one uses the exception-handling mechanism, and one does not.

The first solution does not use the exception-handling mechanism.

```java
public class PurchaseOrder {
    public static final double ERROR_CODE1 = . . . ;
    public double calculateItemTotal(double unitPrice, int quantity) {
        if (quantity < 0) {
            // exception
            return ERROR_CODE1;
        } else {
            // normal condition
            return unitPrice * quantity;
        }
    }
    // . . .
}
```

The caller might catch the exception as follows:

```
PurchaseOrder anOrder;
// . . .
double total = anOrder.calculateItemTotal(. . .  );
if (total == PurchaseOrder.ERROR_CODE1) {
    // handle the exception
    . . .
} else {
    // the normal condition
    . . .     total . . .
    // . . .
}
```

This solution is rather inelegant. Various error conditions might complicate what started as a simple calculation. Moreover, the error condition is returned to the caller through a programmer-defined error code named ERROR_CODE1, which must be carefully chosen. Otherwise, it could be confused with a legitimate value. In addition, the caller must check the return value for the error code before it can be used. Otherwise, it could cause more serious problems by treating the error code as a regular value and using it in other computations.

Using the exception-handling mechanism, we have a simpler and more elegant solution.

```
public class PurchaseOrder {
    public double calculateItemTotal(double unitPrice, int quantity) {
        if (quantity < 0) {
            // exception
            throw new IllegalArgumentException("negative quantity");
        }

        // normal condition
        return unitPrice * quantity;
    }
    // . . .
}
```

Now the caller can catch the exception.

```
PurchaseOrder anOrder;
try {
    // . . .
    double total = anOrder.calculateItemTotal( . . .   );
    . . .     total . . .
    // . . .
} catch (IllegalArgumentException e) {
    // handle exception
}
```

Now, the code for handling normal conditions is separated from the code that handles exceptions. The logic flow under the normal condition can be written more clearly and succinctly.

EXAMPLE 4.11   The Maximum of Two Integers with Exception Handling

PURPOSE

To illustrate the handling of exceptions in the `Maximum` program in Example 4.8.

DESCRIPTION

The `Maximum` program in Example 4.8 does not handle the exception when the input values are invalid. For example, invoking the program with noninteger arguments will cause a `NumberFormatException` to be thrown.

```
venus% java Maximum  eleven twelve
Exception in thread "main" java.lang.NumberFormatException: eleven
        at java.lang.Integer.parseInt(Integer.java:426)
        at java.lang.Integer.parseInt(Integer.java:476)
        at Maximum.main(Maximum.java:13)
```

A more robust version of the program is to catch and handle the exception. In this case, there is no reasonable way to continue when an invalid input value is encountered. So we cannot recover from the exception, but we can at least give a meaningful message in the exception handler.

SOLUTION

The maximum of two integer arguments: `Maximum2.java`

```java
public class Maximum2 {

    public static void main(String[] args) {
        if (args.length >= 2) {
            try {
                int i1 = Integer.parseInt(args[0]);
                int i2 = Integer.parseInt(args[1]);
                System.out.println("The maximum of " + i1 + " and " +
                                  i2 + " is: " + ((i1 >= i2) ? i1 : i2));
            } catch (NumberFormatException e) {
                System.out.println("Invalid input value: " +
                                  e.getMessage());
                System.out.println("The input values must be integers.");
            }
        } else {
            System.out.println("Usage: java Maximum integer1 integer2");
        }
    }
}
```

Running the program with proper arguments produces the following results:

```
venus% java Maximum2 12 11
The maximum of 12 and 11 is: 12
```

Running the program with invalid arguments produces the following results:

```
venus% java Maximum2 eleven twelve
Invalid input value: eleven
The input values must be integers.
```

Finally, a word of caution on using the exception-handling mechanism. The exception-handling mechanism is intended for handling rare and abnormal conditions in programs. Using the exception-handling mechanism to handle normal or typical conditions will have severe negative impact on the performance of programs.

4.7   A SIMPLE ANIMATION APPLET

Java programming is quite different from conventional programming in many aspects. Not only it is object-oriented, but it also is framework-based.

Framework-Based Programming

A *framework* provides the basic structure and utilities for applications, allowing the application development effort to be reduced significantly. A framework is extensible and flexible and hence can accommodate a broad range of application requirements and functionalities. However, using a framework also means that the conventions and styles adopted by the framework must be followed and that applications do not have full control of the system. The top-level control of the system usually resides in the framework, which is often called the *inversion of control*. Applications must cooperate with the framework to perform their tasks.

Interaction Styles

The way in which typical Java programs interact with users can be categorized in the following manner:

> *Active:* Programs in this category run actively without input or intervention from the user. The most common type of active programs consists of animation programs, such as the applet that we present in Example 4.12.

> *Reactive:* Programs in this category perform tasks in reaction to user input, such as keystrokes, mouse clicks, and menu selections. The *Drawing Pad* program discussed in Chapter 9 is an example of such a program.

> *Hybrid:* Hybrid programs combine features from the first two categories. These programs function by themselves and also react to user input. The *Bouncing Ball with Controls* program discussed in Chapter 8 [p. 305] is an example of a hybrid program.

EXAMPLE 4.12 A Digital Clock Applet—The Initial Version

PURPOSE

To illustrate the basics of the Java applet framework and simple animation.

DESCRIPTION

This applet displays the current time in hours, minutes, and seconds in the following format (Figure 4.3):

HH:MM:SS

SOLUTION

An applet does not require a `main()` method, but it must be a subclass of `java.applet.Applet`. The `Applet` class is actually a skeletal implementation of an applet. An applet goes through a life cycle as illustrated in Figure 4.4. The following methods are invoked at various points of the life cycle:

Method	Purpose	Invoked
`init()`	Initializes the applet	When the applet is initially loaded
`start()`	Activates the applet	When entering the Web page that contains the applet
`stop()`	Deactivates the applet	When leaving the Web page that contains the applet
`destroy()`	Destroys the applet	When the Web page that contains the applet is discarded

Figure 4.3

The digital clock applet.

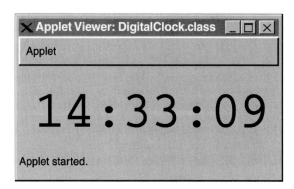

Figure 4.4

The life cycle of
applets.

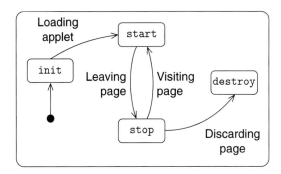

An applet may override some of these methods. In the digital clock example, we
override three of these four methods, `init()`, `start()`, and `stop()`, and define two
other methods: `paint()` and `run()`.

All applets are graphical applications, so the graphical appearance of the applet
must be defined. One way of doing so is to use the `paint()` method to paint the
appearance of the applet directly. Because this is an active applet, it requires a thread
to drive the animation. One way to create a thread is to implement the `Runnable`
interface and define the `run()` method, which is the main body of the thread. The
`run()` method of a thread is analogous to the `main()` method of an application class.

We begin with the following class declaration, which shows the overall structure
of the program. We present the details of the methods separately.

Digital clock applet: `DigitalClock.java`

```
import java.awt.*;
import java.util.Calendar;

public class DigitalClock
        extends java.applet.Applet implements Runnable {
    protected Thread clockThread = null;
    protected Font    font = new Font("Monospaced", Font.BOLD, 48);
    protected Color   color = Color.GREEN;
    ⟨start() and stop() methods on page 151⟩
    ⟨run() method on page 151⟩
    ⟨paint() method on page 152⟩
}
```

The notation

⟨Code segment on page *nnn*⟩

indicates a placeholder of a code segment that is defined elsewhere. The page number
indicates where the code segment is defined for easy reference.

The `font` and `color` fields specify the font and color to be used in drawing the
numbers. We use a 48-point boldface monospace font and the color green. The field

`clockThread` is the thread that keeps the clock running. We discuss threads in detail in Chapter 11 [p. 547]. However, the use of threads in all animation applets is nearly identical and can be captured as an idiom (see Section 5.6.2).

The `start()` and `stop()` methods activate and deactivate the applet by creating and killing the thread.

Methods of class `DigitalClock`: `start()` and `stop()`

```
public void start() {
   if (clockThread == null) {
      clockThread = new Thread(this);
      clockThread.start();
   }
}

public void stop() {
   clockThread = null;
}
```

It is important to deactivate the applet by killing the animation thread. Otherwise, the applet would keep running and consuming CPU and memory resources even after you leave the Web page that contains the applet.

The `run()` method contains an infinite loop that periodically invokes the `repaint()` method. The rate of update, also called the *refresh rate*, is controlled by the argument of the `sleep()` method. It specifies the sleep duration in milliseconds. As the digital clock shows only hours, minutes, and seconds, it needs to be updated only once every second. Therefore, the animation thread can sleep 1 second (1,000 milliseconds) after each update. Also note that the `sleep()` method may throw an `InterruptedException`; therefore, the `sleep()` method must be invoked inside a try-catch statement.

Method of class `DigitalClock`: `run()`

```
public void run() {
   while (Thread.currentThread() == clockThread) {
      repaint();
      try {

         Thread.currentThread().sleep(1000);
      } catch (InterruptedException e){}
   }
}
```

Note that the `run()` method, calls the `repaint()` method, not `paint()`, and the `paint()` method is not explicitly invoked. The missing link is provided by the framework. The `paint()` method will be invoked indirectly when `repaint()` is invoked. We discuss the details of the interaction between these methods in Section 5.5 [p. 193]. The following conventions are important:

- Call the `repaint()` method, not `paint()`, to change the applet's appearance.
- Override the `paint()` method, not `repaint()`, to describe how the applet should be drawn.

We use the `Calendar` class in our `paint()` method to obtain the current hour, minute, and second. For obvious reasons, `Calendar` is a singleton class. An instance of `Calendar` must be obtained with the `getInstance()` method, not the `new` operator.

Method of class `DigitalClock`: `paint()`

```java
public void paint(Graphics g) {
    Calendar calendar = Calendar.getInstance();
    int hour = calendar.get(Calendar.HOUR_OF_DAY);

    int minute = calendar.get(Calendar.MINUTE);
    int second = calendar.get(Calendar.SECOND);
    g.setFont(font);
    g.setColor(color);
    g.drawString(hour +
            ":" + minute / 10 + minute % 10 +
            ":" + second / 10 + second % 10,
            10, 60);
}
```

The `drawString()` method takes three arguments:

drawString(*str*, *x*, *y*)

where *str* is the string to be drawn and (*x*, *y*) specifies the *x* and *y* coordinates of the left end of the string on the baseline, as illustrated in the following diagram.:

The HTML source code for the `DigitalClockDemo` page follows:

HTML source: `DigitalClockDemo.html`

```html
<!--DigitalClockDemo.html-->
<html>
    <head>
        <title>Digital Clock Applet</title>
    </head>
```

```
<body bgcolor=white>
<h1>The Digital Clock Applet</h1><p>
<applet code=DigitalClock.class
        width=250 height=80>
</applet>
<p><hr>
<a href=DigitalClock.java>The source</a>
</body>
</html>
```

The `java.awt.Color` Class

Instances of the `Color` class represent colors. The `Color` class is capable of representing roughly 1.6 million 24-bit colors. The following common colors are predefined as constants:

Constant	Description
BLACK	The color black
BLUE	The color blue
CYAN	The color cyan
DARK_GRAY	The color dark gray
GRAY	The color gray
GREEN	The color green
LIGHT_GRAY	The color light gray
MAGENTA	The color magenta
ORANGE	The color orange
PINK	The color pink
RED	The color red
WHITE	The color white
YELLOW	The color yellow

We can create an arbitrary color with

```
new Color(r, g, b)
```

where r, g, and b are the values of the red, green, and blue components, respectively. They fall in the range 0 to 255.

The `java.awt.Font` Class

We can create a font with

`new Font(`*name*`,` *style*`,` *size*`)`

where *name*, *style*, and *size* are the font family name, font style, and font size, respectively. If a font that exactly matches the description cannot be found, an available font that closely matches the description will be returned. The attributes of fonts are as follows.

Name: A string indicating the name of the font. The font name can be either the *physical font name* or the *logical font name*. The physical font names refer to the actual names of the fonts installed on a particular machine. The physical font names are platform specific and often machine specific. The logical font names refer to families of fonts with certain common characteristics. The logical font names are mapped to physical fonts with matching characteristics available on a given machine. The following logical font names are available[10]:

  `Serif   Sans-serif   Monospaced   Dialog   DialogInput`

Programs using logical font names should be able to run on any platform on any machine without change. Programs using physical font names may need to be customized to use the physical fonts available on a particular machine.

Style: An integer indicating the style of the font. It can be one of the following constants, defined in the `Font` class:

  `Font.PLAIN   Font.BOLD   Font.ITALIC`

Combination styles can be obtained by joining two or more of the style constants using bitwise-or. For example, the bold and italic style can be specified as:

  `Font.BOLD | Font.ITALIC`

Size: A positive integer indicating the size of the font in printer's points. A point is approximately $\frac{1}{72}$ inch on printed media and roughly one pixel on monitor screens.

---

10. For backward compatibility, the following logical font names are also available, but deprecated, `TimesRoman`, `Helvetica`, and `Courier`.

CHAPTER SUMMARY

- Java supports two kinds of types: primitive types and reference types. A primitive type variable holds a value of the type. A reference type variable holds a reference to an object or array. Wrapper classes convert values of primitive types to objects.

- Java supports the primitive types `boolean`, `byte`, `short`, `int`, `long`, `char`, `float`, and `double`. Each type has default initial values for initializing variables.

- Conversion of a type of a narrower range to a type of a broader range is called widening. Conversion of a type of a broader range to a type of a narrower range is called narrowing.

- Java expression and statement syntax is very similar to that of C++.

- Objects and arrays are stored on a garbage-collected heap. They must always be created explicitly by using the `new` operator, array initializer, or string literals.

- Arrays are objects and are bound-checked.

- Equality of references and equality of object states are two distinct concepts. For the reference variables `r1` and `r2`, `r1 == r2` refers to the equality of the references, and `r1.equals(r2)` refers to the equality of the state of the two objects.

- The `goto` statement was eliminated in Java. Multilevel breaking and the exception mechanism are used to handle situations in which `goto` may have been used in other languages.

- Classes are the basic building blocks of Java programs. A Java program consists of one or more class declarations. A class declaration defines a class. Each class defines a reference type. A class declaration comprises declarations of fields, methods, and inner classes.

- Class fields can be initialized via explicit initializers, default initial values, initialization blocks, and constructors.

- Parameters are passed by value. Values of primitive types must be wrapped inside a class in order to serve as in–out parameters.

- Strings are objects, not `char` arrays. The `String` class is immutable, and the `StringBuffer` class is mutable.

- The `toString()` method of each class is implemented to convert the instances of the class to string representations.

- Interfaces declare features but do not provide implementation. Abstract classes are classes with partial implementation.

- Packages are used to organize large programs into logical and manageable units. A package may contain classes, interfaces, or other packages.

- Exceptions are unexpected conditions in programs. The exception-handling mechanism facilitates recovery from unexpected conditions or failures. A statement that may throw an exception must be placed inside a try-catch statement that catches the exception or in a method that declares the exception in its `throws` clause.

EXERCISES

4.1 Write a Java application to calculate the factorial of an integer n, using iteration (not recursion). The factorial function $n!$ is defined as

$$0! = 1$$
$$n! = n * (n - 1)!$$

The input value is given as a command-line argument to the Java application.

4.2 Write a Java application to calculate the average of a list of integers. The input data is stored in a text file, in which each line contains a single integer. The name of the input data file is given as a command-line argument to the Java application. The output should include the number of integers and their average.

4.3 Write a Java application that uses the data from a text file named students.txt to create a file called studentemail.txt. The input file consists of a number of lines, with each line containing the data of a student in colon-delimited format:

Last Name : First Name : Social Security Number

For example:

    Owen:Michael:326502626

The output file contains student e-mail IDs generated from the information in the input file. Each input record will be converted to an e-mail ID in the following format:

    the first character of the first name +
    the first character of the last name +
    the last 4 digits of the social security number +
    "@" +
    "se.depaul.edu"

For example, Michael Owen's new e-mail ID would be

    mo2626@se.depaul.edu

Note that no uppercase letters are allowed in the new e-mail IDs and that the output file should contain one e-mail ID per line.

4.4 Define two Java classes:

Point, with the x and y coordinates, both of which are double values, as the fields.

Circle, with the center, an instance of Point, and radius, a double value, of the circle as the fields.

Write two methods of the Circle class to do the following:

(a) Given a point p and a circle centered at c with radius r, determine whether p is inside the circle.

(b) Given the center and radius of two circles, determine whether the two circles touch or overlap.

Write a main() method of the Circle class to test each of these methods.

4.5 Implement the toString() method for the Card class in Section 4.4.2. Each suit of cards should be represented by a single letter:

   S for ♠   H for ♡   D for ◇   C for ♣

When the rank of a card is no higher than 10, it should be represented by its numeric value. When the rank of a card is higher than 10, it should be represented as

   J for Jack   Q for Queen
   K for King   A for Ace

For example, the ♠ King should be represented as SK.

4.6 Implement a shuffle() method for the Deck class in Section 4.4.2 to shuffle the deck of cards. Use Math.random() to emulate the randomness of shuffling. Then implement a deal() method to deal the cards in the shuffled deck to four hands, and use the toString() method in Exercise 4.5 to print out the hands.

4.7 Using packages.

(a) Move each of the Java applications in Exercises 4.1–4.3 to a package named myprog.single. Compile and run each of the applications.

(b) Move both `Point` and `Circle` classes in Exercise 4.4 to a package named `myprog.multi`. Compile and run the application.

4.8 Run the Java application in Exercise 4.2 with invalid input:

(a) Provide an incorrect file name; that is, the file named does not exist.

(b) Provide a correct file name, but the input file contains invalid contents; for example, a line contains a noninteger or multiple integers.

Write an improved version of the program using exception handling. This program should give a meaningful message when the input file name is incorrect, and ignore any lines in the input file that are other than a single integer.

4.9 The `Calendar` class also provides methods to get the current year, month, date, and day of the week. Enhance the digital clock applet to do the following:

(a) Display the current year, month, date, and day of week.

(b) Display the time using the 12-hour format instead of the 24-hour format.

For example, the display might be

```
3:05:28 PM
5 May 2002 Tue
```

PROJECT

4.1 Assume that you have a student record file. It is a text file in which each line contains a single record, and each record consists of the following colon-delimited fields:

last name:*first name*:*project 1*:*project 2*: *project 3*:*midterm exam*:*final exam*

The scores of the projects and exams are recorded as integers between 0 and 100, as in the record

```
Johnson:Phil:100:90:95:84:91
```

The total score of each student is calculated by using the formula

Total = (Project 1) × 10% + (Project 2) × 10% + (Project 3) × 10% + (Midterm exam) × 30% + (Final exam) × 40%

The total score is then converted to a letter grade by using the chart

Total ≥ 90	A
90 > Total ≥ 80	B
80 > Total ≥ 70	C
70 > Total ≥ 60	D
Total < 60	F

Write a Java application that will read the student record file from standard input and do the following:

(a) Calculate the total score and the letter grade for each student. Print the results to standard output in the format

last name   first name   total   grade

(b) Calculate the highest, lowest, and average scores of the student projects, exams, and total scores, and print the results to standard output.

(c) Count the number of students in each letter-grade range, and print the count to standard output.

Assume that the input file contains no more than 100 records.

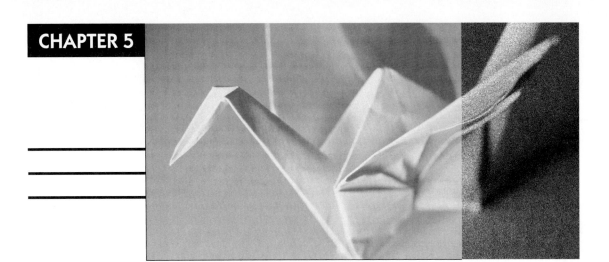

CHAPTER 5

Classes and Inheritance

CHAPTER OVERVIEW

In this chapter, we discuss overloading, inheritance, overriding, hiding, subtypes, polymorphism, and casting. In addition, we examine issues involved in designing and implementing classes and offer some design guidelines. We also present several more sophisticated animation applets to illustrate techniques and idioms commonly used in animation.

5.1 OVERLOADING METHODS AND CONSTRUCTORS

The methods and constructors of a class can be overloaded.

Definition 5.1 *Overloading*

Overloading refers to the ability to allow different methods or constructors of a class to share the same name. The name is said to be *overloaded* with multiple implementations.

159

The legality of overloading depends on the *signatures* of the methods or constructors being overloaded. The *signature* of a method or constructor consists of the name of the method and a list of the types of its parameters. Note that the return type, parameter names, and `final` designations of parameters are not part of the signature. Parameter order, however, is significant. The following are some examples of methods and their signatures:

Method	Signature
`String toString()`	`toString()`
`void move(int dx, int dy)`	`move(int, int)`
`void move(final int dx, final int dy)`	`move(int, int)`
`void paint(Graphics g)`	`paint(Graphics)`

The condition under which overloading is allowed is stated as the following rule:

The Rule of Overloading

Two methods or constructors in the same class can be overloaded, i.e., sharing the same name, if they have either different numbers of parameters or the same number of parameters but of different types. In other words, no two methods or constructors in the same class may have identical signatures.

The following class declaration illustrates overloaded constructors and overloaded methods:

```
public class Point {
   protected double x, y;

   public Point() {
      x = 0.0; y = 0.0;
   }

   public Point(double x, double y) {
      this.x = x; this.y = y;
   }

   /** calculate the distance between this point and the other point */
   public double distance(Point other) {
      double dx = this.x - other.x;
      double dy = this.y - other.y;
      return Math.sqrt(dx * dx + dy * dy);
   }
```

```
/** calculate the distance between this point and (x,y) */
public double distance(double x, double y) {
    double dx = this.x - x;
    double dy = this.y - y;
    return Math.sqrt(dx * dx + dy * dy);
}

/** calculate the distance between this point and (x,y) */
public double distance(int x, int y) {
    double dx = this.x - (double) x;
    double dy = this.y - (double) y;
    return Math.sqrt(dx * dx + dy * dy);
}

/** calculate the distance between this point and the origin */
public double distance() {
    return Math.sqrt(x * x + y * y);
}

// other methods
}
```

When an overloaded method is called, the number and the types of the arguments are used to determine the signature of the method that will be invoked. Overloading is resolved at compile time, as in the following code segment:

```
Point p1 = new Point();       // invoke Point()
Point p2 = new (20.0, 30.0);  // invoke Point(double,double)
p2.distance(p1);              // invoke distance(Point)
p2.distance(50.0, 60.0);      // invoke distance(double,double)
p2.distance(50, 60);          // invoke distance(int,int)
p2.distance();                // invoke distance()
```

Operator Overloading

Operator overloading is a generalization of overloading of methods. It allows operators, such as +, *, and ==, etc., to operate on different types of parameters, i.e., operands. In Java, operators are overloaded only on built-in operations on primitive types. For example, the arithmetic operators (+, -, *, /, %) are overloaded on all numeric types. The only exception is that the operator + and += are also overloaded on class String for concatenation. No other classes are allowed to overload operators.

Operator overloading is an important characteristic of C++. When used properly, it allows computations to be expressed naturally and succinctly while maintaining the conventional meaning of the operator. Operators should be defined in accordance with their usual and conventional meanings. However, there is nothing to prevent operators from being overloaded in misleading ways. Furthermore, as we learned from C++, overuse of operator overloading can hamper the readability of programs. Thus the potential pitfalls of operator overloading overshadow any possible benefits. For this reason, Java restricts operator overloading to its primitive data types and strings.

To Overload or Not to Overload

Overloading is, for the most part, a convenience, not a necessity. It allows methods to be named naturally and logically. However, the same functionality can often be accomplished without the use of overloading. Care must be exercised not to overuse or misuse overloading, which hampers the readability of programs.

Design Guideline   *Use Overloading Judiciously*

Overloading should be used only in two situations:

1. When there is a general, nondiscriminative description of the functionality that fits all the overloaded methods.
2. When all the overloaded methods offer the same functionality, with some of them providing default arguments.

In the first case, all the overloaded methods have the same number of parameters but with different types. An example is the overloaded append() methods in the class StringBuffer.

```
public class StringBuffer {
    public StringBuffer append(String str) { . . . }
    public StringBuffer append(boolean b) { . . . }
    public StringBuffer append(char c) { . . . }
    public StringBuffer append(int i) { . . . }
    public StringBuffer append(long l) { . . . }
    public StringBuffer append(float f) { . . . }
    public StringBuffer append(double d) { . . . }
    // . . .
}
```

All the overloaded methods fit the following general description:

> A string representation of the argument is appended to the end of the current contents of the string buffer.

Another example in this category is the overloaded max() method in the class Math.

```
public class Math {
    public static int max(int a, int b) { . . . }
    public static long max(long a, long b) { . . . }
    public static float max(float a, float b) { . . . }
    public static double max(double a, double b) { . . . }
    // . . .
}
```

Again, all the overloaded methods fit the following general description:

> The result is the maximum of the two arguments.

In the second case, the overloaded methods have different numbers of parameters. Usually the one with the most parameters is the base method, which implements the actual functionality. All other overloaded methods simply delegate the task to the base method. An example is the overloaded `substring` method in the class `String`.

```
public class String {
   public String substring(int i, int j) {
      // base method: return substring [i .. j − 1]
   }
   public String substring(int i) {
      // provide default argument
      return substring(i, length());
   }
   // . . .
}
```

Both methods provide the same functionality: They return a substring. The method with two parameters is the base method. The method with a single parameter simply delegates the task to the base method by supplying a default second argument. Overloading should be avoided in all other situations.

5.2 EXTENDING CLASSES

Inheritance defines a relationship among classes. When class C2 *inherits* from, or *extends*, class C1, class C2 is called a *subclass* or an *extended class* of class C1, and class C1 is called a *superclass* of C2. Inheritance is a mechanism for reusing the implementation and extending the functionalities of superclasses. All the public and protected members of the superclass are accessible in the extended classes.

The extension relationship among classes is the strict form of inheritance, in the sense that the implementation of the superclass is actually inherited or reused in the subclasses. Two other relationships can be viewed as weak forms of inheritance: interface extension and interface implementation (see Section 5.3 [p. 176]). Java supports only single inheritance for class extension; that is, each class may not have more than one superclass. The extension relation among classes forms a hierarchy with the class `Object` as its root. Every class other than `Object` has a unique superclass. If no superclass is explicitly declared, `Object` is assumed to be the superclass. The `Object` class is the only class with no superclass. Multiple inheritance is supported for interface extension and implementation. We discuss the extension and implementation of interfaces in Section 5.3 [p. 176].

Again, the syntax of class declaration is as shown in the following fragment. The `extends` clause specifies the superclass, and the `implements` clause specifies the interfaces implemented by the class.

```
[ClassModifiers] class ClassName
      [extends SuperClass]
      [implements Interface₁, Interface₂ . . . ] {
   ClassMemberDeclarations
}
```

5.2.1 Constructors of Extended Classes

The initialization of an extended class consists of two phases: (1) the initialization of the fields inherited from the superclass and (2) the initialization of the fields declared in the extended class. One of the constructors of the superclass must be invoked to initialize the fields inherited from the superclass. The constructors of the extended class are responsible for initializing the fields declared in the extended class. The following code fragment illustrates the use of several typical constructors of extended classes. The ColoredPoint class extends the Point class to include a new color field.

```
import java.awt.Color;
public class ColoredPoint extends Point {
    public Color color;

    public ColoredPoint(final double x, final double y,
                        final Color color) {
        super(x, y);
        this.color = color;
    }

    public ColoredPoint(final double x, final double y) {
        this(x, y, Color.black); // default value of color
    }

    public ColoredPoint() {
        color = Color.black;
    }
}
```

The fields inherited from the superclass, x and y, should be initialized by invoking one of the constructors of the Point class. The new field in the extended class, color, should be initialized in the constructors of the ColoredPoint class. The constructors of the superclass are invoked with the keyword super.

- In the first constructor of the ColoredPoint class, super(x, y) invokes the constructor of the Point class with a matching signature: Point(double, double). The invocation of super(. . .) must be the first statement in the constructor of the extended class.

- The second constructor of the ColoredPoint class supplies a default value for the color field. It invokes another constructor of the same class with the keyword this. The constructor invoked is the one with the matching signature: ColoredPoint(double, double, Color). The invocation of this(. . .) must be the first statement in the constructor.

- In the third constructor of the ColoredPoint class, no explicit invocation using super or this is made. In this case, the no-arg constructor of the superclass is invoked implicitly.

If no constructor is defined in the extended class, the no-arg constructor is provided by default. The default no-arg constructor simply invokes the no-arg constructor of the superclass. For example, the following no-arg constructor will be provided implicitly for the Extended class when no constructor is provided explicitly:

```
public class ExtendedClass extends SuperClass {
    public ExtendedClass() {
        super();
    }
    // methods and fields
}
```

If the SuperClass does not provide a no-arg constructor, a compilation error will result. If another constructor of the ExtendedClass is present, the no-arg constructor is *not* provided implicitly.

The extended class may also use explicit initializers or the default initial values to initialize the fields. The following order of initialization applies to the fields in both the superclass and the extended class:

1. The fields of the superclass are initialized, using explicit initializers or the default initial values.
2. One of the constructors of the superclass is executed.
3. The fields of the extended class are initialized, using field initializers or the default initial values.
4. One of the constructors of the extended class is executed.

For example, let us consider the classes Super and Extended.

```
public class SuperClass {
    int x = . . . ; // executed first
    public SuperClass() {
        x = . . . ; // executed second
    }
    // . . .
}
public class ExtendedClass extends SuperClass {
    int y = . . . ; // executed third
    public ExtendedClass() {
        super();
        y = . . . ; // executed fourth
    }
    // . . .
}
```

When new Extended() is invoked to create an instance of the extended class, initialization proceeds as indicated by the comments.

5.2.2 Subtypes and Polymorphism

One of the most important characteristics of object-oriented programming languages is the dynamic binding of methods. *Dynamic binding of methods* refers to the binding of a method invocation to a specific implementation of the method at *run time* rather than at *compile time*.

Variables and Types, Objects and Classes

Before getting into the details of dynamic binding, we need to take a closer look at some commonly used terms: variable, object, class, and type. A *variable* is a storage location having an associated *type*. The type of a variable is determined at compile time, that is, statically, based on the declaration of the variable. The type of a variable is also known as its *declared type*. An *object* is an *instance* of a *class*. The class of an object is determined when the object is *created*, at run time. A variable of reference type holds a reference to an object. As we will demonstrate shortly, the variable may hold references to objects of different *classes*, subject to the *substitutability of subtypes*. The class of the object referred to by a reference variable cannot always be determined at compile time. Sometimes it can be determined only at run time.

Subtypes

The inheritance relationship can be viewed in various ways, as illustrated in Figure 5.1(a). A subclass *extends* the capability of its superclass; the subclass inherits features from its superclass and adds more features. Moreover, a subclass is a *specialization* of its superclass; every instance of a subclass is an instance of the superclass, not vice versa. For example, every line is a shape but not every shape is a line. Some features are available in the subclass but not in the superclass. There is yet another view of classes and inheritance: Each class defines a type. All the instances of the class constitute the set of the legitimate values of that type. As every instance of a subclass is also an instance of its superclass, the type defined by the subclass is a proper subset of the type defined by its superclass. The set of all the instances of a subclass is included in the set of all the instances of its superclass, as shown in Figure 5.1(b). The subset relation between the value set of types is known as the *subtype* relation.

Definition 5.2 *Subtype*

Type T_1 is a *subtype* of type T_2 if every legitimate value of T_1 is also a legitimate value of T_2. In this case, T_2 is the *supertype* of T_1.

Figure 5.1

Different views of inheritance: (a) Extending the superclass; and (b) inclusion of instance sets.

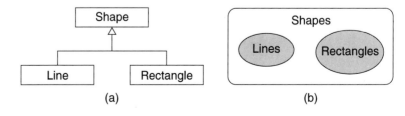

(a)

(b)

That T_1 is a subtype of T_2 is not the same as T_1 and T_2 being compatible. The compatible type relation is symmetric, whereas the subtype relation is not. If T_1 is a subtype of T_2 and T_2 is also a subtype of T_1, then T_1 and T_2 are compatible.

The inheritance relation among classes is a subtype relation. Moreover, each interface also defines a type, and the interface extension and implementation relations are also subtype relations (see Section 5.3 [p. 176]). The subtype relation applies to class types and interface types, as well as primitive types. For example, int is a subtype of long, since the set of all int values is a subset of the set of all long values.

Substitutability of Subtypes

A value of a subtype can appear wherever a value of its supertype is expected. In other words, a value of a subtype can always substitute for a value of its supertype.

To rephrase this rule in the context of classes and objects: An instance of a subclass can appear wherever an instance of its superclass is expected. An instance of a subclass can always substitute for an instance of its superclass.

Conversion of Reference Types

The conversion of reference types is governed by the subtype relation. The concept of widening and narrowing can be extended to reference types.

Definition 5.3 *Widening and Narrowing (Reference Type)*

The conversion of a subtype to one of its supertypes is called *widening*. The conversion of a supertype to one of its subtypes is called *narrowing*.

The widening of reference types is always allowed and is carried out implicitly whenever necessary. In other words, a reference to an object of class C can be implicitly converted to a reference to an object of one of the superclasses of C. The narrowing of reference types requires explicit casts. Thus, the narrowing of reference types is also known as *downcasting*. Narrowing is always allowed at compile time. However, it is not always safe, and it may result in run-time exceptions.

There is also an important difference between the conversions of primitive types and reference types. The conversion of primitive types results in a change of the representation of the values being converted. For example, converting an int to double results in representing the int value in double format. The conversion of an object reference *does not* affect the representation of the object. Its identity and state remain the same.

Polymorphic Assignment

In static programming languages, such as C, the rule of assignments is that the left-hand side and the right-hand side of an assignment must be of compatible types. In object-oriented languages a more powerful form of assignment, known as *polymorphic assignment*, is allowed.

Rule of Assignment

The type of the expression at the right-hand side of an assignment must be a subtype of the type of the variable at the left-hand side of the assignment.

This rule means that the variable on the left-hand side may hold objects of different classes. In other words, if class E extends class B, any instance of E can *act as* an instance of B. In the following code fragment the Student class has two subclasses, Undergraduate and Graduate:

```
class Student { . . . }
class Undergraduate extends Student { . . . }
class Graduate extends Student { . . . }
```

Now we create two instances.

```
Student student1, student2;
student1 = new Undergraduate(); // polymorphic assignment, okay
student2 = new Graduate();       // polymorphic assignment, okay
```

In the assignments shown, the types of the expressions on the right-hand side are Undergraduate and Graduate, respectively. They are subtypes of the type of the variable on the left-hand side, Student. Therefore, no explicit cast is necessary. However, attempting to do the following will result in a compilation error.

```
Graduate student3;
student3 = student2; // compilation error
```

An error will be generated because the right-hand side type is Student and the left-hand side type is Graduate. Even though student2 actually holds a reference to an instance of Graduate, the declared type of student2 is Student, which is not a subtype of the left-hand side type Graduate. Type checking is carried out at compile time and is based on the declared types of variables. An explicit cast is necessary here:

```
student3 = (Graduate) student2; // explicit cast, okay
```

Casting a reference variable to a subtype of its declared type is called *downcasting*. Java allows explicit casting of any reference type to any other reference type at compile time. The validity of an explicit cast is always checked at run time. If the cast is invalid, a ClassCastException will be thrown.

In the preceding example, a run-time check will be performed to determine whether `student2` actually holds a reference to an object that is an instance of `Graduate` or its subclasses. If not, a `ClassCastException` will be thrown. In this case, it is okay. Now, let us consider the following:

```
student3 = (Graduate) student1; // compilation okay, run-time exception
```

This statement will not result in a compilation error. However, as `student1` actually holds an instance of `Undergraduate`, which is not a subtype of `Graduate`, a `ClassCastException` will be thrown at run time.

Since downcasting may result in exceptions being thrown, it should be done with proper care. There are two proper ways of downcasting:

1. The pessimistic approach. Use the `instanceof` operator to check the class of an object before downcasting. The expression

   exp `instanceof` *Type*

   returns `true` if *exp* is an instance of a class or an interface type named *Type*. It returns `false` otherwise. The following program segment uses `instanceof` to prevent a potential run-time exception:

   ```
   if (student1 instanceof Graduate) {
      Graduate gradStudent = (Graduate) student1;
   } else {
      // student1 is not a graduate student
   }
   ```

2. The optimistic approach. Catch the `ClassCastException` exception, as follows:

   ```
   try {
      // . . .
      Graduate gradStudent = (Graduate) student1;
      // . . .
   } catch (ClassCastException e) {
      // student1 is not a graduate student
   }
   ```

Failing to downcast in either of these ways may lead to run-time failure of the program.

Why Is Downcasting Needed?

Let us assume that the `Graduate` class defines a method `getResearchTopic()` that is not defined in the `Student` class.

```
Student student1 = new Graduate();
// . . .
student1.getResearchTopic(); // compilation error
// . . .
```

Invocation of the getResearchTopic() method through student1 results in a compilation error because the declared type of student1 is Student—not Graduate—even though student1 holds an instance of Graduate.

The validity of method invocation is checked statically at compile time and is based on the declared types of variables, not the actual classes of the objects. Therefore, student1 must be downcast to Graduate before the getResearchTopic() method can be invoked.

```
Student student = new Graduate();
// . . .
if (student instanceof Graduate) {
   Graduate gradStudent = (Graduate) student;
   gradStudent.getResearchTopic(); // okay
   // . . .
}
```

Then the question is, Why not declare student to be Graduate in the first place? The possible reasons are as follows:

- The variable student is a parameter. The actual object referenced by student is created in some other part of the program and may be an instance of any subclass of Student.
- The variable student references to an element retrieved from a collection object, such as a Map or a Set. The declared type of elements in collections is usually Object. Downcasting the elements retrieved from a collection to their actual classes is often necessary (see Section 8.2 [p. 308]).
- The variable student references a object returned by the clone() method. The return type of the clone() method is declared as Object. Hence a cloned object needs to be downcast to its actual class.

Array Types

Java arrays are objects. The subtype relationships among array types are defined as follows. First, all array types are subtypes of Object (e.g., int [] and double[] are subtypes of Object). Second, if class or interface Y is a subtype of class or interface type X, then Y[] is also a subtype of X[].

The following diagram illustrates the subtype relation among array types:

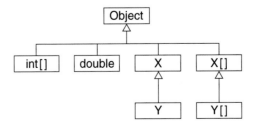

The following sequence is allowed:

```
Student sa1[];
Graduate sa2[] = new Graduate[40];
// ...
sa1 = sa2; // polymorphic assignment
Student student4 = sa1[0];
Graduate student5 = sa2[0];
```

However,

```
Graduate student6 = sa1[0]; // compilation error
```

causes a compilation error, so an explicit downcast is necessary:

```
Graduate student6 = (Graduate) sa1[0]; // okay
```

5.2.3 Overriding Methods

Methods defined in a superclass can be *overridden* by methods defined in a subclass. Here is the definition:

Definition 5.4 *Overriding*

Overriding refers to the introduction of an instance method in a subclass that has the same name, signature, and return type of a method in the superclass. Implementation of the method in the subclass *replaces* the implementation of the method in the superclass.

Overriding is different from overloading. Overriding is concerned with methods of *different* classes that have an inheritance relationship. In overriding, methods share the *same* name, signature, and return type. In contrast, overloaded methods are part of the *same* class, but have *different* signatures.

We can illustrate the distinction between overloading and overriding in the following manner. In

```
class A {
    public void m1() {. . . }
    public void m1(int i) {. . . }
}
```

class A contains two *overloaded* methods. An instance of A can access both methods, depending on the arguments of the method invocation, so

```
A a = new A();
a.m1();   // invoke m1()
a.m1(1);  // invoke m1(int)
```

Now, let us assume that we have the two classes

```
class B {
    public void m2() {. . . }
}
class C extends B {
    public void m2() {. . . }
}
```

Implementation of method m2() in class B is *overridden* by another implementation of method m2() in class C. For a given object, one but not both of the implementations of method m2() is available, depending on the class of the object.

```
B b = new B();
C c = new C();
b.m2(); // invoke the m2() in class B
c.m2(); // invoke the m2() in class C
```

Overriding a method with another method of different signature or return type is not allowed. For example, the following code segment will cause a compilation error:

```
class B {
    public void m3(int i) {. . . }
}
class C extends B {
    public void m3(char c) {. . . }
}
```

Method m3() in class B is *not* overloaded with method m3() in class C because they are not in the same class. In C++ this is legal, and it is interpreted as method m3() in class C *hiding* method m3() in class B (see Section 5.4 [p. 184] on hiding). Such permissiveness in C++ offers little help but adds to the complexity of its semantics. Most likely, the signature of m3() in class C is a mistake. It could actually be intended to override method m3() in class B with the same signature. A C++ compiler would let it go unnoticed, but the Java compiler would generate an error message.

Let us consider the following example with the declarations for Student, Graduate, and Undergraduate:

```
public class Student {
    public Student(String name) {
        this.name = name;
    }

    public String toString() {
        return "Student: " + name;
    }
    protected String name;
}

public class Undergraduate extends Student {
    public Undergraduate(String name) {
        super(name);
    }
```

```
      public String toString() {
         return "Undergraduate student: " + name;
      }
   }
   public class Graduate extends Student {
      public Graduate(String name) {
         super(name);
      }
      public String toString() {
         return "Graduate student: " + name;
      }
   }
```

Note that the instance method `toString()` of `Student` is overridden in both its subclasses. Because a variable of `Student` may hold a reference to an instance of `Student`, `Graduate`, or `Undergraduate`, implementation of method `toString()`, which will be invoked in the following method invocation, cannot be determined at compile time.

```
Student student;
// student is assigned some value
student.toString();
```

Which implementation of method `toString()` will be invoked depends on the actual class of the object referenced by the variable at run time, not the declared type of the variable. This is known as a *polymorphic method invocation*, in which implementation of a method is bound to an invocation *dynamically* at run time. For a polymorphic method invocation

```
var.m(. . . );
```

dynamic binding proceeds as follows:

Step 1. currentClass = the class of the object referenced by var.

Step 2. **if** method `m()` is implemented in *currentClass*
  then the implementation of `m()` in *currentClass* is invoked.
  else *currentClass* = the superclass of *currentClass*, and repeat Step 2.

Now, we illustrate the use of polymorphic method invocation in the class `Course`, which provides an `enroll()` method to enroll a student in the course and a list method to list all the students currently enrolled in the course.

```
public class Course {
   public void enroll(Student s) {
      if (s != null && count < CAPACITY)
         students[count++] = s;
   }
   public void list() {
      for (int i = 0; i < count; i++)
         System.out.println(students[i].toString());
   }
```

```
        protected static final int CAPACITY = 40;
        protected Student students[] = new Student[CAPACITY];
        protected int count = 0;
}
```

Figure 5.2 shows the relationship between the classes. Note that the assignment in enroll,

```
students[count++] = s;
```

is a polymorphic assignment and that the method invocation in list,

```
students[i].toString()
```

is a polymorphic method invocation. Now, we enroll some students—both graduate and undergraduate—in a course.

```
Course c = new Course();
c.enroll(new Undergraduate("John"));
c.enroll(new Graduate("Mark"));
c.enroll(new Undergraduate("Jane"));
c.list();
```

The output is

```
Undergraduate student: John
Graduate student: Mark
Undergraduate student: Jane
```

Note that the expression students[i].toString() was executed three times. Twice it was bound to the implementation in the Undergraduate class, and once it was bound to the implementation in the Graduate class.

Final Methods

A method that is declared as final cannot be overridden in a subclass. Final methods are useful in preventing a subclass from accidentally overriding methods that should not be overridden. Usually, such methods collaborate with some other methods or objects and are expected to honor certain conventions and contracts. Accidental overriding of these methods could violate the contracts and cause program failures. Final methods also allow the Java compiler and JVM to optimize byte-code.

Figure 5.2

Students and courses.

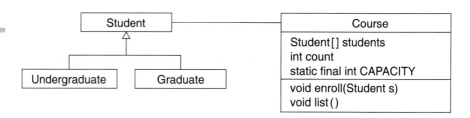

Invoking Overridden Methods

Sometimes it is desirable to invoke the implementation of a method that has been overridden. Suppose that we have defined an `equals()` method for the `Point` class.

```
public class Point {
    public boolean equals(Object other) {
        if (other != null &&
            other instanceof Point) {
          Point p = (Point) other;
          return (x == p.x) && (y == p.y);
        } else {
          return false;
        }
    }

    // other declarations
}
```

Now, we try to define the method `equals()` for the class `ColoredPoint`, which extends the class `Point`. The `equals()` of `ColoredPoint` overrides the `equals()` of `Point`. However, we do not want to repeat implementation of the method `equals()` of `Point`. We want to use the method `equals()` of `Point` to check the equality of the inherited fields and check only the equality of the fields declared in `ColoredPoint` in the `equals()` method of `ColoredPoint`. The `equals()` method of `Point` can be invoked via the super reference.

```
public class ColoredPoint extends Point {
    public boolean equals(Object other) {
        if (other != null &&
            other instanceof ColoredPoint) {
          ColoredPoint p = (ColoredPoint) other;
          return (super.equals(p) && color.equals(p.color));
        } else {
          return false;
        }
    }

    // other declarations
}
```

The keyword `super` represents an object reference having the same value as `this`, but it behaves as if it were a reference to the superclass.

Restriction

In the following scenario, we have a `Polygon` class:

```
public class Polygon {
    public void move(int dx, int dy) { . . . }
    public void scale(double factor) { . . . }
    public void addVertex(Point p) { . . . }
}
```

We want to define a `Rectangle` class, and it is natural to think that `Rectangle` should extend the `Polygon` class. However, the `addVertex()` method clearly does not apply to rectangles because rectangles have a fixed number of vertices. Thus it is reasonable to make the `addVertex()` method unavailable to instances of the `Rectangle` class. Such extensions are called *restrictions*. Although a restriction is desirable in some circumstances, it is also problematic. A restriction is not a subtype of its superclass.

Handling Restrictions in Java

Java does not directly support restrictions. However, restrictions can be handled in Java by overriding the restricted method with an empty body, as in

```
public class Rectangle extends Polygon {
   public void addVertex(Point p) {}
   // . . .
}
```

or by overriding the restricted method and throwing an exception, as in

```
public class Rectangle extends Polygon {
   public void addVertex(Point p)
       throws MethodNotSupported {
      throw new MethodNotSupported("addVertex");
   }
   // . . .
}
```

In the latter case, the `throws` clause must be included in the method declaration of the superclass. (See the discussion of the `throws` clause in Section 4.6 [p. 139].)

5.3   EXTENDING AND IMPLEMENTING INTERFACES

Interfaces declare features but provide no implementation. Classes that implement an interface should provide implementations for all the features (i.e., methods) declared in the interface. Interfaces are intended to capture the common characteristics and behavior of the classes that implement the interfaces. Two relationships involving interfaces may be considered to be weak forms of inheritance. In the *implementation relationship* among classes and interfaces a class may implement zero or more interfaces. A class does not inherit any implementation from an interface; it provides implementation for the features declared in the interface. In the *extension relationship* among interfaces an interface, called a *subinterface,* may extend zero or more interfaces, called *superinterfaces*. The subinterface does not inherit any implementation from the superinterfaces because interfaces contain no implementation. The subinterface contains all the features declared in the superinterfaces. An interface can only extend other interfaces, not classes.

Java allows only *single inheritance* for class extension but *multiple inheritance* for interface extension and interface implementation. A class may implement multiple interfaces, and an interface may extend multiple interfaces. Although the `Object` class is the root of the inheritance hierarchy among classes, there is no single root for the interface extension and implementation relationships.

A class that implements an interface provides implementation for the abstract methods declared in the interface by overriding those methods, as illustrated by the following program fragment:

```
public interface MyInterface {
    void aMethod(int i); // an abstract method
}
public class MyClass implements MyInterface {
    public void aMethod(int i) {
        // implementation
    }
    // . . .
}
```

If a class implements multiple interfaces, it should override all the abstract methods declared in all the interfaces.

5.3.1 Subtypes Revisited

Each interface also defines a type. The interface extension and implementation are also subtype relations. A reference type in Java can be either a class type, an array type, or an interface type. Now, we can define the complete subtype relations among reference types.

▪ If class C_1 extends class C_2, then C_1 is a subtype of C_2.
▪ If interface I_1 extends interface I_2, then I_1 is a subtype of I_2.
▪ If class C implements interface I, then C is a subtype of I.
▪ For every interface I, I is a subtype of `Object`.
▪ For every type T, reference or primitive type, $T[\ ]$ (array of type T) is a subtype of `Object`.
▪ If type T_1 is a subtype of type T_2, then $T_1[\ ]$ is a subtype of type $T_2[\ ]$.

These relations also imply that, for every class C that is not `Object`, C is a subtype of `Object`.

Implementing multiple interfaces allows a class to assume different roles in different contexts. Suppose that we have the following two interfaces, one for students and one for employees:

```
public interface Student {
    float getGPA();
    // . . . other methods
}
public interface Employee {
    float getSalary();
    // . . . other methods
}
```

The FulltimeStudent and FulltimeEmployee classes in the following program segment implement the Student and Employee interfaces, respectively:

```java
public class FulltimeStudent implements Student {
    public float getGPA() {
        // calculate GPA
    }
    protected float gpa;
    // . . . other methods and fields
}

public class FulltimeEmployee implements Employee {
    public float getSalary() {
        // calculate salary
    }
    protected float salary;
    // . . . other methods and fields
}
```

A class can also implement both interfaces:

```java
public class StudentEmployee implements Student, Employee {
    public float getGPA() {
        // calculate GPA
    }
    public float getSalary() {
        // calculate salary
    }
    protected float gpa;
    protected float salary;
    // . . . other methods and fields
}
```

The StudentEmployee class is a subtype of both Student and Employee, as illustrated in Figure 5.3. Hence instances of StudentEmployee can be treated either as students or as employees. In one context, a student employee can be viewed as a student:

```java
Student[] students = new Student[. . . ];
students[0] = new FulltimeStudent();
students[1] = new StudentEmployee(); // a student employee as a student
// . . .
for (int i = 0; i < students.length; i++) {
    . . . students[i].getGPA() . . .
}
```

Figure 5.3

Implementation of interfaces.

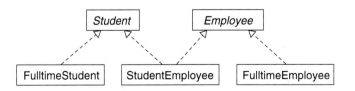

In the other context, a student employee can be viewed as an employee:

```
Employee[] employees = new Employee[. . . ];
employees[0] = new FulltimeEmployee();
employees[1] = new StudentEmployee(); // a student employee as an employee
// . . .
for (int i = 0; i < employees.length; i++) {
   . . . employees[i].getSalary() . . .
}
```

Therefore, a student employee can play two different roles in two different contexts. This dichotomy is the key advantage for allowing a class to have multiple supertypes via interface implementation.

5.3.2 Single Versus Multiple Inheritance

Whether to support single or multiple inheritance is one of the most hotly debated issues in object-oriented programming language design. C++ supports true multiple inheritance, whereas Java supports only a limited form of multiple inheritance through interface extension and implementation. In the preceding example, the `StudentEmployee` class implements two interfaces but inherits no *implementation* from the interfaces, as interfaces have no implementation. As a consequence, the `getGPA()` method is implemented separately in the `FulltimeStudent` and the `StudentEmployee` classes. Similarly, the `getSalary()` method is implemented separately in the `FulltimeEmployee` and the `StudentEmployee` classes. With the type of true multiple inheritance supported by C++, besides the subtype relationship that allows the instances of a subclass to play different roles, a subclass can also *inherit* (i.e., *reuse*) implementation from multiple superclasses. For example, with true multiple inheritance, we could do the following:

```
public class Student {
   public float getGPA() {
      // calculate GPA
   }
   protected float gpa;
   // . . . other methods and fields
}

public class Employee {
   public float getSalary() {
      // calculate salary
   }
   protected float salary;
   // . . . other methods and fields
}

public class FulltimeStudent extends Student {
   // implementation of getGPA() is inherited
   // . . . other methods and fields
}
```

```
public class FulltimeEmployee extends Employee {
    // implementation of getSalary( ) is inherited
    // . . . other methods and fields
}

// the following is illegal in Java!
// multiple inheritance of classes
public class StudentEmployee extends Student, Employee {
    // implementation of both getGPA( ) and getSalary( ) is inherited
    // . . . other methods and fields
}
```

Although multiple inheritance among classes supports implementation reuse in addition to the subtype relation, it is much more complicated than the Java inheritance model. It is more difficult to implement, less efficient, and difficult to use when the inheritance relation becomes complicated. Let us extend the preceding example a bit. Conceivably, both the Student and Employee classes should be subclasses of a more general class Person. This type of inheritance relation is known as *diamond-shaped multiple inheritance*, as illustrated in Figure 5.4, because of its shape. Diamond-shaped multiple inheritance is not a problem, and in fact it is rather common.

```
public class Person {
    public String getName() {
        // . . .
    }
    protected String name;
}

public class Student extends Person {
    public float getGPA() {
        // calculate GPA
    }
    protected float gpa;
    // . . . other methods and fields
}

public class Employee extends Person {
    public float getSalary() {
        // calculate salary
    }
    protected float salary;
    // . . . other methods and fields
}

// the following is illegal in Java!
// multiple inheritance of classes
public class StudentEmployee extends Student, Employee {
    // implementation of both getGPA( ) and getSalary( ) is inherited
    // . . . other methods and fields
}
```

Now, the question is, How many names does a student employee have? Both the Student and Employee classes inherit a copy of the name field from the Person

Figure 5.4

Diamond-shaped
multiple inheri-
tance relationship.

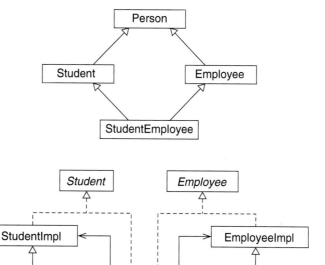

Figure 5.5

Implementation
reuse through
delegation.

class, and the `StudentEmployee` class in turn inherits all the fields from both of its
superclasses. Therefore, each instance of the `StudentEmployee` class contains two
copies of the `name` field. When we try to access the `name` field of a student employee,
which copy is accessed? Is it possible to access both copies? Common sense tells us
that there should be only one copy of the `name` field instead of two for each student
employee. These issues must be addressed when we use true multiple inheritance in
C++, whose semantics are further complicated by name resolution features and virtual
base classes. The complicated semantics of C++ make the implementation and use of
multiple inheritance difficult.

The restricted form of multiple inheritance in Java is much simpler. Furthermore,
the reuse of implementation can be accomplished by using an alternative mechanism,
as shown in Figure 5.5. Assume that we have two interfaces:

```
interface Student {
    public float getGPA();
}
interface Employee {
    public float getSalary();
}
```

We can have two classes to implement these interfaces:

```
public class StudentImpl implements Student {
    public float getGPA() {
        // calculate GPA
    }
    protected float gpa;
}
```

```
public class EmployeeImpl implements Employee {
   public float getSalary() {
      // calculate salary
   }
   protected float salary;
}
```

The implementation in StudentImpl and EmployeeImpl can be directly reused in the full-time student and employee classes by utilizing class extension:

```
public class FulltimeStudent extends StudentImpl {
   // method getGPA() and field gpa are inherited
   // ... other methods and fields
}

public class FulltimeEmployee extends EmployeeImpl {
   // method getSalary() and field salary are inherited
   // ... other methods and fields
}
```

In addition, a student employee class can be implemented as follows to reuse the implementation in StudentImpl and EmployeeImpl:

```
public class StudentEmployee implements Student, Employee {
   public StudentEmployee() {
      studentImpl = new StudentImpl();
      employeeImpl = new EmployeeImpl();
      // ...
   }
   public float getGPA() {
      return studentImpl.getGPA(); // delegation
   }
   public float getSalary() {
      return employeeImpl.getSalary(); // delegation
   }

   protected StudentImpl studentImpl;
   protected EmployeeImpl employeeImpl;

   // ... other methods and fields
}
```

The implementation technique used in the getGPA() and getSalary() methods is known as *delegation* because each method simply delegates the task to another object, studentImpl and employeeImpl, respectively. The implementation in the StudentImpl and EmployeeImpl classes is reused through delegation.

The simple and restricted form of multiple inheritance adopted in Java coupled with the delegation technique can accomplish everything that can be accomplished by using true multiple inheritance.

5.3.3   Name Collisions among Interfaces

In Java, a class may extend one class and implement multiple interfaces, and an interface may extend multiple interfaces. Names inherited from one interface may collide with names inherited from another interface or class. However, name collisions are fairly easy to resolve in Java.

Two methods that have the same name offer the following possibilities:

- If they have different signatures, they are considered to be overloaded.
- If they have the same signature and the same return type, they are considered to be the same method. In other words, the two methods collapse into one.
- If they have the same signature but different return types, a compilation error will result.
- If they have the same signature and the same return type but throw different exceptions, they are considered to be the same method, and the resulting `throws` list is the union of the two original `throws` lists.

For example, let us consider two interfaces and a class that implements both.

```
public interface X {
   public void method1(int i);
   public void method2(int i);
   public void method3(int i);
   public void method4(int i) throws Exception1;
}
public interfaces Y {
   public void method1(double d);
   public void method2(int i);
   public int method3(int i);
   public void method4(int i) throws Exception2;
}
public public class MyClass implements X, Y {
   public void method1(int i) { . . . }      // overrides method1 in X
   public void method1(double d) { . . . }   // overrides method1 in Y
   public void method2(int i) { . . . }      // overrides method2 in X and Y
   public void method4(int i)                // overrides method4 in X and Y
      throws Exception1, Exception2 { . . . }
}
```

The two methods named `method1()` in MyClass are overloaded. The two methods named `method3()` in X and Y will cause a compilation error.

Two constants having the same name is always allowed. They are considered to be two separate constants, as in

```
public interface X {
   static final int a = . . . ;
}
public interfaces Y {
   static final double a = . . . ;
}
```

```
public class MyClass implements X, Y {
   void aMethod() {
      . . . X.a . . .   // the int constant a in X
      . . . Y.a . . .   // the double constant a in Y
   }
}
```

5.3.4 Marker Interfaces

Marker interfaces are empty interfaces, that is, interfaces that declare no methods or constants. They establish a subtype relationship between themselves and the classes that implement them. They are intended to mark classes as having certain properties. The most commonly used marker interface is the `Cloneable` interface. The `Cloneable` interface is used to distinguish classes that can be cloned from those that cannot be cloned. Only those classes that implement the `Cloneable` interface can be cloned.

5.4 HIDING FIELDS AND CLASS METHODS

When a subclass declares a field or class method that is already declared in its superclass, the field or class method in the superclass is not overridden; it is hidden.

Definition 5.5 *Hiding*

Hiding refers to the introduction of a field (instance or class) or a class method in a subclass that has the same name as a field or a class method in the superclass.

Overriding and hiding are different concepts.

■ Instance methods can only be overridden. A method can be overridden only by a method of the same signature and return type.

■ Class methods and fields can only be hidden. A class method or field (instance or class) may be hidden by a class method or a field of any signature or type.

The following example illustrates these differences:

```
public class A {
   int x;
   void y() { . . . }
   static void z() { . . . }
}
public class B extends A {
   float x;                      // hiding
   void y() { . . . }            // overriding
   static int z() { . . . }      // hiding
}
```

There is a crucial distinction between overriding and hiding. When an overridden method is invoked, the implementation that will be executed is chosen at *run time*. However, when a hidden method or field is invoked or accessed, the copy that will be used is determined at *compile time*. In other words, the class methods and fields (instance or class) are *statically bound*, based on the declared type of the variables. Let us consider the following variation of the Point and ColoredPoint example.

```
public class Point {
    public String className = "Point";
    static public String getDescription() {
        return "Point";
    }
    // other declarations
}

public class ColoredPoint extends Point {
    public String className = "ColoredPoint";
    static public String getDescription() {
        return "ColoredPoint";
    }
    // other declarations
}
```

The instance field className of the ColoredPoint class hides the field of the same name of the Point class. The static method getDescription() of the Colored-Point class hides the method of the same name of the Point class.

```
ColoredPoint p1 = new ColoredPoint(10.0, 10.0, Color.blue);
Point p2 = p1;

System.out.println(p1.getDescription());
System.out.println(p2.getDescription());
System.out.println(p1.className);
System.out.println(p2.className);
```

The output is

```
ColoredPoint
Point
ColoredPoint
Point
```

Although, both p1 and p2 refer to the same object, the binding of the static methods and fields is based on the declared types of the variables at compile time. The declared type of p1 and p2 are ColoredPoint and Point, respectively. Hence the result.

If the preceding example looks confusing, that is the reason to avoid hiding. Hiding fields and static methods offers little help but hampers the readability of programs. The rules of hiding are intended to resolve *coincidental* name collisions, that is, un-related features that happen to have the same name in subclasses and superclasses.

Design Guideline *Avoid Hiding*

Avoid hiding fields and class methods. Use different field names and class method names for unrelated features.

Moreover, it is better to invoke class methods through class names instead of object references. So instead of

```
System.out.println(p1.getDescription());
System.out.println(p2.getDescription());
```

we should write

```
System.out.println(ColoredPoint.getDescription());
System.out.println(Point.getDescription());
```

Even though `ColoredPoint.getDescription()` still hides `Point.getDescription()`, at least it is less confusing.

5.5   APPLICATIONS—ANIMATION APPLETS

In this section, we present some animation applets to illustrate the graphics capability of Java and important techniques used in animation.

5.5.1   Parameters of Applets

The initial version of the Digital Clock applet is simple but not very flexible. Nothing can be changed without modifying and recompiling the source code. The flexibility to change the appearance or behavior of applets is desirable in many situations. Applets provide this type of flexibility via the parameters supplied in the applet tag.

EXAMPLE 5.1   The Digital Clock Applet—An Enhancement

PURPOSE

To illustrate the use of parameters in applets and enhancing a class by extension.

DESCRIPTION

In this example, we develop a digital clock that behaves the same as the original version (see Example 4.12) but allows the foreground color to be set as a parameter.

SOLUTION

Because we intend to preserve the behavior of the original digital clock, we extend the original version to obtain the enhanced version. The only method that needs to be overridden is the init() method, in which the display color is set.

Enhanced digital clock applet: `DigitalClock2.java`

```java
import java.awt.Color;
public class DigitalClock2 extends DigitalClock {
    public void init () {
        String param = getParameter("color");
        if ("red".equals(param)) {
          color = Color.red;
        } else if ("blue".equals(param)) {
          color = Color.blue;
        } else if ("yellow".equals(param)) {
          color = Color.yellow;
        } else if ("orange".equals(param)) {
          color = Color.orange;
        } else {
          color = Color.green;
        }
    }
}
```

The getParameter() method is a method of the Applet class. It takes a string argument—the name of the parameter to be retrieved—and returns a string that is the value of the specified parameter. The parameters are expected as part of the <applet> tag in the Web page. If the parameter is not set in the <applet> tag, a null reference is returned by the getParameter() method.

This enhanced digital clock applet allows the foreground color to be set to any of four common colors: red, blue, yellow, and orange. If the color is not specified, the color is set to green by default. The colors can easily be extended to allow more choices.

The following code fragment is a sample applet tag for the enhanced digital clock:

```html
<applet code=DigitalClock2.class width=250 height=80>
<param name=color value=blue>
</applet>
```

In general, the applet tag with parameters takes the following form:

```
<applet code=class_filename
     width=pixels height=pixels>
  <param name=param_name₁ value=param_value₁>

        ⋮

  <param name=param_nameₙ value=param_valueₙ>
</applet>
```

5.5.2 An Idiom for Animation Applets

The basic mechanism of animation is to display a sequence of frames. Each frame shows objects that have moved slightly from their positions in the preceding frame. When the sequence of frames is shown faster than 10 frames per second, human beings will perceive continuous motion of the objects. Motion pictures and television work in the same way but at higher frequencies, typically between 24 and 30 frames per second.

EXAMPLE 5.2   The Scrolling Banner Applet—The Initial Version

PURPOSE

To illustrate animation and text drawing.

DESCRIPTION

In this example, we develop a simple animation applet. It displays a text banner that moves horizontally from right to left. When the banner moves completely off the left end of the viewing area, it reappears at the right end (see Figure 5.6).

SOLUTION

The fields of the `ScrollingBanner` class are summarized in the following table.

Field	Description
bannerThread	The animation thread
text	The text to be displayed
font	The font used to display the text
x, y	The current position of the text
delay	The interval between two consecutive frames in milliseconds
offset	The distance moved between two consecutive frames in pixels
d	The size of the viewing area

Figure 5.6

The scrolling banner applet.

Scrolling banner applet: `ScrollingBanner.java`

```java
import java.awt.*;

public class ScrollingBanner
        extends java.applet.Applet implements Runnable {

    protected Thread bannerThread;
    protected String text;
    protected Font font =
        new java.awt.Font("Sans-serif", Font.BOLD, 24);
    protected int x, y;
    protected int delay = 100;
    protected int offset = 1;
    protected Dimension d;

    ⟨init() method on page 189⟩
    ⟨paint() method on page 190⟩
    ⟨start(), stop(), and run() method on page 190⟩
}
```

The `init()` method handles the initialization of the applet. It retrieves two parameters: `delay` and `text`. The `getSize()` method returns the size of the viewing area in the Web page. The result is of type `Dimension`, which is declared as

```java
public class java.awt.Dimension {
    public int width, height;
}
```

The initial position of the text is set at the rightmost position in the viewing area. The geometry of the drawing is illustrated in Figure 5.7.

Method of `ScrollingBanner` **class:** `init()`

```java
public void init() {
    // get parameters "delay" and "text"
    String att = getParameter("delay");
    if (att != null) {
        delay = Integer.parseInt(att);
    }
    att = getParameter("text");
    if (att != null) {
        text = att;
    } else {
        text = "Scrolling banner.";
    }
```

Figure 5.7

Drawing of the scrolling banner.

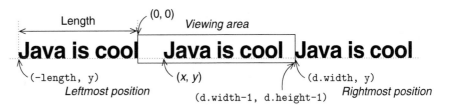

```
    // set initial position of the text
    d = getSize();
    x = d.width;
    y = font.getSize();
}
```

The paint() method paints the current frame. The key to the animation is that the position of the text has to be adjusted from the previous frame. If the text falls out of bounds, it should be repositioned.

Method of ScrollingBanner class: paint()

```
public void paint(Graphics g) {
    // get the font metrics to determine the length of the text
    g.setFont(font);
    FontMetrics fm = g.getFontMetrics();
    int length = fm.stringWidth(text);

    // adjust the position of text from the previous frame
    x -= offset;

    // if the text is completely off to the left end
    // move the position back to the right end
    if (x < -length)
        x = d.width;

    // set the pen color and draw the background
    g.setColor(Color.black);
    g.fillRect(0,0,d.width,d.height);

    // set the pen color, then draw the text
    g.setColor(Color.green);
    g.drawString(text, x, y);
}
```

The control portion of the applet, which consists of the bannerThread variable and the start(), stop(), and run() methods, is nearly identical to that of the digital clock applet.

Methods of ScrollingBanner class: start(), stop(), and run()

```
public void start() {
    bannerThread = new Thread(this);
    bannerThread.start();
}
public void stop() {
    bannerThread = null;
}
public void run() {
    while (Thread.currentThread() == bannerThread) {
        try {
            Thread.currentThread().sleep(delay);
        }
```

```
          catch (InterruptedException e){}
          repaint();
      }
   }
```

Why Use `init()`?

Usually, initialization of an object state is done in the constructors of the class. However, you may have noticed that for applets, the initialization is not done in the constructors but in the method `init()`. Would it be the same if the initialization were moved to a constructor of the applets? The answer is no. The reason is that an applet is not a full-blown program, and it must be invoked by another program referred to as the applet context. The *applet context* is either a Java-enabled Web browser or the `appletviewer`. The applet context is responsible for interpreting the `<applet>` tag in the HTML file and initializing and executing the applet. The key factor here is timing. The applet context first creates an instance of the applet, using its no-arg constructor. At this point, the applet instance has no knowledge of any information specified in the `<applet>` tag. Specifically, a call to `getSize()` from the no-arg constructor of an applet would return a 0×0 dimension, and `getParameter()` would return null. The information specified in the `<applet>` tag will be available to the applet only after it has been created. That is why any initialization that depends on the size and parameters specified in the `<applet>` tag must be done in the method `init()`. The method `init()` is invoked by the applet context *after* the information specified in the `<applet>` tag is processed and made available to the applet.

Idiom: Animation Applets

You may have noticed that the basic structures of the animation applets presented so far are nearly identical. That fact is not a coincidence. The common structure represents a general implementation scheme of animation applets. We capture this scheme as an idiom. An *idiom* is a way to represent a template implementation of a recurring problem that may be customized and adapted in different contexts.

Idiom *Animation Applet*

> *Category:* Behavioral implementation idiom.
>
> *Intent:* For an applet to update continuously its appearance without user input or intervention.
>
> *Also known as:* Active applet.
>
> *Applicability:* Use the animation applet idiom to animate dynamic processes.

The generic structure of the top-level class of an animation applet can be described as follows:

```
public class AnimationApplet
    extends java.applet.Applet implements Runnable {
  Thread  mainThread = null;
  int     delay;
  public void start(){
    if (mainThread == null) {
      mainThread = new Thread(this);
      mainThread.start();
    }
  }
  public void stop() {
    mainThread = null;
  }
  public void run() {
    while (Thread.currentThread() == mainThread) {
      repaint();
      try {
        Thread.currentThread().sleep(delay);
      }
      catch (InterruptedException e) {}
    }
  }
  public void paint(java.awt.Graphics g) {
    ⟨paint the current frame⟩
  }

  ⟨other methods and fields⟩
}
```

When using this idiom to create an animation applet, you should copy the code shown in Courier font verbatim, but you can replace the names shown in italic with any other names. Field *mainThread* is the main control thread. Field *delay* determines the refresh rate.

The java.awt.FontMetrics Class

The FontMetrics class provides the metrics for each font design. The most commonly used metrics are those illustrated in the following diagram, along with the methods for retrieving these metrics:

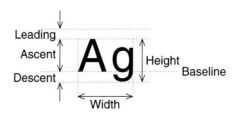

Method	Description
getAscent()	Return the ascent of the font.
getDescent()	Return the descent of the font.
getHeight()	Return the height of the font.
getLeading()	Return the leading of the font.
stringWidth(*str*)	Return the width of string *str* when it is drawn using the font.

It may seem natural for the Font class to provide a method, say, getFontMetrics(), to return an instance of the FontMetrics class corresponding to a given font. However, the getFontMetrics() method is not provided by the Font class, but by the Graphics class instead. The reason is that the metrics of a font depend not only on the font family and the size and style of the font, but also on the resolution of the graphics context in which the characters will be rendered. Therefore, the metrics of a font should be obtained as follows, assuming that g is an instance of Graphics:

```
Font font = new Font(name, style, size);
g.setFont(font);
FontMetrics fm = g.getFontMetrics();
```

5.5.3 Double-Buffered Animation

The ScrollingBanner has a minor glitch. If you pay close attention, you will notice that it flickers. To understand the cause of the flickering, we need to look more closely at how frames are painted. The animation process is controlled by the while loop in the run method. During each iteration, the thread sleeps for a short period of time before calling the repaint() method. The repaint() method calls another method: update(). The default implementation of the update() method

- clears the background by filling it with the background color (usually, the default background color is gray or white),
- sets the pen color to the foreground color, and
- calls the paint() method.

In the paint() method, the background is repainted—this time in black—and then the text is drawn. Because the painting is done directly on the screen, it cannot be completed instantaneously. The background painting may take long enough for the human eye to notice; hence the flickering effect.

EXAMPLE 5.3 The Scrolling Banner Applet—Using Double-Buffering

PURPOSE

To illustrate double-buffered animation and enhancing a class by extension.

DESCRIPTION

This version of the scrolling banner applet behaves basically the same as the initial version but eliminates the flickering.

SOLUTION

The solution to avoid flickering is quite simple. Instead of painting each frame directly on the screen, we first paint it in a temporary buffer in memory. When the frame has been completed, we copy it from the temporary buffer to the screen in a single step. The painting in progress is not visible because it is done in a temporary buffer. Copying an image from memory to the screen is usually supported by graphics hardware so that it can be done fast, resulting in smoother motion from frame to frame. This technique is commonly called *double-buffering*, or *off-screen drawing*.

Now, we try to improve the scrolling banner applet by using double-buffering. The main functionality of the moving text remains the same, so we simply need to extend the original applet.

Double-buffered scrolling banner applet: `ScrollingBanner2.java`

```java
import java.awt.*;
public class ScrollingBanner2 extends ScrollingBanner {
   protected Image image;          // The off-screen image
   protected Graphics offscreen;   // The off-screen graphics

   public void update(Graphics g) {
      // create the offscreen image if it is the first time
      if (image == null) {
         image = createImage(d.width, d.height);
         offscreen = image.getGraphics();
      }
      // draw the current frame into the off-screen image
      // using the paint method of the superclass
      super.paint(offscreen);
      // copy the off-screen image to the screen
      g.drawImage(image, 0, 0, this);
   }

   public void paint(Graphics g) {
      update(g);
   }
}
```

We override the default implementation of the update() method. Our new update() method uses double-buffering, which requires two additional fields:

Field	Description
image	An off-screen image that is the same size as the viewing area
offscreen	A graphics context associated with the off-screen image

An image object is simply a matrix of pixels. We cannot directly draw into an image object. A graphics object must be created for drawing into the image by calling the getGraphics() method. With the graphics object, drawing into an off-screen image is no different from drawing directly on the screen. ▪

EXAMPLE 5.4   The Bouncing Ball Applet

PURPOSE

To illustrate the Animation Applet Idiom, graphics drawing, and double-buffering.

DESCRIPTION

Our new animation applet shows a ball moving inside a rectangular box (see Figure 5.8). The ball reverses direction when it touches any of the four sides of the box.

SOLUTION

The fields of the BouncingBall class are as follows:

Field	Description
color	Color of the ball
radius	Radius of the ball in pixels
x, y	Current position of the ball
dx, dy	Distance moved between two consecutive frames in the x and y directions in pixels
image	Off-screen image
offscreen	Off-screen graphics
d	Size of the viewing area

Figure 5.8

The bouncing ball
applet.

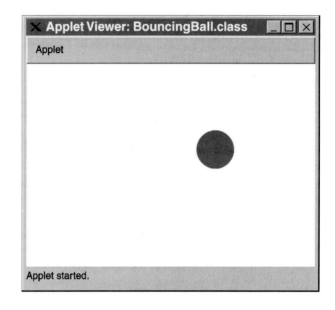

Bouncing ball applet: `BouncingBall.java`

```java
import java.awt.*;

public class BouncingBall
    extends java.applet.Applet implements Runnable {
    protected Color color = Color.green;
    protected int radius = 20;
    protected int x, y;
    protected int dx = -2, dy = -4;
    protected Image image;
    protected Graphics offscreen;
    protected Dimension d;

    public void init() {
        String att = getParameter("delay");
        if (att != null) {
            delay = Integer.parseInt(att);
        }
        d = getSize();
        x = d.width * 2 / 3 ;
        y = d.height - radius;
    }

    public void update(Graphics g) {
        // create the off-screen image buffer
        // if it is invoked the first time
        if (image == null) {
            image = createImage(d.width, d.height);
            offscreen = image.getGraphics();
        }
```

```
    // draw the background
    offscreen.setColor(Color.white);
    offscreen.fillRect(0,0,d.width,d.height);
    // adjust the position of the ball
    // reverse the direction if it touches
    // any of the four sides
    if (x < radius || x > d.width - radius) {
       dx = -dx;
    }
    if (y < radius || y > d.height - radius) {
       dy = -dy;
    }
    x += dx;
    y += dy;
    // draw the ball
    offscreen.setColor(color);
    offscreen.fillOval(x - radius, y - radius,
          radius * 2, radius * 2);
    // copy the off-screen image to the screen
    g.drawImage(image, 0, 0, this);
}

public void paint(Graphics g) {
    update(g);
}

// The animation applet idiom
protected Thread bouncingThread;
protected int delay = 100;
public void start() {
    bouncingThread = new Thread(this);
    bouncingThread.start();
}

public void stop() {
    bouncingThread = null;
}

public void run() {
    while (Thread.currentThread() == bouncingThread) {
      try {
          Thread.currentThread().sleep(delay);
      } catch (InterruptedException e){}
      repaint();
    }
  }
}
```

The java.awt.Graphics Class

The Graphics class is an abstraction of different displaying devices, such as screens, printers, and off-screen images. It encapsulates the details and characteristics of these devices and allows us to treat them uniformly.

The Graphics class is fairly large and provides the basic capabilities for two-dimensional graphics. More sophisticated two-dimensional graphics capabilities are provided in a subclass Graphics2D.

Two groups of methods are commonly used in this class: methods for setting and retrieving attributes and methods for drawing. The methods for setting and retrieving attributes are summarized in the following table. In the parameters of the methods, color is an instance of the class Color and font is an intance of the class Font.

Method	Description
void setColor(*color*)	Set the current color.
void setFont(*font*)	Set the current font.
void setPaintMode()	Switch to the paint or overwrite mode.
void setXORMode(*color*)	Switch to the XOR mode.
Color getColor()	Get the current color.
Font getFont()	Get the current font.
FontMetrics getFontMetrics()	Get the font metrics of the current font.
FontMetrics getFontMetrics(*font*)	Get the font metrics of the specified font.

Drawing methods are divided into two categories: (1) methods that have a draw prefix, which draw the outlines of certain shapes with the current color; and (2) methods that have a fill prefix, which fill the interior areas of certain shapes with the current color. The methods for drawing various shapes are summarized as follows.

Text String

```
drawString(String s, int x, int y)
```

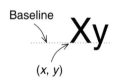

The ordered pair (x, y) specifies the left end of the string on the baseline.

Line Segment

```
void drawLine(int x1, int y1,
              int x2, int y2)
```

(x_1, y_1)

(x_2, y_2)

The ordered pairs (x_1, y_1) and (x_2, y_2) specify the two ends of the line segment.

Rectangle

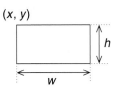

```
void drawRect(int x, int y, int w, int h)
void fillRect(int x, int y, int w, int h)
```

The ordered pair (x, y) specifies the upper-left corner of the rectangle, and w and h specify the width and height, respectively, of the rectangle.

Oval

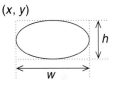

```
void drawOval(int x, int y, int w, int h)
void fillOval(int x, int y, int w, int h)
```

The ordered pair (x, y) specifies the upper-left corner of the surrounding rectangle; and w and h specify the width and height, respectively, of the surrounding rectangle.

Round-Cornered Rectangle

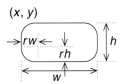

```
void drawRoundRect(int x, int y, int w,
                   int h, int rw, int rh)
void fillRoundRect(int x, int y, int w,
                   int h, int rw, int rh)
```

The ordered pair (x, y) specifies the upper-left corner of the surrounding rectangle; w and h specify the width and the height, respectively, of the surrounding rectangle; and rw and rh specify the width and height, respectively, of the quarter ovals at the corners.

Three-Dimensional Highlighted Rectangle

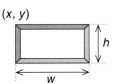

```
void draw3DRect(int x, int y, int w, int h,
                boolean raised)
void fill3DRect(int x, int y, int w, int h,
                boolean raised)
```

The ordered pair (x, y) specifies the upper-left corner of the rectangle; and w and h specify the width and height, respectively, of the rectangle. The boolean parameter raised has the following effects:

- true: Draw a raised three-dimensional rectangle; and
- false: Draw a sunken three-dimensional rectangle.

Arc

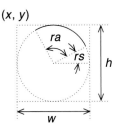

```
void drawArc(int x, int y, int w, int h,
             int rs, int ra)
void fillArc(int x, int y, int w, int h,
             int rs, int ra)
```

The ordered pair (x, y) specifies the upper-left corner of the surrounding rectangle; w and h specify the width and height, respectively, of the surrounding rectangle; and rs and ra specify the starting angle and the angle covered by the arc, respectively, in degrees.

5.5.4   Reading Files in Applets

An applet is not allowed to read or write files on the client machine—the machine on which the applet is executed. However, an applet is allowed to read files from the server host—the host from which the applet is downloaded.

The URL

The URL class represents the *Universal Resource Locator* (URL). A URL takes the following form.[1]

```
http:// java.sun.com:80/document/index.html#section2
```

It consists of the following components, not all of which need be present.

URL Component	Example
Protocol	`http://`
Host address	`java.sun.com`
Port	`:80`
Path	`/document/index.html`
Section reference	`#section2`

---

1. The double slash (//) in a Web site address does not indicate a comment as it does in program code. When it appears in program code, it must be enclosed by double quotes, as in: `"http://java.sun.com/index.html"`.

URLs can be constructed by using one of the following constructors of the URL class.

URL Constructor	Description
URL (*spec*)	Construct a URL represented by a string *spec*.
URL (*url, path*)	Construct a URL by giving a base URL *url* and a relative path *path* to the base URL.

For example,

```
URL url1 = new URL("http://java.sun.com/index.html");
    // Construct URL: http://java.sun.com/index.html

URL url2 = new URL(url1, "document/intro.html");
    // Construct URL: http://java.sun.com/document/intro.html
```

The following two methods of the `Applet` class return the URL of the document page and the Java class file, respectively:

Method	Description
`getDocumentBase()`	Return the URL of the Web page in which the applet is emdedded.
`getCodeBase()`	Return the URL of the applet class file.

An applet can read a file by first constructing a URL, using the relative path of the file to be read. A text file named `filename` can be read as follows:

```
URL url = new URL(getDocumentBase(), filename);
BufferedReader in =
   new BufferedReader(new InputStreamReader(
                         url.openStream()));
String line;
try {
   while ((line = in.readLine()) != null) {
      // process line
   }
} catch (IOException e) {}
```

We discuss the `BufferedReader` and `InputStreamReader` classes in Section 8.4 [p. 366].

Images and Audio Clips

The `Applet` class also provides methods to easily access image and audio files by giving their URLs.

Method	Description
getImage(*url*)	Retrieve the image stored at *url*.
play(*url*)	Retrieve and play the audio clip stored at *url*.

COMMON PROBLEMS AND SOLUTIONS

Symptoms	Possible Causes and/or Fixes
Applets run fine with the applet viewer but do not run in a browser.	The most likely cause is that all the byte-code files (`.class` files) were not transfered to the Web server.
	Unlike C and C++ compilers, which generate a single object file for each source file, the Java compiler may generate multiple byte-code files for each source file. The Java compiler generates a `.class` file for each *class*, even when several classes are put in the same source file.

CHAPTER SUMMARY

- Java allows methods and constructors to be overloaded. Operator overloading is limited to operations on primitive types and string concatenation. Methods or constructors of the same class but with different signatures can be overloaded.
- Inheritance is a mechanism for reusing the implementation as well as extending the functionality of a superclass. The class extension relation is the strict form of

inheritance, in which the implementation of the superclass is actually inherited or reused in the subclasses. The interface extension and implementation relations can be considered as weaker forms of inheritance, in which no implementation is inherited from the interfaces. Only single inheritance is allowed for class extension. Multiple inheritance is allowed for interface extension and implementation.

- Subtypes are relations among types. Every legitimate value of a subtype is also a legitimate value of its supertypes. A value of a subtype can appear wherever a value of its supertype is expected. The subtype relation is defined by class extension, interface extension, and implementation. Downcasting refers to casting a reference type explicitly to one of its subtypes.

- Polymorphic assignment refers to the kind of assignments allowed in object-oriented programming languages, in which the right-hand-side expression of an assignment can be an object of many different types, so long as the type is a subtype of the type of the left-hand-side expression of the assignment. Polymorphic method invocation refers to method invocations that can be bound to different implementations at run time. Such binding occurs when a method is overidden in subclasses.

- Overriding is different from overloading. Overriding has to do with methods in different classes having the same signature and return type. Overloading deals with methods in the same class having different signatures. Overriding is also different from hiding. Instance methods can only be overridden. Static methods and fields can only be hidden. A static method or field may be hidden by a static method or a field of a different signature or type.

- Interfaces declare class features but provide no implementation.

- Java does not support the kind of true multiple inheritance supported by C++. Java supports only a restricted form of multiple inheritance through interface extension and implementation. The Java inheritance model allows a type to have multiple supertypes. The reuse of implementation from multiple superclasses can be emulated in Java through delegation.

- Classes should be designed, organized, and implemented in a way that is easy to understand, is safe to use, and provides complete functionality. Public fields should be avoided. Public classes should conform to the canonical form described in Section 6.3.

- Basic graphics capabilities are provided by the Graphics class, along with the supporting classes Color, Font, FontMetrics, and Dimension.

- Applets cannot read or write files from the client machine; they can only read files from the host server.

- Double-buffering refers to a technique used in animation to reduce flickering. This technique is also called off-screen drawing. Double-buffering improves the quality of animation significantly.

EXERCISES

5.1 A polymorphic array of shapes.

(a) Implement a simple class hierarchy of *shapes*, which consists of an interface.

Shape	Attributes
LineSegment	The coordinates of two end points
Rectangle	The coordinates of the upper-left corner, the width, and the height
Circle	The coordinates of the center and the radius

Shape and three classes, LineSegment, Rectangle, and Circle, that implement the Shape interface. Each shape has the following attributes:

All attributes are integers, and the unit is pixel. The toString() method should be defined for all shapes to give string representations of the shapes.

(b) Write a Java app to do the following:

(i) Read a text file that contains descriptions of different shapes from standard input. Each line of the input file is a description of a shape in one of the following formats:

LineSegment (x_1, y_1) and (x_2, y_2)

Rectangle x and y (*width* and *height*)

Circle (x, y) (*radius*)

All numbers are integer literals. Fields are delimited by white spaces.

(ii) Create instances of the shapes described in the input file and store them in an array of Shapes.

(iii) Print the string representations of all the shapes stored in the array to standard output.

Assume that the input file contains no more than 100 shapes.

5.2 Modify the BouncingBall applet so that it contains documentation comments that can be processed by the javadoc utility. Then use javadoc to generate HTML pages from your modified version of the BouncingBall applet. You should document every class, method, return type, field, and parameter. Use the tags author, version, since, param, returns, and see.

5.3 Write a java applet that uses the getCode-Base() and getDocumentBase() methods to display the applet's code base and document base, respectively. *Hint:* Use the toString() method of the URL class.

5.4 Enhance the digital clock applet to allow the font to be customized via another parameter in the applet tag.

5.5 Write an animation applet that shows an analog clock.

5.6 Enhance the ScrollingBanner applet with the following functionalities:

(a) Allow the font and color to be set by parameters.

(b) Allow the banner to move in different directions: left to right, upward, downward, and diagonally.

PROJECTS

5.1 Write an applet that retrieves a text file containing a list of points, and produce a scatterplot in a two-dimensional coordinate system. Each line of the input file contains a single point, and each point is represented by two integers that specify the x and y coordinates and are separated by white spaces.

5.2 Write an applet that retrieves sales data as parameters, and display the data on a pie chart. The format of the parameters is the following:

```
<param name=categories value="cat₁. . . catₙ">
<param name=cat₁ value=amount₁>
    ⋮
<param name=catₙ value=amountₙ>
```

The amount for each category is represented as an integer. For example, the following are sample sales data for a software superstore:

```
<param name=categories
    value="education utility
           entertainment reference"
<param name=education value=10000>
<param name=utility value=12000>
<param name=entertainment value=30000>
<param name=reference value=9000>
```

5.3 Write an applet that retrieves sales data as parameters in the same format as in Project 5.2, and display the data using a bar chart.

5.4 Extend Exercise 5.1 by adding a `draw()` method to each of the shape classes that draws the respective shape. Write an applet that reads a file that contains descriptions of different shapes, and draw the shapes using the `draw()` method.

CHAPTER 6

From Building Blocks to Projects

CHAPTER OVERVIEW

In this chapter, we examine the issues involved in designing classes: organizing files and classes, and using the canonical form of public classes. We present a number of important design guidelines. We also briefly discuss the documentation of classes and methods and the use of the javadoc utility. We introduce the concepts of contracts, preconditions, postconditions, and invariants, and using the assertion facility to check preconditions, postconditions, and invariants at run time. Finally, we briefly discuss two useful tools: JUnit for unit testing of classes and Ant for project building.

6.1 DESIGN AND IMPLEMENTATION OF CLASSES

6.1.1 Public and Helper Classes

There are two kinds of classes. The first kind comprises classes for general use, known as *public classes*. A public class must be declared public and reside in a file whose name coincides with the class name. For example, the public class Point must reside in a file named Point.java. The second kind comprises classes that are used solely for implementing other classes. These classes are called *auxiliary*, or *helper*, classes. They should not be declared public. If an auxiliary class supports a single public class,

Figure 6.1

The List interface.

```
public interface List {
    public int size();
    public boolean isEmpty();
    public Object element(int i);
    public Object head();
    public Object last();
    public void insert(Object item, int i);
    public void insertHead(Object item);
    public void insertLast(Object item);
    public Object remove(int i);
    public Object removeHead();
    public Object removeLast();
}
```

it should then reside in a separate file. It should reside in the same file as the class it supports. If an auxiliary class supports a multiple public class in the same package, it may reside in a separate file.

Throughout this chapter, we use an interface List as shown in Figure 6.1 and a class LinkedList, which implements the List interface using a doubly linked list, as examples.[1] Now, let us first consider the organization of the LinkedList.java class. The LinkedList.java class is a public class and resides in a file named LinkedList.java. Since the implementation uses a doubly linked list, the LinkedList class requires an auxiliary class Node, which represents the nodes in the doubly linked list. The Node class is used only in implementation and should not be exposed to clients. The Node class should not be public and should reside in the same file as the LinkedList class (i.e., the LinkedList.java file). There are two options for the Node class:

1. The Node class can be a separate class. In file LinkedList.java,

```
public class LinkedList implements List {
    protected Node head, tail;
    protected int count;
    // ...
    // implementation of linked list
}
class Node {
    Object element;
    Node next, prev;
}
```

2. The Node class can be a nested class of the LinkedList class. In file Linked List.java,

```
public class LinkedList implements List {
    protected Node head, tail;
```

1. The List interface and the LinkedList class discussed in this chapter are not the same as and should not be confused with the List interface and the LinkedList in the Java Collection Framework, which is discussed later in Chapter 8.

```
        protected int count;
        static protected class Node {
            Object element;
            Node next, prev;
        }
        // . . .
        // implementation of linked list
}
```

The difference between the two is that in option 1 the Node class is not accessible to any subclass of LinkedList not in the same package, whereas in option 2 the Node class is accessible to subclasses of LinkedList.

6.1.2 Class Members

In Java, the order of the class members is insignificant. In other words, reordering the members of a class does not alter the semantics of the class. This characteristic allows the members of classes to be ordered to maximize the readability.

The fields and methods of a class should be ordered according to their accessibility and roles. The methods of a class should be organized into groups appearing in the following order:

- Public constructors
- Public accessors, or selectors, which are methods that do not modify the state of objects
- Public mutators, or modifiers, which are methods that modify the state of objects
- Nonpublic constructors and auxiliary methods

A recommended organization of a public class is as follows:

```
public class AClass {
    ⟨public constants⟩
    ⟨public constructors⟩
    ⟨public accessors⟩
    ⟨public mutators⟩
    ⟨nonpublic fields⟩
    ⟨nonpublic auxiliary methods or nested classes⟩
}
```

Figure 6.2 shows the organization of the LinkedList class.

6.1.3 Design Guidelines

In this section we examine the issues involved in designing classes. We discuss a number of basic guidelines for class and package design.

Figure 6.2

**Organization of the
LinkedList class.**

```
package mylist;

public class LinkedList implement List {
    // constructor
    public LinkedList() { . . . }

    // accessors
    public int size() { . . . }
    public boolean isEmpty() { . . . }
    public Object element(int i) { . . . }
    public Object head() { . . . }
    public Object last() { . . . }

    // canonical form methods
    public boolean equals(Object other) { . . . }
    public int hashCode() { . . . }
    public Object clone() { . . . }
    public String toString() { . . . }

    // mutators
    public void insert(Object item, int i) { . . . }
    public void insertHead(Object item) { . . . }
    public void insertLast(Object item) { . . . }
    public Object remove(int i) { . . . }
    public Object removeHead() { . . . }
    public Object removeLast() { . . . }

    // fields
    protected Node head, tail;
    protected int count;

    // auxiliary nested class
    static protected class Node {
        Object element;
        Node next, prev;
    }
}
```

Avoid Public Fields

Design Guideline *Avoid Public Fields*

There should be no nonfinal public fields, except when a class is final *and* the field is unconstrained.

For a field named *attr*, an accessor, also known as a getter, named *getAttr( )* should be provided to access the value of the field. Optionally, a mutator of the field, also known as a setter, named *setAttr( )* may be provided to modify the value of the field. When a field is of type boolean, its accessor should be named *isAttr( )*.

Figure 6.3

Rectangular and
polar coordinates.

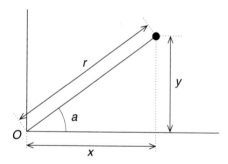

According to this guideline, in the Point class, instead of making x and y public, they should be nonpublic, and accessors and mutators should be provided for them.

```
public class Point {
   public Point() {}

   public Point(final double x, final double y) {
      this.x = x; this.y = y;
   }
   public double getX() {
   return x;
   }
   public double getY() {
      return y;
   }
   public void setX(final double x) {
      this.x = x;
   }

   public void setY(final double y) {
      this.y = y;
   }
   protected double x, y;
}
```

One may think that public fields such as x and y in Point are straightforward and harmless and that accessors and mutators for such simple fields are overkill. However, that assumption is not correct. Let us consider the class PolarPoint. It extends the Point class and represents a point in both rectangular coordinates (x, y) and polar coordinates (r, a), where r is the radius (the distance from the point to the origin) and a is the angle between the x axis and the line that connects the point and the origin, as depicted in Figure 6.3.

```
public class PolarPoint extends Point {
   public PolarPoint() {}
   public PolarPoint(final double r, final double a) {
      this.r = r; this.a = a;
      polarToRectangular();
   }
```

```
        public double getRadius() {
            return r;
        }
        public double getAngle() {
            return a;
        }
        public void setRadius(final double r) {
            this.r = r;
            polarToRectangular();
        }
        public void setAngle(final double a) {
            this.a = a;
            polarToRectangular();
        }
        public void setX(final double x) {
            this.x = x;
            rectangularToPolar();
        }
        public void setY(final double y) {
            this.y = y;
            rectangularToPolar();
        }
        protected double r, a;
        protected void polarToRectangular() {
            x = r * Math.cos(a);
            y = r * Math.sin(a);
        }
        protected void rectangularToPolar() {
            r = Math.sqrt(x * x + y * y);
            a = Math.atan2(y, x);
        }
    }
```

Now, the fields in `PolarPoint` are *constrained* by the following invariant:

$$x = r * \cos(a) \land y = r * \sin(a)$$

If the fields r and a were public, a client would be able to do the following and leave the object in an inconsistent state:

```
PolarPoint p = new PolarPoint();
p.r = 100.0; // p could be inconsistent
```

Using mutators `setR()` and `setA()`, we can maintain the invariant by adjusting fields x and y accordingly when field r or a is modified. Making fields r and a nonpublic and requiring clients to use `setR()` and `setA()` to modify these fields ensures that the instances of `PolarPoint` remain in consistent states.

```
PolarPoint p = new PolarPoint();
p.setR(100.0); // p remains consistent
```

If the fields x and y were public in `Point`, the `Point` class itself would not be harmed because x and y are unconstrained. However, that would allow the clients of `PolarPoint` to modify directly the fields x and y, resulting in an inconsistent state.

```
PolarPoint p = new PolarPoint();
p.x = 100.0;  // p could be inconsistent
```

Thus seemingly harmless public fields can hinder the ability of subclasses to maintain consistency. However, when the x and y fields are nonpublic, their modifiers, `setX()` and `setY()`, can be overridden in `PolarPoint` to ensure consistency.

If a class has no public fields, the clients of the class can only access the functionality or services provided by the class via its public methods. Therefore, a corollary of the *avoid public field* design guideline is the following design guideline:

Design Guideline *Completeness of the Public Interface*

The set of public methods defined in the class should provide full and convenient access to the functionality of the class.

Separating Interface from Implementation

Now, assume that we want to design and implement a list, which is an ordered collection of elements that can be accessed through an index. The size of the list can grow as needed. Such a list can be implemented in various ways, such as a linked list or dynamically resizable array. In this case, we should separate the list interface from the list implementation.

Design Guideline *Separate Interface from Implementation*

When the functionality supported by a class can be implemented in different ways, it is advisable to separate the interface from the implementation.

The advantages of separating interface from implementation are that the implementation details are completely hidden from the clients, so changes in implementation will not affect clients. The `List` interface shown in Figure 6.1 defines the interface of the list we want to implement.

Implementation of the list can be provided in several different classes, all of which implement the `List` interface. For example, both of the following classes,

LinkedList and DynamicArray, implement the List interface, but their implementation can be entirely different:

```
public class LinkedList implements List {
   ⟨body of LinkedList⟩
}

public class DynamicArray implements List {
   ⟨body of DynamicArray⟩
}
```

Separating an interface from the implementation of a class in Java is similar to separating a class into a header file and an implementation file in C++. However, there are a few subtle differences between Java and C++ in this regard. In C++, the header and the implementation files are two parts of a class. In Java, however, the interface and the class are two separate entities that have an implementation relation. In C++, the header file contains the interface and some of the implementation of the class. All the fields—even protected or private—must be declared in the header file. In-line methods must also be defined in the header file. In Java, however, an interface contains no implementation. The implementation is entirely encapsulated in the class that implements the interface.

6.1.4 Documenting the Source Code

A common problem in software development is that as software evolves, the documentation and the actual code of the software could easily become out of sync. As more and more changes are being made to the software code, the documentation and the code could drift farther and farther apart. Eventually, the documentation could become unusable, making further changes to the software code very difficult. Java supports an excellent and unique approach for combining source code with documentation and other reference materials together, in the form of *documentation comments* (*doc comments* for short) in the source code. The goal is to make it easier to keep the documentation and the code in sync by keeping them close to one another.

With the help of a Java utility tool called javadoc, a full set of reference documentation can be built in two steps. First, a set of specially formatted comments can be added to document each class, method, and field in a program. Then the javadoc tool can be used to generate documentation of either individual classes or entire packages. The javadoc utility, which comes with the JDK, parses the declarations and doc comments embedded in Java source files and generates a corresponding set of HTML pages for each class and each package. The generated HTML documetation contains declaration of the classes, methods, and fields, along with doc comments provided in the source code. In addition, the tool generates indices of all the features and an inheritance tree for each package depicting the inheritance hierarchy of all the classes in the package.

Each doc comment describes a feature, which can be a class, a field, a method, a constructor, or a nested class. The doc comment must immediately precede the feature it describes. A doc comment consists of a description of the feature, which will be copied verbatim to the documentation page, followed by a list of *tags*, which will be formatted by javadoc in a consistent style. The commonly used tags are summarized in the following table:

Tag	Description
@author	The author(s) of the feature. Multiple author tags are allowed.
@version	The current version of the feature.
@since	When or in which version the feature first appeared.
@param	The meaning and the acceptable values of a parameter of a method. A method may have multiple param tags.
@return	The meaning and the possible values of the return value of a method.
@see	A link to the documentation of other related classes or methods.
@throws	An unhandled exception that might be thrown by a method

For each public class or interface, a doc comment documenting the class or interface should be provided. The following is an example of doc comment describing the LinkedList class:

```
/**
 * Class LinkedList implements the interface List, which is an
 * ordered collection of elements that can be accessed through
 * an index. The size of a LinkedList can grow as needed.
 *
 * @author Xiaoping Jia
 * @version 1.0  06/25/02
 * @since   JDK1.1
 */
public class LinkedList implements List {
    // . . .
}
```

A doc comment should be provided for each public method or constructor. The @param tag should be used to describe each parameter of the method, and the @return tag should be used to describe the return value, if any. The following is an example of doc comment describing the element() method of the LinkedList class:

```
/**
 * Retrieves the i-th element from the linked list.
 *
 * @param i    The position of the element to be retrieved.
 * @return     Returns the i-th element in the list.
```

```
 * @see        #insert(Object item, int i)
 */
public Object element(int i)  {
   // ...
}
```

6.2   CONTRACTS AND INVARIANTS

6.2.1   Contracts of Methods

Each interface or class defines a set of services, i.e., the public methods, to be provided by an implementor of the interface or by the class itself. The method declarations only specify the *type* of the methods, not the *behavior*. A *contract* of a method is a specification of the behavior of the method, i.e., what service is to be provided by the method. Contracts of methods are often specified informally or even left unspecified. Informal or missing contracts are major contributors of problems in software development. The potential problems of informally specified contracts include these:

- ▪ Incompleteness and silence on some aspects of the behavior.
- ▪ Ambiguity and multiple interpretations.
- ▪ Contradictions with other contracts.

Informal contracts often lead to misunderstandings and misuses of the services. An alternative is to specify the contracts of methods formally, i.e., mathematically. The advantages of formally specified contracts include the following:

- ▪ Precision and unambiguousness.
- ▪ Run-time checking to catch violations of the contract by the implementation as well as misuses of the services by the clients.
- ▪ Facilitation of reasoning about the behavior of both the implementation and the clients.

There are specification languages that support formally specifying the complete behavior of software systems, including the algebraic specification language Larch and model-based specification languages Z and VDM. However, the effective use of these formal specification languages requires extensive skills in mathematics. Its high cost is only justifiable for highly critical applications. Nevertheless, limited use of formally specified contracts can be easy and very cost-effective. We advocate the use of formal contracts to define the behavior of all methods in all classes. The formal contracts do not necessarily need to be complete. Their main goal is to ensure that certain constraints of the services are met and that certain conditions of the implementations are maintained.

The contract of a method can be specified using preconditions and postconditions of the method. A *precondition* of a method is a boolean expression that must hold when the method is invoked. In other words, a method may not be invoked when its precondition is false. A *postcondition* of a method is a boolean expression that holds when the method invocation returns. We document the precondition and postcondition of a method in the doc comments with the special tags @pre and @post.[2]

```
/**
 * @pre precondition
 * @post postcondition
 */
public void aMethod()  {
    // ...
}
```

The preconditions and postconditions must be boolean expressions. The @pre and @post may occur multiple times. The precondition or postcondition of a method defined by mutltiple @pre or @post tags is the conjunction of all the boolean expressions in the @pre or @post tags, respectively.

The preconditions and postconditions can be specified using the Java expression syntax. However, the Java expression syntax is too limited for specifying the preconditions and postconditions in some situations. Therefore, we introduce some minor extension to the Java expression syntax so that the preconditions and postconditions can be more expressive. The following two special names can be used in preconditions and postconditions:

@result   A variable holding the return value of a method.

@nochange   A boolean expression stipulating that the state of the object is not changed by the method.

The following two boolean operators are often quite useful and can be used in preconditions and postconditions.

==>   logical implication, i.e., *a* => *b*, if and only if *a* is false or both *a* and *b* are true.

<=>   logical equivalence, i.e., *a* <=> *b*, if and only if both *a* and *b* are true or both *a* and *b* are false.

Let us have a look at the formal contracts of some of the methods of the List interface:

```
/**
 * Returns the number of elements in the list.
 *
 * @pre true
 * @post @nochange
 */
public int size();
```

---

2. The @pre and @post tags and other tags for documenting contracts and invariants are not supported by the standard javadoc tool. However, there are third-party tools that provide various levels of support for these tags.

```
/**
 * Returns true if and only if the list is empty.
 *
 * @pre true
 * @post @result <=> size() > 0
 * @post @nochange
 */
public boolean isEmpty();
```

A precondition of `true` means that the precondition is always satisfied. Therefore, the `size()` and `isEmpty()` methods can be invoked any time. A postcondition
`@nochange` means that the method does not modify the state of the object; i.e., it is
an accessor. Both `size()` and `isEmpty()` methods are accessors.

```
/**
 * Returns the i-th element in the list.
 *
 * @pre i >= 0 && i < size()
 * @post @nochange
 */
public Object element(int i);
```

The `element()` method has a precondition. It means that the method can only
be invoked when the precondition is `true`. Otherwise, an exception will be thrown.
The postcondition only specifies that the state of the list does not change when this
method is invoked. However, it does not completely specify the behavior of the
method. The simple specification language we use here is inadequate to completely
specify some of the behaviors of the methods. A number of full-blown specification
languages, including Larch, VDM, and Z, are capable of completely specifying the
behaviors of programs and facilitating reasoning about their behaviors. However,
our goal of using formally specified contracts is much more modest. We only try
to formally constrain the behavior as much as possible for the purpose of precisely
documenting the behavior and instrumenting the source code with assertions derived
from the contracts. Such assertions can be extremely effective in assisting the testing
and debugging of programs.

The following are the contracts for methods `head()` and `last()`. They use the
`element()` method to constrain their results.

```
/**
 * Returns the first element in the list.
 *
 * @pre !isEmpty()
 * @post @result == element(0)
 * @post @nochange
 */
public Object head();
```

```
/**
 * Returns the last element in the list.
 *
 * @pre !isEmpty()
 * @post @result == element(size() - 1)
 * @post @nochange
 */
public Object last();
```

When specifying the postcondition of a mutator, i.e., a method that changes the state of the object, it is necessary to distinguish the state of the object before and after the method invocation. By default, the values of the expressions in the postcondition are evaluated with respect to the after state of the object, i.e., the state of the object immediately after the method returns. To refer to the values of expressions evaluated in the before state, i.e., the state of the object immediately before the method is invoked, we use the following *prestate* notation.

Expression @pre	The value of *Expression* evaluated in the state just before the method is invoked, i.e., the prestate.

When specifying contracts involving a collection of objects, such as a list, it is often necessary to use *quantified expressions*, which define conditions on a collection of objects, rather than on an individual object. There are two types of quantified expressions. A *universally* quantified expression stipulates that a predicate holds on every object in a given collection of objects. An *existentially* quantified expression stipulates that a predicate holds on at least one object in a given collection of objects. We introduce the following extensions of quantified expressions that can be used in preconditions and postconditions:

@forall *x* : *Range* @ *Expression*	Universally quantified expression
@exists *x* : *Range* @ *Expression*	Existentially quantified expression

where x is a new variable name, *Range* is a range expression, which specifies a collection of objects, and *Expression* is a boolean expression. The range expression can be one of the following:

[*m* .. *n*]	Both m and n are integer expressions. It defines an integer range from m to n, inclusive.
Expression	The *Expression* must evaluate to a Collection, Enumeration, or Iterator object (see Section 8.2). It defines a range that consists of all the objects in the collection, enumeration, or iterator, respectively.
ClassName	It defines a range consisting of all the instances of the class.

The contract of the `insert()` method is as follows:

```
/**
 * Inserts a new element into the list at the i-th position.
 *
 * @pre item != null && i >= 0 && i <= size()
 * @post size() == size()@pre + 1
 * @post @forall k : [0 .. size() - 1] @
 *                  (k < i ==> element(k)@pre == element(k)) &&
 *                  (k == i ==> item@pre == element(k)) &&
 *                  (k > i ==> element(k - 1)@pre == element(k)
 */
public void insert(Object item, int i);
```

The precondition of the `insert()` method specifies the possible range of the insertion positions, from 0 to `size()`. The postconditions of the `insert()` method are the following:

1. The size of the list will increase by 1 after the insertion.
2. The universally quantified expression specifies that
   a. all the elements before the insertion position remain unchanged.
   b. the element at the insertion position is the new item, after the insertion.
   c. all the elements after the insertion position shift one position toward the end.

The `insertHead()` and `insertLast()` methods are special cases of the `insert()` method, where the insertion position is at the begining and the end of the list, respectively.

```
/**
 * Inserts a new element at the head of the list.
 *
 * @pre item != null
 * @post size() == size()@pre + 1
 * @post item@pre == element(0)
 * @post @forall k : [1 .. size() - 1] @ element(k - 1)@pre == element(k)
 */
public void insertHead(Object item);

/**
 * Inserts a new element at the end of the list.
 *
 * @pre item != null
 * @post size() == size()@pre + 1
 * @post item@pre == element(size() - 1)
 * @post @forall k : [0 .. size() - 2] @ element(k)@pre == element(k)
 */
public void insertLast(Object item);
```

The preconditions of the `remove()` method are these:

1. The list must not be empty.
2. The position of the element to be removed must be in the valid range of the list, i.e., from 0 to `size() - 1`.

The postconditions of the `remove()` method are these:

1. The return value is the element at the *i*th before the method is invoked, i.e., the element being removed.
2. The size of the list will decrease by 1 after the removal.
3. All the elements before the removal position remain unchanged, and all the elements after the removal position shift one position toward the front.

```
/**
 * Remove the element at the i-th position.
 *
 * @pre size() > 0
 * @pre i >= 0 && i < size()
 * @post @result = element(i)@pre
 * @post size() == size()@pre - 1
 * @post @forall k : [0 .. size() - 1] @
 *                  (k < i ==> element(k)@pre == element(k)) &&
 *                  (k >= i ==> element(k + 1)@pre == element(k))
 */
public Object remove(int i);
```

The `removeHead()` and `removeLast()` methods are special cases of the `remove()` method, where the removal position is at the begining and the end of the list, respectively.

```
/**
 * Remove the element at the head.
 *
 * @pre size() > 0
 * @post @result = element(0)@pre
 * @post @forall k : [1 .. size() - 1] @ element(k + 1)@pre == element(k)
 */
public Object removeHead();

/**
 * Remove the element at the end.
 *
 * @pre size() > 0
 * @post @result = element(size() - 1)@pre
 * @post @forall k : [0 .. size() - 1] @ element(k)@pre == element(k)
 */
public Object removeLast();
```

Specifying the contacts of the methods in the `List` interface requires that all classes that implement the `List` interface must honor these contracts. In other words, the preconditions and postconditions of the methods in the interface should become the preconditions and postconditions of the corresponding methods in the classes implementing the interface.

6.2.2 Invaraints of Classes

The state of an object is *transient* if it is being manipulated, i.e., if one or more of the methods of its class are being executed. The state of an object is *stable* if it has been initialized and is not being manipulated, i.e., if one of the constructors of its class has been invoked on the object and none of the methods of its class are being executed. An *invaraint* of a class is a formally specified condition that always holds on any object of the class whenever it is in a stable state. Given the invariants of a class, an object of the class is in a *well-formed* state if the invariants hold on that state.

Invariants of a class are usually concerned with the soundness of the implementation of the class. Consider the LinkedList class shown in Figure 6.2, which implements the List interface. It uses a doubly linked list to represent a list. The key characteristics of the doubly linked list representation can be captured by the following conditions on the implementation:

1. If the list is empty, both head and tail should be null.
2. If the list is not empty, the head field points to the first node in the list, and the tail field points to the last node in the list.
3. The count field should be equal to the number of nodes that are reachable by following the next link from the head of the list, i.e., the node pointed to by the head field.
4. For each node that is reachable from the head of the list, the following conditions hold:
   a. The prev field points to the preceding node in the list, and the next field points to the succeeding node in the list. In other words, given a node in the list, the next field of its preceding node should point to the node itself, and the prev field of its succeeding node should also point to the node itself.
   b. The prev field of the first node in the list is null, and the next field of the last node in the list is null.

The doubly linked list representation is accessed or manipulated by the methods of the class to perform various operations. The doubly linked list representation is well formed if all the preceding conditions hold whenever a linked list object is in a stable state. These conditions are the invariants of the doubly linked list representation used to implement the LinkedList class. We can write an auxiliary method of the LinkedList class to check whether the invariants hold.

```
/**
 * Invaraiants of the linked list implementation.
 */
protected boolean _wellformed() {
    int n = 0;
```

```
for (Node p = head; p != null; p = p.next) {
    n++;
    if (p.prev != null) {
        if (p.prev.next != p) return false;
    } else {
        if (head != p) return false;
    }
    if (p.next != null) {
        if (p.next.prev != p) return false;
    } else {
        if (tail != p) return false;
    }
}
return n == count;
}
```

We introduce a new documentation tag for documenting the invariants of a class.

```
/**
 * @invariant Expression
 */
public class AClass {
    // ...
}
```

The expression in the @invariant tag must be a boolean expression. The @invariant tag may occur multiple times. The invariant defined by multiple occurrences of the @invariant tag is the conjunction of all the boolean expressions in these @invariant tags. The implication and equivalence operators, as well as the quantified expressions, can also be used in invariants. Since invariants always deal with the state of objects at a given moment, the prestate notation is not meaningful in invariants.

The invariant for the LinkedList class can be expressed as follows:

```
/**
 * @invariant   _wellformed()
 */
public class LinkedList implements List {
    // ...
    // implementation of linked list

    protected boolean _wellformed() {
        //  . . .
    }

    protected Node head, tail;
    protected int count;
    static protected class Node {
        Object element;
        Node next, prev;
    }
}
```

The implementer of a class is responsible for ensuring that all public methods preserve the invariants concerning the well-formedness of the implementation. The requirements are stated in the following design guideline:

Design Guideline   *Preserving Invariants*

Given a class and its invariants, the obligations for the implementation to preserve the invariants are the following:

Establishing invariants by public constructors: For each public constructor of the class, the invariant must be the postcondition of the constructor or implied by its postcondition.

Preserving invariants by public methods: For each public method of the class, the invariant can be assumed to be a precondition of the method, and the invariant must be the postcondition of the method or implied by its postcondition.

If these requirements are satisfied, then the invocation of any public method in any order should always result in a well-formed state.

6.2.3   Assertions

An *assertion* is a boolean condition at a given location of a program that should be true whenever the flow of execution reaches that location. Java supports *assertion statements*,[3] which check assertions at run time. The syntax of the assertion statement is the following:

```
assert Assertion ;
```

where *Assertion* is a boolean expression. An assertion statement evaluates the assertion first. If the assertion is `true`, the statement has no other effects. If the assertion is `false`, an `AssertionError` exception is thrown.

Assertions can be used to perform run-time checking of preconditions and postconditions of methods and invariants of classes.

- Assertions on the preconditions should be placed at the entry point of each method, i.e., the beginning of the method body.
- Assertions on the postconditions should be placed at every exit point of each method, i.e., the end of the method body and before each `return` statement.
- Assertions on the invariants of the class should be placed at the entry point and every exit point of each public method.

The following is an implementation of the `head()` method of the doubly linked list class. The precondition is translated into an assertion at the beginning of the

---

3. Assertions are introduced in JDK 1.4. A JDK 1.4 or later is necessary to use assertions.

methods, and the postcondition is translated into an assertion just before the `return` statement.

```
/**
 * Returns the first element in the list.
 *
 * @pre !isEmpty()
 * @post @result == element(0)
 */
public Object head() {
  assert !isEmpty();
  Object result = (head != null ? head.item : null);
  assert result == element(0);
  return result;
}
```

The following is an implementation of the `insert()` method. In addition to the assertions derived from the precondition and the postcondition of the method, the invariant of the doubly linked list class is also translated into assertions at the beginning of the methods and just before the `return` statement.

```
/**
 * Inserts a new element into the list at the i-th position.
 *
 * @pre item != null && i >= 0 && i <= size()
 * @post size() == size()@pre + 1
 */
public void insert(Object item, int i) {
    assert item != null && i >= 0 && i <= size();
    assert _wellformed();
    int size_pre = size();
    if (i <= 0) {
       insertHead(item);
    }  else if (i >= count) {
       insertLast(item);
    }  else {
       // i > 0 && i < count;
       Node n = head;
       for (int j = 0; n != null && j < i - 1; j++) {
          n = n.next;
       }
       Node node = new Node();
       node.item = item;
       node.next = n.next;
       node.prev = n;
       node.next.prev = node;
       n.next = node;
       count++;
    }
    int size_post = size();
    assert size_post == size_pre + 1;
    assert _wellformed();
}
```

To compile a program with assertions requires JDK 1.4 or higher and the -source switch must be used, as follows:

```
venus% javac -source 1.4 LinkedList.java
```

You may notice that not all the postconditions are being asserted. Postconditions that deal with the prestate of objects are usually more complicated to assert. It is often necessary to clone the object before it is modified. We will show another version of this method that asserts the postcondition involving the object in prestate (see p. 233).

Using assertions derived from the preconditions for all methods is known as *defensive programming*. Its aim is to prevent a component from being misused. An assertion failure of a precondition indicates that a client attempted to use the service improperly. In the case of an error, assertions on preconditions can help to establish whether the error is caused by the implementation of the service or the improper use of the service.

Using assertions derived from the postconditions and the invariants of classes can be extremely effective in assisting the unit testing and debugging of the implementation of classes. Incorrect test results can show the symptoms of errors. It is often a tedious, time-consuming, and nontrivial process to locate the source of the errors. An assertion failure of a postcondition or invariant usually identifies the source of an error.

Design Guideline *Use Assertions Aggressively*

Each method should include assertions on the preconditions and postconditions of the method and invariants of the class.

6.2.4 Design by Contract

An important principle of the object-oriented approach is that the extension and implementation relation model the *is-a* relation in the real world. This means that if class *S* is a subclass of class *C*, then an instance of *S* *is an* instance of *C*, and an instance of *S* can be substituted for an instance of *C*. The type compatibility rules on object-oriented languages allow such substitutability. However, the type compatibility rules do not ensure that such substitutions will be well behaved at run time, i.e., whether the instance of *S* will *behave* in a way that is consistent with how an instance of *C* would. To ensure that such substitutions are well behaved at run time, the implementation of class S must honor the contract of class C. This requirement can be stated as the following important design guideline:

Design Guideline *Design by Contract*

Each method in a class must honor the contract of the respective method in its superclass and/or the interfaces implemented by the class. Specifically:

- The precondition of each method in a subclass must be *no stronger* than the precondition of the respective method in its superclass and/or the interfaces implemented by the class. In other words, the method in the subclass cannot be more restrictive than the respective methods in its superclass.
- The postcondition of each method in a subclass must be *no weaker* than the postcondition of the respective method in its superclass and/or the interfaces implemented by the class. In other words, the methods in the subclass cannot do less than the respective methods in its superclass.

6.3   THE CANONICAL FORM OF CLASSES

The *canonical form* of public classes ensures that instances of those classes will be well behaved when they are manipulated by the Java run-time environment and many other classes, such as those classes in the collection framework (see Section 8.2 [p. 308]).

Design Guideline *Canonical Form of Public Classes*

Classes designed for general use should follow the *canonical form* of public classes, which consists of the following elements:

  No-arg constructor: Providing a public no-arg constructor.

  Object equality: Overriding the equals() and hashCode() methods.

  String representation: Overriding the toString() method.

  Cloning: Implementing the Cloneable interface, and overriding the clone() method.

  Serialization: Implementing the java.io.Serializable interface and overriding the readObject() and writeObject() methods, when the instances of the class may need to be saved in files or transferred over the network.

The relevant methods involved in the canonical form are discussed in the following subsections.

6.3.1 No-Argument Constructor

The no-arg constructor of a class is useful because it allows instances of the class to be created dynamically by the Java virtual machine at run time. As a result, the objects are not created by using the `new` operator directly or indirectly anywhere in the program. The program that uses the object may not have any reference to the class or any knowledge of the existence of the class. The class will be made available to the program at run time, and the objects will be created by the Java virtual machine. Many important Java applications and frameworks depend on the ability to load classes and create instances at run time. Therefore, to make your class as widely reusable as possible, it should provide a no-arg constructor.

The dynamic loading mechanism is one of the more useful features of Java. However, a full discussion of the mechanism is beyond the scope of this book.

6.3.2 Object Equality

The `equals()` method defines the equality of object states on a per-class basis. The default implementation of the `equals()` method in the `Object` class tests the identity of objects; that is, `o1.equals(o2)` if and only if both o1 and o2 refer to the same object. Most classes should override this method and define the notion of equality based on the contents, i.e., the states, of the objects, not their identities.

The contract of the `equals()` method is that all implementation must satisfy the following conditions:

- *Reflexivity:* For any object x, `x.equals(x)` is always `true`.
- *Symmetry:* For any objects x and y, `x.equals(y)` is `true` if and only if `y.equals(x)` is `true`.
- *Transitivity:* For any objects x, y, and z, if both `x.equals(y)` and `y.equals(z)` are `true`, then `x.equals(z)` should also be `true`.
- *Consistency:* For any objects x and y, `x.equals(y)` should consistently return `true` or consistently return `false`, if the states of x and y are unchanged.
- *Nonnullity:* For any object x, `x.equals(null)` should always be `false`.

The following is a template of a typical implementation of the `equals()` method of a class *C:*

```
public boolean equals(Object other) {
    if (this == other)
        return true;
    if (other instanceof C) {
        C otherObj = (C) other;
        (compare each field, and return false if not equal)
```

```
        return true;
    }
    return false;
}
```

The comparison of the fields can be done as follows:

- For a field p of primitive type:

```
    if (p != otherObj.p)
        return false;
```

- For a field r of reference type:

```
    if (r == null ? otherObj.r != null : !r.equals(otherObj.r))
        return false;
```

The values of some fields may be temporary, derived from other fields, or nonessential. These fields are called insignificant fields. They can be excluded from the comparison for equality.

The following is an implementation of the equals() method of the LinkedList class. Two lists are considered equal if they are of the same length and the elements at the same position of the two lists are pairwise equal. Note that the list referenced by parameter other does not need to be a linked list.

```
public boolean equals(Object other) {
    if (this == other)
        return true;
    if (other instanceof List) {
        List otherList = (List) other;
        if (this.getCount() == otherList.getCount()) {
            for (int i = 0; i < this.getCount(); i++) {
                Object thisElement = this.elementAt(i);
                Object otherElement = otherList.elementAt(i);
                if (thisElement == null) {
                    if (otherElement != null) {
                        return false;
                    }
                } else {
                    if (!thisElement.equals(otherElement)) {
                        return false;
                    }
                }
            }
            return true;
        }
    }
    return false;
}
```

6.3.3 Hash Code of Objects

The hashCode() method is used by collection classes that implement hash tables such as HashMap and HashSet (see Section 8.2 [p. 308]). Overriding the equals() method requires overriding the hashCode() method also.

The contract of the hashCode() method is that if two objects are equal according to the equals() method, they must return the same hashcode; i.e., for any objects x and y, x.equals(y) must imply x.hashCode() == y.hashCode(). It is not required for two objects that are not equal according to the equals() method to return different hash codes. However, returning different hash codes for objects that are not equal usually improves the performance of hash tables.

In general, the hash code can be computed as follows:

1. Computing a hash code for each significant field. The significant fields are the fields that are compared in the equals() method. For a field of primitive type, the hash code can be computed by converting the value to an integer. For a field of reference type, the hash code can be computed by calling the hashCode() method on the field, if it is nonnull.

2. Combining the hash codes of all significant fields. The key is to include all the hash codes while computing the final hash code.

The following is a template of a typical implementation of the hashCode() method of a class C.

```
public boolean hashCode() {
    int hash = 0;  // the accumulative hash code
    int c;  // the hash code for a field
    (for each field compute and combine the hash code)
    return hash;
}
```

The following are a few ways to combine the hash codes of individual fields:

1. *Bitwise-or*

```
hash = hash << n | c
```

where n is an arbitary integer constant, for example, 8.

2. *Addition*

```
hash = hash * p + c
```

where p is a prime number, for example, 37.

The following is an implementation of the hashcode() method for the Linked-List class that is consistent with the equals() method.

```
public int hashCode() {
    int sum = 0;
    int i = 0;
    Node node = head;
```

```
        while (i < 4 && node != null) {
            if (node.element != null) {
                sum <<= 8;
                sum |= node.element.hashCode() & 0xFF;
            }
            node = node.next;
        }
        return sum;
    }
```

6.3.4 Cloning Objects

The clone() method returns a clone of the object itself. It is analogous to the copy constructor in C++. The contract of the clone() method is the following:

- The cloned object must not be the same object as the original; i.e., o.clone() != o.
- The cloned object and the original object are instances of the same class.
- The cloned object must be equal to the original object; i.e., o.clone().equals(o).

The Object class provides a default implementation of the clone() method. The clone() method in the Object class is protected. The default implementation of the clone() method in the Object class behaves as follows:

- For a class that implements the marker interface Cloneable, it creates a *shallow copy* of the original object.
- For a class that does not implement the marker interface Cloneable, it throws a CloneNotSupportedException.

A shallow copy means that the value of each field of the original object is copied to the corresponding field of the cloned object, whether the field is of primitive type or reference type. Shallow copying is adequate for fields of primitive types. For fields of reference types, only the references are copied, and the actual objects referenced by the fields are not cloned. A deep copy means that the objects referenced by the fields of reference types are also cloned. The difference between shallow and deep copies is illustrated in Figure 6.4 for the LinkedList example.

For a class to support cloning, it is necessary to implement the Cloneable interface, override the clone() method, and declare it public. The following is another version of the Point class that supports cloning. Since all the fields of the Point class are of primitive types, the default shallow copy implementation in the Object class is sufficient.

```
public class Point implements Cloneable {
    public Object clone() throws CloneNotSupportedException {
        return super.clone();
    }
```

```
    // . . .
    }
    // client code
    Point p1 = new Point();
    Point p2 = (Point) p1.clone();
```

The following program fragment is an implementation of the `clone()` method of the `LinkedList` class that creates a deep copy of the list:

```
public class LinkedList implements List, Cloneable {
    // . . .
    public Object clone()
        throws CloneNotSupportedException {
        LinkedList list = (LinkedList) super.clone();
        list.head = list.tail = null;
        list.count = 0;
        for (Node node = head; node != null; node = node.next) {
            if (node.item != null) {
                list.insertLast(node.item);
            }
        }
        return list;
    }
}
```

An important rule in implementing the `clone()` method is that the cloned object should not be created using the `new` operator, unless it is a final class. This rule exists because of the requirement that the cloned object and the original object are instances of the same class. If the `new` operator were used to create the cloned objects, and if there were a subclass that did override the `clone()` method, then a clone of an object

Figure 6.4

Copies in cloning:
(a) shallow copy;
(b) deep copy.

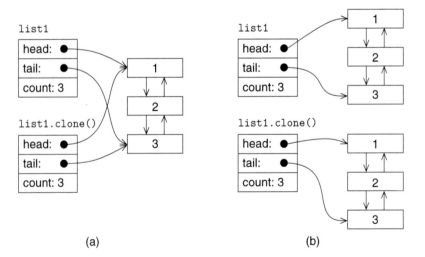

(a)   (b)

of that subclass would be an instance of its superclass, since the inherited `clone()` method was used. The right way to create the cloned objects of a nonfinal class *C* is

```
public Object clone()
   throws CloneNotSupportedException {
   C clonedObject = (C) super.clone();
   (Clone reference type fields, if a deep copy is desired)
   return clonedObject;
}
```

Using Clones in Assertions

Using the `clone()` method, we can assert postconditions involving objects in the prestate. The following is another version of the `insert()` method of the LinkedList class using the `clone()` method to retain a copy of an object in the prestate.

```
/**
 * Inserts a new element into the list at the i-th position.
 *
 * @pre item != null && i >= 0 && i <= size()
 * @post size() == size()@pre + 1
 * @post @forall k : [0 .. size() - 1] @
 *           (k < i ==> element(k)@pre == element(k)) &&
 *           (k == i ==> item@pre == element(k)) &&
 *           (k > i ==> element(k - 1)@pre == element(k)
 */
public void insert(Object item, int i) {
    assert item != null && i >= 0 && i <= size();
    assert _wellformed();
    int size_pre = size();
    LinkedList this_pre = null;
    try {
        this_pre = (LinkedList) clone();
    } catch (CloneNotSupportedException e) {}
    if (i <= 0) {
        insertHead(item);
    }   else if (i >= count) {
        insertLast(item);
    }   else {
        // i > 0 && i < count;
        Node n = head;
        for (int j = 0; n != null && j < i - 1; j++) {
            n = n.next;
        }
        Node node = new Node();
        node.item = item;
        node.next = n.next;
        node.prev = n;
```

```
            node.next.prev = node;
            n.next = node;
            count++;
        }
        int size_post = size();
        assert size_post == size_pre + 1;
        boolean insertOK = true;
        for (int k = 0; insertOK && k < size(); k++) {
            if (k < i) {
                insertOK = (this_pre.element(k) == element(k));
            } else if (k == i) {
                insertOK = (item == element(k));
            } else {
                insertOK = (this_pre.element(k - 1) == element(k));
            }
        }
        assert insertOK;
        assert _wellformed();
    }
```

6.3.5   String Representation of Objects

We have previously discussed the `toString()` method (see Section 4.4.8 [p. 122]). It returns a string representation of an object. The `toString()` method is very useful in many situations, especially for testing and debugging programs. The result of the `toString()` method should include all the fields of the object.

The following code fragment implements the `toString()` method of the `LinkedList` class:

```
    public String toString() {
        StringBuffer s = new StringBuffer();
        int i = 0;
        for (Node node = head; node != null; node = node.next, i++) {
            s.append("[" + i + "] = " + node.element + "\n");
        }
        return s.toString();
    }
```

6.3.6   Serialization

Serialization is the process of transforming an object into a stream of bytes. *Deserialization* is the reverse process. Serialization allows objects to be easily saved to files or sent to remote hosts over a network. Objects of classes that implement the `java.io.Serializable` interface can be serialized and deserialized. Classes whose instances need to be stored in files or sent to remote hosts should implement the `java.io.Serializable` interface. A default implementation for serialization and deserialization is provided for all classes that implement the `java.io.Serializable` interface. Often, this is all that needs to be done to support serialization. A class may customize the way its instances are serialized by implementing the methods `read-Object()` and `writeObject()`. Serialization is discussed further in Section 8.4.1 [p. 367].

6.4   UNIT TESTING

The testing of software systems is usually divided into several phases:

> *Unit testing:* To test each unit, or component, independently, before the units are integrated into the whole system.
>
> *Integration and system testing:* To integrate all the components of a system and to test the system as a whole.
>
> *Acceptance testing:* To validate that the system functions and performs as expected by the customers or the users.

Unit testing is important because (1) for the whole system to function properly, each of its components, or units, must function properly individually; and (2) since units are much smaller than the whole system, it is much easier to find errors in each unit individually. Thorough unit testing will significantly reduce the effort and cost required for integration and system testing. In this book we focus on unit testing only, since unit testing is usually the responsibility of the developer(s) of the unit, while integration and system testing and acceptance testing are usually the responsibility of a separate testing or quality assurance team.

In object-oriented software development, the unit for unit testing is often a single public class along with its helper classes, if any. Each class should include methods that facilitate unit testing. Some simple unit tests can be carried out in the `main()` method of the class. More extensive and complete tests are usually written in separate classes for testing purposes only.

6.4.1   Simple Unit Testing

The following is a simple unit test of the `LinkedList` class:

```
package test;
import mylist.*;

public class LinkedListTest1 {

    public static void main(String args[]) {
        LinkedList l = new LinkedList();
        l.insertHead(new Integer(1));
        l.insertHead(new Integer(2));
        l.insertLast(new Integer(3));
        l.insertLast(new Integer(4));
        l.insert(new Integer(5), 3);
```

```
        l.insert(new Integer(6), 3);
        l.insert(new Integer(7), 3);

        System.out.println("First pass");
        System.out.println(l);

        l.removeHead();
        l.removeLasr();
        l.removeElementAt(2);

        System.out.println("Second pass");
        System.out.println(l);

        LinkedList 12 = (LinkedList) l.clone();
        System.out.println("Cloned list");
        System.out.println(12);

        12.removeHead();
        System.out.println("Original list");
        System.out.println(l);
        System.out.println("Cloned list");
        System.out.println(12);
    }
}
```

The test invokes most of the methods of the LinkedList class. However, the test is rather ad hoc. It only prints out the results without any indication of the correctness of the test results. It requires a visual inspection of the results by a human tester to determine the correctness of the results. A complete test of nontrivial classes is usually much more extensive and often needs to be repeated many times. Depending on human visual inspection to determine the correctness of the results is extemely time-consuming, unreliable, and often impractical.

The testing results can be automatically verified in the testing program. The following is another vision of the program testing the implementation of LinkedList class. In this version, the expected results after each testing step are included in the test program, as a two-dimentional integer array results. The actual results and the expected results are compared, and any discrepencies are reported.

```
package test;

import mylist.*;

public class LinkedListTest2 {

  protected static int[][] results = {
    { 2, 1, 3, 7, 6, 5, 4 }, // result after insertion
    { 1, 3, 6, 5 },          // result after removal
    { 1, 3, 6, 5 },          // the cloned list
    { 1, 3, 6, 5 },          // the original list after removing the
                             //    head from the cloned list
    { 3, 6, 5 },             // the cloned list after removing the
                             //    head from the cloned list
  };
```

```
public static void main(String args[])
  throws CloneNotSupportedException {
  boolean testPassed = true;

  LinkedList l = new LinkedList();
  l.insertHead(new Integer(1));
  l.insertHead(new Integer(2));
  l.insertLast(new Integer(3));
  l.insertLast(new Integer(4));
  l.insert(new Integer(5), 3);
  l.insert(new Integer(6), 3);
  l.insert(new Integer(7), 3);

  System.out.println("First pass");
  System.out.println(l);
  if (!TestUtil.match(l, TestUtil.toIntegerArray(results[0]))) {
    System.out.println("Result mismatch");
    testPassed = false;
  }

  l.removeHead();
  l.removeLast();
  l.remove(2);

  System.out.println("Second pass");
  System.out.println(l);
  if (!TestUtil.match(l, TestUtil.toIntegerArray(results[1]))) {
    System.out.println("Result mismatch");
    testPassed = false;
  }

  LinkedList l2 = (LinkedList) l.clone();
  System.out.println("Cloned list");
  System.out.println(l2);
  if (!TestUtil.match(l2, TestUtil.toIntegerArray(results[2]))) {
    System.out.println("Result mismatch");
    testPassed = false;
  }

  l2.removeHead();
  System.out.println("Original list");
  System.out.println(l);
  if (!TestUtil.match(l, TestUtil.toIntegerArray(results[3]))) {
    System.out.println("Result mismatch");
    testPassed = false;
  }
  System.out.println("Cloned list");
  System.out.println(l2);
  if (!TestUtil.match(l2, TestUtil.toIntegerArray(results[4]))) {
    System.out.println("Result mismatch");
    testPassed = false;
  }
```

```
      if (testPassed) {
        System.out.println("Test passed.");
      } else {
        System.out.println("Test failed.");
      }

    }

  }
```

The TestUtil class provides two auxiliary methods that are used to compare the lists against the expected results:

- The toIntegerArray() method converts an array of integer values to an array of integer objects,
- The match() method tests whether the contents of a list match the contents of an array of objects.

```
package test;

import mylist.*;

public class TestUtil {
  public static boolean match(List list, Object[] array) {
    boolean result = false;
    if (list != null &&
        array != null) {
      int n = list.size();
      if (n == array.length) {
        for (int i = 0; i < n; i++) {
          Object item = list.element(i);
          if (item != null) {
            if (!item.equals(array[i])) {
              return false;
            }
          } else {
            if (array[i] != null) {
              return false;
            }
          }
        }
        result = true;
      }
    } else if (list == null &&
               array == null) {
      result = true;
    }
    return result;
  }

  public static Object[] toIntegerArray(int[] intArray) {
    if (intArray != null) {
      int n = intArray.length;
```

```
      Object[] resultArray = new Object[n];
      for (int i = 0; i < n; i++) {
        resultArray[i] = new Integer(intArray[i]);
      }
      return resultArray;
    } else {
      return null;
    }
  }
}
```

This test program compares the lists to their expected results after each testing step. It also prints out a simple message at the end indicating whether all the test results are correct.

6.4.2 JUnit—A Unit-Testing Tool

When dealing with a large and extensive set of test cases, it is usually more convenient to use a unit-testing tool. JUnit[4] is a flexible, easy-to-use, and open-source unit-testing tool for Java programs. The following is a template of typical JUnit test programs:

```
public class MyTest extends TestCase {
    public MyTest(String name) {
        super(name);
    }
    public void testCase_1() {
        ⟨test and compare results⟩
    }
    . . .
    public void testCase_n() {
        ⟨test and compare results⟩
    }
    public static Test suite() {
        return new TestSuite(MyTest.class);
    }
}
```

Each test program, that is, test suite, is written as a subclass of the TestCase class. The constructor with the test suite name is required. Each test case is written as a separate test method. The names of test methods must begin with the prefix test. The suite() method in the test program is required. It aggregates all the test cases in the class into a test suite.

The LinkedListUnitTest class that follows is a simple test program using JUnit to test the implementation of the LinkedList class. It consists of three test cases as the following three methods of the test class: testInsert(),

---

4. JUnit is available at www.junit.org. Documentation and other information about JUnit can be found at the site.

testRemove(), and testClone(). The assertTrue() method in the test cases asserts that the boolean expression argument must be true, otherwise an error is recorded.

```java
package unittest;

import junit.framework.*;
import mylist.*;
import test.TestUtil;

public class LinkedListUnitTest extends TestCase {
  public LinkedListUnitTest(String name) {
    super(name);
  }

  public void testInsert() {
    LinkedList l = new LinkedList();
    l.insertHead(new Integer(1));
    l.insertHead(new Integer(2));
    l.insertLast(new Integer(3));
    l.insertLast(new Integer(4));
    l.insert(new Integer(5), 3);
    l.insert(new Integer(6), 3);
    l.insert(new Integer(7), 3);

    assertTrue(TestUtil.match(l,
        TestUtil.toIntegerArray(new int[] {2, 1, 3, 7, 6, 5, 4 })));
  }

  public void testRemove() {
    LinkedList l = new LinkedList();
    for (int i = 1; i <= 7; i++) {
      l.insertLast(new Integer(i));
    }
    l.removeHead();
    l.removeLast();
    l.remove(2);

    assertTrue(TestUtil.match(l,
        TestUtil.toIntegerArray(new int[] {2, 3, 5, 6})));
  }

  public void testClone() throws CloneNotSupportedException {
    LinkedList l1 = new LinkedList();
    for (int i = 1; i <= 7; i++) {
      l1.insertLast(new Integer(i));
    }

    int[] ia1 = {1, 2, 3, 4, 5, 6, 7};
    int[] ia2 = {2, 3, 4, 5, 6, 7};

    LinkedList l2 = (LinkedList) l1.clone();
    assertTrue("Clone is not identity", l2 != l1);
    assertTrue("Clone equals to original", l1.equals(l2));
    assertTrue("Match 1", TestUtil.match(l1, TestUtil.toIntegerArray(ia1)));
    assertTrue("Match 2", TestUtil.match(l2, TestUtil.toIntegerArray(ia1)));
```

```
      l2.removeHead();
      assertTrue("Match 3", TestUtil.match(l1, TestUtil.toIntegerArray(ia1)));
      assertTrue("Match 4", TestUtil.match(l2, TestUtil.toIntegerArray(ia2)));
      assertTrue("Not equal", !l1.equals(l2));
    }

    public static Test suite() {
      return new TestSuite(LinkedListUnitTest.class);
    }
  }
```

To compile and run the test program, JUnit must be installed and the library file junit.jar must be included in the CLASSPATH. The following command compiles the JUnit test class:[5]

```
venus% javac -classpath .:JUnit home/junit.jar -source 1.4
        unittest/LinkedListUnitTest.java
```

where *JUnit home* is the installation directory of JUnit on your computer. JUnit provides test runners to execute the test cases. The text-based JUnit test runner can be invoked as follows:[5]

```
venus% java -classpath .:JUnit home/junit.jar -ea junit.textui.TestRunner
        unittest.LinkedListUnitTest
```

The GUI-based JUnit test runner can be invoked as follows:[5]

```
venus% java -classpath .:JUnit home/junit.jar -ea junit.swingui.TestRunner
        unittest.LinkedListUnitTest
```

The result of running the GUI-based JUnit test runner is shown in Figure 6.5.

6.4.3 Testing Coverage Criteria

A thorough and effective unit test of a class must

1. systematically test all aspects of the implementation based on certain established criteria; and
2. automatically check the correctness of the test results.

There are two approaches to deriving test cases and measuring the completeness of a set of test cases: the *black-box* and the *white-box* approaches. The black-box testing approach derives test cases based on the specifications of a component alone, without any consideration of the implementation of the component. The white-box testing approach derives test cases based on the structure of the code implementing the component. The black-box tests can be derived independently from the implementation of the component, and even before the implementation starts. As a key practice in Extreme Programming, it is strongly recommended that the black-box tests of a component be written before the implementation of the component starts.

---

5. The command should be typed on one line.

Figure 6.5

GUI-based JUnit test runner.

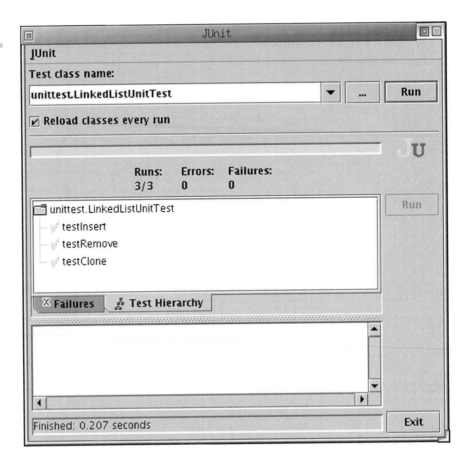

One of the most important methods of black-box testing is *equivalence partitioning of input space*. In this approoch, the input space of a program is partitioned into a number of *equivalence partitions*. The input space should include both valid and invalid input data. Elements in the same equivalence partition are the input data that should be processed by the program in an equivalent way. Therefore, we can reasonably deduce the behavior of the program on all the input data in an equivalence partition by testing a single representative from the equivalence partition. Using this approach, a set of test cases is considered adequate if it tests at least one representative from each equivalence partition.

The white-box testing approach defines a number of coverage criteria of unit testing. Given a set of test cases of a unit, the completeness of the test cases can be measured by the following different levels of coverage they satisfy:

Statement coverage: Every statement in the program must be executed at least once.

Branch coverage: Every branch of the program must be executed at least once.

Condition coverage: Every boolean condition in the control statements of the program must be evaluated to `true` and `false` at least once, respectively.

Combination condition coverage: For every compound boolean condition in the control statements of the program, every combination of the truth value of the individual boolean conditions must be exercised.

The statement coverage represents the minimum unit-testing criterion, and the combination condition coverage represents the most thorough unit-testing criterion.

A thorough unit testing should include test cases systematically derived using both white-box and black-box approaches.

6.5 PROJECT BUILD

The term *project build* refers to both the process and the result of producing an executable deliverable of the project. In an iterative development process, delivering a new project build is a key element in every iteration, starting from the very beginning. Each build process often involves many repetitive tasks, such as compiling, testing, generating documentation, and packaging source or binary files, and so forth. A large-scale software system usually consists of numerous subsystems and components. Each of the subsystems and components could be built separately. Thus, the number of repetitive tasks involved in a build could multiply. It is also quite common that many of the tasks are interdependent. We say task T_2 depends on task T_1, if task T_1 must be completed before task T_2 can be carried out.

A build tool offers assistance in managing the build process in the following ways:

1. Allowing repetitive tasks to be carried out with as little effort as possible.
2. Automatically determining and enforcing the dependencies among the tasks while carrying out the tasks.

6.5.1 Ant—A Build Tool

Ant[6] is a powerful, easy-to-use, open-source build tool for Java projects. The process of project building is specified in a *build file* in XML syntax. By default, the build file is named `build.xml`. The following is a template of typical build files:

```
<project name="project-name" default="default-target-name">
    ... property definitions ...
    ... target definitions ...
</project>
```

6. Ant available at `jakarta.apache.org`. Documentation and other information about Ant can be found at the site.

Each build file defines the process for building a single project. The main body of the build file consists of a set of *property definitions* and a set of *target definitions*. A property is simply a name-value pair. The property name must be unique. A property definition associates a value to a property name.

```
<property name="property-name"value="property-value"/>
```

The value of a defined property can be referenced in the rest of the build file as ${*property-name*}.

A *target* is a step in the build process, which consists of a list of *tasks* that should be performed together. Each target has a name and may also have a dependency list, which is a comma-separated list of the names of other targets that this target depends on. Target t_1 depends on another target t_2 if target t_2 must be successfully completed before target t_1 can be executed. A typical task definition is in the following form:

```
<target name="target-name" depends="dependent₁, . . . , dependentₙ">
    . . . task definitions . . .
</target>
```

Ant supports an extensive set of built-in tasks for building projects. Each task has a name and various parameters. Commonly used tasks include the following:

Task Name	Description
javac	Compile Java source code
java	Execute Java byte-code
javadoc	Create documentation pages
copy	Copy files
move	Move files
mkdir	Create a directory
exec	Run an operating system command or a program
mail	Send an e-mail
jar	Package and compress files in JAR format
zip	Package and compress files in ZIP format

Consult the Ant documentation for the details of using these tasks.

The following is an example of Ant build files for performing various tasks related to the linked list classes and the test suites.

```
<project name="LinkedList" default="dist">

  <!-- set global properties for this build -->
  <property name="src" value="."/>
  <property name="classes" value="classes"/>
```

```
      <property name="test" value="test"/>
      <property name="dist" value="dist"/>
      <property name="junit" value="/home/jia/JUnit/junit3.7"/>

      <target name="init">
        <!-- Create the directory structure used by compile -->
        <mkdir dir="${classes}"/>
      </target>

      <target name="compile" depends="init">
        <!-- Compile the java code from ${src} into ${classes} -->
        <javac srcdir="${src}"
               destdir="${classes}"
               includes="mylist/*"
               source="1.4"/>
      </target>

      <target name="dist" depends="compile">
        <!-- Create the distribution directory -->
        <mkdir dir="${dist}/lib"/>

        <!-- Pack the classes into the LinkedList.jar file -->
        <jar jarfile="${dist}/lib/LinkedList.jar"
             basedir="${classes}"
             includes="mylist/*" />
      </target>

      <target name="clean">
        <!-- Delete the ${classes} and ${dist} directory trees -->
        <delete dir="${build}"/>
        <delete dir="${dist}"/>
      </target>

  </project>
```

This example contains a number of typical targets in build files:

Target Name	Description
init	Prepare for the build
compile	Compile all source code
dist	Package the program for distribution
clean	Delete all nonessential, generated files

To perform a build using Ant, you invoke Ant with the desired build target name as the argument as follows:

```
venus% ant target-name
```

For more details on using Ant, consult the Ant documentation.

CHAPTER SUMMARY

- The members of classes should be ordered to maximize the readability.

- The javadoc tool is very useful for generating documentation of classes and packages. For each public class or interface, a doc comment documenting the class or interface should be provided, and a doc comment should be provided for each public method or constructor.

- A contract of a method is a specification of the behavior of the method. The contract of a method can be specified using preconditions and postconditions of the method. A precondition of a method is a boolean expression that must hold when the method is invoked. A postcondition of a method is a boolean expression that holds when the method invocation returns.

- An invariant of a class is a formally specified condition that always holds on any object of the class whenever it is not manipulated by any methods. Invariants of a class are usually concerned with the soundness of the implementation of the class.

- An assertion is a boolean condition at a given location of a program that should be true whenever the flow of execution reaches that location. Java supports an assertions statement, which checks assertions at run time.

- The canonical form of public classes ensures that instances of those classes will be well behaved when they are manipulated by the Java run-time environment and many other classes, such as those classes in the collection framework. The canonical form of public classes consists of the following elements:

  No-arg constructor
  Object equality
  String representation
  Cloning
  Serialization

- There should be no nonfinal public fields, except when a class is final *and* the field is unconstrained.

- The set of public methods defined in the class should provide full and convenient access to the functionality of the class.

- When the functionality supported by a class can be implemented in different ways, it is advisable to separate the interface from the implementation.

- Each method in a class must honor the contract of the respective method in its superclass and/or the interfaces implemented by the class.

- Unit testing is carried out in order to test each unit, or component, independently, before the units are integrated into the whole system.

- The term "project build" refers to both the process and the result of producing an executable deliverable of the project.

FURTHER READINGS

Binder, R. V. (1999). *Testing Object-Oriented Systems: Models, Patterns, and Tools.* Addison-Wesley.

Burke, E. M., and J. E. Tilly (2002). *Ant: The Definitive Guide.* O'Reilly.

Meyer, B. (2000). *Object-Oriented Software Construction*, 2nd ed., Prentice Hall.

Sykes, D. A., and J. D. McGregor (2001). *Practical Guide to Testing Object-Oriented Software.* Addison-Wesley.

EXERCISES

6.1 Design and implement the classes discussed in the case study of Chapter 2: `Customer` and `Address`. You should follow the principles discussed in Section 6.1 and adopt the canonical form discussed in Section 6.3.

6.2 Make the `LineSegment`, `Rectangle`, and `Circle` classes in Exercise 5.1 conform to the canonical form discussed in Section 6.3.

6.3 Define an interface for a *stack*, which supports the following methods:

- *push:* adds a new object onto the top of the stack.
- *pop:* removes the object at the top of the stack and returns the object.
- *size:* returns the number of objects currently in the stack.
- *top:* returns the object at the top of the stack without removing it from the stack.

Formally specify the contract of each method.

6.4 Define an interface for a *queue*, which supports the following methods:

- *enqueue:* adds a new object at the end of the queue.
- *dequeue:* removes the object at the front of the queue and returns the object.
- *size:* returns the number of objects currently in the queue.
- *first:* returns the object at the front of the queue without removing it from the queue.
- *last:* returns the object at the end of the queue without removing it from the queue.

Formally specify the contract of each method.

6.5 Design and implement a class that implements the `Stack` interface defined in Exercise 6.3 using an array.

(a) Formally specify the invariants of the class.

(b) Use assertions to ensure that the invariants and contracts hold at run time.

(c) Design and implement test cases for unit testing using JUnit.

6.6 Design and implement a class that implements the `Queue` interface defined in Exercise 6.4 using an array.

(a) Formally specify the invariants of the class.

(b) Use assertions to ensure that the invariants and contracts hold at run time.

(c) Design and implement test cases for unit testing using JUnit.

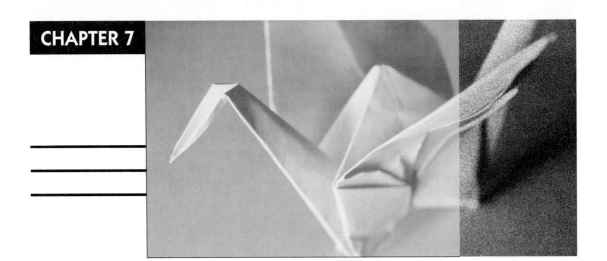

CHAPTER 7

Design by Abstraction

CHAPTER OVERVIEW

In this chapter, we introduce design patterns. The main focus of this chapter is designing reusable and extensible components, using abstract classes, interfaces, and design patterns. We discuss several important design patterns for abstraction: the Template Method, Strategy, Factory, and Iterator. We also present a case study on the animation of sorting algorithms.

One of the promises of object-oriented software development is reusability. Although reuse of implementations through inheritance is relatively easy, reuse on a larger scale (i.e., reuse of system designs and architectures) has proven rather difficult. Among the most important recent developments of object-oriented technologies is the emergence of *design patterns* and *frameworks*, which are intended to address the reuse of software design and architectures.

7.1   DESIGN PATTERNS

The concept of *patterns* was originally articulated by Christopher Alexander and his colleagues to describe architectural designs. In searching for the essence of great buildings, great towns, and beautiful places, Alexander proposed in *The Timeless Way of Building* [Alexander 1979] and *A Pattern Language—Towns, Buildings, Construction* [Alexander et al. 1977] that *the* timeless way of building, which "is thousands of years old, and the same today as it has always been," can be captured in 253 *patterns*. He went on to say:

> Each pattern describes a *problem* which occurs over and over again in our environment, and then describes the core of the *solution* to that problem, in such a way that you can use this solution a million times over, without ever doing it the same way twice. [Alexander et al. 1977]

In other words, each pattern represents a *generic* (i.e., reusable) solution to a recurring problem. Only a relatively small number of patterns are needed to capture the essence of all architectural designs, and they can be adapted and combined in many different ways to generate endless possibilities.

In some aspects, software design resembles architectural design. Similarities between the two include the following:

- Both are creative processes that unfold within a large design space, which comprises all possible designs.
- The resulting design must satisfy the customer's needs.
- The resulting design must be feasible to engineer.
- The designers must balance many competing constraints and requirements.
- The designers must seek certain intrinsic yet unquantifiable qualities, such as elegance and extensibility.

Therefore, it is natural to adapt the concept of architectural patterns to software design. *Software design patterns* are schematic descriptions of solutions to recurring problems in software design. The main purposes of using software design patterns are (1) to capture and document the experience acquired in software design in a relatively small number of design patterns to help designers acquire design expertise; (2) to support reuse in design and boost confidence in software systems that use established design patterns that have been proven effective; and (3) to provide a common vocabulary for software designers to communicate about software design.

The pioneering work in software design patterns was done by Gamma et al., who published the first software design patterns catalog, *Design Patterns* [Gamma et al. 1995]. It includes 23 of the most commonly used general-purpose design patterns that are application domain independent. These design patterns are classified into three categories:

1. *Creational patterns*, which deal with the process of object creation.
2. *Structural patterns*, which deal primarily with the static composition and structure of classes and objects.
3. *Behavioral patterns*, which deal primarily with dynamic interaction among classes and objects.

The *Design Patterns* catalog also popularized a common style for describing design patterns. The description of each design pattern consists of some or all of the following sections:

Pattern name: The essence of the pattern.

Category: Creational, structural, or behavioral.

Intent: A short description of the design issue or problem addressed.

Also known as: Other well-known names of the pattern.

Applicability: Situations in which the pattern can be applied.

Structure: A class or object diagram that depicts the participants of the pattern and the relationships among them.

Participants: A list of classes and/or objects participating in the pattern.

The *singleton class* discussed in Chapter 4 [p. 114] is one of the creational patterns in the *Design Patterns* catalog. We use the Singleton pattern to illustrate the format for describing design patterns.

7.1.1 Design Pattern: Singleton

Design Pattern *Singleton*

Category: Creational design pattern.

Intent: Ensure that a class has only one instance and provide a global point of access to it.

Applicability: Use the Singleton pattern when there must be exactly one instance of a class and it must be accessible to clients from a well-known access point.

The structure of the Singleton pattern is shown in the following diagram.[1]

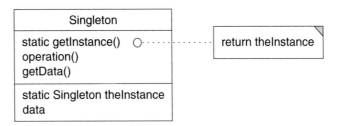

---

1. The rectangular box with a shaded corner denotes a note.

There is only one participant in the Singleton pattern:

▪ **Singleton**

declares the unique instance of the class as a static variable, and
defines a static method getInstance() for clients to access the unique
instance.

The following program segment is an implementation of the Singleton pattern in
Java.

```
public class Singleton {
    public static Singleton getInstance() {
        return theInstance;
    }

    private Singleton() {
        ⟨initialize instance fields⟩
    }

    ⟨other fields and methods⟩

    private static Singleton theInstance = new Singleton();
}
```

In this book, we focus on domain-neutral design patterns. However, the concept
of patterns can also be applied to other aspects of software development, such as
patterns for software architecture [Shaw 1996] and object-oriented analysis [Fowler
1997], and to specific domains of software systems, such as patterns for concurrent
programming in Java [Lea 2000]. Patterns concerning implementation techniques in
a specific programming language are also known as *idioms*. Bloch [2001] discusses
the use of a variety of idioms in Java.

7.2 DESIGNING GENERIC COMPONENTS

By *generic components*, we mean program components, usually in the form of classes
or packages, that can be extended, adapted, and reused in many different contexts
without having to modify the source code. Generic components are also known as
reusable components. In this section we discuss two basic techniques of designing
generic components: refactoring and generalizing. The mechanisms used to build
generic components are inheritance and delegation. Abstract classes and interfaces
play important roles in implementing generic components.

7.2.1 Refactoring

One way to discover possible generic components is by identifying recurring code
segments that are identical or nearly identical. Examples of such recurring code
segments are the nearly identical methods start(), stop(), and run() that appear
in every animation applet.

Refactoring consists of the following tasks:

- Identifying code segments in a program that implement the same logic, often in the same exact code, in many different places.
- Capturing this logic in a generic component that is defined once.
- Restructuring the program so that every occurrence of the code segment is replaced with a reference to the generic component.

Refactoring thus eliminates duplicate code segments, which are hazardous for maintenance. It ensures that a bug fix or logic enhancement need be implemented only once—in the generic component. Without refactoring, every change to a recurring code segment must be repeated everywhere the code segment occurs, some instances of which may be overlooked or forgotten. Recurring code segments can easily "drift apart," making them harder and harder to maintain.

Refactoring must be applied only to code that actually duplicates underlying logic, however. Not all code that looks alike is alike.

Design Guideline *Refactoring Recurring Code Segments*

Recurring code segments based on the same logic are hazardous to maintenance. They should be refactored so that the code segment occurs only once. Other occurrences of the code segment should be replaced with references to the common code.

The simplest form of refactoring can be done through the use of *function* or *method invocation*. For example, in the following class, the highlighted code segment occurs in two different contexts:

```
class Computation {
    void method1(. . . ) {
        // . . .
        computeStep1();
        computeStep2();
        computeStep3();
        // . . .
    }
    void method2(. . . ) {
        // . . .
        computeStep1();
        computeStep2();
        computeStep3();
        // . . .
    }
    // . . .
}
```

The common code sequence can be refactored by introducing a new method com-puteAll() that contains the recurring code segment. The class can be restructured as follows:

```
class RefactoredComputation {
    void computeAll() {
        computeStep1();
        computeStep2();
        computeStep3();
    }
    void method1(. . . ) {
        // ...
        computeAll();
        // ...
    }
    void method2(. . . ) {
        // ...
        computeAll();
        // ...
    }
    // ...
}
```

The refactored version is functionally identical to the original version. If the code in the common code segment needs to be modified, it now has to be modified in only one place (in computeAll()) instead of several places, as in the original version.

Refactoring by method invocation is effective only when each occurrence of the recurring code segment is contained within a single method and all the methods that contain the recurring code segment belong to the same class. When the recurring code segment involves several methods, such as the methods start(), stop(), and run() in animation applets—or when the recurring code segment occurs in several classes—refactoring can be accomplished by using inheritance or delegation.

Refactoring by Inheritance

The refactoring of recurring code segments in different classes can be done through *inheritance*. Consider the following example, in which an identical computation sequence occurs in two different classes:

```
class ComputationA {                      class ComputationB {
    void method1(. . . ) {                    void method2(. . . ) {
        // ...                                    // ...
        computeStep1();                           computeStep1();
        computeStep2();                           computeStep2();
        computeStep3();                           computeStep3();
        // ...                                    // ...
    }                                         }
    // ...                                    // ...
}                                         }
```

A common superclass of ComputationA and ComputationB is introduced. The recurring computation sequence is placed in a method computeAll() in the superclass.

```
class Common {
   void computeAll(. . . ) {
      computeStep1();
      computeStep2();
      computeStep3();
   }
}
```

Each occurrence of the code sequence in the original methods can now be replaced by an invocation of the method computeAll().

```
class ComputationA                 class ComputationB
      extends Common {                   extends Common {
   void method1(. . . )  {          void method2(. . . )  {
      // . . .                         // . . .
      computeAll();                    computeAll();
      // . . .                         // . . .
   }                                }
   // . . .                         // . . .
}                                 }
```

When extracting common code segments to a superclass, all the fields involved in the computation must also be extracted and moved to the superclass.

Refactoring by Delegation

Refactoring of recurring code segments in different classes can also be done through *delegation*. To refactor the recurring code sequence in the preceding example using delegation, we can introduce a helper class and place the refactored code sequence in the computeAll() method of the helper class.

```
class Helper {
   void computeAll(. . . ) {
      computeStep1();
      computeStep2();
      computeStep3();
   }
}
```

Both ComputationA and ComputationB need to contain a reference to the helper class, and each occurrence of the recurring code sequence in the original methods can be replaced by a call to helper.computeAll().

```
class ComputationA {              class ComputationB {
   void compute(. . . )  {           void compute(. . . )  {
      // . . .                         // . . .
      helper.computeAll();             helper.computeAll();
      // . . .                         // . . .
   }                                }
```

```
        Helper helper;              Helper helper;
        // ...                      // ...
    }                           }
```

Refactoring by inheritance and by delegation can achieve rather similar effects. Refactoring by inheritance is usually simpler than by delegation. Refactoring by delegation is more flexible, since a class that wants access to the refactored method does not need to be related via inheritance to the class of the method. This consideration is important because of the restriction of single inheritance among classes in Java. Refactoring by inheritance may not be possible at times. When either ComputationA or ComputationB must be a subclass of a class that is not Object, for example, refactoring by inheritance is not possible. In contrast, refactoring can always be achieved through delegation.

EXAMPLE 7.1   A Generic Animation Applet

PURPOSE

This example demonstrates refactoring by inheritance.

DESCRIPTION

A generic animation applet class AnimationApplet is defined by extracting the common elements in animation applets: the methods start(), stop(), and run(). The digital clock applet presented in Example 4.10 [p. 149] is reimplemented, using the AnimationApplet class.

SOLUTION

The relationship among the classes Applet, AnimationApplet (the generic animation applet class), and DigitalClock3 (the reimplemented digital clock applet using the generic animation applet) are shown in Figure 7.1. The methods of AnimationApplet are summarized in the following table:

Method	Description
start(), stop(), and run()	The common methods in animation applets
setDelay() and getDelay()	Accessor and mutator of the delay field, which specifies the interval between two consecutive animation frames in milliseconds

The setDelay() and getDelay() methods are introduced to make the generic animation applet class more extensible, allowing each concrete animation to set its own refresh rate. Extensibility is essential to all generic components.

Figure 7.1

A generic anima-
tion applet.

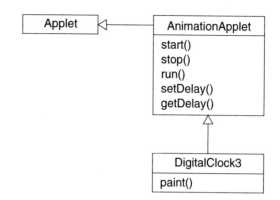

Design Guideline   *Maximize Extensibility*

Rarely can components be reused without adaptation. Extensibility allows components to be extended and adapted to different contexts. The more extensible a component is, the better the chance that it may be reused.

The `AnimationApplet` class is defined as follows:

Generic animation applet: `AnimationApplet`

```
import java.awt.*;

public class AnimationApplet
    extends java.applet.Applet
    implements java.lang.Runnable {
  public void start() {
    animationThread = new Thread(this);
    animationThread.start();
  }
  public void stop() {
    animationThread = null;
  }
  public void run() {
    while (Thread.currentThread() == animationThread) {
      try {
        Thread.currentThread().sleep(delay);
      } catch (InterruptedException e){}
      repaint();
    }
  }
  final public void setDelay(int delay) {
    this.delay = delay;
  }
```

```
      final public int getDelay() {
         return delay;
      }
      protected Thread animationThread;
      protected int delay = 100;
   }
```

Note that the fields used by the methods `start()`, `stop()`, and `run()` are also extracted to the superclass. The `AnimationApplet` class avoids duplication of the `start()`, `stop()`, and `run()` methods in every animation applet. A specific, or concrete, animation applet can simply extend `AnimationApplet` and override the `paint()` method to draw animation frames.

```
public class MyAnimationApplet extends AnimationApplet {
   public void paint(Graphics g) {
      ⟨paint a frame⟩
   }
   ⟨other fields and methods⟩
}
```

Using `AnimationApplet`, we can reimplement the digital clock applet in Section 4.7 [p. 149].

Concrete animation applet: `DigitalClock3`

```
import java.awt.*;
import java.util.Calendar;

public class DigitalClock3 extends AnimationApplet {
   public DigitalClock3() {
      setDelay(1000);
   }
   public void paint(Graphics g) {
      ⟨the body is identical to that of the paint() method in
         DigitalClock in Section 4.7⟩
   }
   protected Font font = new Font("Monospaced", Font.BOLD, 48);
   protected Color color = Color.green;
}
```

The refactoring in Example 7.1 is rather straightforward. However, in reality refactoring is often more complicated. Let us try to take the generic animation example one step further. Another code segment that also recurs in many animation applets deals with double-buffering. We can enhance the generic animation applet so that it can handle double-buffering when necessary. However, several aspects of double-buffering must be determined by the specific animation classes, which are subclasses of the generic animation applet.

EXAMPLE 7.2   A Double-Buffered Generic Animation Applet

PURPOSE

This example illustrates how to resolve the complications involved in refactoring by inheritance. It also addresses issues of extensibility and adaptability in the generic animation applet.

DESCRIPTION

A double-buffered generic animation applet class DBAnimationApplet is defined, using refactoring by inheritance. The bouncing ball applet in Example 5.4 [p. 195] is reimplemented, using the DBAnimationApplet class.

KEY ISSUES

- Accommodating various sizes of the view area.
- Allowing the subclasses to decide whether to use double-buffering.
- Refactoring common code segments that contain changeable parts.

SOLUTION

With regard to the first key issue, in order to initialize the off-screen image buffer, we need to know the dimensions of the viewing area. The problem is that the dimensions of the viewing area are not known until the init() method is invoked. A simplistic solution to this problem is to override the init() method in the generic animation applet.

```
public class DBAnimationApplet extends AnimationApplet {
   protected Dimension dim;
   protected Image im;
   protected Graphics offscreen;

   public void init() {
      dim = getSize();
      im = createImage(dim.width, dim.height);
      offscreen = im.getGraphics();
   }
   // . . .
}
```

This approach properly initializes the off-screen image buffer. However, a problem arises if a subclass of DBAnimationApplet requires additional initialization to be done in the init() method, such as getting parameters. Then it is necessary for the init() method in the subclass to call super.init() to initialize the off-screen image buffer properly.

```
public class MyAnimation extends DBAnimationApplet {
   public void init() {
      // additional initialization specific to MyAnimation
      String param = getParameter(. . .);
      // . . .
```

```
        // the following line is necessary
        super.init();
    }
    // . . .
}
```

Not invoking `super.init()` will cause a null-pointer exception. The burden of following this convention is entirely on the implementer of subclasses because its violation will not be detected by the Java compiler. For various reasons, violations of such conventions are very common, and they often lead to faults, or bugs, that are difficult to trace. Although using a component without following the proper conventions is a misuse of the component, designers of reusable components must do their best to prevent the components being misused.

Design Guideline *Prevent Misuses by Clients*

Well-designed classes should prevent possible misuses by making violations of the conventions of using the classes compilation errors, or using assertions to detect the violations at run time (i.e., defensive programming).

A better solution for initializing the off-screen image buffer is to introduce a new method `initAnimator()` for subclasses to perform subclass-specific initializations. The `init()` method is made *final*, so that it cannot be accidentally overridden by the subclasses. This approach ensures that initializations of `dim`, `im`, and `offscreen` will always be done properly. A null implementation is provided for `initAnimator()`. A subclass needs to override this method only when there are subclass-specific initializations.

```
public class DBAnimationApplet extends AnimationApplet {
    protected Dimension dim;
    protected Image im;
    protected Graphics offscreen;

    final public void init(Graphics g) {
        dim = getSize();
        im = createImage(dim.width, dim.height);
        offscreen = im.getGraphics();
        initAnimator();
    }

    protected void initAnimator() {}
}

public class MyAnimation extends DBAnimationApplet {

    protected void initAnimator() {
        // additional initialization specific to MyAnimation
```

```
        String param = getParameter(. . . );
        // . . .
    }
    // . . .
}
```

The second key issue involves giving the subclasses the flexibility to decide whether to use double-buffering. Hence the generic animation applet should accommodate two scenarios:

1. When double-buffering is not needed, the default implementation of `update()` should be used and the `paint()` method should be overridden by the subclass to paint a frame.

2. When double-buffering is needed, the `update()` method should be overridden to paint a frame.

The generic animation class should unify the two scenarios so that it can handle both. A boolean variable can be used to control the behavior of the `update()` method.

```
public class DBAnimationApplet extends AnimationApplet {
    protected boolean doubleBuffered;

    void update(Graphics g) {
        if (doubleBuffered) {
            // do double-buffering
        } else {
            super.update(g); // use the default implementation
        }
    }
    // . . .
}
```

The third key issue involves the use of double-buffering. The part of the update() method that deals with double-buffering is common to all animation applets, whereas the part that deals with painting the frames varies from applet to applet. The generic animation class should refactor the common part and allow its subclasses to provide the variable part.

The refactoring here is a bit more complicated than before, since the common code segments are intermixed with context-specific code. Let us consider a more general situation. Two methods, method1() and method2(), have some common code segments that are intermixed with some context-specific code:

```
class ContextA {                    class ContextB {
    void method(. . . ) {               void method(. . . ) {
        ⟨common code segment 1⟩             ⟨common code segment 1⟩
        ⟨context-specific code A⟩           ⟨context-specific code B⟩
        ⟨common code segment 2⟩             ⟨common code segment 2⟩
    }                                   }
    // . . .                            // . . .
}                                   }
```

How can the common code segments be refactored? Two approaches are available. The first approach is to refactor each common code segment into a separate method by using the refactoring by inheritance technique [p. 254].

```
class Common {
   void commonCode1() {
      (common code segment 1)
   }
   void commonCode2() {
      (common code segment 2)
   }
}
```

```
class ContextA                        class ContextB
    extends Common {                      extends Common {
   void method(. . . ) {                 void method(. . . ) {
      commonCode1()                          commonCode1()
      (context-specific code A)             (context-specific code B)
      commonCode2()                         commonCode2()
   }                                     }
   // . . .                              // . . .
}                                     }
```

This approach works, and it is a perfectly good solution when the two common code segments are relatively independent. However, this approach is error-prone when the two common code segments are closely related and are merely pieces of a larger process. Breaking the common code segments into two separate methods breaks the logical flow and hampers the readability of the code. The invocation of common-Code1() and commonCode2() in each context must be carefully coordinated. If one of them is omitted or they are invoked in a different order, unpredictable outcomes may result.

The second, more generic, approach is to extract the entire method that contains both common and context-specific code to a superclass and then refactor the context-specific code by introducing a new method as a placeholder, which is intended to be overridden and customized in each subclass.

```
class Common {
   void method(. . . ) {
      (common code segment 1)
      contextSpecificCode();
      (common code segment 2)
   }
   void contextSpecificCode() { . . . }
}

class ContextA extends Common {
   void contextSpecificCode() {
      (context-specific code A)
   }
   // . . .
}
```

```
class ContextB extends Common {
   void contextSpecificCode() {
      ⟨context-specific code B⟩
   }
   // . . .
}
```

The `contextSpecificCode()` method serves as a placeholder in the `Common` class. The question is, What implementation should be provided for `contextSpe-cificCode()` in class `Common`? The answer is that no implementation is appropriate, as `Common` has no knowledge of the specific context. Only the subclasses can provide sensible implementation for this method. Methods that serve as placeholders are declared *abstract methods*. The `Common` class in the preceding code fragment is an abstract class with an abstract method. It can be declared as follows:

```
abstract class Common {
   void method( . . . ) {
      ⟨common code segment 1⟩
      contextSpecificCode();
      ⟨common code segment 2⟩
   }
   abstract void contextSpecificCode();
}
```

An abstract superclass provides a generic approach to the problem of refactoring recurring code segments intermixed with context-specific code. The recurring code is extracted, as before, and an abstract method is declared to serve as a placeholder for the context-specific code. The Java compiler will compel the implementor of every derived class to implement the abstract method, allowing for the insertion of context-specific code. This approach achieves a high level of encapsulation of the otherwise common and recurring code segment. All maintenance of the common code may be performed in one place, out of view and without concern to the designers of the subclasses, who may focus their attention instead on the context-specific code that is germane to their problem.

This approach can be used to refactor double-buffering in the `update()` method in the generic `DBAnimationApplet`. An abstract method `paintFrame()` is introduced for the subclasses to override and to paint the frames. When we put all the pieces together, we get the following program, which is the complete generic animation applet class that supports double-buffering. The structure of the program is shown in Figure 7.2.

Double-buffered generic animation applet: `DBAnimationApplet`

```
import java.awt.*;

public abstract class DBAnimationApplet
      extends AnimationApplet {
```

```
final public void update(Graphics g) {
   if (doubleBuffered) {
      paintFrame(offscreen);
      g.drawImage(im, 0, 0, this);
   } else {
      super.update();
   }
}

final public void paint(Graphics g) {
   paintFrame(g);
}

final public void init() {
   d = getSize();
   im = createImage(d.width, d.height);
   offscreen = im.getGraphics();
   initAnimator();
}

protected void initAnimator() {}

abstract protected void paintFrame(Graphics g);

protected DBAnimationApplet(boolean doubleBuffered) {
   this.doubleBuffered = doubleBuffered;
}

protected DBAnimationApplet() {
   this.doubleBuffered = true;
}

protected boolean doubleBuffered;
protected Dimension d;
protected Image im;
protected Graphics offscreen;
}
```

Figure 7.2

A double-buffered generic animation applet.

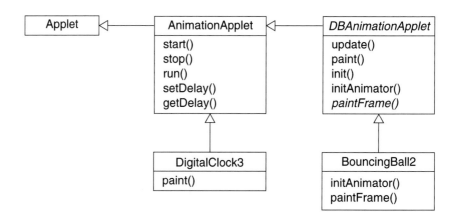

The `initAnimator()` and `paintFrame()` methods are protected, as they are intended only for the subclasses to override. The `update()`, `paint()`, and `init()` methods are final so that the subclasses cannot alter their implementation. The conventions for using the double-buffered generic animation applet class are as follows:

- A concrete animation applet should extend the `DBAnimationApplet` class. The boolean parameter of the constructor indicates whether double-buffering is needed.
- Each concrete animation applet must override the `paintFrame()` method to paint the frames for each animation.
- The `initAnimator()` method may be overridden to provide subclass-specific initializations.

The bouncing ball applet developed in Chapter 5 can be reimplemented by using the `DBAnimationApplet` class.

Concrete double-buffered animation applet: `BouncingBall2`

```java
import java.awt.*;

public class BouncingBall2 extends DBAnimationApplet {

    public BouncingBall2() {
        super(true); // double buffering
    }

    protected void initAnimator() {
        String att = getParameter("delay");
        if (att != null)
            setDelay(Integer.parseInt(att));
        x = d.width * 2 / 3 ;
        y = d.height - radius;
    }

    protected void paintFrame(Graphics g) {
        g.setColor(Color.white);
        g.fillRect(0,0,d.width,d.height);
        if (x < radius || x > d.width - radius) {
            dx = -dx;
        }
        if (y < radius || y > d.height - radius) {
            dy = -dy;
        }
        x += dx; y += dy;
        g.setColor(color);
        g.fillOval(x - radius, y - radius, radius * 2, radius * 2);
    }

    protected int x, y;
    protected int dx = -2, dy = -4;
    protected int radius = 20;
    protected Color color = Color.green;
}
```

The commonalities in animation and double-buffering can also be refactored by using delegation.

7.2.2 Design Pattern: Template Method

The preceding example illustrates the use of an abstract class that serves as a template for classes with shared functionality. An abstract class contains behavior that is common to all of its subclasses. The common behavior is encapsulated in nonabstract methods, which may even be declared final to prevent any modification. Using an abstract class ensures that all subclasses will inherit the same common behavior (i.e., implementation). The abstract methods in such templates require that context-specific behavior be implemented for each concrete subclass.

The abstract method `paintFrame()` acts as a placeholder for the behavior that is implemented differently for each specific context. We call such methods *hook* methods, upon which context-specific behavior may be hung, or implemented. The `paintFrame()` hook is placed, i.e., invoked, within the method `update()`, which is common to all concrete animation applets. Methods containing hooks are called *template* methods.

The double-buffered generic animation applet we just discussed illustrates the Template Method design pattern. The abstract method `paintFrame()` represents the behavior that is changeable, and its implementation is deferred to the concrete animation applets. The `paintFrame()` method is a hook method. Using the hook method, we are able to define the `update()` method, which represents a behavior common to all the concrete animation applets. The `update()` method is a template method. A template method uses hook methods to define a common behavior. Template methods describe the fixed behaviors of a generic class, which are sometimes called *frozen spots*. Hook methods indicate the changeable behaviors of a generic class, which are sometimes called *hot spots*.

Design Pattern *Template Method*

Category: Behavioral design pattern.

Intent: To define the skeleton of an algorithm in a method, deferring some steps to subclasses, thus allowing the subclasses to redefine certain steps of the algorithm.

Applicability: The Template Method pattern should be used

- to implement the invariant parts of an algorithm once and leave it to the subclasses to implement behavior that can vary.
- to refactor and localize the common behavior among subclasses to avoid code duplication.

The structure of the Template Method design pattern is as follows:

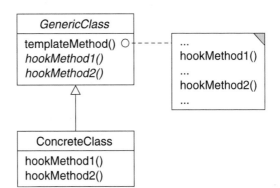

The participants in the Template Method design pattern are these:

- *GenericClass* (e.g., DBAnimationApplet), which defines abstract hook methods (e.g., paintFrame()) that concrete subclasses (e.g., BouncingBall2) override to implement steps of an algorithm and implements a template method (e.g., update()) that defines the skeleton of an algorithm by calling the hook methods.
- *ConcreteClass* (e.g., BouncingBall2), which implements the hook methods (e.g., paintFrame()) to carry out subclass-specific steps of the algorithm defined in the template method.

In the Template Method design pattern, hook methods do not have to be abstract. The generic class may provide default implementations for the hook methods. Thus, the subclasses have the option of overriding the hook methods or using the default implementation. The initAnimator() method in DBAnimationApplet is a non-abstract hook method with a default implementation. The init() method is another template method.

The following example illustrates the use of abstract classes and the Template Method design pattern:

EXAMPLE 7.3   A Generic Function Plotter

PURPOSE

To illustrate the use of the Template Method design pattern.

DESCRIPTION

Design and implement a generic function plotter applet Plotter for plotting arbitrary single-variable functions on a two-dimensional space. The generic plotter should capture the common behavior related to drawing and leave only the definition of the function to be plotted to its subclasses. A concrete plotter `PlotSine` will be implemented to plot the function

$$y = \sin x$$

A screen shot of running the `PlotSine` applet is shown in Figure 7.3.

KEY ISSUE

To represent an arbitrary single-variable function.

SOLUTION

The Template Method pattern offers a reasonable solution. The single-variable function to be plotted can be represented as a hook method in the generic plotter class. The function-plotting method can then be defined in the generic plotter class as a template method. The generic plotter class is outlined in the following program segment:

```
public abstract class Plotter {
    // the hook method
    public abstract double func(double x);

    // the template method
    protected void plotFunction(Graphics g) {
        // ...
    }
    // ...
}
```

Figure 7.3

A screen shot of PlotSine.

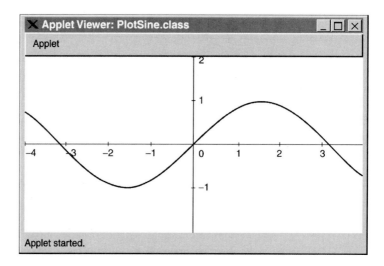

Figure 7.4

A generic function
plotter.

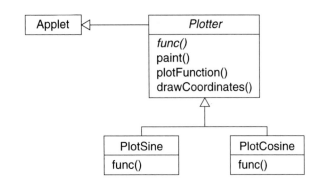

The concrete plotter will only need to extend the generic plotter and define the function to be plotted by overriding the hook method. The program structure is shown in Figure 7.4.

The generic function plotter `Plotter` is implemented as an applet. It has the following methods:

Method	Description
init()	Initialization method to get the parameters
func()	Hook method representing the function to be plotted
paint()	Method to paint the image
plotFunction()	Template method, invoked by paint() to plot the function
drawCoordinates()	Auxiliary function called by paint() to draw the *x*- and *y*-axes and tick marks.

The `Plotter` applet takes the following parameters set in the `applet` tag:

xorigin	The *x* coordinate of the origin on the canvas
yorigin	The *y* coordinate of the origin on the canvas
xratio	The number of pixels in the unit length on the *x*-axis
yratio	The number of pixels in the unit length on the *y*-axis

Generic function plotter: `Plotter`

```java
import java.awt.*;

public abstract class Plotter extends java.applet.Applet {

    public abstract double func(double x); // hook method

    public void paint(Graphics g) {
        drawCoordinates(g);
        plotFunction(g);
    }

    protected void plotFunction(Graphics g) {
        for (int px = 0; px < dim.width; px++) {
            try {
                double x = (double)(px - xorigin) / (double)xratio;
                double y = func(x);
                int py = yorigin - (int) (y * yratio);
                g.fillOval(px - 1, py - 1, 3, 3);
            } catch (Exception e) {}
        }
    }

    public void init() {
        ⟨Get the parameters and initialize the fields⟩
    }

    protected void drawCoordinates(Graphics g) {
        ⟨Draw the x- and y-axes and tick marks⟩
    }

    protected Dimension dim;
    protected Color color = Color.black;
    protected int xorigin, yorigin;
    protected int xratio = 100, yratio = 100;
}
```

The bodies of the `init()` and `drawCoordinates()` methods are left as an exercise. The complete source code is available online.

The class `PlotSine` is a concrete function plotter that simply extends the `Plotter` class and implements the method `func()`.

Concrete function plotter: `PlotSine`

```java
public class PlotSine extends Plotter {
    public double func(double x) {
        return Math.sin(x);
    }
}
```

A screen shot of running the concrete function plotter `PlotSine` is shown in Figure 7.3.

7.2.3 Generalizing

Generalizing is a process that takes a solution to a specific problem and restructures it so that it not only solves the original problem but also solves a category of problems that are similar to the original problem.

EXAMPLE 7.4   A Generic Function Plotter That Plots Multiple Functions

PURPOSE

This example demonstrates the generalizing technique and illustrates the use of the Strategy design pattern.

DESCRIPTION

In this example, the generic function plotter class `Plotter` is generalized to plot multiple single-variable functions overlaid on the same two-dimensional space. The new generic multiple function plotter is named `MultiPlotter`. A concrete subclass `PlotSineCosine` is implemented to plot

$$y = \sin x \qquad \text{and} \qquad y = \cos x$$

A screen shot of running the `PlotSineCosine` applet is shown in Figure 7.5.

KEY ISSUE

How to separate the functions to be plotted from the plotter.

Figure 7.5

A screen shot of PlotSineCosine.

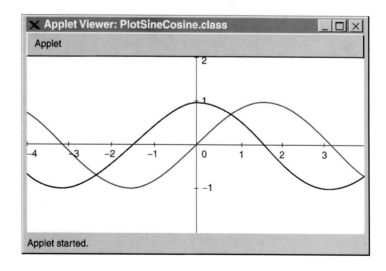

SOLUTION

One way the generic `Plotter` class can be generalized to plot multiple functions is by adding more hook methods, one for each function to be plotted.

```
public class Plotter2 {
   abstract double func1(double x);
   abstract double func2(double x);
   abstract double func3(double x);
   // . . .
}
```

This approach is rather inflexible and inelegant, allowing only a fixed number of functions. Segments of nearly identical code will be duplicated to plot each function. The problem of this approach is that the functions to be plotted and the mechanism to plot the functions are coupled into the same class. Although the coupling is harmless for a single-function plotter, it hampers the extensibility of the plotter. A more elegant solution is to decouple the functions to be plotted from the mechanism to plot them. Instead of representing each function as a method, we can represent each function as an *object*.[2] Different functions are instances of different *function classes*. To allow uniform manipulation of the functions, all the function classes implement the following common interface:

Interface Function

```
interface Function {
   double apply(double x);
}
```

The functions sin x and cos x can be represented simply as follows:

Concrete functions `Sine` and `Cosine`

```
public class Sine implements Function {
   public double apply(double x) {
      return Math.sin(x);
   }
}
public class Cosine implements Function {
   public double apply(double x) {
      return Math.cos(x);
   }
}
```

The structure of the generic multiple function plotter is shown in Figure 7.6. The `MultiPlotter` class extends `Plotter`. It uses a pair of parallel arrays to store the

---

2. Objects that represent functions are sometimes called *functors*.

Figure 7.6

Generic multiple function plotter.

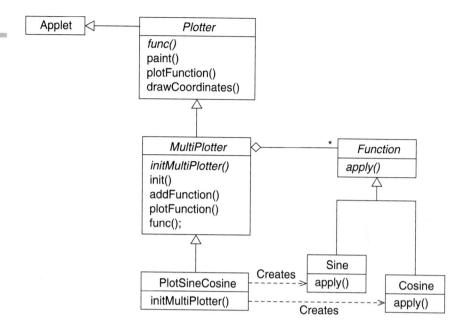

functions to be plotted and the colors used to plot the functions. Although there is a limit to the number of functions, MAX_FUNCTIONS, this limit can be easily removed without affecting any other parts of the program by using an unbounded container, such as List or Set (see Section 8.2 [p. 308]). The methods of MultiPlotter are summarized in the following table:

Method	Description
initMultiPlotter()	Hook method for the subclasses to set up the functions to be plotted
init()	Template method for initialization, which calls the hook method initMultiPlotter()
addFunction()	Method to add a function to be plotted
plotFunction()	Auxiliary function called by paint() to plot the functions
func()	Method inherited from class Plotter that is no longer useful in this class

Implementation of `MultiPlotter` is as follows:

Generic multiple function plotter: `MultiPlotter`

```java
import java.awt.*;
public abstract class MultiPlotter extends Plotter {

    abstract public void initMultiPlotter();

    public void init() {
        super.init();
        initMultiPlotter();
    }

    final public void addFunction(Function f, Color c) {
        if (numOfFunctions < MAX_FUNCTIONS &&
                f != null) {
            functions[numOfFunctions] = f;
            colors[numOfFunctions++] = c;
        }
    }

    protected void plotFunction(Graphics g) {
        for (int i = 0; i < numOfFunctions; i++) {
            if (functions[i] != null) {
                Color c = colors[i];
                if (c != null)
                    g.setColor(c);
                else
                    g.setColor(Color.black);
                for (int px = 0; px < d.width; px++) {
                    try {
                        double x = (double) (px - xorigin) / (double) xratio;
                        double y = functions[i].apply(x);
                        int py = yorigin - (int) (y * yratio);
                        g.fillOval(px - 1, py - 1, 3, 3);
                    } catch (Exception e) {}
                }
            }
        }
    }

    public double func(double x) {
        return 0.0;
    }

    protected static int MAX_FUNCTIONS = 5;
    protected int numOfFunctions = 0;
    protected Function functions[] = new Function[MAX_FUNCTIONS];
    protected Color colors[] = new Color[MAX_FUNCTIONS];

}
```

The following concrete subclass of `MultiPlotter` class plots two functions:

$$y = \sin x \qquad \text{and} \qquad y = \cos x$$

utilizing the `Sine` and `Cosine` classes:

Concrete multiple function plotter: `MultiPlotter`

```java
import java.awt.Color;

public class PlotSineCosine extends MultiPlotter {
    public void initMultiPlotter() {
        addFunction(new Sine(), Color.green);
        addFunction(new Cosine(), Color.blue);
    }
}
```

7.2.4 Design Pattern: Strategy

The preceding generic plotter of multiple functions illustrates the Strategy design pattern. The structure of the Strategy design pattern is shown in the following diagram:

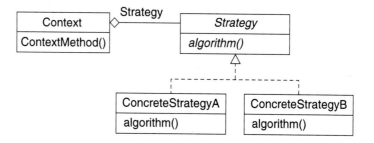

The participants in the Strategy design pattern are as follows:

- *Strategy* (e.g., `Function`), which declares an interface common to all supported algorithms.
- *ConcreteStrategy* (e.g., `Sine` and `Cosine`), which implements the algorithm using the *Strategy* interface.
- *Context* (e.g., `MultiPlotter`), which maintains references to one or more Strategy objects (e.g., `functions` in `MultiPlotter`).

The Strategy design pattern can be considered as a variation of the Template Method design pattern, in which the hook method and the template method reside in two different classes. The abstract methods declared in the `Strategy` class are the hook methods, and the methods in the `Context` class that call the hook methods are the template methods.

Design Pattern *Strategy*

Category: Behavioral design pattern.

Intent: To define a family of algorithms, encapsulate each one, and make them interchangeable.

Applicability: The Strategy pattern should be used when

- many related classes differ only in their behavior (e.g., plot different functions).
- different variants of an algorithm are needed (e.g., the sort algorithms in the case study in Section 7.4 [p. 284]).
- an algorithm uses data that clients should not know about (e.g., the LayoutManager in AWT—see Section 8.3.3 [p. 338]).
- a class defines many behaviors, which appear as multiple conditional statements in its methods (e.g., the TwoEndsTool in the case study in Chapter 9 [p. 439]).

In the MultiPlotter example, we used the Strategy design pattern to represent functions as objects (i.e., functors). Functors can be passed as parameters. This ability obviates the need for pointers to functions, which are commonly used in C and C++ to pass functions as parameters.

7.3 ABSTRACT COUPLING

The Strategy design pattern is an example of abstract coupling. *Abstract coupling* refers to a way in which clients couple with service providers. A client accesses a service through an interface or an abstract class without knowing the actual concrete class that provides the service.

Let us again use the telephone service analogy. The clients are the telephone customers, and the telephone service providers are the telephone companies. Customers can be coupled to the telephone companies directly or through abstract coupling, as illustrated in Figure 7.7. Direct coupling uses each telephone company's proprietary equipment and protocols to provide services to its customers. Each customer has to choose a company for telephone service. Switching to a different company would be difficult because doing so would require replacing equipment and changing the way customers make phone calls.

Abstract coupling is accomplished by requiring all telephone companies to use the same standard equipment and protocols. Doing so would make telephone service interchangeable and allow customers to switch easily among different companies. Customers would receive the same service without having to replace equipment or change the way they make phone calls.

Figure 7.7

(a) **Direct coupling versus (b) abstract coupling.**

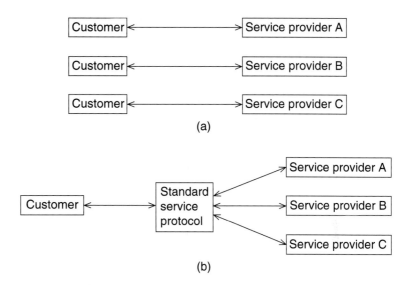

(a)

(b)

Abstract coupling is an important mechanism for enhancing extensibility and reusability in object-oriented design and occurs in many design patterns. Abstract coupling is also an application of the following important guideline of object-oriented design:

Design Guideline *Program to an Interface, Not to an Implementation*

Separate interface from implementation. Clients of a class should access only the functionalities of the class via its interface. Implementation should be hidden and irrelevant to the client.

Programming to an implementation yields ad hoc, context-specific, and inflexible solutions. Programming to an interface yields general, extensible, and reusable solutions.

In Java, implementations are defined as the fields and methods in *classes*, and the interfaces of the implementations can be declared separately as the abstract methods in *abstract classes* or *interfaces*. An abstract method declares only the service or the feature to be provided but defines no implementation. Each abstract method also defines a *contract* of the service to be provided. The contract of an abstract method is a specification that defines the service the clients can expect but without giving an implementation. The contract also defines the responsibilities of the implementations of the service.

7.3.1 Enumerating Elements

Enumerating the elements in a collection object, such as a list, is one of the most common operations on any collection. Although it may seem to be a rather trivial problem, it actually is not. Let us use the simple linked list class LinkedList discussed in Section 6.1.1 [p. 207] as an example. Suppose that we have populated a list with instances of the Course class shown in the following code fragment. The instances of the Course class represent courses offered at a university. The isPrerequisiteOf() method returns true when the receiving object represents a course that is a prerequisite of the course represented by the argument other.

Class Course

```
public class Course {
    public Course(String dept, String code, String title, int level) {
        this.dept = dept;
        this.code = code;
        this.title = title;
        this.level = level;
    }

    public String toString() {
        return (dept + " " + code + " " + title);
    }

    public boolean isPrerequisiteOf(Course other) {
        if (other != null &&
                this.dept == other.dept &&
                this.level < other.level)
            return true; {
        } else {
            return false;
        }
    }

    public String dept, code, title;
    public int level;
}
```

What we want to do is simply iterate through the list and print out the courses in the list.

Solution A: Direct Access

People who are familiar with procedural programming could easily come up with the following solution:

```
LinkedList list;
// populate the courses list
for (LinkedList.Node cur = list.head;
        cur != null;
        cur = cur.next) {
    System.out.println(cur.element);
}
```

This simple solution works only if the fields of LinkedList and the inner class Node are accessible to the clients of LinkedList, and such accessibility means that the fields and the inner class must be public. As we discussed earlier, exposing implementation details by making the fields public not only violates the principle of encapsulation but could also compromise the integrity of the class. This solution is a poor design.

Solution B: Iterate via Method Invocation

A better alternative is to keep the fields and the inner class Node nonpublic and provide public methods for iterating through the list. The IterList class extends LinkedList by adding a field cur that points to the current position of the iteration and providing the following methods for iterating through the list:

Method	Description
reset()	Moves the current position to the beginning of the list
next()	Retrieves the current element in the list and advances the current position
hasNext()	Returns true if the current position is not at the end of the list

Class IterList

```
public class IterList extends LinkedList {

    public void reset() {
        cur = head;
    }

    public Object next() {
        Object obj = null;

        if (cur != null) {
            obj = cur.element;
            cur = cur.next;
        }
        return obj;
    }

    public boolean hasNext() {
        return (cur != null);
    }

    protected Node cur;
}
```

Now, a client can iterate through the list as follows:

```
IterList list;
// populate the courses list . . .
for (list.reset(); list.hasNext();) {
   System.out.println(list.next());
}
```

This solution is clean and simple and is adequate for many situations. However, what if we want to print a table of course prerequisites that lists all the pairs of courses c1 and c2, in which c1 is a prerequisite of c2. To print out the prerequisite table requires nested loops. A logical solution seems to be the following:

```
for (list.reset(); list.hasNext();) {
   Course c1 = (Course) list.next();
   for (list.reset(); list.hasNext();) {
      Course c2 = (Course) list.next();
      if (c1.isPrerequisiteOf(c2)) {
         System.out.println(c1 + " is a prerequisite of " + c2);
      }
   }
}
```

Unfortunately, this solution does not work. The outer loop terminates after the first iteration. The reason is that both the outer and inner loops iterate through the same list, and when the inner loop completes one pass through the list, the cur index of the list has been moved to the end of the list, causing the outer loop to terminate. This type of iteration works only when two or more nested iterations are not on the same list.[3]

Solution C: Separate the Iterator from the List

When there are simultaneous iterations through the same list, each iteration must have its own current position index. In other words, the current position index should be decoupled from the list. The following solution uses a separate *iterator* class that contains the methods for iterating through the list and the current position index. It contains a reference to the original list.

Iterator for linked lists: LinkedListIterator

```
public class LinkedListIterator {

   public LinkedListIterator(LinkedList list) {
      this.list = list;
      cur = list.head;
   }

   public Object next() {
      Object obj = null;
      if (cur != null) {
```

---

3. Simultaneous iterations may arise in unexpected situations and in much less obvious forms, such as recursion.

```
            obj = cur.element
            cur = cur.next;
        }
        return obj;
    }

    public boolean hasNext() {
        return (cur != null);
    }

    protected LinkedList.Node cur;
    protected LinkedList list;
}
```

Now, the following code segment prints the prerequisite table properly:

```
LinkedListIterator iter1 = new LinkedListLiterator(list);
LinkedListIterator iter2 = new LinkedListLiterator(list);
while (iter1.hasNext()) {
   Course c1 = (Course) iter1.next();
   while (iter2.hasNext()) {
      Course c2 = (Course) iter2.next();
      if (c1.isPrerequisiteOf(c2)) {
         System.out.println(c1 + " is a prerequisite of " + c2);
      }
   }
}
```

Solution D: A Generalization

If all we needed to deal with were LinkedList, Solution C would be perfect. However, iterating through a collection is a rather common problem, and the collection could be a list, a hash table, or a set. The implementation in Solution C is tied to a specific class—LinkedList—whereas the principle is applicable to iterating through all kinds of collections. We can develop a uniform way to iterate through all kinds of collections by using *abstract coupling*. In other words, clients will not deal directly with iterators tied to specific implementations; instead, clients will deal with *abstract iterators*. The Java Class Library provides two interfaces for abstract iterators.[4]

```
interface Iterator {
   boolean hasNext();
   Object next();
   void remove();
}

interface Enumeration {
   boolean hasMoreElements();
   Object nextElement();
}
```

---

4. The reason for having two abstract iterator interfaces in Java 2 is to ensure backward compatibility. The Enumeration interface was provided by Java 1.0. The Iterator interface was introduced in Java 2 and subsumes the Enumeration interface. The Enumeration interface is used mainly in Java 1.0.x classes, such as Vector and Hashtable.

The contracts for the methods of `Iterator` and `Enumeration` are as follows:

Method	Description
`next()`	Retrieves the current element in the list and advances the current position
`hasNext()`	Returns `true` if the current position is not at the end of the list
`remove()`	Removes the current element in the list and advances the current position
`nextElement()`	Same as `next()` in `Iterator`
`hasMoreElements()`	Same as `hasNext()` in `Iterator`

Each collection class that supports iteration should provide a *concrete iterator* that implements the `Iterator` interface. Clients will deal only with the abstract iterator and need no knowledge of the concrete iterators. They can iterate through any collection in a uniform way by using the abstract iterator.

To illustrate the implementation of an iterator, we first add the following method to the `List` interface:

```
public interface List {
    public Iterator iterator();
    // other methods . . .
}
```

The `iterator()` method returns an iterator to iterate through a list. In the implementation of the `LinkedList` class, we add the implementation of the `iterator()` method, which returns a concrete iterator—an instance of the private inner class `LinkedListIterator`.

Linked list class with an abstract iterator

```
public class LinkedList implements List {

    // other methods and constructors

    public Iterator iterator() {
        return new LinkedListIterator();
    }

    private class LinkedListIterator implements Iterator {

        public boolean hasNext() {
            return cur != null;
        }
```

```
public Object next() {
    Object obj = null;
    if (cur != null) {
        obj = cur.element;
        cur = cur.next;
    }
    return obj;
}

public void remove() {
    throw new UnSupportedOperationException();
}

private LinkedList.Node cur;

LinkedListIterator() {
    cur = head;
}
    }
}
```

Clients iterate through a list by using abstract iterators.

```
List list = new LinkedList();
// populate the course list
Iterator iter1 = list.iterator();
for (; iter1.hasNext(); ) {
  Course c1 = (Course) iter1.next();
  Iterator iter2 = list.iterator();
  for (; iter2.hasNext(); ) {
    Course c2 = (Course) iter2.next();
    if (c1.isPrerequisiteOf(c2)) {
      System.out.println(c1 + " is a prerequisite of " + c2);
    }
  }
}
```

Note that the concrete iterator class is private. Clients of the LinkedList class need to know nothing about the concrete iterator.

7.3.2 Design Pattern: Iterator

The use of abstract iterators to iterate uniformly through different concrete collections is expressed as the following design pattern:

Design Pattern *Iterator*

Category: Behavioral design pattern.

Intent: To provide a way to access the elements of a collection sequentially.

Applicability: The Iterator design pattern should be used

- to access the contents of a collection without exposing its internal representation.
- to support multiple traversals of collections (e.g., the nested traversal of the course list).
- to provide a uniform interface for traversing different collections (i.e., to support polymorphic iteration).

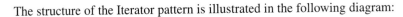

The structure of the Iterator pattern is illustrated in the following diagram:

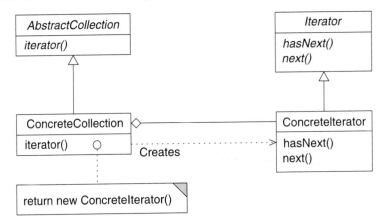

The participants of the Iterator pattern are as follows:

- ▪ *Iterator* (e.g., `Iterator`), which defines an interface for accessing and traversing the elements.
- ▪ *ConcreteIterator* (e.g., `LinkedListIterator`), which implements the iterator interface and keeps track of the current position in the traversal of the collection.
- ▪ *AbstractCollection* (e.g., `List`), which defines an interface for creating a concrete iterator (e.g., the `iterator()` method).
- ▪ *ConcreteCollection* (e.g., `LinkedList`), which implements the `iterator()` method to return an instance of a proper concrete iterator.

The Iterator design pattern is used in the Java Collections Framework to provide a uniform way of iterating through a variety of collection classes. See Section 8.2.3 [p. 315] for discussion of the Java Collections Framework.

7.4 DESIGN CASE STUDY—ANIMATION OF SORTING ALGORITHMS

In this section, we develop an applet to animate different sorting algorithms. A screen shot of the animation is shown in Figure 7.8. We first develop a straightforward and monolithic implementation (i.e., the entire program is implemented as a single class).

Figure 7.8

A screen shot of sort animation applet Sort.

We then discuss the shortcomings of the initial implementation. Finally, we apply design patterns to address the shortcomings and accomplish greater extensibility.

7.4.1 The Initial Implementation

We would like to use the generic animation applet DBAnimationApplet that we developed in Example 7.2. Unfortunately, it is not quite suited for animating sorting algorithms because it requires that the adjustment between two consecutive frames be done in the paintFrame() method, immediately before or after a frame is painted. Most sorting algorithms involve nested loops. Unwinding the loops so that each call to paintFrame() advances one iteration of the inner loop would be rather awkward. A better way to animate a complex algorithm is to let the algorithm control the progress of the animation and pause when a new frame needs to be painted. The algorithm animator class AlgorithmAnimator extends DBAnimationApplet. Again, the Template Method design pattern is used, and the AlgorithmAnimator class defines the following three methods:

Method	Description
algorithm()	Hook method for subclasses to define the algorithm to be animated
run()	Template method, which simply calls the algorithm() method to start the animation
pause()	Method to be called inside method algorithm() of the subclasses when a frame needs to be painted, painting a frame and pausing for a duration specified by delay

Each subclass of `AlgorithmAnimator` is required to define the following methods:

Method	Description
algorithm()	Define the algorithm to be animated. It should call the pause() method when some progress is made and a new frame needs to be painted.
paintFrame()	Paint a frame.

Generic algorithm animation applet: `AlgorithmAnimator`

```java
public abstract class AlgorithmAnimator
       extends DBAnimationApplet {

   // the hook method
   abstract protected void algorithm();

   // the template method
   public void run() {
      algorithm();
   }

   final protected void pause() {
      if (Thread.currentThread() == animationThread) {
         try {
            Thread.sleep(delay);
         } catch (InterruptedException e) {}
         repaint();
      }
   }
}
```

The Monolithic Sort

Now, we are ready to use the generic algorithm animator to animate sorting algorithms. The entire program is a single class Sort. In this animation, we sort an array of nonnegative integers. The array to be sorted is declared as a field of Sort: `protected int arr[];`. The methods of Sort are summarized in the following table:

Method	Description
scramble()	Initialize and scramble the array to be sorted
paintFrame()	Paint a frame

`bubbleSort()`	Bubble sort algorithm
`quickSort()`	Quick sort algorithm
`initAnimator()`	Initialize the animator
`algorithm()`	Sorting algorithm to be animated
`swap()`	Auxiliary method used by sorting algorithms to swap two numbers in the array to be sorted

The following is the overall structure of `Sort`:

Animation of sorting algorithms: `Sort`

```java
import java.awt.*;

public class Sort extends AlgorithmAnimator {

    (Method scramble() on page 287)
    (Method paintFrame() on page 288)
    (Method bubbleSort() on page 288)
    (Method quickSort() on page 288)
    (Method initAnimator() on page 289)
    (Method algorithm() on page 289)
    (Method swap() on page 289)

    protected int arr[];         // the array to be sorted
    protected String algName;    // the name of the algorithm to be animated
}
```

The `scramble()` method first determines the size of the array to be sorted. Then it initializes the array and scrambles the numbers in the array. The array size is determined by the height of the viewing area. Because each number in the array will be represented by a horizontal line that is 1 pixel wide—and adjacent lines are separated by a 1-pixel-wide gap—the size of the array is half the height of the viewing area in pixels. Suppose that n is the size of the array and that the array contains numbers from 0 to $n - 1$.

Method of `Sort` class: `Scramble()`

```java
protected void scramble() {
    arr = new int[getSize().height / 2];
    for (int i = arr.length; --i >= 0;) {
        arr[i] = i;
    }
    for (int i = arr.length; --i >= 0;) {
        int j = (int)(i * Math.random());
        swap(arr, i, j);
    }
}
```

The paintFrame() method paints a frame based on the current contents of the array arr. Each number in the array is represented by a horizontal line that is 1 pixel wide. The length of each line is proportional to the number it represents, with the longest line proportioned to occupy the entire width of the viewing area.

Method of Sort class: paintFrame()

```
protected void paintFrame(Graphics g) {
   Dimension d = getSize();
   g.setColor(Color.white);
   g.fillRect(0, 0, d.width, d.height);
   g.setColor(Color.black);
   int y = d.height - 1;
   double f = d.width / (double) arr.length;
   for (int i = arr.length; --i >= 0; y -= 2) {
      g.drawLine(0, y, (int)(arr[i] * f), y);
   }
}
```

The bubbleSort() and quickSort() methods are the two algorithms to be animated. Each time the program is invoked, one of them will be animated. The implementation of the algorithms is rather straightforward, except that method pause() is called whenever progress is made during the sorting process, to briefly pause the execution of the program and display the current state of the array.

Method of Sort class: bubbleSort()

```
protected void bubbleSort(int a[]) {
   for (int i = a.length; --i >= 0; )
      for (int j = 0; j < i; j++) {
         if (a[j] > a[j+1]) {
            swap(a, j, j + 1);
         }
         pause();
      }
}
```

Method of Sort class: quickSort()

```
protected void quickSort(int a[], int lo0, int hi0) {
   int lo = lo0, hi = hi0, mid;
   pause();
   if (hi0 > lo0) {
      mid = a[(lo0 + hi0) / 2];
      while(lo <= hi) {
         while ((lo < hi0) && (a[lo] < mid)) {
            ++lo;
         }
         while ((hi > lo0) && (a[hi] > mid)) {
            --hi;
         }
         if(lo <= hi) {
            swap(a, lo, hi);
```

```
            pause();
            ++lo;
            --hi;
         }
      }
      if(lo0 < hi) {
         quickSort(a, lo0, hi);
      }
      if(lo < hi0) {
         quickSort(a, lo, hi0);
      }
   }
}
```

Which of the two algorithms to be animated is determined by the parameter `alg` set in the `<applet>` tag. The `initAnimator()` method initializes the animation by first retrieving the parameter `alg`, storing it in the field `algName`, and then calling `scramble()` to set up the array to be sorted.

Method of Sort class: `initAnimator()`

```
protected void initAnimator() {
   algName = "BubbleSort";
   String at = getParameter("alg");
   if (at != null) {
      algName = at;
   }
   setDelay(20);
   scramble();
}
```

The `algorithm()` method simply chooses one of the algorithms to animate, based on the value of the field `algName`.

Method of Sort class: `algorithm()`

```
protected void algorithm() {
   if ("BubbleSort".equals(algName)) {
      bubbleSort(arr);
   } else if ("QuickSort".equals(algName)) {
      quickSort(arr, 0, arr.length - 1);
   } else {
      bubbleSort(arr);
   }
}
```

Finally, the auxiliary method `swap()` swaps two numbers in the array.

Method of Sort class: `swap()`

```
private void swap(int a[], int i, int j) {
   int temp = a[i]; a[i] = a[j]; a[j] = temp;
}
```

7.4.2 Separating Algorithms

The initial version of the sorting algorithm animation applet works, except that the design of the program is *not* object oriented. It lumps everything into a single class, which for those who are accustomed to procedural programming is a natural thing to do. However, this approach usually results in huge classes that contain a wide variety of functionalities, and thus lack of cohesion. The resulting programs are overly complex, inflexible, and difficult to maintain in the long run.

Large classes usually contain loosely coupled elements. Such elements in a class usually address different concerns in the problem to be solved. Separating these concerns into different classes can reduce the complexity of the design and enhance its extensibility and maintainability.

Design Guideline *Separate Functionalities That Address Different Concerns*

If a class contains components that address different concerns, these components are candidates for separation from the original class.

By separating different concerns in a loosely coupled class, we end up with classes that are smaller and tightly coupled (i.e., all their components are closely related and highly interdependent). When separation is combined with the Template Method and Strategy design patterns, the resulting design can offer great extensibility in solving each aspect of the problem.

The initial version of the sorting algorithm animation Sort is rather loosely coupled. The sorting algorithms are good candidates for separating because they should be independent of the animation mechanism. Adding or replacing sorting algorithms should have little impact on the animation mechanism. The algorithms can be separated from the animation class, and the Strategy design pattern can be used to make the algorithms to be animated interchangeable. The structure of the new design is shown in Figure 7.9.

The Abstract Sorting Algorithm

The abstract class sortAlgorithm is the *strategy* in the Strategy design pattern. It represents an abstract sorting algorithm. The sort() method is the hook method. The pause() and swap() methods are to be invoked by the subclasses of SortAlgorithm.

Abstract sorting algorithm: SortAlgorithm

```
public abstract class SortAlgorithm {
   abstract public void sort(int a[]);

   protected SortAlgorithm(AlgorithmAnimator animator) {
     this.animator = animator;
   }
```

```
protected void pause() {
   if (animator != null) {
      animator.pause();
   }
}

protected static void swap(int a[], int i, int j) {
   int temp;
   temp = a[i]; a[i] = a[j]; a[j] = temp;
}

private AlgorithmAnimator animator;
}
```

The implementation of the SortAlgorithm class shows some interesting and common variations of the Strategy design pattern. The first variation is that the abstract strategy, SortAlgorithm, is an abstract class instead of an interface. Using an abstract class for the abstract strategy allows some utility methods needed by concrete strategy classes to be implemented in the abstract strategy class. In the SortAlgorithm class, two utility methods, pause() and swap(), are implemented. The second variation is that the abstract strategy class SortAlgorithm contains a reference to the client, the AlgorithmAnimator class. This reference allows the abstract and concrete strategy classes to access the client's interface. In this example, the reference to AlgorithmAnimator is used in the pause() method to delegate the invocation of pause().

The Concrete Algorithms

The algorithms to be animated are represented as *concrete strategies*. The Bubble-SortAlgorithm and QuickSortAlgorithm classes both extend SortAlgorithm. They define the bubble sort and the quick sort algorithms, respectively.

Figure 7.9

Separating and en-capsulating sorting algorithms, using the Strategy design pattern.

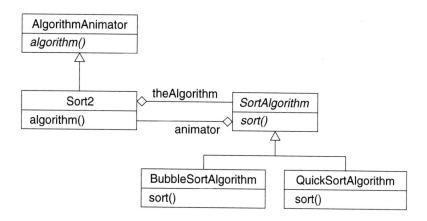

Concrete sorting algorithm: `BubbleSortAlgorithm`

```java
public class BubbleSortAlgorithm extends SortAlgorithm {
    public void sort(int a[]) {
        for (int i = a.length; --i >= 0; ) {
            for (int j = 0; j < i; j++) {
                if (a[j] > a[j+1]) {
                    swap(a, j, j+1);
                }
                pause();
            }
        }
    }
    public BubbleSortAlgorithm(AlgorithmAnimator animator) {
        super(animator);
    }
}
```

Concrete sorting algorithm: `QuickSortAlgorithm`

```java
public class QuickSortAlgorithm extends SortAlgorithm {
    protected void qsort(int a[], int lo0, int hi0) {
        int lo = lo0;
        int hi = hi0;
        int mid;
        pause();
        if (hi0 > lo0) {
            mid = a[(lo0 + hi0) / 2];
            while (lo <= hi) {
                while ((lo < hi0) && (a[lo] < mid)) {
                    lo++;
                }
                while ((hi > lo0) && (a[hi] > mid)) {
                    hi--;
                }
                if (lo <= hi) {
                    swap(a, lo, hi);
                    pause();
                    lo++;
                    hi--;
                }
            }
            if (lo0 < hi) {
                qsort(a, lo0, hi);
            }
            if (lo < hi0) {
                qsort(a, lo, hi0);
            }
        }
    }
    public void sort(int a[]) {
        qsort(a, 0, a.length - 1);
    }
```

```
    public QuickSortAlgorithm(AlgorithmAnimator animator) {
        super(animator);
    }
}
```

Creating Instances of Concrete Algorithms

We utilize the concrete algorithms in a new version of sort animation—Sort2. The question is, Where are instances of these concrete algorithms to be created? One option is to create the instances in the initAnimator() method of Sort2.

```
public class Sort2 extends AlgorithmAnimator {

    protected SortAlgorithm theAlgorithm;

    protected void initAnimator() {
        algName = "BubbleSort";
        String at = getParameter("alg");
        if (at != null) {
            algName = at;
        }
        if ("BubbleSort".equals(algName)) {
            theAlgorithm = new BubbleSortAlgorithm(this);
        } else if ("QuickSort".equals(algName)) {
            theAlgorithm = new QuickSortAlgorithm(this);
        } else { // default algorithm
            theAlgorithm = new BubbleSortAlgorithm(this);
        }
        setDelay(20);
        scramble();
    }

    // other methods and fields . . .
}
```

Although this solution works, it leaves the client (the Sort2 class) of the Strategy design pattern (the SortingAlgorithm class) to deal directly with the concrete strategies (the BubbleSortAlgorithm and QuickSortAlgorithm classes). This result negates one of the key advantages of using the Strategy design pattern—that is, to make concrete strategies interchangeable by decoupling the clients from the strategies. The client should be completely unaware of the concrete strategies.

A better alternative is to use a separate class whose sole responsibility is to create instances of concrete sorting algorithms. We call this class a *factory*. Using the factory, the client (the Sort2 class) can be completely decoupled from the concrete sorting algorithms.

The factory class can be implemented in several different ways. To allow the flexibility of using different factories and to insulate the client from future changes in them, the Strategy design pattern once again can be applied to make different factories interchangeable. The revised design of the sorting algorithm animation is shown in Figure 7.10. The abstract algorithm factory, AlgorithmFactory, is defined as an interface. The contract of the hook method makeSortAlgorithm() is

> Given the name of a sorting algorithm, return an instance of a subclass of Sort
> Algorithm that implements the named sorting algorithm.

Figure 7.10

A revised design of sort animation, using factories.

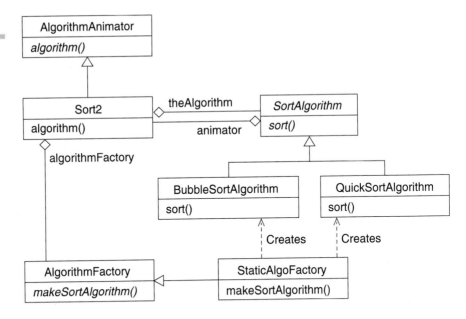

```
public interface AlgorithmFactory {
    public SortAlgorithm makeSortAlgorithm(String algName);
}
```

A straightforward implementation of a concrete algorithm factory is the `StaticAlgoFactory` class.

Concrete algorithm factory: `StaticAlgoFactory`

```
public class StaticAlgoFactory implements AlgorithmFactory {

    public StaticAlgoFactory(AlgorithmAnimator animator) {
        this.animator = animator;
    }

    public SortAlgorithm makeSortAlgorithm(String algName) {
        if ("BubbleSort".equals(algName)) {
            return new BubbleSortAlgorithm(animator);
        } else if ("QuickSort".equals(algName)) {
            return new QuickSortAlgorithm(animator);
        } else {
            return new BubbleSortAlgorithm(animator);
        }
    }

    protected AlgorithmAnimator animator;

}
```

This static algorithm factory is tightly coupled with concrete sorting algorithms. Adding or changing concrete sorting algorithms requires changes to this factory. However, using Java's dynamic class-loading capability, we can build a *dynamic* sorting algorithm factory that is completely decoupled from the concrete sorting algorithms; that is, adding or changing concrete sorting algorithms does not affect the dynamic factory![5]

The Revised Sort Animation

The revised sorting algorithm animation applet Sort2 is now completely decoupled from the concrete sorting algorithms.

Revised sorting algorithm animation applet: Sort2

```
public class Sort2 extends AlgorithmAnimator {
    protected SortAlgorithm theAlgorithm;
    protected SortAlgorithmFactory algorithmFactory;

    protected void initAnimator() {
        algName = "BubbleSort";
        String at = getParameter("alg");
        if (at != null) {
            algName = at;
        }
        algorithmFactory = new StaticAlgoFactory(this);
        theAlgorithm = algorithmFactory.makeSortAlgorithm(algName);

        setDelay(20);
        scramble();
    }

    protected void algorithm() {
        if (theAlgorithm != null)
            theAlgorithm.sort(arr);
    }

    protected void scramble() {
        (The body is identical to that of scramble() in Sort on page 287)
    }

    protected void paintFrame(Graphics g) {
        (The body is identical to that of paintFrame() in Sort on page 288)
    }

    protected int arr[];
    protected String algName;
}
```

---

5. An implementation of a dynamic factory is included in the *Online Supplement* to this book.

7.4.3 Design Pattern: Factory

The use of factories to create concrete sorting algorithms illustrates another useful design pattern—Factory.

Design Pattern *Factory*

Category: Creational design pattern.

Intent: To define an interface for creating objects but let subclasses decide which class to instantiate and how.

Applicability: The Factory design pattern should be used when a system should be independent of how its products are created.

The structure of the Factory design pattern is shown in the following diagram:

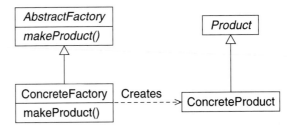

The participants in the Factory design pattern are the following:

- *Product* (e.g., `SortAlgorithm`), which defines an interface of the objects that the factory will create.
- *ConcreteProduct* (e.g., `QuickSortAlgorithm`), which implements the `Product` interface.
- *AbstractFactory* (e.g., `AlgorithmFactory`), which defines a factory method (e.g., `makeSortAlgorithm()`) that returns an object of type `Product`.
- *ConcreteFactory* (e.g., `StaticSortAlgorithmFactory`), which overrides the factory method to return an instance of `ConcreteProduct`.

The Factory design pattern is closely related to but distict from two other creational design patterns: Abstract Factory and Factory Method, which will be discussed in Section 10.2.2 [p. 484] and Section 9.5.6 [p. 447], respectively.

7.4.4 Separating Display Strategies

If we examine the revised sorting algorithm animation applet `Sort2` closely, we find there is another loosely coupled component—the display strategy (i.e., the visual representation) of the array. The display strategy should be independent of the algorithms being animated and the animation mechanism. Changing the display strategy should not affect the algorithms and the animation mechanism. The display strategy can be decoupled from the animation mechanism and the algorithms by using the Strategy and Factory design patterns so that different display strategies become interchangeable. The revised design is shown in Figure 7.11.

Three Design Options

The key issue here is the design of the interface of the display strategy—the SortDisplay interface, which represents an abstract display strategy. We start by designing the interface.

```
public interface SortDisplay {
    public void display(int a[], Graphics g, Dimension d);
}
```

The interface defines a single method for displaying the array. The parameters of the method are necessary for displaying the array. This solution is rather straightforward, and the interface is small, resulting in low coupling. The change needed in the main class Sort3 is for the paintFrame() method to delegate the painting responsibility to the display strategy.

```
public class Sort3 extends Sort2 {

    protected SortDisplay theDisplay;

    public void paintFrame(Graphics g) {
        theDisplay.display(arr, g, getSize());
    }
    // ...
}
```

This solution works, but it is inflexible because there is a subtle coupling between the display strategy and the display size. In the preceding implementation, the size of the array is determined in the scramble() method of the Sort class based on the height of the viewing area. As a result, the scramble() method is tightly coupled to the displaying scheme.

Figure 7.11

Encapsulating the display strategies, using the Strategy design pattern.

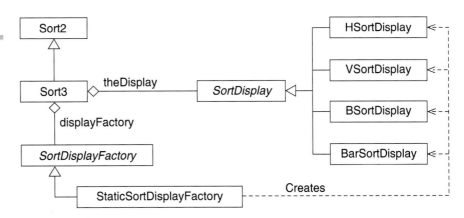

The second design option is to move the scramble() method to the SortDis-play interface so that tightly coupled functionalities are in the same class.

```
public interface SortDisplay {
    public void scramble(int a[], Dimension d);
    public void display(int a[], Graphics g, Dimension d);
}
```

The new scramble() method of Sort3 will now also delegate the responsibility of initializing the array to the display strategy.

```
public class Sort3 extends Sort2 {

    protected SortDisplay theDisplay;

    public void scramble() {
        theDisplay.scramble(arr, getSize());
    }

    public void paintFrame(Graphics g) {
        theDisplay.display(arr, g, getSize());
    }
    // ...
}
```

Now, coupling between the display strategy and its client is reduced. However, SortDisplay is not very cohesive, as initializing the array and scrambling it have nothing to do with displaying it. These are basically independent functionalities, except that they both must agree on the size of the array. So, the third and best design option is to move scramble()'s functionality back into the Sort3 class. We introduce a new method, getArraySize(), in the SortDisplay interface to capture the interdependency among these methods.

Abstract display strategy: SortDisplay

```
import java.awt.*;

public interface SortDisplay {
    public int getArraySize(Dimension d);
    public void display(int a[], Graphics g, Dimension d);
}
```

The design of the SortDisplay interface illustrates the following design guide-line:

Design Guideline *Minimize the Interface*

Design the smallest possible interface that provides the needed functionality. Interface size is determined by the number of methods and their parameters. Large interfaces usually indicate high levels of coupling with collaborating classes and high complexity.

Concrete Display Strategies

The original display strategy that uses 1-pixel horizontal lines can be reimplemented as a concrete strategy HSortDisplay that implements the SortDisplay interface.

Concrete display strategy: HSortDisplay

```java
import java.awt.*;

public class HSortDisplay implements SortDisplay {
   public int getArraySize(Dimension d) {
      return d.height / 2;
   }

   public void display(int a[], Graphics g, Dimension d) {
      double f = d.width / (double) a.length;
      g.setColor(Color.white);
      g.fillRect(0, 0, d.width, d.height);
      int y = d.height - 1;
      g.setColor(Color.black);
      y = d.height - 1;
      for (int i = a.length; --i >= 0; y -= 2)
         g.drawLine(0, y, (int)(a[i] * f), y);
   }
}
```

The revised design allows us to introduce new display strategies easily. Two variations of the original display strategy are implemented:

- VSortDisplay: Use vertical lines, with all lines flush against the top edge and extending downward, as shown in Figure 7.12(a).
- BSortDisplay: Use vertical lines, with all lines flush against the bottom edge and extending upward, as shown in Figure 7.12(b).

The implementations follow:

Concrete display strategy: VSortDisplay

```java
import java.awt.*;

public class VSortDisplay implements SortDisplay {

   public int getArraySize(Dimension d) {
      return d.width / 2;
   }

   public void display(int a[], Graphics g, Dimension d) {
      g.setColor(Color.white);
      g.fillRect(0, 0, d.width, d.height);
      int x = d.width - 1;
      double f = d.height / (double) a.length;
      g.setColor(Color.black);
      for (int i = a.length; --i >= 0; x -= 2)
         g.drawLine(x, 0, x, (int)(a[i] * f));
   }
}
```

Figure 7.12

Screen shots of
Sort3 showing
various display
strategies.

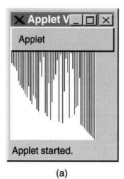

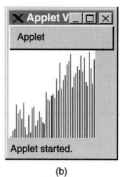

(a)   (b)

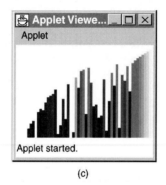

(c)

Concrete display strategy: BSortDisplay

```java
import java.awt.*;

public class BSortDisplay implements SortDisplay {

  public int getArraySize(Dimension d) {
    return d.width / 2;
  }

  public void display(int a[], Graphics g, Dimension d) {
    g.setColor(Color.white);
    g.fillRect(0, 0, d.width, d.height);
    double f = d.height / (double) a.length;
    int x = d.width - 1;
    g.setColor(Color.black);
    for (int i = a.length; --i >= 0; x -= 2)
      g.drawLine(x, d.height, x, d.height - (int)(a[i] * f));
  }
}
```

A more interesting display strategy is the BarSortDisplay, shown in Figure 7.12(c). The vertical lines are 3 pixels wide, the heights of the lines are proportional to the numbers they represent, and different colors are used to represent different numbers.

Concrete display strategy: `BarSortDisplay`

```java
public class BarSortDisplay implements SortDisplay {
  public int getArraySize(Dimension d) {
    return d.width / 3;
  }
  public void display(int a[], Graphics g, Dimension d) {
    g.setColor(Color.white);
    g.fillRect(0, 0, d.width, d.height);
    double f = d.height / (double) a.length;
    double cf = 255.0 / (double) a.length;
    int x = d.width - 3;
    for (int i = a.length; --i >= 0; x -= 3) {
      g.setColor(new Color((int)(a[i]*cf/1.5), (int)(a[i]*cf), 0));
      g.fillRect(x, d.height - (int)(a[i]*f), 3, (int)(a[i]*f));
    }
  }
}
```

Display Factory

The instances of concrete display strategies are also created by a factory. The structure is similar to the algorithm factories. Implementation of a simple static factory is as follows:

Abstract display factory: `SortDisplayFactory`

```java
public interface SortDisplayFactory {
  SortDisplay makeSortDisplay(String name);
}
```

Concrete display factory: `StaticSortDisplayFactory`

```java
public class StaticSortDisplayFactory
    implements SortDisplayFactory {
  public SortDisplay makeSortDisplay(String name) {
    if ("horizontal".equals(name))
      return new HSortDisplay();
    else if ("vertical".equals(name))
      return new VSortDisplay();
    else if ("bottom".equals(name))
      return new BSortDisplay();
    else if ("bar".equals(name))
      return new BarSortDisplay();
    else
      return new HSortDisplay();
  }
}
```

Putting All the Pieces Together

Sorting algorithm animation applet: Sort3

```java
import java.awt.*;

public class Sort3 extends Sort2 {

    protected SortDisplay theDisplay;
    protected SortDisplayFactory displayFactory;

    protected void initAnimator() {
        String att = getParameter("dis");
        displayFactory = new StaticSortDisplayFactory();
        theDisplay = displayFactory.makeSortDisplay(att);
        super.initAnimator();
    }

    protected void scramble() {
        int n = theDisplay.getArraySize(getSize());
        arr = new int[n];
        for (int i = arr.length; --i >= 0;)
            arr[i] = i;
        for (int i = arr.length; --i >= 0;) {
            int j = (int)(i * Math.random());
            SortAlgorithm.swap(arr, i, j);
        }
    }

    protected void paintFrame(Graphics g) {
        theDisplay.display(arr, g, getSize());
    }
}
```

CHAPTER SUMMARY

- Design patterns are schematic descriptions of solutions to recurring problems in software design. Each pattern represents a generic (i.e., reusable) solution to a recurring problem. Only a relatively small number of patterns are needed to capture the essence of the design process, and they can be adapted and combined in countless ways to generate endless possibilities.

- Generic components are program components, usually classes and packages, that can be adapted and used in many different contexts without modification of the source code. Generic components are also known as reusable components.

- Refactoring is used to identify recurring, identical, or nearly identical code segments and to restructure a program so that the recurring code segments are captured as a generic component that is defined once and is usable in many different contexts. Refactoring can be accomplished by inheritance or delegation.

- Generalization is a process that takes a solution to a specific problem and restructures it so that it not only solves the original problem but also solves a category of problems that are similar to the original problem. Generalization is often accomplished by using abstract classes or interfaces and design patterns, such as Template Method and Strategy.

▪ An abstract method is a method whose implementation is deferred to its subclasses. Abstract methods are also known as deferred methods. An abstract class is a class that includes or inherits at least one abstract method.

▪ The Template Method design pattern defines the skeleton of an algorithm in a method, deferring some steps to subclasses and thus allowing the subclasses to redefine certain steps of the algorithm. The Template Method design pattern should be used to implement the invariant parts of an algorithm or to refactor and localize common behavior among subclasses.

▪ The Strategy design pattern defines a family of algorithms, encapsulates each one, and makes them interchangeable. The Strategy design pattern should be used when many related classes differ only in their behavior or when different variants of an algorithm are needed.

▪ The Factory design pattern defines an interface for creating objects but lets subclasses decide which class to instantiate and how. The Factory design pattern should be used when a system should be independent of how its products are created.

▪ Important design guidelines include the following:

Refactor recurring code segments: Recurring code segments based on the same logic are hazardous to maintenance. They should be refactored so that the code segment occurs only once. Other occurrences of the code segment should be replaced with references to the common code.

Maximize extensibility: Rarely can components be reused without adaptation. Extensibility allows components to be extended and adapted to different contexts. The more extensible a component is, the better the chance that it may be reused.

Prevent misuses by clients: Well-designed classes should prevent possible misuses by making violations of the conventions of using the classes compilation errors, or using assertions to detect the violations at run time (i.e., defensive programming).

Program to an interface, not to an implementation: Separate interface from implementation. Clients of a class should access only the functionalities of the class via its interface. Implementation should be hidden and irrelevant to the client.

Separate functionalities that address different concerns: If a class contains components that address different concerns, these components are candidates for separation from the original class.

Minimize the interface: Design the smallest possible interface that provides the needed functionality. Interface size is determined by the number of methods and their parameters. Large interfaces usually indicate high levels of coupling with collaborating classes and high complexity.

FURTHER READINGS

Gamma, E., et al. (1995). *Design Patterns—Elements of Reusable Object-Oriented Software*. Addison-Wesley.

Metsker, S. J. (2002). *Design Patterns Java Workbook*. Addison-Wesley.

Shalloway, A., and J. R. Trott (2001). *Design Patterns Explained: A New Perspective on Object-Oriented Design*. Addison-Wesley.

EXERCISES

7.1 Extend the generic function plotter class `Plotter` to plot the following functions:

(a) $y = \sqrt{x}$

(b) $y = \ln x$

(c) $y = \tan x$

(d) $y = x^3 - 3x^2 + 5x + 8$

7.2 Write a generic plotter applet that takes a parameter `func` that represents a single-variable polynomial function and plots the function. For example, the input might be in the form

```
x^3 - 3 * x^2 + 5 * x + 8
```

7.3 Extend the generic multiple function plotter `MultiPlotter` to plot the following functions in the same two-dimensional canvas:

(a) $y = 5x$

(b) $y = 2x^2$

(c) $y = 0.5x^3$

(d) $y = 0.2e^x$

(e) $y = \ln x$

7.4 Write an applet that combines the applets in Exercises 5.7 and 5.8. It should support two display strategies: a bar chart or a pie chart. The user should be able to choose either of the two display strategies by setting a parameter. The display strategies are to be implemented by using the Strategy design pattern.

7.5 Write an animated applet with two bouncing balls by extending the `DBAnimationApplet`

class. The balls should bounce off each other when they collide. *Bonus:* Allow the user to add more balls.

7.6 Enhance the latest version of the animation applet `Sort3` by adding the following capabilities:

(a) New sorting algorithms, such as *insertion sort*.

(b) New display strategies.

7.7 Refactor the bouncing ball applet in Example 7.2 to separate the ball object from the animator. Extend the applet so that the object being bounced around can be any shape or image.

PROJECT

7.1 Develop animation applets to animate graph algorithms. Candidates include the following:

(a) Kruskal's and Prim's algorithms for minimum spanning trees [Thomas, Corman, and Rivest 1990]. Animate the process of adding edges to the minimum spanning tree.

(b) Dijkstra's algorithm for single-source shortest path [Thomas, Corman, and Rivest 1990]. Animate the process of discovering the edges on the shortest path.

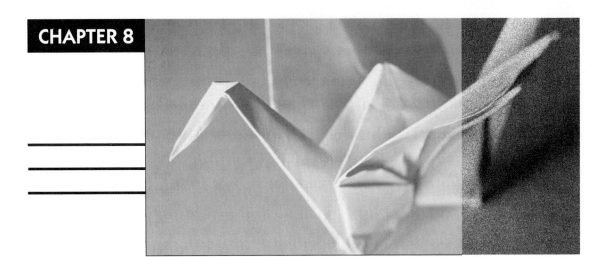

CHAPTER 8

Object-Oriented Application Frameworks

CHAPTER OVERVIEW

In this chapter, we discuss the design of application frameworks and the use of design patterns. We present three important frameworks in the Java Class Library—the collections framework, the input/output framework, and the graphical user interface (GUI) framework using AWT and Swing.

8.1   APPLICATION FRAMEWORKS

An *object-oriented application framework*, or *framework* for short, is a set of co-operating classes that represent reusable designs of software systems in a particular application domain. An application framework typically consists of a set of abstract classes and interfaces that are parts of semicomplete applications that can be specialized to produce custom applications. An application framework often prescribes a set of conventions for extending the abstract classes, implementing the interfaces, and allowing their instances to interact with one another. The main goal of application frameworks is to support the reuse of designs and implementations in particular application domains and thereby greatly simplify them.

The generic animation applet classes that we developed in Chapter 7 (`AnimationApplet` and `DBAnimationApplet`) can be considered as mini-frameworks. They exhibit some of the characteristics of application frameworks in that they are reusable and extensible, they are semicomplete programs, and the reusable design and implementation is captured in abstract classes with hook methods to be overridden by the subclasses.

Real application frameworks are of much larger scale. Some examples are graphical user interface (GUI) frameworks such as the Abstract Windows Toolkit (AWT) and Swing portion of the Java Foundation Classes (JFC), and the Microsoft Foundation Classes (MFC) for C++; and distributed computing frameworks such as the Java Remote Method Invocation (RMI) and the Common Object Request Broker Architecture (CORBA).

8.1.1 Characteristics

Key characteristics of application frameworks are discussed under the following headings.

Extensibility

An application framework typically consists of a set of abstract classes and interfaces to be extended and specialized. Its changeable aspects, also known as the *hot spots* of the framework, are often represented as hook methods. Custom applications use the framework by extending or implementing the classes and interfaces in the framework and by overriding the hook methods to provide customized behaviors.

For example, a concrete animation applet, such as `BouncingBall2`, simply extends the `DBAnimationApplet` class and overrides the hook methods `paintFrame()` and `initAnimator()`.

Inversion of Control

When we use a conventional library of routines and classes, the applications usually control the flow of execution. In other words, the applications are acting as the masters, whereas the routines and classes in the libraries are acting as servants to provide services. When we use an application framework, the control of the flow of execution often resides in the framework, not in the applications. In other words, the framework is acting as the master, whereas the applications are acting as servants to fill in the hot spots.

For example, with the `LinkedList` class, the applications are in control, and the `LinkedList` class simply provides services. That approach is quite different from using the `Applet` class, which can be considered a mini-framework. The control resides in the `Applet` class and the applet context. A specific applet extends the `Applet` class and overrides the hook methods, `init()`, `start()`, and the like, which represent the hot spots of the applet framework.

Design Patterns as Building Blocks

Although both design patterns and frameworks are mechanisms used to capture reusable designs, they are quite different. On the one hand, design patterns are schematic descriptions of reusable designs that are not concrete programs and that are language independent. On the other hand, frameworks are compilable programs written in a specific programming language and often contain abstract classes and interfaces. Design patterns are the architectural building blocks of application frameworks. They help make application frameworks extensible and reusable. Frameworks usually contain implementations of many cooperating design patterns. For example, the design patterns Template Method and Strategy are used in almost all application frameworks.

8.1.2 Design Requirements

Designing application frameworks is more challenging than designing specific applications. A designer of application frameworks must foresee the potential changes and the variabilities required by potential applications that may use the frameworks. Booch [1994] has suggested the following design requirements of application frameworks.

Completeness

The framework must provide a family of classes, united by a shared interface but each employing a different representation. Developers can then select the classes having the time and space semantics most appropriate to their given application.

Adaptability

All platform-specific aspects of the framework must be clearly identified and isolated. Doing so permits local substitutions to be made.

Efficiency

Components must be easily assembled (efficient in terms of compilation resources). They must impose minimal run-time and memory overhead (efficient in execution resources). And they must be more reliable than hand-built mechanisms (efficient in developer resources).

Safety

Each abstraction must be type-safe so that static assumptions about the behavior of a class may be enforced by the compilation system. Exceptions should be used to signify run-time violations of the contract concerning the dynamic semantics of the class. Raising an exception must not corrupt the state of the object that threw the exception.

Simplicity

The framework must have a clear and consistent organization that makes it easy to identify and select appropriate concrete classes.

Extensibility

Developers must be able to add new classes independently. At the same time they must be able to preserve the architectural integrity of the framework.

8.1.3   Specific Frameworks Considered

To use application frameworks effectively, you must understand the interfaces, conventions, and restrictions of a framework. In return, using well-designed frameworks can significantly simplify the design and implementation of applications. The Java 2 Platform class library includes several well-designed and powerful application frameworks. In the remainder of this chapter, we discuss the interfaces, conventions, and designs of the following Java application frameworks:

The collections framework: Collections are also known as containers.[1] The collections framework is a set of interfaces and classes that support storing and retrieving objects in collections of varying data structures, algorithms, and time-space complexities.

The graphical user interfaces framework: The graphical user interfaces framework consists of the Abstract Windows Toolkit (AWT) and the Swing portion of the Java Foundation Classes. It is a set of interfaces and classes that support the construction of graphical user interfaces with a great deal of versatility.

The input/output framework: The input/output framework is a set of interfaces and classes that support the input and output of different types of objects to and from different media with varying capabilities.

8.2   THE COLLECTIONS FRAMEWORK

A *collection* is an object that contains other objects, which are called the *elements* of the collection. Based on their structures and capabilities, collections can be classified in a few major categories known as *abstract collections*.

---

1. Not to be confused with the `Container` class in AWT. They are unrelated.

8.2.1 Abstract Collections

There are four major types of collections: bags, sets, lists, and maps.

Bags

A *bag* is an unordered collection of elements that may contain duplicate elements. Bags are also known as *multisets*. Bags are the least restrictive and most general form of collections. In the Java collections framework, bags are represented by the `Collection` interface. Bags are rarely used directly. More restrictive forms of collections, such as sets and lists, are used much more often.

Sets

A *set* is an unordered collection of elements. No duplicate elements are allowed in sets. In other words, inserting the same elements in a set twice is the same as inserting the element just once. A set is denoted

$$\{e_1, e_2, \ldots, e_n\}$$

where $e_1, e_2, \ldots, e_n$ are the elements of the set. For example, the following is a set of languages:

```
{ "English", "Chinese", "German" }
```

A variation of sets is *sorted sets*, whose elements are automatically sorted according to a certain order. Sorted sets are also known as *ordered sets*. For example, the following is an ordered set of languages sorted in alphabetical order:

```
{ "Chinese", "English", "German" }
```

In the Java collections framework, sets are represented by the `Set` interface, and sorted sets are represented by the `SortedSet` interface.

Lists

A *list* is an ordered collection of elements. Lists are also known as *sequences*. Elements in a list are indexed sequentially starting from 0. Duplicate elements are allowed in lists. A list is denoted

$$\langle e_1, e_2, \ldots, e_n \rangle$$

where $e_1, e_2, \ldots, e_n$ are the elements of the list. For example, the following are three different lists:

```
⟨ "Chinese", "German", "English" ⟩
⟨ "English", "Chinese", "German" ⟩
⟨ "English", "Chinese", "English", "German" ⟩
```

In the Java collections framework, lists are represented by the `List` interface.

Maps

A *map* is an unordered collection of key-value pairs, denoted *key* $\mapsto$ *value*. Maps are also known as *functions*, *dictionaries*, or *associative arrays*. The keys in a map must be unique (i.e., each key can map to at most one value). A map is denoted

$$\{k_1 \mapsto v_1, k_2 \mapsto v_2, \ldots, k_n \mapsto v_n\}$$

where $k_1, k_2, \ldots, k_n$ are the keys and $v_1, v_2, \ldots, v_n$ are the values of the map. For example, the following is a very small English-Chinese dictionary:

{ "welcome" $\mapsto$ "欢迎", "software" $\mapsto$ "软件", "coffee" $\mapsto$ "咖啡" }

A variation of maps is *sorted maps*, whose elements are automatically sorted by keys according to a certain order. Sorted maps are also known as *ordered maps*. In the Java collections framework, maps are represented by the Map interface, and sorted maps are represented by the SortedMap interface.

8.2.2 Interfaces of Collections

The abstract collections are represented by a set of interfaces, as shown in Figure 8.1. The implementations of these collections are defined as classes that implement the abstract collection interfaces. The following design guideline is important to the design of the Java collections framework:

Design Guideline *Maximize the Uniformity of Common Aspects of Related Classes/Interfaces*

The common aspects of related classes should be handled in a uniform way. These common aspects are usually captured as interfaces or abstract classes. The greater the uniformity, the simpler and more useful is the design.

Figure 8.1

The abstract collections.

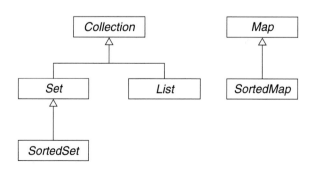

Although each kind of abstract collection has its unique characteristics, together they have a lot in common. For example, all collections support insertion and deletion of elements. It is simpler if the insertion and deletion of different collections can be expressed by using the same methods and following the same conventions. More important, different implementations of an abstract collection will all implement the same interface. Thus, knowing the interface of an abstract collection is adequate for use of all the implementations of an abstract collection. For example, the Set interface can be implemented by using an array, a linked list, a tree, and so on. A user needs to study only the Set interface in order to use all its implementations, and switching from one implementation to another is easy. However, we often need to know about the concrete implementation classes so that we can make informed decisions on the most suitable implementation, depending on a number of factors, such as performance, memory consumption, thread safety, and so on.

The Collection Interface

The Collection interface represents a bag. The methods of the Collection interface are summarized in Table 8.1. In these methods, parameter o is of type Object and parameter c is of type Collection.

TABLE 8.1

Methods of Interface Collection

Method	Description
add(o)	Adds a new element o to this collection
addAll(c)	Adds all the elements in the collection c to this collection
clear()	Removes all the elements from this collection
contains(o)	Returns true if this collection contains an element that equals o
containsAll(c)	Returns true if this collection contains all the elements in the collection c
isEmpty()	Returns true if this collection contains no elements
iterator()	Returns an iterator over the elements in this collection (see Section 8.2.4 [p. 319])
remove(o)	Removes an element that equals o from this collection if such an element exists
removeAll(c)	Removes from this collection all the elements that are contained in the collection c
retainAll(c)	Retains only the elements in this collection that are contained in the collection c, and removes all other elements
size()	Returns the number of elements in this collection

The elements of a collection can be any objects (i.e., the elements can be of any reference type). Values of primitive types cannot be directly stored in collections. To be stored in a collection, the values of primitive types must be wrapped in an object of a suitable wrapper class (see Section 4.4.9). In the methods `contains()`, `containsAll(c)`, `remove(o)`, `removeAll(c)`, and `retainAll(c)`, the notion of equality between two elements is defined by the `equals()` method of the class of the elements.

The `Set` Interface

The `Set` interface extends the `Collection` interface and represents a set. All the methods of the `Collection` interface are inherited, so the `Set` interface introduces no new methods. However, some of the methods have different semantics, or contracts, than those in the `Collection` interface, owing to the restriction of sets. The methods with altered semantics in the `Set` interface are summarized in Table 8.2. In these methods, parameter o is of type `Object` and parameter c is of type `Collection`.

Here is an example of using sets:

```
Set set = new HashSet();  // HashSet is the class that implements Set
set.add("foo");           // the set is { foo }
set.add("bar");           // the set is { foo, bar }
int n = set.size();       // n is 2
if (set.contains("foo"))  // is true
    System.out.println("foo is in");
```

The `SortedSet` interface further extends the `Set` interface. We discuss it in Section 8.2.5 [p. 325].

The `List` Interface

The `List` interface also extends the `Collection` interface, and the `List` interface introduces some new methods and also alters the semantics of many of the methods inherited from the `Collection` interface because of the ordering imposed by lists.

TABLE 8.2

Methods of Interface `Set`

Method	Description
add(o)	Adds the element o to this set if it is not already present
addAll(c)	Adds all the elements in the collection c to this set if they are not already present

The new methods and the methods with altered semantics in the List interface are summarized in Table 8.3. In these methods, parameter o is of type Object, parameter c is of type Collection, and parameters i and j are integers representing indices.

The Map Interface

The Map interface represents a map. Although maps are conceptually sets of key-value pairs and are often implemented as sets, the Map interface does not extend the Collection interface; nor does it extend the Set interface. Maps are more restrictive than sets because maps contain only key-value pairs and do not allow duplicate keys. Therefore, some of the methods in the Set and Collection interfaces cannot be

TABLE 8.3

Methods of Interface List

Method	Description
add(i, o)	Inserts the element o at the i-th position in this list
add(o)	Appends the element o to the end of this list
addAll(c)	Appends all the elements in the collection c to the end of this list, in the order that they are returned by the iterator of c
addAll(i, c)	Inserts all the elements in the collection c into this list, starting at the i-th position
get(i)	Returns the element at the i-th position in this list
indexOf(o)	Returns the index in this list of the first occurrence of the element o, or −1 if the element is not present in this list
lastIndexOf(o)	Returns the index in this list of the last occurrence of the element o, or −1 if the element is not present in this list
listIterator()	Returns a ListIterator of the elements in this list (see Section 8.2.4 [p. 319])
listIterator(i)	Returns a ListIterator of the elements in this list, starting from the i-th position (see Section 8.2.4 [p. 319])
remove(i)	Removes the element at the i-th position in this list and returns the removed element
remove(o)	Removes the first occurrence of the element o in this list
set(i, o)	Replaces the element at the i-th position in this list with the element o, and returns the element that was replaced
subList(i, j)	Returns a sublist of this list from the i-th position, inclusive, to the j-th position, exclusive

TABLE 8.4

Methods of Interface Map

Method	Description
clear()	Removes all entries from this map
containsKey(k)	Returns true if this map contains an entry for the key k
containsValue(v)	Returns true if this map contains one or more entries with the value v
entrySet()	Returns the entry set view of this map
get(k)	Returns the value to which this map maps the key k
isEmpty()	Returns true if this map contains no entries (i.e., key-value pairs)
keySet()	Returns the key set view of this map
put(k, v)	Maps the key k to the value v in this map
putAll(m)	Copies all the entries from map m to this map
remove(k)	Removes the entry for key k from this map if present
size()	Returns the number of entries (i.e., key-value pairs) in this map
values()	Returns the value collection view of this map

supported by maps. Maps are not sets, but they can be viewed as sets if so desired. The Map interface provides the following views of maps:

- *The entry set view:* The set of all the entries (i.e., key-value pairs) of the map.
- *The key set view:* The set of all the keys contained in the map. It is a set because keys are unique.
- *The value collection view:* The collection of all the values contained in the map. It is a collection rather than a set because different keys can be mapped to the same value, in which case the value occurs multiple times in the value collection.

The methods of the Map interface are summarized in Table 8.4. In these methods, parameter k is of type Object and represents a key, parameter v is also of type Object and represents a value, and parameter m is of type Map.

The keys and values of a map can be of any reference type. Here is an example of using maps:

```
Map map = new HashMap();    // HashMap is class that implements Map
map.put("a", "X");          // the map is { a -> X }
map.put("b", "Y");          // the map is { a -> X, b -> Y }
map.put("c", "X");          // the map is { a -> X, b -> Y, c -> X }
```

```
map.put("a", "Z");                // the map is { a -> Z, b -> Y, c -> X }
Object val = map.get("a"); // val is "Z"
map.remove("a");                  // the map is { b -> Y, c -> X }
```

The SortedMap interface extends the Map interface. We discuss it in Section 8.2.5 [p. 324].

8.2.3 Implementations of Collections

Each of the abstract collections can be implemented with various data structures and algorithms. An implementation of the abstract collections is called a *concrete collection*. The implementations may vary in many respects, including the following:

- Whether the collection is *bounded* (i.e., has a fixed maximum size) or is *unbounded* (i.e., may grow and shrink dynamically as needed).
- The time and space complexity of various operations, such as searching, insertion, deletion, and iteration.

Common data structures used to implement the abstract collections include arrays, linked lists, trees, and hash tables.

Each concrete collection is a class that implements the interface of an abstract collection. This characteristic makes different implementations of the same abstract collection interchangeable. For example, an array implementation of a list can be switched to a linked list implementation without affecting the clients. The concrete collections supported by the collections framework are summarized in Table 8.5. All these concrete collections support unbounded collections. The collections can grow and shrink dynamically as needed.

Choosing Implementations of Collections

Implementations for Set   Three different implementations of the Set interface are provided:

- The HashSet implementation stores the elements in a hash table. The HashSet implementation is very efficient in insertion (add()) and membership checking (contains()). The time complexity of these operations is $O(1)$. However, the HashSet implementation does not maintain any particular order among the elements. The iteration order is unpredictable and determined by the hash function of the elements.
- The LinkedHashSet implementation is very similar to the HashSet implementation, except the iteration order is predictable and usually is the insertion order.
- The TreeSet implementation stores the elements in a red-black tree, a form of balanced binary tree. The TreeSet class implements the SortedSet interface. The elements are ordered based on either their natural order or a user-defined order (see Section 8.2.5 [p. 324]). The TreeSet implementation is less efficient than the HashSet implementation in insertion and membership checking. The time complexity of these operations is $O(\log n)$, where n is the size of the set.

TABLE 8.5

Concrete Collections

Concrete Collection	Interface Implemented	Data Structure/ Description
HashSet	Set	Hash table
LinkedHashSet	Set	Hash table and doubly linked list Ensures predictable iteration order
TreeSet	SortedSet	Balanced binary tree Ensures elements are in ascending order
ArrayList	List	Resizable array
LinkedList	List	Doubly linked list
Vector	List	Resizable array Supports legacy methods that are available since JDK 1.0
HashMap	Map	Hash table
IdentityHashMap	Map	Hash table Comparison on keys is based on identity not equality
LinkedHashMap	Map	Hash table Ensures predictable iteration order
TreeMap	SortedMap	Balanced binary tree Ensures entries are in ascending key order
Hashtable	Map	Hash table Supports legacy methods that are available since JDK 1.0

When choosing a concrete set implementation, if the elements should maintain a certain order, then the TreeSet should be used. Otherwise, HashSet should be used for the sake of efficiency.

The HashSet implementation requires that the equals() and hashCode() methods be defined properly in the class of the elements.

Implementations for List   Two different implementations of the List interface are provided. The ArrayList implementation uses an array to store the elements, whereas `LinkedList` implementation uses a doubly linked list to store the elements. The main differences are as follows:

- The `ArrayList` uses an array that is large enough to store all the elements. Often, a large portion of the array is unused. The `LinkedList` wastes no space.

- The `ArrayList` incurs a significant penalty of performance when the size of the list exceeds the size of the array, in which case a new larger array must be allocated and all the elements copied to the new array. The `LinkedList` incurs no extra penalty on performance when the list grows.

- The `ArrayList` is more efficient than the `LinkedList` for methods involving indices, such as `get()` and `set()` methods. The time complexity of these operations is $O(1)$ for `ArrayList` and $O(n)$ for `LinkedList`, where n is the size of the list.

The `Vector` implementation is the same as the `ArrayList` implementation. The main difference is that the `Vector` class supports additional "legacy methods" that predate the collection framework. The `Vector` class is also thread-safe; i.e., its objects are always well behaved even in the presence of multiple threads manipulating the same object (see discussion in Chapter 11). As a consequence, the `Vector` implementation incurs a significant overhead in performance. When you are choosing a concrete list implementation, the volatility of the list is the main factor. The `LinkedList` implementation is more suitable for volatile lists (i.e., lists that grow and shrink a lot). The `ArrayList` is more efficient for relatively stable lists.

Implementations for Map   Four different implementations of the Map interface are provided:

- The `HashMap` implementation stores the entries in a hash table. The `HashMap` implementation is very efficient in insertion (`put()`) and mapping (`get()`). The time complexity of these operations is $O(1)$. However, the `HashSet` implementation does not maintain any particular order among the entries. The iteration order is unpredictable and determined by the hash function of the keys.

- The `LinkedHashMap` implementation is very similar to the `HashMap` implementation, except the iteration order is predictable and usually is the insertion order.

- The `IdentityHashMap` implementation is also very similar to the `HashMap` implementation, except that the comparison on keys is based on reference identity not object equality. This fact makes the implementation more efficient than the `HashMap` implementation, when it is appropriate to use identity comparison instead of equality comparison.

- The `TreeMap` implementation stores the entries in a red-black tree. The `TreeMap` class implements the `SortedMap` interface. The entries are ordered based on either the natural order or a user-defined order of the keys (see Section 8.2.5 [p. 324]). The `TreeMap` implementation is less efficient than the `HashMap` implementation insertion and mapping. The time complexity of these operations is $O(\log n)$, where n is the size of the set.

When choosing a concrete map implementation, if the entries should maintain a certain order according to their keys, then the `TreeMap` should be used. Otherwise, the `HashMap` should be used for the sake of efficiency. The `HashMap` implementation requires that the `equals()` and `hashCode()` methods be defined properly in the class of the keys.

The `Hashtable` class is implemented the same way as the `HashMap` class. The main difference is that the `Hashtable` class supports additional "legacy methods" that predate the collection framework. Similar to the `Vector` class, the `Hashtable` class is also thread-safe. As a consequence, the `Hashtable` implementation incurs a significant overhead in performance.

EXAMPLE 8.1   Count the Number of Different Words

PURPOSE
This example demonstrates the use of a set.

DESCRIPTION
This program reads a piece of text as input. It counts the total number of words and the number of different words in the text input.

SOLUTION
This example is an extension of the program `Words` in Example 4.7 [p. 127]. In `Words`, we break the text input into words. In this example, we first add a simple counter to count the total number of words in the text input. If a word occurs multiple times, it will be counted multiple times. To count the number of different words in the text input, we must remember the words that have already occurred. A set serves this purpose well. We use a `HashSet` to store the different words in the text input. Each word occurs only once in the set even if it occurs multiple times in the input text.

Class CountWords

```
import java.util.*;
import java.io.*;

public class CountWords {
    static public void main(String[] args) {
        Set words = new HashSet();
        BufferedReader in = new BufferedReader(
                        new InputStreamReader(System.in));
        String delim = " \t\n.,:;?!-/()[]\"\'";
        String line;
        int count = 0;
        try {
            while ((line = in.readLine()) != null) {
                StringTokenizer st = new StringTokenizer(line, delim);
```

```
                while (st.hasMoreTokens()) {
                    count++;
                    words.add(st.nextToken().toLowerCase());
                }
            }
        } catch (IOException e) {
            e.printStackTrace();
        }
        System.out.println("Total number of words: " + count);
        System.out.println("Number of different words: " +
                        words.size());
    }
}
```

Using President Lincoln's *Gettysburg Address* as the input, we have the following output:

```
Total number of words: 270
Number of different words: 140
```

8.2.4   Iterators of Collections

The Iterator pattern is used to provide a uniform way to iterate through different concrete collections (i.e., polymorphic iteration). Two iterator interfaces are defined: Iterator and ListIterator. Instances of Iterator support traversal of collections in one direction (forward), and instances of ListIterator support traversal of lists in forward and backward directions. The methods of the Iterator interface are summarized in Table 8.6.

TABLE 8.6

Methods of Interface Iterator

Method	Description
hasNext()	Returns true if the iteration has more elements
next()	Returns the next element in the iteration
remove()	Removes the last element returned by the iterator from the underlying collection

The return type of next() is Object. Usually, the elements returned by the iterator must be downcast to their actual classes before they can be manipulated. Here is an example of iterating through a set:

```
Iterator iter = set.iterator();
while (iter.hasNext()) {
    // assume the elements are strings
    String s = (String) iter.next();
    // . . .
}
```

The ListIterator interface extends the Iterator interface. The methods of the ListIterator interface are summarized in Table 8.7. In these methods, parameter o is of type Object.

Iterations on all collections are done uniformly using these two abstract iterator interfaces. Each concrete collection provides a concrete iterator that implements the Iterator interface. Furthermore, each concrete collection that implements the List interface provides a concrete list iterator that implements the ListIterator

TABLE 8.7

Methods of Interface ListIterator

Method	Description
add(o)	Inserts the element o into the list at the current position
hasNext()	Returns true if this list iterator has more elements when traversing the list in the forward direction
hasPrevious()	Returns true if this list iterator has more elements when traversing the list in the reverse direction
next()	Returns the next element in the list
nextIndex()	Returns the index of the element that would be returned by a subsequent call to next()
previous()	Returns the previous element in the list
previousIndex()	Returns the index of the element that would be returned by a subsequent call to previous()
remove()	Removes from the list the last element that was returned by next() or previous()
set(o)	Replaces the last element returned by next() or previous() with the element o

interface. Instances of concrete iterators are obtained through one of the following methods defined in the `Collection` and `List` interfaces, respectively:

- Defined in the `Collection` interface:

  ```
  Iterator iterator()
  ```

- Defined in the `List` interface:

  ```
  ListIterator listIterator()
  ```

Iterate through the Views of Maps

Usually, figuring out the classes of the elements in a collection is straightforward. In the case of views created by maps, the classes of the elements in these views are the following:

View	Type of Elements
Key set	The class of keys
Value collection	The class of values
Entry set	`Map.Entry`

Here is an example of iterating through the key set view of a map:

```
Set keys = map.keySet();
Iterator iter = keys.iterator();
while (iter.hasNext()) {
    // assume the keys are strings
    String key = (String) iter.next();
    // ...
}
```

The interface `Map.Entry` is defined inside the `Map` interface as a nested interface. The elements in the entry set view of maps are instances of `Map.Entry`. The methods of the `Map.Entry` interface are summarized in the following table. In these methods, parameter v is of type `Object` and represents a value in a key-value pair.

Method	Description
`getKey()`	Returns the key corresponding to this entry
`getValue()`	Returns the value corresponding to this entry
`setValue(v)`	Replaces the value corresponding to this entry with the value v

Here is an example of iterating through the entry set view of a map:

```
Set entries = map.entrySet();
Iterator iter = entries.iterator();
while (iter.hasNext()) {
    Map.Entry entry = (Map.Entry) iter.next();
    // assume the keys and values are strings
    String key = (String) entry.getKey();
    String value = (String) entry.getValue();
    // . . .
}
```

EXAMPLE 8.2   Count the Number of Occurrences of Each Word

PURPOSE

This example demonstrates iterating through the entry set of a map.

DESCRIPTION

This program reads a piece of text as input. It counts the number of occurrences of each word in the text input.

SOLUTION

In order to count the number of occurrences of each word, we need a map that maps each word to the number of its occurrences. To print out the result, we first obtain the entry set view of the map. We then iterate through the entry set and print out each entry.

The values in the map are instances of the following classes:

Class Count

```
public class Count {
    public Count(String word, int i) {
        this.word = word;
        this.i = i;
    }

    public String word;
    public int i;
}
```

Class WordFrequency

```
import java.util.*;
import java.io.*;

public class WordFrequency {
    static public void main(String[]args) {
        Map words = new HashMap();
```

```
String delim = " \t\n.,:;?!-/()[]\"\'";
BufferedReader in = new BufferedReader(
                    new InputStreamReader(System.in));
String line, word;
Count count;
try {
    while ((line = in.readLine()) != null) {
        StringTokenizer st = new StringTokenizer(line, delim);
        while (st.hasMoreTokens()) {
            word = st.nextToken().toLowerCase();
            count = (Count) words.get(word);
            if (count == null) {
                words.put(word, new Count(word, 1));
            } else {
                count.i++;
            }
        }
    }
} catch (IOException e) {
  e.printStackTrace();
}

Set set = words.entrySet();
Iterator iter = set.iterator();
while (iter.hasNext()) {
    Map.Entry entry = (Map.Entry) iter.next();
    word = (String) entry.getKey();
    count = (Count) entry.getValue();
    System.out.println(word +
                    (word.length() < 8 ? "\t\t" : "\t") +
                    count.i);
}
        }
    }
}
```

Using President Lincoln's *Gettysburg Address* as the input, we have the following output:

```
devotion    2           . . .
years       1       men         2
civil       1       remember    1
place       1       who         3
gave        2       did         1
they        3       work        1
struggled   1       rather      2
. . .               fathers     1
```

Note that the words in the output are not in any particular order.

8.2.5 Ordering and Sorting

An *order*, more precisely a *partial order*, is a binary relation between two objects that is transitive. Let $\prec$ denote a partial order; then, for any three objects a, b, and c, $a \prec b$ and $b \prec c$ implies $a \prec c$. If a partial order ensures that for any two objects a and b, $a \prec b$ and $b \prec a$ implies $a = b$, then it is called a *total order*. A partial order that is not a total order is called a *strictly partial order*. A *sorted collection* is one that orders its elements according to a certain order. *Sorting* arranges the elements of a collection so that they are ordered according to a certain order.

There are two ways to define orders on objects:

1. Each class can define a *natural order* among its instances by implementing the Comparable interface.
2. Arbitrary orders among different objects can be defined by *comparators*, or classes that implement the Comparator interface.

Defining Natural Orders

The natural order of a class can be defined by implementing the Comparable interface and providing an implementation for the only method compareTo() declared in the interface. The Comparable interface is defined as follows:

```
public interface Comparable {
    public int compareTo(Object o);
}
```

The compareTo() method compares the receiving object this with the parameter o. The result of the comparison is an integer. The contract of the method is

Result < 0, if this precedes o;
Result 0, if neither this precedes o, nor o precedes this; or
Result > 0, if o precedes this.

The compareTo() method must properly define a total order. For any two objects a and b,

a.compareTo $(b) > 0$ implies that b.compareTo $(a) < 0$,
a.compareTo $(b) < 0$ implies that b.compareTo $(a) > 0$, and
a.compareTo $(b) = 0$ implies that b.compareTo $(a) = 0$.

Also, the definition of the compareTo() method must be consistent with the definition of the equals() method. For any two objects a and b,

a.equals (b) is true if and only if a.compareTo (b) is 0.

The natural order of many classes in JDK, such as String, is already defined.

Defining User-Defined Orders

User-defined orders among objects can be defined using *comparators*. User-defined orders can be used to sort collections with elements for which no natural order is defined, or to sort the elements in an order different from the natural order of the elements. A comparator implements the Comparator interface and provides an implementation for the only method, compare(), declared in the interface. The Comparator interface is defined as follows:

```
public interface Comparator {
    int compare(Object o1, Object o2);
}
```

The compare() method compares the two parameters. The result of the comparison is an integer. The contract of the method is

Result < 0,   if o1 precedes o2;

Result 0,   if neither o1 precedes o2, nor o2 precedes o1; or

Result > 0,   if o2 precedes o1.

Similar to the preceding compareTo() method, the compare() method must properly define a total order. For any two objects a and b, and a comparator c,

c.compare $(a, b) > 0$ implies that c.compare $(b, a) < 0$;

c.compare $(a, b) < 0$ implies that c.compare $(b, a) > 0$; and

c.compare $(a, b) = 0$ implies that c.compare $(b, a) = 0$.

Also, the definition of the compare() method must be consistent with the definition of the equals() method in the class of objects being compared. For any two objects a and b, and a comparator c,

c.compare (a, b) is 0 if and only if both a.equals (b) and b.equals (a) are true;

a.equals (b) is true implies c.compare (a, b) is 0; and

c.compare $(a, b) > 0$ implies c.compare $(b, a) < 0$, and c.compare $(a, b) < 0$ implies c.compare $(b, a) > 0$.

Sorted Collections

There are two sorted abstract collections: SortedSet and SortedMap. The SortedSet interface extends the Set interface. All the methods of the Set interface are inherited. The new methods in the SortedSet interfaces are summarized in the following table. The parameters of the methods, o, o1, and o2, are all Objects representing elements.

Method	Description
comparator()	Returns the comparator associated with this sorted set, or null if the natural order is used
first()	Returns the first (lowest) element currently in this sorted set
headSet(o)	Returns a set view of the portion of this sorted set whose elements are strictly less than o
last()	Returns the last (highest) element currently in this sorted set
subSet(o1, o2)	Returns a set view of the portion of this sorted set whose elements range from o1, inclusive, to o2, exclusive
tailSet(o)	Returns a set view of the portion of this sorted set whose elements are greater than or equal to o

The SortedMap interface extends the Map interface. All the methods of the Map interface are inherited. The new methods in the SortedMap interface are summarized in the following table. The parameters of the methods, k, k1, and k2, are all of type Object representing keys.

Method	Description
comparator()	Returns the comparator associated with this sorted map, or null if the natural order is used
firstKey()	Returns the first (lowest) key currently in this sorted map
headMap(k)	Returns a map view of the portion of this sorted map whose keys are strictly less than k
lastKey()	Returns the last (highest) key currently in this sorted map
subMap(k1, k2)	Returns a map view of the portion of this sorted map whose keys range from k1, inclusive, to k2, exclusive
tailMap(k)	Returns a map view of the portion of this sorted map whose keys are greater than or equal to k

A concrete sorted collection *SC* that implements the SortedSet or SortedMap interface provides at least two constructors:

- *SC*() creates a sorted collection that is sorted according to the natural order of the elements.
- *SC*(Comparator c) creates a sorted collection that is sorted according to the order defined by the specified comparator.

EXAMPLE 8.3   List Word Count in Alphabetical Order

PURPOSE

This example demonstrates the use of a sorted map ordered according to the natural order of its keys.

DESCRIPTION

This program reads a piece of text as input. It counts the number of occurrences of each word in the text input and prints out the results as a list sorted according to the alphabetical order of the words.

SOLUTION

This is a variation of Example 8.2 [p. 322]. The words are the keys of the map, and the alphabetical order of words is the natural order of `String`. So we can simply use a `TreeMap`, which by default maintains its entries according to the natural order of its keys.

Class WordFrequency2

```
import java.util.*;
import java.io.*;

public class WordFrequency2 {
    static public void main(String[] args) {
        Map words = new TreeMap();
        String delim = " \t\n.,:;?!-/()[]\"\'";
        BufferedReader in = new BufferedReader(
                            new InputStreamReader(System.in));
        String line, word;
        Count count;
        try {
            while ((line = in.readLine()) != null) {
                StringTokenizer st = new StringTokenizer(line, delim);
                while (st.hasMoreTokens()) {
                    word = st.nextToken().toLowerCase();
                    if (words.containsKey(word)) {
                        count = (Count) words.get(word);
                        count.i++;
                    } else {
                        words.put(word, new Count(word, 1));
                    }
                }
            }
        } catch (IOException e) {
            e.printStackTrace();
        }
        Set set = words.entrySet();
        Iterator iter = set.iterator();
```

```
            while (iter.hasNext()) {
                Map.Entry entry = (Map.Entry) iter.next();
                word = (String) entry.getKey();
                count = (Count) entry.getValue();
                System.out.println(word +
                                (word.length() < 8 ? "\t\t" : "\t") +
                                count.i);
            }
        }
    }
```

Note that the class WordFrequency2 is nearly identical to class WordFre-quency in Example 8.2 [p. 322]; the exception is the line in boldface, where the TreeMap implementation is used instead of the HashMap implementation. Using President Lincoln's *Gettysburg Address* as the input, we have the following output:

```
a          7        . . .
above      1        whether   1
add        1        which     2
address    1        who       3
advanced   1        will      1
ago        1        work      1
all        1        world     1
. . .               years     1
```

EXAMPLE 8.4   List Word Count in Reverse Alphabetical Order

PURPOSE

This example demonstrates the use of a sorted map ordered according to a user-defined order on the keys.

DESCRIPTION

This program reads a piece of text as input. It counts the number of occurrences of each word in the text input and prints out the results as a list sorted according to the reverse alphabetical order of the words.

SOLUTION

This is another variation of Example 8.2 [p. 322]. To sort the entries according to an order other than the natural order of the keys, we need to define a user-defined order. An instance of TreeMap can be instantiated by specifying the user-defined comparator in the constructor.

The following program contains the comparator for the reverse alphabetical order of strings. To obtain the reverse alphabetical order, we simply negate the sign of the result of the compareTo() method of the String class.

Comparator for reverse alphabetical order: `StringComparator`

```java
public class StringComparator implements Comparator {
   public int compare(Object o1, Object o2) {
      if (o1 != null &&
          o2 != null &&
          o1 instanceof String &&
          o2 instanceof String) {
        String s1 = (String) o1;
        String s2 = (String) o2;
        return - (s1.compareTo(s2));

      } else {
        return 0;
      }
   }
}
```

Class `WordFrequency3`

```java
import java.util.*;
import java.io.*;

public class WordFrequency3 {
   static public void main(String[] args) {
      Map words = new TreeMap(new StringComparator());
      String delim = " \t\n.,:;?!-/()[]\"\'";
      BufferedReader in = new BufferedReader(
                       new InputStreamReader(System.in));
      String line, word;
      Count count;
      try {
        while ((line = in.readLine()) != null) {
          StringTokenizer st = new StringTokenizer(line, delim);
          while (st.hasMoreTokens()) {
            word = st.nextToken().toLowerCase();
            if (words.containsKey(word)) {
              count = (Count) words.get(word);
              count.i++;
            } else {
              words.put(word, new Count(word, 1));
            }
          }
        }
      } catch (IOException e) {
        e.printStackTrace();
      }

      Set set = words.entries();
      Iterator iter = set.iterator();
      while (iter.hasNext()) {
        Map.Entry entry = (Map.Entry) iter.next();
        word = (String) entry.getKey();
```

```
                       count = (Count) entry.getValue();
                       System.out.println(word +
                                        (word.length() < 8 ? "\t\t" : "\t") +
                                        count.i);
                 }
             }
         }
```

Again, note that the class WordFrequency3 is also nearly identical to class WordFrequency in Example 8.2 [p. 322]; the exception is the line in boldface, where a user-defined comparator is provided as the parameter of the constructor of the TreeMap. Using President Lincoln's *Gettysburg Address* as the input, we obtain the following output:

```
    years      1        . . .
    world      1        all        1
    work       1        ago        1
    will       1        advanced   1
    who        3        address    1
    which      2        add        1
    whether    1        above      1
    . . .               a          7
```

Utilities on Collections

Besides the sorted collections, the collection framework also provides a set of useful utilities and algorithms related to ordering and sorting. They are provided as static methods of the Collections class. These methods are summarized in Table 8.8. Parameter 1 is of type List, parameter c is of type Collection, parameter k is of type Object, and parameter comp is of type Comparator.

EXAMPLE 8.5   List Word Count in the Order of Frequency

PURPOSE

This example demonstrates the use of sorting utilities to sort collections according to user-defined orders.

DESCRIPTION

This program reads a piece of text as input. It counts the number of occurrences of each word in the text input and prints out the results as a list sorted by the frequencies of occurrences of the words.

SOLUTION

This is another variation of Example 8.2 [p. 322]. In this case, the desired order is not based on keys but on values, so sorted maps offer no help. We use a HashMap to store the word counts. After all the words have been counted, we obtain a collection view of the values contained in the map and then sort the value collection according to a user-defined comparator CountComparator.

The comparator is used to sort the frequency list.

TABLE 8.8

Utility Methods of the Collections Class

Method	Description
sort(l)	Sorts the list l according to the natural order of the elements
sort(l, comp)	Sorts the list l according to the order defined by the comparator comp
binarySearch(l, k)	Searches for the element k in the list l, using the binary search algorithm. The list l is sorted according to the natural order of the elements. The return value is the index of element k if it is present in the list, or (*insertion point*) − 1. The insertion point is the index at which the element should be inserted.
binarySearch(l, k, comp)	Same as preceding, except that the list l is sorted according to the order defined by the comparator comp
min(c)	Returns the minimum element in the collection c according to the natural order of the elements in the collection
min(c, comp)	Returns the minimum element in the collection c according to the order defined by the comparator comp
max(c)	Returns the maximum element in the collection c according to the natural order of the elements in the collection
max(c, comp)	Returns the maximum element in the collection c according to the order defined by the comparator comp

Comparator for word count: CountComparator

```
public class CountComparator implements Comparator {
    public int compare(Object o1, Object o2) {
        if (o1 != null &&
            o2 != null &&
            o1 instanceof Count &&
            o2 instanceof Count) {
            Count c1 = (Count) o1;
            Count c2 = (Count) o2;
            return (c2.i - c1.i);
        } else {
            return 0;
        }
    }
}
```

Class WordFrequency4

```java
import java.util.*;
import java.io.*;

public class WordFrequency4 {
    static public void main(String[] args) {
        Map words = new HashMap();
        String delim = " \t\n.,:;?!-/()[]\"\'";
        BufferedReader in = new BufferedReader(
                        new InputStreamReader(System.in));
        String line, word;
        Count count;
        try {
            while ((line = in.readLine()) != null) {
                StringTokenizer st = new StringTokenizer(line, delim);
                while (st.hasMoreTokens()) {
                    word = st.nextToken().toLowerCase();
                    count = (Count) words.get(word);
                    if (count == null) {
                        words.put(word, new Count(word, 1));
                    } else {
                        count.i++;
                    }
                }
            }
        } catch (IOException e) {
            e.printStackTrace();
        }
        List list = new ArrayList(words.values());
        Collections.sort(list, new CountComparator());
        Iterator iter = list.iterator();
        while (iter.hasNext()) {
            count = (Count) iter.next();
            word = count.word;
            System.out.println(word +
                        (word.length() < 8 ? "\t\t" : "\t") +
                        count.i);
        }
    }
}
```

Using President Lincoln's *Gettysburg Address* as the input, we have the following output:

the	13	. . .	
that	12	consecrate	1
we	10	world	1
here	8	consecrated	1
to	8	remember	1
a	7	did	1
and	6	work	1
. . .		fathers	1

8.3 THE GRAPHICAL USER INTERFACE FRAMEWORK—AWT AND SWING

Java provides an extensive framework for building high-quality graphical user interfaces (GUI). The graphical user interface framework is part of the *Java Foundation Classes* (JFC). We focus on two important packages in the JFC: the *Abstract Windows Toolkit* (AWT) and *Swing*.

The Java GUI framework consists of several categories of classes. The main categories are the following:

GUI components: Components, also known as widgets, are the building blocks of the visual aspect of graphical user interfaces. Each GUI component is characterized by its its visual appearance, the *look*, and its behavior pattern in response to user input, the *feel*. Each type of GUI component is defined by a GUI component class. Examples of the GUI component classes include `Button`, `Label`, `Checkbox`, `Scrollbar`, `Frame`, and `Dialog`.

Layout managers: Layout managers define strategies for laying out GUI components in windows. Commonly used layout managers include `FlowLayout` and `BorderLayout`.

Events and event listeners: Events represent user input or actions. Each event class represents a particular type of user input, such as the `KeyEvent` class for keyboard input and the `MouseEvent` class for mouse actions. Each event class is associated with an event listener class responsible for handling this type of event. For example, the `KeyListener` class is associated with the `KeyEvent` class, and the `MouseListener` class is associated with the `MouseEvent` class.

Graphics and imaging classes: These classes allow components to draw their visual appearances and include graphics (`Color`, `Font`, `Graphics`, etc.), geometry (`Point`, `Rectangle`, `Dimension`, etc.), and imaging (`Image`, `Icon`, etc.).

The Abstract Windows Toolkit (AWT) package provides the basic support for building graphical user interfaces. The Swing package is an extension of AWT, which provides extensive support for building sophisticated-looking and high-quality graphical user interfaces.

8.3.1 The GUI Components

The inheritance hierarchy of GUI component classes in AWT is shown in Figure 8.2. All classes shown in the class diagram belong to the package `java.awt`, except the `Applet` class, which belongs to package `java.applet`. All Java GUI component classes are subclasses of the `Component` class. The `Component` class is an abstract class that defines the characteristics and behaviors that are common to all the GUI

Figure 8.2

The GUI compo-
nent classes in
AWT.

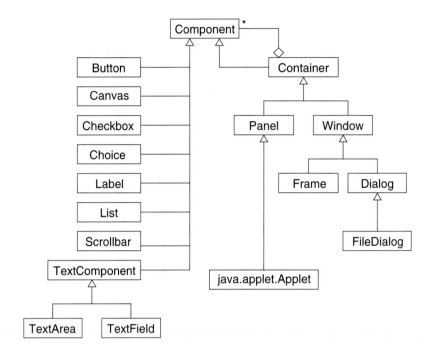

components. The subclasses of Component class are divided into two groups: *primitive components*, which do not contain other components, and *containers*, which may contain other primitive components and containers.

The Container class is an abstract class that defines the characteristics and behaviors common to all the containers. In Figure 8.2, the left branch of the Component class consists of the primitive components, and the right branch of the Component class consists of the containers. Using containers, we can construct graphical user interfaces by organizing components into tree structures, in which the primitive components are the leaves and the containers are the interior nodes. Furthermore, as both primitive components and containers are subclasses of the Component class, they can be treated uniformly.

The AWT and Swing Components

The primitive components and containers in AWT are summarized in Table 8.9.

The Swing package supports building high-quality graphical user interfaces. It is an extension of AWT and provides many more varieties of more sophisticated components than AWT. A major difference between the AWT components and the Swing components is that most of the Swing components are *lightweight*, whereas all the components in AWT are *heavyweight*. Heavyweight components are associated with *native* components created by the underlying window system, such as Win32 or X-Window. The native component associated with an AWT component is known

TABLE 8.9

Component and Container Classes in AWT

AWT Component	Description
Button	Text labeled "push" button that responds to mouse clicks
Canvas	Blank rectangular area of the screen onto which the application can draw or from which the application can trap input events from the user
Checkbox	A two-state component that can be either "on" (true) or "off" (false)
Choice	Pop-up menu of text choices from which the user can choose
Label	Component with a text that does not respond to any user input
List	Scrolling list of text items from which the user can choose
Scrollbar	Scroll bar
TextComponent	Superclass of any component that allows the editing of some text
TextField	Text component that allows for the editing of a single line of text
TextArea	Multiline region that displays text and allows editing of multiline text

AWT Container	Description
Dialog	Window that takes input from the user
FileDialog	Dialog window from which the user can select a file
Frame	Top-level window with a title and a border
Panel	Borderless, titleless, and transparent container
Window	Borderless and titleless top-level window

as its *peer* component. The appearance of the AWT component is determined by its peer component and is thus platform dependent. In other words, a GUI application written in Java with AWT can run on different platforms with the same behavior but different looks. Lightweight components have no peers. Their looks are determined by the Java run-time environment, not the underlying window system. Lightweight components eliminate the overhead associated with peer components and ensure that GUI applications written in Java will not only run on different platforms with the same behavior, but also have the same look. Furthermore, lightweight components emulate the looks of various window systems regardless of the underlying window

Figure 8.3

Swing counterparts
of AWT compo-
nents.

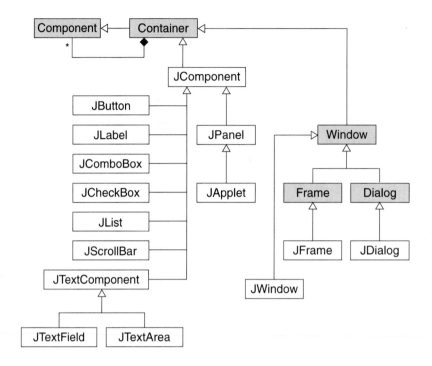

system. For example, a Java GUI application using Swing can have a Motif look even when it is running on a Win32 platform. This capability is known as the *pluggable* look and feel.

The Swing package consists of several hundred classes and numerous subpackages, of which we cover only a few. The most straightforward part of Swing consists of classes with counterparts in AWT. These classes are shown in Figure 8.3, with the shaded boxes being classes in AWT. The names of Swing component classes begin with a prefix J followed by the name of their counterparts in AWT.[2] The subclasses of JComponent represent lightweight components. Note that JWindow, JFrame, and JDialog are not lightweight components. The differences between these Swing components and their AWT counterparts are summarized in Table 8.10.

8.3.2   Design Pattern: Composite

The design of the GUI components hierarchy illustrates a commonly used design pattern: the Composite pattern.

---

2. There are some exceptions to this naming convention.

TABLE 8.10

Component and Container Classes in Swing

Swing Component	Description
JButton	Allows an image icon and a text label; supports keyboard accelerators
JCheckBox	Allows user-defined icons for the on and off states
JComboBox	An extension of Choice. The items are not limited to text. They can be icons or components. The choices can be editable.
JLabel	Allows an image icon and a text label
JList	The items are not limited to text. They can be icons or components.
JScrollbar	Lightweight scroll bar
JTextComponent	Superclass of lightweight components for text editing
JTextField	Lightweight single-line text component; supports multilingual text displaying and editing
JTextArea	Lightweight multiline text component; supports multilingual text displaying and editing
JPanel	Lightweight container
JDialog	Dialog tailored for lightweight components
JFrame	Frame tailored for lightweight components
JWindow	Window tailored for lightweight components

Design Pattern *Composite*

Category: Structural design pattern.

Intent: Compose objects into tree structures to represent a part-whole hierarchy. Composite lets clients treat individual objects and composite objects uniformly.

Applicability: Use the Composite pattern

- when you want to represent a part-whole hierarchy of objects.
- when you want clients to be able to ignore the difference between composite objects and individual objects (clients will treat all objects in the composite structure uniformly).

The structure of the Composite design pattern is shown in the following diagram:

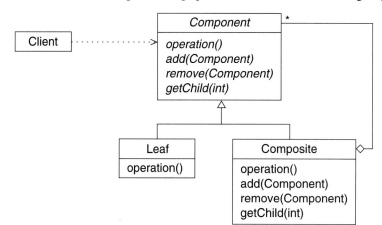

The participants of the Composite design pattern are the following:

- *Component* (e.g., `Component`), which declares the common interface for all classes in the composite; implements default behavior common to all classes, as appropriate; and (optionally) defines an interface for accessing a component's parent in the hierarchy.
- *Leaf* (e.g., `Button`, `Label`, and `Checkbox`), which defines behavior for primitive objects in the composition.
- *Composite* (e.g., `Container` and `Panel`), which declares an interface for accessing and managing its child components, defines behavior for components having children, stores child components, and implements child-related operations in the `Component` interface.
- *Client*, which manipulates objects in the composition through the `Component` interface.

8.3.3 Layout Managers

Each container has a *layout manager*, which handles the layout of the components contained in the container. Several layout managers are provided in the JDK, as illustrated in Figure 8.4. Each layout manager defines a layout strategy. One of the advantages of using layout managers is that we do not have to specify the absolute coordinates and dimensions of each component. The components in the container are displayed based on their *relative positions*. The relative positions of components can be specified explicitly with *positional constraints* or implicitly by the order in which they are inserted in the container. The positions and sizes of the components are computed by the layout manager based on the dimensions of the container and automatically adjusted whenever the dimensions of the container change, which is usually caused by resizing the top-level window.

Figure 8.4

The layout managers.

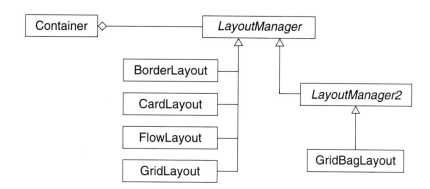

We discuss and illustrate the use of several commonly used layout managers: FlowLayout, GridLayout, and BorderLayout. We also demonstrate how to do customized layout without using the layout managers.

Using Layout Managers

The design of layout managers uses the Strategy design pattern, with each layout manager implemented as a strategy. Different layout managers can be used uniformly and interchangeably. The following methods of the Container class deal with the use of layout managers. In the parameters of the methods, lm represents a layout manager, comp represents a component, and cst represents a positional constraint.

Method	Description
setLayout(lm)	Sets lm as the layout manager of this container
add(comp)	Adds component comp to this container
add(comp, cst)	Adds component comp to this container with a positional constraint cst (e.g., the position key in BorderLayout)

Flow Layout

The flow layout is the most straightforward layout strategy. It arranges the components in a left-to-right flow, in the order in which they were inserted in the container. If the container is not wide enough for all the components, it breaks the flow into several lines. Each line is centered by default, and each component is sized to its *natural size*.

A flow layout manager can be created by using one of the following constructors of the `FlowLayout` class:

Constructor	Description
`FlowLayout(align, hGap, vGap)`	Creates a flow layout manager with the alignment set to `align` and the horizontal and vertical gaps set to `hGap` and `vGap`, respectively
`FlowLayout(align)`	Creates a flow layout manager with the alignment set to `align` and the horizontal and vertical gaps set to the default value
`FlowLayout()`	Creates a flow layout manager with the alignment and the horizontal and vertical gaps all set to their respective default values

The alignment of the flow layout can be one of the following:

`FlowLayout.LEFT`   The components are flush left.
`FlowLayout.CENTER`   The components are centered.
`FlowLayout.RIGHT`   The components are flush right.

The default alignment is centered. The horizontal and vertical gaps are the gaps between the adjacent components, specified in pixels. The defaults are 5 pixels for both the horizontal and vertical gaps.

EXAMPLE 8.6   Using Flow Layout

PURPOSE

This example demonstrates the use of the flow layout and the creation of buttons.

DESCRIPTION

The `Applet` class is a subclass of `Panel`, so the drawing area of an applet is actually a container. We can add any component to the panel. Here, we simply create and add six buttons to the panel. The results are shown in Figure 8.5. The layout shown in Figure 8.5(a) is the result of using the flow layout in a panel that is 400 pixels wide and 50 pixels high. The layout shown in Figure 8.5(b) is the result of using the same flow layout in a panel that is 100 pixels wide and 120 pixels high. Note the correspondence between the order of insertion and order of buttons in the layouts.

Figure 8.5

Flow layouts.

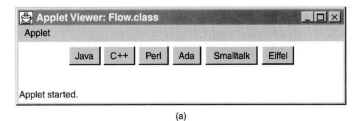

(a)

(b)

SOLUTION

A FlowLayout object is created first and is set as the layout manager of the container (i.e., the Panel object) using the setLayout() method of the Container class. A button can be created as follows:

```
new Button(label)
```

where *label* is the label of the button. Each button is added to the container using the add() method of the Container class. Since the order of the components in a flow layout is determined by the insertion order, no positional constraints are necessary for the add() method when using FlowLayout.

Flow layout applet: Flow

```java
import java.awt.*;
import java.applet.Applet;

public class Flow extends Applet {
    public Flow () {
        setLayout(new FlowLayout());
        add(new Button("Java"));
        add(new Button("C++"));
        add(new Button("Perl"));
        add(new Button("Ada"));
        add(new Button("Smalltalk"));
        add(new Button("Eiffel"));
    }
}
```

Grid Layout

The grid layout arranges components in a rectangular grid, and all components are given the same size. The components can be stretched vertically and horizontally, if necessary, to fill the entire space of the container. A grid layout manager can be created by using one of the following constructors of the GridLayout class:

Constructor	Description
GridLayout(r, c, hGap, vGap)	Creates a grid layout manager with r rows and c columns and with the horizontal and vertical gaps set to hGap and vGap, respectively
GridLayout(r, c)	Creates a grid layout manager with r rows and c columns and with the horizontal and vertical gaps set to 0
GridLayout()	Creates a grid layout manager with a single row and with the horizontal gap set to 0

When the first two constructors are used, r and c must be nonnegative integers. One of them, but not both, can be 0. If r is 0, the grid may have any number of rows, depending on the number of components in the container. Similarly, if c is 0, the grid may have any number of columns, also depending on the number of components in the container.

EXAMPLE 8.7   Using Grid Layout

PURPOSE

This example demonstrates the use of the grid layout.

DESCRIPTION

This program is similar to the one in Example 8.6. The main difference is that a grid layout manager is used here. The numbers of rows and columns of the grid are specified as the parameters of the applet.

Figure 8.6 shows the effects of grid layout in a panel with six buttons. The layout shown in Figure 8.6(a) is the result of specifying 1 row and 0 column, or (1, 0). The layout shown in Figure 8.6(b) is the result of specifying 3 rows and 2 columns, or (3, 2). The layout shown in Figure 8.6(c) is the result of specifying 0 row and 1 column, or (0, 1).

SOLUTION

First, the numbers of rows and columns of the grid are determined based on the values of two parameters specified in the <applet> tag: row and col. Second, a

Figure 8.6

Grid layouts.

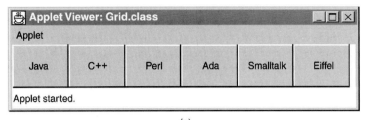

(a)

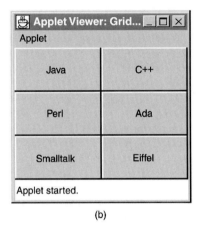

(b)

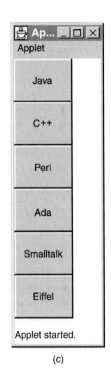

(c)

GridLayout object is created with the given number of rows and columns and is set as the layout manager of the container. Third, a number of buttons are inserted into the container. The position of components in a grid layout is also determined by the order of insertion, so no positional constraints are necessary for the add() method when using GridLayout.

Grid layout applet: Grid

```
import java.awt.*;
import java.applet.Applet;

public class Grid extends Applet {
   public void init () {
      int row = 0, col = 0;
```

```
            String att = getParameter("row");
            if (att != null)
                row = Integer.parseInt(att);
            att = getParameter("col");
            if (att != null)
                col = Integer.parseInt(att);
            if (row == 0 && col == 0) {
                row = 3; col = 2;
            }
            setLayout(new GridLayout(row, col));
            add(new Button("Java"));
            add(new Button("C++"));
            add(new Button("Perl"));
            add(new Button("Ada"));
            add(new Button("Smalltalk"));
            add(new Button("Eiffel"));
        }
    }
```

Border Layout

The border layout is one of the most versatile layout managers. It arranges as many as five components in five positions identified as *North*, *South*, *East*, *West*, and *Center*, as illustrated in Figure 8.7. The North and South components are placed at the top and bottom of the container, respectively. They are set to their natural heights and may be stretched horizontally to fill the entire width of the container. The East and West components are placed at the right and left sides of the container, respectively. They are set to their natural widths and may be stretched vertically to fill the space between the North and South components. The Center component may be stretched horizontally and vertically to fill the space left in the center. If one or more of the components, except the Center component, are absent, the remaining components will be stretched vertically and/or horizontally to fill the space left by the missing components. A border layout manager can be created by using one of the following constructors of the BorderLayout class:

Method	Description
BorderLayout(hGap, vGap)	Creates a border layout manager with the horizontal and vertical gaps set to hGap and vGap, respectively
BorderLayout()	Creates a border layout manager with the horizontal and vertical gaps set to 0

Figure 8.7

Border layout.

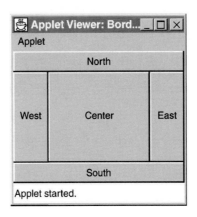

The components managed by a border layout manager should be inserted with one of the following positional constraints, which are symbolic constants defined in the BorderLayout class:

BorderLayout.NORTH   Places the component in the North position
BorderLayout.SOUTH   Places the component in the South position
BorderLayout.EAST   Places the component in the East position
BorderLayout.WEST   Places the component in the West position
BorderLayout.CENTER   Places the component in the Center position

EXAMPLE 8.8   Using Border Layout

PURPOSE

This example demonstrates the use of the border layout.

DESCRIPTION

This applet uses a border layout manager and simply inserts a button in each of the five positions.

SOLUTION

The buttons are inserted using the add() method with a positional constraint.

Border layout applet: Border

```
import java.awt.*;
import java.applet.Applet;

public class Border extends Applet {
    public Border () {
        setLayout(new BorderLayout());
```

```
                        add(new Button("North"),  BorderLayout.NORTH);
                        add(new Button("South"),  BorderLayout.SOUTH);
                        add(new Button("East"),   BorderLayout.EAST);
                        add(new Button("West"),   BorderLayout.WEST);
                        add(new Button("Center"), BorderLayout.CENTER);
                }
        }
```

EXAMPLE 8.9   Nested Border Layouts

PURPOSE

This example demonstrates the nesting of containers and creation of choices and labels.

DESCRIPTION

This applet yields the layout shown in Figure 8.8. The outer panel contains two nested panels and uses a border layout manager. Three buttons are inserted in the North, East, and West positions of the outer panel. The center position contains another panel, which also uses a border layout manager. A button is inserted in each of the five positions of the panel at the center. The South position of the outer panel contains yet another panel, which uses a flow layout manager. A button, a choice, and a label are inserted in the panel in the South position.

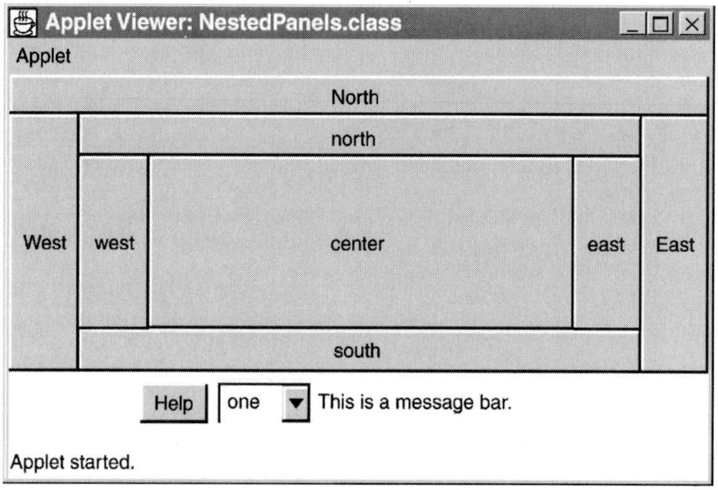

Figure 8.8

Nested border layout.

SOLUTION

Nested panel applet: `NestedPanels`

```java
import java.awt.*;
import java.applet.Applet;

public class NestedPanels extends Applet {

    public NestedPanels () {
        // set up the center panel
        Panel center = new Panel();
        center.setLayout(new BorderLayout());
        center.add(new Button("south"),  BorderLayout.SOUTH);
        center.add(new Button("north"),  BorderLayout.NORTH);
        center.add(new Button("east"),   BorderLayout.EAST);
        center.add(new Button("west"),   BorderLayout.WEST);
        center.add(new Button("center"), BorderLayout.CENTER);

        // set up the south panel
        Panel south = new Panel();
        south.setLayout(new FlowLayout());
        south.add(new Button("Help"));
        choice = new Choice();
        choice.addItem("one");
        choice.addItem("two");
        choice.addItem("three");
        choice.addItem("four");
        choice.addItem("five");
        south.add(choice);
        messageBar = new Label("This is a message bar.");
        south.add(messageBar);

        // set up the outer panel
        setLayout(new BorderLayout());
        add(new Button("North"), BorderLayout.NORTH);
        add(new Button("East"),  BorderLayout.EAST);
        add(new Button("West"),  BorderLayout.WEST);
        add(south, BorderLayout.SOUTH);
        add(center, BorderLayout.CENTER);
    }

    protected Label messageBar;
    protected Choice choice;
}
```

Other layout managers in JDK include the `GridBagLayout` and `CardLayout` in AWT and the `BoxLayout` in Swing. For details about the use of these layout managers see Chan and Lee [1998] and Walrath and Campione [1999].

8.3.4 Handling Events

GUI components communicate with the rest of the applications through *events*, which represent user inputs or actions. The *source* of an event is the component from which the event is originated. A *listener* of an event is an object that receives and processes the event. Events are classified into different types, each of which is represented by an event class, which is a subclass of `AWTEvent`. The class hierarchy of event classes is shown in Figure 8.9. Each type of event is associated with a listener interface, which is implemented by the listeners of that event type. The listener interfaces and their associations with event classes are also shown in Figure 8.9. Listeners must be registered to their respective sources before they can receive events from their sources.

Event handling in Java programs involves the following steps:

- Determine the types of events to be handled and their associated listener interfaces. For example, to handle button clicks, the event class is the `ActionEvent` and the associated listener interface is `ActionListener`.
- Define listener classes that implement the listener interfaces and implement all the methods of the interfaces. For example, to handle button clicks, the listener class must implement the `ActionListener` interface.

```java
class MyButtonHandler implements ActionListener {
    public void actionPerformed(ActionEvent event) {
        //... handle button click
    }
}
```

Naming Convention *Events and Listeners*

The following conventions are used throughout AWT and Swing:

- The names of event classes end with the suffix `Event`.
- For event class *Xyz*`Event`, the associated listener interface is usually named *Xyz*`Listener`. If there is also an associated adapter class, it will be named *Xyz*`Adapter`.
- For a listener that implements interface *Xyz*`Listener`, the name of the method to register the listener to its source is add*Xyz*`Listener`.

- Create instances of the components, which are the sources of the events. For example,

```java
Button button1 = new Button("One");
```

Figure 8.9

The event classes and listeners.

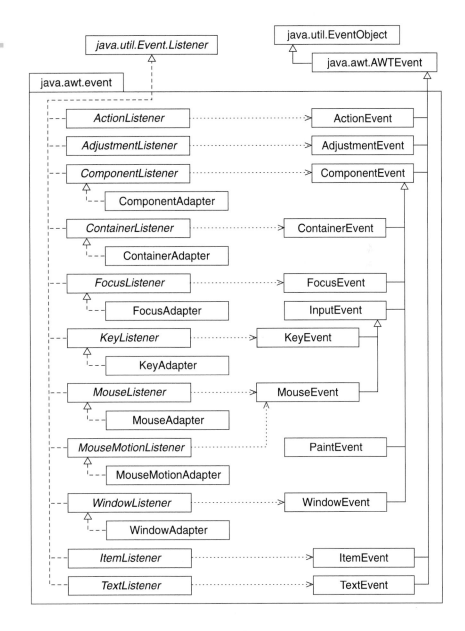

- Create instances of the listeners, and register the listeners to their sources. For example, to handle button clicks using MyButtonHandler use

```
MyButtonHandler handler = new MyButtonHandler();
button1.addActionListener(handler);
```

A listener may listen to several sources, and a source can have multiple listeners. Continuing with the preceding example, we can create another button, button2, and let the listener handler handle clicks on both buttons:

```
Button button2 = new Button("Two");
button2.addActionListener(handler);
```

A listener may also listen to different types of events by simply implementing multiple listener interfaces.

Event *adapters* are classes that implement listener interfaces and provide null implementations for all the methods. They are provided for listener interfaces with more than one method, for the sake of convenience. A listener class may implement the appropriate listener interface or extend the corresponding event adapter. The difference is that implementing a listener interface requires all methods declared in the interface to be implemented in the listener class, while extending the event adapter saves the effort of implementing methods of no interest in a particular context.

The event-handling process can roughly be described as follows:

1. When an event is triggered, the Java run time first determines its source and type.
2. If a listener for this type of event is registered with the source, then an event object is created.
3. For each listener that listens to this type of event, the Java run time invokes the appropriate event-handling method of the listener and passes the event object as the parameter.

The interaction among the source, its listeners, and the event objects is shown in Figure 8.10.

Figure 8.10

The event handling.

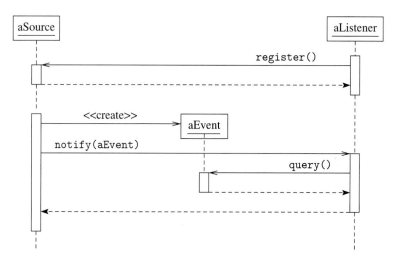

EXAMPLE 8.10 Handling Events

PURPOSE

This example demonstrates event handling.

DESCRIPTION

This program extends the `NestedPanel` class presented in Example 8.9 by adding event handling. When one of the buttons is clicked or one of the items in the choice is selected, a message is displayed in the message bar, which is a label. The class `NestedPanels2` listens for both types of events and listens to all the buttons and the choice contained in the nested panel.

SOLUTION

The event class for button click is `ActionEvent`, and the associated listener interface is `ActionListener`. The event class for choice item selection is `ItemEvent`, and the associated listener interface is `ItemListener`.

Nested panels applet with event handling: `NestedPanels2`

```
import java.awt.*;
import java.awt.event.*;

public class NestedPanels2 extends NestedPanels
        implements ActionListener, ItemListener {
    public NestedPanels2() {
        super(); // create all the components
        choice.addItemListener(this); // register item listener
        registerButtonHandler(this); // register action listener
    }

    (Event handling methods on page 351)
    (Method registerButtonHandler() on page 352)
}
```

The method `itemStateChanged()` is declared in the `ItemListener` interface for handling choice item selections. The method `actionPerformed()` is declared in the `ActionListener` interface for handling button clicks.

Event handling methods of class `NestedPanels2`

```
public void itemStateChanged(ItemEvent event) {
    if (event.getStateChange() == ItemEvent.SELECTED) {
        messageBar.setText("Choice selected: " + event.getItem());
    }
}

public void actionPerformed(ActionEvent event) {
    Button source = (Button) event.getSource();
    messageBar.setText("Button pushed: " + source.getLabel());
}
```

The registerButtonHandler() method registers this object to all the buttons contained in the component comp. If comp is a container, it recursively registers this object to all the components contained in the container. This method is invoked in the constructor of the NestedPanels2 class [p. 351] with the top-level panel as the argument.

Method of class NestedPanels2: registerButtonHandler

```
protected void registerButtonHandler(Component comp) {
    if (comp != null) {
        if (comp instanceof Button) {
            Button button = (Button) comp;
            button.addActionListener(this);
        } else if (comp instanceof Container) {
            Container container = (Container) comp;
            int n = container.getComponentCount();
            for (int i = 0; i < n; i++)
                registerButtonHandler(container.getComponent(i));
        }
    }
}
```

Event listener classes are usually very small classes. To avoid unnecessary proliferation of small classes and files, event listener classes are commonly defined as nested classes. Furthermore, being nested classes also gives the listener classes access to the nonpublic fields of the enclosing class, which is often needed for handling the events.

EXAMPLE 8.11 Event Handlers as Nested Classes

PURPOSE

This example demonstrates the use of nested classes as event listener classes.

DESCRIPTION

This program behaves the same as the program in Example 8.10. It uses two nested classes: one handles the button clicks, and the other handles the choice item selections.

SOLUTION

Nested panels applet using nested class event listeners: NestedPanels3

```
import java.awt.*;
import java.awt.event.*;

public class NestedPanels3
        extends NestedPanels {
    public NestedPanels3() {
        super();
        ChoiceEventHandler cHandler = new ChoiceEventHandler();
```

```
            choice.addItemListener(cHandler);
            ButtonEventHandler bHandler = new ButtonEventHandler();
            bHandler.registerButtonHandler(this);
        }

    (Nested class ChoiceEventHandler on page 353)
    (Nested class ButtonEventHandler on page 353)
}
```

Nested class of `NestedPanels3`: `ChoiceEventHandler`

```
class ChoiceEventHandler implements ItemListener {
    public void itemStateChanged(ItemEvent event) {
        if (event.getStateChange() == ItemEvent.SELECTED) {
            messageBar.setText("Choice selected: " + event.getItem());
        }
    }
}
```

Nested class of `NestedPanels3`: `ButtonEventHandler`

```
class ButtonEventHandler implements ActionListener {
    public void actionPerformed(ActionEvent event) {
        Button source = (Button) event.getSource();
        messageBar.setText("Button pushed: " + source.getLabel());
    }

    protected void registerButtonHandler(Component comp) {
        if (comp != null) {
            if (comp instanceof Button) {
                Button button = (Button) comp;
                button.addActionListener(this);
            } else if (comp instanceof Container) {
                Container container = (Container) comp;
                int n = container.getComponentCount();
                for (int i = 0; i < n; i++)
                    registerButtonHandler(container.getComponent(i));
            }
        }
    }
}
```

EXAMPLE 8.12   Bouncing Ball Applet with Controls

PURPOSE

This example demonstrates factorization by delegation and the use of buttons and choices to control animations.

DESCRIPTION

This is an enhancement of the bouncing ball applet in Example 5.4 using Swing components. The layout of the applet is shown in Figure 8.11. Three GUI components are added to the original applet to control the animation:

- A *start* button to start the animation.
- A *stop* button to stop the animation.
- A *choice* to choose the color of the ball.

SOLUTION

In the original bouncing ball applet, the animation occupies the entire viewing area. The program consists of only one GUI component, the top-level panel. All methods dealing with animation belong to the applet class. In the reusable animation applet class `AnimationApplet` in Example 7.1 [p. 256], we assumed that the animation component occupies the entire viewing area. However, in the present case, the animation component occupies only a portion of the viewing area. We need a reusable animation component that is not tied to the top-level panel of an applet but that can be associated with any GUI component. In this case, it is better to use delegation to refactor the animation component so that the concrete animation class does not have to be the subclass of the reusable animation class. This approach permits multiple instances of the reusable animation class in a single program. The structure of the delegation-

Figure 8.11

The bouncing ball applet with controls.

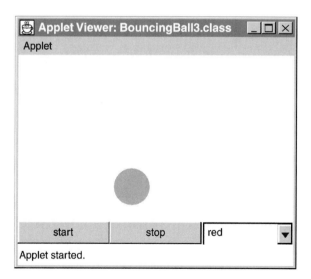

based reusable animation class is shown in Figure 8.12. The implementation is shown in the following program:

Delegation-based generic animator: `Animator`

```java
import java.awt.*;

public class Animator implements Runnable {
  public Animator(Component comp) {
    this.comp = comp;
  }
  final public void setDelay(int delay) {
    this.delay = delay;
  }
  final public int getDelay() {
    return delay;
  }
  public void start() {
    animationThread = new Thread(this);
    animationThread.start();
  }
  public void stop() {
    animationThread = null;
  }
  public void run() {
    while (Thread.currentThread() == animationThread) {
      try {
        Thread.sleep(delay);
      } catch (InterruptedException e) {}
      comp.repaint();
    }
  }

  protected Component comp; // the component to be animated
  protected int delay = 100;
  protected Thread animationThread;
}
```

Figure 8.12

The delegation-based reusable animation class.

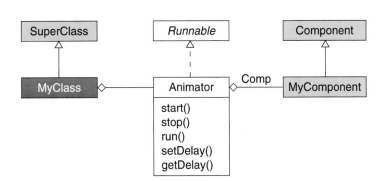

Figure 8.13

The structure of the bouncing ball applet with controls.

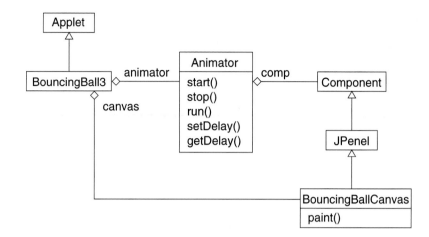

In the bouncing ball applet with controls, the animation component is the BouncingBallCanvas class, which extends the JPanel class in Swing. The JPanel class supports double-buffering. The top-level applet is the BouncingBall3 class. The structure of the entire program is shown in Figure 8.13.

Double-buffered canvas: BouncingBallCanvas

```java
import java.awt.*;
import javax.swing.*;

public class BouncingBallCanvas
  extends JPanel {

  public BouncingBallCanvas() {
    super(true); // double-buffered
  }

  public void initCanvas() {
    d = getSize();
    x = d.width * 2 / 3 ;
    y = d.height - radius;
  }

  public void paint(Graphics g) {
    g.setColor(Color.white);
    g.fillRect(0, 0, d.width, d.height);
    if (x < radius || x > d.width - radius)
      dx = -dx;
    if (y < radius || y > d.height - radius)
      dy = -dy;
    x += dx; y += dy;
    g.setColor(ballcolor);
    g.fillOval(x - radius, y - radius, radius * 2, radius * 2);
  }
```

```
  public void setBallColor(Color c) {
    ballcolor = c;
  }

  public void setBallPosition(int x, int y) {
    this.x = x; this.y = y;
  }

  protected int x, y, dx = -2, dy = -4, radius = 20;
  protected Color ballcolor = Color.red;
  protected Dimension d;

}
```

The BouncingBall3 class contains two nested classes for handling the events from the start and stop buttons and the color-choice box.

Bouncing ball applet with controls: `BouncingBall3.java`

```
import java.awt.*;
import java.awt.event.*;
import javax.swing.*;

public class BouncingBall3
        extends java.applet.Applet {
  public BouncingBall3() {
    setLayout(new BorderLayout());
    canvas = new BouncingBallCanvas();
    add("Center", canvas);
    animator = new Animator(canvas);
    Dimension d;

    controlPanel = new JPanel();
    controlPanel.setLayout(new GridLayout(1,0));
    JButton startButton = new JButton("start");
    controlPanel.add(startButton);
    JButton stopButton = new JButton("stop");
    controlPanel.add(stopButton);
    JComboBox choice = new JComboBox();
    choice.addItem("red");
    choice.addItem("green");
    choice.addItem("blue");
    controlPanel.add(choice);
    add("South", controlPanel);

    startButton.addActionListener(
              new ButtonHandler(ButtonHandler.START_ANIMATION));
    stopButton.addActionListener(
              new ButtonHandler(ButtonHandler.STOP_ANIMATION));
    choice.addItemListener(new ColorChoiceHandler());
  }
```

```java
    public void init() {
      String att = getParameter("delay");
      if (att != null) {
        int delay = Integer.parseInt(att);
        animator.setDelay(delay);
      }
      canvas.initCanvas();
    }

    public void start() {
      animator.start();
    }

    public void stop() {
      animator.stop();
    }

    protected BouncingBallCanvas canvas;
    protected Animator animator;
    protected JPanel controlPanel;

    protected class ButtonHandler implements ActionListener {

      static final int START_ANIMATION = 1;
      static final int STOP_ANIMATION = 2;

      public ButtonHandler(int cmd) {
        this.cmd = cmd;
      }

      public void actionPerformed(ActionEvent event) {
        switch (cmd) {
        case START_ANIMATION: start(); break;
        case STOP_ANIMATION: stop(); break;
        }
      }

      protected int cmd;
    }

    protected class ColorChoiceHandler implements ItemListener {
      public void itemStateChanged(ItemEvent event)  {
        JComboBox choice = (JComboBox) event.getSource();
        if (choice != null) {
          if ("red".equals(event.getItem()))
            canvas.setBallColor(Color.red);
          else if ("green".equals(event.getItem()))
            canvas.setBallColor(Color.green);
          else if ("blue".equals(event.getItem()))
            canvas.setBallColor(Color.blue);
          canvas.repaint();
        }
      }
    }
  }
```

8.3.5 Frames and Dialogs

A GUI application starts with a frame. A *frame* is a top-level window with a border, a title bar, and control buttons located at the upper corners of the frame. The main work area of a GUI app is usually contained within a frame. A *dialog* is a pop-up window that usually appears for only a short period of time and requires the immediate attention of the user. Dialog windows are used for displaying messages or getting input.

EXAMPLE 8.13 A Simple Online-Ordering GUI Application Using Swing

PURPOSE

This example demonstrates building GUI apps with frames and dialogs; the use of Swing components, including image labels, borders, and button groups; and customized layout.

DESCRIPTION

The frame of the online ordering app contains two components: an image label, which consists of an image and a text, and the Order button. When the Order button is pushed, a dialog box pops up. The dialog box has three compartments, as shown in Figure 8.14.

- The top compartment contains text labels and text fields. The layouts of the labels and the fields are not handled by a layout manager. Rather, a customized layout is specified, using the absolute position and dimension of each component.
- The middle compartment has a titled border with the title Credit Card. It contains three check boxes that are exclusive.
- The bottom compartment has an etched border. It contains the OK and Cancel buttons. An order is completed when the OK button is pushed, and the order information will be printed to the standard output.

The structure of the online-ordering app is shown in Figure 8.15. The Order class is the top-level class of the GUI application. It extends the JFrame class.

SOLUTION

The online shopping app: Order

```
import java.awt.*;
import java.awt.event.*;
import javax.swing.*;

public class Order extends JFrame {
    public Order(String imageFile) {
        setTitle(imageFile);
        getContentPane().setLayout(new BorderLayout());
        Icon image = new ImageIcon(imageFile);
```

Figure 8.14

The online
ordering form.

Frame control menu   Frame title bar   Frame control buttons

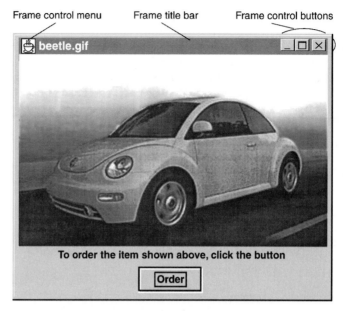

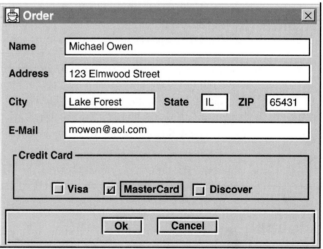

```
    JLabel center =
        new JLabel("To order the item shown above, click the button",
                   image,
                   SwingConstants.CENTER);
    center.setHorizontalTextPosition(SwingConstants.CENTER);
    center.setVerticalTextPosition(SwingConstants.BOTTOM);
    JPanel bottom = new JPanel();
    JButton orderButton = new JButton("Order");
    bottom.add(orderButton);
    orderButton.addActionListener(makeOrderHandler());
    getContentPane().add(center, BorderLayout.CENTER);
    getContentPane().add(bottom, BorderLayout.SOUTH);
    addWindowListener(new AppCloser());
}

ActionListener makeOrderHandler() {
    return new OrderHandler();
}

⟨Nested class AppCloser on page 362⟩
⟨Nested class OrderHandler on page 362⟩
⟨The main() method on page 362⟩
}
```

The AppCloser is an event listener that listens to the *window events*—the events triggered by the frame menus and control buttons that usually are located at the upper left and upper right corners of the window frame, respectively (see Figure 8.14). The AppCloser simply terminates the program when the close window (**X**) button is pushed. Without the AppCloser, pushing the close window button will not close the window. The implementation of AppCloser here is simplistic. In real applications, before terminating the program the user should be prompted to confirm the action, and any unsaved data should be saved to disk to prevent data loss. Note that the AppCloser extends the WindowAdapter class instead of implementing the WindowListener interface.

Figure 8.15

The structure of the online shopping app.

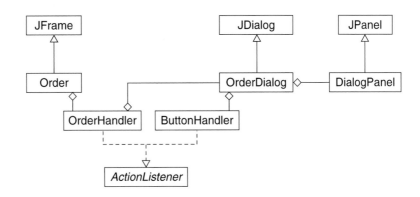

Nested class of Order: AppCloser

```
static class AppCloser extends WindowAdapter {
    public void window Closing(WindowEvent e) {
        System.exit(0);
    }
}
```

The `OrderHandler` is the listener class of the Order button. The first time the Order button is pushed, an instance of `OrderDialog`, which represents the order dialog box, is created with the invocation of

```
new OrderDialog(Order.this)
```

The order dialog box becomes visible when `dialog.show()` is invoked. The order dialog box is created only once. Subsequently, pushing the Order button causes the order dialog box to reappear by invoking `dialog.show()`.

Nested class of Order: OrderHandler

```
class OrderHandler implements ActionListener {
    JDialog dialog;
    public void actionPerformed(ActionEvent evt) {
        if (dialog == null) {
            dialog = new OrderDialog(Order.this);
        }
        dialog.show();
    }
}
```

The `main()` method creates an instance of the order frame. The order frame becomes visible when `frame.show()` is invoked.

The main() method of Order class

```
public static void main(String[] args) {
    if (args.length > 0) {
        Order frame = new Order(args[0]);
        frame.show();
    }
}
```

The `OrderDialog` class represents a dialog box that pops up when the Order button in the order frame is pushed. It contains the OK and Cancel buttons and the order information panel.

The order dialog class: OrderDialog

```
import java.awt.*;
import java.awt.event.*;
import javax.swing.*;

public class OrderDialog extends JDialog {
    JPanel bottom;
    JButton okButton, cancelButton;
```

```
  DialogPanel dialogPanel;

  public OrderDialog(JFrame owner) {
    super(owner, true);
    setTitle("Order");
    okButton = new JButton("Ok");
    cancelButton = new JButton("Cancel");
    ButtonHandler bHandler = new ButtonHandler();
    okButton.addActionListener(bHandler);
    cancelButton.addActionListener(bHandler);
    bottom = new JPanel();
    bottom.add(okButton);
    bottom.add(cancelButton);
    bottom.setBorder(BorderFactory.createEtchedBorder());
    dialogPanel = new DialogPanel();
    getContentPane().setLayout(new BorderLayout());
    getContentPane().add(bottom, BorderLayout.SOUTH);
    getContentPane().add(dialogPanel, BorderLayout.CENTER);
  }

  ⟨Nested class ButtonHandler on page 366⟩
}
```

The `DialogPanel` class represents the order-information panel that contains text fields for the customer's name, address, and e-mail. Each text field is accompanied by a text label. It also contains three check boxes for choosing a credit card. The selection of the check boxes is exclusive; i.e., only one of them can be selected. The check boxes are contained in another nested panel.

An auxiliary class: `DialogPanel`

```
class DialogPanel extends JPanel {
  JLabel nameLabel;
  JTextField nameField;
  JLabel addressLabel;
  JTextField addressField;
  JLabel cityLabel;
  JTextField cityField;
  JLabel stateLabel;
  JTextField stateField;
  JLabel zipLabel;
  JTextField zipField;
  JLabel emailLabel;
  JTextField emailField;
  JCheckBox visaBox, mcBox, discoverBox;
  JPanel creditCard;
  ButtonGroup group;

  ⟨The constructor on page 364⟩
  ⟨The layout methods on page 365⟩
  ⟨The reset() method on page 365⟩
}
```

The constructor creates instances of the text fields and labels. Swing components may have borders. The panel for check boxes has a titled border. The three check boxes are added to the same button group, so that they are exclusive.

The constructor of `DialogPanel` class

```
DialogPanel() {
    nameLabel = new JLabel("Name");
    nameField = new JTextField();
    addressLabel = new JLabel("Address");
    addressField = new JTextField();
    cityLabel = new JLabel("City");
    cityField = new JTextField();
    stateLabel = new JLabel("State");
    stateField = new JTextField();
    zipLabel = new JLabel("ZIP");
    zipField = new JTextField();
    emailLabel = new JLabel("E-Mail");
    emailField = new JTextField();
    creditCard = new JPanel();
    visaBox = new JCheckBox("Visa", true);
    mcBox = new JCheckBox("MasterCard");
    discoverBox = new JCheckBox("Discover");
    creditCard.add(visaBox);
    creditCard.add(mcBox);
    creditCard.add(discoverBox);
    creditCard.setBorder(BorderFactory.createTitledBorder(
                            "Credit Card"));
    group = new ButtonGroup();
    group.add(visaBox);
    group.add(mcBox);
    group.add(discoverBox);

    add(nameLabel);
    add(nameField);
    add(addressLabel);
    add(addressField);
    add(cityLabel);
    add(cityField);
    add(stateLabel);
    add(stateField);
    add(zipLabel);
    add(zipField);
    add(emailLabel);
    add(emailField);
    add(creditCard);
}
```

The layout of the components contained in a container is handled by the doLayout() method. By default, the doLayout() method delegates the responsibility to the layout manager associated with the container. To create a customized layout, you need to override the doLayout() method. Furthermore, you should also override the getPreferredSize() and getMinimumSize() methods to return the preferred and minimum sizes of the container, respectively. The sizes returned by the get-PreferredSize() and getMinimumSize() methods should be determined by the layout strategy implemented in the doLayout() method. The actual layout is done in the doLayout() method. The position and dimension of each component are set using the setBounds() methods defined in the Component class.

The layout methods of `DialogPanel` class

```
public Dimension getPreferredSize() {
    return new Dimension(350, 200);
}

public Dimension getMinimumSize() {
    return new Dimension(350, 200);
}

public void doLayout() {
    nameLabel.setBounds(10, 10, 60, 30);
    nameField.setBounds(70, 15, 270, 20);
    addressLabel.setBounds(10, 40, 60, 30);
    addressField.setBounds(70, 45, 270, 20);
    cityLabel.setBounds(10, 70, 60, 30);
    cityField.setBounds(70, 75, 100, 20);
    stateLabel.setBounds(180, 70, 40, 30);
    stateField.setBounds(220, 75, 30, 20);
    zipLabel.setBounds(260, 70, 30, 30);
    zipField.setBounds(290, 75, 50, 20);
    emailLabel.setBounds(10, 100, 60, 30);
    emailField.setBounds(70, 105, 270, 20);
    creditCard.setBounds(10, 140, 330, 50);
}
```

The reset() method clears the text fields so the same dialog panel can be used by the next customer.

Method of class `DialogPanel`: `reset()`

```
public void reset() {
    nameField.setText("");
    addressField.setText("");
    cityField.setText("");
    stateField.setText("");
    zipField.setText("");
    emailField.setText("");
    visaBox.setSelected(true);
}
```

The ButtonHandler class is the event listener class for the buttons in the order dialog box. If the OK button is pushed, the order information is printed to the standard output. When either the OK or the Cancel button is pushed, the text fields are cleared, and the dialog box is closed.

Nested class of `OrderDialog`: `ButtonHandler`

```java
class ButtonHandler implements ActionListener {
   public void actionPerformed(ActionEvent evt) {
      JButton button = (JButton) evt.getSource();
      String label = button.getText();
      if ("Ok".equals(label)) {
         System.out.println("An order is received:");
         System.out.println("\tName:    " +
                            dialogPanel.nameField.getText());
         System.out.println("\tAddress: " +
                            dialogPanel.addressField.getText());
         System.out.println("\tCity:    " +
                            dialogPanel.cityField.getText());
         System.out.println("\tState:   " +
                            dialogPanel.stateField.getText());
         System.out.println("\tZIP:     " +
                            dialogPanel.zipField.getText());
         System.out.println("\tE-Mail:  " +
                            dialogPanel.emailField.getText());
         System.out.print("\tCredit card: ");
         if (dialogPanel.visaBox.isSelected()) {
            System.out.println("Visa");
         } else if (dialogPanel.mcBox.isSelected()) {
            System.out.println("MasterCard");
         } else if (dialogPanel.discoverBox.isSelected()) {
            System.out.println("Discover");
         }
      }
      dialogPanel.reset();
      setVisible(false);  // close the dialog box
   }
}
```

8.4   THE INPUT/OUTPUT FRAMEWORK

The Java input/output framework is designed to be flexible and easily configurable. Java supports two types of input/output (I/O):

1. *Stream I/O:* A stream is a sequence of bytes. Stream-based I/O supports reading or writing data *sequentially*, that is, reading or writing data successively in one direction. A stream may be opened for reading *or* writing, but not for both reading *and* writing.

2. *Random Access I/O:* Random access I/O supports reading and writing data at any position of a file. A random access file may be opened for both reading and writing.

There are two kinds of streams: *byte streams* and *character streams*. Byte streams support reading and writing data of any type, including strings, in the binary format. Character streams support reading and writing of text, using locale-dependent character encodings.

8.4.1 Byte Streams

The most basic and primitive stream I/O capabilities are declared in two abstract classes: InputStream and OutputStream. They support reading and writing of a single byte and a sequence of bytes in an array. The methods for reading and writing are summarized in the following table. In these methods, b is a byte, ba is a byte array, off and len are integers that specify a segment of an array; off represents the offset (i.e., the starting index of the segment), and len represents the length (i.e., the number of bytes in the segment); n is a long integer.

Input Method	Output Method	Description
read()	write(b)	Reads/writes a single byte
read(ba)	write(ba)	Reads/writes an entire byte array
read(ba,off,len)	write(ba,off,len)	Reads/writes a segment of the byte array
skip(n)		Skips over n bytes
close()	close()	Closes the stream

Two of the concrete classes for byte stream I/O, which extend the two abstract classes, are FileInputStream and FileOutputStream, as shown in Figure 8.16. Instances of these two classes can be constructed by specifying the filename.

Figure 8.16

The file input stream and the file output stream.

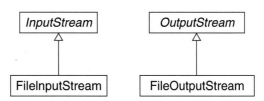

Constructor	Description
`FileInputStream(filename)`	Create, an input stream reading from the file named `filename`. An `IOException` is thrown if the file does not exist.
`FileOutputStream(filename)`	Create, an output stream writing to the file named `filename`. If the file does not exist, a new file is created. If the file already exists, the original file is overwritten.
`FileOutputStream(filename, append)`	Create, an output stream writing to the file named `filename`. If the file does not exist, a new file is created. If the file already exists, the new data will be appended to the end of the original file if the boolean flag append is `true`; otherwise, the original file is overwritten.

The primitive I/O capabilities provided in these classes make reading and writing data of any type possible, but hardly convenient.

EXAMPLE 8.14 Using Basic Byte I/O Streams

PURPOSE

This example demonstrates reading and writing a two-dimensional matrix using the primitive I/O capabilities provided in the `FileInputStream` and `FileOutput-Stream` classes.

DESCRIPTION

`WriteMatrix1` writes a 2 × 3 matrix to a file. It first writes the number of rows and columns of the matrix, followed by the numbers in the matrix. `ReadMatrix1` reads the file written by `WriteMatrix1` and restores the matrix.

SOLUTION

The data to be written to file are defined in the following interface:

Matrix data

```
public interface MatrixData {
    double[][] data = {
```

```
            { Math.exp(2.0), Math.exp(3.0), Math.exp(4.0) },
            { Math.exp(-2.0), Math.exp(-3.0), Math.exp(-4.0) },
        };
    }
```

In the following WriteMatrix1 class, the writeInt() method converts an integer value to a byte array and writes the byte array to the output stream. Similarly, the writeDouble() method converts a double value to a byte array and writes the byte array to the output stream.

Class WriteMatrix1

```java
import java.io.*;

public class WriteMatrix1 implements MatrixData {
    public static void main(String[] args) {
        int row = data.length;
        int col = data[0].length;
        int i, j;
        for (i = 0; i < row; i++) {
          for (j = 0; j < col; j++) {
            System.out.println("data[" + i + "][" + j + "] = " +
                                    data[i][j]);
          }
        }

        if (args.length > 0) {
          try {
            FileOutputStream out = new FileOutputStream(args[0]);
            writeInt(row, out);
            writeInt(col, out);
            for (i = 0; i < row; i++) {
              for (j = 0; j < col; j++) {
                writeDouble(data[i][j], out);
              }
            }
            out.close();
          } catch (IOException e) {
             e.printStackTrace();
          }
        }
    }

    public static void writeInt(int i, OutputStream out)
        throws IOException {
      byte[] buf = new byte[4];
      for (int k = 3; k >= 0; k--) {
         buf[k] = (byte)(i & 0xFF);
         i >>>= 8;
      }
      out.write(buf);
    }
```

```
        public static void writeDouble(double d, OutputStream out)
           throws IOException {
          byte[] buf = new byte[8];
          long l = Double.doubleToLongBits(d);
          for (int k = 7; k >= 0; k--) {
             buf[k] = (byte)(l & 0xFF);
             l >>>= 8;
          }
          out.write(buf);
        }
}
```

Running this program creates a file named data1.out and produces the following output:

```
venus% java WriteMatrix1 data1.out
data[0][0] = 7.38905609893065
data[0][1] = 20.085536923187668
data[0][2] = 54.598150033144236
data[1][0] = 0.1353352832366127
data[1][1] = 0.049787068367863944
data[1][2] = 0.01831563888873418
```

In the following ReadMatrix1 class, the readInt() method reads 4 bytes from the input stream into a byte array and converts the byte array to an integer value. Similarly, the readDouble() method reads 8 bytes from the input stream into a byte array and converts the byte array to a double value.

Class ReadMatrix1

```
import java.io.*;

public class ReadMatrix1 {
   static double[][] data;
   public static void main(String[] args) {
      if (args.length > 0) {
         try {
            FileInputStream in = new FileInputStream(args[0]);
            int row = readInt(in);
            System.out.println("row = " + row);
            int col = readInt(in);
            System.out.println("col = " + col);
            data = new double[row][col];
            for (int i = 0; i < row; i++) {
               for (int j = 0; j < col; j++) {
                  data[i][j] = readDouble(in);
                  System.out.println("data[" + i + "][" + j + "] = " +
                                    data[i][j]);
               }
            }
```

```
        } catch (IOException e) {
            e.printStackTrace();
        }
    }
}

public static int readInt(InputStream in)
    throws IOException {
  byte[] buf = new byte[4];
  in.read(buf);
  int i = 0;       for (int k = 0; k < 4; k++) {
    i <<= 8;
    i += (((int) buf[k]) & 0xFF);
  }
  return i;
}

public static double readDouble(InputStream in)
      throws IOException {
  byte[] buf = new byte[8];
  in.read(buf);
  long l = 0;
  for (int k = 0; k < 8; k++) {
    l <<= 8;
    l += (((int) buf[k]) & 0xFF);
  }
  return Double.longBitsToDouble(l);
}
}
```

Running this program with the `data1.out` file produced by `WriteMatrix1` as the input produces the following output:

```
venus% java ReadMatrix1 data1.out
row = 2
col = 3
data[0][0] = 7.38905609893065
data[0][1] = 20.085536923187668
data[0][2] = 54.598150033144236
data[1][0] = 0.1353352832366127
data[1][1] = 0.049787068367863944
data[1][2] = 0.01831563888873418
```

Data Input and Data Output Streams

Such laboring of reading and writing data by using bytes is rarely necessary. The methods for reading and writing data of various types are declared in two interfaces,

DataInput and DataOutput, respectively. These methods are summarized in the following table:

Input Method	Output Method	Description
readBoolean()	writeBoolean(b)	Reads/writes a boolean value
readByte()	writeByte(b)	Reads/writes a byte value
readChar()	writeChar(c)	Reads/writes a char value
readDouble()	writeDouble(d)	Reads/writes a double value
readFloat()	writeFloat(f)	Reads/writes a float value
readInt()	writeInt(i)	Reads/writes an int value
readLong()	writeLong(l)	Reads/writes a long value
readShort()	writeShort(s)	Reads/writes a short value
readUTF()	writeUTF(s)	Reads/writes a String value

Two concrete classes, DataInputStream and DataOutputStream, implement the DataInput and DataOutput interfaces, respectively, as illustrated in Figure 8.17. The DataInputStream and DataOutputStream are defined as filters, or

Figure 8.17

The data input stream and the data output stream.

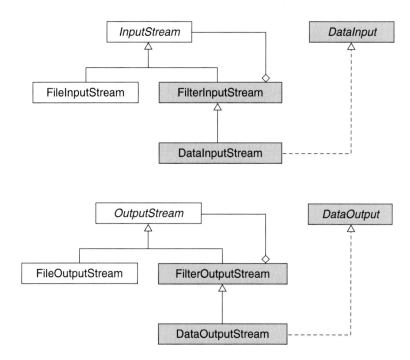

decorators; that is, they take I/O streams with primitive I/O capabilities and transform them into I/O streams with data input and output capabilities. The Decorator design pattern is discussed on page 380.

Constructor	Description
DataInputStream(in)	Creates a data input stream that reads data from the specified input stream in
DataOutputStream(out)	Creates a data output stream that writes data to the specified output stream out

EXAMPLE 8.15 Using DataInput and DataOutput Streams

PURPOSE

This example demonstrates reading and writing a two-dimensional matrix using the I/O decorators DataInputStream and DataOutputStream.

DESCRIPTION

The WriteMatrix2 and ReadMatrix2 classes perform the same tasks as the WriteMatrix1 and ReadMatrix1 classes in Example 8.14. The main differences are the construction of the data input and output streams, which are shown in boldface in the following programs. The writeInt(), writeDouble(), readInt(), and readDouble() methods in the previous examples are no longer needed.

SOLUTION

Class WriteMatrix2

```java
import java.io.*;

public class WriteMatrix2 implements MatrixData {
    public static void main(String[] args) {
        int row = data.length;
        int col = data[0].length;
        int i, j;
        for (i = 0; i < row; i++) {
            for (j = 0; j < col; j++) {
                System.out.println("data[" + i + "][" + j + "] = " +
                                data[i][j]);
            }
        }

        if (args.length > 0) {
            try {
                DataOutputStream out =
                    new DataOutputStream(new FileOutputStream(args[0]));
```

```
      out.writeInt(row);
      out.writeInt(col);
      for (i = 0; i < row; i++) {
        for (j = 0; j < col; j++) {
          out.writeDouble(data[i][j]);
        }
      }
      out.close();
    } catch (IOException e) {
      e.printStackTrace();
    }
   }
  }
}
```

Class ReadMatrix2

```
import java.io.*;

public class ReadMatrix2 {

  static double[][] data;

  public static void main(String[] args) {
    if (args.length > 0) {
      try {
        DataInputStream in =
              new DataInputStream(new FileInputStream(args[0]));
        int row = in.readInt();
        System.out.println("row = " + row);
        int col = in.readInt();
        System.out.println("col = " + col);
        data = new double[row][col];
        for (int i = 0; i < row; i++) {
          for (int j = 0; j < col; j++) {
            data[i][j] = in.readDouble();
            System.out.println("data[" + i + "][" + j + "] = " +
                               data[i][j]);
          }
        }
      } catch (IOException e) {
        e.printStackTrace();
      }
    }
  }
}
```

This example produces the same output as Example 8.14.

Buffered Input and Output Streams

The `BufferedInputStream` and `BufferedOutputStream` classes are filter streams that support buffered I/O. The relationships among the related classes are shown in Figure 8.18. They take I/O streams and transform them into buffered I/O streams. The constructors are shown in the following table:

Constructor	Description
`BufferedInputStream(in)`	Creates a buffered input stream that reads data from the specified input stream `in`
`BufferedOutputStream(out)`	Creates a buffered output stream that writes data to the specified output stream `out`

Figure 8.18

The buffered input stream and the buffered output stream.

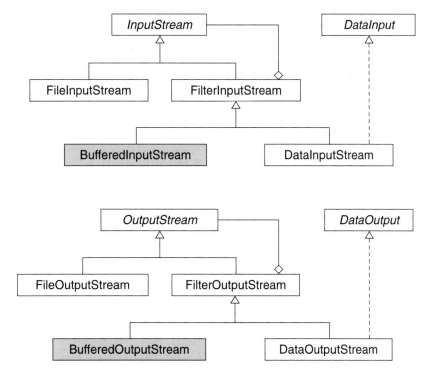

EXAMPLE 8.16 Using Buffered I/O Streams

PURPOSE
This example demonstrates the use of buffered input and output streams.

DESCRIPTION
The WriteMatrix3 and ReadMatrix3 classes perform the same tasks as in Examples 8.14 and 8.15. The main differences are the construction of the buffered input and output streams, which are shown in boldface in the following programs.

SOLUTION

Class WriteMatrix3

```java
import java.io.*;

public class WriteMatrix3 implements MatrixData {
   public static void main(String[] args) {
      int row = data.length;
      int col = data[0].length;
      int i, j;
      for (i = 0; i < row; i++) {
        for (j = 0; j < col; j++) {
          System.out.println("data[" + i + "][" + j + "] = " +
                             data[i][j]);
        }
      }

      if (args.length > 0) {
        try {
          DataOutputStream out =
             new DataOutputStream(
             new BufferedOutputStream(
             new FileOutputStream(args[0])));
          out.writeInt(row);
          out.writeInt(col);
          for (i = 0; i < row; i++) {
            for (j = 0; j < col; j++) {
              out.writeDouble(data[i][j]);
            }
          }
          out.close();
        } catch (IOException e) {
          e.printStackTrace();
        }
      }
   }
}
```

Class ReadMatrix3

```java
import java.io.*;

public class ReadMatrix3 {

    static double[][] data;

    public static void main(String[] args) {
        if (args.length > 0) {
            try {
                DataInputStream in =
                    new DataInputStream(
                    new BufferedInputStream(
                    new FileInputStream(args[0])));
                int row = in.readInt();
                System.out.println("row = " + row);
                int col = in.readInt();
                System.out.println("col = " + col);
                data = new double[row][col];
                for (int i = 0; i < row; i++) {
                    for (int j = 0; j < col; j++) {
                        data[i][j] = in.readDouble();
                        System.out.println("data[" + i + "][" + j + "] = " +
                                            data[i][j]);
                    }
                }
            } catch (IOException e) {
                e.printStackTrace();
            }
        }
    }
}
```

This example produces the same output as Example 8.14.

Object Streams

Java supports object serialization. It involves two processes:

1. *Serializing:* To write an object and all the objects that are directly or indirectly referenced by the object[3] to a stream (i.e., a sequence of bytes).
2. *Deserializing:* To restore an object and all the objects that are directly or indirectly referenced by the object from a stream that is the result a serialization.

Instances of classes that implement the Serializable interface can be serialized. Many classes in the Java 2 Platform class libraries can be serialized, including most

---

3. All the objects that are directly or indirectly referenced by a given object *o* along with the reference relation among these objects form what is known as the object graph of *o*.

Figure 8.19

The object input stream and the object output stream.

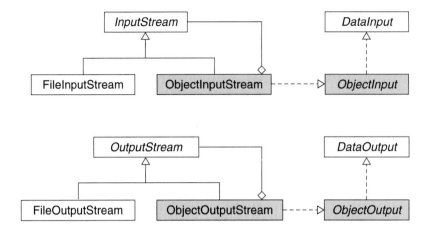

of the classes in `java.lang` and the collection classes. Arrays can also be serialized as long as the elements are serializable.

The methods for serializing and deserializing are declared in the `ObjectInput` and `ObjectOutput` interfaces, which extend `DataInput` and `DataOutput`, respectively. The input method is `readObject()`; the output method is `writeObject()`.

The `ObjectInputStream` and `ObjectOutputStream` are two I/O filter classes that implement the `ObjectInput` and `ObjectOutput` interfaces, respectively, as shown in Figure 8.19. The constructors are described in the following table:

Constructor	Description
`ObjectInputStream(in)`	Creates an object input stream that reads data from the specified input stream `in`
`ObjectOutputStream(out)`	Creates an object output stream that writes data to the specified output stream `out`

EXAMPLE 8.17 Using Object Serialization

PURPOSE

This example demonstrates reading and writing a two-dimensional matrix using object serialization.

DESCRIPTION

The `WriteMatrix3` and `ReadMatrix3` classes perform the same tasks as in Examples 8.14–8.16.

SOLUTION

Using object serialization, we can easily read and write the entire array with a single method invocation.

Class WriteMatrix4

```java
import java.io.*;

public class WriteMatrix4 implements MatrixData {
   public static void main(String[] args) {
     int row = data.length;
     int col = data[0].length;
     int i, j;
     for (i = 0; i < row; i++) {
       for (j = 0; j < col; j++) {
         System.out.println("data[" + i + "][" + j + "] = " +
                            data[i][j]);
       }
     }
     if (args.length > 0) {
       try {
         ObjectOutputStream out =
           new ObjectOutputStream(new FileOutputStream(args[0]));

         out.writeObject(data);
         out.close();
       } catch (IOException e) {
         e.printStackTrace();
       }
     }
   }
}
```

Class ReadMatrix4

```java
import java.io.*;

public class ReadMatrix4 {
   static double[][] data;

   public static void main(String[] args) {
     if (args.length > 0) {
       try {
         ObjectInputStream in =
           new ObjectInputStream(new FileInputStream(args[0]));
         data = (double[][]) in.readObject();
         int row = data.length;
         int col = data[0].length;
         for (int i = 0; i < row; i++){
           for (int j = 0; j < col; j++){
             System.out.println("data[" + i + "][" + j + "] = " +
                                data[i][j]);
           }
         }
```

```
            } catch (Exception e) {
                e.printStackTrace();
            }
        }
    }
}
```

8.4.2 Design Pattern: Decorator

The design of the Java input/output framework illustrates the Decorator design pattern. The basic byte-based I/O capability is provided by the `InputStream` and `Output-Stream` classes. Also, there are many *add-on* features that enhance the basic I/O capability, such as reading and writing data of primitive types, read and write objects, buffered read and write, compression and decompression of data, encryption and decryption of data, and so on. These add-on features can be combined in many different ways, and in different contexts we may need to use different combinations of them. One approach to satisfying all the potential needs is to extend the `InputStream` and `OutputStream` classes to add these features. A large number of classes are necessary to cover every possible combination of these add-on features, such as

- `BufferedDataInputStream`,
- `EncryptedDataInputStream`,
- `CompressedInputStream`,
- `EncryptedCompressedDataInputStream`,
- and so on.

An alternative approach is to define each add-on feature as a separate class known as a *decorator*, or *filter*,[4] that adds a feature to the basic I/O capability through object composition. A particular combination of the add-on features is composed by adding the corresponding decorators of these add-on features to the basic I/O capability, as in

> **new** *Decorator2*(**new** *Decorator1* (*inputStream*))

This approach avoids an explosion of the number of classes and provides flexibility through object composition.

Design Pattern *Decorator*

Category: Structural design pattern.

Intent: Attach additional responsibilities or capabilities to an object dynamically. Decorators provide a flexible alternative to subclassing for extending functionality.

---

4. *Decorator* seems to be a better name than *filter* because *decorate* connotes adding, whereas *filter* connotes removing.

Applicability: The Decorator design pattern should be used
- to add responsibilities to individual objects dynamically without affecting other objects in the same class.
- for responsibilities that can be withdrawn.
- when extension by subclassing is impractical owing to a large number of possible independent extensions, which would produce an explosion of subclasses to support every combination.

The structure of the Decorator design pattern is shown in the following diagram:

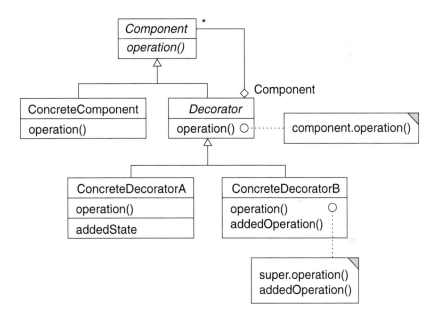

The participants of the Decorator design pattern are as follows:

Component (e.g., `InputStream`), which defines the interface for objects that can have responsibilities added to them dynamically.

ConcreteComponent (e.g., `FileInputStream`), which defines an object to which additional responsibilities can be added.

Decorator (e.g., `FilterInputStream`), which maintains a reference to a component object and defines an interface that conforms to the component's interface.

ConcreteDecorator (e.g., `DataInputStream` and `BufferedOutputStream`), which adds responsibilities to the component.

For a detailed discussion of the Decorator design pattern, see Gamma et al. [1995].

8.4.3 Character Streams

In Java programs, strings are represented internally in Unicode, in which all characters are encoded in two bytes. Externally, text files are stored in various character encodings supported by the platform on which the programs are running. The default character encoding of a machine is often determined by the machine's locale. A *locale* is a geographic region that shares the same language and customs. For example, in the United States, the default character encoding is ISO-8859-1, commonly known as the ASCII code, in which all characters are encoded in a single byte. In the People's Republic of China, the default character encoding is GB-2312, in which all Latin characters are encoded in a single byte, and all Chinese ideographs are encoded in two bytes.

The character-based I/O streams perform conversions between the Unicode and the locale-sensitive character encodings when reading and writing strings. In other words, character streams are locale sensitive, but byte streams are not.

Two abstract classes, `Reader` and `Writer`, are the roots of inheritance hierarchies of the character-based input and output streams, respectively. The relationships among the key character I/O streams are shown in Figure 8.20. The `Reader` and `Writer` classes provide the basic capabilities for reading and writing characters. Their methods are summarized in the following table. The parameter c represents a character, ca represents a character array, and off and len are integers that specify a

Figure 8.20

The character-based readers and writers.

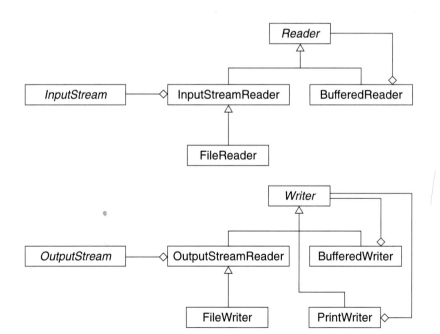

segment of an array; `off` represents the offset (i.e., the starting index of the segment), and `len` represents the length (i.e., the number of elements in the segment).

Input Method	Output Method	Description
`read()`	`write(c)`	Reads/writes a single character
`read(ca)`	`write(ca)`	Reads/writes an entire character array
`read(ca,off,len)`	`write(ca,off,len)`	Reads/writes a segment of the character array
`close()`	`close()`	Closes the stream

The `InputStreamReader` and `OutputStreamWriter` are two filters that serve as bridges between byte-based I/O and character-based I/O. The constructors of these two classes are summarized in the following table. The parameter `encoding` is a string that denotes the character encoding used by the reader/writer. For example, the ISO-8859-1 encoding for English is denoted `"8859_1,"` and the GB-2312 encoding for simplified Chinese is denoted `"GB2312."`

Constructor	Description
`InputStreamReader(in)`	Creates an input stream reader that reads data from the specified input stream `in` and uses the default character encoding
`InputStreamReader(in, encoding)`	Creates an input stream reader that reads data from the specified input stream `in` and uses the specified character encoding
`OutputStreamWriter(out)`	Creates an output stream writer that writes data to the specified output stream `out` and uses the default character encoding
`OutputStreamWriter(out, encoding)`	Creates an output stream writer that writes data to the specified output stream `out` and uses the specified character encoding

The FileReader and FileWriter are two concrete character streams that provide the basic character-based I/O capabilities. The constructors of these two classes are summarized in the following table:

Constructor	Description
FileReader(filename)	Creates a file reader reading from the file named filename. An IOException is thrown if the file does not exist.
FileWriter(filename)	Creates a file writer writing to the file named filename. If the file does not exist, a new file is created. If the file already exists, the original file is overwritten.
FileWriter(filename, append)	Creates a file writer writing to the file named filename. If the file does not exist, a new file is created. If the file already exists, the new data will be appended to the end of the original file if the boolean flag append is true; otherwise, the original file is overwritten.

The BufferedReader and BufferedWriter are two filters that support buffered character-based I/O. The constructors of these two classes are summarized in the following table:

Constructor	Description
BufferedReader(reader)	Creates a buffered reader that reads data from the specified reader
BufferedWriter(writer)	Creates a buffered writer that writes data to the specified writer

The BufferedReader class adds the method readLine(), which reads a line of text.

PrintWriter is a useful filter class that supports writing values of various data types by converting them to their string representations. The PrintWriter class has the following constructor:

```
PrintWriter(writer)
```

which creates a print writer that writes data to the specified writer. The `PrintWriter` class provides the following two methods, which are overloaded on all data types; i.e., the parameter v can be of any type.

Method	Description
`print(v)`	Prints the string representation of v
`println(v)`	Prints the string representation of v followed by a new line

The string representations of values of primitive types are formatted according to the usual and customary conventions. The string representations of objects are defined by the `toString()` method of their classes.

EXAMPLE 8.18 Using Character Streams

PURPOSE

This example demonstrates reading and writing a two-dimensional matrix using character-based I/O streams.

DESCRIPTION

To read and write data using strings, all data must be converted to and from their string representations. To write data, we must insert delimiters between consecutive values.

SOLUTION

The `WriteMatrix5` class writes the two-dimensional array to a text file. Each line contains a single value. The first two lines contain the number of rows and columns followed by the values in the matrix.

Class `WriteMatrix5`

```java
import java.io.*;

public class WriteMatrix5 implements MatrixData {

    public static void main(String[] args) {
        int row = data.length;
        int col = data[0].length;
        int i, j;
        for (i = 0; i < row; i++) {
            for (j = 0; j < col; j++) {
                System.out.println("data[" + i + "][" + j + "] = " +
                                data[i][j]);
            }
        }
    }
```

```
        if (args.length > 0) {
          try {
            PrintWriter out =
                new PrintWriter(
                new BufferedWriter(
                new FileWriter(args[0])));
            out.println(row);
            out.println(col);
            for (i = 0; i < row; i++) {
              for (j = 0; j < col; j++) {
                out.println(data[i][j]);
              }
            }
            out.close();
          } catch (IOException e) {
            e.printStackTrace();
          }
        }
      }
    }
  }
```

The ReadMatrix5 class reads the text file written by WriteMatrix5 and restores the array.

Class ReadMatrix5

```
import java.io.*;

public class ReadMatrix5 {
    static double[][] data;
    public static void main(String[] args) {
      if (args.length > 0) {
        try {
          BufferedReader in =
              new BufferedReader(
              new FileReader(args[0]));
          String line;
          line = in.readLine();
          int row = Integer.parseInt(line);
          System.out.println("row = " + row);
          line = in.readLine();
          int col = Integer.parseInt(line);
          System.out.println("col = " + col);
          data = new double[row][col];
          for (int i = 0; i < row; i++){
            for (int j = 0; j < col; j++){
              line = in.readLine();
              data[i][j] = Double.valueOf(line).doubleValue();
              System.out.println("data[" + i + "][" + j + "] = " +
                                 data[i][j]);
            }
          }
```

```
      } catch (IOException e) {
        e.printStackTrace();
      }
    }
  }
}
```

Character streams are also able to use character encodings that are different from the default character encoding.

EXAMPLE 8.19 A Universal Text Viewer

PURPOSE

This example demonstrates the use of character-based readers to view text files in any character encoding.

DESCRIPTION

This GUI application makes use of Swing components. It consists of an instance of JTextArea inside an instance of JScrollPane, which allows the text area to be scrolled both vertically and horizontally. The program expects two arguments: the text file name and the character encoding.

SOLUTION

Class UniversalTextViewer

```java
import java.awt.*;
import java.awt.event.*;
import java.io.*;
import javax.swing.*;

public class UniversalTextViewer extends JPanel {
    public UniversalTextViewer(String filename, String enc) {
        setLayout(new BorderLayout());
        JTextArea textArea = new JTextArea(40, 80);
        textArea.setEditable(false);
        textArea.setFont(new Font("Monospaced", Font.BOLD, 16));
        add(new JScrollPane(textArea), BorderLayout.CENTER);
        try {
            BufferedReader in =
                new BufferedReader(
                new InputStreamReader(new FileInputStream(filename),
                                      enc));
            String line;
            while ((line = in.readLine()) != null) {
                textArea.append(line + "\n");
            }
        } catch (IOException e) {
            e.printStackTrace();
        }
    }
```

```
public static void main(String args[]) {
  if (args.length >= 2) {
    JFrame frame = new JFrame();
    frame.setTitle("Universal Text Viewer: " +
                   args[0] + " [" + args[1] + "]");
    frame.getContentPane().setLayout(new BorderLayout());
    frame.getContentPane().add(new UniversalTextViewer(args[0],
                               args[1]), BorderLayout.CENTER);
    frame.addWindowListener(new AppCloser());
    frame.setSize(600, 400);
    frame.show();
  }
}

protected static final class AppCloser extends WindowAdapter {
  public void windowClosing(WindowEvent e) {
    System.exit(0);
  }
}
}
```

The universal text viewer can be invoked as

```
venus% java UniversalTextViewer filename encoding
```

Figure 8.21 shows a screen shot of the universal text viewer presenting a text file in simplified Chinese (GB2312 encoding).[5]

5. For the Chinese characters to be displayed properly, Chinese fonts must be installed and the `font.properties` file of the JDK or JRE must be configured to use the appropriate fonts. See the online supplement of the book for details of setting up the fonts.

Figure 8.21

The universal text viewer.

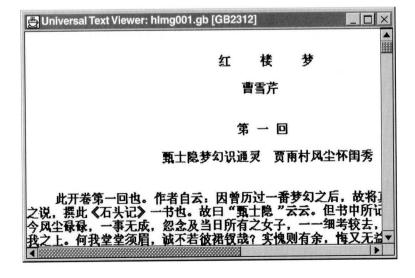

8.4.4 Random Access Files

Random access files support reading and writing data at any position in the files and can support reading and writing at the same time. The RandomAccessFile class provides the basic capabilities of random-access I/O. The constructor of the RandomAccessFile class is the following:

Constructor	Description
RandomAccessFile(filename, mode)	Creates a random-access file that reads from, and optionally writes to, the file named filename. The mode argument is a string whose value must be either "r", for read-only, or "rw", for read–write.

The RandomAccessFile class implements both DataInput and DataOutput interfaces. Moreover, it supports the following methods for moving the current read/write position. The read/write position is the location in the file where the next read or write operation will occur. In the parameters of the following methods, i is an integer, and l is a long integer.

Method	Description
seek(l)	Moves the read/write position to the l-th byte counting from the beginning of the file
skipBytes(i)	Moves the read/write position i bytes relative to the current position; moves forward if $i > 0$ and moves backward if $i < 0$

EXAMPLE 8.20 Store Serialized Objects in Random-Access Files

PURPOSE

This example demonstrates the use of a random-access file.

DESCRIPTION

The RandomAccessFile class does not implement the ObjectInput and the ObjectOutput interfaces. So serialized objects cannot be directly written to random-access files. In this example, we extend the RandomAccessFile to support reading and writing serialized objects in random-access files.

SOLUTION

Because serialized objects vary in size, for each object, we first store its size as an integer (4-byte) and then store the serialized object itself. The `writeObject()` method first serializes the object in a byte array and copies the array to the file, and then the total number of bytes written to the file (including the size count) is returned. The `readObject()` method reads a serialized object at the current read/write position. It first reads the size count and then reads the serialized object into a byte array and deserializes the object.

Class `ObjectRandomAccessFile`

```java
import java.io.*;

public class ObjectRandomAccessFile extends RandomAccessFile {
    protected ByteArrayOutputStream bOut;
    protected byte[] buf;
    public ObjectRandomAccessFile(String name, String mode)
            throws IOException {
        super(name, mode);
        bOut = new ByteArrayOutputStream();
    }

    public int writeObject(Object obj) throws IOException {
        if (obj != null &&
            obj instanceof Serializable) {
            ObjectOutputStream objOut = new ObjectOutputStream(bOut);
            objOut.writeObject(obj);
            int count = bOut.size();
            byte[] buf = bOut.toByteArray();
            writeInt(count);
            write(buf, 0, count);
            bOut.reset();
            return count + 4;
        } else {
            return 0;
        }
    }

    public Object readObject() throws IOException,
                                      ClassNotFoundException {
        int count = readInt();
        if (buf == null ||
            count > buf.length) {
            buf = new byte[count];
        }
        read(buf, 0, count);
        ObjectInputStream objIn =
            new ObjectInputStream(new ByteArrayInputStream(buf, 0, count));
        Object obj = objIn.readObject();
        objIn.close();
        return obj;
    }
}
```

The following simple test program writes three serialized strings into a random access file:

Test of the `writeObject()` method of `ObjectRandomAccessFile`

```java
import java.io.*;

public class TestWrite {
   public static void main(String[] args) {
      if (args.length > 0) {
         try {
            ObjectRandomAccessFile out =
                new ObjectRandomAccessFile(args[0], "rw");
            Object[] obj = {"Tic", "Tac", "Toe" };
            long offset = 0;
            int count;
            for (int i = 0; i < obj.length; i++) {
               count = out.writeObject(obj[i]);
               System.out.println(obj[i] + " written at offset " +
                                  offset + " size = " + count);
               offset += count;
            }
         } catch (IOException e) {
            e.printStackTrace();
         }
      }
   }
}
```

The output is

```
venus% java TestWrite obj.out
Tic written at offset 0 size = 14
Tac written at offset 14 size = 14
Toe written at offset 28 size = 14
```

The following is a simple test program that reads the random-access file created by TestWrite. It expects the first argument to be the file name and the following arguments to be integers specifying the offsets at which the objects are to be read.

Test of the `readObject()` method of `ObjectRandomAccessFile`

```java
import java.io.*;

public class TestRead {
   public static void main(String[] args) {
      if (args.length > 0) {
         try {
            ObjectRandomAccessFile in =
                new ObjectRandomAccessFile(args[0], "r");
            Object obj;
            long offset;
            for (int i = 1; i < args.length; i++) {
               offset = Long.parseLong(args[i]);
               in.seek(offset);
```

```
        obj = in.readObject();
        System.out.println(obj + " read at offset " + offset);
      }
    } catch (Exception e) {
      e.printStackTrace();
    }
  }
 }
}
```

The output is

```
venus% java TestRead obj.out 28 14 0
Toe read at offset 28
Tac read at offset 14
Tic read at offset 0
```

CHAPTER SUMMARY

- An object-oriented application framework is a set of cooperating classes that represent reusable designs of software systems in a particular application domain. It typically consists of a set of abstract classes and interfaces that are parts of semi-complete applications that can be specialized to produce custom applications. The key characteristics of application frameworks are extendability, inversion of control, and use of design patterns.

- Although both design patterns and frameworks are mechanisms used to capture reusable designs, they are quite different. Design patterns are schematic descriptions of reusable designs that are not concrete programs and are language independent. In contrast, frameworks are semicomplete applications that are written in a specific programming language.

- A collection is an object that contains other objects, which are called the elements of the collection. The collections framework is a set of interfaces and classes that support storing and retrieving objects in collections of varying structures, algorithms, and time-space complexities. The collections can be grouped in the following abstract collection categories:

   A bag is an unordered collection of elements that may contain duplicate elements. Bags are also known as multisets.
   A set is an unordered collection of elements with no duplicate elements.
   A sorted set is a set whose elements are automatically sorted according to a certain sequence.

A list is an ordered collection of elements that allows duplicate elements. Lists are also known as sequences.

A map is an unordered collection of key-value pairs. The keys in a map must be unique. Maps are also known as functions, dictionaries, or associative arrays.

Each of the abstract collections can be implemented by using different data structures and algorithms.

- The Iterator design pattern is used to provide a uniform way to iterate through different concrete collections (i.e., polymorphic iteration). Two iterator interfaces are defined: `Iterator` and `ListIterator`.

- The graphical user interface (GUI) framework consists of the Abstract Windows Toolkit (AWT) and the Swing portion of the Java Foundation Classes. It is a set of interfaces and classes that support the construction of graphical user interfaces with a great deal of versatility.

- GUI components are the building blocks of the visual aspect of graphical user interfaces. All Java GUI component classes are subclasses of the `Component` class. These subclasses are divided into two groups: primitive components, which do not contain other components, and containers, which may contain other primitive components and containers.

- Each container has a layout manager, which handles the layout of the components contained in the container. Each layout manager defines a layout strategy. Commonly used layout managers include `FlowLayout`, `BorderLayout`, and `GridLayout`.

- GUI components communicate with other applications through events, which represent user input or actions. The source of an event is the component from which the event originated. A listener of an event is an object that receives and processes the event. Events are classified as different types, with each type of event represented by an event class. Each type of event is also associated with a listener interface, which the listeners of this type of event must implement. Listeners must be registered to their respective sources before they can receive events from their sources.

- The input/output framework is a set of interfaces and classes that support the input and output of different types of objects to and from different media with varying capabilities.

- Java supports two types of I/O: stream I/O and random-access I/O. A stream is a sequence of bytes. Stream-based I/O supports reading or writing data sequentially. A stream may be opened for reading or writing, but not reading and writing. There are two kinds of streams: byte streams and character streams. Byte streams support reading and writing data of any type, including strings, in the binary format. Character streams support reading and writing of text using locale-dependent character encodings. Random-access I/O supports reading and writing data at any position of a file. A random-access file may be opened for both reading and writing.

- Serialization is the process of writing an object and all the objects that are directly or indirectly referenced by the object to a stream. Deserialization is the process of restoring an object and all the objects that are directly or indirectly referenced by the object that have been serialized.

- The Composite design pattern composes objects into tree structures to represent a part-whole hierarchy. The Composite design pattern lets clients treat individual objects and compositions of objects uniformly. The Composite design pattern should be used to represent a part-whole hierarchy of objects or to allow clients to treat all objects in the composite structure uniformly.

- The Decorator design pattern attaches additional responsibilities to an object dynamically. Decorators provide a flexible alternative to subclassing for extending functionality. The Decorator design pattern should be used to add responsibilities to individual objects dynamically without affecting other objects in the same class, or to avoid an explosion of subclasses caused by an extension by subclassing.

- The common aspects of related classes should be handled uniformly. These common aspects are usually interfaces or abstract classes. The greater the uniformity, the simpler and more useful is the design.

FURTHER READING

Walrath, K., and M. Campione (1999). *The JFC Swing Tutorial: A Guide to Constructing GUIs*. Addison-Wesley.

EXERCISES

8.1 The Set interface defines only the most basic operations on sets. Some of the common operations on sets that are not included in the Set interface and their definitions are the following:

- The union of two sets:

$$S_1 \cup S_2 \equiv \{x \mid x \in S_1 \vee x \in S_2\}$$

- The intersection of two sets:

$$S_1 \cap S_2 \equiv \{x \mid x \in S_1 \wedge x \in S_2\}$$

- The nonsymmetric difference of two sets:

$$S_1 \setminus S_2 \equiv \{x \mid x \in S_1 \wedge x \notin S_2\}$$

Define and implement a class that supports these operations on sets as algorithms that can be applied to any concrete classes that implement the Set interface.

8.2 Design and implement a class Car that describes the key characteristics of a car, such as model, model year, manufacturer, color, horsepower, number of cylinders, and so on. The Car class should implement the Comparable interface. The natural order of the car objects is based on the ascending orders of the following attributes of the cars in descending significance:

- The manufacturer
- The model
- The model year

Write a program `SortCars` that instantiates a number of instances of the `Car` class, inserts them into a list, sorts the cars in the list, and prints out the cars in their natural order.

8.3 Extend the `Car` class in the previous exercise by defining a comparator for each attribute of a car. Write a program `SortCars2` similar to the program `SortCars` in the previous exercise, except that it can sort the cars based on different attributes of the cars in either ascending or descending order using different comparators. The program takes a command-line argument indicating the attribute to be sorted on and whether in ascending or descending order. For example, the program can be invoked as follows:

```
java SortCars2 model ascend
```

8.4 Hash tables are often used to build indices for fast access to objects in a large collection. Use the `Customer` and `Address` classes defined in Exercise 6.1 to build a list of customers. Then use hash tables to build indices on customer names, customer IDs, and the postal code of the shipping addresses. Note that the customer ID of each customer is unique and that the name and the postal code of the shipping address of each customer are not unique.

8.5 Write a simple calculator applet. It should contain buttons for the digits, the operators (+, −, *, and /), and the equals sign (=). The results can be displayed by using a text field.

8.6 Enhance the digital clock applet so that it can display the time of any time zone around the world. Use a choice component for choosing the time zone.

8.7 Java supports compression and decompression of data in ZIP or GZIP format. Write a program to read a text file, compress the contents, and write a file with the compressed contents. The compression format is either ZIP or GZIP specified by a command-line argument. Write another program to read a compressed file, decompress the contents, and write a text file with the decompressed text. (*Hint:* Find out the details of the compression/decompression classes by reading the J2SE API documentation on package `java.util.zip`.)

PROJECTS

8.1 Enhance the applets developed in Projects 5.2 and 5.3. Use a button to dynamically switch between the pie chart display and the bar chart display. Flip the button labels as well.

8.2 Enhance the bouncing ball applet in Example 8.12 so that there can be several balls. Use a pair of buttons to increase or decrease the number of balls. If two balls collide, change the direction of their movement.

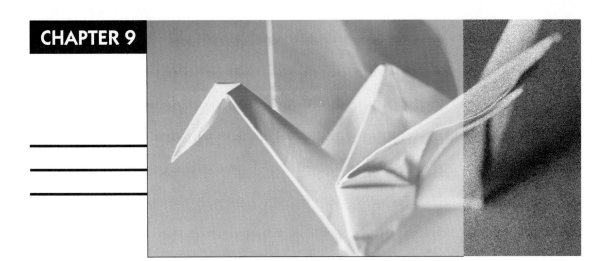

CHAPTER 9

Design Case Study: A Drawing Pad

CHAPTER OVERVIEW

In this chapter, we present a case study in developing graphical user interfaces (GUIs), using the Java Foundation Class (JFC). We also demonstrate the iterative development process by designing and implementing a graphical drawing pad in successive increments. We introduce two new design patterns: Factory Method and State.

9.1   PLANNING

In this chapter, we develop a complete GUI application using the lightweight components in the Swing package. The GUI application to be developed is a drawing tool that supports the following:

- Scribbling and drawing various shapes
- Saving the drawings to files and loading the drawings from files
- Typing from the keyboard
- Choosing colors and fonts

The aim of this case study is to illustrate the iterative development process and the use of design patterns. The use of design patterns plays a crucial role in the iterative development process because each increment must be designed to be extensible to accommodate design changes and enhancements in subsequent iterations.

The plan is to divide the development process into six iterations:

Iteration 1: Creating a simple scribble pad, which consists of only a canvas for scribbling.

Iteration 2: Adding support for saving and loading drawings, a menu bar, various dialogs.

Iteration 3: Refactoring to support various tools for drawing various shapes.

Iteration 4: Adding tools for drawing lines, rectangles, and ovals.

Iteration 5: Refactoring and adding tools for drawing filled rectangles and ovals.

Iteration 6: Adding a tool for typing text.

In order for students to study the changes between iterations, the code produced in each iteration is placed in a separate package.

9.2   ITERATION 1: A SIMPLE SCRIBBLE PAD

The goal of the first iteration is to deliver an initial version of the application that contains a minimum subset of features. In order to keep it as simple as possible, the initial version of the drawing tool only supports scribbling. The application consists of a frame that contains the canvas for scribbling only. A screen shot of the initial version of the simple scribble pad is shown in Figure 9.1.

Figure 9.1

The simple scribble pad.

Figure 9.2

The design of the
scribble pad—
iteration 1.

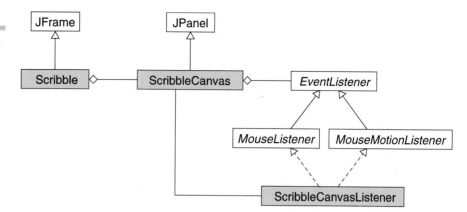

The initial design of the simple scribble pad is shown in Figure 9.2. The UML
diagrams in this chapter contain shaded classes to indicate that these classes are the
ones to be developed in the current iteration, and the rest are classes and interfaces
either in the Java 2 Class Library or developed in previous iterations. The classes
to be developed in the first iteration are in the package scribble1, and they are
summarized in the following table:

Class	Description
Scribble	The main application
ScribbleCanvas	The canvas for scribble
ScribbleCanvasListener	The event listener that listens to mouse events for scribbling

9.2.1 The Scribbling Canvas and Its Listener

Let us first take a look at the ScribbleCanvas class. This is the GUI component on
which all the drawing takes place. It extends the javax.swing.JPanel class, which
is the Swing counterpart of the Panel in AWT. The fields of the ScribbleCanvas
class are as follows:

Fields	Description
mouseButtonDown	Whether one of the mouse buttons is being pressed down
x, y	The current mouse position in the canvas
listener	Mouse event listener of the canvas

Class `scribble1.ScribbleCanvas`

```
package scribble1;

import java.awt.*;
import java.awt.event.*;
import java.util.EventListener;
import javax.swing.*;

public class ScribbleCanvas extends JPanel {

    public ScribbleCanvas() {
        listener = new ScribbleCanvasListener(this);
        addMouseListener((MouseListener) listener);
        addMouseMotionListener((MouseMotionListener) listener);
    }

    protected EventListener listener;
    protected boolean mouseButtonDown = false;
    protected int x, y;

}
```

The `ScribbleCanvasListener` class handles the mouse events that occur in the canvas. The desired behavior of scribbling involves the following actions:

- A stroke begins when any mouse button is pressed.
- The stroke continues when the mouse is dragged, that is, when the user moves the mouse while pressing one of the buttons.
- The stroke finishes when the mouse button is released.

There are two event listener interfaces that deal with mouse events:

1. `java.awt.event.MouseListener`, for events related to the actions on the buttons of the mouse, such as button press and release.
2. `java.awt.event.MouseMotionListener`, for events related to the movement of the mouse, such as mouse move or drag.

The `ScribbleCanvasListener` class must handle button press, button release, and mouse drag actions, so it must implement both the `MouseListener` and `MouseMotionListener` interfaces. The relevant methods of the `ScribbleCanvasListener` class are summarized in the following table:

Methods	Description
mousePressed()	Notified when a mouse button is pressed
mouseReleased()	Notified when a mouse button is released
mouseDragged()	Notified while the mouse is being dragged

The other methods declared in the MouseListener and MouseMotionListener interfaces are of no interest here, so empty implementations are provided for
them.

Class scribble1.ScribbleCanvasListener

```java
package scribble1;

import java.awt.*;
import java.awt.event.*;

public class ScribbleCanvasListener
        implements MouseListener, MouseMotionListener {

    public ScribbleCanvasListener(ScribbleCanvas canvas) {
        this.canvas = canvas;
    }

    public void mousePressed(MouseEvent e) {
        Point p = e.getPoint();
        canvas.mouseButtonDown = true;
        canvas.x = p.x;
        canvas.y = p.y;
    }

    public void mouseReleased(MouseEvent e) {
        canvas.mouseButtonDown = false;
    }

    public void mouseDragged(MouseEvent e) {
        Point p = e.getPoint();
        if (canvas.mouseButtonDown) {
            canvas.getGraphics().drawLine(canvas.x, canvas.y, p.x, p.y);
            canvas.x = p.x;
            canvas.y = p.y;
        }
    }

    public void mouseClicked(MouseEvent e) {}
    public void mouseEntered(MouseEvent e) {}
    public void mouseExited(MouseEvent e) {}
    public void mouseMoved(MouseEvent e) {}

    protected ScribbleCanvas canvas;
}
```

The mousePressed() method handles the beginning of a stroke. It sets the
boolean flag mouseButtonDown of the ScribbleCanvas to true and stores
the current mouse position. The current mouse position is obtained by invoking
e.getPoint(). The position is relative to the upper-left corner of the source component (i.e., the canvas).

While the mouse is being dragged, a series of mouse drag events are generated
by the Java run time. Each event indicates the current mouse position. The mouse-
Dragged() method handles the continuation of a stroke. It draws a line from the

previous mouse position to the current position and updates the current mouse position in `ScribbleCanvas`.

The `mouseReleased()` method handles the end of a drawing stroke. It sets the boolean flag `mouseButtonDown` of the canvas to `false`.

The constructor of `ScribbleCanvas` class [p. 400] creates an instance of `ScribbleCanvasListener` and registers the listener as both `MouseListener` and `MouseMotionListener` of the canvas.

9.2.2 The Application

The `Scribble` class is the main application class of the initial version of the scribble pad. It extends the `javax.swing.JFrame` class. A frame is created in the `main()` method, and an instance of the `ScribbleCanvas` is placed at the center of the frame.

Class `scribble1.Scribble`

```java
package scribble1;

import java.awt.*;
import java.awt.event.*;
import javax.swing.*;

public class Scribble extends JFrame {

    public Scribble() {
        setTitle("Scribble Pad");
        canvas = new ScribbleCanvas();
        canvas.setBackground(Color.white);
        getContentPane().setLayout(new BorderLayout());
        getContentPane().add(canvas, BorderLayout.CENTER);
        addWindowListener(new WindowAdapter() {
            public void windowClosing(WindowEvent e) {
                System.exit(0);
            }
        });
    }

    public static void main(String[] args) {
        int width = 600;
        int height = 400;
        JFrame frame = new Scribble();
        frame.setSize(width, height);
        Dimension screenSize = java.awt.Toolkit.getDefaultToolkit()
            .getScreenSize();
        // place the application frame at the center of the screen
        frame.setLocation(screenSize.width/2 - width/2,
                          screenSize.height/2 - height/2);
        frame.show();
    }

    protected ScribbleCanvas canvas;

}
```

This completes the first iteration of the drawing pad. The result is a simple but completely functional GUI application.

9.3   ITERATION 2: MENUS, OPTIONS, AND FILES

The aim of this iteration is to enhance the scribble in a number of aspects:

- Storing the drawings internally so that they can be redrawn
- Saving the drawings into files and loading drawings from files
- Building a menu bar
- Using the file dialogs
- Creating a dialog box for selecting colors

A screen shot of the scribble pad built in this iteration is shown in Figure 9.3. The design of this iteration of the simple scribble pad is shown in Figure 9.4. The classes of this iteration are in package `scribble2`.

9.3.1   Strokes

One of the deficiencies of the initial version is that the drawings are directly painted onto the canvas by the `ScribbleCanvasListener` object, and they are not stored internally. As a result, if the application frame is moved, covered, or minimized, the drawings disappear. To retain the drawings after the application frame is moved,

Figure 9.3

The scribble pad—iteration 2.

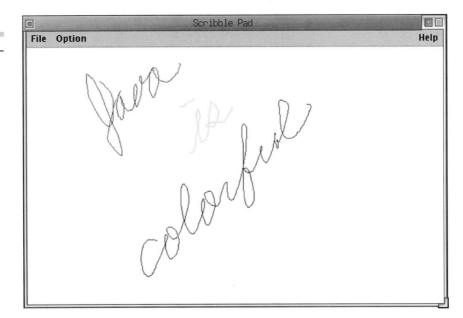

Figure 9.4

The design of the scribble pad—iteration 2.

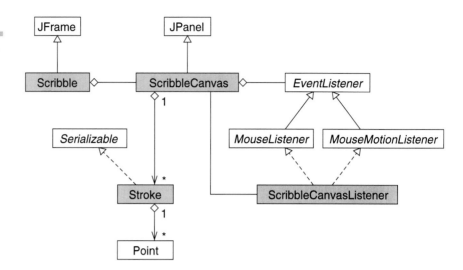

covered, or minimized, the drawings must be stored internally and repainted whenever necessary.

The drawings are stored in the following structure:

- Each drawing consists of a list of *strokes*.
- Each stroke consists of a list of points and the color of the stroke.

The scribble2.Stroke class represents a single stroke in a drawing. Since we want to be able to save the drawings in files, we make Stroke class serializable so that we can use the serialization mechanism to save and load drawings. The fields of the Stroke class are as follows:

Fields	Description
points	The list of points that form the stroke
color	The color of the stroke

The methods of the Stroke class are these:

Methods	Description
setColor()	Set the color of the stroke.
getColor()	Get the color of the stroke.
addPoint()	Append a point to the stroke.
getPoints()	Return the list of points.

Class `scribble2.Stroke`

```java
package scribble2;

import java.util.*;
import java.io.Serializable;
import java.awt.Point;
import java.awt.Color;

public class Stroke implements Serializable {

    public Stroke() {}
    public Stroke(Color color) {
        this.color = color;
    }
    public void setColor(Color color) {
        this.color = color;
    }
    public Color getColor() {
        return color;
    }
    public void addPoint(Point p) {
        if (p != null) {
            points.add(p);
        }
    }
    public List getPoints() {
        return points;
    }
    protected List points = new ArrayList();
    protected Color color = Color.black;
}
```

9.3.2 The Scribble Canvas

The `scribble2.ScribbleCanvas` class is an enhancement to the `scribble1`
`.ScribbleCanvas` class. It stores the drawing as a list of strokes and repaints the
drawings onto the canvas whenever necessary. In addition to the fields declared in
`scribble1.ScribbleCanvas`, the `scribble2.ScribbleCanvas` class contains
the following fields:

Fields	Description
strokes	The list of strokes
curStroke	The current stroke, while the stroke is being drawn
curColor	The color of the current stroke

The methods of the `scribble2.ScribbleCanvas` class are summarized in the following table:

Methods	Description
setCurColor()	Set the current color.
getCurColor()	Get the current color.
startStroke()	Invoked by the listener to start a new stroke. A new current stroke is created.
addPointToStroke()	Invoked by the listener to append a point to the current stroke. A new point is appended to the current stroke.
endStroke()	Invoked by the listener to end a new stroke. The current stroke is added to the list of strokes.
paint()	Invoked by the Java run time whenever the canvas needs to be painted. The drawing is repainted onto the canvas by retracing the strokes stored internally.
newFile()	Create a new drawing and a new file.
saveFile()	Save the current drawing to a file using object serialization.
openFile()	Load a drawing from a file by deserializing the object stored in the file and repaint the canvas.

Class `scribble2.ScribbleCanvas`

```
package scribble2;

import java.awt.Color;
import java.awt.Dimension;
import java.awt.Graphics;
import java.awt.Point;
import java.util.*;
import java.io.*;
import java.awt.event.*;
import java.util.EventListener;
import javax.swing.*;

public class ScribbleCanvas extends JPanel {

    public ScribbleCanvas() {
        listener = new ScribbleCanvasListener(this);
        addMouseListener((MouseListener) listener);
        addMouseMotionListener((MouseMotionListener) listener);
    }
```

```java
public void setCurColor(Color curColor) {
   this.curColor = curColor;
}

public Color getCurColor() {
   return curColor;
}

public void startStroke(Point p) {
   curStroke = new Stroke(curColor);
   curStroke.addPoint(p);
}

public void addPointToStroke(Point p) {
   if (curStroke != null) {
      curStroke.addPoint(p);
   }
}

public void endStroke(Point p) {
   if (curStroke != null) {
      curStroke.addPoint(p);
      strokes.add(curStroke);
      curStroke = null;
   }
}

public void paint(Graphics g) {
   Dimension dim = getSize();
   g.setColor(Color.white);
   g.fillRect(0, 0, dim.width, dim.height);
   g.setColor(Color.black);
   if (strokes != null) {
      Iterator iter1 = strokes.iterator();
      while (iter1.hasNext()) {
         Stroke stroke = (Stroke) iter1.next();
         if (stroke != null) {
            g.setColor(stroke.getColor());
            Point prev = null;
            List points = stroke.getPoints();
            Iterator iter2 = points.iterator();
            while (iter2.hasNext()) {
               Point cur = (Point) iter2.next();
               if (prev != null) {
                  g.drawLine(prev.x, prev.y, cur.x, cur.y);
               }
               prev = cur;
            }
         }
      }
   }
}
```

```java
public void newFile() {
    strokes.clear();
    repaint();
}

public void saveFile(String filename) {
    try {
        ObjectOutputStream out =
            new ObjectOutputStream(new FileOutputStream(filename));
        out.writeObject(strokes);
        out.close();
        System.out.println("Save drawing to " + filename);
    } catch (IOException e) {
        System.out.println("Unable to write file: " + filename);
    }
}

public void openFile(String filename) {
    try {
        ObjectInputStream in =
            new ObjectInputStream(new FileInputStream(filename));
        strokes = (List) in.readObject();
        in.close();
        repaint();
    } catch (IOException e1) {
        System.out.println("Unable to open file: " + filename);
    } catch (ClassNotFoundException e2) {
        System.out.println(e2);
    }
}

protected List strokes = new ArrayList();

protected Stroke curStroke = null;
protected Color curColor = Color.black;

protected EventListener listener;
protected boolean mouseButtonDown = false;
protected int x, y;
}
```

9.3.3   The Canvas Listener

The scribble2.ScribbleCanvasListener class is very similar to the scribble1.ScribbleCanvas class in the previous iteration. The only difference is that in addition to drawing the points of a stroke onto the canvas, the points must also be stored in strokes. Method startStroke(), addPointToStroke(), or endStroke() of the canvas is invoked by method mousePressed(), mouseReleased(), or mouseDragged() of the listener, respectively.

Class `scribble2.ScribbleCanvasListener`

```java
package scribble2;

import java.awt.*;
import java.awt.event.*;

public class ScribbleCanvasListener
        implements MouseListener, MouseMotionListener {

   public ScribbleCanvasListener(ScribbleCanvas canvas) {
      this.canvas = canvas;
   }

   public void mousePressed(MouseEvent e) {
      Point p = e.getPoint();
      canvas.mouseButtonDown = true;
      canvas.startStroke(p);
      canvas.x = p.x;
      canvas.y = p.y;
   }

   public void mouseReleased(MouseEvent e) {
      Point p = e.getPoint();
      canvas.endStroke(p);
      canvas.mouseButtonDown = false;
   }

   public void mouseDragged(MouseEvent e) {
      Point p = e.getPoint();
      if (canvas.mouseButtonDown) {
         canvas.addPointToStroke(p);
         Graphics g = canvas.getGraphics();
         g.setColor(canvas.getCurColor());
         g.drawLine(canvas.x, canvas.y, p.x, p.y);
         canvas.x = p.x;
         canvas.y = p.y;
      }
   }

   public void mouseClicked(MouseEvent e) {}
   public void mouseEntered(MouseEvent e) {}
   public void mouseExited(MouseEvent e) {}
   public void mouseMoved(MouseEvent e) {}

   protected ScribbleCanvas canvas;

}
```

9.3.4 The Application

The `scribble2.Scribble` class is the main application class. This version of the scribble pad has a menu bar. The `scribble2.Scribble` class contains a number of nested classes, which are the listeners of the menu items in the menu bar. The methods of the `scribble2.Scribble` class are summarized in the following table:

Methods	Description
createMenuBar()	Create the menu bar.
newFile()	Start a new drawing and a new file.
openFile()	Load a drawing from the specified file.
saveFile()	Save the current drawing to the current file.
saveFileAs()	Save the current drawing to the specified file.

The nested classes of the `scribble2.Scribble` class are summarized in the following table:

Nested Classes	Description
NewFileListener	Action for the "New" menu item
OpenFileListener	Action for the "Open" menu item
SaveFileListener	Action for the "Save" menu item
SaveAsFileListener	Action for the "Save As" menu item
ExitListener	Action for the "Exit" menu item
ColorListener	Action for the "Color" menu item
AboutListener	Action for the "About" menu item

Class `scribble2.Scribble`

```java
package scribble2;

import java.awt.*;
import java.awt.event.*;
import java.io.*;
import javax.swing.*;

public class Scribble extends JFrame {
    public Scribble() {
        setTitle("Scribble Pad");
        canvas = new ScribbleCanvas();
        getContentPane().setLayout(new BorderLayout());
        getContentPane().add(createMenuBar(), BorderLayout.NORTH);
        getContentPane().add(canvas, BorderLayout.CENTER);
```

```
        addWindowListener(new WindowAdapter() {
            public void windowClosing(WindowEvent e) {
                if (exitAction != null) {
                    exitAction.actionPerformed(new ActionEvent
                                                (Scribble.this, 0, null));
                }
            }
        });
    }

    〈createMenuBar() method on page 411〉
    〈newFile(), openFile(), saveFile(), and saveFileAs() methods on page 416〉
    〈Nested class NewFileListener on page 413〉
    〈Nested class OpenFileListener on page 413〉
    〈Nested class SaveFileListener on page 414〉
    〈Nested class SaveAsFileListener on page 415〉
    〈Nested class ExitListener on page 415〉
    〈Nested class ColorListener on page 417〉
    〈Nested class AboutListener on page 413〉

    public static void main(String[] args) {
        int width = 600;
        int height = 400;
        JFrame frame = new Scribble();
        frame.setSize(width, height);
        Dimension screenSize =
            java.awt.Toolkit.getDefaultToolkit().getScreenSize();
        // place the application frame at the center of the screen
        frame.setLocation(screenSize.width/2 - width/2,
                          screenSize.height/2 - height/2);
        frame.show();
    }

    protected String currentFilename = null;
    protected ScribbleCanvas canvas;
    protected ActionListener exitAction;
    protected JFileChooser chooser = new JFileChooser(".");

}
```

In the constructor of the Scribble class, the menu bar is created and placed
above the canvas. The menu bar is created by the following createMenuBar()
method:

Method of scribble2.Scribble class: createMenuBar()

```
protected JMenuBar createMenuBar() {
    JMenuBar menuBar = new JMenuBar();
    JMenu menu;
    JMenuItem mi;

    // File menu
    menu = new JMenu("File");
    menuBar.add(menu);
```

```java
        mi = new JMenuItem("New");
        menu.add(mi);
        mi.addActionListener(new NewFileListener());

        mi = new JMenuItem("Open");
        menu.add(mi);
        mi.addActionListener(new OpenFileListener());

        mi = new JMenuItem("Save");
        menu.add(mi);
        mi.addActionListener(new SaveFileListener());

        mi = new JMenuItem("Save As");
        menu.add(mi);
        mi.addActionListener(new SaveAsFileListener());

        menu.add(new JSeparator());

        exitAction = new ExitListener();
        mi = new JMenuItem("Exit");
        menu.add(mi);
        mi.addActionListener(exitAction);

        // option menu
        menu = new JMenu("Option");
        menuBar.add(menu);

        mi = new JMenuItem("Color");
        menu.add(mi);
        mi.addActionListener(new ColorListener());

        // horizontal space
        menuBar.add(Box.createHorizontalGlue());

        // Help menu
        menu = new JMenu("Help");
        menuBar.add(menu);

        mi = new JMenuItem("About");
        menu.add(mi);
        mi.addActionListener(new AboutListener());

        return menuBar;
    }
```

Note that each menu item has an associated action listener to handle the action of the menu item. The action listeners are all defined as nested classes of the Scribble class.

The simplest action listener is the AboutListener, which handles the action of the *About* menu item in the *Help* menu. It displays a simple dialog box using the javax.swing.JOptionPane class as shown in Figure 9.5. The JOptionPane class provides various static methods to display the most commonly used dialog boxes with a single method invocation.[1]

---

1. See API documentations on the javax.swing.JOptionPane class for details.

Figure 9.5

The "About" dialog
of the scribble pad.

Nested class of `scribble2.Scribble` class: `AboutListener`

```
class AboutListener implements ActionListener {

   public void actionPerformed(ActionEvent e) {
      JOptionPane.showMessageDialog(null,
            "DrawingPad version 1.0\nCopyright (c) Xiaoping Jia 2002",
               "About",
            JOptionPane.INFORMATION_MESSAGE);
   }

}
```

The `NewFileListener` class handles the action of the *New* menu item in the *File* menu. The action is delegated to the `newFile()` method, as follows:

Nested class of `scribble2.Scribble` class: `NewFileListener`

```
class NewFileListener implements ActionListener {

   public void actionPerformed(ActionEvent e) {
      newFile();
   }

}
```

The `OpenFileListener` class handles the action of the *Open* menu item in the *File* menu. It uses the `javax.swing.JFileChooser` class to display a file dialog as shown in Figure 9.6. After a file name is selected using the file dialog, the action is delegated to the `openFile()` method with the selected file name, as follows:

Nested class of `scribble2.Scribble` class: `OpenFileListener`

```
class OpenFileListener implements ActionListener {

   public void actionPerformed(ActionEvent e) {
      int retval = chooser.showDialog(null, "Open");
      if (retval == JFileChooser.APPROVE_OPTION) {
         File theFile = chooser.getSelectedFile();
         if (theFile != null) {
            if (theFile.isFile()) {
```

```
                        String filename =
                            chooser.getSelectedFile().getAbsolutePath();
                        openFile(filename);
                    }
                }
            }
        }
    }
```

The SaveFileListener class handles the action of the *Save* menu item in the *File* menu. The action is delegated to the saveFile() method, as follows:

Nested class of scribble2.Scribble class: SaveFileListener

```
class SaveFileListener implements ActionListener {

    public void actionPerformed(ActionEvent e) {
        saveFile();
    }
}
```

The SaveAsFileListener class handles the action of the *Save As* menu item in the *File* menu. It also uses the javax.swing.JFileChooser class to display a file dialog similar to the one shown in Figure 9.6. After a file name is selected using

Figure 9.6

The file dialog of the scribble pad.

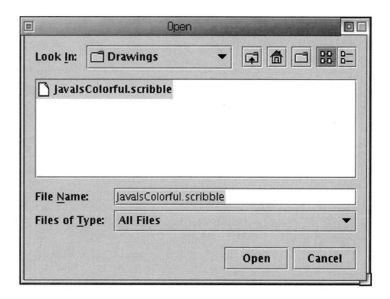

the file dialog, the action is delegated to the `saveFileAs()` method with the selected file name, as follows:

Nested class of `scribble2.Scribble` class: `SaveAsFileListener`

```
class SaveAsFileListener implements ActionListener {

    public void actionPerformed(ActionEvent e) {
        int retval = chooser.showDialog(null, "Save As");
        if (retval == JFileChooser.APPROVE_OPTION) {
            File theFile = chooser.getSelectedFile();
            if (theFile != null) {
                if (!theFile.isDirectory()) {
                    String filename =
                        chooser.getSelectedFile().getAbsolutePath();
                    saveFileAs(filename);
                }
            }
        }
    }

}
```

The `ExitListener` class handles the action of the *Exit* menu item in the *File* menu. It displays a simple dialog box using the `javax.swing.JOptionPane` class as shown in Figure 9.7 to prompt the user to save the current drawing.

Nested class of `scribble2.Scribble` class: `ExitListener`

```
class ExitListener implements ActionListener {

    public void actionPerformed(ActionEvent e) {
        int result = JOptionPane.showConfirmDialog(null,
                        "Do you want to exit Scribble Pad?",
                        "Exit Scribble Pad?",
                        JOptionPane.YES_NO_OPTION);
        if (result == JOptionPane.YES_OPTION) {
            saveFile();
            System.exit(0);
        }
    }
}
```

Figure 9.7

The "Exit" dialog of the scribble pad.

The methods dealing with files maintain the current file name and delegate most of the work to the corresponding method in the `scribble2.ScribbleCanvas` class [p. 406].

Methods of `scribble2.Scribble` class: `newFile()`, `openFile()`, `saveFile()`, and `saveFileAs()`

```java
protected void newFile() {
    currentFilename = null;
    canvas.newFile();
    setTitle("Scribble Pad");
}

protected void openFile(String filename) {
    currentFilename = filename;
    canvas.openFile(filename);
    setTitle("Scribble Pad [" + currentFilename + "]");
}

protected void saveFile() {
    if (currentFilename == null) {
        currentFilename = "Untitled";
    }
    canvas.saveFile(currentFilename);
    setTitle("Scribble Pad [" + currentFilename + "]");
}

protected void saveFileAs(String filename) {
    currentFilename = filename;
    canvas.saveFile(filename);
    setTitle("Scribble Pad [" + currentFilename + "]");
}
```

9.3.5 Choosing Colors

The nested `ColorListener` class handles the action of the *Color* menu item in the *Option* menu. It displays a custom dialog box as shown in Figure 9.8. The custom color dialog is defined in the `scribble2.ColorDialog` class.

Figure 9.8

The color dialog of the scribble pad.

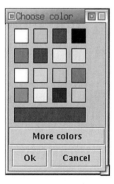

Nested class of `scribble2.Scribble` class: `ColorListener`

```java
class ColorListener implements ActionListener {

    public void actionPerformed(ActionEvent e) {
        Color result = dialog.showDialog();
        if (result != null) {
            canvas.setCurColor(result);
        }
    }

    protected ColorDialog dialog =
        new ColorDialog(Scribble.this, "Choose color",
                        canvas.getCurColor());

}
```

Class `scribble2.ColorDialog`

```java
package scribble2;

import java.awt.*;
import java.awt.event.*;
import javax.swing.*;

public class ColorDialog extends JDialog implements
    ActionListener {

    public ColorDialog(JFrame owner, String title) {
        this(owner, title, Color.black);
    }

    public ColorDialog(JFrame owner, String title,
                        Color color) {
        super(owner, title, true);
        this.color = color;

        getContentPane().setLayout(new BorderLayout());

        JPanel topPanel = new JPanel();
        topPanel.setLayout(new BorderLayout());
        colorPanel = new ColorPanel(20, 20, 8, 8);
        topPanel.add(colorPanel, BorderLayout.CENTER);
        moreColorButton = new JButton("More colors");
        moreColorButton.addActionListener(this);
        topPanel.add(moreColorButton, BorderLayout.SOUTH);
        getContentPane().add(topPanel, BorderLayout.CENTER);

        JPanel bottomPanel = new JPanel();
        bottomPanel.setLayout(new FlowLayout(FlowLayout.RIGHT));
        okButton = new JButton("Ok");
        okButton.addActionListener(this);
        bottomPanel.add(okButton);
        cancelButton = new JButton("Cancel");
        cancelButton.addActionListener(this);
```

```
        bottomPanel.add(cancelButton);
        getContentPane().add(bottomPanel, BorderLayout.SOUTH);

        pack();
    }

    public Color showDialog() {
        result = null;
        colorPanel.setColor(color);
        Dimension screenSize =
            Toolkit.getDefaultToolkit().getScreenSize();
        Dimension dialogSize = getSize();
        setLocation(screenSize.width / 2 - dialogSize.width / 2,
                    screenSize.height / 2 - dialogSize.height / 2);
        show();
        if (result != null) {
            color = result;
        }
        return result;
    }

    public void actionPerformed(ActionEvent e) {
        Object source = e.getSource();
        if (source == okButton) {
            result = colorPanel.getColor();
        } else if (source == moreColorButton) {
            Color selectedColor = chooser.showDialog(ColorDialog.this,
                                                     "Choose color",
                                                     color);

            if (selectedColor != null) {
                colorPanel.setColor(selectedColor);
                colorPanel.repaint();
            }
            return;
        }
        setVisible(false);
    }

    protected JButton okButton;
    protected JButton cancelButton;
    protected JButton moreColorButton;
    protected ColorPanel colorPanel;
    protected JColorChooser chooser = new JColorChooser();
    protected Color color = null;

    protected Color result = null;

    class ColorPanel extends JPanel {

        ColorPanel(int cellWidth, int cellHeight, int xpad, int ypad) {
            if (cellWidth < 5) {
                cellWidth = 5;
            }
```

```java
        if (cellHeight < 5) {
            cellHeight = 5;
        }
        if (xpad < 2) {
            xpad = 2;
        }
        if (ypad < 2) {
            ypad = 2;
        }
        this.cellWidth = cellWidth;
        this.cellHeight = cellHeight;
        this.xpad = xpad;
        this.ypad = ypad;
        rowCount = colorGrid.length;
        columnCount = colorGrid[0].length;
        dimension = new Dimension((cellWidth + xpad) *
                                   columnCount + xpad,
                                   (cellHeight + ypad) *
                                   (rowCount + 1) + ypad);
        addMouseListener(new MouseAdapter() {
            public void mousePressed(MouseEvent event) {
                Point p = event.getPoint();
                int i = (p.y / (ColorPanel.this.cellHeight +
                            ColorPanel.this.ypad));
                int j = (p.x / (ColorPanel.this.cellWidth +
                            ColorPanel.this.xpad));
                if (i < rowCount &&
                    j < columnCount) {
                    color = colorGrid[i][j];
                    repaint();
                }
            }
        });
    }

    public void setColor(Color color) {
        this.color = color;
    }

    public Color getColor() {
        return color;
    }

    public Dimension getMinimumSize() {
        return dimension;
    }

    public Dimension getPreferredSize() {
        return dimension;
    }
```

```java
    public void paint(Graphics g) {
        Dimension dim = getSize();
        g.setColor(Color.lightGray);
        g.fillRect(0, 0, dim.width, dim.height);
        int x, y;
        for (int i = 0; i < rowCount; i++) {
            for (int j = 0; j < columnCount; j++) {
                x = (cellWidth + xpad) * j + xpad;
                y = (cellHeight + ypad) * i + ypad;
                g.setColor(colorGrid[i][j]);
                g.fillRect(x, y, cellWidth, cellHeight);
                g.setColor(Color.black);
                g.drawRect(x, y, cellWidth, cellHeight);
            }
        }
        x = xpad;
        y = (cellHeight + ypad) * rowCount + ypad;
        int width = (cellWidth + xpad) * columnCount - xpad;
        g.setColor(color);
        g.fillRect(x, y, width, cellHeight);
        g.setColor(Color.black);
        g.drawRect(x, y, width, cellHeight);
    }

    protected Color color;

    protected int cellWidth;
    protected int cellHeight;
    protected int rowCount;
    protected int columnCount;
    protected int xpad;
    protected int ypad;
    protected Dimension dimension;

    protected Color[][] colorGrid = {
        { Color.white, Color.lightGray, Color.darkGray,
          Color.black },
        { Color.gray, Color.blue, Color.cyan,
          Color.green },
        { Color.yellow, Color.orange, Color.pink,
          Color.red },
        { Color.magenta, new Color(230, 230, 250),
          new Color(0, 0, 128),
          new Color(64, 224, 208) } };

}

}
```

It uses the `javax.swing.ColorChooser` class to display a color chooser dialog as shown in Figure 9.9.

This completes the second iteration of the drawing pad.

Figure 9.9

The Swing color chooser.

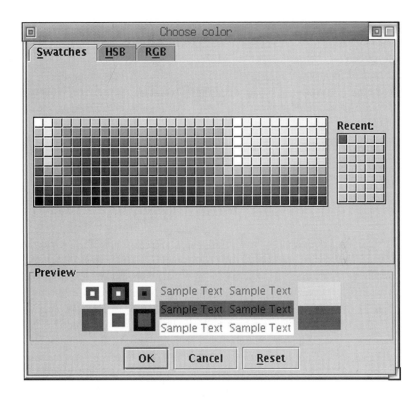

9.4 ITERATION 3: REFACTORING

The ultimate goal of the drawing pad is to support the drawing of various types of shapes, such as lines, ovals, and rectangles. The current version of the drawing pad supports only scribbling. The design of the current version of the drawing pad is also rather simpleminded to support scribbling only. In order to support the drawing of various types of shapes, the design of the drawing pad must be improved to accommodate such extensions. The aim of this iteration is to refactor the design to improve its extensibility. The functionality of the resulting application is identical to that of the previous iteration.

9.4.1 The Shapes

The first step in refactoring the design of the drawing pad is to generalize the notion of shapes that can be drawn in the drawing pad. Currently, the only shape that can be drawn is a stroke as defined in the previous iteration. To generalize the notion

Figure 9.10

Refactoring the
scribble pad—the
shapes.

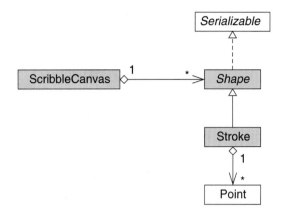

of shapes, we introduce an abstract class Shape to represent all shapes that can be drawn, with stroke being one of such shapes. The refactored design concerning the shapes is shown in Figure 9.10. Other shapes include lines, ovals, and rectangles. The subclasses representing these other shapes are introduced in the next iteration (see Figure 9.13).

The reason for Shape being an abstract class instead of an interface is that there are some features, that is, fields and methods, that are common to all shapes, for example, the color of each shape. It is more appropriate to define these common features in a common superclass. The field color and the associated methods previously defined in the Stroke class are moved to the superclass Shape. The abstract method draw() is intended for each subclass to define how each shape should be drawn.

Abstract class scribble3.Shape

```
package scribble3;

import java.awt.*;
import java.io.Serializable;

public abstract class Shape implements Serializable {

    public Shape() {}

    public Shape(Color color) {
        this.color = color;
    }

    public void setColor(Color color) {
        this.color = color;
    }

    public Color getColor() {
        return color;
    }

    public abstract void draw(Graphics g);

    protected Color color = Color.black;

}
```

The scribble3.Stroke class in this iteration is identical to the version in the previous iteration, except the field color and related methods are moved to the superclass Shape.

Class scribble3.Stroke

```java
package scribble3;

import java.util.*;
import java.awt.Point;
import java.awt.Color;
import java.awt.Graphics;

public class Stroke extends Shape {

    public Stroke() {}

    public Stroke(Color color) {
        super(color);
    }

    public void addPoint(Point p) {
        if (p != null) {
            points.add(p);
        }
    }

    public List getPoints() {
        return points;
    }

    public void draw(Graphics g) {
        if (color != null) {
            g.setColor(color);
        }
        Point prev = null;
        Iterator iter = points.iterator();
        while (iter.hasNext()) {
            Point cur = (Point) iter.next();
            if (prev != null) {
                g.drawLine(prev.x, prev.y, cur.x, cur.y);
            }
            prev = cur;
        }
    }

    // The list of points on the stroke
    // elements are instances of java.awt.Point
    protected List points = new ArrayList();

}
```

The refactoring of the design concerning the shapes is an application of the Strategy design pattern. The Shape class is the abstract strategy, and the Stroke class is a concrete strategy.

9.4.2 The Tools

In order to draw different shapes, such as lines, ovals, and rectangles, the behavior of the canvas listener must be different when drawing different shapes. One possible approach is outlined in the following code fragments. First, we define a set of constants to represent possible shapes that need to be drawn and use a field `currentShape` to indicate the currently selected shape:

```java
public class DrawingPad {
    // constants representing shapes
    public static final int SCRIBBLE = 0;
    public static final int LINE = 1;
    public static final int RECTANGLE = 2;
    public static final int OVAL = 3;
    // the currently selected shape
    protected int currentShape = SCRIBBLE;
    public void setCurrentShape(int shape) {
        currentShape = shape;
    }
    public int getCurrentShape() {
        return currentShape;
    }
    // other fields and methods
}
```

Second, the canvas listener will be extended as follows:

```java
public class DrawingCanvasListener
        implements MouseListener, MouseMotionListener {

    public void mousePressed(MouseEvent e) {
        switch (drawingPad.getCurrentShape()) {
        case DrawingPad.SCRIBBLE:
            // handle mouse pressed event for scribbling break;
        case DrawingPad.LINE:
            // handle mouse pressed event for drawing a line break;
        case DrawingPad.RECTANGLE:
            // handle mouse pressed event for drawing a rectangle break;
        case DrawingPad.OVAL:
            // handle mouse pressed event for drawing an oval break;
        }
    }

    public void mouseDragged(MouseEvent e) {
        switch (drawingPad.getCurrentShape()) {
        case DrawingPad.SCRIBBLE:
            // handle mouse dragged event for scribbling break;
        case DrawingPad.LINE:
            // handle mouse dragged event for drawing a line break;
        case DrawingPad.RECTANGLE:
            // handle mouse dragged event for drawing a rectangle break;
        case DrawingPad.OVAL:
            // handle mouse dragged event for drawing an oval break;
        }
    }
```

```
public void mouseReleased(MouseEvent e) {
  switch (drawingPad.getCurrentShape()) {
  case DrawingPad.SCRIBBLE:
    // handle mouse released event for scribbling break;
  case DrawingPad.LINE:
    // handle mouse released event for drawing a line break;
  case DrawingPad.RECTANGLE:
    // handle mouse released event for drawing a rectangle break;
  case DrawingPad.OVAL:
    // handle mouse released event for drawing an oval break;
  }
}
// . . .
}
```

This design works. However, it is rather cumbersome, inflexible, and inelegant, for the following reasons. First, the use of the constants to represent shapes causes the coupling between the DrawingPad and DrawingPadListener classes to be very high. The labels of the switch statements in the DrawingPadListener class must exactly match the constants defined in the DrawingPad class. Adding new shapes or removing existing shapes requires carefully coordinated changes in both classes. Second, the behavior of drawing each shape is defined in three separate methods— mousePressed(), mouseReleased(), and mouseDragged()—intermixed with the behaviors of dealing with other shapes. Thus, changing the behavior of handling a particular shape or adding or removing a shape requires coordinated changes in all three methods. This requirement is a severe hindrance to the readability of the code and makes changes to the code very difficult and error-prone.

A better design is to encapsulate the behavior of handling the drawing of a particular shape in a class, which we call a *tool*. The behavior of each tool is defined by its response to the following events: mouse button pressed, mouse button released, and mouse dragged. The following interface Tool represents an abstraction of the tools. The behavior of drawing a particular shape is defined in a class that implements the Tool interface, such as the ScribbleTool class. The refactored design concerning the tools is shown in Figure 9.11. It becomes clear in the next iteration that this design allows much easier extensions of additional shapes and tools (see Figure 9.14).

Figure 9.11

Refactoring the
scribble pad—the
tools.

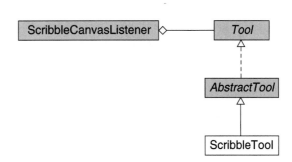

Interface `scribble3.Tool`

```
package scribble3;

import java.awt.*;

public interface Tool {

    public String getName();
    public void startShape(Point p);
    public void addPointToShape(Point p);
    public void endShape(Point p);

}
```

The `AbstractTool` class implements the `Tool` interface and provides default implementation to features that are shared by all tools.

Abstract class `scribble3.AbstractTool`

```
package scribble3;

public abstract class AbstractTool implements Tool {

    public String getName() {
        return name;
    }

    protected AbstractTool(ScribbleCanvas canvas, String name) {
        this.canvas = canvas;
        this.name = name;
    }

    protected ScribbleCanvas canvas;
    protected String name;

}
```

The `ScribbleTool` class is a concrete tool that defines the behavior for scribbling. Note that the implementation of the `ScribbleTool` class is identical to portions of the implementation that were previously in the `scribble2.ScribbleCanvasListener` class.

Class `scribble3.ScribbleTool`

```
package scribble3;

import java.awt.*;

public class ScribbleTool extends AbstractTool {

    public ScribbleTool(ScribbleCanvas canvas, String name) {
        super(canvas, name);
    }

    public void startShape(Point p) {
        curStroke = new Stroke(canvas.getCurColor());
        curStroke.addPoint(p);
    }
```

```
public void addPointToShape(Point p) {
    if (curStroke != null) {
        curStroke.addPoint(p);
        Graphics g = canvas.getGraphics();
        g.setColor(canvas.getCurColor());
        g.drawLine(canvas.x, canvas.y, p.x, p.y);
    }
}

public void endShape(Point p) {
    if (curStroke != null) {
        curStroke.addPoint(p);
        canvas.addShape(curStroke);
        curStroke = null;
    }
}

protected Stroke curStroke = null;
}
```

The behavior of drawing each shape is now encapsulated in a tool for that shape. The scribble3.ScribbleCanvasListener class contains a reference to the current tool being used for drawing, that is, the scribble tool in this iteration, since it is the only tool supported. It is to this tool that responses to events of the scribble3.ScribbleCanvasListener class are delegated.

Class scribble3.ScribbleCanvasListener

```
package scribble3;
import java.awt.*;
import java.awt.event.*;

public class ScribbleCanvasListener
        implements MouseListener, MouseMotionListener {

    public ScribbleCanvasListener(ScribbleCanvas canvas) {
        this.canvas = canvas;
        tool = new ScribbleTool(canvas, "Scribble");
    }

    public void mousePressed(MouseEvent e) {
        Point p = e.getPoint();
        tool.startShape(p);
        canvas.mouseButtonDown = true;
        canvas.x = p.x;
        canvas.y = p.y;
    }

    public void mouseDragged(MouseEvent e) {
        Point p = e.getPoint();
        if (canvas.mouseButtonDown) {
            tool.addPointToShape(p);
            canvas.x = p.x;
            canvas.y = p.y;
        }
    }
```

```
public void mouseReleased(MouseEvent e) {
    Point p = e.getPoint();
    tool.endShape(p);
    canvas.mouseButtonDown = false;
}

public void mouseClicked(MouseEvent e) {}
public void mouseEntered(MouseEvent e) {}
public void mouseExited(MouseEvent e) {}
public void mouseMoved(MouseEvent e) {}

protected ScribbleCanvasListener(ScribbleCanvas canvas, Tool tool) {
    this.canvas = canvas;
    this.tool = tool;
}

protected ScribbleCanvas canvas;
protected Tool tool;

}
```

The refactoring concerning the tools is also an application of the Strategy design pattern. In the next iteration, the design will be further extended to support multiple tools, in which case the Strategy pattern concerning the tools here will become a part of a new design pattern—State (see Section 9.5.3).

9.4.3 Extending Components

The various components of the drawing pad will be enhanced and extended in several iterations. Enhancements can usually be accomplished in two ways:

1. Modifying the original class
2. Building a new class that extends the original class

Usually the same enhancement can be accomplished in either way. However, enhancement by extending the original class has several advantages:

- It is nondestructive. The original implementation is untouched, and the enhancements or changes can be easily reversed.
- It is more suited for iterative development, in which systems are built in small increments. The separate classes form the natural boundaries of the increments.
- It is the only option when the source code of the original class is not available or the original class should not be modified for some reason; e.g., it is used by other programs that should not be affected by the enhancements or changes to the class.

In iterations 2 and 3, we modified the original code in classes Scribble, Scribble-Canvas, and ScribbleCanvasListener to implement enhancements and changes. In all the subsequent iterations, we will use the extension technique to implement enhancements and changes. Specifically, new versions of the canvas and canvas listener classes will extend the previous version of the canvas and canvas listener classes, respectively.

The `scribble3.Scribble` class is nearly identical to the `scribble2.Scribble` class. The only difference is that in `scribble3.Scribble` the canvas is not created directly by using the `new` operator; rather it is created indirectly by using a *factory method*—`makeCanvas()`. Using a factory method instead of the `new` operator allows subclasses of the `Scribble` class to instantiate instances of subclasses of `ScribbleCanvas`, which represent enhanced versions of the canvas. To replace the canvas with an enhanced canvas, a subclass of the `Scribble` class can override the factory methods to create instances of the enhanced canvas. No change in the `Scribble` class would be necessary. The benefits of using factory methods will become clear in iteration 4 [p. 445].

Class `scribble3.Scribble`

```java
package scribble3;

import java.awt.*;
import java.awt.event.*;
import java.io.*;
import javax.swing.*;

public class Scribble extends JFrame {

    public Scribble() {
        super("Scribble Pad");
        // calling the factory method
        canvas = makeCanvas();
        getContentPane().setLayout(new BorderLayout());
        menuBar = createMenuBar();
        getContentPane().add(menuBar, BorderLayout.NORTH);
        getContentPane().add(canvas, BorderLayout.CENTER);
        addWindowListener(new WindowAdapter() {
            public void windowClosing(WindowEvent e) {
                if (exitAction != null) {
                    exitAction.actionPerformed(new ActionEvent
                                        (Scribble.this, 0, null));
                }
            }
        });
    }

    // the factory method
    protected ScribbleCanvas makeCanvas() {
        return new ScribbleCanvas();
    }
```

⟨createMenuBar() method on page 411⟩
⟨newFile(), openFile(), saveFile(), and saveFileAs() methods on page 416⟩
⟨Nested class NewFileListener on page 413⟩
⟨Nested class OpenFileListener on page 413⟩
⟨Nested class SaveFileListener on page 414⟩

⟨Nested class SaveAsFileListener on page 415⟩
⟨Nested class ExitListener on page 415⟩
⟨Nested class ColorListener on page 417⟩
⟨Nested class AboutListener on page 413⟩
}

The scribble3.ScribbleCanvas class is also very similar to scribble2 .ScribbleCanvas. The main differences in the scribble3.ScribbleCanvas class are these:

- The canvas listener is also created using a factory method—makeCanvas-Listener().
- The drawings are stored as a list of *shapes* instead of a list of *strokes*. The strokes field in scribble2.ScribbleCanvas is replaced by the shapes field in scribble3.ScribbleCanvas. Corresponding changes are also made in methods newFile(), openFile(), saveFile(), and paint().

Class scribble3.ScribbleCanvas

```java
package scribble3;

import java.awt.Color;
import java.awt.Dimension;
import java.awt.Graphics;
import java.awt.Point;
import java.util.*;
import java.io.*;
import java.awt.event.*;
import java.util.EventListener;
import javax.swing.*;

public class ScribbleCanvas extends JPanel {

    public ScribbleCanvas() {
        // calling the factory method
        listener = makeCanvasListener();
        addMouseListener((MouseListener) listener);
        addMouseMotionListener((MouseMotionListener) listener);
    }

    public void setCurColor(Color curColor) {
        this.curColor = curColor;
    }

    public Color getCurColor() {
        return curColor;
    }

    public void addShape(Shape shape) {
        if (shape != null) {
            shapes.add(shape);
        }
    }
}
```

```java
public void paint(Graphics g) {
    Dimension dim = getSize();
    g.setColor(Color.white);
    g.fillRect(0, 0, dim.width, dim.height);
    g.setColor(Color.black);
    if (shapes != null) {
        Iterator iter = shapes.iterator();
        while (iter.hasNext()) {
            Shape shape = (Shape) iter.next();
            if (shape != null) {
                shape.draw(g);
            }
        }
    }
}

public void newFile() {
    shapes.clear();
    repaint();
}

public void openFile(String filename) {
    try {
        ObjectInputStream in =
            new ObjectInputStream(new FileInputStream(filename));
        shapes = (List) in.readObject();
        in.close();
        repaint();
    } catch (IOException e1) {
        System.out.println("Unable to open file: " + filename);
    } catch (ClassNotFoundException e2) {
        System.out.println(e2);
    }
}

public void saveFile(String filename) {
    try {
        ObjectOutputStream out =
            new ObjectOutputStream(new FileOutputStream(filename));
        out.writeObject(shapes);
        out.close();
        System.out.println("Save drawing to " + filename);
    } catch (IOException e) {
        System.out.println("Unable to write file: " + filename);
    }
}

// the factory method
protected EventListener makeCanvasListener() {
    return new ScribbleCanvasListener(this);
}
```

```
        protected List shapes = new ArrayList();

        protected Color curColor = Color.black;

        protected EventListener listener;

        public boolean mouseButtonDown = false;
        public int x, y;

    }
```

This completes the third iteration of the drawing pad, which is concerned with refactoring only to improve extensibility without enhancement in functionality.

9.5 ITERATION 4: ADDING SHAPES AND TOOLS

In this iteration, we enhance the functionality of the drawing pad. The refactoring of the design in the last iteration allows these enhancements to be added easily and incrementally. A screen shot of this version of the drawing pad is shown in Figure 9.12. The drawing pad has a tool bar at the left, with each tool button representing a different tool. Clicking on the tool button selects the tool for the drawing. The tools supported by this drawing pad are the scribbling tool, the line-drawing tool, the rectangle-drawing tool, and the oval-drawing tool. This version also adds a new menu—*Tools*—on the menu bar. A drawing tool can also be selected from the menu item corresponding to the tool.

Figure 9.12

The drawing pad—
iteration 4.

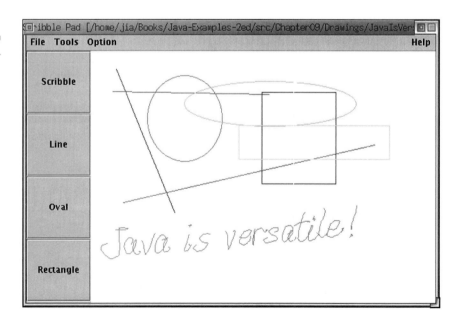

The key issues addressed in this iteration are the following:

- Use of the State design pattern to support the different behaviors associated with different tools and to switch among different tools dynamically.
- Use of the Factory Method design pattern to allow flexibility in creating instances of different subclasses.

9.5.1 The Shapes

In this iteration, the drawing of the following types of shapes will be supported: line, oval, and rectangle. These three types of shapes share a common characteristic—each of these shapes can be completely defined by two points: the two end points for lines and the two diagonally opposite corners for rectangles and ovals. We call these two points the *end points*. An abstract class named TwoEndsShape is introduced to capture this common feature. The design concerning the shapes in this iteration is shown in Figure 9.13.

The methods of the TwoEndsShape class are summarized in the following table:

Methods	Description
setEnds()	Set both end points.
setEnd1()	Set the first end point.
setEnd2()	Set the second end point.
getX1()	Return the *x* coordinate of the first end point.
getY1()	Return the *y* coordinate of the first end point.
getX2()	Return the *x* coordinate of the second end point.
getY2()	Return the *y* coordinate of the second end point.
drawOutline()	Draw a temporary frame of the shape.

Figure 9.13

The design of the drawing pad—the shapes.

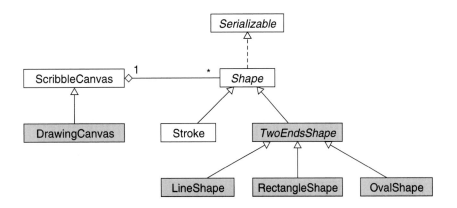

Abstract class `draw1.TwoEndsShape`

```java
package draw1;

import java.awt.Graphics;
import java.awt.Color;

public abstract class TwoEndsShape extends scribble3.Shape implements
    Cloneable {

    public TwoEndsShape() {}

    public TwoEndsShape(Color color) {
        super(color);
    }

    public Object clone() throws CloneNotSupportedException {
        return super.clone();
    }

    public void setEnds(int x1, int y1, int x2, int y2) {
        this.x1 = x1;
        this.y1 = y1;
        this.x2 = x2;
        this.y2 = y2;
    }

    public void setEnd1(int x1, int y1) {
        this.x1 = x1;
        this.y1 = y1;
    }

    public void setEnd2(int x2, int y2) {
        this.x2 = x2;
        this.y2 = y2;
    }

    public int getX1() {
        return x1;
    }

    public int getY1() {
        return y1;
    }

    public int getX2() {
        return x2;
    }

    public int getY2() {
        return y2;
    }

    abstract public void drawOutline(Graphics g, int x1, int y1,
                                      int x2, int y2);

    protected int x1;
    protected int y1;
```

```
    protected int x2;
    protected int y2;

}
```

The three types of concrete shapes are defined as concrete subclasses of the TwoEndsShape class.

Class draw1.LineShape

```java
package draw1;
import java.awt.*;

public class LineShape extends TwoEndsShape {

    public void draw(Graphics g) {
        if (color != null) {
            g.setColor(color);
        }
        g.drawLine(x1, y1, x2, y2);
    }

    public void drawOutline(Graphics g, int x1, int y1,
                            int x2, int y2) {
        g.drawLine(x1, y1, x2, y2);
    }
}
```

Class draw1.OvalShape

```java
package draw1;
import java.awt.*;

public class OvalShape extends TwoEndsShape {

    public void draw(Graphics g) {
        int x = Math.min(x1, x2);
        int y = Math.min(y1, y2);
        int w = Math.abs(x1 - x2) + 1;
        int h = Math.abs(y1 - y2) + 1;
        if (color != null) {
            g.setColor(color);
        }
        g.drawOval(x, y, w, h);
    }

    public void drawOutline(Graphics g, int x1, int y1,
                            int x2, int y2) {
        int x = Math.min(x1, x2);
        int y = Math.min(y1, y2);
        int w = Math.abs(x1 - x2) + 1;
        int h = Math.abs(y1 - y2) + 1;
        g.drawOval(x, y, w, h);
    }
}
```

Class draw1.RectangleShape

```
package draw1;

import java.awt.*;

public class RectangleShape extends TwoEndsShape {
    public void draw(Graphics g) {
        int x = Math.min(x1, x2);
        int y = Math.min(y1, y2);
        int w = Math.abs(x1 - x2) + 1;
        int h = Math.abs(y1 - y2) + 1;
        if (color != null) {
            g.setColor(color);
        }
        g.drawRect(x, y, w, h);
    }

    public void drawOutline(Graphics g, int x1, int y1,
                            int x2, int y2) {
        int x = Math.min(x1, x2);
        int y = Math.min(y1, y2);
        int w = Math.abs(x1 - x2) + 1;
        int h = Math.abs(y1 - y2) + 1;
        g.drawRect(x, y, w, h);
    }
}
```

9.5.2 The Toolkit

The design concerning the tools in this iteration is shown in Figure 9.14. The drawing pad provides a set of different drawing tools. Each tool extends the abstract class `AbstractTool` in the previous iteration. The `Toolkit` class represents a set of tools supported by the drawing pad and keeps track of the currently selected tool. The responses to a mouse button press or release and mouse dragging on the drawing

Figure 9.14

The design of the drawing pad—the tools.

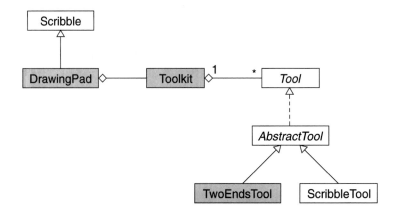

canvas depend on which tool is currently selected. In the Toolkit class, each tool can be identified either by its name or by its position in the toolkit. In the DrawingPad class, an integer field is used to indicate the position of the tool to be selected. The methods of the Toolkit class are summarized in the following table:

Methods	Description
addTool()	Add a new tool to the toolkit.
getToolCount()	Return the number of tools in the toolkit.
getTool(i)	Return the i-th tool in the toolkit.
findTool(name)	Return the tool with the given name.
setSelectedTool(i)	Set the i-th tool to be the current tool.
setSelectedTool(name)	Set the tool with the given name to be the current tool.
setSelectedTool()	Set the specified tool to be the current tool.
getSelectedTool()	Return the selected tool.

Class draw1.ToolKit

```java
package draw1;

import java.util.*;
import scribble3.Tool;

public class ToolKit {

    public ToolKit() {}

    public int addTool(Tool tool) {
        if (tool != null) {
            tools.add(tool);
            return (tools.size() - 1);
        }
        return -1;
    }

    public int getToolCount() {
        return tools.size();
    }

    public Tool getTool(int i) {
        if (i >= 0 &&
                i < tools.size()) {
            return (Tool) tools.get(i);
        }
        return null;
    }
```

```
                public Tool findTool(String name) {
                    if (name != null) {
                        for (int i = 0; i < tools.size(); i++) {
                            Tool tool = (Tool) tools.get(i);
                            if (name.equals(tool.getName())) {
                                return tool;
                            }
                        }
                    }
                    return null;
                }
                public void setSelectedTool(int i) {
                    Tool tool = getTool(i);
                    if (tool != null) {
                        selectedTool = tool;
                    }
                }

                public Tool setSelectedTool(String name) {
                    Tool tool = findTool(name);
                    if (tool != null) {
                        selectedTool = tool;
                    }
                    return tool;
                }

                public void setSelectedTool(Tool tool) {
                    selectedTool = tool;
                }

                public Tool getSelectedTool() {
                    return selectedTool;
                }

                protected List tools = new ArrayList(16);
                protected Tool selectedTool = null;

            }
```

9.5.3 Design Pattern: State

The refactoring concerning the toolkit illustrates the State design pattern, which allows encapsulation of the behavior of each tool in a separate class and decouples the tools from the DrawingPad class.

Design Pattern *State*

Category: Behavioral design pattern.

Intent: Allow an object to alter its behavior when its internal state changes.

Also Known As: Objects for states.

Applicability: Use the State design pattern

- when an object's behavior depends on its state and it must change its behavior at run time, depending on that state (e.g., selecting among several tools).
- when methods have large, multipart conditional statements that depend on the object's state (e.g., the switch statements in the `DrawingPadLis-tener` class [p. 424]).

The structure of the State design pattern is shown in the following diagram.

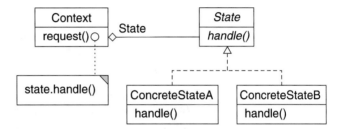

The participants of the State design pattern are as follows:

- *Context* (e.g., `DrawingPad`), which maintains an instance of a `ConcreteState` that defines the current state (e.g., the `currentTool` field in the `DrawingPad` class).
- *State* (e.g., `Tool`), which defines an interface for encapsulating the behavior associated with a particular state of the `Context`.
- *ConcreteState* (e.g., `ScribbleTool`), in which each subclass implements a behavior associated with a state of `Context`.

9.5.4 A Concrete Tool—TwoEndsTool

When we select the line-drawing, rectangle-drawing, or oval-drawing tool, we can use the mouse to draw a line, a rectangle, or a circle. Although these shapes have little in common, the ways in which they are drawn are quite similar—by defining the two end points. These shapes are drawn as follows:

- When the mouse button is pressed, the current mouse position defines the first end point of the selected shape.
- When the mouse is dragged, temporary frames of the selected shape are drawn. These temporary frames follow the mouse as it is being dragged. This process is commonly known as *rubber banding* because dragging the mouse is like stretching a rubber band.
- When the mouse button is released, the current mouse position defines the second end point of the selected shape. The selected shape defined by the two end points is drawn.

Because of the similarities in drawing lines, rectangles, and ovals, we design a single tool, the TwoEndsTool, to handle all three shapes. Each shape is identified by an integer constant: LINE, OVAL, or RECT. The fields of the TwoEndsTool are summarized in the following table:

Field	Description
shape	Shape to be drawn
xStart, yStart	Coordinates of the first end point

Class draw1.TwoEndsTool

```
package draw1;
import java.awt.*;
import scribble3.*;

public class TwoEndsTool extends AbstractTool {
    public static final int LINE = 0;
    public static final int OVAL = 1;
    public static final int RECT = 2;

    public TwoEndsTool(ScribbleCanvas canvas, String name, int shape) {
        super(canvas, name);
        this.shape = shape;
    }
    public void startShape(Point p) {
        canvas.mouseButtonDown = true;
        xStart = canvas.x = p.x;
        yStart = canvas.y = p.y;
        Graphics g = canvas.getGraphics();
        g.setXORMode(Color.darkGray);
        g.setColor(Color.lightGray);
        switch (shape) {
        case LINE:
            drawLine(g, xStart, yStart, xStart, yStart);
            break;
        case OVAL:
            drawOval(g, xStart, yStart, 1, 1);
            break;
        case RECT:
            drawRect(g, xStart, yStart, 1, 1);
            break;
        }
    }
```

```java
public void addPointToShape(Point p) {
    if (canvas.mouseButtonDown) {
        Graphics g = canvas.getGraphics();
        g.setXORMode(Color.darkGray);
        g.setColor(Color.lightGray);
        switch (shape) {
        case LINE:
            drawLine(g, xStart, yStart, canvas.x, canvas.y);
            drawLine(g, xStart, yStart, p.x, p.y);
            break;
        case OVAL:
            drawOval(g, xStart, yStart, canvas.x - xStart + 1,
                    canvas.y - yStart + 1);
            drawOval(g, xStart, yStart, p.x - xStart + 1,
                    p.y - yStart + 1);
            break;
        case RECT:
            drawRect(g, xStart, yStart, canvas.x - xStart + 1,
                    canvas.y - yStart + 1);
            drawRect(g, xStart, yStart, p.x - xStart + 1,
                    p.y - yStart + 1);
            break;
        }
        canvas.x = p.x;
        canvas.y = p.y;
    }
}

public void endShape(Point p) {
    canvas.mouseButtonDown = false;
    TwoEndsShape newShape = null;
    switch (shape) {
    case LINE:
        newShape = new LineShape();
        break;
    case OVAL:
        newShape = new OvalShape();
        break;
    case RECT:
        newShape = new RectangleShape();
    }
    if (newShape != null) {
        newShape.setColor(canvas.getCurColor());
        newShape.setEnds(xStart, yStart, p.x, p.y);
        canvas.addShape(newShape);
    }
    Graphics g = canvas.getGraphics();
    g.setPaintMode();
    canvas.repaint();
}

protected int shape = LINE;
protected int xStart, yStart;
```

```java
// helper methods
public static void drawLine(Graphics g,
                            int x1, int y1, int x2, int y2) {
    g.drawLine(x1, y1, x2, y2);
}

public static void drawRect(Graphics g,
                            int x, int y, int w, int h) {
    if (w < 0) {
        x = x + w;
        w = -w;
    }
    if (h < 0) {
        y = y + h;
        h = -h;
    }
    g.drawRect(x, y, w, h);
}

public static void drawOval(Graphics g, int x, int y, int w,
                            int h) {
    if (w < 0) {
        x = x + w;
        w = -w;
    }
    if (h < 0) {
        y = y + h;
        h = -h;
    }
    g.drawOval(x, y, w, h);
}

}
```

The `mousePressed()` method records the coordinates of the first end point and prepares for rubber banding. Rubber banding is accomplished by using the *exclusive-or* (XOR) mode of the graphics context. When the XOR mode is used in a graphics context and a figure is drawn once, the figure is visible. However, the color of the figure depends not only on the current pen color, but also on the colors of the pixels that the figure covers. When the same figure is drawn twice in the same position, the figure disappears. The `mouseDragged()` method performs the rubber banding. The values `canvas.x` and `canvas.y` are the coordinates of the intermediate preceding location of the mouse. The `mouseReleased()` method records the second end point of the shape. It sets the mode of the graphics context to the default paint mode. A new instance of the selected shape is created, and the selected shape is drawn on the canvas.

9.5.5 Extending Components

In this iteration, the main application, the canvas, and the canvas listener classes all extend their counterparts in the previous iteration. Factory methods are used in the extended classes to create instances of the extended classes. The design is shown in Figure 9.15.

Figure 9.15

The overall design of the drawing pad—iteration 4.

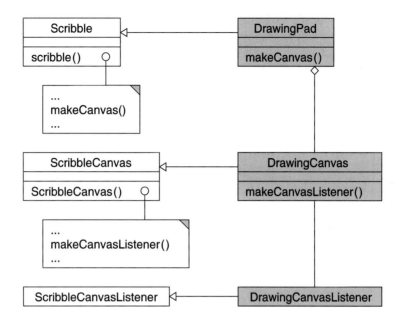

The draw1.DrawingCanvasListener class extends the scribble3
.ScribbleCanvasListener class in the previous iteration. In the scribble3
.ScribbleCanvasListener class, only one tool, the scribble tool, is supported. In
the draw1.DrawingCanvasListener class, the tool can be set to any tool supported
by the drawing pad.

Class draw1.DrawingCanvasListener

```
package draw1;

import java.awt.*;
import java.awt.event.*;
import scribble3.*;

public class DrawingCanvasListener extends ScribbleCanvasListener {

    public DrawingCanvasListener(DrawingCanvas canvas) {
        super(canvas, null);
    }

    public Tool getTool() {
        return tool;
    }

    public void setTool(Tool tool) {
        this.tool = tool;
    }

}
```

The `draw1.DrawingCanvas` class extends the `scribble3.Scribble` class. The factory method `makeCanvasListener()` is used to create an instance of the enhanced canvas listener.

Class `draw1.DrawingCanvas`

```java
package draw1;

import java.awt.Color;
import java.awt.Dimension;
import java.awt.Graphics;
import java.awt.Point;
import java.util.*;
import java.io.*;
import java.awt.event.*;
import java.util.EventListener;
import javax.swing.*;
import scribble3.*;

public class DrawingCanvas extends ScribbleCanvas {

    public DrawingCanvas() {
    }

    public void setTool(Tool tool) {
        drawingCanvasListener.setTool(tool);
    }

    public Tool getTool() {
        return drawingCanvasListener.getTool();
    }

    // the factory method
    protected EventListener makeCanvasListener() {
        return (drawingCanvasListener =
            new DrawingCanvasListener(this));
    }

    protected DrawingCanvasListener drawingCanvasListener;

}
```

The `draw1.DrawingPad` class is the main application class. It manages the toolkit and is responsible for creating the tool bar on the left and the tool menu on the menu bar for selecting the current drawing tool. The methods of the `DrawingPad` class are summarized in the following table:

Methods	Description
`initTools()`	Create the tools and initialize the toolkit.
`getSelectedTool()`	Return the currently selected drawing tool.

`makeCanvas()`	Create the canvas (the factory method).
`createToolBar()`	Create the tool bar on the left side.
`createToolMenu()`	Create the tool menu on the menu bar.

The factory method `makeCanvas()` is used to create an instance of the enhanced canvas. An anonymous nested class is used as the action listener for both the tool bar and the tool menu for selecting the drawing tool. The menu bar is constructed incrementally. The menu bar is first constructed in the constructor of the superclass without the tool menu. The tool menu is created by the `createToolMenu()` method and then inserted into the menu bar.

Class `draw1.DrawingPad`

```
package draw1;
import java.awt.*;
import java.awt.event.*;
import java.io.*;
import javax.swing.*;
import scribble3.*;

public class DrawingPad extends Scribble {

    public DrawingPad(String title) {
        super(title);
        initTools();
        // an anonymous nested class to select the current tool
        ActionListener toolListener = new ActionListener() {
            public void actionPerformed(ActionEvent event) {
                Object source = event.getSource();
                if (source instanceof AbstractButton) {
                    AbstractButton button = (AbstractButton) source;
                    Tool tool =
                        toolkit.setSelectedTool(button.getText());
                    drawingCanvas.setTool(tool);
                }
            }
        };
        // create the tool bar
        JComponent toolbar = createToolBar(toolListener);
        getContentPane().add(toolbar, BorderLayout.WEST);

        // create the tool menu
        JMenu menu = createToolMenu(toolListener);
        // insert the tool menu into the menu bar
        menuBar.add(menu, 1); // insert at index position 1
    }

    public Tool getSelectedTool() {
        return toolkit.getSelectedTool();
    }
```

```
// create the drawing tools and initialize the toolkit
protected void initTools() {
    toolkit = new ToolKit();
    toolkit.addTool(new ScribbleTool(canvas, "Scribble"));
    toolkit.addTool(new TwoEndsTool(canvas, "Line", TwoEndsTool.LINE));
    toolkit.addTool(new TwoEndsTool(canvas, "Oval", TwoEndsTool.OVAL));
    toolkit.addTool(new TwoEndsTool(canvas, "Rectangle",
                                    TwoEndsTool.RECT));
    drawingCanvas.setTool(toolkit.getTool(0));
}

// the factory method
protected ScribbleCanvas makeCanvas() {
    return (drawingCanvas = new DrawingCanvas());
}

protected JComponent createToolBar(ActionListener toolListener) {
    JPanel toolbar = new JPanel(new GridLayout(0, 1));
    // create a button for each tool
    int n = toolkit.getToolCount();
    for (int i = 0; i < n; i++) {
        Tool tool = toolkit.getTool(i);
        if (tool != null) {
            JButton button = new JButton(tool.getName());
            button.addActionListener(toolListener);
            toolbar.add(button);
        }
    }
    return toolbar;
}

protected JMenu createToolMenu(ActionListener toolListener) {
    JMenu menu = new JMenu("Tools");
    // create a menu item for each tool
    int n = toolkit.getToolCount();
    for (int i = 0; i < n; i++) {
        Tool tool = toolkit.getTool(i);
        if (tool != null) {
            JMenuItem menuitem = new JMenuItem(tool.getName());
            menuitem.addActionListener(toolListener);
            menu.add(menuitem);
        }
    }
    return menu;
}

protected ToolKit toolkit;
protected DrawingCanvas drawingCanvas;

public static void main(String[] args) {
    JFrame frame = new DrawingPad("Drawing Pad");
    frame.setSize(width, height);
    Dimension screenSize =
        java.awt.Toolkit.getDefaultToolkit().getScreenSize();
```

```
          // place the application frame at the center of the screen
          frame.setLocation(screenSize.width/2 - width/2,
                            screenSize.height/2 - height/2);
          frame.show();
       }

    }
```

This completes the fourth iteration of the drawing pad.

9.5.6 Design Pattern: Factory Method

Design Pattern *Factory Method*

Category: Creational design pattern.

Intent: To define an interface for creating an object but defer instantiation to the subclasses.

Also Known As: Virtual constructor.

Applicability: Use the Factory Method design pattern

- when a class cannot anticipate the class of objects it must create.
- when a class defers to its subclasses to specify the objects it creates.

The structure of the Factory Method design pattern is shown in the following diagram:

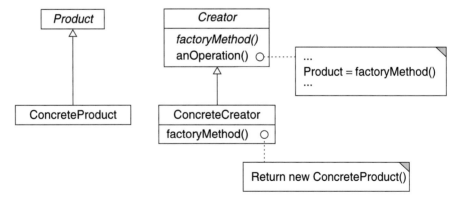

The participants of the Factory Method design pattern are the following:

- *Product* (e.g., EventListener), which defines the interface of the objects to be created.
- *ConcreteProduct* (e.g., ScribbleCanvasListener and ToolListener), which implements the *Product* interface, and may provide default implementation.

- *Creator* (e.g., Scribble), which defines one or more factory methods (e.g. makeCanvasListener()) that create abstract products, that is, objects of type *Product*. The *Creator* may provide a default implementation (e.g., the implementation of the makeCanvasListener() method in the Scribble class) and may call factory methods to create *Product* objects (e.g., invocation of the makeCanvasListener() method in the constructor of the Scribble class).
- *ConcreteCreator* (e.g., DrawingPad), which overrides the factory method to return an instance of a ConcreteProduct (e.g., implementation of the makeCanvasListener() method in the DrawingPad class).

Factory Method and Factory (see Section 7.4.3 [p. 296]) are different design patterns. The Factory design pattern involves a factory class whose sole responsibility is to create objects. The Factory Method is for a class to defer the creation of certain objects to its subclasses.

9.6 ITERATION 5: MORE DRAWING TOOLS

The goal of this iteration is rather simple. We want to further enhance the drawing pad by adding tools for drawing filled ovals and rectangles. An ad hoc extension is rather straightforward, but it is inelegant and difficult to maintain. We refactor the design of the TwoEndsTool class to make it more extensible.

9.6.1 Filled Shapes

First, we define two new shapes, FilledOvalShape and FilledRectangleShape, by extending OvalShape and RectangleShape, respectively:

Class draw2.FilledOvalShape

```
package draw2;

import java.awt.*;
import draw1.*;

public class FilledOvalShape extends OvalShape {

    public void draw(Graphics g) {
        int x = Math.min(x1, x2);
        int y = Math.min(y1, y2);
        int w = Math.abs(x1 - x2) + 1;
        int h = Math.abs(y1 - y2) + 1;
        if (color != null) {
            g.setColor(color);
        }
        g.fillOval(x, y, w, h);
    }
```

```
}
```

Class draw2.FilledRectangleShape

```
package draw2;

import java.awt.*;
import draw1.*;

public class FilledRectangleShape extends RectangleShape {

    public void draw(Graphics g) {
        int x = Math.min(x1, x2);
        int y = Math.min(y1, y2);
        int w = Math.abs(x1 - x2) + 1;
        int h = Math.abs(y1 - y2) + 1;
        if (color != null) {
            g.setColor(color);
        }
        g.fillRect(x, y, w, h);
    }
}
```

9.6.2 Drawing Filled Shapes

Drawing filled rectangles and ovals is very similar to drawing unfilled rectangles and ovals. A simple ad hoc approach to support the drawing of filled rectangles and ovals is to modify the TwoEndsTool as follows:

```
public class TwoEndsTool implements Tool {
    public static final int LINE = . . . ;
    public static final int OVAL = . . . ;
    public static final int RECT = . . . ;
    public static final int FILLED_OVAL = . . . ;
    public static final int FILLED_RECT = . . . ;
    public void mousePressed(Point p, ScribbleCanvas canvas) {
        //...
        switch (shape) {
        case LINE: //...
        case OVAL: //...
        case RECT: //...
        case FILLED_OVAL: //...
        case FILLED_RECT: //...
        }
    }

    public void mouseDragged(Point p, ScribbleCanvas canvas) {
        //...
        switch (shape) {
        case LINE: //...
        case OVAL: //...
        case RECT: //...
```

```
                   case FILLED_OVAL: // ...
                   case FILLED_RECT: // ...
                   }
             }
             public void mouseReleased(Point p, ScribbleCanvas canvas) {
                   // ...
                   switch (shape) {
                   case LINE: // ...
                   case OVAL: // ...
                   case RECT: // ...
                   case FILLED_OVAL: // ...
                   case FILLED_RECT: // ...
                   }
             }
       }
```

In this approach, modification is required for each new shape. The relevant code segments for each shape are scattered in three different methods: mousePressed(), mouseDragged(), and mouseReleased(). Modifications to these methods must be carefully coordinated because the shapes to be drawn are tightly coupled with the two-ends tool. It is rather cumbersome and error-prone to add new shapes using this approach. Adding new shapes would be much simpler if the shapes to be drawn could be decoupled from the two-ends tool.

Figure 9.16

The design of the drawing pad— iteration 5.

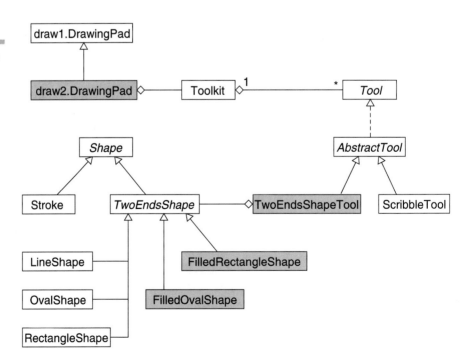

A better design is to separate the shape from the tool for drawing that shape using the Strategy design pattern. The TwoEndsShapeTool class, instead of using an integer value to indicate the shape to be drawn, contains a reference to TwoEndsShape, which represents the abstract strategy; the classes that implement the TwoEndsShape interface represent the concrete strategies. Using the Strategy pattern, the switch statements that are tightly coupled with the shapes are eliminated. The TwoEndsShapeTool class does not contain code that is specific to any particular shape. The design is shown in Figure 9.16

The prototype object serves as a representative of the shape to be drawn. The mousePressed(), mouseDragged(), and mouseReleased() methods delegate actions specific to each shape to the prototype object. The new shape object to be added to the drawing is created by cloning the prototype object.

Class draw2.TwoEndsShapeTool

```java
package draw2;

import java.awt.*;
import scribble3.*;
import draw1.*;

public class TwoEndsShapeTool extends AbstractTool {

    public TwoEndsShapeTool(ScribbleCanvas canvas, String name,
                            TwoEndsShape prototype) {
        super(canvas, name);
        this.prototype = prototype;
    }

    public void startShape(Point p) {
        if (prototype != null) {
            canvas.mouseButtonDown = true;
            xStart = canvas.x = p.x;
            yStart = canvas.y = p.y;
            Graphics g = canvas.getGraphics();
            g.setXORMode(Color.darkGray);
            g.setColor(Color.lightGray);
            prototype.drawOutline(g, xStart, yStart, xStart, yStart);
        }
    }

    public void addPointToShape(Point p) {
        if (prototype != null &&
            canvas.mouseButtonDown) {
            Graphics g = canvas.getGraphics();
            g.setXORMode(Color.darkGray);
            g.setColor(Color.lightGray);
            prototype.drawOutline(g, xStart, yStart, canvas.x, canvas.y);
            prototype.drawOutline(g, xStart, yStart, p.x, p.y);
        }
    }
```

```
            public void endShape(Point p) {
               canvas.mouseButtonDown = false;
               if (prototype != null) {
                  try {
                     TwoEndsShape newShape = (TwoEndsShape) prototype.clone();
                     newShape.setColor(canvas.getCurColor());
                     newShape.setEnds(xStart, yStart, p.x, p.y);
                     canvas.addShape(newShape);
                  } catch (CloneNotSupportedException e) {}
                  Graphics g = canvas.getGraphics();
                  g.setPaintMode();
                  canvas.repaint();
               }
            }

            protected int xStart, yStart;
            protected TwoEndsShape prototype;

         }
```

9.6.3   The Application

The main application class `draw2.DrawingPad` overrides the `initTools()` method to include two additional drawing tools for filled ovals and filled rectangles. No other changes are necessary.

Class `draw2.DrawingPad`

```
package draw2;

import java.awt.*;
import java.awt.event.*;
import java.io.*;
import javax.swing.*;
import scribble3.*;
import draw1.*;

public class DrawingPad extends draw1.DrawingPad {

   public DrawingPad(String title) {
      super(title);
   }

   // create the drawing tools and initialize the toolkit
   protected void initTools() {
      toolkit = new ToolKit();
      toolkit.addTool(new ScribbleTool(canvas, "Scribble"));
      toolkit.addTool(new TwoEndsShapeTool(canvas, "Line",
                                    new LineShape()));
      toolkit.addTool(new TwoEndsShapeTool(canvas, "Oval",
                                    new OvalShape()));
      toolkit.addTool(new TwoEndsShapeTool(canvas, "Rect",
                                    new RectangleShape()));
      toolkit.addTool(new TwoEndsShapeTool(canvas, "Filled Oval",
                                    new FilledOvalShape()));
```

```
        toolkit.addTool(new TwoEndsShapeTool(canvas, "Filled Rect",
                                     new FilledRectangleShape())));
        drawingCanvas.setTool(toolkit.getTool(0));
    }
    public static void main(String[] args) {
        JFrame frame = new draw2.DrawingPad("Drawing Pad");
        frame.setSize(width, height);
        Dimension screenSize =
            java.awt.Toolkit.getDefaultToolkit().getScreenSize();
        // place the application frame at the center of the screen
        frame.setLocation(screenSize.width/2 - width/2,
                          screenSize.height/2 - height/2);
        frame.show();
    }

}
```

This completes the fifth iteration of the drawing pad.

9.7 ITERATION 6: THE TEXT TOOL

In this iteration, we further enhance the drawing pad by adding a different type of tool: a tool for typing text using the keyboard. A screen shot of the new drawing pad is shown in Figure 9.17. The design is shown in Figure 9.18 The key issues addressed in this iteration are handling keyboard input and keyboard focus.

Figure 9.17

The drawing pad—iteration 6.

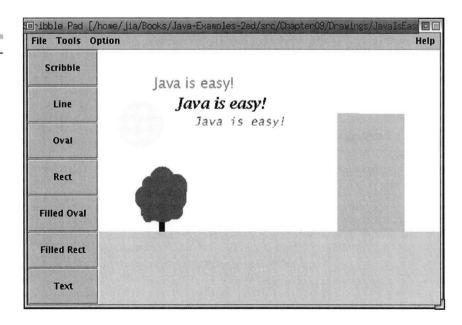

Figure 9.18

The design of the drawing pad—iteration 6.

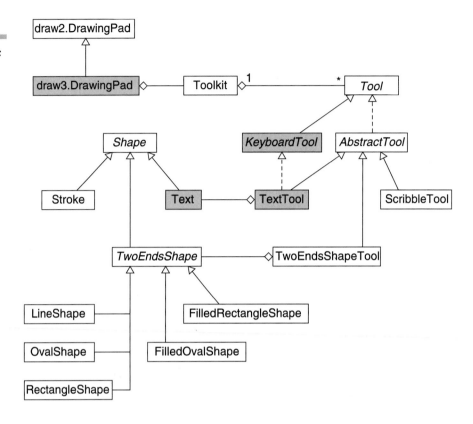

9.7.1 The Text Shape

The draw3.Text class is a subclass of the Shape class representing a text string. The field text represents the keys typed. The field font indicates the font to be used to draw the text. The fields x and y represent the location of the text.

Class draw3.Text

```java
package draw3;

import java.awt.*;

public class Text extends scribble3.Shape {

    public Text() {}

    public Text(Color color) {
        super(color);
    }

    public void setLocation(int x, int y) {
        this.x = x;
        this.y = y;
    }
```

```java
    public int getX() {
        return x;
    }

    public int getY() {
        return y;
    }

    public void setText(String text) {
        this.text = text;
    }

    public String getText() {
        return text;
    }

    public Font getFont() {
        return font;
    }

    public void setFont(Font font) {
        this.font = font;
    }

    public void draw(Graphics g) {
        if (text != null) {
            if (color != null) {
                g.setColor(color);
            }
            if (font != null) {
                g.setFont(font);
            } else {
                g.setFont(defaultFont);
            }
            g.drawString(text, x, y);
        }
    }

    protected int x;
    protected int y;
    protected String text;
    protected Font font;

    protected static Font defaultFont =
        new Font("Serif", Font.BOLD, 24);

}
```

9.7.2   The Keyboard Input Tool

The Tool interface defined earlier is intended to handle the input from a mouse. It is inadequate to handle input from a keyboard. To define tools that handle key presses from a keyboard, we introduce an extended interface KeyboardTool.

```
package draw3;

import scribble3.Tool;

public interface KeyboardTool extends Tool {

    public void addCharToShape(char c);

}
```

The TextTool class represents a concrete tool that handles input from the keyboard. The text field stores the characters that have been typed. Because the text field needs to be updated whenever a key is pressed, we use StringBuffer instead of String for the sake of efficiency. The behavior of the text tool is as follows:

- A mouse press indicates the position in the canvas where the text will be displayed.
- Whenever a key is pressed, the corresponding character is appended to text, and it is drawn in the canvas.

This way of handling keyboard input is rather primitive. It does not support editing capabilities, such as deleting characters and moving the cursor.

```
package draw3;

import java.awt.*;
import scribble3.*;

public class TextTool extends AbstractTool implements KeyboardTool {

    public TextTool(ScribbleCanvas canvas, String name) {
        super(canvas, name);
        text = new StringBuffer();
    }

    public void startShape(Point p) {
        text.delete(0, text.length());
        curShape = new Text();
        curShape.setColor(canvas.getCurColor());
        curShape.setLocation(p.x, p.y);
        if (canvas instanceof KeyboardDrawingCanvas) {
            curShape.setFont(((KeyboardDrawingCanvas) canvas).getFont());
        }
        canvas.addShape(curShape);
    }

    public void addCharToShape(char c) {
        text.append(c);
        curShape.setText(text.toString());
        canvas.repaint();
    }
```

```
    public void addPointToShape(Point p) {}
    public void endShape(Point p) {}

    protected StringBuffer text;
    protected Text curShape;

}
```

The event listener of the canvas must also be extended to receive and handle the events originating from the keyboard. The listener interface for keyboard events is `KeyListener`. The method `keyPressed()` of a key listener is invoked when one or more keys on the keyboard are pressed. In the following implementation, if the current tool is an instance of `KeyEventTool`, the `keyPressed()` method of the current tool is invoked; otherwise, the key press is ignored:

Class draw3.KeyDrawingCanvasListener

```
package draw3;

import java.awt.*;
import java.awt.event.*;
import draw1.*;

public class KeyboardDrawingCanvasListener
        extends DrawingCanvasListener implements KeyListener {

    public KeyboardDrawingCanvasListener(DrawingCanvas canvas) {
        super(canvas);
    }

    public void keyPressed(KeyEvent e) {
        if (tool instanceof KeyboardTool) {
            KeyboardTool keyboardTool = (KeyboardTool) tool;
            keyboardTool.addCharToShape((char) e.getKeyChar());
        }
    }

    public void keyReleased(KeyEvent e) {}
    public void keyTyped(KeyEvent e) {}

    public void mouseClicked(MouseEvent e) {
        canvas.requestFocus();
    }

}
```

When dealing with input from the keyboard, we face another complication: keyboard focus. Often several windows are open on the screen, and multiple components could accept input from the keyboard. However, only one component will receive keyboard input at any moment: the component that currently has the *keyboard focus*. The component having the keyboard focus is determined by a focus manager, which provides a set of conventions for navigating the focus. In our drawing pad, we specify that whenever the mouse is clicked on a component, that component will have the keyboard focus. Therefore, clicking the mouse on the canvas ensures that the canvas has the keyboard focus. The implementation of the method `mouseClicked()` of the event listener of the canvas accomplishes this purpose by requesting the keyboard focus when a mouse click event occurs on the canvas.

In the canvas class, in order to receive the keyboard input, it is necessary to define the `isFocusable()` method to return `true`.

Class `draw3.KeyDrawingCanvas`

```java
package draw3;

import java.awt.*;
import java.awt.event.*;
import java.util.EventListener;
import draw1.*;

public class KeyboardDrawingCanvas extends DrawingCanvas {

    public KeyboardDrawingCanvas() {
        addKeyListener((KeyListener) listener);
        font = new Font(fontFamily, fontStyle, fontSize);
    }

    public Font getFont() {
        return font;
    }

    public String getFontFamily() {
        return fontFamily;
    }

    public void setFontFamily(String fontFamily) {
        if (fontFamily != null &&
                !fontFamily.equals(this.fontFamily)) {
            this.fontFamily =fontFamily;
            font = new Font(fontFamily, fontStyle, fontSize);
        }
    }

    public int getFontSize() {
        return fontSize;
    }

    public void setFontSize(int fontSize) {
        if (fontSize > 0 &&
                fontSize != this.fontSize) {
            this.fontSize = fontSize;
            font = new Font(fontFamily, fontStyle, fontSize);
        }
    }

    public int getFontStyle() {
        return fontStyle;
    }
```

```
        public void setFontStyle(int fontStyle) {
            if (fontStyle != this.fontStyle) {
                this.fontStyle = fontStyle;
                font = new Font(fontFamily, fontStyle, fontSize);
            }
        }

        // necessary for keyboard input
        public boolean isFocusable() {
            return true;
        }

        // factory method
        protected EventListener makeCanvasListener() {
            return (drawingCanvasListener =
                new KeyboardDrawingCanvasListener(this));
        }

        protected String fontFamily = "Serif";
        protected int fontSize = 24;
        protected int fontStyle = Font.PLAIN;
        protected Font font;

    }
```

9.7.3 The Font Option Menu

The main application class `draw3.DrawingPad` adds the new text tool to the toolkit and adds a cascading menu to the menu bar for selecting the font family, font size, and font style:

Class `draw3.DrawingPad`

```
package draw3;
import java.awt.*;
import java.awt.event.*;
import java.io.*;
import javax.swing.*;
import draw2.*;
import scribble3.*;

public class DrawingPad extends draw2.DrawingPad {

    public DrawingPad(String title) {
        super(title);
        JMenu optionMenu = menuBar.getMenu(2);
        addFontOptions(optionMenu);
    }

    // factory method
    protected ScribbleCanvas makeCanvas() {
        return (drawingCanvas = keyboardDrawingCanvas =
                                new KeyboardDrawingCanvas());
    }
```

```
protected void initTools() {
   super.initTools();
   toolkit.addTool(new TextTool(canvas, "Text"));
}

protected void addFontOptions(JMenu optionMenu) {
   String[] fontFamilyNames = {
      "Serif",
      "Sans-serif",
      "Monospaced",
      "Dialog",
      "DialogInput"
   };

   int[] fontSizes = {
      8, 10, 12, 16, 20, 24, 28, 32, 40, 48, 64
   };

   String[] fontStyleNames = {
      "plain",
      "bold",
      "italic",
      "bold italic"
   };

   int i;
   ActionListener fontFamilyAction = new ActionListener() {
         public void actionPerformed(ActionEvent event) {
            Object source = event.getSource();
            if (source instanceof JCheckBoxMenuItem) {
               JCheckBoxMenuItem mi = (JCheckBoxMenuItem) source;
               String name = mi.getText();
               keyboardDrawingCanvas.setFontFamily(name);
            }
         }
      };
   JMenu fontFamilyMenu = new JMenu("Font family");
   ButtonGroup group = new ButtonGroup();
   for (i = 0; i < fontFamilyNames.length; i++) {
      JCheckBoxMenuItem mi =
         new JCheckBoxMenuItem(fontFamilyNames[i]);
      fontFamilyMenu.add(mi);
      mi.addActionListener(fontFamilyAction);
      group.add(mi);
   }
   optionMenu.add(fontFamilyMenu);

   ActionListener fontSizeAction = new ActionListener() {
         public void actionPerformed(ActionEvent event) {
            Object source = event.getSource();
            if (source instanceof JCheckBoxMenuItem) {
               JCheckBoxMenuItem mi = (JCheckBoxMenuItem) source;
               String size = mi.getText();
```

```
                    try {
                        keyboardDrawingCanvas.setFontSize(
                            Integer.parseInt(size));
                    } catch (NumberFormatException e) {
                        e.printStackTrace();
                    }
                }
            }
        };
    JMenu fontSizeMenu = new JMenu("Font size");
    group = new ButtonGroup();
    for (i = 0; i < fontSizes.length; i++) {
        JCheckBoxMenuItem mi =
            new JCheckBoxMenuItem(Integer.toString(fontSizes[i]));
        fontSizeMenu.add(mi);
        mi.addActionListener(fontSizeAction);
        group.add(mi);
    }
    optionMenu.add(fontSizeMenu);

    ActionListener fontStyleAction = new ActionListener() {
            public void actionPerformed(ActionEvent event) {
                Object source = event.getSource();
                if (source instanceof JCheckBoxMenuItem) {
                    JCheckBoxMenuItem mi = (JCheckBoxMenuItem) source;
                    String styleName = mi.getText();
                    int style = Font.PLAIN;
                    if (styleName.equals("bold")) {
                        style = Font.BOLD;
                    } else if (styleName.equals("italic")) {
                        style = Font.ITALIC;
                    } else if (styleName.equals("bold italic")) {
                        style = Font.BOLD | Font.ITALIC;
                    }
                    keyboardDrawingCanvas.setFontStyle(style);
                }
            }
        };
    JMenu fontStyleMenu = new JMenu("Font style");
    group = new ButtonGroup();
    for (i = 0; i < fontStyleNames.length; i++) {
        JCheckBoxMenuItem mi =
            new JCheckBoxMenuItem(fontStyleNames[i]);
        fontStyleMenu.add(mi);
        mi.addActionListener(fontStyleAction);
        group.add(mi);
    }
    optionMenu.add(fontStyleMenu);
}

protected KeyboardDrawingCanvas keyboardDrawingCanvas;
```

```
public static void main(String[] args) {
    JFrame frame = new draw3.DrawingPad("Drawing Pad");
    frame.setSize(width, height);
    Dimension screenSize =
        java.awt.Toolkit.getDefaultToolkit().getScreenSize();
    // place the application frame at the center of the screen
    frame.setLocation(screenSize.width/2 - width/2,
                        screenSize.height/2 - height/2);
    frame.show();
    }

}
```

This completes the last iteration of this case study.

CHAPTER SUMMARY

- The iterative process is used to develop large-scale software systems in a succession of iterations. Each iteration builds on the result of the preceding iteration and enhances functionality in small increments. Each iteration involves a complete development cycle, including conceptualization, analysis and modeling, design, and implementation. Each iteration results in a completely functional intermediate product.

- Design patterns, such as Strategy, Template Method, Factory Method, and State, are often used in the iterative development process to allow the functionality of systems to be enhanced incrementally and changed dynamically.

- The State design pattern allows an object to alter its behavior when its internal state changes. The State design pattern should be used when an object's behavior depends on its state and it must change its behavior at run time, depending on that state, or when methods have large, multipart conditional statements that depend on the object's state.

- The Factory Method design pattern defines an interface for creating an object but lets subclasses decide which class to instantiate. The Factory Method design pattern should be used when a class cannot anticipate the class of objects it must create or when a class wants its subclass to specify the objects it creates.

FURTHER READINGS

Bloch, J. (2001). *Effective Java Programming Language Guide*. Addison-Wesley.

Gamma, E., et al. (1995). *Design Patterns—Elements of Reusable Object-Oriented Software*. Addison-Wesley.

Metsker, S. J. (2002). *Design Patterns Java Workbook*. Addison-Wesley.

Shalloway, A., and J. R. Trott (2001). *Design Patterns Explained: A New Perspective on Object-Oriented Design*. Addison-Wesley.

PROJECT

9.1 Use the iterative development approach to add some of the following enhancements to the drawing pad program:

(a) Add new drawing tools to draw different shapes, such as diamonds, polygons, splines, and so on.

(b) Support selecting different background colors. Refactor the code to avoid code duplication with the selecting-pen-colors function.

(c) Support selecting image files as the background.

(d) Support a zoom-in and zoom-out function.

(e) Support moving and deleting shapes.

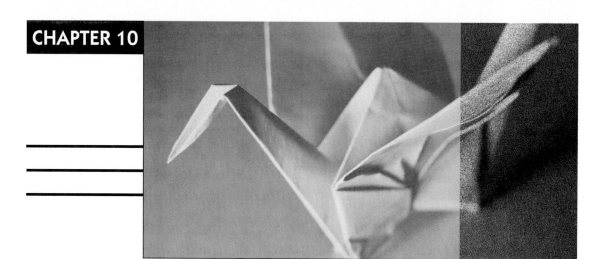

CHAPTER 10

More Design Patterns

CHAPTER OVERVIEW

In this chapter, we first present an idiom for type-safe enumeration types. We then discuss a number of important design patterns, including Abstract Factory, Prototype, Builder, Command, and Adapter. These design patterns will be illustrated in the context of several complete programs.

10.1   TYPE-SAFE ENUMERATION TYPES

10.1.1   A Simple Maze Game

In this chapter, we use a simple maze game as shown in Figure 10.1 to illustrate an implementation idiom and a number of important design patterns. The following is a very brief description of the maze game:

> The board of the maze game is an $n \times m$ grid. Figure 10.1 shows two instances of the maze game: a small, 1×2 maze game, and a large, 3×3 maze game. Each square on the board is a room. Adjacent rooms are separated by either a wall or a door between them. The doors can be either open or closed. Each maze game contains a player represented by a dot. The player can move from room to room through open doors.

> Various aspects of the game will be further elaborated later on.

Figure 10.1

A simple maze game.

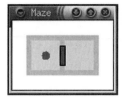

10.1.2 Enumeration Types

Before we discuss the design of the maze game, we first present a useful implementation idiom for enumeration types in Java. An enumeration type consists of a finite set of distinct values. To implement the maze game, we need to deal with a couple of simple enumeration types:

- *Orientation*, with values of horizontal and vertical. A wall or a door on the maze board is in either horizontal or vertical position.
- *Direction*, with values of north, south, east, and west. Each room has four sides, one in each direction.

Some languages, such as C/C++, provide language support for enumeration types. In these languages, enumeration types are distinct from all other types, and their values are all distinct and noninterchangeable. Proper use of enumeration type variables and values can be type checked at compile time.

Java does not support enumeration types. One simple and common approach to implement enumeration types in Java is to treat enumeration types as integer types and define integer constants for the values of enumeration types. For example, the orientation and direction type can be defined as follows:

```java
public interface Orientation {
    public static final int HORIZONTAL = 0;
    public static final int VERTICAL   = 1;
}

public interface Direction {
    public static final int NORTH = 0;
    public static final int EAST  = 1;
    public static final int SOUTH = 2;
    public static final int WEST  = 3;
}
```

This is a workable solution. However, it has a number of shortcomings. First, it is not type-safe, and second, it is quite error-prone. For example, consider the following variables of these enumeration types:

```
int orientation; // an enumeration type variable for orientation
int direction;   // an enumeration type variable for direction

orientation = Orientation.VERTICAL; // okay
direction = Direction.EAST;         // okay
```

However, the following statements clearly make no sense, but are legal:

```
orientation = Direction.WEST;
direction = Orientation.HORIZONTAL;

orientation = 6;
direction = -1;
```

In this approach, variables and values of different enumeration types are interchangeable, and the values may not even be meaningful. Second, the values of enumeration types are numbers. When directly printing these values, they are cryptic. For example,

```
direction = Direction.EAST;
System.out.println("The current direction is: " + direction);
```

This prints out the following message, which is cryptic and unreadable:

```
The current direction is: 1
```

To make the printout more readable, the printing of values must be handled as follows:

```
public interface Orientation {
    public static final int HORIZONTAL = 0;
    public static final int VERTICAL   = 1;

    public static String name(int v) {
        if (v == HORIZONTAL)
            return "Horizontal";
        else if (v == VERTICAL)
            return "Vertical";
        else
            return null;
    }
}
// ...
direction = Direction.EAST;
System.out.println("The current direction is: " +
                    Orientation.name(direction));
```

10.1.3   Unordered Type-Safe Enumeration Idiom

In Java, there is a better approach to implementing enumeration types using the *type-safe enumeration* idiom, as illustrated in the following definition of the enumeration type Orientation:

Enumeration type maze.Orientation

```
package maze;
public class Orientation {

    public static final Orientation VERTICAL =
        new Orientation("Vertical");
    public static final Orientation HORIZONTAL =
        new Orientation("Horizontal");

    public String toString() {
        return name;
    }

    private Orientation(String name) {
        this.name = name;
    }

    private final String name;
}
```

Using this idiom, each enumeration type is defined as a class. Each value of the enumeration type is associated with a descriptive name rather than an integer value. Each value of the enumeration type is defined as a constant that references an instance of the class. The toString() method returns the descriptive name of each value. The constructor of the class is *private*. It prevents any other instances of the class from being created outside the class, since an enumeration type consists of only a fixed finite number of distinct values. In other words, the instances referenced by the constants defined in this class are the only instances of this class in existence. This idiom ensures that

- each enumeration type may only have a fixed number of distinct values.
- the enumeration types are type-safe; that is, variables and values of different enumeration types are not interchangeable.
- the values can be printed with descriptive names.

For example,

```
Orientation orientation = Orientation.VERTICAL;
System.out.println("The current orientation is: " + orientation);
```

This prints out the following message:

```
The current orientation is: Vertical
```

Furthermore, since the enumeration type has only a fixed number of distinct values, equality of two values (instances) is the same as the identity of the two values (instances). So, identity comparison, that is, equality of references, can be used for comparing the equality of values:

```
Orientation orientation1 = . . . ;
Orientation orientation2 = . . . ;
if (orientation1 == orientation2) {
   // both have the same orientation
}
```

Comparison of the identities is usually more efficient than comparison of the contents.

10.1.4 Ordered Type-Safe Enumeration Idiom

An extension of the type-safe enumeration idiom deals with an *ordered* enumeration type; that is, there is an order among the values of an enumeration type. The following is a definition of the ordered enumeration type `Direction` using the extended idiom:

Ordered enumeration type `maze.Direction`

```
package maze;

public class Direction implements Comparable {

   public static final Direction NORTH = new Direction("North");
   public static final Direction EAST  = new Direction("East");
   public static final Direction SOUTH = new Direction("South");
   public static final Direction WEST  = new Direction("West");

   public String toString() {
      return name;
   }
   public int getOrdinal() {
      return ordinal;
   }
   public int compareTo(Object o) {
      if (o instanceof Direction) {
         return ordinal - ((Direction) o).getOrdinal();
      }
      return 0;
   }
   public static Direction first() {
      return values[0];
   }
   public Direction next() {
      if (ordinal < values.length - 1) {
         return values[ordinal + 1];
      } else {
         return null;
      }
   }
}
```

```
public Direction opposite() {
    return values[(ordinal + 2) % 4];
}

private Direction(String name) {
    this.name = name;
}

private static int nextOrdinal = 0;
private final String name;
private final int ordinal = nextOrdinal++;
private static final Direction[] values =
    {NORTH, EAST, SOUTH, WEST };
}
```

In this ordered enumeration type, each value is also associated with an ordinal number, which is automatically assigned when the instances are created. This class implements the Comparable interface and defines the compareTo() method to compare with other instances of this class based on the ordinal numbers.

This class also provides a number of methods that are specific to handling the directions: the opposite() method returns the opposite direction, and the first() and next() methods support iteration through the directions, as illustrated here:

```
for (Direction dir = Direction.first(); dir != null; dir = dir.next()) {
    // process each direction
}
```

10.2   CREATIONAL DESIGN PATTERNS

10.2.1   A Simple Design of the Maze Game

In this section, we present a simple design of the maze game that supports only a default style of the maze game. The design is shown in Figure 10.2. Later, we present several improved designs using various design patterns to support different styles of the maze game.

Figure 10.2

The design of the simple maze game.

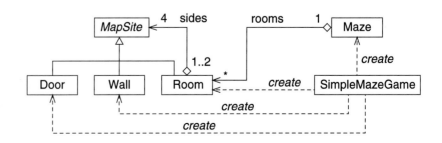

The Map Sites

The interface `MapSite` defines the common behavior of the map sites, that is, the fixed objects that comprise the maze board: rooms, walls, and doors. The `draw()` method draws the visual appearance of each map site, and the `enter()` method defines the reaction of each map site when the player attempts to enter the map site. The specific behaviors are defined in the classes implementing the `MapSite` interface, that is, classes representing specific types of map sites: Room, Door, and `Wall`.[1]

Interface `maze.MapSite`

```java
package maze;

import java.awt.*;

public interface MapSite extends Cloneable {

    public Object clone() throws CloneNotSupportedException;
    public void enter(Maze maze);
    public void draw(Graphics g, int x, int y, int w, int h);

}
```

The Room class represents rooms on the maze board. Each room has a room number. Each room also has four sides, which must be either walls or doors. When a player enters a room, a sound will be played.

Class `maze.Room`

```java
package maze;

import java.awt.*;
import java.applet.AudioClip;

public class Room implements MapSite {

    public static final Color ROOM_COLOR = new Color(152, 251, 152);
    public static final Color PLAYER_COLOR = Color.red;

    public Room(int roomNumber) {
        this.roomNumber = roomNumber;
    }

    public Object clone() throws CloneNotSupportedException {
        Room room = (Room) super.clone();
        room.sides = new MapSite[4];
        for (int i = 0; i < 4; i++) {
            if (sides[i] != null) {
                room.sides[i] = (MapSite) sides[i].clone();
            }
        }
        return room;
    }
}
```

---

1. Some of the details of drawing the maze board are not essential in illustrating the design patterns and are thus omitted in the source code listings that follow. The complete source code is available in the supplement package.

```
public MapSite getSide(Direction dir) {
   if (dir != null) {
      return sides[dir.getOrdinal()];
   }
   return null;
}

public void setSide(Direction dir, MapSite site) {
   if (dir != null) {
      sides[dir.getOrdinal()] = site;
      if (site instanceof Door) {
         Door door = (Door) site;
         if (dir == Direction.NORTH ||
             dir == Direction.SOUTH) {
            door.setOrientation(Orientation.HORIZONTAL);
         } else {
            door.setOrientation(Orientation.VERTICAL);
         }
      }
   }
}

public void setRoomNumber(int roomNumber) {
   this.roomNumber = roomNumber;
}

public int getRoomNumber() {
   return roomNumber;
}

public Point getLocation() {
   return location;
}

public void setLocation(Point location) {
   this.location = location;
}

public void enter(Maze maze) {
   maze.setCurrentRoom(this);
   gong.play();
}

public boolean isInRoom() {
   return inroom;
}

public void setInRoom(boolean inroom) {
   this.inroom = inroom;
}

public void draw(Graphics g, int x, int y, int w, int h) {
   g.setColor(ROOM_COLOR);
   g.fillRect(x, y, w, h);
```

```
            if (inroom) {
                g.setColor(PLAYER_COLOR);
                g.fillOval(x + w / 2 - 5, y + h / 2 - 5, 10, 10);
            }
        }

        protected int roomNumber = 0;
        protected boolean inroom = false; // whether the play is in this room
        protected MapSite[] sides = new MapSite[4];
        protected Point location = null;

        protected static AudioClip gong =
            util.AudioUtility.getAudioClip("audio/gong.au");

    }
```

The Door class represents doors on the maze board. Each door connects two rooms, one on each side. When the player tries to enter a door that is open, the player will enter the room on the other side of the door. When a player tries to enter a door that is closed, the player will remain in the current room and a smashing sound will be played.

Class `maze.Door`

```
package maze;

import java.awt.*;
import java.applet.AudioClip;

public class Door implements MapSite {

    public Door(Room room1, Room room2) {
        this.room1 = room1;
        this.room2 = room2;
    }

    public Object clone() throws CloneNotSupportedException {
        return super.clone();
    }

    public boolean isOpen() {
        return open;
    }

    public void setOpen(boolean open) {
        this.open = open;
    }

    public void setRooms(Room room1, Room room2) {
        this.room1 = room1;
        this.room2 = room2;
    }

    public Orientation getOrientation() {
        return orientation;
    }
```

```
      public void setOrientation(Orientation orientation) {
         this.orientation = orientation;
      }
      public Room otherSideFrom(Room room) {
         if (room != null) {
            if (room == room1) {
               return room2;
            } else if (room == room2) {
               return room1;
            }
         }
         return null;
      }

      public void enter(Maze maze) {
         if (open) {
            Room otherRoom = otherSideFrom(maze.getCurrentRoom());
            if (otherRoom != null) {
               otherRoom.enter(maze);
            }
         } else {
            ding.play();
         }
      }

      public void draw(Graphics g, int x, int y, int w, int h) {
         g.setColor(Wall.WALL_COLOR);
         g.fillRect(x, y, w, h);
         if (orientation == Orientation.VERTICAL) {
            y += 2 * w; h -= 4 * w;
         } else {
            x += 2 * h; w -= 4 * h;
         }
         if (open) {
            g.setColor(Room.ROOM_COLOR);
            g.fillRect(x, y, w, h);
         } else {
            g.setColor(Color.red);
            g.fillRect(x, y, w, h);
            g.setColor(Color.black);
            g.drawRect(x, y, w, h);
         }
      }

      protected Room room1;
      protected Room room2;
      protected boolean open;
      protected Orientation orientation;

      protected static AudioClip ding =
         util.AudioUtility.getAudioClip("audio/ding.au");

}
```

The Wall class represents walls on the maze board. A wall could be between two rooms or on the edge of the maze board. Walls are impassable. So when a player tries to enter a wall, the player will remain in the current room and a smashing sound will be played.

Class maze.Wall

```java
package maze;

import java.awt.*;
import java.applet.AudioClip;

public class Wall implements MapSite {

    public static final Color WALL_COLOR = Color.orange;

    public Object clone() throws CloneNotSupportedException {
        return super.clone();
    }

    public void enter(Maze maze) {
        hurts.play();
    }

    public void draw(Graphics g, int x, int y, int w, int h) {
        g.setColor(WALL_COLOR);
        g.fillRect(x, y, w, h);
    }

    protected static AudioClip hurts =
        util.AudioUtility.getAudioClip("audio/that.hurts.au");

}
```

The Maze Board

The Maze class represents the maze board. The maze board consists of a list of rooms, represented by the field rooms. The current room, which is represented by the field curRoom, is the room where the player is. The Maze class has two major responsibilities: (1) to draw the maze board, and (2) to control the movement of the player. We first use this maze game to illustrate various creational design patterns, so we focus only on the first responsibility here. The code concerning the second responsibility is omitted here and will be discussed in Section 10.3.1 to illustrate a behavioral design pattern Command.

Class maze.Maze

```java
package maze;

import java.util.*;
import java.awt.*;
import java.awt.event.*;
import javax.swing.*;
```

```java
public class Maze implements Cloneable {

   public Object clone() throws CloneNotSupportedException {
      return super.clone();
   }

   public void addRoom(Room room) {
      if (room != null) {
         rooms.add(room);
      }
   }

   public Room findRoom(int roomNumber) {
      for (int i = 0; i < rooms.size(); i++) {
         Room room = (Room) rooms.get(i);
         if (roomNumber == room.getRoomNumber()) {
            return room;
         }
      }
      return null;
   }

   public void setCurrentRoom(int roomNumber) {
      Room room = findRoom(roomNumber);
      setCurrentRoom(room);
   }

   public void setCurrentRoom(Room room) {
      if (room != curRoom) {
         if (curRoom != null) {
            curRoom.setInRoom(false);
         }
         if (room != null) {
            room.setInRoom(true);
            curRoom = room;
         }
         if (view != null) {
            view.repaint();
         }
      }
   }

   public Room getCurrentRoom() {
      return curRoom;
   }

   public void draw(Graphics g) {
      〈draw the maze board on the view component〉
   }

   protected List rooms = new ArrayList();  // the list of rooms that comprise
                                            // the board
   protected Room curRoom = null;           // the room in which the player is
```

```
protected Component view; // the GUI component representing the board
```
⟨Methods, fields, and nested classes for handling the movement of the player.
  See Section 10.3.1 [p. 507]⟩

```
}
```

The `SimpleMazeGame` class is the main driver of the maze program. It is responsible for creating the layout of maze games. The `createMaze()` method creates a small maze board with two rooms, and the `createLargeMaze()` method creates a large maze board with nine rooms. Note that the code to create a large maze game is lengthy, ad hoc, and hard to change.

Class `maze.SimpleMazeGame`

```java
package maze;

import java.awt.*;
import javax.swing.*;

public class SimpleMazeGame {
    /**
     * Creates a 1 x 2 small maze board with 2 rooms.
     */
    public static Maze createMaze() {
        Maze maze = new Maze();
        Room room1 = new Room(1);
        Room room2 = new Room(2);
        Door door = new Door(room1, room2);

        room1.setSide(Direction.NORTH, new Wall());
        room1.setSide(Direction.EAST, door);
        room1.setSide(Direction.SOUTH, new Wall());
        room1.setSide(Direction.WEST, new Wall());

        room2.setSide(Direction.NORTH, new Wall());
        room2.setSide(Direction.EAST, new Wall());
        room2.setSide(Direction.SOUTH, new Wall());
        room2.setSide(Direction.WEST, door);

        maze.addRoom(room1);
        maze.addRoom(room2);

        return maze;
    }
    /**
     * Creates a 3 x 3 large maze board with 9 rooms.
     */
    public static Maze createLargeMaze() {
        Maze maze = new Maze();
        Room room1 = new Room(1);
        Room room2 = new Room(2);
        Room room3 = new Room(3);
```

```
Room room4 = new Room(4);
Room room5 = new Room(5);
Room room6 = new Room(6);
Room room7 = new Room(7);
Room room8 = new Room(8);
Room room9 = new Room(9);
Door door1 = new Door(room1, room2);
Door door2 = new Door(room2, room3);
Door door3 = new Door(room4, room5);
Door door4 = new Door(room5, room6);
Door door5 = new Door(room5, room8);
Door door6 = new Door(room6, room9);
Door door7 = new Door(room7, room8);
Door door8 = new Door(room1, room4);

door1.setOpen(true);
door2.setOpen(false);
door3.setOpen(true);
door4.setOpen(true);
door5.setOpen(false);
door6.setOpen(true);
door7.setOpen(true);
door8.setOpen(true);

room1.setSide(Direction.NORTH, door8);
room1.setSide(Direction.EAST, new Wall());
room1.setSide(Direction.SOUTH, new Wall());
room1.setSide(Direction.WEST, door1);

room2.setSide(Direction.NORTH, new Wall());
room2.setSide(Direction.EAST, door1);
room2.setSide(Direction.SOUTH, new Wall());
room2.setSide(Direction.WEST, door2);

room3.setSide(Direction.NORTH, new Wall());
room3.setSide(Direction.EAST, door2);
room3.setSide(Direction.SOUTH, new Wall());
room3.setSide(Direction.WEST, new Wall());

room4.setSide(Direction.NORTH, new Wall());
room4.setSide(Direction.EAST, new Wall());
room4.setSide(Direction.SOUTH, door8);
room4.setSide(Direction.WEST, door3);

room5.setSide(Direction.NORTH, door5);
room5.setSide(Direction.EAST, door3);
room5.setSide(Direction.SOUTH, new Wall());
room5.setSide(Direction.WEST, door4);

room6.setSide(Direction.NORTH, door6);
room6.setSide(Direction.EAST, door4);
room6.setSide(Direction.SOUTH, new Wall());
room6.setSide(Direction.WEST, new Wall());
```

```
        room7.setSide(Direction.NORTH, new Wall());
        room7.setSide(Direction.EAST, new Wall());
        room7.setSide(Direction.SOUTH, new Wall());
        room7.setSide(Direction.WEST, door7);

        room8.setSide(Direction.NORTH, new Wall());
        room8.setSide(Direction.EAST, door7);
        room8.setSide(Direction.SOUTH, door5);
        room8.setSide(Direction.WEST, new Wall());

        room9.setSide(Direction.NORTH, new Wall());
        room9.setSide(Direction.EAST, new Wall());
        room9.setSide(Direction.SOUTH, door6);
        room9.setSide(Direction.WEST, new Wall());

        maze.addRoom(room1);
        maze.addRoom(room2);
        maze.addRoom(room3);
        maze.addRoom(room4);
        maze.addRoom(room5);
        maze.addRoom(room6);
        maze.addRoom(room7);
        maze.addRoom(room8);
        maze.addRoom(room9);

        return maze;
    }
    public static void main(String[] args) {
        Maze maze;
        // choose the size of the maze board
        if (args.length > 0 &&
            "Large".equals(args[0])) {
          maze = createLargeMaze();
        } else {
          maze = createMaze();
        }
        maze.setCurrentRoom(1);
        maze.showFrame("Maze");  // build and create frame
    }

}
```

The `SimpleMazeGame` class can be invoked with an optional argument `Large`. The `main()` method creates a small or large maze board depending on the command-line argument. If the command argument `Large` is present, the large maze board will be created; otherwise, the small maze board will be created (see Figure 10.1).

The Themes

To make the maze game more interesting, we want to support different looks or themes of the game. In different themes, the rooms, walls, and doors could be drawn in different shapes or colors, and the reactions to entering rooms, walls, and doors

Figure 10.3

Two themes of the
maze game.

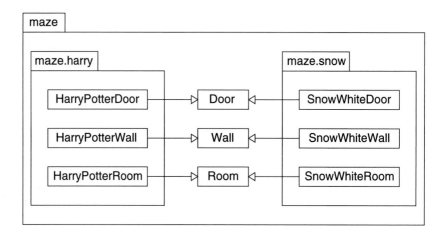

could also have different sound or animation effects. Each theme consists of a set of
rooms, walls, and doors. For the purpose of illustration, we build two new themes of
the maze game in addition to the default theme: a *Harry Potter* theme and a *Snow
White* theme. For each theme, a set of subclasses of room, wall, and door are defined.
The subclasses of different themes are placed in separate packages; see Figure 10.3.

The classes for the Harry Potter theme are in a subpackage named maze.harry.
The rooms, doors, and walls in the Harry Potter theme are represented by classes
HarryPotterRoom, HarryPotterDoor, and HarryPotterWall, respectively.

Class maze.harry.HarryPotterRoom

```
package maze.harry;

import java.awt.*;
import java.applet.AudioClip;
import maze.*;

class HarryPotterRoom extends Room {

    public static final Color ROOM_COLOR = new Color(85, 107, 47);
    public static final Color PLAYER_COLOR = Color.black;

    public HarryPotterRoom(int roomNumber) {
        super(roomNumber);
    }

    public void enter(Maze maze) {
        maze.setCurrentRoom(this);
        adapt.play();
    }

    public void draw(Graphics g, int x, int y, int w, int h) {
        g.setColor(ROOM_COLOR);
        g.fillRect(x, y, w, h);
        if (inroom) {
            g.setColor(PLAYER_COLOR);
```

```
            g.fillOval(x + w / 2 - 5, y + h / 2 - 5, 10, 10);
        }
    }

    protected static AudioClip adapt =
        util.AudioUtility.getAudioClip("audio/adapt-or-die.au");
}
```

Class maze.harry.HarryPotterDoor

```
package maze.harry;

import java.awt.*;
import maze.*;

class HarryPotterDoor extends Door {

    public HarryPotterDoor(Room room1, Room room2) {
        super(room1, room2);
    }

    public void draw(Graphics g, int x, int y, int w, int h) {
        g.setColor(HarryPotterWall.WALL_COLOR);
        g.fillRect(x, y, w, h);
        if (orientation == Orientation.VERTICAL) {
            y += 2 * w; h -= 4 * w;
        } else {
            x += 2 * h; w -= 4 * h;
        }
        if (open) {
            g.setColor(HarryPotterRoom.ROOM_COLOR);
            g.fillRect(x, y, w, h);
        } else {
            g.setColor(new Color(139, 69, 0));
            g.fillRect(x, y, w, h);
            g.setColor(Color.black);
            g.drawRect(x, y, w, h);
        }
    }

}
```

Class maze.harry.HarryPotterWall

```
package maze.harry;

import java.awt.*;
import maze.*;

class HarryPotterWall extends Wall {

    public static final Color WALL_COLOR = new Color(178, 34, 34);

    public void draw(Graphics g, int x, int y, int w, int h) {
        g.setColor(WALL_COLOR);
        g.fillRect(x, y, w, h);
    }

}
```

The classes for the Snow White theme are in a subpackage named `maze.snow`. The rooms, doors, and walls in the Snow White theme are represented by classes `SnowWhiteRoom`, `SnowWhiteDoor`, and `SnowWhiteWall`, respectively.

Class `maze.snow.SnowWhiteRoom`

```java
package maze.snow;

import java.awt.*;
import java.applet.AudioClip;
import maze.*;

class SnowWhiteRoom extends Room {
    public static final Color ROOM_COLOR = new Color(255, 218, 185);
    public static final Color PLAYER_COLOR = Color.white;

    public SnowWhiteRoom(int roomNumber) {
        super(roomNumber);
    }

    public void enter(Maze maze) {
        maze.setCurrentRoom(this);
        tiptoe.play();
    }

    public void draw(Graphics g, int x, int y, int w, int h) {
        g.setColor(ROOM_COLOR);
        g.fillRect(x, y, w, h);
        if (inroom) {
            g.setColor(PLAYER_COLOR);
            g.fillOval(x + w / 2 - 5, y + h / 2 - 5, 10, 10);
        }
    }

    protected static AudioClip tiptoe =
        util.AudioUtility.getAudioClip("audio/tiptoe.thru.the.tulips.au");
}
```

Class `maze.snow.SnowWhiteDoor`

```java
package maze.snow;

import java.awt.*;
import maze.*;

class SnowWhiteDoor extends Door {
    public SnowWhiteDoor(Room room1, Room room2) {
        super(room1, room2);
    }

    public void draw(Graphics g, int x, int y, int w, int h) {
        g.setColor(SnowWhiteWall.WALL_COLOR);
        g.fillRect(x, y, w, h);
```

```
        if (orientation == Orientation.VERTICAL) {
            y += 2 * w; h -= 4 * w;
        } else {
            x += 2 * h; w -= 4 * h;
        }
        if (open) {
            g.setColor(SnowWhiteRoom.ROOM_COLOR);
            g.fillRect(x, y, w, h);
        } else {
            g.setColor(Color.orange);
            g.fillRect(x, y, w, h);
            g.setColor(Color.black);
            g.drawRect(x, y, w, h);
        }
    }

}
```

Class `maze.snow.SnowWhiteWall`

```
package maze.snow;

import java.awt.*;
import maze.*;

class SnowWhiteWall extends Wall {

    public static final Color WALL_COLOR = new Color(255, 20, 147);

    public void draw(Graphics g, int x, int y, int w, int h) {
        g.setColor(WALL_COLOR);
        g.fillRect(x, y, w, h);
    }

}
```

Now we have defined the classes in the new themes. The question is how to make the themes easily interchangeable without affecting other aspects of the maze game, and to make it easy to add additional themes. Switching between themes means replacing one set of rooms, walls, and doors from one theme with another set of rooms, walls, and doors from another theme. A straightforward solution is to create the maze boards of different themes in a way similar to the `createMaze()` and `createLargeMaze()` in `SimpleMazeGame` [p. 477]. Using the small maze board as an example, the maze boards in the two new themes can be created as follows:

```
public static Maze createHarryPotterMaze() {
    Maze maze = new Maze();
    Room room1 = new HarryPotterRoom(1);
    Room room2 = new HarryPotterRoom(2);
    Door door = new HarryPotterDoor(room1, room2);

    room1.setSide(Direction.NORTH, new HarryPotterWall());
    room1.setSide(Direction.EAST, door);
```

```
        room1.setSide(Direction.SOUTH, new HarryPotterWall());
        room1.setSide(Direction.WEST, new HarryPotterWall());

        room2.setSide(Direction.NORTH, new HarryPotterWall());
        room2.setSide(Direction.EAST, new HarryPotterWall());
        room2.setSide(Direction.SOUTH, new HarryPotterWall());
        room2.setSide(Direction.WEST, door);

        maze.addRoom(room1);
        maze.addRoom(room2);

        return maze;
    }
    public static Maze createSnowWhiteMaze() {
        Maze maze = new Maze();
        Room room1 = new SnowWhiteRoom(1);
        Room room2 = new SnowWhiteRoom(2);
        Door door = new SnowWhiteDoor(room1, room2);

        room1.setSide(Direction.NORTH, new SnowWhiteWall());
        room1.setSide(Direction.EAST, door);
        room1.setSide(Direction.SOUTH, new SnowWhiteWall());
        room1.setSide(Direction.WEST, new SnowWhiteWall());

        room2.setSide(Direction.NORTH, new SnowWhiteWall());
        room2.setSide(Direction.EAST, new SnowWhiteWall());
        room2.setSide(Direction.SOUTH, new SnowWhiteWall());
        room2.setSide(Direction.WEST, door);

        maze.addRoom(room1);
        maze.addRoom(room2);

        return maze;
    }
```

This is obviously an undesirable solution, since it involves duplication of largely identical code segments. The duplicated code segments perform the identical task with merely different parts. If we were to create the large maze board and to handle more themes, the code duplication would be much more substantial. This is a serious maintenance hazard, since it is tedious and error-prone to modify the code and to ensure that the same changes are made to all the duplicated code. There are a number of better solutions to create the objects in different themes and to switch easily between themes using various creational design patterns, including Abstract Factory, Factory Method, Prototype, and Builder.

10.2.2   Design Pattern: Abstract Factory

Abstract Factory is a creational design pattern for creating a set of related and compatible products from several interchangeable product families. The product instances are not created using the new operator. They are created using a set of methods defined in a factory class, which represents a product family. The different factories representing different product families share a common interface—the abstract factory interface. Therefore, a client can easily switch from one factory, or product family, to another.

Design Pattern *Abstract Factory*

> *Category:* Creational design pattern.
>
> *Intent:* To provide an interface for creating a family of related or dependent objects without specifying their concrete classes.
>
> *Also Known As:* Kit.
>
> *Applicability:* Use the Abstract Factory design pattern
>
> - when a system should be independent of how its components or products are created.
> - when a system should be configurable with one of multiple interchangeable families of products.
> - when a family of related products should not be mixed with similar products from different families.
> - when only the interfaces of the products are exposed, while the implementation of the products is not revealed.

The structure of the Abstract Factory design pattern is shown in the following diagram:

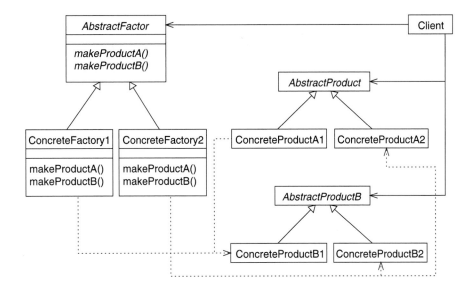

The participants of the Abstract Factory design pattern are the following:

- *AbstractFactory* (e.g., MazeFactory), which defines methods that create abstract products (e.g. makeRoom(), makeWall(), makeDoor()) and may provide default implementation.
- *ConcreteFactory* (e.g., HarryPotterMazeFactory, SnowWhiteMazeFactory), which implements the methods to create concrete instances of *ConcreteProduct*. Each *ConcreteFactory* creates products in the same product family.
- *AbstractProduct* (e.g., Room, Wall, Door), which defines an interface for a type of product and may provide default implementation.
- *ConcreteProduct* (e.g., HarryPotterRoom, HarryPotterWall, HarryPotterDoor, SnowWhiteRoom, SnowWhiteWall, SnowWhiteDoor), which defines a product to be created by the corresponding concrete factory and implements the *AbstractProduct* interface.
- *Client* (e.g., Maze), which uses only *AbstractFactory* and *AbstractProduct*.

In the SimpleMazeGame class [p. 477], map site objects are created using the new operator. So it is inflexible and inextensible. Using the Abstract Factory design pattern, map site objects in different themes can be created using interchangeable factories for the themes. The design of the maze game using the Abstract Factory design pattern is shown in Figure 10.4.

The abstract products in this design of the maze game are the map site classes Room, Wall, and Door. More precisely, these are abstract products with default implementations. The concrete products are the map site classes defined in the different themes, that is, HarryPotterRoom, HarryPotterWall, and HarryPotterDoor in the Harry Potter theme, and SnowWhiteRoom, SnowWhiteWall, and SnowWhiteDoor in the Snow White theme. Each theme represents a product family. The MazeFactory class defines the abstract factory. It also provides a default implementation that returns the map site objects in the default theme.

Abstract factory `maze.MazeFactory`

```java
package maze;

public class MazeFactory {

    public Maze makeMaze() {
        return new Maze();
    }

    public Wall makeWall() {
        return new Wall();
    }

    public Room makeRoom(int roomNumber) {
        return new Room(roomNumber);
    }

    public Door makeDoor(Room room1, Room room2) {
        return new Door(room1, room2);
    }

}
```

Figure 10.4

A design of the
maze game using
the Abstract Fac-
tory pattern.

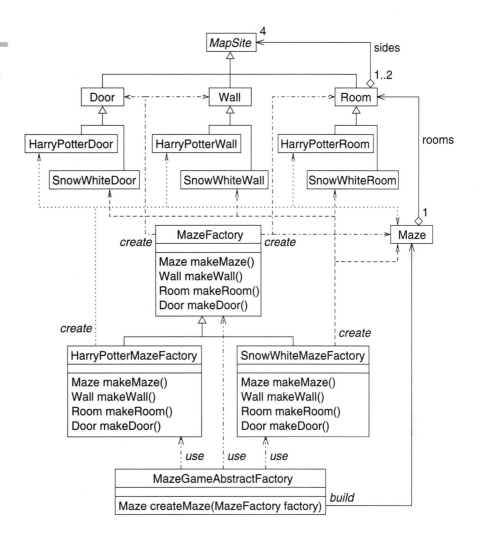

The `HarryPotterMazeFactory` and `SnowWhiteMazeFactory` are the two
concrete factories, which return the map site objects in the two respective themes.

Concrete factory `maze.HarryPotterMazeFactory`

```
package maze;

public class HarryPotterMazeFactory extends MazeFactory {

    public Wall makeWall() {
        return new HarryPotterWall();
    }

    public Room makeRoom(int roomNumber) {
        return new HarryPotterRoom(roomNumber);
    }
```

```
    public Door makeDoor(Room room1, Room room2) {
        return new HarryPotterDoor(room1, room2);
    }

}
```

Concrete factory `maze.SnowWhiteMazeFactory`

```
package maze;

public class SnowWhiteMazeFactory extends MazeFactory {

    public Wall makeWall() {
        return new SnowWhiteWall();
    }

    public Room makeRoom(int roomNumber) {
        return new SnowWhiteRoom(roomNumber);
    }

    public Door makeDoor(Room room1, Room room2) {
        return new SnowWhiteDoor(room1, room2);
    }

}
```

The `MazeGameAbstractFactory` class is the main class of this implementation of the maze game using the Abstract Factory pattern, and it is also the client role in the Abstract Factory pattern. The `createMaze()` method creates a 3 × 3 maze board. It takes a parameter of `MazeFactory` object—the abstract factory. The map site objects are created using the abstract factory interface. This method can be invoked with one of the several different concrete factories. Switching between different themes means using different concrete factories, which causes no code duplication. It is also easy to introduce new themes, a task that involves defining a new set of concrete products and a new concrete factory.

Maze game (client) `maze.MazeGameAbstractFactory`

```
package maze;

public class MazeGameAbstractFactory {

    // build a 3 x 3 maze board using abstract factory
    public static Maze createMaze(MazeFactory factory) {
        Maze maze = factory.makeMaze();
        Room room1 = factory.makeRoom(1);
        Room room2 = factory.makeRoom(2);
        Room room3 = factory.makeRoom(3);
        Room room4 = factory.makeRoom(4);
        Room room5 = factory.makeRoom(5);
        Room room6 = factory.makeRoom(6);
        Room room7 = factory.makeRoom(7);
        Room room8 = factory.makeRoom(8);
        Room room9 = factory.makeRoom(9);
        Door door1 = factory.makeDoor(room1, room2);
        Door door2 = factory.makeDoor(room2, room3);
```

```
Door door3 = factory.makeDoor(room4, room5);
Door door4 = factory.makeDoor(room5, room6);
Door door5 = factory.makeDoor(room5, room8);
Door door6 = factory.makeDoor(room6, room9);
Door door7 = factory.makeDoor(room7, room8);
Door door8 = factory.makeDoor(room1, room4);

door1.setOpen(true);
door2.setOpen(false);
door3.setOpen(true);
door4.setOpen(true);
door5.setOpen(false);
door6.setOpen(true);
door7.setOpen(true);
door8.setOpen(true);

room1.setSide(Direction.NORTH, door8);
room1.setSide(Direction.EAST, factory.makeWall());
room1.setSide(Direction.SOUTH, factory.makeWall());
room1.setSide(Direction.WEST, door1);

room2.setSide(Direction.NORTH, factory.makeWall());
room2.setSide(Direction.EAST, door1);
room2.setSide(Direction.SOUTH, factory.makeWall());
room2.setSide(Direction.WEST, door2);

room3.setSide(Direction.NORTH, factory.makeWall());
room3.setSide(Direction.EAST, door2);
room3.setSide(Direction.SOUTH, factory.makeWall());
room3.setSide(Direction.WEST, factory.makeWall());

room4.setSide(Direction.NORTH, factory.makeWall());
room4.setSide(Direction.EAST, factory.makeWall());
room4.setSide(Direction.SOUTH, door8);
room4.setSide(Direction.WEST, door3);

room5.setSide(Direction.NORTH, door5);
room5.setSide(Direction.EAST, door3);
room5.setSide(Direction.SOUTH, factory.makeWall());
room5.setSide(Direction.WEST, door4);

room6.setSide(Direction.NORTH, door6);
room6.setSide(Direction.EAST, door4);
room6.setSide(Direction.SOUTH, factory.makeWall());
room6.setSide(Direction.WEST, factory.makeWall());

room7.setSide(Direction.NORTH, factory.makeWall());
room7.setSide(Direction.EAST, factory.makeWall());
room7.setSide(Direction.SOUTH, factory.makeWall());
room7.setSide(Direction.WEST, door7);

room8.setSide(Direction.NORTH, factory.makeWall());
room8.setSide(Direction.EAST, door7);
room8.setSide(Direction.SOUTH, door5);
room8.setSide(Direction.WEST, factory.makeWall());
```

```
        room9.setSide(Direction.NORTH, factory.makeWall());
        room9.setSide(Direction.EAST, factory.makeWall());
        room9.setSide(Direction.SOUTH, door6);
        room9.setSide(Direction.WEST, factory.makeWall());

        maze.addRoom(room1);
        maze.addRoom(room2);
        maze.addRoom(room3);
        maze.addRoom(room4);
        maze.addRoom(room5);
        maze.addRoom(room6);
        maze.addRoom(room7);
        maze.addRoom(room8);
        maze.addRoom(room9);

        return maze;
    }

    public static void main(String[] args) {
        Maze maze;
        MazeFactory factory = null;

        // choose a theme by creating an appropriate concrete factory
        if (args.length > 0) {
            if ("Harry".equals(args[0])) {
                factory = new maze.harry.HarryPotterMazeFactory();
            } else if ("Snow".equals(args[0])) {
                factory = new maze.snow.SnowWhiteMazeFactory();
            }
        }
        if (factory == null) {
            factory = new MazeFactory();
        }
        maze = createMaze(factory);
        maze.setCurrentRoom(1);
        maze.showFrame("Maze -- Abstract Factory");
    }

}
```

The MazeGameAbstractFactory class can be invoked with an optional argument: Harry for the Harry Potter theme, or Snow for the Snow White theme. The main() method first creates a concrete factory for the specified theme, or the default theme if the command-line argument is absent. The maze board is then created by the createMaze() method using the appropriate concrete factory.

Another benefit of the Abstract Factory pattern is that it allows the implementation of the concrete products to be hidden from the client. Note that in this design the classes representing concrete products are in separate packages, maze.harry and maze.snow, respectively, and these classes are nonpublic. Only the concrete factory in the respective package needs to be public, since the client only accesses the factories directly. This is an important application of the encapsulation principle at the package level.

10.2.3 Design Pattern: Factory Method

An alternative solution, which is similar to the Abstract Factory pattern, is to use the Factory Method pattern discussed in Section 9.5.6 [p. 447]. The two solutions are similar in the sense that both define methods (factory methods) for creating instances of products, and different themes are represented by subclasses that override the factory methods to create concrete products in respective themes. There are also differences between the two patterns. The sole responsibility of the factories in the Abstract Factory pattern is to create products. However, creating products is only one of the responsibilities of the creators in the Factory Method pattern. The creators in the Factory Method pattern are also responsible for building a structure using the products created by the factory methods. For example, in the maze game, the Abstract Factory pattern separates the responsibilities for creating the map sites, that is, the parts, and building the maze board using the parts, and assigns them to two classes. The Factory Method pattern, however, combines these two responsibilities into one class—the MazeGameCreator class.

The design of the maze game using the Factory Method design pattern is shown in Figure 10.5. The MazeGameCreator class is the creator in the Factory Method

Figure 10.5

A design of the maze game using the Factory Method pattern.

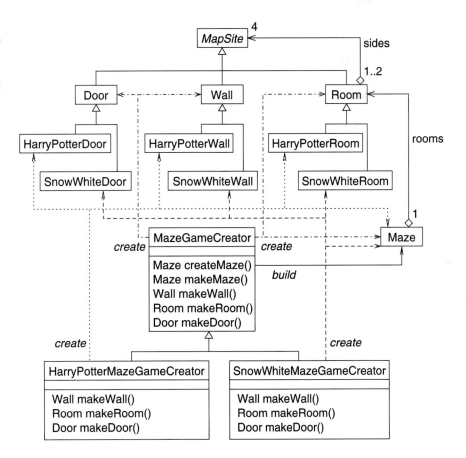

pattern. The `makeMaze()`, `makeWall()`, `makeRoom()`, and `makeDoor()` methods are the factory methods. The `createMaze()` method builds the maze board using the parts created by the factory methods.

Class `maze.MazeGameCreator`

```java
package maze;

import java.awt.*;
import javax.swing.*;

public class MazeGameCreator {

    public Maze createMaze() {
        Maze maze = makeMaze();
        Room room1 = makeRoom(1);
        Room room2 = makeRoom(2);
        Room room3 = makeRoom(3);
        Room room4 = makeRoom(4);
        Room room5 = makeRoom(5);
        Room room6 = makeRoom(6);
        Room room7 = makeRoom(7);
        Room room8 = makeRoom(8);
        Room room9 = makeRoom(9);
        Door door1 = makeDoor(room1, room2);
        Door door2 = makeDoor(room2, room3);
        Door door3 = makeDoor(room4, room5);
        Door door4 = makeDoor(room5, room6);
        Door door5 = makeDoor(room5, room8);
        Door door6 = makeDoor(room6, room9);
        Door door7 = makeDoor(room7, room8);
        Door door8 = makeDoor(room1, room4);

        door1.setOpen(true);
        door2.setOpen(false);
        door3.setOpen(true);
        door4.setOpen(true);
        door5.setOpen(false);
        door6.setOpen(true);
        door7.setOpen(true);
        door8.setOpen(true);

        room1.setSide(Direction.NORTH, door8);
        room1.setSide(Direction.EAST, makeWall());
        room1.setSide(Direction.SOUTH, makeWall());
        room1.setSide(Direction.WEST, door1);

        room2.setSide(Direction.NORTH, makeWall());
        room2.setSide(Direction.EAST, door1);
        room2.setSide(Direction.SOUTH, makeWall());
        room2.setSide(Direction.WEST, door2);
```

```
        room3.setSide(Direction.NORTH, makeWall());
        room3.setSide(Direction.EAST, door2);
        room3.setSide(Direction.SOUTH, makeWall());
        room3.setSide(Direction.WEST, makeWall());

        room4.setSide(Direction.NORTH, makeWall());
        room4.setSide(Direction.EAST, makeWall());
        room4.setSide(Direction.SOUTH, door8);
        room4.setSide(Direction.WEST, door3);

        room5.setSide(Direction.NORTH, door5);
        room5.setSide(Direction.EAST, door3);
        room5.setSide(Direction.SOUTH, makeWall());
        room5.setSide(Direction.WEST, door4);

        room6.setSide(Direction.NORTH, door6);
        room6.setSide(Direction.EAST, door4);
        room6.setSide(Direction.SOUTH, makeWall());
        room6.setSide(Direction.WEST, makeWall());

        room7.setSide(Direction.NORTH, makeWall());
        room7.setSide(Direction.EAST, makeWall());
        room7.setSide(Direction.SOUTH, makeWall());
        room7.setSide(Direction.WEST, door7);

        room8.setSide(Direction.NORTH, makeWall());
        room8.setSide(Direction.EAST, door7);
        room8.setSide(Direction.SOUTH, door5);
        room8.setSide(Direction.WEST, makeWall());

        room9.setSide(Direction.NORTH, makeWall());
        room9.setSide(Direction.EAST, makeWall());
        room9.setSide(Direction.SOUTH, door6);
        room9.setSide(Direction.WEST, makeWall());

        maze.addRoom(room1);
        maze.addRoom(room2);
        maze.addRoom(room3);
        maze.addRoom(room4);
        maze.addRoom(room5);
        maze.addRoom(room6);
        maze.addRoom(room7);
        maze.addRoom(room8);
        maze.addRoom(room9);

        return maze;
    }

    public Maze makeMaze() {
        return new Maze();
    }

    public Wall makeWall() {
        return new Wall();
    }
```

```java
    public Room makeRoom(int roomNumber) {
        return new Room(roomNumber);
    }

    public Door makeDoor(Room room1, Room room2) {
        return new Door(room1, room2);
    }

    public static void main(String[] args) {
        Maze maze;
        MazeGameCreator creator = null;

        // choose a theme by creating an appropriate concrete creator
        if (args.length > 0) {
            if ("Harry".equals(args[0])) {
                creator = new HarryPotterMazeGameCreator();
            } else if ("Snow".equals(args[0])) {
                creator = new SnowWhiteMazeGameCreator();
            }
        }
        if (creator == null) {
            creator = new MazeGameCreator();
        }
        maze = creator.createMaze();
        maze.setCurrentRoom(1);
        maze.showFrame("Maze -- Factory Method");
    }

}
```

The `HarryPotterMazeGameCreator` and `SnowWhiteMazeGameCreator` classes are the concrete creators. They extend the creator class, `MazeGameCreator`, and override the factory methods to create concrete map site objects in the respective themes.

Class `maze.HarryPotterMazeGameCreator`

```java
package maze;

public class HarryPotterMazeGameCreator extends MazeGameCreator {

    public Wall makeWall() {
        return new HarryPotterWall();
    }

    public Room makeRoom(int roomNumber) {
        return new HarryPotterRoom(roomNumber);
    }

    public Door makeDoor(Room room1, Room room2) {
        return new HarryPotterDoor(room1, room2);
    }

}
```

Class maze.SnowWhiteMazeGameCreator

```
package maze;

public class SnowWhiteMazeGameCreator extends MazeGameCreator {

    public Wall makeWall() {
        return new SnowWhiteWall();
    }

    public Room makeRoom(int roomNumber) {
        return new SnowWhiteRoom(roomNumber);
    }

    public Door makeDoor(Room room1, Room room2) {
        return new SnowWhiteDoor(room1, room2);
    }

}
```

The MazeGameCreator class can be also invoked with an optional argument: Harry for the Harry Potter theme, or Snow for the Snow White theme. The main() method first creates a concrete creator for the specified theme, or the default theme if the command-line argument is absent. The maze board is then created by the createMaze() method using the polymorphic factory methods provided by the respective concrete creator.

10.2.4 Design Pattern: Prototype

One of the shortcomings of the Abstract Factory and Factory Method patterns is that each product family is represented by a subclass. Therefore, if there are many product families, there will also be many subclasses. Furthermore, if it is possible to mix products from different product families, then the potential number of combinations and the number of subclasses could explode. An alternative solution that would prevent the explosion of the number of subclasses is to use the Prototype pattern. Using the Prototype pattern, objects are created by cloning a set of prototypes. Objects in different product families can be created by using a different set of prototypes. Using the Prototype pattern, product families can be defined or altered at run time by choosing the desired prototype. While using the Abstract Factory or Factory Method patterns, product families are defined in the form of a class and thus cannot be altered or configured at run time.

Design Pattern *Prototype*

Category: Creational design pattern.

Intent: To specify the kinds of objects to create using a prototypical instance and create new instances by cloning this prototype.

Applicability: Use the Prototype design pattern

- when a system should be independent of how its components or products are created.
- when the classes to instantiate are specified at run time.
- to avoid building a class hierarchy of factories that parallels the class hierarchy of products.

The structure of the Prototype design pattern is shown in the following diagram:

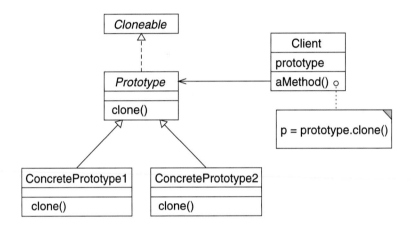

The participants of the Prototype design pattern are the following:

- *Prototype* (e.g., Room, Wall, Door), which defines interfaces of objects to be created, implements the java.lang.Cloneable interface and defines a public clone() method.
- *ConcretePrototype* (e.g., HarryPotterRoom, HarryPotterWall, HarryPotterDoor, SnowWhiteRoom, SnowWhiteWall, SnowWhiteDoor), which implements the *Prototype* interface and implements the clone() method.
- *Client* (e.g., MazePrototypeFactory), which creates new instances by cloning the prototype.

The design of the maze game using the Prototype design pattern is shown in Figure 10.6. This design is also an extension of the design using the Abstract Factory pattern. The MazePrototypeFactory is a concrete factory in the Abstract Factory pattern, and it creates the map site objects using the Prototype pattern. It contains a set of prototypes of the concrete map sites to be created. The concrete map site objects are created by cloning the corresponding prototypes. To allow the cloning of the prototypes, the concrete product classes must implement the java.lang.Cloneable interface and define a public clone() method (see Section 6.3.4 [p. 231]).

Figure 10.6

A design of the maze game using the Prototype pattern.

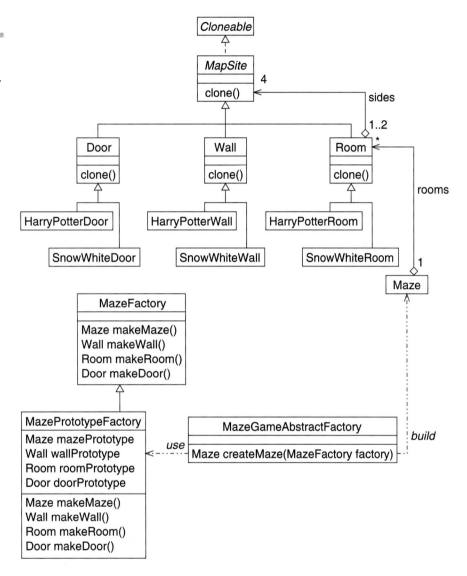

Class maze.MazePrototypeFactory

```
package maze;

import java.awt.*;
import javax.swing.*;

public class MazePrototypeFactory extends MazeFactory {
```

```
public MazePrototypeFactory(Maze mazePrototype,
                            Wall wallPrototype,
                            Room roomPrototype,
                            Door doorPrototype) {
   this.mazePrototype = mazePrototype;
   this.wallPrototype = wallPrototype;
   this.roomPrototype = roomPrototype;
   this.doorPrototype = doorPrototype;
}

public Maze makeMaze() {
   try {
      return (Maze) mazePrototype.clone();
   } catch (CloneNotSupportedException e) {
      System.err.println("CloneNotSupportedException: " + e.getMessage());
   }
   return null;
}

public Wall makeWall() {
   try {
      return (Wall) wallPrototype.clone();
   } catch (CloneNotSupportedException e) {
      System.err.println("CloneNotSupportedException: " + e.getMessage());
   }
   return null;
}

public Room makeRoom(int roomNumber) {
   try {
      Room room = (Room) roomPrototype.clone();
      room.setRoomNumber(roomNumber);
      return room;
   } catch (CloneNotSupportedException e) {
      System.err.println("CloneNotSupportedException: " + e.getMessage());
   }
   return null;
}

public Door makeDoor(Room room1, Room room2) {
   try {
      Door door = (Door) doorPrototype.clone();
      door.setRooms(room1, room2);
      return door;
   } catch (CloneNotSupportedException e) {
      System.err.println("CloneNotSupportedException: " + e.getMessage());
   }
   return null;
}

protected Maze mazePrototype;
protected Wall wallPrototype;
protected Room roomPrototype;
protected Door doorPrototype;
```

```
public static void main(String[] args) {
   Maze maze;
   MazePrototypeFactory factory = null;
   MazeFactory prototypeFactory = null;
   if (args.length > 0) {
      if ("Harry".equals(args[0])) {
         prototypeFactory = new maze.harry.HarryPotterMazeFactory();
      } else if ("Snow".equals(args[0])) {
         prototypeFactory = new maze.snow.SnowWhiteMazeFactory();
      }
   }
   if (prototypeFactory == null) {
      prototypeFactory = new MazeFactory();
   }
   factory = new MazePrototypeFactory(prototypeFactory.makeMaze(),
                            prototypeFactory.makeWall(),
                            prototypeFactory.makeRoom(0),
                            prototypeFactory.makeDoor(null, null));
   maze = MazeGameAbstractFactory.createMaze(factory);
   maze.setCurrentRoom(1);
   maze.showFrame("Maze -- Prototype");
}

}
```

The MazePrototypeFactory class can be also invoked with an optional argument: Harry for the Harry Potter theme, or Snow for the Snow White theme. The main() method first creates a concrete factory, prototypeFactory, for the specified theme, or the default theme if the command-line argument is absent. The prototype factory is used to create prototypes. Then an instance of MazePrototype-Factory, the Prototype pattern–based factory, is created using the prototypes. The Prototype pattern–based factory is used as a concrete factory in the createMaze() method of the MazeGameAbstractFactory class to build the maze board.

Configurable Universal Factory

One of the advantages of using factories is reconfigurability. In practice, the configuration settings can be passed to programs in several different ways:

1. Command-line arguments
2. Operating system environment variables
3. Java properties

In the previous examples the configuration, or the theme, is set using command line arguments. Most operating systems allow users to set global properties in environment variables, which are accessible to all programs. Environment variables are often used in C/C++ and other programs. Although Java applications can also access environment variables, this approach is often avoided because environment variables are platform dependent. Java programs often use properties to configure programs.

Properties are represented as a mapping whose keys and values are all strings. Properties can be stored in a text file, which can be easily edited.

The following `UniversalMazeFactory` class can build maze games with various schemes and using various styles of factories. It selects the scheme and factory based on the following two properties:

- `maze.theme` indicates the theme of the game board, one of `Harry`, `Snow`, or `Simple`.
- `maze.prototype` indicates whether to use prototype-based factory, either `true` or `false`.

These properties can be specified in two ways:

1. In a properties file named `maze.properties`. The properties can be specified in the properties file as follows:

   ```
   maze.theme=Harry
   maze.prototype=true
   ```

2. Using the −D command-line option. The properties can be specified on the command line as follows:

   ```
   java −Dmaze.theme=Harry −Dmaze.prototype=true maze.UniversalMazeFactory
   ```

The `UniversalMazeFactory` class is implemented as a singleton. The static initialization block is executed before the singleton instance is created. During the initialization, it tries to find the properties file named `maze.properties`. If the file is found, the properties specified in the file will be used. Otherwise, it tries to use the system properties. In the `getInstance()` method, it creates a factory based on the values of properties read in the initialization.

Class `maze.UniversalMazeFactory`

```java
package maze;

import java.util.*;
import java.io.*;
import java.awt.*;
import javax.swing.*;

public class UniversalMazeFactory extends MazeFactory {

    public static MazeFactory getInstance() {
        if (theInstance == null) {
            if (usePrototype) {
                MazeFactory factory = null;
                switch (theme) {
                case HARRY_PORTER_THEME:
                    factory = new maze.harry.HarryPotterMazeFactory();
                    break;
                case SNOW_WHITE_THEME:
                    factory = new maze.snow.SnowWhiteMazeFactory();
                    break;
                }
```

```
           if (factory == null) {
               factory = new MazeFactory();
           }
           theInstance =
               new MazePrototypeFactory(factory.makeMaze(),
                                        factory.makeWall(),
                                        factory.makeRoom(0),
                                        factory.makeDoor(null, null));
       } else {
           switch (theme) {
           case HARRY_PORTER_THEME:
               theInstance = new maze.harry.HarryPotterMazeFactory();
               break;
           case SNOW_WHITE_THEME:
               theInstance = new maze.snow.SnowWhiteMazeFactory();
               break;
           default:
               theInstance = new MazeFactory();
               break;
           }
       }
   }
   return theInstance;
}

protected UniversalMazeFactory() {}

private static MazeFactory theInstance = null;

private static final int SIMPLE_THEME = 0;
private static final int HARRY_PORTER_THEME = 1;
private static final int SNOW_WHITE_THEME = 2;
private static boolean usePrototype = true;
private static int theme = SIMPLE_THEME;

static {
   Properties configProperties = new Properties();
   try {
       configProperties.load(new FileInputStream("maze.properties"));
   } catch (IOException e) {
       e.printStackTrace();
   }
   String value;
   value = System.getProperty("maze.theme");
   if (value == null) {
       value = configProperties.getProperty("maze.theme");
   }
   if (value != null) {
       if ("Harry".equals(value)) {
           theme = HARRY_PORTER_THEME;
       } else if ("Snow".equals(value)) {
           theme = SNOW_WHITE_THEME;
       }
   }
}
```

```
            value = System.getProperty("maze.prototype");

            if (value == null) {
                value = configProperties.getProperty("maze.prototype");
            }

            if (value != null) {
                usePrototype = Boolean.getBoolean(value);
            }
        }
        public static void main(String[] args) {
            MazeFactory factory = UniversalMazeFactory.getInstance();
            Maze maze = MazeGameAbstractFactory.createMaze(factory);
            maze.setCurrentRoom(1);
            maze.showFrame("Maze -- Universal Factory");
        }

    }
```

10.2.5 Design Pattern: Builder

In the previous examples, the method `createMaze()` constructs a maze board. It is lengthy and contains many code segments that perform identical tasks such as creating similar components of the maze board. The Builder design pattern can be used to simplify the construction process by avoiding the duplication of similar code and shortening the code for the construction.

Design Pattern *Builder*

Category: Creational design pattern.

Intent: To separate the construction of a complex object from the implementation of its parts so that the same construction process can create complex objects from different implementations of parts.

Applicability: Use the Builder design pattern

- when the process for creating a complex object should be independent of the parts that make up the object.
- when the construction process should allow various implementations of the parts used for construction.

The structure of the Builder design pattern is shown in the following diagram:

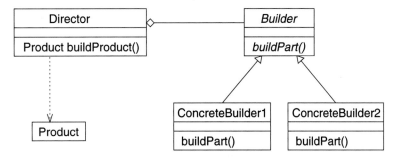

The participants of the Builder design pattern are the following:

- *Builder* (e.g., MazeBuilder), which defines an interface for creating parts of a *Product* object.
- *ConcreteBuilder* (e.g., SimpleMazeBuilder, FactoryMazeBuilder), which constructs and assembles parts of the product by implementing the *Builder* interface.
- *Director* (e.g., MazeGameBuilder), which constructs a *Product* object using the *Builder* interface.
- *Product* (e.g., Maze), which represents the complex object under construction.

The design of the maze game using the Builder design pattern is shown in Figure 10.7. In this design, we define a builder interface MazeBuilder to build

Figure 10.7

A design of the maze game using the Builder pattern.

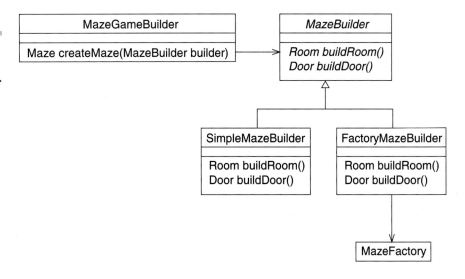

components of the maze board from the basic parts. The methods of the `MazeBuilder` class are summarized in the following table:

Methods	Description
newMaze()	Start to build a new maze board.
getMaze()()	Retrieve the maze boards that have been completely built.
buildRoom()	Build a new room with walls on all four sides.
buildDoor()	Build a door between two rooms.

Class `maze.MazeBuilder`

```
package maze;

public interface MazeBuilder {

    public void newMaze();
    public Maze getMaze();
    public void buildRoom(int roomNumber);
    public void buildDoor(int roomNumber1, int roomNumber2,
                          Direction dir, boolean open);
}
```

Two concrete builders are implemented. The `SimpleMazeBuilder` class constructs the map site objects in the default themes using the `new` operator.

Class `maze.SimpleMazeBuilder`

```
package maze;
public class SimpleMazeBuilder implements MazeBuilder {

    public void newMaze() {
        maze = new Maze();
    }

    public Maze getMaze() {
        return maze;
    }

    public void buildRoom(int roomNumber) {
        if (maze == null) {
            newMaze();
        }
        Room room = new Room(roomNumber);
        for (Direction dir = Direction.first(); dir != null;
            dir = dir.next()) {
            room.setSide(dir, new Wall());
        }
        maze.addRoom(room);
    }
```

```
    public void buildDoor(int roomNumber1, int roomNumber2,
                          Direction dir, boolean open) {
        if (maze == null) {
            newMaze();
        }
        Room room1 = maze.findRoom(roomNumber1);
        Room room2 = maze.findRoom(roomNumber2);
        if (room1 != null &&
            room2 != null &&
            dir != null) {
            Door door = new Door(room1, room2);
            room1.setSide(dir, door);
            room2.setSide(dir.opposite(), door);
            door.setOpen(open);
        }
    }

    protected Maze maze;

}
```

The FactoryMazeBuilder class uses a factory to construct the map site objects, so that different themes can be supported.

Class maze.FactoryMazeBuilder

```
package maze;

public class FactoryMazeBuilder implements MazeBuilder {
    public FactoryMazeBuilder(MazeFactory factory) {
        this.factory = factory;
    }

    public void newMaze() {
        maze = factory.makeMaze();
    }

    public Maze getMaze() {
        return maze;
    }

    public void buildRoom(int roomNumber) {
        if (maze == null) {
            newMaze();
        }
        Room room = factory.makeRoom(roomNumber);
        for (Direction dir = Direction.first(); dir != null;
             dir = dir.next()) {
            room.setSide(dir, factory.makeWall());
        }
        maze.addRoom(room);
    }
```

```
        public void buildDoor(int roomNumber1, int roomNumber2,
                         Direction dir, boolean open) {
    if (maze == null) {
       newMaze();
    }
    Room room1 = maze.findRoom(roomNumber1);
    Room room2 = maze.findRoom(roomNumber2);
    if (room1 != null &&
        room2 != null &&
        dir != null) {
       Door door = factory.makeDoor(room1, room2);
       room1.setSide(dir, door);
       room2.setSide(dir.opposite(), door);
       door.setOpen(open);
    }
  }
}

  protected MazeFactory factory;
  protected Maze maze;

}
```

The MazeGameBuilder class is the director in the Builder pattern. It constructs the maze board from the components built by the builder. The createMaze() method constructs the same 3 × 3 maze board constructed in the previous examples. Using the Builder pattern, the createMaze() method becomes much simpler and shorter.

Class maze.MazeGameBuilder

```
package maze;

import java.awt.*;
import javax.swing.*;

public class MazeGameBuilder {

  public static Maze createMaze(MazeBuilder builder) {
    builder.newMaze();
    builder.buildRoom(1);
    builder.buildRoom(2);
    builder.buildRoom(3);
    builder.buildRoom(4);
    builder.buildRoom(5);
    builder.buildRoom(6);
    builder.buildRoom(7);
    builder.buildRoom(8);
    builder.buildRoom(9);

    builder.buildDoor(1, 2, Direction.WEST, true);
    builder.buildDoor(2, 3, Direction.WEST, false);
    builder.buildDoor(4, 5, Direction.WEST, true);
    builder.buildDoor(5, 6, Direction.WEST, true);
    builder.buildDoor(5, 8, Direction.NORTH, false);
    builder.buildDoor(6, 9, Direction.NORTH, true);
```

```
            builder.buildDoor(7, 8, Direction.WEST, true);
            builder.buildDoor(1, 4, Direction.NORTH, true);

            return builder.getMaze();
        }
    public static void main(String[] args) {
        Maze maze;
        MazeBuilder builder;
        MazeFactory factory = null;

        if (args.length > 0) {
            if ("Harry".equals(args[0])) {
                factory = new HarryPotterMazeFactory();
            } else if ("Snow".equals(args[0])) {
                factory = new SnowWhiteMazeFactory();
            } else if ("Default".equals(args[0])) {
                factory = new MazeFactory();
            }
        }
        if (factory != null) {
            builder = new FactoryMazeBuilder(factory);
        } else {
            builder = new SimpleMazeBuilder();
        }
        maze = createMaze(builder);
        maze.setCurrentRoom(1);
        maze.showFrame("Maze -- Builder");
    }

}
```

The MazeGameBuilder class can be invoked with an optional argument. If the argument is present, the FactoryMazeBuilder will be used and the argument specifies the theme: Harry for the Harry Potter theme, Snow for the Snow White theme, or Default for the default theme. If the argument is absent, the SimpleMazeBuilder will be used.

10.3 BEHAVIORAL PATTERNS

10.3.1 Design Pattern: Command

In the previous section, we focused on constructing the maze board. In this section, we focus on the behavior of the maze game. The player starts in a specified room of the maze board. The player can be moved with the arrow keys: left, right, up, and down. The player can move to an adjacent room through an open door. Furthermore, we support the undoing of moves by the player.

An object-oriented approach to supporting the undoing of actions is to use the Command pattern, which is a behavioral design pattern that treats actions as objects.

Design Pattern *Command*

Category: Behavioral design pattern.

Intent: To encapsulate an action as an object, so that actions can be passed as parameters, queued, and possibly undone.

Also Known As: Action.

Applicability: Use the Command design pattern

- when actions need to be passed as parameters.
- when actions need to be queued and then executed later.
- when actions can be undone.

The structure of the Command design pattern is shown in the following diagram:

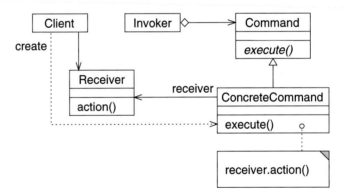

The participants of the Command design pattern are the following:

- *Command* (e.g., Command, UndoableCommand), which defines an interface to perform or undo an action.
- *Receiver* (e.g., Maze), which knows how to perform the actions.
- *ConcreteCommand* (e.g., MazeMoveCommand), which implements the *Command* interface and delegates the execution of the action to the *Receiver*.
- *Client* (e.g., Maze.MazeKeyListener), which creates the concrete commands and binds the concrete commands to their receivers.
- *Invoker* (e.g., Maze), which asks the command to carry out the action.

10.3.2 Supporting Undo

The design of the maze game with undoable moves using the Command pattern is shown in Figure 10.8.

The Command Interfaces

The `Command` interface defines the basic interface of command objects. The `execute()` method performs the action represented by the command object.

Class `maze.Command`

```java
package maze;

public interface Command {

    public void execute();

}
```

The `UndoableCommand` interface extends the `Command` interface to define an `undo()` method, which undoes the action performed by the `execute()` method.

Class `maze.UndoableCommand`

```java
package maze;

public interface UndoableCommand extends Command {

    public void undo();

}
```

Figure 10.8

Undoable moves in the maze game using the Command pattern.

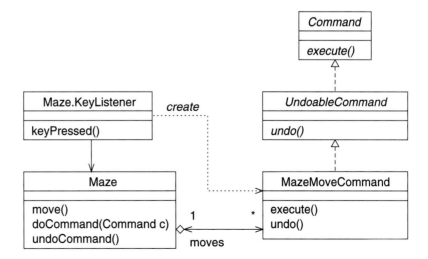

The Receiver and Invoker of Command

The receiver in the Command pattern is the class that is responsible for actually carrying out the actions represented by the command objects. The invoker is the class that invokes the command, that is, that has the action of the command object carried out. In the maze game, the role of the receiver and the invoker are played by the same class: Maze. The move() method of the Maze class fulfills the responsibility of the receiver. It attempts to move the player in the specified direction. If there is an open door in the specified direction, the player enters the room on the other side of the door. Otherwise, the player stays in the current room. The doCommand() and undoCommand() methods of the Maze class fulfill the responsibility of the invoker. The doCommand() method executes the command and saves the command in a stack named moves for possible undoing of the command. The undoCommand() method pops the command at the top of the moves stack and attempts to undo the command.

Class maze.Maze

```
public class Maze implements Cloneable {
    ⟨Methods for building the maze board. See Section 10.2.1 [p. 475]⟩
    public void move(Direction direction) {
        if (curRoom != null) {
            MapSite side = curRoom.getSide(direction);
            if (side != null) {
                side.enter(this);
            }
        }
    }

    protected void doCommand(Command command) {
        if (command != null) {
            moves.push(command);
            command.execute();
        }
    }

    protected void undoCommand() {
        if (!moves.empty()) {
            Object top = moves.peek();  // looking at the top element
                                        // without popping it
            if (top instanceof UndoableCommand) {
                moves.pop();
                UndoableCommand undoableCommand = (UndoableCommand) top;
                undoableCommand.undo();
            }
        }
    }

    protected List rooms = new ArrayList();
    protected Room curRoom = null;
    protected Stack moves = new Stack();
    ⟨Nested class MazeKeyListener on page 511⟩
}
```

The Concrete Commands

The concrete command in the maze game is the MazeMoveCommand class, which implements the UndoableCommand interface. The execute() method attempts to move the player in the specified direction, and the undo() method attempts to move the player in the direction opposite to the specified direction.

Class maze.MazeMoveCommand

```
package maze;

public class MazeMoveCommand implements UndoableCommand {

   public MazeMoveCommand(Maze maze, Direction direction) {
      this.maze = maze;
      this.direction = direction;
   }
   public void execute() {
      maze.move(direction);
   }
   public void undo() {
      maze.move(direction.opposite());
   }
   protected Maze maze;
   protected Direction direction;

}
```

The Client of Command

The client of the Command pattern is the class that is responsible for creating the command objects. In the maze game, this client is the nested class Maze.MazeKey-Listener, which listens for key strokes. For the arrow keys (left, right, up, and down) it creates a MazeMoveCommand object and sends the command object to the maze object.

Nested class of maze.Maze: MazeKeyListener

```
static class MazeKeyListener extends KeyAdapter {

   MazeKeyListener(Maze maze) {
      this.maze = maze;
   }
   public void keyPressed(KeyEvent e) {
      System.out.println("Key pressed");
      Command command = null;
      int code = e.getKeyCode();
      switch (code) {
      case KeyEvent.VK_UP:
         command = new MazeMoveCommand(maze, Direction.NORTH);
         break;
      case KeyEvent.VK_DOWN:
         command = new MazeMoveCommand(maze, Direction.SOUTH);
         maze.move(Direction.SOUTH);
```

```
            break;
        case KeyEvent.VK_LEFT:
            command = new MazeMoveCommand(maze, Direction.WEST);
            break;
        case KeyEvent.VK_RIGHT:
            command = new MazeMoveCommand(maze, Direction.EAST);
            break;
        }
        if (command != null) {
            maze.doCommand(command);
        }
    }

    Maze maze;
}
```

The Undoable Maze Game

The maze.UndoableMazeGame class is the main class of the maze game that supports undo commands. The main() method is similar to the main() method of the MazeGameBuilder class, except that it also builds a menu bar that contains an *undo* menu item. The undo command can be invoked from the *undo* menu item.

Class maze.UndoableMazeGame

```java
package maze;

import java.awt.*;
import java.awt.event.*;
import javax.swing.*;

public class UndoableMazeGame {
    public static void main(String[] args) {
        Maze maze;
        MazeBuilder builder;
        MazeFactory factory = null;

        if (args.length > 0) {
            if ("Harry".equals(args[0])) {
                factory = new HarryPotterMazeFactory();
            } else if ("Snow".equals(args[0])) {
                factory = new SnowWhiteMazeFactory();
            } else if ("Default".equals(args[0])) {
                factory = new MazeFactory();
            }
        }
        if (factory != null) {
            builder = new FactoryMazeBuilder(factory);
        } else {
            builder = new SimpleMazeBuilder();
        }
        maze = MazeGameBuilder.createMaze(builder);
        maze.setCurrentRoom(1);
```

```
                    JMenuBar menubar = new JMenuBar();
                    JMenu menu = new JMenu("Command");
                    JMenuItem undoMenuItem = new JMenuItem("undo");
                    undoMenuItem.addActionListener(new MazeCommandAction(maze));
                    menu.add(undoMenuItem);
                    menubar.add(menu);

                    JFrame frame;
                    frame = new JFrame("Maze -- Builder");
                    frame.getContentPane().setLayout(new BorderLayout());
                    frame.getContentPane().add(menubar, BorderLayout.NORTH);
                    frame.getContentPane().add(new Maze.MazePanel(maze),
                                        BorderLayout.CENTER);
                    frame.pack();
                    Dimension frameDim = frame.getSize();
                    Dimension screenSize = Toolkit.getDefaultToolkit().getScreenSize();
                    frame.setLocation(screenSize.width / 2 - frameDim.width / 2,
                                    screenSize.height / 2 - frameDim.height / 2);
                    frame.setDefaultCloseOperation(WindowConstants.EXIT_ON_CLOSE);
                    frame.setVisible(true);
                }

            static class MazeCommandAction implements ActionListener {
                public MazeCommandAction(Maze maze) {
                    this.maze = maze;
                }

                public void actionPerformed(ActionEvent event) {
                    maze.undoCommand();
                }

                protected Maze maze;
            }
        }
```

10.4 STRUCTURAL PATTERNS

10.4.1 Design Pattern: Adapter

The Adapter design pattern is another very commonly used design pattern. We often find some classes that provide functionality that can be reused. However, the interface providing the functionality is not the interface expected by the client. The Adapter pattern addresses the issue of adapting an interface to accommodate the needs of a client that hopes to reuse the functionality but expects a different interface.

Design Pattern *Adapter*

Category: Structural design pattern.

Intent: To convert the interface of a class into another interface that clients expect.

Also Known As: Wrapper.

Applicability: Use the Adapter design pattern

- to use an existing class with an interface different from the desired interface.

There are two forms of the Adapter pattern:

- *Class adapter*, which relies on inheritance. The structure of the class adapter is shown in the following diagram:

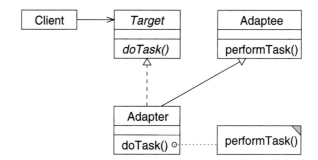

- *Object adapter*, which relies on delegation, or object composition. The structure of the object adapter is shown in the following diagram:

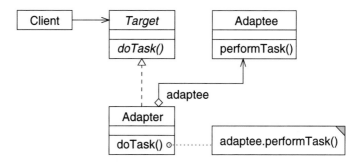

The participants of the Adapter design pattern are the following:

- *Target* (e.g., `TableEntry`), which defines the interface used by the *Client*.
- *Client* (e.g., `Table`), which uses objects conforming to the *Target* interface.
- *Adaptee* (e.g., `Student`), which defines the interface of an existing class to be reused.
- *Adapter* (e.g., `StudentEntry`, `StudentEntry2`), which adapts the interface of *Adaptee* to *Target*.

To illustrate the Adapter pattern, we design a generic table to display a list of objects of any class in tabular form. An example of a table with entries of student

Figure 10.9

The table of entries of student information.

ID	First Name	Last Name	Street Address	State	City	Country	Postal ...	Telephone	GPA	Total..
1006	Thomas	Jackson	543 Lake Ave.	IL	Plainville	USA	80108	103-367-4105	2.1	72
1007	Jim	Barksdale	789 Bay Street	CA	Any Town	USA	34191	156-303-8166	2.5	84
1020	Mitchell	Kapor	4328 Central Bl...	MA	Sea Side	USA	71126	230-525-1849	3.1	44
1017	Ralph	Johnson	446 Main Street	IL	Middle Town	USA	93686	252-438-9179	3.8	64
1011	Chris	Galvin	768 My Street	IL	Northfield	USA	37857	272-666-5555	2.9	32
1002	Steve	Jobs	100 Next Drive	CA	Orchidville	USA	79910	321-654-4567	3.7	24
1014	Jerry	Young	748 Hillside Blvd.	CA	Yahooville	USA	91578	397-716-6169	3.5	104
1008	Marc	Andreesen	333 Westgate A...	IL	Old Town	USA	33081	430-488-0931	3.7	24
1015	Eric	Gamma	897 Central Str...	NM	Any Town	USA	27351	431-878-7706	3.6	136
1005	Paul	Allen	51 Garden Street	OR	Protland	USA	36845	455-757-7311	3.9	144
1010	James	Gosling	1 Oak Street	CA	Java Island	USA	98650	516-192-9406	4.0	64
1001	Bill	Gates	1 Microsoft Way	WA	Redmond	USA	65432	555-123-4567	3.9	32
1003	Scott	McNealy	123 Main Street	CA	Sunnyville	USA	90715	590-298-4262	3.5	48

information is shown in Figure 10.9. When you click on the header of a column, the list of objects will be sorted based on the values in that column.

Our table class, `adapter.Table`, extends the `JTable` class in swing. The design of the generic table is shown in Figure 10.10.

The key to the design of the generic table is that the data entries shown in the table must be instances of a class that conforms to the `TableEntry` interface.

Class `adapter.TableEntry`

```java
package adapter;

import java.util.Comparator;

public interface TableEntry {

    public int getColumnCount();
    public String getColumnName(int col);
    public Object getColumnValue(int col);
    public String getColumnTip(int col);
    public Class getColumnClass(int col);
    public Comparator getColumnComparator(int col);
    public int getColumnWidth(int col);

}
```

Figure 10.10

The design of the generic table with sorting capability.

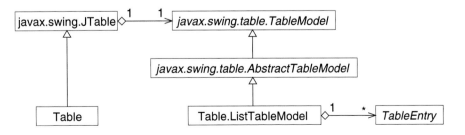

Each entry represents a row in the table. The methods of the `TableEntry` interface are summarized in the following table:

Methods	Description
getColumnCount()	Returns the number of columns
getColumnName(col)	Returns the name of column col, which will be displayed on the header of the column
getColumnValue(col)	Returns the value of column col, which will be displayed in the cell of the column
getColumnTip(col)	Returns the text of pop-up tips for column col, which will be displayed when the mouse moves over the header of the column
getColumnClass(col)	Returns the class of the values in column col
getColumnComparator(col)	Returns a Comparator object for sorting column col
getColumnWidth()	Returns the minimum width of column col

The implementation of the `Table` class is shown in the following code. However, the implementation of the `Table` class is immaterial to the discussion of the Adapter pattern.

Class `adapter.Table`

```java
package adapter;

import java.awt.Color;
import java.awt.Point;
import java.awt.event.*;
import javax.swing.*;
import javax.swing.table.*;
import javax.swing.event.*;
import java.util.*;

public class Table extends JTable {

    public Table() {
        this(null);
    }

    public Table(List entries) {
        super(new ListTableModel(entries));
        model = (ListTableModel) dataModel;
```

```
getTableHeader().addMouseListener(new MouseAdapter() {
    public void mousePressed(MouseEvent e) {
        Point p = e.getPoint();
        JTableHeader header = (JTableHeader) e.getSource();
        int column = header.columnAtPoint(p);
        if (model.sort(column)) {
            clearSelection();
            updateUI();
        }
    }
});

setSelectionMode(ListSelectionModel.SINGLE_SELECTION);

int columnCount = model.getColumnCount();
for (int i = 0; i < columnCount; i++) {
    TableColumn column = getColumnModel().getColumn(i);
    DefaultTableCellRenderer renderer =
        new DefaultTableCellRenderer();
    String tip = model.getColumnTip(i);
    renderer.setToolTipText(tip);
    column.setCellRenderer(renderer);
    int w = model.getColumnWidth(i);
    if (w > 0) {
        column.setPreferredWidth(w);
    }
}
}

protected ListTableModel model;

static class ListTableModel extends AbstractTableModel {

    public ListTableModel(List entries) {
        if (entries != null &&
            entries.size() > 0) {
            Object obj = entries.get(0);
            if (obj != null &&
                obj instanceof TableEntry) {
                this.prototype = (TableEntry) obj;
                setData(entries);
            }
        }
    }

    public ListTableModel(TableEntry prototype) {
        this.prototype = prototype;
    }
```

```
public int getColumnCount() {
   if (prototype != null) {
      return prototype.getColumnCount();
   }
   return 0;
}

public int getRowCount() {
   if (entries != null) {
      return entries.size();
   } else {
      return 0;
   }
}

public String getColumnName(int col) {
   if (prototype != null) {
      return prototype.getColumnName(col);
   }
   return null;
}

public Object getValueAt(int row, int col) {
   if (entries != null) {
      TableEntry entry = getTableEntry(row);
      if (entry != null) {
         return entry.getColumnValue(col);
      }
   }
   return null;
}

public Class getColumnClass(int col) {
   if (prototype != null) {
      return prototype.getColumnClass(col);
   }
   return String.class;
}

public String getColumnTip(int col) {
   if (prototype != null) {
      return prototype.getColumnTip(col);
   }
   return null;
}

public Comparator getColumnComparator(int col) {
   if (prototype != null) {
      return prototype.getColumnComparator(col);
   }
   return null;
}
```

```
public int getColumnWidth(int col) {
   if (prototype != null) {
      return prototype.getColumnWidth(col);
   }
   return -1;
}

public boolean isCellEditable(int row, int col) {
   return false;
}

public void setValueAt(Object value, int row, int col) {
}

public void clearData() {
   entries = null;
}

public void setData(List entries) {
   this.entries = entries;
}

public boolean sort(int col) {
   if (entries != null &&
      col >=0 &&
      col < getColumnCount()) {
      Comparator c = getColumnComparator(col);
      if (c != null) {
         Collections.sort(entries, c);
         return true;
      }
   }
   return false;
}

public TableEntry getTableEntry(int i) {
   if (entries != null &&
      i >= 0 &&
      i < entries.size()) {
      return (TableEntry) entries.get(i);
   }
   return null;
}

protected TableEntry prototype;
protected List entries; // elements are instance of TableEntry

}

}
```

Now, given the following Student class, we want to display the student information using the generic table.

Class adapter.Student

```
package adapter;

public class Student implements Cloneable {
    public Student() {}

    public Student(String ID,
                   String firstName,
                   String lastName,
                   String streetAddress,
                   String state,
                   String city,
                   String country,
                   String postalCode,
                   String telephone,
                   float GPA,
                   int totalCredits) {
        this.ID = ID;
        this.firstName = firstName;
        this.lastName = lastName;
        this.streetAddress = streetAddress;
        this.state = state;
        this.city = city;
        this.country = country;
        this.postalCode = postalCode;
        this.telephone = telephone;
        this.GPA = GPA;
        this.totalCredits = totalCredits;
    }

    public Object clone()
            throws CloneNotSupportedException {
        return super.clone();
    }

    public String getCity() {
        return city;
    }

    public String getCountry() {
        return country;
    }

    public String getFirstName() {
        return firstName;
    }

    public float getGPA() {
        return GPA;
    }
```

```java
public String getID() {
   return ID;
}

public String getLastName() {
   return lastName;
}

public String getPostalCode() {
   return postalCode;
}

public String getState() {
   return state;
}

public String getStreetAddress() {
   return streetAddress;
}

public String getTelephone() {
   return telephone;
}

public int getTotalCredits() {
   return totalCredits;
}

public void setCity(String city) {
   this.city = city;
}

public void setCountry(String country) {
   this.country = country;
}

public void setFirstName(String firstName) {
   this.firstName = firstName;
}

public void setGPA(float GPA) {
   this.GPA = GPA;
}

public void setID(String ID) {
   this.ID = ID;
}

public void setLastName(String lastName) {
   this.lastName = lastName;
}

public void setPostalCode(String postalCode) {
   this.postalCode = postalCode;
}
```

```
public void setState(String state) {
   this.state = state;
}

public void setStreetAddress(String streetAddress) {
   this.streetAddress = streetAddress;
}

public void setTelephone(String telephone) {
   this.telephone = telephone;
}

public void setTotalCredits(int totalCredits) {
   this.totalCredits = totalCredits;
}

public String toString() {
   StringBuffer s = new StringBuffer();
   s.append("Student [");
   s.append("totalCredits=");
   s.append(totalCredits);
   s.append("; ");
   s.append("GPA=");
   s.append(GPA);
   s.append("; ");
   s.append("telephone=");
   s.append(telephone);
   s.append("; ");
   s.append("postalCode=");
   s.append(postalCode);
   s.append("; ");
   s.append("country=");
   s.append(country);
   s.append("; ");
   s.append("city=");
   s.append(city);
   s.append("; ");
   s.append("state=");
   s.append(state);
   s.append("; ");
   s.append("streetAddress=");
   s.append(streetAddress);
   s.append("; ");
   s.append("lastName=");
   s.append(lastName);
   s.append("; ");
   s.append("firstName=");
   s.append(firstName);
   s.append("; ");
   s.append("ID=");
   s.append(ID);
   s.append("]");
   return s.toString();
}
```

```
        protected int totalCredits;
        protected float GPA;
        protected String telephone;
        protected String postalCode;
        protected String country;
        protected String city;
        protected String state;
        protected String streetAddress;
        protected String lastName;
        protected String firstName;
        protected String ID;

    }
```

The problem is that the Table class expects the entries to be instances of a class that conforms to the TableEntry interface, while the Student class does not conform to the TableEntry interface. Instead of rewriting the Student class to make it conform to the TableEntry interface, we can use the Adapter pattern. We can use either form of the Adapter to accomplish the task. The design using the class adapter form is shown in Figure 10.11. The StudentEntry class is the adapter, the Student class is the adaptee, and the TableEntry interface is the target.

Class adapter.StudentEntry

```
package adapter;

import java.util.Comparator;

/**
 * Adapter design pattern
 */
public class StudentEntry extends Student implements TableEntry {

    // position of each column
    public static final int ID_COLUMN              = 0;
    public static final int FIRST_NAME_COLUMN      = 1;
    public static final int LAST_NAME_COLUMN       = 2;
    public static final int STREET_ADDRESS_COLUMN  = 3;
    public static final int STATE_COLUMN           = 4;
    public static final int CITY_COLUMN            = 5;
    public static final int COUNTRY_COLUMN         = 6;
    public static final int POSTAL_CODE_COLUMN     = 7;
```

Figure 10.11

Class adapter: adapt by inheritance.

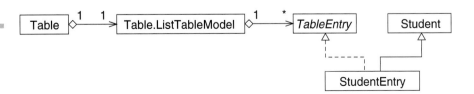

```java
    public static final int TELEPHONE_COLUMN      = 8;
    public static final int GPA_COLUMN            = 9;
    public static final int TOTAL_CREDITS_COLUMN  = 10;

    public static final String[] columnNames = {
       "ID",
       "First Name",
       "Last Name",
       "Street Address",
       "State",
       "City",
       "Country",
       "Postal Code",
       "Telephone",
       "GPA",
       "Total Credits",
    };

    public static final String[] columnTips = {
       "ID",
       "First Name",
       "Last Name",
       "Street Address",
       "State",
       "City",
       "Country",
       "Postal Code",
       "Telephone",
       "GPA",
       "Total Credits",
    };

    public static final Comparator[] comparators = {
       new StudentEntryComparator(ID_COLUMN),
       new StudentEntryComparator(FIRST_NAME_COLUMN),
       new StudentEntryComparator(LAST_NAME_COLUMN),
       new StudentEntryComparator(STREET_ADDRESS_COLUMN),
       new StudentEntryComparator(STATE_COLUMN),
       new StudentEntryComparator(CITY_COLUMN),
       new StudentEntryComparator(COUNTRY_COLUMN),
       new StudentEntryComparator(POSTAL_CODE_COLUMN),
       new StudentEntryComparator(TELEPHONE_COLUMN),
       new StudentEntryComparator(GPA_COLUMN),
       new StudentEntryComparator(TOTAL_CREDITS_COLUMN),
    };

    public StudentEntry(String ID,
                        String firstName,
                        String lastName,
                        String streetAddress,
                        String state,
                        String city,
                        String country,
                        String postalCode,
```

```
                              String telephone,
                              float GPA,
                              int totalCredits) {
    super(ID, firstName, lastName, streetAddress, state, city,
        country, postalCode, telephone, GPA, totalCredits);
}

public StudentEntry(Student student) {
    if (student != null) {
        this.ID = student.ID;
        this.firstName = student.firstName;
        this.lastName = student.lastName;
        this.streetAddress = student.streetAddress;
        this.state = student.state;
        this.city = student.city;
        this.country = student.country;
        this.postalCode = student.postalCode;
        this.telephone = student.telephone;
        this.GPA = student.GPA;
        this.totalCredits = student.totalCredits;
    }
}

public int getColumnCount() {
    return columnNames.length;
}

public String getColumnName(int col) {
    if (col >= 0 &&
        col < columnNames.length) {
        return columnNames[col];
    }
    return null;
}

public Object getColumnValue(int col) {
    if (col >= 0 &&
        col < columnNames.length) {
        switch (col) {
        case ID_COLUMN:             return ID;
        case FIRST_NAME_COLUMN:     return firstName;
        case LAST_NAME_COLUMN:      return lastName;
        case STREET_ADDRESS_COLUMN: return streetAddress;
        case STATE_COLUMN:          return state;
        case CITY_COLUMN:           return city;
        case COUNTRY_COLUMN:        return country;
        case POSTAL_CODE_COLUMN:    return postalCode;
        case TELEPHONE_COLUMN:      return telephone;
        case GPA_COLUMN:            return new Float(GPA);
        case TOTAL_CREDITS_COLUMN:  return new Integer(totalCredits);
        }
    }
    return null;
}
```

```java
public String getColumnTip(int col) {
   if (col >= 0 &&
       col < columnTips.length) {
     return columnTips[col];
   }
   return null;
}

public Class getColumnClass(int col) {
   if (col == GPA_COLUMN) {
     return Float.class;
   } else if (col == TOTAL_CREDITS_COLUMN) {
     return Integer.class;
   } else {
     return String.class;
   }
}

public Comparator getColumnComparator(int col) {
   if (col >= 0 &&
       col < comparators.length) {
     return comparators[col];
   }
   return null;
}

public int getColumnWidth(int col) {
   return -1;
}

static public class StudentEntryComparator implements Comparator {
   public StudentEntryComparator(int col) {
     this.col = col;
   }

   public int compare(Object o1, Object o2) {
     if (o1 != null &&
         o2 != null &&
         o1 instanceof StudentEntry &&
         o2 instanceof StudentEntry) {
       StudentEntry e1 = (StudentEntry) o1;
       StudentEntry e2 = (StudentEntry) o2;
       if (col == GPA_COLUMN) {
         return (int) (e1.getGPA() * 1000 - e2.getGPA() * 1000);
       } else if (col == TOTAL_CREDITS_COLUMN) {
         return (e1.getTotalCredits() - e2.getTotalCredits());
       } else {
         return ((String) e1.getColumnValue(col)).compareTo
                 (e2.getColumnValue(col));
       }
     }
     return 0;
   }
```

```
        protected int col;
    }
}
```

The design using the object adapter form is shown in Figure 10.12. The
StudentEntry2 class is the adapter, the Student class is the adaptee, and the
TableEntry interface is the target.

Class adapter.StudentEntry2

```java
package adapter;
import java.util.Comparator;

/**
 * Adapter design pattern
 */
public class StudentEntry2 implements TableEntry {

    // position of each column
    public static final int ID_COLUMN             = 0;
    public static final int FIRST_NAME_COLUMN     = 1;
    public static final int LAST_NAME_COLUMN      = 2;
    public static final int STREET_ADDRESS_COLUMN = 3;
    public static final int STATE_COLUMN          = 4;
    public static final int CITY_COLUMN           = 5;
    public static final int COUNTRY_COLUMN        = 6;
    public static final int POSTAL_CODE_COLUMN    = 7;
    public static final int TELEPHONE_COLUMN      = 8;
    public static final int GPA_COLUMN            = 9;
    public static final int TOTAL_CREDITS_COLUMN  = 10;

    public static final String[] columnNames = {
        "ID",
        "First Name",
        "Last Name",
        "Street Address",
        "State",
        "City",
        "Country",
        "Postal Code",
        "Telephone",
        "GPA",
        "Total Credits",
    };
```

Figure 10.12

Object adapter: adapt by delegation.

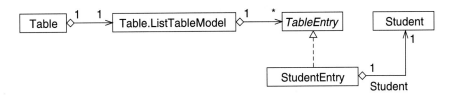

```java
    public static final String[] columnTips = {
       "ID",
       "First Name",
       "Last Name",
       "Street Address",
       "State",
       "City",
       "Country",
       "Postal Code",
       "Telephone",
       "GPA",
       "Total Credits",
    };

    public static final Comparator[] comparators = {
       new StudentEntryComparator(ID_COLUMN),
       new StudentEntryComparator(FIRST_NAME_COLUMN),
       new StudentEntryComparator(LAST_NAME_COLUMN),
       new StudentEntryComparator(STREET_ADDRESS_COLUMN),
       new StudentEntryComparator(STATE_COLUMN),
       new StudentEntryComparator(CITY_COLUMN),
       new StudentEntryComparator(COUNTRY_COLUMN),
       new StudentEntryComparator(POSTAL_CODE_COLUMN),
       new StudentEntryComparator(TELEPHONE_COLUMN),
       new StudentEntryComparator(GPA_COLUMN),
       new StudentEntryComparator(TOTAL_CREDITS_COLUMN),
    };

    public StudentEntry2(String ID,
                         String firstName,
                         String lastName,
                         String streetAddress,
                         String state,
                         String city,
                         String country,
                         String postalCode,
                         String telephone,
                         float GPA,
                         int totalCredits) {
       student = new Student(ID, firstName, lastName,
                         streetAddress, state, city, country,
                         postalCode, telephone, GPA,
                         totalCredits);
    }

    public StudentEntry2(Student student) {
       this.student= student;
    }

    public int getColumnCount() {
       return columnNames.length;
    }
```

```
public String getColumnName(int col) {
   if (col >= 0 &&
       col < columnNames.length) {
     return columnNames[col];
   }
   return null;
}
public Object getColumnValue(int col) {
   if (student != null &&
       col >= 0 &&
       col < columnNames.length) {
     switch (col) {
     case ID_COLUMN:              return student.getID();
     case FIRST_NAME_COLUMN:      return student.getFirstName();
     case LAST_NAME_COLUMN:       return student.getLastName();
     case STREET_ADDRESS_COLUMN:  return student.getStreetAddress();
     case STATE_COLUMN:           return student.getState();
     case CITY_COLUMN:            return student.getCity();
     case COUNTRY_COLUMN:         return student.getCountry();
     case POSTAL_CODE_COLUMN:     return student.getPostalCode();
     case TELEPHONE_COLUMN:       return student.getTelephone();
     case GPA_COLUMN:             return new Float(student.getGPA());
     case TOTAL_CREDITS_COLUMN:   return new Integer
                                         (student.getTotalCredits());
     }
   }
   return null;
}

public String getColumnTip(int col) {
   if (col >= 0 &&
       col < columnTips.length) {
     return columnTips[col];
   }
   return null;
}

public Class getColumnClass(int col) {
   if (col == GPA_COLUMN) {
     return Float.class;
   } else if (col == TOTAL_CREDITS_COLUMN) {
     return Integer.class;
   } else {
     return String.class;
   }
}

public Comparator getColumnComparator(int col) {
   if (col >= 0 &&
       col < comparators.length) {
     return comparators[col];
   }
   return null;
}
```

```
        public int getColumnWidth(int col) {
            return -1;
        }

        protected Student student;

        static public class StudentEntryComparator implements Comparator {

            public StudentEntryComparator(int col) {
                this.col = col;
            }

            public int compare(Object o1, Object o2) {
                if (o1 != null &&
                    o2 != null &&
                    o1 instanceof StudentEntry2 &&
                    o2 instanceof StudentEntry2) {
                    StudentEntry2 e1 = (StudentEntry2) o1;
                    StudentEntry2 e2 = (StudentEntry2) o2;
                    if (col == GPA_COLUMN) {
                        return (int) (e1.student.getGPA() * 1000 -
                                        e2.student.getGPA() * 1000);
                    } else if (col == TOTAL_CREDITS_COLUMN) {
                        return (e1.student.getTotalCredits() -
                                e2.student.getTotalCredits());
                    } else {
                        return ((String) e1.getColumnValue(col)).compareTo
                                (e2.getColumnValue(col));
                    }
                }
                return 0;
            }

            protected int col;
        }

    }
```

The Main class creates a list of instances of the Student class and displays the instances using the generic table via either of the adapters. The adapters are selected by an optional command-line argument. If the command-line argument Delegation is present, the object adapter will be used; otherwise, the class adapter will be used.

Class adapter.Main

```
package adapter;

import java.awt.Dimension;
import java.awt.Toolkit;
import java.util.*;
import javax.swing.*;

public class Main {

    static Student[] students = {
```

```
            new Student("1001", "Bill", "Gates",
                    "1 Microsoft Way", "WA", "Redmond", "USA", "65432",
                    "555-123-4567", 3.9f, 32),
        // ... more instances of Students ...
    };

    public static final int INITIAL_FRAME_WIDTH = 800;
    public static final int INITIAL_FRAME_HEIGHT = 400;

    public static void main(String[] args) {
        boolean useDelegation = false;
        if (args.length > 0 &&
            "Delegation".equals(args[0])) {
          useDelegation = true;
        }

        List entries = new ArrayList(students.length);
        for (int i = 0; i < students.length; i++) {
           if (useDelegation) {
               entries.add(new StudentEntry2(students[i]));
           } else {
               entries.add(new StudentEntry(students[i]));
           }
        }

        Table table = new Table(entries);

        JFrame frame = new JFrame("Students");
        frame.setContentPane(new JScrollPane(table));
        frame.setSize(INITIAL_FRAME_WIDTH, INITIAL_FRAME_HEIGHT);
        Dimension screenSize = Toolkit.getDefaultToolkit().getScreenSize();
        frame.setLocation(screenSize.width / 2 - INITIAL_FRAME_WIDTH / 2,
                    screenSize.height / 2 - INITIAL_FRAME_HEIGHT / 2);
        frame.setDefaultCloseOperation(WindowConstants.EXIT_ON_CLOSE);
        frame.setVisible(true);
    }

}
```

10.4.2 Design Pattern: Composite

The Composite design pattern was discussed in Section 8.3.2 [page 336]. Here, we present another example to illustrate the Composite pattern.

The Composite pattern is used to build a hierarchical structure of objects. An example of such a hierarchy can be found in various e-mail programs:

▪ A mailbox consists of a number of *mail folders*.

▪ A mail folder consists of a number of *mails* and/or sub-mail folders; that is, mail folders can be nested any number of levels.

Therefore, the mail folders form a hierarchy. The Composite pattern can be used to represent such a hierarchical structure. The design of the e-mail manager program using the Composite pattern is shown in Figure 10.13.

Figure 10.13

A design of the mail application using the Composite pattern.

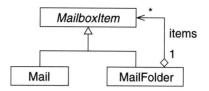

The `MailboxItem` class is the component role in Composite pattern.

Class `mail.MailboxItem`

```java
package mail;

public abstract class MailboxItem {

    public String getName() {
        return name;
    }

    public void setName(String name) {
        this.name = name;
    }

    public MailFolder getOwner() {
        return owner;
    }

    public void setOwner(MailFolder owner) {
        this.owner = owner;
    }

    public String toString() {
        return name;
    }

    public abstract int count();
    public abstract int countNewMail();

    protected MailboxItem(String name, MailFolder owner) {
        this.name = name;
        this.owner = owner;
    }

    protected String name;
    protected MailFolder owner;

}
```

The `MailFolder` class is the composite role in Composite pattern.

Class `mail.MailFolder`

```java
package mail;

import java.util.*;

public class MailFolder extends MailboxItem {
```

```java
public MailFolder(String name) {
  super(name, null);
}

public MailFolder(String name, MailFolder owner) {
   super(name, owner);
}

public List getItems() {
   return items;
}

public List getSubFolders() {
   List folders = new ArrayList();
   Iterator iterator = items.iterator();
   while (iterator.hasNext()) {
      Object item = iterator.next();
      if (item instanceof MailFolder) {
         folders.add(item);
      }
   }
   return folders;
}

public List getMails() {
   List mails = new ArrayList();
   Iterator iterator = items.iterator();
   while (iterator.hasNext()) {
      Object item = iterator.next();
      if (item instanceof Mail) {
         mails.add(item);
      }
   }
   return mails;
}

public void add(MailboxItem item) {
   items.add(item);
   item.setOwner(this);
}

public void add(MailboxItem[] items) {
   if (items != null) {
      for (int i = 0; i < items.length; i++) {
         add(items[i]);
      }
   }
}

public int count() {
   int count = 0;
   Iterator iterator = items.iterator();
   while (iterator.hasNext()) {
      Object item = iterator.next();
      if (item instanceof MailboxItem) {
```

```
                    count += ((MailboxItem) item).count();
            }
        }
        return count;
    }

    public int countNewMail() {
        int count = 0;
        Iterator iterator = items.iterator();
        while (iterator.hasNext()) {
            Object item = iterator.next();
            if (item instanceof MailboxItem) {
                count += ((MailboxItem) item).countNewMail();
            }
        }
        return count;
    }

    protected List items = new ArrayList();

}
```

The `Mail` class is the leaf role in Composite pattern.

Class `mail.Mail`

```
package mail;

import java.util.*;

public class Mail extends MailboxItem {

    public Mail(String from,
                String subject,
                Date date,
                MailPriority priority,
                MailStatus status) {
        this(from, subject, null, date, priority, status, null, null);
    }

    public Mail(String from,
                String subject,
                MailFolder owner,
                Date date,
                MailPriority priority,
                MailStatus status,
                String message,
                List attachments) {
        super(subject, owner);
        this.from = from;
        this.date = date;
        this.priority = priority;
        this.status = status;
        this.message = message;
        this.attachments = attachments;
    }
```

```java
public String getSubject() {
   return name;
}

public void setSubject(String subject) {
   name = subject;
}

public Date getDate() {
   return date;
}

public void setDate(Date date) {
   this.date = date;
}

public MailPriority getPriority() {
   return priority;
}

public void setPriority(MailPriority priority) {
   this.priority = priority;
}

public MailStatus getStatus() {
   return status;
}

public void setStatus(MailStatus status) {
   this.status = status;
}

public String getFrom() {
   return from;
}

public void setFrom(String from) {
   this.from = from;
}

public String getMessage() {
   return message;
}

public void setMessage(String message) {
   this.message = message;
}

public List getAttachments() {
   return attachments;
}

public void addAttachment(Object attachment) {
   if (attachment != null) {
      attachments.add(attachment);
   }
}
```

```
      public int count() {
         return 1;
      }

      public int countNewMail() {
         return (status == MailStatus.NEW ? 1 : 0);
      }

      public String toString() {
         return "From: " + from + "; Subject: " + name + ";\n
                  Received: " + date + "; Priority: " + priority + ";
                  Status: " + status + ";";
      }

      protected Date date;
      protected MailPriority priority;
      protected MailStatus status;
      protected String from;
      protected String message;
      protected List attachments;

   }
```

Two ordered enumeration types are used in the Mail class: MailPriority and MailStatus.

Class mail.MailPriority

```
package mail;

public class MailPriority implements Comparable {

   public static final MailPriority LOW = new MailPriority("Low");
   public static final MailPriority MEDIUM = new MailPriority("Medium");
   public static final MailPriority HIGH = new MailPriority("High");
   public static final MailPriority VERY_HIGH =
      new MailPriority ("Very high");

   public String toString() {
      return name;
   }

   public int getOrdinal() {
      return ordinal;
   }

   public int compareTo(Object o) {
      if (o instanceof MailPriority) {
         return ordinal - ((MailPriority) o).getOrdinal();
      }
      return 0;
   }

   private MailPriority(String name) {
      this.name = name;
   }
```

```
    private static int nextOrdinal = 0;
    private final String name;
    private final int ordinal = nextOrdinal++;
}
```

Class `mail.MailStatus`

```java
package mail;

public class MailStatus implements Comparable {

    public static final MailStatus NEW = new MailStatus("New");
    public static final MailStatus READ = new MailStatus("Read");
    public static final MailStatus REPLIED = new MailStatus("Replied");
    public static final MailStatus FORWARDED = new MailStatus("Forwarded");

    public String toString() {
        return name;
    }

    public int getOrdinal() {
        return ordinal;
    }

    public int compareTo(Object o) {
        if (o instanceof MailStatus) {
            return ordinal - ((MailStatus) o).getOrdinal();
        }
        return 0;
    }

    private MailStatus(String name) {
        this.name = name;
    }

    private static int nextOrdinal = 0;
    private final String name;
    private final int ordinal = nextOrdinal++;

}
```

The `mail.Main` class is a simple test of the mail manager program. It populates the mailbox hierarchy by creating a number of mail folders, subfolders, and mails. Then it gets a count of the total number of mails and the total number of new e-mail messages in all folders, including nested subfolders, of the in box.

Class `mail.Main`

```java
package mail;

import java.util.*;

public class Main {

    static Mail[] se450 = {
        new Mail("Bill Gates", "Need extension for final project",
                getTime(2001, Calendar.NOVEMBER, 20, 23, 50),
                MailPriority.VERY_HIGH, MailStatus.REPLIED),
```

```
        new Mail(. . . ), . . .
    };
    static Mail[] se452 = {
        new Mail(. . . ), . . .
    };
    static Mail[] work = {
        new Mail(. . . ), . . .
    };
    static Mail[] news = {
        new Mail(. . . ), . . .
    };
    static Mail[] junks = {
        new Mail(. . . ), . . .
    };
    public static MailFolder buildInbox() {
        MailFolder inboxFolder = new MailFolder("Inbox");
        MailFolder coursesFolder = new MailFolder("Courses");
        MailFolder se450Folder = new MailFolder("SE450");
        se450Folder.add(se450);
        MailFolder se452Folder = new MailFolder("SE452");
        se452Folder.add(se452);
        coursesFolder.add(se450Folder);
        coursesFolder.add(se452Folder);
        MailFolder workFolder = new MailFolder("Work");
        workFolder.add(work);
        MailFolder newsFolder = new MailFolder("News");
        newsFolder.add(news);
        MailFolder junksFolder = new MailFolder("Junk Mails");
        junksFolder.add(junks);
        inboxFolder.add(coursesFolder);
        inboxFolder.add(workFolder);
        inboxFolder.add(newsFolder);
        inboxFolder.add(junksFolder);
        return inboxFolder;
    }

    public static void main(String[] args) {
        MailFolder inboxFolder = buildInbox();
        System.out.println("You " + inboxFolder.count() + " mails in Inbox");
        System.out.println("You " + inboxFolder.countNewMail() +
                            " new mails in Inbox");
    }

    protected static Date getTime(int year, int month, int date, int hour,
                                  int minute) {
        Calendar calendar = Calendar.getInstance();
        calendar.set(year, month, date, hour, minute, 0);
        return calendar.getTime();
    }

}
```

Figure 10.14

A mail application.

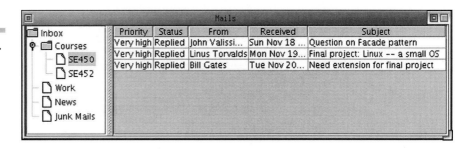

A GUI Implementation

The next step in developing the mail manager program is to build a GUI interface. The hierarchy of folders is represented by a tree structure using the JTree class in Swing. The mail in each folder is displayed using the generic table discussed in the previous section. A screen shot of the GUI interface is shown in Figure 10.14. The object Adapter pattern is used to adapt the Mail to TableEntry. The design is shown in Figure 10.15.

The MailEntry class is the adapter, the Mail class is the adaptee, and the TableEntry interface is the target.

Class mail.gui.MailEntry

```
package mail.gui;

import java.util.Date;
import java.util.Comparator;
import adapter.TableEntry;
import mail.*;
```

Figure 10.15

A design of the GUI interface for the mail application using the Adapter pattern.

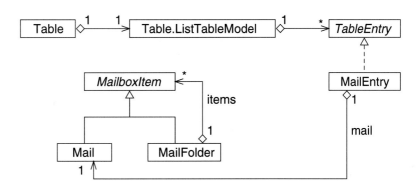

```java
public class MailEntry implements TableEntry {
    // position of each column
    public static final int PRIORITY_COLUMN = 0;
    public static final int STATUS_COLUMN   = 1;
    public static final int FROM_COLUMN     = 2;
    public static final int RECEIVED_COLUMN = 3;
    public static final int SUBJECT_COLUMN  = 4;

    public static final String[] columnNames = {
        "Priority",
        "Status",
        "From",
        "Received",
        "Subject",
    };

    public static final String[] columnTips = {
        "Priority",
        "Status",
        "From",
        "Received",
        "Subject",
    };

    public static final Comparator[] comparators = {
        new MailEntryComparator(PRIORITY_COLUMN),
        new MailEntryComparator(STATUS_COLUMN),
        new MailEntryComparator(FROM_COLUMN),
        new MailEntryComparator(RECEIVED_COLUMN),
        new MailEntryComparator(SUBJECT_COLUMN),
    };

    public static final int[] columnWidths = { 50, 50, 100, 150, 200 };

    public MailEntry(Mail mail) {
        this.mail = mail;
    }

    public int getColumnCount() {
        return columnNames.length;
    }

    public String getColumnName(int col) {
        if (col >= 0 &&
            col < columnNames.length) {
            return columnNames[col];
        }
        return null;
    }

    public Object getColumnValue(int col) {
        if (mail != null &&
            col >= 0 &&
            col < columnNames.length) {
```

```
        switch (col) {
        case PRIORITY_COLUMN: return mail.getPriority();
        case STATUS_COLUMN:   return mail.getStatus();
        case FROM_COLUMN:     return mail.getFrom();
        case RECEIVED_COLUMN: return mail.getDate();
        case SUBJECT_COLUMN:  return mail.getSubject();
        }
    }
    return null;
}

public String getColumnTip(int col) {
    if (col >= 0 &&
        col < columnTips.length) {
        return columnTips[col];
    }
    return null;
}

public Class getColumnClass(int col) {
    if (col == PRIORITY_COLUMN) {
      return MailPriority.class;
    } else if (col == STATUS_COLUMN) {
      return MailStatus.class;
    } else if (col == RECEIVED_COLUMN) {
      return Date.class;
    } else {
      return String.class;
    }
}

public Comparator getColumnComparator(int col) {
    if (col >= 0 &&
        col < comparators.length) {
        return comparators[col];
    }
    return null;
}

public int getColumnWidth(int col) {
    if (col >= 0 &&
        col < columnWidths.length) {
        return columnWidths[col];
    }
    return -1;
}

protected Mail mail;

static public class MailEntryComparator implements Comparator {

    public MailEntryComparator(int col) {
       this.col = col;
    }
```

```
        public int compare(Object o1, Object o2) {
            if (o1 != null &&
                o2 != null &&
                o1 instanceof MailEntry &&
                o2 instanceof MailEntry) {
              MailEntry e1 = (MailEntry) o1;
              MailEntry e2 = (MailEntry) o2;
              if (col == PRIORITY_COLUMN) {
                  return -((Comparable) e1.getColumnValue(col)).compareTo
                          (e2.getColumnValue(col));
              } else if (col == STATUS_COLUMN) {
                  return ((Comparable) e1.getColumnValue(col)).compareTo
                          (e2.getColumnValue(col));
              } else if (col == RECEIVED_COLUMN) {
                  return ((Date) e1.getColumnValue(col)).compareTo
                          (e2.getColumnValue(col));
              } else {
                  return ((String) e1.getColumnValue(col)).compareTo
                          (e2.getColumnValue(col));
              }
            }
            return 0;
        }

        protected int col;
    }

}
```

The `mail.gui.Main` class constructs the GUI interface using a `JTree` object
for the folder hierarchy and a `Table` object for displaying the mail in the current
folder.

Class `mail.gui.Main`

```
package mail.gui;

import java.awt.Dimension;
import java.awt.Toolkit;
import java.util.*;
import javax.swing.*;
import javax.swing.tree.*;
import javax.swing.event.*;

import mail.*;
import adapter.*;

public class Main {

    public static final int INITIAL_FRAME_WIDTH = 800;
    public static final int INITIAL_FRAME_HEIGHT = 400;

    public static void main(String[] args) {
        MailFolder inboxFolder = mail.Main.buildInbox();
```

```
    JTree tree = new JTree(buildMailFolderTree(inboxFolder));
    JSplitPane splitPane = new JSplitPane();
    splitPane.setLeftComponent(new JScrollPane(tree));
    splitPane.setRightComponent(new JPanel());
    tree.addTreeSelectionListener(new MailFolderTreeSelectionListener
                            (tree, splitPane));

    JFrame frame = new JFrame("Mails");
    frame.setContentPane(splitPane);
    frame.setSize(INITIAL_FRAME_WIDTH, INITIAL_FRAME_HEIGHT);
    Dimension screenSize = Toolkit.getDefaultToolkit().getScreenSize();
    frame.setLocation(screenSize.width / 2 - INITIAL_FRAME_WIDTH / 2,
                    screenSize.height / 2 - INITIAL_FRAME_HEIGHT / 2);
    frame.setDefaultCloseOperation(WindowConstants.EXIT_ON_CLOSE);
    frame.setVisible(true);
}

static class MailFolderTreeSelectionListener implements
            TreeSelectionListener {

    MailFolderTreeSelectionListener(JTree tree, JSplitPane splitPane) {
        this.tree = tree;
        this.splitPane = splitPane;
    }

    public void valueChanged(TreeSelectionEvent ev) {
        DefaultMutableTreeNode node =
            (DefaultMutableTreeNode) tree.getLastSelectedPathComponent();
        if (node != null) {
            Object item = node.getUserObject();
            if (item instanceof MailFolder) {
                splitPane.setRightComponent(new JScrollPane(buildTable
                                    ((MailFolder) item)));
            }
        }
    }

    JTree tree;
    JSplitPane splitPane;
}

protected static DefaultMutableTreeNode buildMailFolderTree
                                    (MailFolder folder) {
    if (folder != null) {
        DefaultMutableTreeNode root = new DefaultMutableTreeNode(folder);
        List subfolders = folder.getSubFolders();
        Iterator iterator = subfolders.iterator();
        while (iterator.hasNext()) {
            Object item = iterator.next();
            if (item instanceof MailFolder) {
                root.add(buildMailFolderTree((MailFolder) item));
            }
        }
```

```
            return root;
        }
        return null;
    }

    protected static Table buildTable(MailFolder folder) {
        if (folder != null) {
            List mails = folder.getMails();
            List entries = new ArrayList(mails.size());
            for (int i = 0; i < mails.size(); i++) {
                entries.add(new MailEntry((Mail) mails.get(i)));
            }
            return new Table(entries);
        }
        return null;
    }

}
```

CHAPTER SUMMARY

- The type-safe enumeration type idiom defines an enumeration type as a class. Each value of the enumeration type is associated with a descriptive name and is defined as a constant that references an instance of the class. This idiom ensures that
  - each enumeration type may only have a fixed number of distinct values.
  - the enumeration types are type-safe; that is, variables and values of different enumeration types are not interchangeable.
  - the values can be printed with descriptive names.
- The Abstract Factory design pattern is for creating a set of related and compatible products from several interchangeable product families. The product instances are not created using the new operator. They are created using a set of methods defined in a factory class, which represents a product family. The different factories representing different product families share a common interface—the abstract factory interface. Therefore, a client can easily switch from one factory, or product family, to another.
- The Prototype design pattern creates objects by cloning a set of prototypes. Objects in different product families can be created by using a different set of prototypes. Using the Prototype pattern, product families can be defined or altered at run time by choosing a desired prototype. While using the Abstract Factory or Factory Method patterns, product families are defined in the form of a class and thus cannot be altered or configured at run time.
- The Builder design pattern separates the construction of a complex object from the implementation of its parts so that the same construction process can create complex objects from different implementations of the parts. The Builder design

pattern can be used to simplify the construction process by avoiding duplication of similar code and shortening the code for the construction.

- The Command design pattern encapsulates an action as an object, so that actions can be passed as parameters, queued, and possibly undone.

- The Adapter design pattern converts the interface of a class into an interface that clients expect. There are two forms of the Adapter pattern: *Class adapter*, which relies on inheritance, and *Object adapter*, which relies on delegation, or object composition.

FURTHER READINGS

Gamma, E., et al. (1995). *Design Patterns—Elements of Reusable Object-Oriented Software*. Addison-Wesley.

Metsker, S. J. (2002). *Design Patterns Java Workbook*. Addison-Wesley.

Shalloway, A., and J. R. Trott (2001). *Design Patterns Explained: A New Perspective on Object-Oriented Design*. Addison-Wesley.

CHAPTER 11

Concurrent Programming

CHAPTER OVERVIEW

In this chapter, we introduce concurrent, or multithreaded, programming. We discuss the mechanisms that Java provides to support concurrent programming. We also address the issues of synchronization and cooperation among threads.

11.1 THREADS

Concurrent programming is also known as *multithreaded programming*. A *thread* is a single sequential flow of control within a program. Most conventional programming languages are single-threaded, or sequential. A single-threaded program can handle only one task at any given moment during its execution. In contrast, a *multithreaded*, or *concurrent*, program has multiple threads running simultaneously and so may handle multiple tasks at the same time during its execution. It is not necessary to have multiprocessor systems to run multithreaded programs. Most modern operating systems support *multitasking*, which allows multithreaded programs to run on single-processor systems on a time-sharing basis.

Multithreaded programming offers some important advantages over single-threaded programming:

- It is suitable for developing *reactive systems*, which continuously monitor arrays of sensors and react to control systems according to the sensor readings. Examples of reactive systems include autopilot systems, which control modern aircraft from takeoff to landing, and patient monitoring systems, which monitor patients' vital signs.
- It makes applications more responsive to user input. For example, it allows a GUI application to respond to user input immediately even if the application is engaged in a time-consuming computation task.
- It allows a server to handle multiple clients simultaneously.
- It may take advantage of the availability of multiple processors by executing the threads on different processors in parallel.

However, multithreaded programming is more difficult than single-threaded programming because each thread proceeds independently from the others. The exact order of execution of different threads is nondeterministic. Interaction and cooperation among different threads often become complicated. Such complications may lead to *safety* and *liveness* problems, which are unique to multithreaded programs. Multithreaded programs also involve significant overhead, owing to the cost of thread creation, context switching, and synchronization.

Threads are different from *processes*. A process is a heavyweight independent flow that executes concurrently with other processes. Processes are managed by the operating systems, and there is no shared memory space among different processes. Different processes can only communicate with one another via interprocess communication channels, such as pipes on Unix platforms. A thread is a lightweight flow that executes concurrently with other threads within a single process. Java threads are managed by the Java virtual machine. All threads managed by the same Java virtual machine share common memory space. Therefore, different threads managed by the same Java virtual machine can communicate with one another via shared variables and objects.

11.1.1 Creation of Threads

A thread is an instance of the `java.lang.Thread` class. A `Thread` object is also known as an *active object*. The graphical notation for active objects is shown in Figure 11.1.

Threads can be created and declared in one of two ways: by directly extending the `java.lang.Thread` class or by implementing the `java.lang.Runnable` interface.

Extending the `Thread` Class

All threads are instances of the `Thread` class. Therefore, the most straightforward way of defining a new thread is by directly extending the `Thread` class. The `run()` method

Figure 11.1

Graphical notation
for active objects
(i.e., threads).

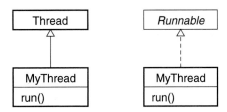

of the Thread class is a hook method, which must be overridden in the subclass. The run() method defines the body of the thread and is similar to the main() method of a sequential program. The run() method of a thread is invoked when execution starts. Execution of a thread ends when the run() method returns. A template for defining a new thread class is presented in the following program segment:

```
public class MyThread extends Thread {
    public void run() {
        // the thread body
    }
    // other methods and fields
}
```

To start a new thread defined by MyThread, we have to create an instance of the MyThread class and invoke the start() method, which indirectly invokes the run() method:

```
new MyThread().start();
```

Conversely, the run() method should not be invoked directly. Doing so would cause the method to be executed in the thread of the caller, not in a new thread.

EXAMPLE 11.1 A Simple Infinite Counter

PURPOSE

This example demonstrates thread creation by extending the Thread class.

DESCRIPTION

The infinite counter starts from an initial value, and the counter will be incremented by a specified amount at a given pace.

SOLUTION

The following is the thread class that implements the infinite counter. It extends the Thread class. This class defines a thread whose body consists of an infinite loop. It maintains a counter, which is incremented by the amount of inc in each iteration. Each iteration of the loop sleeps a duration specified by the field delay in milliseconds.

A simple thread class: `Counter1`

```java
public class Counter1 extends Thread {

    protected int count;
    protected int inc;
    protected int delay;

    public Counter1(int init, int inc, int delay) {
        this.count = init;
        this.inc = inc;
        this.delay = delay;
    }

    public void run() {
        try {
            for (;;) {
                System.out.print(count + " ");
                count += inc;
                sleep(delay);
            }
        } catch (InterruptedException e) {
            e.printStackTrace();
        }
    }

    public static void main(String[] args) {
        new Counter1(0, 1, 33).start();
        new Counter1(0, -1, 100).start();
    }
}
```

Two threads are started in the `main()` method. Both start counting from 0, but in different directions. The second thread, the one with a negative increment, receives a longer delay. Note in the following output that the output from the two threads is interleaved:

```
venus% java Counter1
0 0 1 2 -1 3 4 5 -2 6 7 8 -3 9 10 -4 11 12 13 -5 14 15 16 -6 17 18
-7 19 20 21 -8 22 23 24 -9 25 26 -10 27 28 -11 29 30 31 -12 32 33
34 -13 35 36 37 -14 38 39 -15 40 41 42 -16 43 44 45 -17 46 47 -18
48 49 50 -19 51 52 -20 53 54 55 -21 56 57 -22 58 59 60 -23 61 62 63
-24 64 65 -25 66 67 68 -26 69 70 -27 71 72 73 -28 74 75 -29 76 77
-30 78 79 80 -31 81 82 83 -32 84 85 -33 86 87 88 -34 89 90 91 -35
92 93 -36 94 95 96 -37 97 98 -38 99 100 -39 101 102 103 -40 104 105
106 -41 107 108 -42 109 -43 110 111 -44 112 113 114 -45 115 116 -46
. . .
```

Execution of this program actually involves three threads: the thread that executes the `main()` method and the two `Counter1` threads created inside the `main()` method. The thread that executes the `main()` method terminates when the `main()` method returns from creating the two `Counter1` threads. The two `Counter1` threads will run concurrently and indefinitely until they are explicitly killed.

EXAMPLE 11.2 Stock Quote Generator

PURPOSE

This is another example that demonstrates thread creation by extending the Thread class.

DESCRIPTION

This program generates a series of quotes for the price of a given stock by simulating the fluctuation of stock prices.

SOLUTION

The following class implements an infinite loop that generates stock quotes. It simulates the fluctuation of stock prices using a random number generation function Math.random().

```
Stock quote generator: Quote

public class Quote extends Thread {

    protected int value;

    public Quote(int init) {
        value = init;
    }

    public void run() {
        try {
          for (;;) {
             System.out.println(value);
             value += (Math.random() - 0.4) * (10.0 * Math.random());
             sleep(100);
          }
        } catch (InterruptedException e) {
          e.printStackTrace();
        }
    }

    public static void main(String[] args) {
        new Quote(100).start();
    }
}
```

The program is started with the initial price set at 100. The following is the output:

```
venus% java Quote
100
99
97
98
99
99
100
100
```

```
100
101
104
103
102
101
. . .
```

Implementing the `Runnable` Interface

Defining threads by directly extending the `Thread` class is only one of the options. Sometimes, however, it may be impossible to use this option, because Java only supports single inheritance among classes. For example, applets are required to extend the class `java.applet.Applet`. Thus applets cannot also extend the `Thread` class at the same time. Java provides an alternative means of defining threads—by implementing the `Runnable` interface.

The Runnable interface is simple. It consists of a single method, `run()`:

```java
public interface Runnable {
    public abstract void run();
}
```

A template for defining a new thread class by implementing the `Runnable` interface is shown in the following code fragment. As in the first approach, the `run()` method defines the body of the thread.

```java
public class MyThread extends AnotherClass implements Runnable {
    public void run() {
        // the thread body
    }
    // other methods and fields
}
```

To start a new thread defined in this way, we must first create an instance of `MyThread`. We use the `MyThread` instance to create an instance of `Thread` and then invoke the `start()` method:

```java
new Thread(new MyThread()).start();
```

EXAMPLE 11.3 A Simple Infinite Counter II

PURPOSE

This example demonstrates thread creation by implementation of the `Runnable` interface.

DESCRIPTION

This class defines a thread that behaves the same as the one in Example 11.1.

SOLUTION

A simple thread class: `Counter2`

```java
public class Counter2 implements Runnable {

    protected int count;
    protected int inc;
    protected int delay;

    public Counter2(int init, int inc, int delay) {
        this.count = init;
        this.inc = inc;
        this.delay = delay;
    }

    public void run() {
        try {
            for (;;) {
                System.out.print(count + " ");
                count += inc;
                Thread.sleep(delay);
            }
        } catch (InterruptedException e) {
            e.printStackTrace();
        }
    }

    public static void main(String[] args) {
        new Thread(new Counter2(0, 1, 33)).start();
        new Thread(new Counter2(0, -1, 100)).start();
    }
}
```

The following is the output:

```
venus% java Counter2
0 0 1 2 -1 3 4 5 -2 6 7 8 -3 9 10 -4 11 12 13 -5 14 15 16 -6 17 18
-7 19 20 21 -8 22 23 24 -9 25 26 -10 27 28 -11 29 30 31 -12 32 33
34 -13 35 36 -14 37 38 39 -15 40 41 42 -16 43 44 45 -17 46 47 -18
48 49 50 -19 51 52 -20 53 54 55 -21 56 57 -22 58 59 60 -23 61 62 63
-24 64 65 -25 66 67 68 -26 69 70 -27 71 72 -28 73 74 -29 75 76 77
-30 78 79 -31 80 81 82 -32 83 84 -33 85 86 87 -34 88 89 90 -35 91
92 -36 93 94 95 -37 96 97 -38 98 99 -39 100 101 102 -40 103 104 105
-41 106 107 -42 108 109 110 -43 111 112 -44 113 114 115 -45 116 117
. . .
```

11.1.2 Controlling Threads

Programmers have only high-level control of thread execution by controlling the states of the life cycle of threads. The execution of threads is ultimately controlled by the Java virtual machine. Programmers may also influence the execution of threads by manipulating the priorities of threads.

The Life Cycle of a Thread

The life cycle of a thread is shown in Figure 11.2 on a state chart. A thread can be in one of the following states:

New   A thread is in the New state after its creation (that is, new MyThread()) and before the start() method is invoked.

Alive   When the start() method is invoked on a thread, it enters the Alive state. The run() method is invoked implicitly, and the execution of the thread begins. The Alive state has two substates:

Runnable   Threads in the Runnable state are ready to run. Threads in this state may be running or waiting for their turn to run.

Blocked   A thread in the Blocked state is not ready to run. It is blocked until a certain event happens, at which time it may become runnable.

Dead   A thread enters the Dead state when the run() method returns. A dead thread cannot be restarted.

The methods of the Thread class for controlling threads are summarized in Table 11.1. The wait(), notify(), and notifyAll() methods defined in the Object class can also affect the states of threads. Invoking the wait() method on an object will cause the thread to be blocked until either the notify() or notifyAll() method is invoked on the same object, at which time the thread will be returned to the Runnable state. The wait(), notify(), and notifyAll() methods are discussed in more detail in Section 11.2.2 [p. 564].

Figure 11.2

The life cycle of threads.

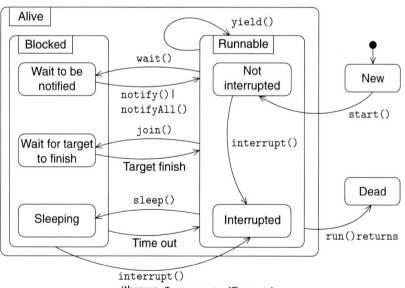

TABLE 11.1

Methods of `java.lang.Thread` **Class**

Method	Description
`start()`	The thread should be in the New state. The `start()` method causes the thread to enter the Alive state and start execution.
`sleep()`	The thread should be in the Runnable state. The `sleep()` method causes the thread to enter the Blocked state and sleep a given amount of time. It will be awakened when the specified duration of time expires and returned to the Runnable state.
`join()`	The thread should be in the Runnable state. The `join()` method causes the thread to enter the Blocked state and wait for another thread to finish, at which time it will be returned to the Runnable state.
`yield()`	The thread should be in the Runnable state and will remain in the Runnable state. The `yield()` method gives other runnable threads an opportunity to run.
`interrupt()`	If the thread is in the Runnable state, the interrupted flag will be set. If the thread is in the Blocked state, it is awakened and enters the Runnable state, and an `InterruptedException` is thrown.
`isAlive()`	Returns `true` if the thread is in the Alive state.
`isInterrupted()`	Returns `true` if the interrupted flag is set.

Thread Priority and Scheduling

The Java virtual machine implements a rather simple scheduling strategy to determine which of the runnable threads should be running. It is based on the *priority* of each runnable thread. Each thread contains a priority attribute, which is an integer value assigned when the thread is created. By default, a new thread has the same priority as the one that creates it. The priority of a thread may be changed during its lifetime.

The Java virtual machine will select the runnable threads with the highest priority for execution. If more than one runnable thread has the same highest priority, one of them will be selected *arbitrarily*. In other words, the Java virtual machine is not required to guarantee *fairness*. A thread of higher priority will also preempt a thread of lower priority. In other words, while a thread is being executed, if a thread with higher priority becomes runnable, the current thread will stop running (but remain runnable) and the higher priority thread will start running. A thread that is currently running relinquishes control when one of the following occurs:

- Yielding, that is, invoking the `yield()` method on the thread.
- Blocking, that is, invoking the `sleep()`, `join()`, or `wait()` method on the thread.
- Preempting, when a thread with a higher priority becomes runnable.
- Switching, when its time-slice has expired.

The following guideline is an important constraint on the use of priorities:

Design Guideline *Thread Priority*

Use priorities only to tune the performance of programs. The correctness of programs should not depend on the priorities of the threads involved.

11.2 THREAD SAFETY AND LIVENESS

Safety properties are conditions that should hold throughout the lifetime of a program. They stipulate that nothing bad should ever happen. An important safety property is the consistency of object states. While an object is being modified, it may go through a series of intermediate states that are *inconsistent* or *invalid*. If the thread that is modifying the object is interrupted, it may leave the object in an inconsistent state. When another thread tries to access an object in an inconsistent state, this action may lead to incorrect, perhaps disastrous, behavior. Let us consider an example of a simplified bank account class. The `withdraw()` method attempts to withdraw a specified amount of money from an account. It succeeds when the withdrawal amount is less than or equal to the balance in the account.

```java
public class Account {
    // ...
    public boolean withdraw(long amount) {
        if (amount <= balance) {
            long newBalance = balance - amount;
            balance = newBalance;
            return true;
        } else {
            return false;
        }
    }
    private long balance;
}
```

This implementation is valid when used in single-thread programs. However, this class cannot safely be used with multithreaded programs. Consider the following scenario:

> Assume that the initial balance is $1,000,000. Two withdrawal requests of $1,000,000 each are issued almost simultaneously, and they are executed on separate threads.

The following is a plausible, although highly unlikely, sequence of events, which would lead to both withdrawal requests being successful, albeit incorrect:

Balance	Withdrawal 1	Withdrawal 2
1000000	`amount <= balance`	
1000000		`amount <= balance`
1000000	`newBalance = . . . ;`	
1000000		`newBalance = . . . ;`
0	`balance = . . . ;`	
0		`balance = . . . ;`
0	`return true;`	
0		`return true;`

This problem, which is common in multithreaded programs, is known as a *race hazard* or *race condition*. A class is said to be *thread-safe* if it ensures the consistency of the states of the objects and the results of method invocations upon these objects in the presence of multiple threads. As we have demonstrated, the Account class is not thread-safe.

To maintain the consistency of object states and the results of method invocations, more than one thread must be prevented from simultaneously entering certain program regions, known as *critical regions*, which are segments of code that should be executed by only one thread at a time on a given object. Java provides a *synchronization* mechanism to ensure that, while a thread is executing the statements in a critical region, no other threads can execute statements in the same critical region at the same time on a given object.

11.2.1 Synchronization

An operation that cannot be interrupted is known as an *atomic operation*. In Java the reading and assignment of variables of primitive types, except `long` and `double`, are atomic. All other operations should be explicitly *synchronized* to ensure atomicity.

Synchronization can be applied to methods or a block of statements. A synchronized instance method can be declared as in the following code segment:

```
class MyClass {

    synchronized void aMethod() {
        ⟨do something⟩
    }
}
```

In this case, the entire body of the method is the critical region. A synchronized statement takes the following form:

```
synchronized(exp) {
    ⟨do something⟩
}
```

where the expression *exp* must be of reference type. The statements enclosed in the synchronized block comprise the critical region.

The synchronization mechanism is implemented by associating each object with a *lock*. A thread must obtain *exclusive possession* of the appropriate lock before entering the critical region.

- For a synchronized instance method, the lock associated with the receiving object `this` is used.
- For a synchronized statement, the lock associated with the result of the expression *exp* is used.

The lock is released when the thread leaves the critical region. The lock may also be released temporarily before leaving the critical region, when the `wait()` method is invoked (see Section 11.2.2 [p. 564]).

The synchronized method in the following code fragment:

```
class MyClass {

    synchronized void aMethod() {
        ⟨do something⟩
    }

}
```

is equivalent to the following synchronized statement:

```
class MyClass {

    void aMethod() {
        synchronized(this) {
            ⟨do something⟩
        }
    }
}
```

As only one thread can have exclusive possession of the lock of a critical region, only one thread at a time can execute the statements in the critical region. Moreover, different critical regions may share the same lock. For example, all the synchronized instance methods use the lock associated with the receiving object. Consider the following example:

```
public class A {
    synchronized void m1() { . . . }
    synchronized void m2() { . . . }
    void m3() { . . . } // unsynchronized
}
```

Given an instance a of class A, when one thread is executing a.m1(), another thread will be prohibited from executing a.m1() or a.m2(). A synchronized method is allowed to invoke another synchronized method of the same class because the invocation will be on the same thread. In the preceding example, m2() may be invoked inside the body of method m1(). A synchronized method may execute concurrently with unsynchronized methods on the same object. In the preceding example, when one thread is executing a.m1(), another thread may execute a.m3() concurrently.

EXAMPLE 11.4   Bounded Queue (Sequential Version)

PURPOSE

This example shows a simple bounded queue implementation that is not thread-safe. Therefore, it is only suitable for sequential, that is, single-threaded, applications.

DESCRIPTION

A bounded queue is a first-in, first-out queue with a fixed capacity.

SOLUTION

The following program for the BoundedQueue class is implemented with a circular array. The capacity of the queue is specified by the argument to the constructor. The capacity of the queue may not be changed. The methods of the BoundedQueue class are summarized in the following table:

Method	Description
isEmpty()	Returns true if the queue is empty
isFull()	Returns true if the queue is full
getCount()	Returns the number of elements in the queue
put()	Inserts an element at the end of the queue
get()	Removes the element at the head of the queue and returns the element

Bounded queue (sequential version)

```
public class BoundedQueue {

    protected Object rep[];
    protected int front = 0;
    protected int back = -1;
    protected int size = 0;
    protected int count = 0;
```

```
public BoundedQueue(int size) {
    if (size > 0) {
        this.size = size;
        rep = new Object[size];
        back = size - 1;
    }
}

public boolean isEmpty() {
    return (count == 0);
}

public boolean isFull() {
    return (count == size);
}

public int getCount() {
    return count;
}

public void put(Object e) {
    if (e != null && !isFull()) {
        back++;
        if (back >= size)
            back = 0;
        rep[back] = e;
        count++;
    }
}

public Object get() {
    Object result = null;
    if (!isEmpty()) {
        result = rep[front];
        rep[front] = null;
        front++;
        if (front >= size)
            front = 0;
        count--;
    }
    return result;
}

public static void main(String args[]) {
    BoundedQueue queue = new BoundedQueue(10);
    for (int i = 0; !queue.isFull(); i++) {
        queue.put(new Integer(i));
        System.out.println("put: "+i);
    }
    while (!queue.isEmpty()) {
        System.out.println("get: "+queue.get());
    }
}
}
```

This implementation of the bounded queue has two shortcomings. The put() method ignores the new element when the queue is full, and the get() method returns null when the queue is empty. When used with sequential programs, however, this implementation is reasonable.

The main() method carries out a simple test of the BoundedQueue class, giving the following output:

```
put: 0
put: 1
put: 2
put: 3
put: 4
put: 5
put: 6
put: 7
put: 8
put: 9
get: 0
get: 1
get: 2
get: 3
get: 4
get: 5
get: 6
get: 7
get: 8
get: 9
```

The result in Example 11.4 is exactly what we expected. However, the sequential version of the BoundedQueue class is not thread-safe. An easy way to make a class thread-safe is to synchronize all the methods of the class.

EXAMPLE 11.5 Bounded Queue (Fully Synchronized Version)

PURPOSE

This example demonstrates the use of synchronization to ensure thread safety.

SOLUTION

The SyncBoundedQueue class is identical to the the BoundedQueue in Example 11.4, except that it is fully synchronized and thread-safe.

Bounded queue (fully synchronized version)

```java
public class SyncBoundedQueue extends BoundedQueue {

    public SyncBoundedQueue(int size) {
        super(size);
    }
```

```
        synchronized public boolean isEmpty() {
            return super.isEmpty();
        }

        synchronized public boolean isFull() {
            return super.isFull();
        }

        synchronized public int getCount() {
            return super.getCount();
        }

        synchronized public void put(Object e) {
            super.put(e);
        }

        synchronized public Object get() {
            return super.get();
        }

        (Method main() for testing on page 563)
}
```

A typical use of the SyncBoundedQueue class is to serve as a buffer between a producer and a consumer, both of which are threads. The producer produces items and puts them in the bounded queue, and the consumer retrieves items from the bounded queue and consumes them. The relationships among the producer, the consumer, and the bounded queue are shown in Figure 11.3.

The Producer class

```
public class Producer extends Thread {

    protected BoundedQueue queue;
    protected int n;

    public Producer(BoundedQueue queue, int n) {
        this.queue = queue;
        this.n = n;
    }
```

Figure 11.3

The producer, consumer, and bounded queue.

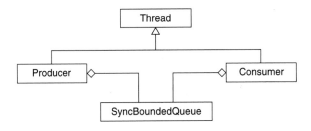

```
        public void run() {
           for (int i = 0; i < n; i++) {
              queue.put(new Integer(i));
              System.out.println("produce: " + i);
              try {
                 sleep((int)(Math.random() * 100));
              } catch (InterruptedException e) {
                 e.printStackTrace();
              }
           }
        }
    }
```

The Consumer class

```
public class Consumer extends Thread {

    protected BoundedQueue queue;
    protected int n;

    public Consumer(BoundedQueue queue, int n) {
        this.queue = queue;
        this.n = n;
    }

    public void run() {
        for (int i = 0; i < n; i++) {
           Object obj = queue.get();
           if (obj != null)
              System.out.println("\tconsume: "+obj);
           try {
              sleep((int)(Math.random() * 400));
           } catch (InterruptedException e) {
              e.printStackTrace();
           }
        }
    }
}
```

The main() method of SyncBoundedQueue first creates a bounded queue of size 5. It then creates and starts two threads: one for the producer and one for the consumer.

The main() method of class SyncBoundedQueue

```
public static void main(String args[]) {
    SyncBoundedQueue queue = new SyncBoundedQueue(5);
    new Producer(queue, 15).start(); // produce 15 items
    new Consumer(queue, 10).start(); // consume 10 items
}
```

The following is the output:

```
produce: 0
        consume: 0
produce: 1
produce: 2
produce: 3
produce: 4
produce: 5
        consume: 1
produce: 6
produce: 7
        consume: 2
produce: 8
produce: 9
produce: 10
produce: 11
        consume: 3
produce: 12
produce: 13
produce: 14
        consume: 4
        consume: 5
        consume: 6
        consume: 8
        consume: 12
```

Note that the producer produces items faster than the consumer consumes the items. This implementation of the bounded queue causes some of the items to be lost.

11.2.2   Cooperation Among Threads

Synchronization ensures the mutual exclusion of two or more threads in the critical regions, but it does not address cooperation among threads. The SyncBoundedQueue in the preceding example is thread-safe. However, the producer and the consumer threads are not cooperating very well, and this lack of cooperation leads to a loss of items in the queue. The producer and the consumer should cooperate in the following ways:

- When the producer attempts to put a new item into the queue while the queue is full, it should wait for the consumer to consume some of the items in the queue, making room for the new item.
- When the consumer attempts to retrieve an item from the queue while the queue is empty, it should wait for the producer to produce items and put them in the queue.

Thread cooperation is a requirement in many applications and can be accomplished with guarded suspension. A *guard* is the precondition for a certain action to

TABLE 11.2

Thread-Controlling Methods

Method	Description
wait()	The current thread is temporarily blocked and is placed in the *wait* queue associated with the receiving object. The lock associated with the receiving object is temporarily released. The thread will resume execution when it is awakened by notify() or notifyAll().
notify()	One of the threads in the wait queue associated with the receiving object will be awakened and removed from the wait queue. The awakened thread must reobtain the lock before it can resume at the point immediately following the invocation of the wait() method.
notifyAll()	This method is the same as the notify() method, except that all threads that are in the wait queue associated with the receiving object will be awakened and removed from the wait queue.

complete successfully. *Guarded suspension* is a requirement for threads to cooperate in the following way:

- Before a method is executed, the guard is tested.
- Execution continues only when the guard is true, ensuring the successful completion of the method invocation.
- Execution is temporarily suspended until the guard becomes true, at which time execution may continue.

Guarded suspension can be implemented by using the wait(), notify(), and notifyAll() methods of the Object class. The wait() method should be invoked when a thread is temporarily unable to continue and we want to let other threads proceed. The notify() or notifyAll() method should be invoked when we want a thread to notify other threads that they may proceed. These three methods can be invoked only by a thread that currently owns the lock of the receiving object. The methods are summarized in Table 11.2.

EXAMPLE 11.6 Bounded Queue with Guarded Suspension

PURPOSE

This example demonstrates the use of the wait() and notify() methods to implement guarded suspension and ensure cooperation among threads.

DESCRIPTION

This version of bounded queue supports the cooperation between the producer and the consumer in the way described previously.

SOLUTION

The BoundedQueueWithGuard class extends the BoundedQueue class. It is fully synchronized. The put() and get() methods are overridden to support cooperation between the producer and the consumer.

Bounded queue with guarded suspension

```
public class BoundedQueueWithGuard extends BoundedQueue {

    public BoundedQueueWithGuard(int size) {
        super(size);
    }

    synchronized public boolean isEmpty() {
        return super.isEmpty();
    }

    synchronized public boolean isFull() {
        return super.isFull();
    }

    synchronized public int getCount() {
        return super.getCount();
    }

    ⟨Method put() on page 566⟩

    ⟨Method get() on page 567⟩

    ⟨Method main() for testing on page 568⟩

}
```

The guard of the put() method ensures that *the queue is not full*, and the guard of the get() method ensures that *the queue is not empty*. The put() method invokes the wait() method to suspend the producer thread temporarily when the queue is full. Similarly, the get() method invokes the wait() method to suspend the consumer thread temporarily when the queue is empty. Both methods invoke the notify() method at the end to wake up a suspended thread, if any.

The put() method of BoundedQueueWithGuard

```
synchronized void put(Object obj) {
    try {
        while (isFull()) {
            wait();
        }
    } catch (InterruptedException e) {
        e.printStackTrace();
    }
    super.put(obj);
    notify();
}
```

The get() method of BoundedQueueWithGuard

```
synchronized Object get() {
    try {
        while (isEmpty()) {
            wait();
        }
    } catch (InterruptedException e) {
        e.printStackTrace();
    }
    Object result = super.get();
    notify();
    return result;
}
```

The interaction between the put() and get() methods, which are invoked by the producer and consumer threads, respectively, is best illustrated by two scenarios:

Scenario A:

The producer produces items faster than the consumer consumes them.

1. The producer thread acquires the lock associated with the queue and invokes the put() method, but the queue is full.
2. The wait() method is invoked, and the producer thread is suspended. The lock associated with the queue is temporarily released by the producer thread.
3. The consumer thread acquires the lock associated with the queue and invokes the get() method. The queue must not be empty; indeed, it is full. So the guard of the get() method returns true, and one item is removed from the queue.
4. The notify() method is invoked to awaken the suspended producer thread. The consumer thread completes the invocation of the get() method and releases the lock associated with the queue.
5. The producer thread is awakened in the put() method and reacquires the lock associated with the queue. The guard of the put() method is true this time, and execution resumes where it left off.

Scenario B:

The producer produces items more slowly than the consumer consumes them.

1. The consumer thread acquires the lock associated with the queue and invokes the get() method when the queue is empty.
2. The wait() method is invoked, and the consumer thread is suspended. The lock associated with the queue is temporarily released by the consumer thread.
3. The producer thread acquires the lock associated with the queue and invokes the put() method. The queue is not full; indeed, it is empty. So the guard of the put() method returns true, and one item is inserted into the queue.

4. The `notify()` method is invoked to awaken the suspended consumer thread. The producer thread completes the invocation of the `put()` method and releases the lock associated with the queue.

5. The consumer thread is awakened in the `get()` method and reacquires the lock associated with the queue. The guard of the `get()` method returns `true` this time, and execution resumes where it left off.

The `main()` method performs a simple test of the bounded queue, with the producer and the consumer running on separate threads.

The `main()` method of `BoundedQueueWithGuard`

```
public static void main(String args[]) {
    BoundedQueueWithGuard queue =
        new BoundedQueueWithGuard(5);
    new Producer(queue, 15).start(); // produce 15 items
    new Consumer(queue, 15).start(); // consume 15 items
}
```

The following is the output:

```
produce: 0
        consume: 0
produce: 1
produce: 2
        consume: 1
produce: 3
        consume: 2
produce: 4
produce: 5
        consume: 3
produce: 6
produce: 7
produce: 8
        consume: 4
produce: 9
        consume: 5
produce: 10
        consume: 6
produce: 11
        consume: 7
produce: 12
        consume: 8
produce: 13
        consume: 9
produce: 14
        consume: 10
        consume: 11
        consume: 12
        consume: 13
        consume: 14
```

11.2.3 Liveness Failures

Liveness refers to desirable conditions that will come about during the lifetime of a program. In other words, liveness properties stipulate that something positive will eventually happen. For example, common liveness properties include the following: (1) A certain task will be completed eventually; (2) a thread should always respond to user input until the thread is terminated; and (3) the status of certain systems must be displayed and updated constantly.

Safety properties can be ensured locally, but liveness properties are context dependent. Ensuring liveness properties is a much more difficult task than ensuring safety properties. Some common types of liveness failures are contention, dormancy, deadlock, and premature termination.

Contention

Contention (also known as *starvation* or *indefinite postponement*) occurs when a runnable thread never gets a chance to run. This can occur when there are always one or more runnable threads with higher priorities or when there is a runnable thread with the same priority but it never yields.

Let us consider the `run()` method of a typical animation applet:

```
public class AnAnimation {

    protected Thread animationThread;

    public void run() {
        while (Thread.currentThread() == animationThread) {
            repaint();
            try {
                Thread.currentThread().sleep(delay);
            } catch (InterruptedException e){
                e.printStackTrace();
            }
        }
    }
    // other fields and methods . . .

}
```

The `repaint()` method draws the current frame on a separate thread having the same priority as the animation thread. If the `sleep()` method were not invoked, the repaint thread would never get a chance to run and the animation would appear as a blank area.

To avoid contention, the thread with the highest priority must periodically invoke the `sleep()` or `yield()` method to provide other cooperating threads having the same or lower priorities with a chance to run.

Dormancy

Dormancy occurs when a thread that is blocked never becomes runnable. A common cause of dormancy is that a thread blocked by an invocation of the `wait()` method is never awakened by `notify()` or `notifyAll()`. For example, in the

BoundedQueueWithGuard class [p. 566], if the invocation of the notify() method in either the put() or get() method were omitted, the consumer and the producer threads could both become dormant. If the invocation of notify() in the put() method were omitted, the following scenario could occur:

1. The queue becomes empty. The consumer thread invokes the wait() method inside the get() method and becomes blocked.
2. The producer thread puts items into the queue, but the consumer thread is not awakened because the invocation of the notify() method is omitted. The consumer thread remains blocked.
3. The queue becomes full. The producer thread invokes the wait() method inside the put() method and becomes blocked.

At this point, both the consumer and producer threads are blocked. If there are no other threads to awaken them, they become dormant.

To avoid dormancy caused by waiting, be sure that each thread that can be blocked by the wait() method will be awakened by another thread that invokes the notify() or notifyAll() method. When in doubt, use the notifyAll() method, which awakens all the waiting threads and makes the system less dormancy-prone.

Deadlock

Deadlock occurs when two or more threads block each other and none can make progress. It is usually caused by two or more threads competing for multiple shared resources and each thread requiring exclusive possession of those resources simultaneously. Consider the following oversimplified example. The DiskDrive class represents a disk drive, and the copy() method copies a file from this disk drive to another drive.

```
public class DiskDrive {

    public synchronized void copy(DiskDrive destination, String filename) {
        InputStream in = openFile(filename);
        destination.writeFile(filename, in);
    }

    public synchronized InputStream openFile(String filename) {
        // ...
    }

    public synchronized void writeFile(String filename, InputStream in) {
        // copy the contents read from the parameter into a file
    }
}
```

To maintain the integrity of the file being copied, all the methods are synchronized. The copy() method needs to acquire the locks associated with both the source and destination disk drives. Let us assume that we have two disk drives, c and d. On one thread we do `c.copy(d, file1)`, and on another thread we do `d.copy(c, file2)`. The following is a possible scenario:

Thread 1: `c.copy(d, file1)`   **Thread 2:** `d.copy(c, file2)`
Invoke `c.copy( . . . )`
Obtain lock of c

                                               Invoke `d.copy( . . . )`
                                               Obtain lock of d

Invoke `c.openFile( . . . )`

                                               Invoke `d.openFile( . . . )`

Invoke `d.writeFile( . . . )`
Unable to obtain lock of d

                                               Invoke `c.writeFile( . . . )`
                                               Unable to obtain lock of c

Neither thread is able to obtain the lock needed to proceed, so they are in a "deadlock."

In general, detecting and preventing deadlock is difficult. An extensive body of work on deadlock detection and prevention is available. A more detailed discussion on this topic is presented in Lea [2000].

Premature Termination

Premature termination occurs when a thread is terminated before it should be, impeding the progress of other threads. For example, in the `BoundedQueueWithGuard` class [p. 566], premature termination of either the producer or the consumer thread causes the other thread to be blocked forever (that is, to become dormant).

11.3   DESIGN CASE STUDY—TIC-TAC-TOE GAME

In this section, we will develop a simple game: tic-tac-toe. Here we implement it as a two-player game on a 3×3 board, but it is designed so that it can be extended to a k-player ($k \geq 2$) game on an $m \times n$ board. The program is multithreaded, and each player is represented as a separate thread. Two types of players are implemented:

- A human player, which waits for a human to make moves by clicking the mouse on the game board.
- A machine player, which automatically generates moves (not necessarily good ones).

The game can be played by two human players, two machine players, or a human and a machine player. The structure of the program is shown in Figure 11.4.

Figure 11.4

Structure of the tic-tac-toe game.

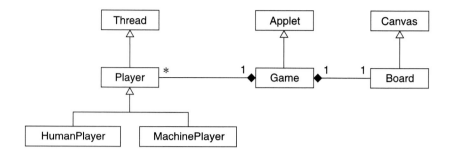

11.3.1 The Game Board

The class Board represents the game board.

> **Class Board**

```
import java.awt.*;
import java.awt.event.*;

public class Board extends Canvas {

    protected Game game;
    protected int row, col;
    protected int rowHeight, colWidth;
    protected int board[][];
    protected int maxMoves;
    protected int moves;
    protected boolean over = false;
    protected int winner = 0;

    ⟨Constructor Board() on page 572⟩
    ⟨Accessors of fields on page 573⟩
    ⟨Method paint() on page 574⟩
    ⟨Method recordMove() on page 575⟩
    ⟨Method isLegalMove() on page 575⟩
    ⟨Method checkGame() on page 576⟩
    ⟨Auxiliary methods checkRow(), checkCol(), and checkDiagonal() on page 576⟩
    ⟨Inner class MouseHandler on page 577⟩

}
```

The fields of the Board class are described in Table 11.3. The constructor of the Board class simply initializes the fields.

> **Constructor of the Board class**

```
public Board(Game game, int row, int col) {
    this.game = game;
    this.row = row;
    this.col = col;
    maxMoves = row * col;
```

```
        moves = 0;
        board = new int[row][col];
        addMouseListener(new MouseHandler());
    }
```

The following accessors of the Board class return the values of the corresponding fields:

Accessors of Board class

```
public int getRow() {
    return row;
}

public int getCol() {
    return col;
}

public boolean isOver() {
    return over;
}

public int getWinner() {
    return winner;
}
```

TABLE 11.3

Fields of the Board Class

Methods	Description
game	The Game object with which this game board is associated
row, col	The number of rows and columns on the game board
rowHeight	The height of each row
colWidth	The width of each column
board	The two-dimensional array that records the state of the game board, each cell containing the ID of the player who occupies the cell and the player ID starting at 1
moves	The number of moves that have been made
maxMoves	The maximum number of moves allowed in the game
over	The boolean flag that is set to true if the game is over
winner	The ID of the player who won the game, which is 0 while the game is in progress

Figure 11.5

The tic-tac-toe
game board.

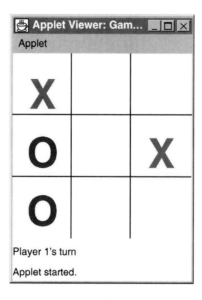

The paint() method paints the game board. A screen shot of the game board is shown in Figure 11.5. The paint() method first draws the grid. It then draws an *X* for each cell occupied by player 1 and an *O* for each cell occupied by player 2.

The paint() method of the Board class

```
public void paint(Graphics g) {
    Dimension d = getSize();
    rowHeight = d.height / row;
    colWidth = d.width / col;
    int i, j;
    for (i = 1; i < row; i++)
        g.drawLine(0, i * rowHeight, d.width, i * rowHeight);
    for (j = 1; j < col; j++)
        g.drawLine(j * colWidth, 0, j * colWidth, d.height);

    Font font = new Font("Sans-serif", Font.BOLD, 48);
    g.setFont(font);
    for (i = 0; i < row; i++) {
        for (j = 0; j < col; j++) {
            if (board[i][j] != 0) {
                int x = i * colWidth + 12;
                int y = j * rowHeight + 60;
                switch (board[i][j]) {
                case 1:
                    g.setColor(Color.red);
                    g.drawString("X", x, y);
                    break;
```

```
            case 2:
                g.setColor(Color.blue);
                g.drawString("O", x, y);
                break;
            }
        }
    }
  }
}
```

The `recordMove()` method records a move made by the specified player. A move is an instance of the following Move class, which indicates the cell the player intends to occupy:

Class Move

```
public class Move {
    public int row, col;
}
```

Before a move is recorded, the `recordMove()` method checks to determine whether the move is a legal move. It returns `true` if the move is legal and `false` if the move is illegal.

The `recordMove()` method of the Board class

```
public boolean recordMove(Move move, int playerId) {
    if (isLegalMove(move)) {
        moves++;
        board[move.row][move.col] = playerId;
        repaint();
        return true;
    } else {
        return false;
    }
}
```

The `isLegalMove()` method returns `true` if the specified move is legal. A move is legal if the cell is unoccupied.

The `isLegalMove()` method of the Board class

```
public boolean isLegalMove(Move move) {
    return (board[move.row][move.col] == 0);
}
```

The `checkGame()` method checks to determine whether the game is over. The game is over if all the cells on the game board are occupied or one of the players has won. It depends on three auxiliary methods—`checkRow()`, `checkCol()`, and `checkDiagonal()`—to determine whether one of the players has won.

The `checkGame()` method of the Board class

```
protected void checkGame(int playerId) {
    if (moves >= maxMoves) {
        over = true;
        return;
    }

    boolean win = false;
    for (int i = 0; i < row; i++) {
        if (checkRow(playerId, i)) {
            win = true;
            break;
        }
    }
    if (!win) {
        for (int i = 0; i < col; i++) {
            if (checkCol(playerId, i)) {
                win = true;
                break;
            }
        }
    }
    if (!win) {
        win = checkDiagonal(playerId);
    }
    if (win) {
        winner = playerId;
        over = true;
    }
}
```

The auxiliary methods `checkRow()`, `checkCol()`, and `checkDiagonal()` check on whether the specified player occupies an entire row, an entire column, or an entire diagonal.

Auxiliary methods of the Board class

```
protected boolean checkRow(int playerId, int row) {
    for (int i = 0; i < col; i++) {
        if (board[row][i] != playerId) {
            return false;
        }
    }
    return true;
}

protected boolean checkCol(int playerId, int col) {
    for (int i = 0; i < row; i++) {
        if (board[i][col] != playerId) {
            return false;
        }
    }
}
```

```
      return true;
   }
   protected boolean checkDiagonal(int playerId) {
      boolean result = true;
      for (int i = 0; i < row; i++) {
         if (board[i][i] != playerId) {
            result = false;
            break;
         }
      }
      if (result) {
         return true;
      }
      result = true;
      for (int i = 0; i < row; i++) {
         if (board[i][col - i - 1] != playerId) {
            result = false;
            break;
         }
      }
      return result;
   }
```

The inner class `MouseHandler` receives mouse clicks on the game board, which indicate moves made by a human player.

The Inner class of the Board class

```
class MouseHandler extends MouseAdapter {
   public void mouseClicked(MouseEvent event) {
      Point p = event.getPoint();
      game.getPlayer().selectCell(p.x / colWidth, p.y / rowHeight);
   }
}
```

11.3.2 The Game

The Game class extends the `Applet` class. It contains a game board and a message bar. The field `player` is an array of players in the game. In this implementation the number of players is fixed at 2. The field `turn` refers to the player who currently has the turn (that is, the player who is supposed to make the next move).

Class Game

```
import java.awt.*;
import java.applet.Applet;

public class Game extends Applet {
   protected Board board;
   protected Label messageBar;
```

```
    protected Player players[];
    protected Player turn;
```

⟨Constructor Game() on page 578⟩
⟨Method init() on page 582⟩
⟨Methods getPlayer(), getBoard(), isOver(),
    and displayMessage() on page 578⟩
⟨Method recordMove() on page 578⟩

```
}
```

The constructor initializes the fields by creating the board and the message bar.

Constructor of the Game class

```
public Game() {
    players = new Player[2];
    board = new Board(this, 3, 3);

    messageBar = new Label("Game begin.");
    setLayout(new BorderLayout());
    add(board, BorderLayout.CENTER);
    add(messageBar, BorderLayout.SOUTH);
}
```

The getPlayer() method returns the player who has the turn. The getBoard() method returns the game board. The isOver() method returns true if the game is over. The displayMessage() method displays a message on the message bar.

Methods of the Game class

```
public Player getPlayer() {
    return turn;
}

public Board getBoard() {
    return board;
}

public boolean isOver() {
    return board.isOver();
}

public void displayMessage(String msg) {
    messageBar.setText(msg);
}
```

The recordMove() method records a move made by a player. It returns true if the move is legal and returns false otherwise. It also displays messages regarding the outcome of the game.

The recordMove() method of the Game class

```
public boolean recordMove(Move move) {
    if (board.recordMove(move, turn.getId())) {
        board.checkGame(turn.getId());
```

```
        if (isOver()) {
            int winner = board.getWinner();
            if (winner >= 1) {
                displayMessage("Player " + winner + " won.");
            } else {
                displayMessage("It's a draw");
            }
            for (int n = 0; n < players.length; n++) {
                players[n].stop();
            }
        }
        return true;
    } else {
        return false;
    }
}
```

11.3.3 The Players

The Player class is an abstract class that represents players in the game. Different types of players are represented by different subclasses of this class. The field game refers to the game the players are in. The field id is the ID of the first player. The field next refers to the player whose turn follows that of the preceding player. In two-player games, next refers to the second player. The field turn refers to the player who currently has the turn. It is this player's turn if turn == this. The turn and next fields of the player objects are initialized in the init() method of the Game class.

Abstract class Player

```
abstract public class Player extends Thread {

    protected Game game;
    protected int id;
    protected Player next;
    protected Player turn;

    public Player(Game game, int id) {
        this.game = game;
        this.id = id;
    }

    public int getId() {
        return id;
    }

    public synchronized void setNext(Player p){
        next = p;
    }

    public synchronized void hasTurn() {
        turn = this;
        game.turn = this;
        notify();
    }
```

```
abstract public Move makeMove();

public void selectCell(int x, int y) {}

public synchronized void run() {
    while (!game.isOver()) {
        while (turn != this) {
            try {
                wait();
            }
            catch (InterruptedException ex) { return; }
        }
        game.displayMessage("Player " + id + "'s turn");
        while (true) {
            Move move = makeMove();
            if (game.recordMove(move)) {
                break;
            } else {
                game.displayMessage("Illegal move!");
            }
        }
        turn = null;
        next.hasTurn();
    }
}
```

The getId() method returns the ID of this player. The setNext() method sets which player is after this player. The hasTurn() method is invoked when this player should have the turn. This method is invoked by the preceding player, and it awakens this player (see the run() method). The makeMove() method is a hook method for the subclasses to override. This method should return the next move to be made by the player. The selectCell() method is invoked by the MouseHandler of the Board class. It informs the player that a mouse click has been received and a cell position given. This method is ignored by the MachinePlayer class, but it is used by the HumanPlayer class to get the move made by a human.

The run() method is the body of the player thread and is also a template method. First, it waits until this player gets the turn. Then it invokes the hook method makeMove() to make a move.

The HumanPlayer class implements the makeMove() method. It simply waits for a mouse click on the game board.

Class HumanPlayer

```
public class HumanPlayer extends Player {
    protected  Move move;

    public HumanPlayer(Game game, int id) {
        super(game, id);
        move = new Move();
    }
```

```
synchronized public Move makeMove() {
   try {
      wait();
   } catch (InterruptedException e) {
      e.printStackTrace();
   }
   return move;
}

synchronized public void selectCell(int x, int y) {
   move.row = x;
   move.col = y;
   notify();
}
}
```

The MachinePlayer also implements the makeMove() method. It randomly generates a move.

Class MachinePlayer

```
public class MachinePlayer extends Player {

   protected int nCells;

   public MachinePlayer(Game game, int id) {
      super(game, id);
      Board board = game.getBoard();
      nCells = board.getRow() * board.getCol();
   }

   public Move makeMove() {
      try {
         Thread.currentThread().sleep(1000);
      } catch (InterruptedException e) {}

      Move move = new Move();
      Board board = game.getBoard();
      int row = game.getBoard().getRow();
      int i = (int)(Math.random() * nCells);
      move.row = i / row;
      move.col = i % row;
      while (!board.isLegalMove(move)) {
         i++;
         if (i >= nCells) {
            i = i % nCells;
         }
         move.row = i / row;
         move.col = i % row;
      }
      return move;
   }
}
```

The init() method of the Game class initializes the players according to the parameter type.

The init() method of the Game class

```
public void init() {
    String gameType = getParameter("type");
    if (gameType.equals("human-human")) {
        players[0] = new HumanPlayer(this, 1);
        players[1] = new HumanPlayer(this, 2);
    } else if (gameType.equals("machine-machine")) {
        players[0] = new MachinePlayer(this, 1);
        players[1] = new MachinePlayer(this, 2);
    } else {
        players[0] = new HumanPlayer(this, 1);
        players[1] = new MachinePlayer(this, 2);
    }
    players[0].start();
    players[1].start();
    players[0].setNext(players[1]);
    players[1].setNext(players[0]);
    players[0].hasTurn();
}
```

11.3.4 Idiom: Taking Turns

The Player class implements a behavior that allows the players taking turns to make moves. This behavior can be generalized by the following idiom that extends to more than two objects, or players, and is applicable to nongame applications:

Idiom *Taking Turns*

Category: Behavioral implementation idiom.

Intent: For each participant in a group of objects to take turns in a fixed order and perform a certain task.

Applicability: This idiom can be used to implement k-player games ($k \geq 2$), or other applications that require the participants to take turns.

Each participant is a thread. The following code comprises the implementation:

```
class Participant extends Thread {

    protected Participant next;
    protected Participant turn;
```

```
public synchronized void run() {
    while (!isDone()) {
        while (turn != this) {
            try {
                wait();
            }
            catch (InterruptedException ex) { return; }
        }
        // perform an action or make a move
        turn = null;
        next.hasTurn();
    }
}

public synchronized void hasTurn() {
    turn = this;
    notify();
}

// other fields and methods
}
```

If there are n participants and they take turns in the order, $p_0, p_1, \ldots, p_{n-1}$, they must be initialized as

```
p₀.next == p₁
p₁.next == p₂
. . .
pₙ₋₂.next == pₙ₋₁
pₙ₋₁.next == p₀
```

To start the process, we do the following:

```
p₀.start();
p₁.start();
. . .
pₙ₋₁.start();
p₀.hasTurn();
```

Using the taking-turns idiom, we can extend the two-player game shown here to multiplayer games. This is left as a project (Project 11.1).

CHAPTER SUMMARY

- Concurrent programs, also known as multithreaded programs, are capable of running several threads simultaneously.
- A thread is a single sequential flow of control within a program. Threads are different from processes. A process is a heavyweight flow that executes concurrently with other processes. A thread is a lightweight flow that executes concurrently with other threads within the same process.

- Threads can be defined by extending the `Thread` class or by implementing the `Runnable` interface.
- The life cycle of a thread includes three main states: new, alive, and dead. Threads in the alive state can be either runnable or blocked.
- The Java virtual machine assigns and maintains a priority for each thread. This priority, which is an integer value, should be manipulated by the programmer only for performance tuning.
- Critical regions are segments of code that should be executed by only one thread at a time. Race hazards occur when more than one thread executes the statements in a critical region at the same time. Race hazards could leave objects in inconsistent or invalid states. Java provides a synchronization mechanism to ensure that, while a thread is executing the statements in a critical region, no other threads can execute statements in that same critical region at the same time.
- A guard is the precondition for a certain action to complete successfully. Guarded suspension is a policy for threads to cooperate in the following way:
  1. Before executing a method, the guard is tested.
  2. Execution continues only when the guard is true, which ensures successful completion of the method invocation.
  3. Execution is temporarily suspended until the guard becomes true, at which time execution may continue.
- Liveness refers to desirable conditions that will come about during the lifetime of a program. Some common types of liveness failures are

  contention (also called *starvation* or *indefinite postponement*), when a runnable thread never gets a chance to run.

  dormancy, when a thread that is blocked never becomes runnable.

  deadlock, when two or more threads block each other and none can progress.

  premature termination, when a thread is terminated before it should be, impeding the progress of other threads.

FURTHER READING

Lea, D. (2000). *Concurrent Programming in Java—Design Principles and Patterns*, 2nd ed. Addison-Wesley.

EXERCISES

11.1 Complete the `Account` class on page 556 and be sure that it is thread-safe. It should contain methods such as `deposit()` and `getBalance()`. All critical regions of the class should be protected with synchronization as needed.

11.2 Implement a thread-safe linked list class based on the LinkedList class in Chapters 6 and 7. All critical regions of the class should be protected with synchronization as needed.

11.3 Using the BoundedQueueWithGuard class as a model, implement a thread-safe Stack class with guarded suspension. The Stack class should contain the methods pop(), push(), isFull(), and isEmpty(). Test the Stack class by using classes similar to the Producer and Consumer classes presented in this chapter.

PROJECTS

11.1 Design and implement a multiplayer tic-tac-toe game. (*Hint:* Use a larger board and design a new scoring system.)

11.2 Develop a Java program that simulates a traffic control system for a four-way intersection. The system controls four sets of traffic lights, facing north, east, south, and west. Each set of lights can be in one of the following states: *green*, *yellow*, and *red*. The goals of the traffic control system are

- never to give green lights simultaneously to traffic flows that may collide.
- to avoid unnecessary blocking of the traffic flows.
- to give green lights to emergency vehicles.

For testing purposes, use independent threads to generate simulated traffic flows, which have emergency vehicles occasionally, in different directions. Develop a GUI program to animate traffic lights and traffic flows. (*Note:* Take precautions so that your program does not deadlock.) *Bonus:* Add a left-turn signal to each set of traffic lights.

11.3 Develop a Java program that simulates an elevator control system for a bank of *m* elevators of an *n*-story building. Each floor, except the top and bottom, has an *Up* and a *Down* button. The top floor has only the *Down* button, and the bottom floor has only the *Up* button. Inside each elevator is a button for each floor. The goal of the system is to ensure that

(a) one of the elevators moving upward will stop at the floor for which the *Up* button is pushed.

(b) one of the elevators moving downward will stop at the floor for which the *Down* button is pushed.

(c) each elevator must stop at the *i*th floor if the button *i* in this elevator is pushed.

Develop a GUI program to animate the status of all the buttons and the movement of the elevators. Two testing modes of the system should be supported:

(a) Use independent threads to simulate the requests of the passengers.

(b) Manually push the buttons on each floor and inside each elevator.

CHAPTER 12

Distributed Computing

CHAPTER OVERVIEW

In this chapter, we first discuss two pure Java mechanisms for distributed computing: socket-based communication and remote method invocation (RMI). We illustrate the design and implementation of distributed applications, using a stock ticker application. We then discuss a Java mechanism, JDBC, for communicating with relational databases. We also briefly discuss a mechanism for interfacing Java applications with non-Java applications in distributed computing environments: the Common Object Request Broker Architecture (CORBA). This chapter serves as an introduction to developing distributed applications in Java.

Today's computing environments are inherently distributed and heterogeneous. Internet and intranet applications often run on different operating systems in different locations. *Distributed applications* consist of collaborating components that reside and execute on different network hosts. The components residing on different hosts do not share storage space (that is, memory and disc). Exchange of information among these components can take place only via communication connections, or links, among the hosts. Furthermore, the hosts can be running different operating systems, forming a heterogeneous network computing environment.

587

In this chapter we discuss two Java mechanisms for distributed computing:

Socket-based communication: Sockets are the end points of two-way connections between two distributed components that communicate with each other. A connection must be explicitly established by both parties.

Remote method invocation: RMI makes the network "transparent." It allows distributed components to be manipulated (almost) as if they were all on the same host. Programmers need not deal with interhost communications at all. All network communication is handled implicitly by the run-time environment supporting the remote method invocation.

We also briefly discuss a mechanism for interfacing Java applications with non-Java applications in distributed computing environments: the *Common Object Request Broker Architecture (CORBA)*. CORBA is an object-oriented framework that supports interoperability among objects written in different languages and running on different platforms. CORBA support is available for most programming languages, including Java, and platforms used for industrial applications. CORBA is especially useful in interfacing applications developed with modern languages, such as Java and C++, with legacy systems.

This chapter serves only as an introduction to developing distributed applications in Java.

12.1   SOCKET-BASED COMMUNICATION

Sockets are the end points of logical connections between hosts and can be used to send and receive data. At the application programming level, it is assumed that the socket connections are reliable; that is, the data sent from one end of the connection will be received at the other end in the same order and with no loss. Sockets are supported by most programming languages and platforms in use today. Java applications can use sockets to communicate with applications written in other languages.

12.1.1   Server and Client Sockets

There are two kinds of sockets: server sockets and client sockets. A server socket waits for requests for connections from clients. A client socket can be used to send and receive data.

Server Sockets

Each server socket listens at a specific *port*. The port number is necessary to distinguish different servers running on the same host, so each server must have a unique port number.

A server socket must be running on the server host before its clients initiate contact. After the server socket is contacted by a client, a connection can be established, and a client socket is created for the application running on the server host to communicate with the client that initiated the contact.

A server socket is an instance of the `ServerSocket` class and can be created with one of these constructors:

```
ServerSocket(int port)
ServerSocket(int port, int backlog)
```

The parameter `port` specifies the port number at which the server socket will be listening to requests from clients. When multiple clients are contacting the same server socket at the same time, they will be put in a waiting queue and will be processed in the order in which they are received. The optional parameter `backlog` specifies the maximum length of the waiting queue. Server sockets can be created only with Java apps, not applets. The commonly used methods of the `ServerSocket` class are summarized in the following table:

Method	Description
`accept()`	Waits for a connection request. The thread that executes the method will be blocked until a request is received, at which time the method returns a client socket.
`close()`	Stops waiting for requests from clients.

The following program segment is a typical use of server sockets:

```
try {
   ServerSocket s = new ServerSocket(port);
   while (true) {
      Socket incoming = s.accept(); // obtain a client socket
      ⟨Handle a client⟩
   }
} catch (IOException e) {
   ⟨Handle exception: fail to create a server socket⟩
}
```

Client Sockets

A client socket is an instance of the `Socket` class and can be obtained in two ways:

1. On the client side, client sockets can be created by using the constructor

   ```
   Socket (String host, int port)
   ```

   The parameter `host` specifies the address of the host, and the parameter `port` specifies the port number. Client sockets can be created and used by both Java apps and applets.
2. On the server side, client sockets are returned by the `accept()` method of the `ServerSocket` class, after requests for connection have been received from clients.

Communication between the server and the client is handled by client sockets at both ends. Each client socket has an `InputStream` object for receiving data and an `OutputStream` object for sending data. When the `InputStream` and `OutputStream` objects are used, sending and receiving data between a client and a server are essentially no different from reading data from and writing data to files. The commonly used methods of the `Socket` class are summarized in the following table:

Method	Description
getInputStream()	Returns an `InputStream` object for receiving data
getOutputStream()	Returns an `OutputStream` object for sending data
close()	Closes the socket connection

The following program segment illustrates the typical use of client sockets for sending and receiving text data:

```
try {
    Socket s = new Socket(host, port); // create a client socket
    PrintWriter out = new PrintWriter(
        new OutputStreamWriter(s.getOutputStream()));
    BufferedReader in = new BufferedReader(
        new InputStreamReader(s.getInputStream()));
    ⟨Send and receive data⟩
    in.close();
    out.close();
    s.close();
} catch (IOException e) {
    ⟨Handle exception: connection fails⟩
}
```

12.1.2 Servers and Clients Using Sockets

In this section, we illustrate client–server programming, using sockets, through a series of examples. Let us start with a simple server that only echoes the messages it receives from its client.

EXAMPLE 12.1 A Simple Echo Server

PURPOSE

This example illustrates the basic elements of a server application.

DESCRIPTION

This server echoes each line of text that it receives from its client. The client can terminate the connection by sending a line that says "BYE."

SOLUTION

Typically, a server is supposed to run for a long time. So a server usually contains an infinite loop of some kind. In this case, each iteration of the loop handles one client. Thus this server can handle multiple clients sequentially (that is, only one client at a time), not simultaneously.

A simple echo server

```java
import java.io.*;
import java.net.*;

public class EchoServer {
    public static void main(String[] args) {
        try {
            ServerSocket s = new ServerSocket(8008);
            while (true) {
                Socket incoming = s.accept();
                BufferedReader in
                    = new BufferedReader(new InputStreamReader(
                                    incoming.getInputStream()));
                PrintWriter out
                    = new PrintWriter(new OutputStreamWriter(
                                    incoming.getOutputStream()));
                out.println("Hello! This is the Java EchoServer.");
                out.println("Enter BYE to exit.");
                out.flush();

                while (true) {
                    String str = in.readLine();
                    if (str == null) {
                        break; // client closed connection
                    } else {
                        out.println("Echo: " + str);
                        out.flush();
                        if (str.trim().equals("BYE")) {
                            break;
                        }
                    }
                }
                incoming.close();
            }
        } catch (Exception e) {
            e.printStackTrace();
        }
    }
}
```

The echo server will listen on port 8008. The method invocation `in.readLine()` attempts to receive a line of text from the client. If the connection is alive but the client does not send anything, the method invocation will be blocked. If the client sends a line of text, the method invocation will return with that line of text. If the client closes the connection, the method invocation will return with `null`. The `flush()` call on the output stream forces the messages to be sent to the client right away.

The server application can be compiled as usual. Let us say that we compile and start the echo server on a host called `saturn`:

```
saturn% java EchoServer
```

Now, the server is ready and is waiting for clients. We can test the echo server with the `telnet` program, which is available on almost all platforms. Let us say that we run `telnet` on a host called `venus`:[1]

```
venus% telnet saturn 8008
Trying 140.192.34.63 . . .
Connected to saturn.
Escape character is '^]'.
Hello! This is the Java EchoServer.
Enter BYE to exit.
Hi, this is from venus
Echo: Hi, this is from venus
BYE
Echo: BYE
Connection closed by foreign host.
```

We can also write a Java client that communicates with the echo server:

EXAMPLE 12.2 A Simple Client Talks to the Echo Server

PURPOSE

This example illustrates the basic elements of a client application.

DESCRIPTION

This client contacts the echo server, sends 10 lines of text to the echo server, and prints out the data it receives from the server.

SOLUTION

A simple client for the echo server

```
import java.io.*;
import java.net.*;

public class EchoClient {

    public static void main(String[] args) {
        try {
            String host;
```

---

1. Although here we run the server and the client on different hosts, it should be okay to test the server and client on the same host. In this case, the host name is `localhost` or `127.0.0.1`.

```
        if (args.length > 0) {
            host = args[0];
        } else {
            host = "localhost";
        }
        Socket socket = new Socket(host, 8008);
        BufferedReader in
            = new BufferedReader(new InputStreamReader(
                            socket.getInputStream()));
        PrintWriter out
            = new PrintWriter(new OutputStreamWriter(
                            socket.getOutputStream()));
        // send data to the server
        for (int i = 1; i <= 10; i++) {
            System.out.println("Sending: line " + i);
            out.println("line " + i);
            out.flush();
        }
        out.println("BYE");
        out.flush();

        // receive data from the server
        while (true) {
            String str = in.readLine();
            if (str == null) {
                break;
            } else {
                System.out.println(str);
            }
        }
    } catch (Exception e) {
        e.printStackTrace();
    }
  }
}
```

The first argument of the program is the name of the host on which the server is running. If the host name is absent, localhost is assumed. This client contacts the server on the given host at port 8008. The method invocation in.readLine() behaves the same on the client side as on the server side. To test this client, we first need to run the echo server on the host saturn: saturn% java EchoServer. Then we compile and run EchoClient on the host called venus. The output is:

```
venus% java EchoClient saturn
Sending: line 1
. . .
Sending: line 10
Hello! This is Java EchoServer.
Enter BYE to exit.
Echo: line 1
. . .
Echo: line 10
Echo: BYE
```

This echo server handles one client at a time. This behavior is not acceptable in some situations. It is more desirable for the server to be able to serve multiple clients simultaneously. To accomplish that purpose, each client should be handled by a separate thread.

EXAMPLE 12.3 An Echo Server That Handles Multiple Clients Simultaneously

PURPOSE
This example illustrates a server that handles multiple clients simultaneously with the use of threads.

DESCRIPTION
The behavior of this echo server is similar to that of the simple echo server; the difference is that each client is handled by a separate thread.

SOLUTION
The `ClientHandler` class defines the threads that handle the clients. Note that the body of the `run()` method is essentially the same as the body of the loop of the echo server.

A thread that handles a client: `ClientHandler`

```java
import java.io.*;
import java.net.*;

public class ClientHandler extends Thread {

    protected Socket incoming;

    public ClientHandler(Socket incoming) {
        this.incoming = incoming;
    }

    public void run() {
        try {
            BufferedReader in
                = new BufferedReader(new InputStreamReader(
                                        incoming.getInputStream()));
            PrintWriter out
                = new PrintWriter(new OutputStreamWriter(
                                        incoming.getOutputStream()));
            out.println("Hello! This is the Java MultiEchoServer.");
            out.println("Enter BYE to exit.");
            out.flush();
            while (true) {
                String str = in.readLine();
                if (str == null) {
                    break;
                } else {
                    out.println("Echo: " + str);
```

```
                    out.flush();
                    if (str.trim().equals("BYE"))
                       break;
                 }
              }
              incoming.close();
          } catch (Exception e) {
              e.printStackTrace();
          }
       }
   }
```

The `MultiEchoServer` class is the server, which creates a server socket. When-ever a client request is received, a new `ClientHandler` object, which is a thread, is created and started.

Echo server that handles multiple clients simultaneously

```
public class MultiEchoServer {

    public static void main(String[] args) {
       try {
          ServerSocket s = new ServerSocket(8009);
          while (true) {
             Socket incoming = s.accept();
             new ClientHandler(incoming).start();
          }
       } catch (Exception e) {
          e.printStackTrace();
       }
    }
}
```

So far, we have developed two servers and a client that are all Java apps. Although only a Java app can be a server in socket-based client–server applications, a client can be written as either an app or an applet. Example 12.4 shows a client that is written as an applet.

EXAMPLE 12.4 Visitor Counter Applet and Server

PURPOSE

This example illustrates a client implemented as an applet.

DESCRIPTION

This applet shows the number of visits, or hits, of the Web page that contains the applet. A screen shot of the applet is shown in Figure 12.1.

Figure 12.1

The visitor counter
applet.

SOLUTION

The CounterServer class is the visitor counter server. It must be running on the
host where the Web server (that is, the HTTP server) is running.

The visitor counter server: CounterServer

```java
import java.io.*;
import java.net.*;

public class CounterServer {

    public static void main(String[] args) {
        System.out.println("CounterServer started.");
        int i = 1;
        try {
            // read count from the file
            InputStream fin = new FileInputStream("Counter.dat");
            DataInputStream din = new DataInputStream(fin);
            i = din.readInt() + 1;
            din.close();
        } catch (IOException e) {
            e.printStackTrace();
        }
        try {
            ServerSocket s = new ServerSocket(8190);
            while (true) {
                Socket incoming = s.accept();
                DataOutputStream out
                    = new DataOutputStream(incoming.getOutputStream());
                System.out.println("Count: " + i);
                out.writeInt(i);
                incoming.close();
                OutputStream fout = new FileOutputStream("Counter.dat");
                DataOutputStream dout = new DataOutputStream(fout);
                dout.writeInt(i);
                dout.close();
                out.close();
                i++;
            }
        } catch (Exception e) {
            e.printStackTrace();
        }
    }
```

```
            System.out.println("CounterServer stopped.");
        }
    }
```

When the server starts up, it attempts to open a data file named `Counter.dat` to retrieve the last count. If the file `Counter.dat` does not exist, an `IOException` will be thrown. The exception will be caught and the count set to 1, the initial value of `i`. The current count is saved to the file every time the count changes so that the count can be restored and continue after the server is shut down and restarted. The data file is written with a `DataOutputStream` object, so it is in binary form. Similarly, the count is sent to the client in binary form.

The `Counter` class is the visitor counter applet. The applet communicates with the server to retrieve the count. In the `init()` method, a client socket is created. Recall that an applet can communicate only with a server that resides on the same host as the Web server. The host name of the client socket can only be the host of the document base.

Visitor counter applet: `Counter`

```java
import java.io.*;
import java.net.*;
import java.awt.*;
import java.applet.Applet;

public class Counter extends Applet {

    protected int count = 0;
    protected Font font = new Font("Serif", Font.BOLD, 24);

    public void init() {
        URL url = getDocumentBase();
        try {
            Socket t = new Socket(url.getHost(), 8190);
            DataInputStream in
                = new DataInputStream(t.getInputStream());
            count = in.readInt();
        } catch (Exception e) {
            e.printStackTrace();
        }
    }

    public void paint(Graphics g) {
        int x = 0, y = font.getSize();
        g.setColor(Color.green);
        g.setFont(font);
        g.drawString("You are visitor: " + count, x, y);
    }
}
```

The servers in all the examples so far deal with each client independently from other clients. No client-to-client communication is supported. The following example illustrates how clients can communicate with each other via the server.

EXAMPLE 12.5 Broadcasting Echo Server

PURPOSE

This example illustrates how clients can interact with one another through the server.

DESCRIPTION

The behavior of this echo server is similar to that of the echo server in Example 12.4; the difference is that this server will broadcast messages received from a client to all other active clients. This capability allows its clients to "chat" online.

SOLUTION

The BroadcastClientHandler class defines a thread that handles the clients. The BroadcastEchoServer class is the server. It contains a set of active clients, which will be used while the server is broadcasting messages.

The broadcasting echo server

```java
public class BroadcastEchoServer {
    static protected Set activeClients = new HashSet();

    public static void main(String[] args) {
        int i = 1;
        try {
            ServerSocket s = new ServerSocket(8010);
            while (true) {
                Socket incoming = s.accept();
                BroadcastClientHandler newClient =
                    new BroadcastClientHandler(incoming, i++);
                activeClients.add(newClient);
                newClient.start();
            }
        } catch (Exception e) {
            e.printStackTrace();
        }
    }
}
```

The BroadcastClientHandler class defines a thread that handles a client. The sendMessage() method sends a message to the client. The key feature in this client-handling thread is the loop that iterates through the active clients set BroadcastEchoServer.activeClients. The message received from this client is also broadcast to all other active clients. Thus the sendMessage() method needs to be synchronized because it will be invoked by all the threads that are handling clients.

A thread that handles a client

```java
public class BroadcastClientHandler extends Thread {

    protected Socket incoming;
    protected int id;
    protected BufferedReader in;
    protected PrintWriter out;

    public BroadcastClientHandler(Socket incoming, int id) {
        this.incoming = incoming;
        this.id = id;
        try {
            if (incoming != null) {
                in = new BufferedReader(new InputStreamReader(
                                        incoming.getInputStream()));
                out = new PrintWriter(new OutputStreamWriter(
                                        incoming.getOutputStream()));
            }
        } catch (Exception e) {
            e.printStackTrace();
        }
    }

    public synchronized void sendMessage(String msg) {
        if (out != null) {
            out.println(msg);
            out.flush();
        }
    }

    public void run() {
        if (in != null &&
            out != null) {
            sendMessage("Hello! This is Java BroadcastEchoServer.");
            sendMessage("Enter BYE to exit.");
            try {
                while (true) {
                    String str = in.readLine();
                    if (str == null) {
                        break;
                    } else {
                        // echo back to this client
                        sendMessage("Echo: " + str );
                        if (str.trim().equals("BYE")) {
                            break;
                        } else {
                            // broadcast to other active clients
                            Iterator iter =
                                BroadcastEchoServer.activeClients.iterator();
```

```
                          while (iter.hasNext()) {
                              BroadcastClientHandler t =
                                  (BroadcastClientHandler) iter.next();
                              if (t != this) {
                                  t.sendMessage("Broadcast(" + id + "): " +
                                                  str);
                              }
                          }
                      }
                  }
              }
              incoming.close();
              // this client is no longer active
              BroadcastEchoServer.activeClients.remove(this);
          } catch (IOException e) {
              e.printStackTrace();
          }
      }
  }
}
```

To test this broadcast server, we first start the server on a host called `neptune`:
`neptune% java BroadcastEchoServer`. Then we start two `telnet` clients on
hosts `venus` and `saturn`, respectively:

Client 1 on venus	**Client 2 on saturn**
venus% telnet neptune 8010	saturn% telnet neptune 8010
Hello! This is	Hello! This is
Java BroadcastEchoServer.	Java BroadcastEchoServer.
Enter BYE to exit.	Enter BYE to exit.
Echo: Hi there!	Broadcast(1): Hi there!
Broadcast(2): Hello!	Echo: Hello!
Echo: I'm on venus. Where are you?	Broadcast(1): I'm on venus.
	Where are you?
Broadcast(2): I'm on saturn.	Echo: I'm on saturn.
. . .	. . .

The broadcasting echo server is a prototype of many useful applications, including multiplayer games and distributed online collaboration.   ▪

12.1.3   Design Case Study—Stock Quotes I

In this section, we develop a stock quote server and stock ticker client applet. The
stock quote server maintains the current quotes of the stocks of various companies.
A random number generator is used to simulate the fluctuation of the quotes (see
Example 11.2 [p. 551]). The stock ticker client applet displays the quotes of a selected
list of companies that are of interest. The ticker symbols and quotes scroll across the

Figure 12.2

The stock ticker client applet.

ticker banner continuously. A screen shot of the stock ticker client applet is shown in Figure 12.2.

This application involves real-time updates of stock quotes. There are generally two strategies for handling real-time updates:

Client pull: The client periodically contacts the server to receive the current quotes from the server.

Server push: The server notifies clients whenever the quote of one of the stocks watched by the clients has changed.

The strategy chosen depends on many factors, including acceptable latency of updates, frequency of changes, and the like. We implement the stock ticker application by using both strategies.

The Client Pull Implementation

The information flow of the client pull implementation is as follows: (1) Periodically, the ticker client connects to the quote server; and (2) the quote server sends the quotes of all the companies in the following format and then disconnects:

$name_1$ $quote_1$
$name_2$ $quote_2$
. . .
$name_n$ $quote_n$

The structure of the design is shown in Figure 12.3. The three shaded classes are the new classes to be implemented here. The `Ticker` class handles the display and animation of the quotes. The display and animation portion of the client is implemented similarly to the `ScrollingBanner` applet in Example 5.3 [p. 194].

Figure 12.3

The client pull design of the stock ticker applet and the quote server.

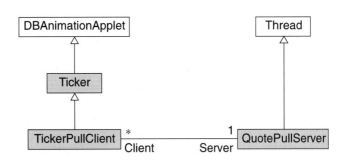

The update strategy of the stock quote is separate from the display and animation of the stock quotes and is implemented in the class `TickerPullClient`. The separation allows the `Ticker` class to be reused in different implementations of the stock ticker client with different update strategies and communication mechanisms.

The Stock Ticker Animator

The `Ticker` class extends the double-buffered generic animation applet class `DBAnimationApplet` in Example 7.2 [p. 259]. The fields are summarized in the following table:

Field	Description
watch	Watch list—a string that consists of a list of the names of the companies to be watched by this client
symbol	Array of names of the companies in the watch list
quote	Array of current quotes of the corresponding companies in the symbol array
prevQuotes	String containing the quotes of the previous cycle
curQuotes	String containing the quotes of the current cycle
url	URL of the quote server

In order to create the appearance of continuously scrolling stock quotes, we use two strings: `prevQuotes` and `curQuotes`. For example, at any given moment, the two strings may have the following values:

```
prevQuotes:"IBM 91 Sun 105 Intel 99"
curQuotes: "IBM 89 Sun 106 Intel 99"
```

The methods of the `Ticker` class are summarized in the following table:

Method	Description
initAnimator()	Initializes the ticker client
initQuotes()	Hook method for retrieving the initial quotes from the quote server
updateQuotes()	Hook method for updating quotes. The prevQuotes and curQuotes strings will be updated and properly formatted after calling this method
paintFrame()	Paints the current frame

The generic ticker banner class `Ticker`

```java
import java.awt.*;
import java.util.*;
import java.net.*;
import java.io.*;

public class Ticker extends DBAnimationApplet {
    protected Font font = new Font("Sans-serif", Font.BOLD, 24);
    protected int offset = 1;
    protected int x, y;
    protected String watch;
    protected String symbol[], quote[];
    protected String prevQuotes, curQuotes;
    protected URL url;
    ⟨The initAnimator() method on page 603⟩
    ⟨The paintFrame() method on page 604⟩
    ⟨The initQuotes() and updateQuotes() methods on page 604⟩
}
```

The `initAnimator()` method initializes the fields of the ticker client. The watch list is obtained from the applet parameter `watch`. The watch list is broken down into single names and then stored in the array `symbol`.

The `initAnimator()` method of the `Ticker` class

```java
public void initAnimator() {
    String att = getParameter("delay");
    if (att != null) {
        setDelay(Integer.parseInt(att));
    }
    watch = getParameter("watch");
    if (att != null) {
        StringTokenizer tk = new StringTokenizer(watch);
        List list = new ArrayList();
        while (tk.hasMoreTokens()) {
            list.add(tk.nextToken());
        }
        int n = list.size();
        symbol = new String[n];
        quote = new String[n];
        for (int i = 0; i < n; i++) {
            symbol[i] = (String) list.get(i);
            quote[i] = "0";
        }
    }
    url = getDocumentBase();
    initQuotes();
    updateQuotes();
    prevQuotes = curQuotes;
    x = d.width;
    y = font.getSize();
}
```

Figure 12.4

Drawing of the
stock ticker string.

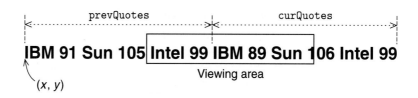

The paintFrame() method implements a behavior similar to that of the scrolling banner. The drawing of the ticker strings is done by concatenating two strings: prevQuotes and curQuotes, as illustrated in Figure 12.4. When the string prevQuote moves completely off the left end of the viewing area, the update-Quotes() method is invoked to retrieve the new quotes of the companies and form a new curQuotes string. The current curQuotes becomes the prevQuotes.

The paintFrame() method of the Ticker class

```
public void paintFrame(Graphics g) {
    g.setColor(Color.black);
    g.fillRect(0,0,d.width,d.height);
    // set the font and color, and draw the text
    g.setFont(font);
    g.setColor(Color.green);
    g.drawString(prevQuotes + curQuotes, x, y);
    // get the font metrics to determine the length of the text
    FontMetrics fm = g.getFontMetrics();
    int length = fm.stringWidth(prevQuotes);
    // adjust the position of the ticker string for the next frame
    x -= offset;
    // if the prevQuotes string is completely off to the left end
    // update the quotes and adjust the position.
    if (x < -length) {
        x = 0;
        prevQuotes = curQuotes;
        updateQuotes();
    }
}
```

The methods initQuotes() and updateQuotes() are hook methods that can be overridden in the subclasses. A null implementation is provided for initQuotes(). The implementation of updateQuotes() simply forms the curQuotes string by concatenating all the symbols and quotes.

The initQuotes() and updateQuotes() methods of the Ticker class

```
public void initQuotes() {}

protected synchronized void updateQuotes() {
    StringBuffer sb = new StringBuffer();
    for (int i = 0; i < quote.length; i++) {
        sb.append(symbol[i] + " " + quote[i] +"   ");
    }
    curQuotes = sb.toString();
}
```

The Stock Ticker Pull Client

The `TickerPullClient` class is the client applet. It extends the `Ticker` class and overrides the `updateQuotes()` method. In the `updateQuotes()` method, a socket connection is established with the quote server to retrieve the current quotes of all the companies in the format

$name_1$ $quote_1$
$name_2$ $quote_2$
. . .
$name_n$ $quote_n$

The client picks out the companies on its watch list and updates the `quote` array. Then a new `curQuotes` string is formed, using the new quotes.

Ticker pull client

```
import java.awt.*;
import java.util.*;
import java.net.*;
import java.io.*;
public class TickerPullClient extends Ticker {

    protected void updateQuotes() {
      int i;
      try {
        Socket t = new Socket(url.getHost(), 8001);
        BufferedReader in =
          new BufferedReader(new InputStreamReader(t.getInputStream()));
        String line;
        while ((line = in.readLine()) != null) {
          StringTokenizer tk = new StringTokenizer(line);
          String name = tk.nextToken();
          for (i = 0; i < quote.length; i++) {
            if (symbol[i].equals(name)) {
              String newQuote = tk.nextToken();
              quote[i] = newQuote;
            }
          }
        }
        t.close();
      } catch (IOException e) {
        e.printStackTrace();
      }
      super.updateQuotes(); // form the curQuotes string
    }
}
```

This completes the implementation of the stock ticker client with the client pull strategy.

The Stock Quote Pull Server

The quote server involves two threads: (1) The main thread listens to incoming clients; and (2) another thread monitors changes in the quotes. In this example, changes are simulated with a random number generator. The array `symbol` contains the names of all the companies, and the array `quote` contains the current quotes of the corresponding companies in the array `symbol`.

The stock quote pull server

```java
import java.io.*;
import java.net.*;

public class QuotePullServer extends Thread {
   static protected String symbol[] =
      { "IBM", "Sun", "Intel", "Apple" };
   static protected int quote[] =
      { 100, 100, 100, 100 };

   ⟨The main() method on page 606⟩
   ⟨The run() method on page 606⟩
}
```

The `main()` method listens to incoming ticker clients. It sends the quotes of all companies to any client that contacts the quote server.

The main() method of the QuotePullServer class

```java
public static void main(String[] args) {
   new QuotePullServer().start();
   try {
      ServerSocket s = new ServerSocket(8001);
      while (true) {
         Socket incoming = s.accept();
         PrintWriter out =
            new PrintWriter(new OutputStreamWriter(
               incoming.getOutputStream()));
         for (int i = 0; i < quote.length; i++) {
            out.println(symbol[i] + " " + quote[i]);
         }
         out.flush();
         out.close();
         incoming.close();
      }
   } catch (Exception e) {
      e.printStackTrace();
   }
}
```

The `run()` method simulates the changes of the quotes with a random number generator and updates the `quote` array.

The run() method of the QuotePullServer class

```java
public void run() {
   while (true) {
      try {
         Thread.currentThread().sleep(10000);
```

```
            for (int i = 0; i < quote.length; i++) {
               quote[i] += (Math.random() - 0.4) * (10.0 * Math.random());
            }
         } catch (Exception e) {
            e.printStackTrace();
         }
      }
   }
}
```

This completes the stock quote server implementation using the client pull strategy.

The Server Push Implementation

The information flow of the server push implementation is as follows:

- The ticker client contacts the quote server initially and provides a watch list in the format WATCH $name_1$ $name_2$ . . . $name_n$.
- The quote server registers the client and sends the quotes of only the companies on the watch list to the client in the format

   $name_1$ $quote_1$
   $name_2$ $quote_2$
   . . .
   $name_n$ $quote_n$
   DONE

- The connection between the ticker client and the quote server is maintained until the client decides to close it.
- Whenever the quote of a company is changed, the quote server sends the quote to those clients who are watching the company, in the format

   name quote

- The client closes the connection by sending the message CLOSE.

The structure of the design is shown in Figure 12.5. The shaded boxes contain the new classes to be implemented here.

The Stock Ticker Push Client

The client involves two classes:

1. The TickerPushClient class extends the Ticker class. It makes the initial contact with the quote server, retrieves the initial quotes, and handles the display of the quotes.
2. The QuoteListener class is a thread that listens to the quote server for updates on the quote. Each client has a QuoteListener object that maintains a connection with the quote server and updates the quotes displayed by the ticker client when changes occur.

Figure 12.5

The server push design of the stock ticker applet and the quote server.

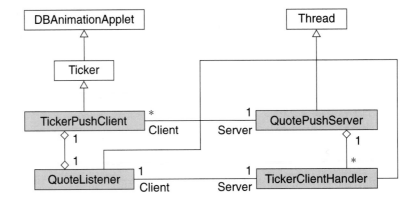

The `TickerPushClient` overrides the `initQuotes()` method of the `Ticker` class. In the `initQuotes()` method, the quote server is contacted to retrieve the initial quotes of the companies on the watch list. Then a `QuoteListener` object, which is a thread, is created and started to listen to the changes in the quotes.

The stock ticker push client

```java
import java.awt.*;
import java.util.*;
import java.net.*;
import java.io.*;

public class TickerPushClient extends Ticker {

    protected Socket socket;
    protected PrintWriter out;
    protected QuoteListener quoteListener;

    public void initQuotes() {
      try {
        socket = new Socket(url.getHost(), 8002);
        // send the watch list
        out = new PrintWriter(new OutputStreamWriter(
          socket.getOutputStream()));
        out.println("WATCH " + watch);
        out.flush();
        // receive the initial quotes
        BufferedReader in =
          new BufferedReader(new InputStreamReader(
            socket.getInputStream()));
        String line;
        while ((line = in.readLine()) != null) {
          if (line.trim().equals("DONE")) {
            break;
          }
```

```
            StringTokenizer tk = new StringTokenizer(line);
            String name = tk.nextToken();
            for (int i = 0; i < quote.length; i++) {
              if (symbol[i].equals(name)) {
                String newQuote = tk.nextToken();
                quote[i] = newQuote;
              }
            }
          }
          quoteListener = new QuoteListener(this, in);
          quoteListener.start();
      } catch (IOException e) {
        e.printStackTrace();
      }
    }

    public void destroy() {
      out.println("CLOSE");
      quoteListener.interrupt();
    }
  }
```

The Quote Listener

A QuoteListener object is a thread that listens to the quote server for changes of the quotes. In contrast to the client pull strategy, a QuoteListener object does not actively contact the quote server but passively waits for the server to send any changes.

Class QuoteListener

```
class QuoteListener extends Thread {

    public QuoteListener(TickerPushClient ticker, BufferedReader in) {
      this.ticker = ticker;
      this.in = in;
    }

    public void run() {
      String line;
      try {
        while ((line = in.readLine()) != null) {
          StringTokenizer tk = new StringTokenizer(line);
          String name = tk.nextToken();
          for (int i = 0; i < ticker.n; i++) {
            if (ticker.symbol[i].equals(name)) {
              String newQuote = tk.nextToken();
              ticker.quote[i] = newQuote;
            }
          }
          if (isInterrupted()) {
            break;
          }
        }
```

```
            in.close();
        } catch (IOException e) {
            e.printStackTrace();
        }
    }

    protected TickerPushClient ticker;
    protected BufferedReader in;
}
```

This completes the implementation of the stock ticker client using the server push strategy.

The Stock Quote Push Server

The quote server implementation consists of two classes:

1. The `QuotePushServer` class involves two threads: one listens to incoming clients, and the other monitors the changes in the quotes.
2. The `TickerClientHandler` class defines a thread that handles a ticker client. A `TickerClientHandler` object maintains a connection with a `QuoteListener` object of a ticker client and pushes the changes of quotes to that client.

The field `clients` is a set that holds handlers for active ticker clients.

The stock quote push server

```
import java.io.*;
import java.util.*;
import java.net.*;

public class QuotePushServer extends Thread {

    static protected String symbol[] =
        { "IBM", "Sun", "Intel", "Apple" };
    static protected int quote[] =
        { 100, 100, 100, 100 };
    static protected Set clients = new HashSet();

    ⟨The main() method on page 610⟩
    ⟨The run() method on page 611⟩
    ⟨The getQuote() method on page 612⟩
}
```

The `main()` method listens to incoming ticker clients, and creates a `Ticker-ClientHandler` object, which is a thread, for each ticker client, adds the client handler to the active clients set `clients`, and starts the thread.

The `main()` method of the `QuotePushServer` class

```
public static void main(String[] args) {
    new QuotePushServer().start();
    try {
        ServerSocket s = new ServerSocket(8002);
```

```
      while (true) {
        Socket incoming = s.accept();
        TickerClientHandler newClient = new TickerClientHandler(incoming);
        clients.add(newClient);
        newClient.start();
      }
    } catch (Exception e) {
      e.printStackTrace();
    }
  }
```

The `run()` method simulates the changes of the quotes with a random number generator and updates the `quote` array. Furthermore, if the quote of a stock is changed, it iterates through the set of handlers of active ticker clients and invokes the `newQuote()` method of the `TickerClientHandler` class to request that the handlers push the change to their respective clients.

The `run()` method of the `QuotePushServer` class

```
public void run() {
    while (true) {
      try {
        Thread.currentThread().sleep(10000);
        for (int i = 0; i < quote.length; i++) {
          int dq = 0;
          if (Math.random() < 0.5) {
            dq = (int) ((Math.random() - 0.4) * (10.0 * Math.random()));
          }
          if (dq != 0) {
            // quote is changed
            quote[i] += dq;
            // push to ticker clients
            Iterator iter = clients.iterator();
            while  (iter.hasNext()) {
              TickerClientHandler t = (TickerClientHandler) iter.next();
              t.newQuote(symbol[i], quote[i]);
            }
          }
        }
      } catch (Exception e) {
        e.printStackTrace();
      }
    }
  }
```

The `getQuote()` method retrieves the current quote of a company by its name. It is used by the `TickerClientHandler` class when sending the initial quotes of companies to the clients on its watch list.

The getQuote() method of the QuotePushServer class

```
static public int getQuote(String name) {
    for (int i = 0; i < n; i++) {
        if (symbol[i].equals(name)) {
            return quote[i];
        }
    }
    return 0;
}
```

The Client Handler for the Stock Quote Push Server

The TickerClientHandler class defines a thread that handles a ticker client.

Class ClientHandler

```
class TickerClientHandler extends Thread {

    protected PrintWriter out;
    protected BufferedReader in;
    protected Socket socket;
    protected String symbol[];

    public TickerClientHandler (Socket socket) {
        this.socket = socket;
        try {
            out = new PrintWriter(new OutputStreamWriter(
                socket.getOutputStream()));
            in = new BufferedReader(new InputStreamReader(
                socket.getInputStream()));
        } catch (IOException e) {
            e.printStackTrace();
        }
    }

    ⟨The run() method on page 613⟩
    ⟨The newQuote() method on page 613⟩
}
```

The run() method defines the body of the thread that handles a ticker client. It waits for messages sent by its client and responds to two messages:

1. WATCH: This watch list is sent by the client at the beginning of the session. The client handler responds by sending to the client the initial quotes of companies on the watch list.
2. CLOSE: This message should be the last one received from the client. The client handler responds by removing itself from the active-clients set QuotePushServer.clients and terminates itself.

The handler thread is blocked during the session.

The `run()` method of the `TickerClientHandler` class

```java
public void run() {
   try {
   String line;
      while ((line = in.readLine()) != null) {
        if (line.startsWith("WATCH")) {
          StringTokenizer tk = new StringTokenizer(line);
          tk.nextToken();
          Vector v = new Vector();
          while (tk.hasMoreTokens()) {
            v.addElement(tk.nextToken());
          }
          int n = v.size();
          String symbol[] = new String[n];
          int i;
          for (i = 0; i < n; i++) {
            symbol[i] = (String) v.elementAt(i);
          }
          this.symbol = symbol;
          for (i = 0; i < n; i++) {
            out.println(symbol[i] + " " +
                        QuotePushServer.getQuote(symbol[i]));
          }
          out.println("DONE");
          out.flush();
        } else if (line.trim().equals("CLOSE")) {
          break;
        }
      }
    socket.close();
    in.close();
    out.close();
   } catch (IOException e) {
    e.printStackTrace();
   }
   QuotePushServer.clients.remove(this);
}
```

The `newQuote()` method pushes a new quote to the ticker client. This method is not invoked by the client handler thread but by the quote-monitoring thread defined in the `run()` method of the `QuotePushServer` class [p. 611].

The `newQuote()` method of `TickerClientHandler` class

```java
public void newQuote(String name, int quote) {
   boolean needToSend = false;
   if (symbol != null) {
      for (int i = 0; i < symbol.length; i++)
```

```
                   if (symbol[i].equals(name)) {
                       needToSend = true;
                       break;
                   }
               } else {
                   needToSend = true;
               }
               if (needToSend) {
                   out.println(name + " " + quote);
                   out.flush();
               }
           }
       }
```

This completes the stock quote server implementation using the server push strategy.

12.2   REMOTE METHOD INVOCATION

Developing distributed applications using socket-based communications requires explicit connections between clients and servers and transmission of data through the connections. Java *remote method invocation* (RMI) is a mechanism that simplifies the programming model of distributed applications. It does not require explicit connections and data transmission. Objects residing on different hosts can be manipulated as if they were all on the same host. Interaction and communication among objects residing on different hosts can be accomplished similarly to regular method invocation in Java. The connections among different hosts and the transmission of data are handled implicitly by JVM.

12.2.1   The Architecture

The key participants of the RMI architecture are the following:

Server: An object that provides services to objects residing on remote hosts.

Service contract: An interface that defines the services provided by the server.

Client: An object that uses the services provided by objects residing on remote hosts.

Stub: An object that resides on the same host as the client and serves as a proxy, or surrogate, for the remote server.

Skeleton: An object that resides on the same host as the server, receiving requests from the stubs and dispatching the requests to the server.

The clients and servers are written by programmers. Stubs and skeletons are automatically generated by the RMI compiler from the server code.

Figure 12.6

The architecture
of remote method
invocation (RMI).

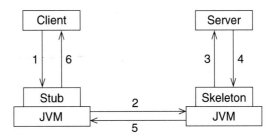

A remote method invocation is simply an invocation of a method of a remote object. Remote method invocation uses the same syntax as regular method invocations. Figure 12.6 is a high-level view of the RMI invocation process.

1. The remote method invocation `server.m()` by the client is carried out as an invocation of a method of the stub: `stub.m()`.

2. The stub marshals[2] the arguments and sends the arguments and call information to the skeleton on the server host.

3. The skeleton unmarshals the call information and the arguments and invokes the method of the server: `server.m()`.

4. The server object executes the method and returns the result to the skeleton.

5. The skeleton marshals the result and sends the result back to the stub.

6. The stub unmarshals the result and returns the result to the client.

Key Issues

In Java, there are actually two types of objects: (1) Objects that are accessible only within the local host are called *local objects* or nonremote objects (by default, objects are local); and (2) objects that are accessible from a remote host are called *remote objects,* and are instances of classes that implement a marker interface called `java.rmi.Remote`.

Remote objects and local objects are similar in the following respects: References to local or remote objects can be passed as arguments and returned as results of method invocation (local or remote). References to local or remote objects can be cast using the same syntax. The `instanceof` operator can be applied to local or remote objects.

One difference between remote and local objects is that the clients of remote objects interact with the stubs representing the remote object, not the actual objects. Another difference between remote and local objects is in the passing of arguments and return values of remote method invocations. If an argument or return value of a remote method invocation is a local object, the object is serialized, sent to the remote host, and deserialized (that is, a copy of the local object is passed to the remote host). If an argument or return value of a remote method invocation is a remote object, a

---

2. *Marshal* in this context means to arrange the information in a linear stream.

remote object reference is passed. A remote object reference can uniquely identify and locate a remote object in the network. In short, in remote method invocation, local objects are passed by value and remote objects are passed by reference.

An important question is, How does a client locate the server that will provide the service? This question is resolved by use of a naming scheme coupled with the RMI *registry*. Each RMI server is identified by a URL with the protocol `rmi`. An RMI registry is like a telephone directory. It contains a mapping between the RMI servers and their names. Each RMI server must be registered to an RMI registry to make it available to remote clients, a process known as *binding*. A client can locate an RMI server by contacting an RMI registry running on a remote host and looking up the server by name. The following URL identifies an RMI server:

> `rmi://`*host*`:`*port*`/`*name*

where *host* is the name or IP address of the host on which the RMI registry is running, *port* is the port number of the RMI registry, and *name* is the name bound to the RMI server.

12.2.2 Using RMI

The classes and interfaces related to RMI are contained in the `java.rmi` package. The programming interface of the RMI registry is provided in the class `Naming`. All the methods of the `Naming` class are static. They are summarized in the following table:

Method	Description
`bind(name, obj)`	Binds the remote object `obj` to the specified name
`rebind(name, obj)`	Binds the remote object `obj` to the specified name, even if the name is already bound. The old binding is discarded
`unbind(name)`	Removes the binding of the specified name
`lookup(url)`	Returns the remote object bound to the specified URL
`list(url)`	Returns a list of the bindings registered in the RMI registry at the specified URL

Using remote method invocation involves the following steps:

1. Define an interface of the remote object. This is the contract between the server and its clients.

```
public interface Contract extends Remote {
    public void aService(. . . ) throws RemoteException;
    // other services . . .
}
```

The `Contract` interface must extend the `Remote` interface. The methods in this interface must declare that they may throw the `RemoteException` exception. The types of the arguments and return values must be serializable.

2. Define a service implementation class that implements the `Contract` interface.

```
public class ServiceProvider extends UnicastRemoteObject,
    implements Contract {

    public String aService(. . . ) throws RemoteException {
        // implementation . . .
    }
    // implementation of other services . . .
}
```

The service implementation class must extend the `UnicastRemoteObject` class.

3. Create an instance of the server, and register that server to an RMI registry:

```
Contract server = new ServiceProvider(. . . );
Naming.rebind(name, server);
```

4. Generate the stub and skeleton classes, using the RMI compiler. The stub class is named `ServiceProvider_Stub`, and the skeleton class is named `ServiceProvider_Skel`. The stub class also implements the `Contract` interface.

5. Develop a client that uses the service provided by the `Contract` interface. The client can be a local or remote object. It must first locate the remote object that provides the service before remote methods can be invoked:

```
Remote remoteObj = Naming.lookup(name);
Contract serverObj = (Contract) remoteObj;
// . . .
serverObj.aService(. . . ); // remote method invocation
// . . .
```

The `remoteObj` is actually an instance of the stub class, which also implements the `Contract` interface. It should be downcast to `Contract` before invoking its methods.

The typical structure of RMI applications is shown in Figure 12.7.

Design Pattern: Proxy

The structure of RMI applications illustrates the Proxy design pattern.

Design Pattern *Proxy*

Category: Structural design pattern.

Intent: To provide a surrogate or placeholder that represents another object.

Applicability: The Proxy design pattern is applicable when there is a need for a more versatile or sophisticated reference to an object than a simple reference (or pointer). Common situations in which the Proxy design pattern is applicable include

- a *remote proxy,* such as the stub in RMI, providing a local representative for an object residing on a remote host.
- a *virtual proxy,* creating space- or time-consuming objects on demand.
- a *protection proxy,* controlling access to the original object to provide different levels of access rights.

The structure of the Proxy design patterns is shown in the following diagram:

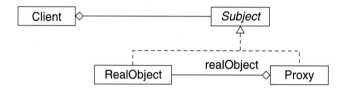

The participants of the Proxy pattern are the following:

- ▪ *Proxy* (e.g., `ServiceProvider_Stub`), which maintains a reference that lets the proxy access the real object and implements the Subject interface so that a proxy can be substituted for a real object.
- ▪ *Subject* (e.g., `Contract`), which defines the common interface for RealObject and Proxy so that a Proxy can be used anywhere a RealObject is expected.
- ▪ *RealObject* (e.g., `ServiceProvider`), which defines the real object that the proxy represents.

For a detailed discussion of the Proxy design pattern see Gamma et al. [1995].

Figure 12.7

The typical structure of RMI applications.

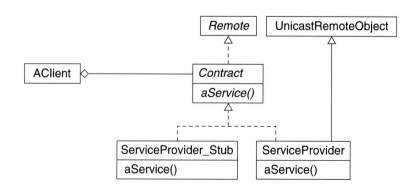

EXAMPLE 12.6 A Simple RMI Program—Hello from Venus!

PURPOSE

This example shows the basic elements and steps involved in building an RMI application.

DESCRIPTION

We develop an RMI server and an RMI client. The server sends a string "Hello from Venus!" to its clients. The client, which is an applet, displays the string it receives from the server.

SOLUTION

The Hello interface defines the service to be provided by the server. The HelloImpl class is the server that implements the Hello interface. The HelloApplet class is the client.

The contract interface for RMI pull server

```
public interface Hello extends java.rmi.Remote {
    String sayHello() throws java.rmi.RemoteException;
}
```

The main() method of the HelloImpl class creates an instance of the server and binds it to the name HelloServer in the RMI registry.

The RMI server implementation

```
import java.rmi.*;
import java.rmi.server.UnicastRemoteObject;
public class HelloImpl
        extends UnicastRemoteObject
        implements Hello {
    private String name;
    public HelloImpl(String s)
            throws java.rmi.RemoteException {
        super();
        name = s;
    }
    public String sayHello() throws RemoteException {
        return   "Hello from Venus!";
    }
    public static void main(String args[]) {
        System.setSecurityManager(new RMISecurityManager());    try {
            HelloImpl obj = new HelloImpl("HelloServer");
            Naming.rebind("HelloServer", obj);
        } catch (Exception e) {
            e.printStackTrace();
        }
    }
}
```

Running the RMI server involves the following steps:

1. Compile the server implementation class `HelloImpl.java`.
2. Generate the stubs and skeletons, using the RMI compiler `rmic`:

```
venus% rmic HelloImpl
```

The compiler `rmic` generates two files: `HelloImpl_Stub.class` (the stub) and `HelloImpl_Skel.class` (the skeleton).

3. Start the RMI registry on the server host:

```
venus% rmiregistry &
```

4. Run the server:

```
venus% java HelloImpl &
```

The `init()` of the client applet looks up the server through the RMI registry on the server host. It downcasts the server to `Hello`, the contract interface, and makes remote method invocation `obj.sayHello()`.

The RMI client

```java
import java.awt.*;
import java.rmi.*;
public class HelloApplet
        extends java.applet.Applet {
  String message = "";
  public void init() {
      try {
          Hello obj = (Hello)
              Naming.lookup("rmi: // " + getCodeBase().getHost() +
                              "/HelloServer");
          message = obj.sayHello();
      } catch (Exception e) {
          e.printStackTrace();
      }
  }
  public void paint(Graphics g) {
      g.drawString(message, 25, 50);
  }
}
```

The client can be compiled and executed as usual on any host.

12.2.3   Design Case Study—Stock Quotes II

In this section we implement the stock ticker application by using RMI. We implement both the client-pull and server-push strategies.

Figure 12.8

The client pull design of stock ticker applet and the quote server, using RMI.

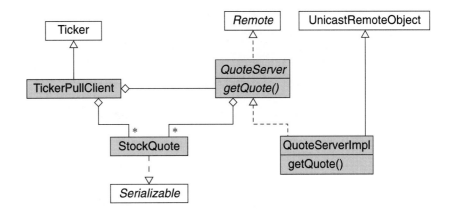

The RMI Client Pull Implementation

In the client pull implementation, the clients periodically contact the server for current quotes. Therefore, only the server needs to be a remote object; the clients are local objects. The structure of the design is shown in Figure 12.8.

The RMI Pull Server Contract Interface

The service provided by the server simply returns an array of quotes, so the service contract interface is quite simple.

Remote interface `QuoteServer`

```
public interface QuoteServer extends java.rmi.Remote {
    StockQuote[] getQuote()
        throws java.rmi.RemoteException;
}
```

The `StockQuote` class is a simple class that represents the quote of a stock. Its instances are passed as the results of the `getQuote()` method, so it must be serializable.

Class `StockQuote`

```
import java.io.*;
public class StockQuote implements Serializable {

    public String name;
    public int quote;

    public StockQuote(String name, int quote) {
        this.name = name;
        this.quote = quote;
    }
}
```

The RMI Stock Quote Pull Server

The RMI server implementation class `QuoteServerImpl` provides an implementation for the `getQuote()` method defined in the `QuoteServer` interface.

The RMI server implementation `QuoteServerImpl`

```
import java.rmi.*;
import java.rmi.server.UnicastRemoteObject;

public class QuoteServerImpl extends UnicastRemoteObject
      implements QuoteServer {

  public QuoteServerImpl() throws java.rmi.RemoteException {}

  protected StockQuote quote[] = {
    new StockQuote("IBM", 100),
    new StockQuote("Sun", 100),
    new StockQuote("Intel", 100),
    new StockQuote("Apple", 100) };

  public StockQuote[] getQuote() throws java.rmi.RemoteException {
    return quote;
  }

  ⟨The main() method on page 622⟩
  ⟨The monitorQuotes() method on page 623⟩
}
```

The `main()` method creates an instance of `QuoteServerImpl` and binds it to the name `QuoteServer`. At the end, the `monitorQuotes()` method is invoked, which continuously monitors the changes in the stock quotes. Unlike a socket server, an RMI server does not need to wait for a client to contact the server. An RMI client will contact the RMI registry first, and a remote reference of the RMI server will be passed to the client.

The `main()` method of the `QuoteServerImpl` class

```
public static void main(String[] args) {
  System.setSecurityManager(new RMISecurityManager());
  try {
    QuoteServerImpl obj = new QuoteServerImpl();
    Naming.rebind("QuoteServer", obj);
    obj.monitorQuotes();
  } catch (Exception e) {
    e.printStackTrace();
  }
}
```

The `monitorQuotes()` method contains an infinite loop that simulates the changes to the quotes with a random number generator.

The `monitorQuotes()` method of the `QuoteServerImpl` class

```
public void monitorQuotes() {
   while (true) {
     try {
       Thread.currentThread().sleep(10000);
       for (int i = 0; i < quote.length; i++) {
         quote[i].quote +=
             (Math.random() - 0.4) * (10.0 * Math.random());
       }
     } catch (Exception e) {
       e.printStackTrace();
     }
   }
}
```

This completes the RMI stock quote server implementation using the client pull strategy.

The RMI Stock Ticker Pull Client

The RMI client `TickerPullClient` class extends the class `Ticker`, which handles the display of the quotes. It contains a reference to the remote server and overrides the `initQuotes()` and the `updateQuotes()` methods.

RMI client `TickerPullClient`

```
import java.awt.*;
import java.util.*;
import java.io.*;
import java.rmi.*;

public class TickerPullClient extends Ticker {
   protected QuoteServer server;

   ⟨The initQuotes() method on page 623⟩
   ⟨The updateQuotes() method on page 624⟩
}
```

In the `initQuotes()` method, the client looks up the quote server.

The `initQuotes()` method of the `TickerPullClient` class

```
public void initQuotes() {
   try {
     server = (QuoteServer)
        Naming.lookup("rmi://" + getCodeBase().getHost() +
        "/QuoteServer");
   } catch (Exception e) {
     e.printStackTrace();
   }
}
```

In the `updateQuotes()` method, the client invokes a remote method, `server.getQuote()`, and updates the `quote` array with the new quotes.

The `updatesQuotes()` method of the `TickerPullClient` class

```
protected void updateQuotes() {
    int i, j;
    try {
        StockQuote newQuote[] = server.getQuote();
        for (j = 0; j < newQuote.length; j ++) {
            for (i = 0; i < quote.length; i++) {
                if (newQuote[j].name.equals(symbol[i])) {
                    quote[i] = Integer.toString(newQuote[j].quote);
                }
            }
        }
    } catch (Exception e) {
        e.printStackTrace();
    }
    super.updateQuotes();
}
```

This completes the implementation of the RMI stock ticker client using the client pull strategy.

The RMI Server Push Implementation

In the server push implementation, a client contacts the server and provides a watch list. The client also retrieves the current quotes of the companies that it watches. The server keeps track of all the active clients. When the quote of a company changes, it contacts (also known as a *call-back*) all the clients that are watching the company. Thus the server and the clients are all remote objects. Each client has a reference to the server, and the server maintains references to all the active clients. We have two remote interfaces: one for the server and one for the clients. The structure of the design is shown in Figure 12.9.

The RMI Push-Server and Client-Contract Interfaces

The contract interface for the push server extends the `QuoteServer` interface. The `watch()` method lets the clients provide their watch lists to the server.

The contract interface for RMI push server

```
import java.rmi.*;

public interface QuotePushServer extends QuoteServer {
    void watch(QuoteClient client, String[] list)
        throws RemoteException;
}
```

The `QuoteClient` interface defines a call-back method supported by the clients. The `newQuote()` method allows the push server to inform the clients of new quotes of the stocks that they are watching.

Figure 12.9

The server push design of the stock ticker applet and the quote server, using RMI.

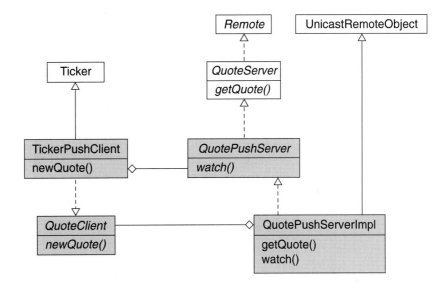

The contract interface for the RMI push client

```
import java.rmi.*;

public interface QuoteClient extends Remote {
    void newQuote(StockQuote newQuote)
        throws RemoteException;
}
```

The RMI Stock Quote Push Server

The `QuotePushServerImpl` class implements the `QuotePushServer` interface. The field `clients` is a set of active clients. Each element in the `clients` set is an instance of the inner class `ClientInfo`, which contains a remote reference to the client and the client's watch list. The `getQuote()` method returns the array of current quotes. The `watch()` method creates a `ClientInfo` object and adds it to the `clients` set.

The push server `QuotePushServerImpl`

```
import java.util.*;
import java.rmi.*;
import java.rmi.server.UnicastRemoteObject;

public class QuotePushServerImpl extends UnicastRemoteObject
    implements QuotePushServer {

    public QuotePushServerImpl() throws java.rmi.RemoteException {}

    protected StockQuote quote[] = {
        new StockQuote("IBM", 100),
        new StockQuote("Sun", 100),
```

```
            new StockQuote("Intel", 100),
            new StockQuote("Apple", 100) };

     protected Set clients = new HashSet();

     class ClientInfo {
        ClientInfo(QuoteClient client, String[] watch) {
           this.client = client;
           this.watch = watch;
        }
        QuoteClient client; // remote reference to a client
        String watch[];
     }

     public StockQuote[] getQuote() throws java.rmi.RemoteException {
        return quote;
     }

     public void watch(QuoteClient client, String[] list)
           throws java.rmi.RemoteException {
        clients.add(new ClientInfo(client, list));
     }

     〈The main() method on page 626〉
     〈The monitorQuotes() method on page 626〉
  }
```

The main() method creates an instance of QuotePushServerImpl and binds it to the name QuotePushServer. At the end, the monitorQuotes() method is invoked, which continuously monitors changes in the stock quotes.

The main() method of the QuotePushServerImpl class

```
public static void main(String[] args) {
   System.setSecurityManager(new RMISecurityManager());
   try {
      QuotePushServerImpl obj = new QuotePushServerImpl();
      Naming.rebind("QuotePushServer", obj);
      monitorQuotes();
   } catch (Exception e) {
      e.printStackTrace();
   }
}
```

The monitorQuotes() method simulates the changes to the quotes with a random number generator. When the quote of a stock is changed, it iterates through the clients set. For each client that is watching the stock, the newQuote() method is invoked through the remote reference to the client.

The monitorQuotes() method of the QuotePushServerImpl class

```
public void monitorQuotes() {
   while (true) {
      try {
         Thread.currentThread().sleep(10000);
```

```
        for (int i = 0; i < quote.length; i++) {
            int dq = 0;
            if (Math.random() < 0.5) {
                dq = (int)((Math.random() - 0.4) * (10.0 * Math.random()));
            }
            if (dq > 0) {
                quote[i].quote += dq;
                Iterator iter = clients.iterator();
                while (iter.hasNext()) {
                    ClientInfo ci = (ClientInfo) iter.next();
                    for (int k = 0; k < ci.watch.length; k++) {
                        if (ci.watch[k].equals(quote[i].name)) {
                            ci.client.newQuote(quote[i]);
                            break;
                        }
                    }
                }
            }
        }
    } catch (Exception e) {
        e.printStackTrace();
    }
  }
}
```

This completes the RMI stock quote server implementation using the server push strategy.

The RMI Stock Ticker Push Client

The TickerPushClient class implements the remote client interface Quote-Client. The newQuote() method is remotely invoked by the quote server. It updates the quote array, which is local to each client. The initQuotes() method locates the quote server and sends the server the watch list by invoking the watch() method of the server. Note that it passes itself, this, as the argument to the remote method invocation. The object reference to a remote object is automatically converted to a remote object reference when it is passed as an argument to a remote method invocation. Furthermore, to allow the server to invoke the client's call-back method newQuote(), the client must be exported as a remote object by calling the static method exportObject() of the UnicastRemoteObject class.

The ticker push client

```
import java.awt.*;
import java.util.*;
import java.io.*;
import java.rmi.*;
import java.rmi.server.*;

public class TickerPushClient extends Ticker
        implements QuoteClient {
```

```
                        public void initQuotes() {
                          try {

                            UnicastRemoteObject.exportObject(this);
                            QuotePushServer obj = (QuotePushServer)
                                Naming.lookup("//" + getCodeBase().getHost() +
                                                "/QuotePushServer");
                            obj.watch(this, symbol);
                            StockQuote newQuote[] = obj.getQuote();
                            for (int j = 0; j < newQuote.length; j ++) {
                              for (int i = 0; i < n; i++) {
                                if (newQuote[j].name.equals(symbol[i])) {
                                  quote[i] = Integer.toString(newQuote[j].quote);
                                }
                              }
                            }
                          } catch (Exception e) {
                              e.printStackTrace();
                          }
                        }

                        public void newQuote(StockQuote newQuote) throws
                              java.rmi.RemoteException {
                          for (int i = 0; i < n; i++) {
                            if (newQuote.name.equals(symbol[i])) {
                              quote[i] = Integer.toString(newQuote.quote);
                            }
                          }
                        }
                      }
                    }
```

This completes the implementation of the RMI stock ticker client using the server push strategy.

12.3 JAVA DATABASE CONNECTIVITY

Java database connectivity (JDBC) allows Java applications to interface with relational databases, which are widely used today. A wealth of information is stored in relational databases. Through JDBC, Java applications can access information stored in existing databases and share information with applications written in other languages.

Java database connectivity is a mechanism that allows Java programs to access relational databases. It is a simple Java interface for Structured Query Language (SQL), the standard language for accessing relational databases. The JDBC interface supports full access to relational databases, including creating new tables, modifying existing tables, inserting and updating data in existing tables, querying a database, and retrieving meta data (information about a database and its contents).

A key component in the implementation of JDBC is the *JDBC driver,* which communicates between Java applications and the databases. The following table summarizes the main characteristics of the four types of JDBC drivers:[3]

Driver	Description
1. JDBC-ODBC bridge	Provides JDBC access via most ODBC drivers
2. Native-API (partially Java)	Converts JDBC calls to DBMS calls
3. Net-protocol (pure Java)	Translates JDBC calls into a DBMS independent net protocol, which is then translated to a DBMS protocol by a net server. The net server can connect all its Java clients to several different databases
4. Native-protocol (pure Java)	Converts JDBC calls to the network protocol used by the DBMS directly

An Overview of the Structured Query Language

The SQL is a programming language for accessing relational databases. Most industrial-strength relational databases support SQL. Some of the commonly used SQL commands are summarized in the following table:

Command	Description
INSERT	Inserts new row(s) in a table
DELETE	Removes row(s) from a table
UPDATE	Modifies the values of existing table row(s)
SELECT	Retrieves database information based on a condition
CREATE	Creates a new database object
DROP	Removes an existing database object
ALTER	Alters the format of an existing database object

3. For more information about JDBC drivers and their availability, capabilities, and limitations, see http://java.sun.com/.

Assume that we want to create the following table in a relational database:

name	address	city	state	zip	email	creditCard	orderno
M. Jordan	549 E. Surf	Chicago	IL	60657	mjordan@nba.com	Visa	102219985502
S. Pippen	11 S. 59th	Oakbrook	IL	60606	spippen@nba.com	Discover	103119983212
D. Rodman	234 N. 3rd	Chicago	IL	60030	drodman@nba.com	MasterCard	103119983223
S. Kerr	4010 Pine	Los Angeles	CA	90507	skerr@nba.com	Visa	010219991201
R. Harper	234 N. 3rd	New York	NY	20304	rharper@nba.com	MasterCard	012019992013

The following SQL statement creates a new table called `Beetles`. It specifies the columns that the table must have and declares a data type for each. For example, the column specification name `VARCHAR(35)` defines a 35-character column called `name`.

```
CREATE TABLE Beetles (name  VARCHAR(35),
                      address VARCHAR(35),
                      city VARCHAR(20),
                      state VARCHAR(2),
                      zip VARCHAR(5),
                      email VARCHAR(30),
                      creditCard VARCHAR(15));
```

Note that the `orderno` column is missing from the `Beetles` table. We can add the column to the table by using the SQL statement

```
ALTER TABLE Beetles ADD orderno VARCHAR(12);
```

After the table is built, rows are added to it with the `INSERT` command. The following SQL statement adds a row to the Beetles table:

```
INSERT INTO Beetles VALUES('Michael Owen',
                           '123 Elmwood Street',
                           'Lake Forest',
                           'IL', '65431',
                           'mowen@aol.com',
                           'MasterCard',
                           '112819981304');
```

The `SELECT` statement retrieves data from a database, based on a specified criterion. When no criterion is supplied, as in the following example, all the rows will be returned from the specified table:

```
SELECT * from Beetles;
```

The following example would *select* every row from the Beetles table *where* the `name` column contained the value "Michael Owen."

```
SELECT * from Beetles WHERE name = 'Michael Owen';
```

For the remainder of this section, familiarity with SQL and relational databases is assumed. For detailed discussions of SQL and relational databases see Bowman et al. [1996] and Darwen and Date [1997].

An Overview of JDBC

The interfaces and classes of JDBC are contained in the `java.sql` package. The commonly used JDBC interfaces and classes are summarized in the following table:

Interface/Class	Description
DriverManager	Manages the loading of JDBC drivers and supports new database connections
Connection	Represents database connections
Statement	Represents SQL statements to be passed to the DBMS via an already established connection
ResultSet	Provides access to the results of a query, as well as information about the database
ResultSetMetaData	Provides information about the columns in a ResultSet

Using JDBC involves establishing a connection with a database, by means of the `DriverManager` and `Connection` classes, using `Statement` objects to pass SQL commands to a DBMS, and processing the results of an SQL query, which are captured as `ResultSet` objects.

Establishing a Connection with a Database

The `DriverManager` class is used for loading and managing JDBC drivers. A JDBC driver must be loaded before any other activities can take place. The JDBC drivers are loaded, using *dynamic class loading,* as follows:

Class.forName(*JDBCDriverName*);

For example, the following statement loads the *JDBC–ODBC Bridge driver* provided by Sun Microsystems:

```
Class.forName("sun.jdbc.odbc.JdbcOdbcDriver");
```

JDBC uses URLs to locate databases. JDBC URLs are presented in one of two formats:

■ For a database on the local machine:

jdbc:*subprotocol*:*subname*

■ For a database on a network host:

jdbc:*subprotocol*: //host [:*port*] /*subname*

The components of a JDBC URL are summarized in the following table:

Component	Description
subprotocol	Specifies a driver or a database connectivity mechanism that may be supported by one or more drivers. A common example of a subprotocol name is odbc
subname	Identifies a database

Instances of the `Connection` class represent open database connections. `Connection` objects are created by using a static method `getConnection()` of the `DriverManager` class. The `getConnection()` method takes a JDBC URL, a user ID, and a password as parameters. In the following example the ODBC subprotocol is used to access a database named `myDatabase`:

```
String url = "jdbc:odbc:myDatabase";
Connection conn =
    DriverManager.getConnection(url, "myID", "myPassword");
```

Once the connection to a database has been established successfully, a `Connection` object is returned. It can be used to query the database. The most commonly used methods of the `Connection` interface are summarized in the following table:

Method	Description
createStatement()	Returns a new `Statement` object for executing SQL statements
commit()	Commits (makes permanent) any database changes that have been made since the last call to *commit*. A call to commit also releases any database locks held by this `Connection` object
close()	Releases the DBMS and any other JDBC resources currently being used by this `Connection` object

Querying the Database

Instances of the `Statement` class are used to compose SQL commands and send them to a DBMS. `Statement` objects can be obtained from an opened database connection:

```
Statement stmt = conn.createStatement();
```

The commonly used methods of the `Statement` interface are summarized in the following table. The parameter `sql` is a string that represents a SQL statement.

Method	Description
executeQuery(sql)	Executes the statement `sql` that retrieves data from the database and returns a `ResultSet` object
executeUpdate(sql)	Executes the statement `sql` that updates the database (that is, one of INSERT, UPDATE, or DELETE statements) and returns an integer indicating the number of rows affected by the statement
close()	Releases the DBMS and any other JDBC resources currently being used by this Statement object, immediately rather than relying on automatic closure by the garbage collector

Using the `Beetles` table example, the following statements create the table, using JDBC:

```
String createString =
"CREATE TABLE Beetles (name VARCHAR(35), " +
                      "address VARCHAR(35), " +
                      "city VARCHAR(20), " +
                      "state VARCHAR(2), " +
                      "zip VARCHAR(5), " +
                      "email VARCHAR(30), " +
                      "creditCard VARCHAR(15))";
stmt.executeUpdate(createString);
```

A query on the Beetles table can be made as

```
ResultSet rset = stmt.executeQuery("SELECT name, email FROM Beetles");
```

It retrieves the `name` and `email` columns of the `Beetles` table.

Processing the Results

The results of a query are stored as a set of rows and columns in a `ResultSet` object. The methods of the `ResultSet` interface are summarized in Table 12.1.

The rows of the `ResultSet` object can be accessed by using a combination of the `next()` method and the `getType()` method. The `next()` method moves the cursor to the next row of a `ResultSet` object and makes that the current row (i.e., the row

---

TABLE 12.1

Methods of the `ResultSet` Interface

Method	Description
`next()`	Advances to the next row of the result set; returns `true` if successful or `false` when there are no more rows in the result set
get*Type*(`i`)	Returns the value of the `i`th column. *Type* is the data type of the column, and it can be one of `Byte`, `Boolean`, `Double`, `Float`, `Int`, `Long`, or `String` among others. The return value is of the corresponding type.
get*Type*(`name`)	Same as the preceding method, except that it retrieves the values of a column by its name
`void close()`	Releases the DBMS and any other JDBC resources currently being used by this `ResultSet` object

---

that is currently available for processing). Initially, the cursor is positioned just above the first row of a `ResultSet` object. Invoking `next()` moves the cursor to the first row and makes it the current row. Subsequent calls to `next()` cause the cursor to be moved down through the result set, one row at a time, from top to bottom. The `next()` method will return `false` when there are no more rows. There are two ways to identify the columns in the current row: by the column name or by the column index. For example, `getString(1)` returns the first column of the result set as a `String` object, and `getString("name")` returns the name column as a `String` object. The following `while` loop iterates through the rows of the `ResultSet` object, displaying the `name` and `email` fields as it goes:

```
while (rset.next()) {
    String name = rset.getString("name");
    String email = rset.getString("email");
    System.out.println(name + ", " + email);
}
```

The following is an example of what the output might look like.

```
M. Jordan, mjordan@nba.com
S. Pippen, spippen@nba.com
D. Rodman, drodman@nba.com
S. Kerr, skerr@nba.com
```

EXAMPLE 12.7 Building a Table with JDBC

PURPOSE

Illustrate the basic concepts of JDBC.

DESCRIPTION

This program builds a new Beetles table, inserts a test record into the table, and queries the table.

SOLUTION

Build JDBC Table

```
import java.sql.*;
import java.io.*;
import java.util.Date;

public class BuildBeetlesTable {
   public static void main(String args[])
               throws SQLException, IOException {

      System.out.print("\n Loading JDBC-ODBC driver...\n\n");
      try {
         Class.forName("sun.jdbc.odbc.JdbcOdbcDriver");
      } catch(ClassNotFoundException e) {
         e.printStackTrace();
         System.exit(1);
      }
      System.out.print("Connecting to Orders database...\n\n");
      String url = "jdbc:odbc:OrdersDriver";
      Connection conn =
               DriverManager.getConnection(url,"rPasenko","mpf98eub");
      System.out.print("Building new Beetles table...\n\n");
      String createString =
               "CREATE TABLE Beetles (name VARCHAR(35), " +
                                     "address VARCHAR(35), " +
                                     "city VARCHAR(20), " +
                                     "state VARCHAR(2), " +
                                     "zip VARCHAR(5), " +
                                     "email VARCHAR(30), " +
                                     "creditCard VARCHAR(15))";
      stmt.executeUpdate(createString);
      System.out.print("Inserting test row in Beetles table...\n\n");
      String insertString =
               "INSERT INTO Beetles VALUES ('Michael Owen', " +
                                          "'123 Elmwood Street', " +
                                          "'Lake Forest', " +
                                          "'IL', " +
                                          "'65431', " +
                                          "'mowen@aol.com', " +
                                          "'MasterCard')";
```

```
                    stmt.executeUpdate(insertString);
                    ResultSet rset = stmt.executeQuery("SELECT * FROM Beetles");

                    while( rset.next() ) {
                       System.out.print("" + rset.getString( "name" ) + ", ");
                       System.out.print(rset.getString( 2 ) + ", " );
                       System.out.print(rset.getString( 3 ) + ", " );
                       System.out.print(rset.getString( 4 ) + ",\n");
                       System.out.print(rset.getString( 5 ) + ", ");
                       System.out.print(rset.getString( 6 ) + ", ");
                       System.out.print(rset.getString( 7 ) + "\n");
                    }
                    System.out.print("\n Closing database connection...");
                    conn.commit();
                    stmt.close();
                    rset.close();
                    conn.close();
                 }
              }
```

Following is the output of the BuildBeetlesTable program:

```
venus% java BuildBeetlesTable
Loading JDBC-ODBC driver...
Connecting to Orders database...
Building new Beetles table...
Inserting test row in Beetles table...
    Michael Owen, 123 Elmwood Street, Lake Forest, IL,
    65431, mowen@aol.com, MasterCard
Closing database connection...
```

EXAMPLE 12.8 Modifying a Table with JDBC

PURPOSE

This example shows how to modify a table with JDBC.

DESCRIPTION

This program modifies the structure of the Beetles table, updates the test record in that table, displays the modified table contents, and then deletes the test record.

SOLUTION

> **JDBC Modify Table**

```
import java.util.Calendar;
import java.sql.*;
import java.io.*;
```

```java
class ModifyBeetlesTable {
   public static void main( String args[] )
      throws SQLException, IOException {
      try {
         Class.forName("sun.jdbc.odbc.JdbcOdbcDriver");
      } catch(ClassNotFoundException e) {
         e.printStackTrace();
         System.exit(1);
      }
      System.out.print("\n Connecting to Beetles table...\n\n");
      String url = "jdbc:odbc:OrdersDriver";
      Connection conn =
         DriverManager.getConnection(url,"rPasenko","mpf98eub");
      Statement stmt = conn.createStatement();
      System.out.print("Modifying Beetles table...\n\n");
      String updateString =
         "ALTER TABLE Beetles ADD ORDERNO VARCHAR(12)";
      stmt.executeUpdate(updateString);
      Calendar cal = Calendar.getInstance();
      String orderNo = String.valueOf(cal.get(cal.MONTH)+1) +
                       String.valueOf(cal.get(cal.DAY_ OF_ MONTH)) +
                       String.valueOf(cal.get(cal.YEAR)) +
                       String.valueOf(cal.get(cal.HOUR)) +
                       String.valueOf(cal.get(cal.MINUTE)) +
                       String.valueOf(cal.get(cal.SECOND));
      updateString = "UPDATE Beetles SET ORDERNO = " +
                     orderNo + " WHERE NAME='Michael Owen'";
      stmt.executeUpdate(updateString);
      ResultSet rset = stmt.executeQuery("SELECT * FROM Beetles");
      System.out.print("Displaying table contents...\n\n");
      while (rset.next()) {
         System.out.println("" +
               rset.getString("name") + ", " +
               rset.getString("address") + ", " +
               rset.getString("city") + ", " +
               rset.getString("state") + "\n" +
               rset.getString("zip") + ", " +
               rset.getString("email") + ", " +
               rset.getString("creditCard") + ", " +
               rset.getString("orderno") );
      }
      System.out.print("\n Deleting test record...\n\n");
      updateString = "DELETE FROM Beetles WHERE NAME='Michael Owen'";
      stmt.executeUpdate(updateString);
      System.out.print("Closing connection...\n\n");
      conn.commit();
      stmt.close();
      rset.close();
      conn.close();
   }
}
```

The following are the results of the `ModifyBeetlesTable` program:

```
venus% java ModifyBeetlesTable
Connecting to Beetles table...
Modifying Beetles table...
Displaying table contents...
    Michael Owen, 123 Elmwood Street, Lake Forest, IL
    65431, mowen@aol.com, MasterCard, 179917556
Deleting test record...
Closing connection...
```

EXAMPLE 12.9 Adding Database Functionality to the Order Applet

PURPOSE

This example demonstrates database updates with JDBC.

DESCRIPTION

This example extends the `Order` applet from Example 8.13 so that it includes database functionality. In this version, the applet writes each order to the `Order` database.

SOLUTION

We extend the `Order` class in Example 8.13. The `OrderDialog` class will be replaced by a new class `JdbcOrderDialog`.

JDBC Order Dialog

```java
import java.util.Calendar;
import java.awt.event.*;
import javax.swing.*;
import java.sql.*;
import java.io.*;

public class JdbcOrderDialog extends OrderDialog {

    public JdbcOrderDialog(JFrame owner) {
        super(owner);
    }

    protected ActionListener makeButtonHandler() {
        return new JdbcButtonHandler();
    }

    class JdbcButtonHandler implements ActionListener {
        public void actionPerformed(ActionEvent evt) {
            JButton button = (JButton) evt.getSource();
            String label = button.getText();
            if ("Ok".equals(label)) {
                try {
                    insertNewOrder();
                } catch(IOException x) {
                    e.printStackTrace();
                }
```

```java
            dialogPanel.reset();
            setVisible(false);
        }
    }

    public void insertNewOrder() throws SQLException, IOException {
        System.out.print( "Loading JDBC OCI driver...\n\n\n" );
        try {
            Class.forName( "sun.jdbc.odbc.JdbcOdbcDriver" );
        } catch (ClassNotFoundException e) {
            e.printStackTrace();
            System.exit(1);
        }
        String url = "jdbc:odbc:OrdersDriver";
        Connection conn =
            DriverManager.getConnection(url,"rpasenko","mpf8eub");
        Statement stmt = conn.createStatement();
        String creditCard = null;
        if (dialogPanel.visaBox.isSelected()) {
            creditCard = "Visa";
        } else if (dialogPanel.mcBox.isSelected()) {
            creditCard = "MasterCard";
        } else if (dialogPanel.discoverBox.isSelected() ) {
            creditCard = "Discover";
        }

        Calendar cal = Calendar.getInstance();
        String orderNo = String.valueOf(cal.get(cal.MONTH)+1) +
                         String.valueOf(cal.get(cal.DAY_ OF_ MONTH)) +
                         String.valueOf(cal.get(cal.YEAR)) +
                         String.valueOf(cal.get(cal.HOUR)) +
                         String.valueOf(cal.get(cal.MINUTE)) +
                         String.valueOf(cal.get(cal.SECOND));

        String insertString;
        insertString = "INSERT INTO Beetles VALUES( " +
                    "'" + dialogPanel.nameField.getText()    + "'," +
                    "'" + dialogPanel.addressField.getText() + "'," +
                    "'" + dialogPanel.cityField.getText()    + "'," +
                    "'" + dialogPanel.stateField.getText()   + "'," +
                    "'" + dialogPanel.zipField.getText()     + "'," +
                    "'" + dialogPanel.emailField.getText()   + "'," +
                    "'" + creditCard                         + "'," +
                    "'" + orderNo                            + "')";
        stmt.executeUpdate(insertString);
        stmt.close();
        conn.commit();
        conn.close();
    }
}
}
```

The `JdbcOrderDialog` class extends the `OrderDialog` class in Example 8.13. The new method `insertNewOrder()` opens a database connection, builds an SQL string for inserting an order in the Beetles table, executes the SQL command, and then closes the database connection and other JDBC resources.

We have now introduced most of the basic aspects of JDBC. For more complete coverage of JDBC, see Hamilton et al. [1997].

12.4 COMMON OBJECT REQUEST BROKER ARCHITECTURE

Socket-based communication and remote method invocation are adequate and effective mechanisms for distributed Java applications. However, the reality of today's computing environment is that the majority of existing applications are written in languages other than Java. In this section we briefly discuss a mechanism for interfacing Java applications with non-Java applications in distributed computing environments: Common Object Request Broker Architecture (CORBA).

CORBA is an open, distributed object-computing infrastructure being standardized by the Object Management Group (OMG), an industrial consortium that comprises 500 software vendors, developers, and users.

CORBA simplifies the development of distributed applications by providing a unified view of all distributed systems. The CORBA application framework provides interoperability between objects in heterogeneous distributed environments, where the objects can be implemented in different languages, such as Java, C/C++, Ada, and COBOL.

The basic architecture of CORBA resembles that of RMI. The participants in a CORBA application are similar to participants in a Java RMI application:

Server: An object that provides services to objects residing on remote hosts.

Service contract: An interface that defines the services provided by the server.

Client: An object that uses services provided by objects residing on remote hosts.

Stub: An object that resides on the same host as the client and serves as a proxy, or surrogate, of the remote server.

Skeleton: An object that resides on the same host as the server, receives requests from the stubs, and dispatches the requests to the server.

The centerpiece of CORBA is the *Interface Definition Language* (IDL). The CORBA clients and servers can be implemented in different languages. The service contract interface of a CORBA server is defined in a language-neutral fashion, using IDL. The IDL compliers translate the interfaces written in IDL to various implementation languages, such as Java and C/C++. The IDL compilers also generate stubs and skeletons in various implementation languages.

A key component of the CORBA architecture is the *Object Request Broker* (ORB). The ORB defines the mechanism and interfaces that enable objects to make requests and receive responses in a distributed environment. The ORB provides an infrastructure allowing objects to communicate independently of specific platforms and implementation languages. The basic structure of a CORBA application is shown in Figure 12.10.

A CORBA application consists of a set of collaborating objects. When a client requests a service, the ORB will first locate a server that implements the requested service. The ORB is also responsible for sending the arguments and call information to the server, invoking the method on the server, and sending the results back to the client. The client need not be concerned with the server object's location, programming language, or operating system.

CORBA provides flexibility and interoperability in today's increasingly complex computing environment. It lets programmers choose the most appropriate operating system, execution environment, and programming language to use for each component that they are constructing. Moreover, CORBA allows the integration of Java applications with existing applications. In a CORBA-based solution, legacy components can be modeled by using IDL. Thus CORBA is a giant step on the road to interoperability in distributed object-oriented applications.

A complete discussion of CORBA is beyond the scope of this book. For more information on CORBA see Orfali and Harkey [1998].

Figure 12.10

The basic structure of a CORBA application.

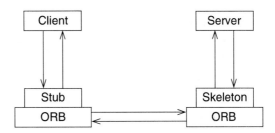

CHAPTER SUMMARY

- Distributed applications consist of components that reside on different network hosts.
- Sockets are the end points of two-way connections between two distributed components that communicate with each other. A connection must be explicitly established by both parties. There are two kinds of sockets: client sockets and server sockets. A client socket can be used to send and receive data. A server socket waits for requests for connections from clients. Server sockets can be created only by Java apps, not by applets. Client sockets can be created and used by both Java apps and applets.
- Remote method invocation (RMI) makes the network "transparent." It allows distributed components to be manipulated (almost) as if they were all on the same host. Programmers need not deal at all with interhost communications. They are

handled implicitly by the run-time environment supporting the remote method invocation. The key participants of RMI architecture are the following:

Server: An object that provides services to objects residing on remote hosts.

Service contract: An interface that defines the services provided by the server.

Client: An object that uses the services provided by objects residing on remote hosts.

Stub: An object that resides on the same host as the client and serves as a proxy, or surrogate, of the remote server.

Skeleton: An object that resides on the same host as the server, receives requests from the stubs, and dispatches the requests to the server.

Clients and servers are written by programmers, whereas stubs and skeletons are automatically generated by the RMI compiler from the server code.

■ Java database connectivity (JDBC) allows Java applications to interface with relational databases, which are widely used today. A wealth of information is stored in relational databases. Through JDBC, Java applications can access information stored in existing databases and share information with applications written in other languages. Using JDBC involves establishing a connection with a database by means of the `DriverManager` and `Connection` classes, using `Statement` objects to pass SQL commands to a DBMS, and processing the results of an SQL query, which are captured as `ResultSet` objects.

■ The Common Object Request Broker Architecture (CORBA) is an object-oriented framework that supports interoperability among objects written in different languages and running on different platforms. CORBA support is available for most programming languages, including Java, and platforms used for industrial applications. CORBA is especially useful in interfacing applications developed in modern languages, such as Java and C++, with legacy systems.

FURTHER READINGS

Farley, J. (1998). *Java Distributed Computing*. O'Reilly.

Reese, G. (2000). *Database Programming with JDBC and Java*, 2nd ed., O'Reilly.

EXERCISES

12.1 Use sockets to implement a two-way chat application consisting of a server and two clients. The client program has a graphical user interface that consists of the following:

- A text area for typing outgoing messages
- Another text area for displaying incoming messages

- A Send button for sending outgoing messages
- A Clear outgoing messages button
- A Clear incoming messages button
- A Quit button

12.2 Enhance Exercise 12.1 to support multiple clients.

12.3 Use RMI to implement Exercises 12.1 and 12.2.

PROJECTS

12.1 Develop a distributed version of the tic-tac-toe game in Section 11.3 [p. 571] using sockets or RMI. It should allow two players on different hosts to play the game remotely.

12.2 Develop a distributed version of the multiplayer tic-tac-toe game in Project 11.1 [p. 585] using sockets or RMI. It should allow multiple players on different hosts to play the game remotely.

12.3 Develop a distributed version of the drawing pad using sockets or RMI. Several drawing pad clients can run simultaneously on different hosts. Drawings by all the clients should be displayed on the same canvas and should be visible to all the clients.

Summary of the APPLET Tag

The `<applet>` tag is used to embed a Java applet in an HTML page. The `<applet>` tag has the following form:

```
<applet
    [align = alignment]
    [alt = alternate-text]
    [archive = archived-file]
    code = applet-filename
    [codebase = applet-url]
    height = pixel-height
    [hspace = horizontal-pixel-space]
    [name = applet-name]
    [vspace = vertical-pixel-space]
    width = pixel-width
>
[<param name = param-name₁ value = param-value₁ >]
. . .
[<param name = param-nameₙ value = param-valueₙ >]
[alternate-html-content]
</applet>
```

The attributes `code`, `width`, and `height` are required. The rest are optional. The attributes of the `<applet>` tag are summarized in the following table:

Attribute	Description
codebase	Specifies the base URL of the applet. It is a relative path to the directory containing the current HTML document. The default value is the same directory as the current HTML document.
code	Specifies the class name of the applet. The location of the class file is specified by the `codebase` attribute.
width	Specifies the width of the applet's display area in pixels.
height	Specifies the height of the applet's display area in pixels.
alt	Specifies alternative text that should be displayed by browsers that understand the `<applet>` tag but do not support Java.
name	Specifies a name for the applet instance, making it possible for applets on the same page to communicate with each other.
align	Specifies the applet's position with respect to surrounding text.
vspace	Specifies the top and bottom margins in pixels.
hspace	Specifies the left and right margins in pixels.
param	Specifies the parameters to the applet. Each parameter is specified by a name–value pair. The `param` attribute may occur multiple times.
archive	Specifies a comma-separated list of Java archives (JAR files) containing classes and other resources.

The *alternate-html-content* section specifies alternative text that should be displayed by browsers that do not understand the `<applet>` tag.

APPENDIX B

Summary of Documentation Tags

Documentation comments are special comments in Java source code that are delimited by /** and */. They are processed by the javadoc utility to generate API documentation. The tags that can be used in the documentation comments are summarized as follows:

@author *name*

Adds an *Author* entry to the generated docs when the -author option of javadoc is used. A doc comment may contain multiple @author tags or multiple names per tag.

@deprecated *description*

Adds a comment indicating that this method has been deprecated since the specified version. The first sentence of the @deprecated description should tell the user when the method was deprecated and what can be used as a replacement. An @link tag should be included that points to the replacement method.

@exception *name description*

Adds an exception description to the *Exceptions* section of the generated API documentation. An @exception tag should be included for each checked exception declared in the throws clause of a method. It is synonymous with the @throws tag.

647

@link *name*

Inserts a link that points to the specified name. Multiple link tags can be used.

@param *name description*

Adds a parameter description to the *Parameters* section of the generated API documentation. An **@param** tag should be included for each parameter of a method.

@return *description*

Adds a *Returns* section to the generated API documentation that describes the return value of a method. The **@return** tag should be used for all methods except methods that return `void` or constructors.

@see *text*

Adds a text entry. No link is generated.

@see *package. class#member*

Adds a link that points to a specific name in the API documentation.

@see `<a href=`*url*`>`*text*`</a>`

Adds a link to the specified URL.

@serial *description*

Describes the serializable fields.

@since *text*

Indicates the release or version number in which the feature was first introduced.

@throws *name description*

Synonymous with the **@exception** tag.

@version *text*

Adds a *Version* section for specifying the version of the software that contains this class or member when the `-version` option of `javadoc` is used. Only one @version tag is allowed per doc comment.

Summary of Java Naming Conventions

The following is a summary of the naming conventions used in Java. Using these conventions can help produce more readable code and avoid name conflicts.

Package Names

The first identifier of a package name consists of two or three letters that name an Internet domain, such as com, edu, gov, mil, net, org, or a two-letter ISO country code such as uk or jp. The following are some examples:

```
com.sun.java.corba
org.npr.pledge.driver
uk.ac.city.rugby.game
```

When defining package names for local use, you should begin the first identifier with a lowercase letter. The first identifier should not be java, because it is reserved for standard Java packages.

Class and Interface Names

Descriptive nouns or noun phrases should be used for class type names and interface type names (adjectives that describe a behavior can also be used as interface names). In addition, capitalize the first letter of each word and use mixed case. The following are some examples:

```
HttpSessionContext
HelloServlet
```

```
ServletInputStream
Thread
PrintStream
Runnable
Cloneable
```

Method Names

Verbs or verb phrases should be used for method names. In addition, method names should consist of mixed case, with a lowercase first letter. The first letter of any subsequent words should be capitalized. The following are examples:

```
write
play
showContent
```

Other conventions for method names include the following:

- When using a method to get or set an attribute thought of as variable Var, use getVar and setVar. Examples are getDate and setDate.
- When a method tests a boolean condition Cond about an object, it should be named isCond. An example is isInterrupted.

Field Names

Field names (other than those that are final) should have names that are nouns, noun phrases, or abbreviations of nouns. They should be in mixed case with a lowercase first letter and the first letters of subsequent words capitalized. Examples include buf, pos, count, and bytesTransferred.

Constant Names

When naming the constants in interface types and the final variables of class types, you should use a sequence of one or more words (or other appropriate parts of speech), acronyms, or abbreviations. In addition, components should be all uppercase, and they should be separated by the underscore character (_). Examples include MIN_VALUE, MAX_VALUE, MIN_RADIX, and MAX_RADIX.

Local Variable and Parameter Names

Local variable and parameter names are often short sequences of lowercase letters that are not complete words, such as

- an acronym, such as bg, for a variable holding a Color object used for the background.
- an abbreviation, such as buf, for a variable referring to a buffer.
- a mnemonic term, such as in and out, for input and output streams.

One-character local variable or parameter names should be used only for temporary and loop control variables, or where a variable holds an undistinguished value of a type. Acceptable one-character names are as follows:

Name	Type
b	byte
c	char
d	double
e	Exception
f	float
i	integer
j	integer
k	integer
l	long
o	Object
s	String
v	any type

You should not use local variable or parameter names that consist of only two or three uppercase letters, as they may conflict with the initial country codes and domain names of unique package names.

abstract class A class that contains at least one abstract method. Abstract classes cannot be instantiated; they must be extended by a class that implements the abstract methods. See also *abstract method*.

abstract method A method that has no implementation. The implementation is deferred to subclasses.

Abstract Windows Toolkit (AWT) A core Java package that provides the basic support for building graphical user interfaces. See also *Swing*.

abstraction The principle of characterizing the behaviors, or functions, of a module in a succinct and precise description known as the contractual interface. See also *contractual interface*.

aggregation A special form of association in which one class is a part of or belongs to another class. It represents the *has-a* or *part-of* relationship. See also *composition*.

app See *Java app*.

applet See *Java applet*.

appletviewer A command-line utility in JDK for viewing Java applets.

application framework A set of cooperating classes that represent reusable designs of software systems in a particular application domain. It is a semicomplete application written in a specific programming language.

ASCII The default character encoding of the United States, officially known as ISO-8859-1, in which all characters are encoded in a single byte.

association A general binary relationship among classes. See also *aggregation* and *composition*.

auxiliary class A class that is nonpublic and is solely used for implementing other classes.

bag An unordered collection of elements that may contain duplicates. Bags are also known as multisets.

byte-code   The instructions of the Java Virtual Machine (JVM). The Java compiler compiles Java source code to Java byte-code and stores this resulting code in files with the extension `.class`. See also *Java Virtual Machine*.

cast (of types)   The explicit conversion of one data type to another. Also known as *coersion*.

class   A set of objects with similar characteristics or behaviors. A class characterizes the structure of states and behaviors that are shared by all its instances.

client   A module that uses the services provided by another module.

cohesion   A measurement of the functional relatedness of the entities within a module.

Common Object Request Broker Architecture (CORBA)   An object-oriented framework that supports interoperability among objects written in different languages and running on different platforms.

compiler   A computer program that translates, or compiles, the source code of a program into machine code, allowing the machine code to be directly executed by the operating system and the hardware.

composition   A stronger form of aggregation, which implies exclusive ownership of the component class by the aggregate class. See also *aggregation*.

concurrent program   See *multithreaded program*.

constructor   An instance method of a class that is invoked with the `new` keyword with the purpose of creating an object. In Java, a constructor has the same name as its class.

contractural interface   A service contract between a module that provides one or more services and its clients.

coupling   A measurement of the interdependency among modules.

CRC cards   A useful technique for deriving complete analysis models. A CRC card is simply a 3 × 5–inch index card describing a class, its responsibilities, and its collaborators.

critical region   A code segment that should be accessible only by one thread at a time.

Decorator   A design pattern that attaches additional responsibilities to an object dynamically. Decorators provide a flexible alternative to subclassing for extending functionality.

deserialization   The process of restoring an object that has been serialized, and all the objects that are directly or indirectly referenced by the object. See also *serialization*.

design pattern   A schematic description of reusable designs. Each pattern describes a recurring problem and the core of the solution to that problem.

distributed application   An application that consists of multiple autonomous programs residing on different computers, or hosts, in a computer network and cooperating with one another.

double-buffering   A technique used in animation to reduce flickering. Also known as *off-screen drawing*.

downcast   Explicit cast of a reference type to one of its subtypes. See also *cast*.

dual application/applet   A Java program that can be invoked as either an applet or an application. In either case, program behavior will be identical.

dynamic binding   The binding of a method invocation to a specific implementation at run time instead of at compile time.

encapsulation   The principle of separating the implementation of an object from its contractual interface and hiding the implementation from its clients. See also *contractual interface*.

event   The occurrence of a stimulus that can trigger a state transition. See also *statechart*.

exception   An unexpected condition in a program that prevents the program from continuing normally.

extended class   See *inheritance*.

extension (of classes)   See *inheritance*.

extension (of interfaces)   A weak form of inheritance, in which an interface may extend multiple interfaces by inheriting all the features declared in them and declaring additional features. See also *inheritance*.

factorization   The process of deriving generic components by identifying recurring code segments that implement the same logic, and capturing this logic in a generic component that is defined once.

Factory Method   A design pattern that defines an interface for creating an object but lets the subclasses decide which class to instantiate and how.

framework   See *application framework*.

garbage collection   A mechanism that automatically detects and deallocates unreferenced or unreachable objects (i.e., garbage).

generic component   A program component, usually in the form of a class or package, that can be adapted and used in different contexts without modification.

helper class   See *auxiliary class*.

heterogeneous network   A computer network that consists of computers with different CPUs running different operating systems, such as the Internet.

hiding   The introduction of a field or a static method in a subclass that has the same name as a field or a static method in the superclass. See also *overriding* and *overloading*.

hook method   A placeholder for context-specific behavior that is implemented differently for each specific context. Hook methods are used in design patterns such as Template Method and are often abstract. See also *Template Method*.

hypertext   A form of text file that contrasts sharply to *linear* text, the form of text seen in almost all printed media, such as books and newspapers, that is intended to be read linearly from the beginning to the end. A hypertext document consists of a set of *nodes* that may contain text, graphics, and/or audio/video clips, and a set of *links* between the nodes that are related in some way. A hypertext document is read by following the links but not in a prescribed linear order.

Hypertext Markup Language (HTML)   An application of the Standard Generalized Markup Language (SGML) for writing hypertext documents. It is the standard language supported by Web browsers.

Hypertext Transfer Protocol (HTTP)   The standard protocol used by Web browsers to transfer HTML documents.

inheritance   The relationship among classes and interfaces that models the *is-a* relationship in the real world; the aspect of the *is-a* relationship that permits the reuse of class definitions. When class C2 inherits from, or extends, class C1, class C2 is known as a subclass or an extended class of class C1, and class C1 is known as a superclass of C2. The extension relationship among interfaces and the implementation relationship between a class and interfaces can be considered as a weak form of inheritance. See also *single inheritance* and *multiple inheritance*.

inner class   A class that is declared inside another class.

instance field   Instance fields are per-object fields that are owned by each instance.

instance method   A method that accesses instance fields or invokes other instance methods.

interface   A special form of class that declares features but provides no implementation. An interface declares only constants and abstract methods. See also *abstract method* and *abstract class*.

interpreter   A computer program that directly parses and executes program source code without generating machine code.

Iterator   A design pattern that uses abstract iterators to iterate through different concrete collections in a uniform way.

Java app (application)   A full-fledged Java program with full access to system resources.

Java applet   A Java program that is embedded in Web pages with restricted access to system resources to prevent break-ins to the hosts that run the applets.

Java chip   A CPU that uses Java byte-code as native machine code.

Java Collections Framework   A set of interfaces and classes that support storing and retrieving objects in collections of varying structures, algorithms, and time–space complexities.

Java Development Kit (JDK)   A collection of tools for developing and running Java programs.

Java Run-Time Environment (JRE)   A subset of JDK that contains the tools for running Java programs.

Java Virtual Machine (JVM)   An abstract computing machine that executes Java byte-code. It can be implemented as interpreters, JIT compilers, or Java chips— hardware implementations of the JVM. See also *byte-code*.

javac   The command that invokes the Java compiler.

javadoc   A JDK utility that builds a full set of reference documentation from tags that are embedded in programs.

Just-in-Time (JIT) compiler   A compiler that compiles Java byte-code to native machine code "on the fly" and then executes the native machine code.

levels of abstraction   The principle of ordering abstractions into different levels through inheritance. See also *inheritance*.

list   An ordered collection of elements in which the elements are indexed sequentially starting from 0. Lists are also known as sequences.

literal   The representation of the constant values of types.

macro process   An iterative software development process that includes the following phases: conceptualization, analysis and modeling, design, implementation, and maintenance.

map   An unordered collection of key-value pairs. Maps are also known as functions, dictionaries, or associative arrays.

marker interface   An empty interface that is intended to signify that all classes implementing the interface share certain common properties.

message passing   The mechanism by which objects communicate. A message consists of an object (the recipient), a method, and optional parameters.

microprocess   A development process that consists of successive iterations of the following phases: identify the classes; identify the semantics (i.e., attributes and behaviors of the classes); identify the relationships among the classes; define the class interfaces; and then implement the classes.

modularity The principle of decomposing complex systems into highly cohesive and loosely coupled modules. It is intended to control the complexity of large-scale systems through the use of the divide-and-conquer technique.

multiple inheritance A form of inheritance that allows a class to have multiple superclasses. Java allows only single inheritance among classes. However, Java allows multiple inheritance for interface extension and interface implementation. A class may implement multiple interfaces, and an interface may extend multiple interfaces.

multithreaded program A program that is capable of running several threads simultaneously. Also known as a *concurrent program*.

narrowing (of types) Conversion of a type of a larger range to a type of a smaller range.

object Anything in the real world that can be distinctly identified. Objects have unique identity, states, behaviors, and relationships with other objects.

object-oriented analysis and modeling The task of describing the essential and relevant aspects of the problem domain and the problems to be solved in terms of objects, classes, and their relationships. See also *object* and *class*.

overloading The ability of allowing different methods or constructors with different signatures of the same class to share the same name. See also *overriding* and *hiding*.

overriding The introduction of an instance method in a subclass that has the same name, signature, and return type of a method in its superclass. The implementation of the method in the subclass replaces the implementation of the method in the superclass. See also *instance method, overloading*, and *hiding*.

package A mechanism for organizing large programs into logical and manageable units. A package may contain classes, interfaces, or other packages.

parameter passing The way parameters are passed to method invocations. In Java, all parameters are passed by value.

platform independence (of programs) The ability to run programs on different platforms without having to modify the programs.

polymorphism The ability to dynamically interchange modules without affecting clients.

polymorphic assignment A form of assignment supported by object-oriented programming languages, where the right-hand-side expression of an assignment can be an object of many different types, as long as the type is a subtype of the type of the left-hand-side expression of the assignment. See also *polymorphism* and *subtype*.

polymorphic method invocation Method invocation that can be bound to different implementations at run time. It occurs when a method is overridden in subclasses.

porting programs   Conversion of the source code of programs to allow them to be run on different platforms.

primitive type   One of `boolean`, `byte`, `short`, `int`, `long`, `char`, `float`, and `double`. A primitive type variable holds a value of that type. See also *reference type*.

process   A heavyweight flow that executes concurrently with other processes. See also *thread*.

reusable component   See *generic component*.

reference type   A class type, an interface type, or an array type. A reference type variable holds an indirect reference to an object or array.

remote method invocation (RMI)   A distributed object model in which the methods of remote Java objects can be invoked from other Java programs, possibly residing on different hosts.

serialization   The process of writing an object, and all the objects that are directly or indirectly referenced by the object, to a stream. See also *deserialization*.

set   An unordered collection of elements in which no duplicates are allowed.

signature   The signature of a method or constructor, consisting of the sequence of types of its parameters.

single inheritance   A form of inheritance in which each class may inherit from only one superclass. See also *multiple inheritance*.

Singleton   A design pattern that ensures that a class has only one instance and provides a global point of access to it.

skeleton   An object that resides on the same host as the server, receives requests from client stubs, and dispatches the requests to the server.

socket   An end point of logical connections between hosts that can be used to send and receive data.

state (statechart)   A condition or situation during the life of an object during which it satisfies some condition, performs some actions, or waits for some events. See also *statechart*.

State (design pattern)   A design pattern that allows an application to dynamically associate behavior with a given object, based on that object's state.

state transition   A relationship between two states indicating that an object in the first state (the source state) will perform certain actions and enter the second state (the destination state) when a specified event occurs and conditions are satisfied. See also *statechart*.

statechart   A diagram that depicts the flow of control using the concepts of states and transitions.

static field   Per-class fields that are shared by all the instances of the same class.

static method   A method that accesses only static fields.

Strategy   A design pattern that defines a family of algorithms, encapsulates each one, and makes them interchangeable.

stub   An object that resides on the same host as the client and serves as a proxy, or surrogate, of the remote server.

subclass   See *inheritance*.

subtype   A relationship among types. Type T1 is a subtype of type T2 if every legitimate value of T1 is also a legitimate value of T2. T2 is also known as the supertype of T1.

superclass   See *inheritance*.

supertype   See *subtype*.

Swing   An extension of AWT that provides extensive support for building sophisticated and high-quality graphical user interfaces. See also *Abstract Windows Toolkit*.

synchronization   A mechanism to ensure that, while a thread is executing the statements in a critical region, no other threads can execute that same critical region at the same time.

Template Method   A design pattern that defines the skeleton of an algorithm in a method, deferring some steps to subclasses using hook methods, thus allowing the subclasses to redefine certain steps of the algorithm. See also *hook method*.

testing   An activity in software development that is intended to discover bugs.

thread   A single sequential flow of control within a program. A thread is a lightweight flow that executes concurrently with other threads within the same process. See also *process*.

type compatibility   Two types are compatible if values of one type can appear wherever values of the other type are expected, and vice versa.

type conversion   The conversion of one data type to another.

Unicode   An international standard of 16-bit character sets that consists of encodings of characters of most languages used in the world today. Java characters are in unicode.

Unified Modeling Language (UML)   A graphical notation for describing object-oriented analysis and design models.

unit testing   An activity that tests each component, usually a class, independently. See also *testing*.

Universal Resource Locator (URL) A mechanism to uniquely identify every resource (e.g., document, program, etc.) on the Internet. A URL consists of the *transfer protocol*, the *host name*, the *path*, and the *port number*. See also *Hypertext Markup Language*.

widening (of types) Conversion of a type of a smaller range to a type of a larger range.

REFERENCES

Alexander, C. (1979). *The Timeless Way of Building*. Oxford University Press.

Alexander, C., et al. (1977). *A Pattern Language—Towns, Buildings, Construction*. Oxford University Press.

Arnold, K., and Gosling, J. (2001). *The Java Programming Language*, 3rd ed. Addison-Wesley.

Beck, K. (2000). *Extreme Programming Explained*. Addison-Wesley.

Bloch, J. (2001). *Effective Java: Programming Language Guide*. Addison-Wesley.

Boehm, B. (1988). A spiral model of software development and enhancement. *IEEE Software*, 21(5):61–72.

Böhm, C., and Jacopini, G. (1966). Flow diagrams, Turing machines and languages with only two formation rules. *Communications of ACM*, 9:366–371.

Booch, G. (1987). *Software Engineering with Ada*, 2nd ed. Benjamin/Cummings.

Booch, G. (1994). *Object-Oriented Analysis and Design with Applications*, 2nd ed. Benjamin/Cummings.

Booch, G., Rumbaugh, J., and Jacobson, I. (1999). *The Unified Modeling Language User Guide*. Addison Wesley Longman.

Bowman, J., Emerson, S., and Darnovsky, M. (1996). *The Practical SQL Handbook: Using Structured Query Language*. Addison-Wesley.

Brooks, Frederick P., Jr. (1975). *The Mythical Man-Month: Essays on Software Engineering*. Addison-Wesley.

Brooks, Frederick P., Jr. (1987). No silver bullet: Essence and accidents of software engineering. *IEEE Software*, 20(4).

Campione, M., and Walrath, K. (1998). *The Java Tutorial. Object-Oriented Programming for the Internet*, 2nd ed. Addison-Wesley.

Darwen, H., and Date, C. (1997). *A Guide to the SQL Standard*, 4th ed. Addison-Wesley.

Ellis, M., and Stroustrup, B. (1990). *The Annotated C++ Reference Manual*. Addison-Wesley.

Fowler, M. (1997). *Analysis Patterns: Reusable Object Models*. Addison-Wesley.

Fowler, M., and Scott, K. (1997). *UML Distilled: Applying the Standard Object Modeling Language*. Addison-Wesley.

Gamma, E., et al. (1995). *Design Patterns: Elements of Reusable Object-Oriented Software*. Addison-Wesley.

Goldberg, A. (1985). *Smalltalk-80: The Interactive Programming Environment*. Addison-Wesley.

Goldberg, A., and Robson, D. (1983). *Smalltalk-80: The Language and Its Implementation*. Addison-Wesley.

Hamilton, G., Cattell, R., and Fisher, M. (1997). *JDBC Dabase Access with Java, A Tutorial and Annotated Reference*. Addison-Wesley.

Harbison, S. (1992). *Modular-3*. Prentice Hall.

IEEE. (1985). *IEEE/ANSI Standard for Binary Floating-Point Arithmetic, IEEE STD 754–1985*.

Jacobson, I., Booch, G., and Rumbaugh, J. (1999). *The Unified Software Development Process*. Addision Wesley Longman.

Kassem, N., and Team, E. (2000). *Designing Enterprise Applications with Java 2 Platform, Enterprise Edition*. Addison-Wesley.

Kruchten, P. (2000). *The Rational Unified Process, An Introduction*, 2nd ed. Addison-Wesley.

Larman, C. (2002). *Applying UML and Patterns*, 2nd ed. Prentice Hall.

Lea, D. (2000). *Concurrent Programming in Java: Design Principles and Patterns*, 2nd ed. Addison-Wesley.

Lindholm, T., and Yellin, F. (1996). *The Java Virtual Machine*. Addison-Wesley.

McGraw, G., and Felten, E. W. (1997). *Java Security: Hostile Applets, Holes, and Antidotes*. John Wiley & Sons.

Metsker, S. J. (2002). *Design Patterns Java Workbook*. Addison-Wesley.

Meyer, B. (1992). *Eiffel: The Language*. Prentice Hall.

Meyer, B. (2000). *Object-Oriented Software Construction*, 2nd ed. Prentice Hall.

Orfali, R., and Harkey, D. (1998). *Client/Server Programming with Java and CORBA*, 2nd ed. John Wiley & Sons.

Pinson, L. J., and Wiener, R. S. (1991). *Objective C: Object-Oriented Programming Techniques*. Prentice Hall.

Pressman, R. S. (1997). *Software Engineering, A Practitioner's Approach*, 4th ed. McGraw-Hill.

Raggett, D., et al. (1998). *Raggett on HTML 4*. Addison-Wesley.

Riggd, R., Taivalsaari, A., and Vandenbrink, M. (2001). *Programming Wireless Devices with the Java 2 Platform, Micro Edition*. Addison-Wesley.

Rumbaugh, J., Jacobson, I., and Booch, G. (1999). *The Unified Modeling Language Reference Manual*. Addison Wesley Longman.

Schneier, B. (1996). *Applied Cryptography*, 2nd ed. John Wiley & Sons.

Shalloway, A., and Trott, J. R. (2001). *Design Patterns Explained: A New Perspective on Object-Oriented Design*. Addison-Wesley.

Shaw, M., and Garlan, D. (1996). *Software Architecture: Perspective on an Emerging Discipline*. Prentice Hall.

Sommerville, I. (2001). *Software Engineering*, 6th ed. Addison-Wesley.

Stroustrup, B. (1994). *The Design and Evolution of C++*. Addison-Wesley.

Stroustrup, B. (1997). *The C++ Programming Language*, 3rd ed. Addison-Wesley.

The Unicode Consortium (1996). *The Unicode Standard, Version 2.0*. Addison-Wesley.

Walrath, K., and Campione, M. (1999). *The JFC Swing Tutorial*. Addison-Wesley.

Zachary, G. P. (1994). *Show-Stopper*. Free Press.

INDEX

— A

Abstract collections, 284, 309–310
Abstract coupling
  enumerating elements and, 278–283
  explanation of, 276–277
  iterator pattern and, 283–284
  use of, 281
Abstract display factory, 301
Abstract display strategy, 298
Abstract Factory design pattern
  explanation of, 484–486
  maze game and, 486–490
  shortcomings of, 495
Abstraction
  explanation of, 10, 27–28
  level of, 31–32
Abstract iterators, 281–284
Abstract Windows Toolkit (AWT), 308
  conventions and, 348
  explanation of, 333
  GUI component classes in, 334
  Swing components and, 334–336
Acceptance testing, 235
Accessibility, of fields, 22
Accessing shadowed fields, 116–117
Accessors, 20
Actions, 38, 39
Active objects, 548
Active programs, Java, 148
Actors
  explanation of, 41
  extension relationships among, 43
  use case and, 41–43
Ada, 75
Adapter design pattern
  explanation of, 513–514
  forms of, 514

implementation of, 516–531
participants of, 514–515
Advisee, 32–33
Adviser, 32–33
Adviser-advisee association, 33, 34
Aggregation, 34–35
Alexander, Christopher, 249–250
Algorithm animator, 286
Algorithms
  abstract sorting, 290–291, 294
  animation of sorting, 284–302
  concrete, 291–295
  real-world, 9
Animation applets. *See also* Bouncing
  ball applets
  double-buffered, 193–200, 259–266
  enhanced, 186–188
  generic, 256–258
  idiom for, 188–193
  simple, 148–154
Ant, 243–245
AppCloser, 361–362
Applets. *See also* Animation applets;
  Bouncing ball applets
  to animate sorting algorithms,
  284–302
  basic structure of, 69–71
  common problems and solutions to,
  202
  explanation of, 63, 64
  life cycle of, 149
  order, 638–639
  reading files in, 200–202
  security issues and, 64–65
  visitor counter, 595–598
Applet tag
  attributes of, 71

summary of, 645–646
Application frameworks. *See*
  Object-oriented application
  frameworks
Applications
  distributed, 587–588 (*See also*
  Distributed computing)
  explanation of, 63
  Java, 63–67
  scribble pad, 402–403, 452–453
Architecture
  common object request broker,
  640–641
  Java run-time, 59–65
  remote method invocation, 614–616
Ariane 5 communication satellite
  launcher, 2
Arithmetic operators, 81, 83–84
ArrayList, 316–317
Arrays
  explanation of, 91
  of integers, 97, 133
  Java, 170
  max-min value of, 133–134
  multidimensional, 93
  one-dimensional, 92–93
  string and character, 123
ASCII, 77
ASCII characters, 79–80
ASCII code, 382
Assertions
  explanation of, 224–226
  using clones in, 233–234
Assignment, 168–169
Assignment operators, 87
Associations
  aggregation as form of, 34–35

Associations *(continued)*
   explanation of, 32–33
   graphical notation of, 33–34
AT&T long-distance telephone
   network, 2
Attributes
   of applet tag, 71
   explanation of, 20, 101
Auxiliary classes, 207–208
AWT. *See* Abstract Windows Toolkit
   (AWT)

— B

Bags, 309
Behavioral patterns. *See also* Design
      patterns
   Command, 507–513
   explanation of, 250
   State, 438–439
   Strategy, 275–276, 290–291
Bitwise operators, 85–86
Black-box tests, 241–242
Boolean expressions, 216–217, 219
Boolean type, 77
BorderLayout, 339, 344–346
Border layout, 344–347
Bouncing ball applets
   with controls, 353–358
   double-buffered animation applet
      and, 265
   illustration of, 195–200, 265
Bounded queue
   fully synchronized version of,
      561–564
   with guarded suspension, 565–568
   producer, consumer and, 562, 563
   sequential version of, 559–561
Break statements, 99–100
BroadcastClientHandler class,
   598–600
Bubble sort, 98, 291–293
Buffered input streams, 376–378
Buffered output streams, 376–378
BufferedReader, 384
BufferedWriter, 384
Builder design pattern
   explanation of, 502–503
   maze game and, 503–507
Build tools, 243–245
Byte-code
   execution of, 62
   explanation of, 62

Java, 62–63, 174
   verification of, 64
Byte streams
   buffered, 376–378
   data input and data output, 371–375
   example using, 368–373
   explanation of, 367, 368

— C

C
   arrays in, 92
   assignment in, 168
   enumeration types and, 466
   environmental variables in, 499
   pointers in, 89
   style comments, 67
C++
   arrays in, 92
   development of, 11
   enumeration types and, 466
   environmental variables in, 499
   features of objects in, 21
   implementation file in, 214
   Java and, 75–76
   multiple inheritance and, 179
   operator overloading and, 161
   pointers in, 89, 106
   style comments, 67
Canvas listener, 408–409
Cellular phones
   Java chips in, 62
   state diagram describing operation
      of, 39–41
Character encoding, 382
Character literals, 79–80
Characters, Java, 76–77
Character streams
   explanation of, 367, 382–385
   universal text viewer and, 387–388
   use of, 385–387
Character type, Java, 79
ClassCastException, 168–169
Class Course, 278
Class declarations
   accessing fields and methods and,
      106–107
   class fields and methods and,
      110–114
   creating and initializing objects and,
      104–106
   explanation of, 101

interfaces and abstract classes and,
   117–118
method invocation and parameter
   passing and, 107–109
object reference this and, 114–117
overloading and, 160–161
strings and, 118–128
syntax of, 101–103, 163
wrapper classes and, 128–134
Class diagrams
   aggregation relationship in, 34
   association relationship in, 33
   dependency relationship in, 35
   elements of, 29
   inheritance relationship in, 31
Classes
   abstract, 118
   canonical form of, 227–235
   design of, 209–214
   documenting source code and,
      214–216
   double, 130–131
   event, 348, 349
   explanation of, 20, 21
   extended, 163–176
   extension relation among, 29
   features of, 48–49
   float, 130–131
   grouped into packages, 25
   identification of, 46–47
   implementation relation among, 30
   instance of, 166
   interfaces and, 117–118, 176–177
   invariants of, 222–224
   members of, 209
   natural orders of, 324
   public and helper, 207–209,
      227–235
   relationships among, 29, 31, 49–51
   singleton, 114
   thread-safe, 557
   UML notation for, 21–24
   wrapper, 128–134
Class fields
   explanation of, 110
   final, 112
   initialization of, 111–112
Class IterList, 279–280
Class modifiers, 101
Class names, 649–650
Client handler, 612–614
Client pull, 601–602
Client pull implementation, 621

Clients
  in RMI, 614
  stock ticker pull, 605
  stock ticker push, 607–609
Client sockets, 589–590
Cloneable interface, 184
Clone() method, 231–234
Code segments, refactoring, 253–255, 262
Cohesion, 26
Collections
  abstract, 284, 308–310
  concrete, 315
  explanation of, 308
  implementations of, 315–319
  interfaces of, 310–315
  iterators of, 319–323
  sorted, 324–330
  types of, 309–310
  utilities on, 330–332
Colon-delimited records, 125–127
Color, for drawing pad, 416–421
ColoredPoint class, 164, 175
Command design pattern
  client of, 511–512
  explanation of, 508
  maze game and, 509–513
Command line arguments, 113
Common object request broker architecture (CORBA), 640–641
Compare(), 325
CompareTo(), 324
Compilation, Java and, 60
Composite design pattern
  explanation of, 336–338, 531
  mail application using, 532–538
Composite states, 39
Composition, 34
Compound statements, 94. See also Statements
Conceptualization, 12
Concrete algorithms
  creating instances of, 293–295
  explanation of, 291–293
ConcreteClass, 267
Concrete collections
  explanation of, 284, 315
  list of, 316
Concrete display factory, 301
Concrete display strategy, 299–301
ConcreteIterator, 284
Concrete plotter, 269, 270

Concurrent programming
  explanation of, 547–548
  thread safety and liveness and, 556–571
  threads and, 547–556 (See also Threads)
  tic-tac-toe game and, 571–583
Conditional operators, 86
Connected, Limited Divice Configuration (CLDC), 58
Connected Device Configuration (CDC), 58
Constant names, 650
Constants, in Java, 112
Constructors
  explanation of, 104–105
  of extended classes, 164–165
  no-arg, 228
  overloading and, 159–160
  signature of, 160
Contention, thread, 569
Continue statements, 99–100
Contract
  design by, 226–227
  of methods, 216–222
Contractual interface, 27
CountComparator, 331
CounterServer class, 596
Coupling
  abstract, 276–284
  direct, 276
  explanation of, 26
Course class, 278
Creational designs. See also Design patterns
  Abstract Factory, 484–490
  Builder, 502–507
  Factory Method, 296, 442, 444–448, 491–495
  for maze game, 470–484
  Prototype, 495–502
Creational patterns
  explanation of, 250
  Prototype, 495–499

— D

Data output streams, 371–375
Data unput streams, 371–375
Deadlock, thread, 570–571
Decorator pattern, 380–381
Decrement operators, 84, 85

Default character encoding, 382
Default initial value, 88, 104
Delegation
  adapt by, 527–531
  explanation of, 182
  refactoring by, 255–266
Dependency
  among use cases, 42, 43
  explanation of, 35–36
Deserialization, 234, 377, 378
Design. See also Object-oriented design
  analysis of, 8
  by contract, 226–227
  detail, 5
  documentation of, 5
  drawing pad (See Drawing pad case study)
  elements of, 4–5
  maze game (See Maze game)
  software vs. architectural, 250
Design patterns
  abstract couping and, 276–284
  Abstract Factory, 484–490, 495
  application framework, 307
  Builder, 502–507
  categories of, 250–251
  Composite, 336–338, 531–538
  Decorator, 380–381
  in drawing pad case study (See Drawing pad case study)
  Factory Method, 296, 442, 444–448, 491–495
  format for describing, 251–252
  generalizing technique and, 271–275
  Iterator, 283–284
  overview of, 249–250
  Prototype, 495–499
  Proxy, 617–618
  refactoring and, 252–266 (See also Refactoring)
  sorting algorithm and, 284–302
  State, 438–439
  Strategy, 275–276, 290–291
  template method for, 266–270
Design Patterns (Gamma), 11
Detail design, 5
Dialog, 349
Diamond-shaped multiple inheritance, 180–181
Digital clock applets
  enhanced, 186–193

Digital clock applets *(continued)*
  initial version of, 149–154
Directory structure, 136–138
Display factory, 301–302
Display strategy
  abstract, 298
  concrete, 299–301
  design options and, 297–298
  explanation of, 296–297
  factory and, 301–302
Distributed computing
  common object request broker
    architecture and, 640–641
  explanation of, 587–588
  Java database connectivity and,
    628–640
  remote method invocation and, 614–
    628 (*See also* Remote method
    invocation [RMI])
  socket-based communications and,
    588–614 (*See also* Socket-based
    communications)
doCommand(), 510
Documentation tags, 647–648
Dormancy, thread, 569–570
Double-buffered animation applets
  bouncing ball, 356–358
  explanation of, 193–200
  generic, 259–266
Double classes, 130–131
do-while loop, 96, 97
Downcasting
  explanation of, 167, 168
  methods for, 169
  need for, 169–170
Drawing pad case study
  iteration 1—simple scribble pad,
    398–403
  iteration 2—menus, options, and
    files, 403–421
  iteration 3—refactoring,
    421–432
  iteration 4—adding shapes and
    tools, 432–448
  iteration 5—additional drawing
    tools, 448–453
  iteration 6—text tools, 453–462
  planning phase of, 397–398
Dynamic behavior modeling
  explanation of, 36
  sequence diagram and, 36–37
  state diagram and, 37–41
Dynamic binding, 165

— E

E-bookstore case study
  conceptualization and, 44
  object models and, 46–51
  use cases and, 44–46
Echo servers
  broadcasting, 598–600
  simple, 590–592
  simple client talks to, 592–594
  that handle multiple clients
    simultaneously, 594–595
Efficiency, 7
Eiffel, 11
e-mail. *See* Mail application
Encapsulation, 28
Enroll association, 33
Entry actions, 39
Enumeration types
  explanation of, 466–467
  ordered type-safe, 469–470
  unordered type-safe, 468–469
Equals() method, 228–229
Equivalence partitioning, 242
Escape sequences, 80
European Space Agency, 2
Event adapters, 350
Event handling
  bouncing ball applet with controls
    and, 353–358
  example of, 351–352
  explanation of, 348
  in Java, 348
  nested classes and, 352–353
  process of, 350
  steps in, 348–350
Events
  explanation of, 38, 333, 348
  listener of, 333, 348–350
  source of, 348
Exceptions
  catching and handling, 144–148
  checked, 142
  explanation of, 139–140
  hierarchy of, 140–143
  sources of, 140
  throwing, 143–144
  unchecked, 142
Exit actions, 39
Explicit initializers, 104
Extended classes
  constructors of, 164–165
  explanation of, 163
  overriding methods and, 171–176

  subtypes and polymorphism and,
    165–171
Extensibility
  animation applets and, 256, 257
  of application frameworks, 306, 308
Extension relationships
  among actors, 42
  among classes, 29
  among interfaces, 30
Extreme Programming (XP)
  explanation of, 11, 15–16
  key practices of, 16

— F

Factories, 499–502
Factory Method design pattern
  explanation of, 296, 442, 444–448
  maze game and, 491–495
  shortcomings of, 495
Features
  of classes, 48–49
  of objects, 20
Field declarations, 22
Field names, 650
Fields
  accessibility of, 22
  accessing, 106–107
  accessing shadowed, 116–117
  class, 104, 110–112
  explanation of, 20, 101
  hiding, 184–186
  instance, 110
  methods of initializing, 104–106
  public, 210–213
  static, 110, 111
  visibility of, 22
File input stream, 367, 368
File output stream, 367, 368
FileReader, 384
Files, 134
FileWriter, 384
Filled shapes, 448–452
Finite state machines (FSM), 37
Flexibility, 7
Float classes, 130–131
Floating-point types, Java, 78–79
FlowLayout, 339–341
Font option menu, 459–462
for loop, 97
Frames
  explanation of, 359

graphical user interface and, 359–366
Frozen spots, 266
Functional requirements, 4
Function invocation, 253–254

— G

Games. *See* Maze game; Tic-tac-toe game
Garbage collection, 90–91
GB-2313 (People's Republic of China), 382
Generalizing
  design patterns and, 271–275
  explanation of, 271
GenericClass, 267
Generic component design
  explanation of, 252
  generalizing method and, 271–275
  refactoring and, 252–266
  strategy pattern and, 275–276
  template method and, 266–270
Generic plotter, 267–274
getParameter () method, 187
Glossary, 653–661
Gosling, James, 55
goto statement, 93–94, 100
Graphical user interfaces (GUI)
  case study in (*See* Drawing pad case study)
  components of, 333–336
  Composite pattern and, 336–338
  events and, 348–349
  explanation of, 308, 333
  frames and dialogs and, 359–366
  layout managers and, 338–347
  mail application and, 539–544
Grid layout, 339, 342–344
Guard, 38
GUI. *See* Graphical user interfaces (GUI)

— H

Has-a relationship, 34
Hash code() method, 230–231
HashMap, 317, 318
Hello from Venus!
  applet, 67–72
  application, 65–67
  RMI program, 619–620
Helper classes. *See* Auxiliary classes

Hiding
  avoidance of, 185–186
  explanation of, 184
  overriding vs., 184–185
Hook methods
  application frameworks and, 306
  explanation of, 266, 272, 273, 275
Hot spots, 266, 306
Hybrid programs, Java, 148

— I

Identifiers, Java, 77
if statement, 96
Immutable objects, 20–21
Implementations
  between class and interface, 30, 213–214
  of collections, 315–319
  explanation of, 5, 12
  for list, 316–317
  for map, 317–319
  programming to, 277
  for set, 315–316
Increment operators, 84, 85
Infinite counters, 549–550, 552–553
Information hiding, 28. *See also* Encapsulation
Inheritance
  adapt by, 523–527
  explanation of, 29–30, 163
  levels of abstraction and, 31–32
  multiple, 176–177, 179
  refactoring by, 254–256
  single, 31, 176, 179–182
  subtypes and, 166, 167
  UML terminology for, 30–31
Initialization block, 105–106
Input/output (I/O)
  byte streams and, 367–380
  character streams and, 382–388
  Decorator pattern and, 380–381
  explanation of, 308
  random access files and, 389–392
  types of, 366–367
InputStreamReader, 383
Instance, 21
Instance fields, 110
Integer intervals, 33
Integers
  minimum of array of, 133
  sum of array of, 97
Integer types, Java, 78

Integration, 5
Interator for linked lists, 280–281
Interface Definition Language (IDL), 640
Interface names, 649–650
Interfaces
  of collections, 310–315
  completeness of public, 213
  explanation of, 177–179
  extending and implementing, 176–184
  extension relation between, 30
  Java, 117–118
  list, 312–313
  map, 313–315
  marker, 184
  name collisions among, 183–184
  set, 312
  single and multiple inheritance and, 179–182
  subtypes and, 177–179
Internet. *See also* World Wide Web
  explanation of, 59
  interplanetary, 65
  security and, 59
Interpretation
  explanation of, 10
  Java and, 60–62
  in real word, 20
Invariants, of classes, 222–224
Inversion of control, 148
ISO-8859-1, 382
Iteration
  abstract, 281, 282
  methods of, 282
  simultaneous, 280
  use of, 279–280
Iterative development processes
  for drawing pad case study, 397–398 (*See also* Drawing pad case study)
  explanation of, 11–12
Iterator design pattern, 283–284
Iterator interface, 117, 319–322

— J

Java, 11. *See also* Type-safe enumeration types
  advantages of, 56
  applets, 67–72, 148–154
  applications, 65–67
  assertion statements and, 224

Java *(continued)*
  boolean type and, 77
  characteristics of, 55–56
  character literals and, 79–80
  character set and, 76–77
  character type and, 79
  class declarations and, 101–134
  collections framework, 309, 310
  common object request broker
    architecture and, 640–641
  common problems and solutions
    with, 72
  enumeration types and, 466, 468
  event handling in, 348
  exceptions and, 139–148
  explanation of, 55, 75–76
  explicit casting and, 168
  features of objects in, 21
  field declaration and, 22
  floating-point type and, 78–79
  graphical user interfaces and,
    333 (*See also* Graphical user
    interfaces [GUI])
  handling restrictions in, 176
  identifiers and, 77
  implementations in, 277
  inheritance and, 31, 176–177,
    179–182
  input/output framework and,
    380–381
  integer type and, 78
  lexical elements and, 76–87
  name collisions in, 183
  naming conventions used in,
    649–651
  operators and expressions, 80–87
  packages and, 134–139
  properties used in, 499–500
  separating interface from
    implementation of class in, 214
  statements and, 93–100
  string literals and, 80
  unique features of, 76
  use of, 12
  variables and types and, 87–93
  visibility and, 22
Java 2 Platform
  Enterprise Edition, 56, 58
  Micro Edition, 56, 58
  overview of, 56–57
  Standard Edition, 56–58, 139
Java archive (JAR), 72
Java byte-code, 62–63

Java chips, 62
Java Class Library
  exceptions and, 140
  organization of, 138–139
Java database connectivity (JDBC)
  building table with, 635–636
  database updates with, 638–640
  establishing connection with
    database and, 631–633
  explanation of, 628–629, 631
  modifying table with, 636–638
  processing results and, 633–634
  querying database and, 633
  structured query language and,
    619–631
Java documentation comments, 67
Java Foundation Classes, 308, 333
Java run-time architecture
  Java virtual machine and, 61–65
  platforms and, 59
  program execution models and,
    60–61
  security and, 59
Java Virtual Machine (JVM)
  byte-code optimization and, 174
  exceptions and, 143
  explanation of, 62–63
  security of, 64–65
  threads and, 555
JDBC. *See* Java database connectivity
  (JDBC)
JDBC driver, 629
JDK 1.0, 56
JDK 1.1, 56
JDK 1.2, 56
JDK 1.4, 226
JDK (Java Development Kit), 77
JUnit, 239–241
Just-in-Time (JIT) compiler, 62

— K

Keyboard input tool, 455–459
K-Virtual Machine (KVM), 58
KVM, 58

— L

Labeled break statement, 99–100
Larch, 216, 218
Layout managers
  border layout and, 344–347
  explanation of, 333, 338–339

  flow layout and, 339–341
  grid layout and, 342–344
  use of, 339
Lexical elements
  character set, 76–77
  explanation of, 76
  identifiers, 77
  operators and expressions, 80–87
  primitive types and literals, 77–80
LinkedList class, 208–209, 235–237,
  282–283, 306
LinkedListIterator, 280–281
Listener
  canvas, 408–409
  of events, 333, 348–350
  scribble canvas and its, 399–402
List interface
  explanation of, 312–313
  implementations for, 316–317
ListIterator, 319, 320
Lists, 309
Liveness
  contention and, 569
  deadlock and, 570–571
  dormancy and, 569–570
  explanation of, 569
  premature termination and, 571
Locale, 382
Local objects, 615
Local variable declarations, 95
Local variable names, 650–651
Logical operators, 85
Loops, 99–100
Loop statements, 96–98

— M

Macro process, 11
Mail application
  UI interface for, 539–544
  using Adapter design pattern, 539
  using Composite design pattern,
    532–538
main () method, 113, 402, 626
Maintainability, 6–7
Maintenance, 5, 13
Map interface
  explanation of, 312–315
  implementations for, 317–319
Maps
  explanation of, 310
  iterate through view of, 321–322
Map sites, 471–475

Marker interfaces, 184
Mathematical constants and functions, 131, 132
Maze board, 475–479. *See also* Creational designs
Maze game
  Abstract Factory design pattern and, 486–490
  Builder design pattern and, 503–507
  Command design pattern and, 509–513
  explanation of, 465
  Factory Method design pattern and, 491–495
  implementation of, 466
  map sites for, 471–475
  maze board for, 475–479
  Prototype design pattern and, 496–499
  simple design of, 470–484
  themes of, 479–484
Method declarations, 22, 103
Method invocation
  explanation of, 253–254
  iterate via, 279–280
Method names, 650
Methods
  contacts of, 216–222
  preconditions of, 216–217
Micro process, 11
Microsoft Windows NT operating system, 2
Mobile Information Device Profile (MIDP), 58
Models, 9–10
Modula3, 75
Modular decomposition, 27
Modularity, 26–27
monitorQuotes() method, 622–623
mouseDragged() method, 401–402
MouseListener, 400, 401
MouseMotionListener, 400, 401
mousePressed() method, 401
mouseReleased() method, 402
Multidimensional arrays, 93
Multiple inheritance
  diamond-shaped, 180–181
  single vs., 179–182
Multiplicity specification, 32–33
MultiPlotter, 273–276
Multisets, 309
Multitasking, 547

Multithreaded programming. *See* Concurrent programming
Mutable objects, 20
Mutators, 20

— N

Name collisions, in Java, 183–184
Natural orders, 324
Nested classes
  event handlers as, 352–353
  explanation of, 101, 102
  of order dialog, 366
Nested state diagrams, 39–41
Nester border layouts, 346–347
New York Stock Exchange (NYSE), 2
No-arg constructor, 164–165, 228
Node class, 208
Nonfunctional requirements, 4

— O

Objective-C
  development of, 11
  Java and, 75, 76
  use of, 55
Object Management Group (OMG), 19n
Object-oriented application frameworks
  characteristics of, 306–307
  collections and, 308–332 (*See also* Collections)
  considerations for, 308
  design requirements for, 307–308
  explanation of, 305–306
  graphical user interfaces framework and, 333–366 (*See also* Graphical user interfaces [GUI])
  input/output framework and, 366–392 (*See also* Input/output [I/O])
Object-oriented design
  by contract, 226–227
  explanation of, 12
Object-oriented modeling
  aggregation and composition and, 34–35
  association and, 32–34
  dependency and, 35–36
  of dynamic behavior, 36–41
  e-bookstore case study of, 44–51
  explanation of, 12

  inheritance and, 29–32
  use cases and, 41–43
Object-oriented programming languages
  dynamic binding of methods and, 165–166
  Java and, 55, 75–76 (*See also* Java)
Object-oriented software development. *See also* Software development
  activities of, 12–13
  Extreme Programming and, 15–16
  historical background of, 10–11
  iterative, 11–12
  modeling real world and, 9–10
  objects and classes and, 20–26
  principles and concepts of, 19, 26–29
  Rational Unified Process and, 13–15
  unit testing of, 235
Object Request Broker (ORB), 640, 641
Objects
  active, 548
  cloning, 231–234
  explanation of, 20
  features of, 20
  hash code of, 230–231
  immutable, 20–21
  Java arrays as, 170
  life of, 38
  local, 615
  mutable, 20
  remote, 615–616
  string representation of, 234
  UML notation for, 24–25
Object serialization
  explanation of, 377–378
  use of, 378–380
Object streams, 377–378
One-dimensional arrays, 92–93, 97, 98
Online ordering GUI application, 359–366
Operations, 20
Operator overloading, 161
Operators and expressions (Java)
  arithmetic, 81, 83–84
  assignment, 87
  bitwise and shift, 85–86
  conditional, 86
  explanation of, 80–81
  increment and decrement, 84–85
  logical, 85
  relational, 85

Operators and expressions
  (Java) *(continued)*
  string concatenation, 84
  summary of, 82
Orders, 324, 325
OutputStreamWriter, 383
Overloading
  decisions regarding use of, 161–163
  explanation of, 159
  legality of, 160
  methods of, 160–161
  operator, 161
  overriding vs., 171–172
  rule of, 160
Overriding
  explanation of, 171–174
  final methods and, 174
  hiding vs., 184–185
  invoking, 175
  overloading vs., 171–172
  restriction and, 175–176

— P

Package declaration, 135
Package names, 25, 649
Packages
  directory structure and, 136–138
  explanation of, 25, 134
  Java Class Library and, 138–139
  partitioning name space and, 136
  UML notation of, 26
  use of, 135–136
Parameter names, 650–651
Parameter passing, 108–109, 115
Parsing method, 130
Partial orders. *See* Orders
Part-of relationship, 34, 35
Patterns. *See* Design patterns
Peer components, 335
Personal Java, 58
Personal Profile, 58
Phase, 5–6
Platforms, 56, 59
Player class, 579–582
Point class
  constructor of, 164
  explanation of, 21, 23, 211
PolarPoint, 211–213
Polymorphic assignment
  example of, 174
  explanation of, 168–169
Polymorphism, 28–29

Porting, 59
Postconditions
  assertions and, 225
  of methods, 217–222
Preconditions
  assertions and, 224–225
  of methods, 216–222
Premature termination, thread, 571
Primitive types
  boolean, 77
  character, 79
  declaring variable of, 91
  floating-point, 78–79
  integer, 78
  parameters of, 108–109
  wrapper classes and, 128–129
Primitive type variable, 88
PrintReader, 384
PrintWriter, 384–385
Programming. *See* Concurrent
  programming
Project build
  Ant, 243–245
  explanation of, 243
Property definitions, 244
Protection proxy, 618
Prototype design pattern
  explanation of, 495–496
  maze game and, 496–499
Proxy design pattern, 617–618
Public classes
  canonical form of, 227–235
  drawing pad, 424–425
  explanation of, 207–208
  organization of, 209
Public fields, 210–213
Pull server contract interface, 621
Push-server and client-contract
  interfaces, 624–625

— Q

QuoteListener class, 607, 609–610
QuotePushServer class, 610, 611
QuotePushServerImpl, 625–627
QuoteServerImpl, 622

— R

Race hazard, 557
Random access files
  explanation of, 389
  use of, 389–392

Random access I/O, 366, 367
Rapid application development (RAD),
  61
Rational Unified Process (RUP)
  explanation of, 11, 13
  phases defined by, 15
  process workflows defined by,
    14–15
  as use case driven, 14
Reactive programs, Java, 148
Readability, 7
Receiving instance, 114
Refactoring
  by delegation, 255–266
  of drawing pad design, 421–432
  explanation of, 252–253
  function invocation and, 253–254
  by inheritance, 254–256
  recurring code segments, 253
  tasks of, 253
Reference types
  conversion of, 167
  creating objects and arrays and,
    91
  explanation of, 89–90
  garbage collection and, 90–91
  Java and, 88
  parameters of, 108–109
Reference type variables, 88, 91
Relational operators, 85
Reliability, 6, 7
Remote method invocation (RMI)
  architecture of, 614–616
  explanation of, 614
  stock quotes II case study and,
    620–628
  use of, 616–620, 640
Remote objects, 615–616
Remote proxy, 618
Representation, in object-oriented
  models, 20
Requirements analysis, 4
Requirements specifications, 4
Restrictions
  explanation of, 175–176
  in Java, 176
Return statement, 95
Reusability, 6, 249
Reusable components. *See* Generic
  component design
Revised sort animation, 295
RMI. *See* Remote method invocation
  (RMI)

RMI registry, 616. *See also* Remote method invocation (RMI)
Role name, 32
Rubber banding, 439, 442
Runnable interface, 117
Run-time architecture, Java, 59–65

— S

Sandbox, 56, 65
scribble1.ScribbleCanvasListener, 401, 408
scribble2.ScribbleCanvas class, 405–408
scribble2.ScribbleCanvasListener, 408–409
scribble2.Scribble class, 409–416
scribble2.Stroke class, 404–405
scribble3.ScribbleCanvasListener, 427–428
ScribbleCanvas class, 399, 402
ScribbleCanvasListener, 400–402
Scribble pad. *See also* Drawing pad case study
  application and, 402–403
  initial design of, 398–399
  refactoring, 421–432
  scribble canvas and its listener and, 399–402
ScribbleTool class, 425, 426
Scrolling banner applet
  initial version of, 188–193
  using double-buffering, 193–202
Security, 59
Security manager, 64
Selection statements, 96
Sequence diagrams, 36–37
Seralizable interface, 234
Serialization
  explanation of, 234–235, 377
  object, 389–392
Server push
  explanation of, 601
  implementation of, 607
Server push implementation, 624
Servers
  broadcasting echo, 598–600
  in RMI, 614
  simple client talks to echo, 592–594
  simple echo, 590–592
  that handle multiple clients simultaneously, 594–595
  visitor counter applet and, 595–598

ServerSocket class, 589
Server sockets, 588–589
Service contract, in RMI, 614
Set interface
  explanation of, 312
  implementations for, 315–316
Sets, 309
Shadowing variables, 117
Shapes
  adding, 433–436
  filled, 448–452
  for refactoring drawing pad, 421–423
Shift operators, 86
Signature, of constructor, 160
Simple scribble pad. *See* Scribble pad
Simple statements, 94. *See also* Statements
Simplicity, of software systems, 7
Single inheritance
  explanation of, 31
  Java and, 176
  multiple vs., 179–182
Singleton class
  explanation of, 114
  structure of, 251–252
Skeletons, 614
Smalltalk
  development of, 10
  Java and, 75, 76
  use of, 55
Socket-based communications
  developing distributed applications using, 614
  explanation of, 588
  server and client sockets and, 588–590
  servers and clients using sockets and, 590–600
  stock quotes case study I, 600–614
  use of, 640
Sockets
  client, 589–590
  server, 588–589
  servers and clients using, 590–600
Software design patterns. *See* Design patterns
Software development. *See also* Object-oriented software development
  background of, 1–2
  challenges of, 2–3
  design as aspect of, 4–5

problems in, 10
  processes of, 5–6
  requirements analysis for, 4
Software engineering
  analysis of designs and, 8
  codification of knowledge and, 9
  explanation of, 4, 8
  failures and, 8–9
Software systems
  complexity of, 3
  desirable qualities of, 6–7
  effects of glitches in, 2
  as engineering process, 8–9
  factors contributing to maintainability of, 7
  longevity of, 3
  unit testing of, 235–243
  use expectations for, 3
Sorted collections, 324–330
SortedMap, 325, 326
Sorted maps, 310
SortedSet, 325, 326
Sorting algorithm animation applet
  development of, 284–285, 302
  display strategy and, 296–302
  factories to create, 296
  initial implementation of, 285–289
  separating, 290–295
Source code, 214–216
Spiral model, 11
State design pattern, 438–439
State diagrams
  explanation of, 37–39
  nested, 39–41
Statement blocks, 94–95, 107
Statement labels, 99
Statements
  break and continue, 99–100
  compound, 94
  expression, 94
  in Java, 93–100
  local variable declaration, 95
  loop, 96–98
  return, 95
  selection, 96
  simple, 94
States, 37, 39
State transitions, 38–39
Static fields, 110, 111
StockQuote class, 621
Stock quote generator, 551–552
Stock quote pull server, 605–607, 622–623

Stock quote push server, 625–626
    client handler for, 612–614
    explanation of, 610–612
Stock quotes case study I
    client handler for stock quote push
        server and, 612–614
    client pull implementation and,
        601–602
    overview of, 600–601
    quote listener and, 609–610
    server push implementation and,
        607
    stock quote pull server and,
        605–607
    stock quote push server and,
        610–612
    stock ticker animator and, 602–604
    stock ticker pull client and, 605
    stock ticker push client and,
        607–609
Stock quotes case study II
    overview of, 620
    RMI client pull implementation
        and, 621
    RMI pull server contract interface
        and, 621
    RMI push-server and client-contract
        interfaces and, 624–625
    RMI server push implementation
        and, 624
    RMI stock quote pull server and,
        622–623
    RMI stock quote push server and,
        625–626
    RMI stock ticker pull client and,
        623–624
    RMI stock ticker push client and,
        627–628
Stock ticker animator, 602–604
Stock ticker pull client, 605, 623–624
Stock ticker push client, 607–609,
    627–628
Strategy design pattern
    abstract sorting algorithm and,
        290–291
    explanation of, 275–276
    use of, 297
Stream I/O, 366, 367. *See also* Byte
    streams; Character streams
Strictly partial orders, 324. *See also*
    Orders
String concatenation, 84
String literals, 80
String representations, 234

Strings
    and character array, 123
    comparison of, 118–122
    explanation of, 118
    in Java programs, 382
    method of operation on, 122–123
    reading and writing, 123–125
    working with, 125–128
StringTokenizer, 127–128
Strokes, 403–405
Structural patterns. *See also* Design
        patterns
    Adapter, 513–531
    Composite, 336–338, 531–538
    Decorator, 380–381
    explanation of, 250
    Proxy, 617–618
Structured Query Language (SQL),
    628–631
Stubs, 614
Subclass
    abstractions and, 32
    classes inheriting from multiple, 31
    explanation of, 29, 163
    Prototype design pattern and, 495
Subinterface, 176
Substates, 39
Subtypes
    array types and, 170–171
    inheritance and, 166, 167
    interface implementation and,
        177–179
    substitutability of, 167
Sun Microsystems, 55
Superclass
    abstractions and, 32
    constructors and, 164, 165
    explanation of, 29, 163
    overriding methods and, 171–174
Superinterface, 176
Superstates, 39
Swing
    conventions and, 348
    explanation of, 333
    graphical user interfaces and,
        334–336, 359–366
    online ordering GUI application
        using, 359–366
switch statement, 96
Synchronization, 557–564
System design, 4–5. *See also*
        Object-oriented design
System specifications, 4
System testing, 5

— T

Tacoma Narrows Bridge, 8
Taking turns, 582–583
Target definitions, 244
Teach association, 33
Template method
    explanation of, 266–267
    illustration of, 267–270
    use of, 285
Testing, 235. *See also* Unit testing
TestUtil class, 238
Text shape, 454–455
Text tool
    explanation of, 453–454
    font option menu and, 459–462
    keyboard input tool and, 455–459
    text shape and, 454–455
this, 114–117
Thread class, 548–549
Threads
    cooperation among, 564–568
    creation of, 548–553
    explanation of, 547–548
    life cycle of, 554, 555
    liveness and, 569–571
    priority and scheduling of, 555–556
    safety properties and, 556–557, 569
    synchronization and, 557–564
Throwable class, 140–141
Ticker class, 602
TickerClientHandler class, 610,
    612–614
TickerPullClient class, 605, 623, 624
TickerPushClient class, 607, 608,
    627–628
Tic-tac-toe game
    game board and, 572–577
    game class and, 579
    players and, 579–582
    structure of, 571, 572
    taking turns and, 582–583
Timeliness, 6
Tokens, 125
Toolkit, 436–438
Tools
    drawing pad, 424–428, 448–453
    explanation of, 425
    for typing text using keyboard,
        453–462
toString() method, 122–123, 234, 385,
    468
Total orders, 324. *See also* Orders
Transitions
    explanation of, 37–38

state, 38–39
triggerless, 38
TreeMap, 327–328
Triggerless transitions, 38
Try-catch statement, 144
TwoEndsShape, 433–436
TwoEndsTool, 439–442
Types
compatibility of, 88
conversion of, 88–89, 167
declared, 166
explanation of, 87, 166
primitive (*See* Primitive types)
reference (*See* Reference types)
Type-safe enumeration types
ordered, 469–470
unordered, 468–469

— U

UML. *See* Unified Modeling Language
(UML)
Unchecked exceptions, 142
UndoableCommand interface, 509
UndoableMazeGame class, 512–513
undoCommand(), 510
Unicode
explanation of, 76, 77
Java and, 382
Unified Modeling Language (UML).
See also Object-oriented
modeling
aggregation relationships and, 34

association relationships and, 32
dependency relationships and,
35–36
explanation of, 11, 19
inheritance relationships and, 30–31
notation for classes, 21–24
notation for objects, 24–25
notation for packages, 26
sequence diagrams and, 36–37
state diagrams and, 38–41
use cases and use case diagrams
and, 41–43
use of, 12, 16
Unit testing
of coverage criteria, 241–243
explanation of, 5, 235
simple, 235–239
using JUnit, 239–241
UniversalMazeFactory class, 500–502
Universal Resource Locator (URL)
JDBC and, 632
reading files in applets and, 200–202
Universal text viewer, 387–388
Use case diagrams
explanation of, 42
types of dependency among, 42–43
use of, 41
Use cases
dependency among, 42, 43
e-bookstore case study and, 44–46
explanation of, 41
modeling requirements with, 41–43
scenarios of, 41

use of, 41
Usefulness, 6
User friendliness, 7
Utilities, 330–332

— V

Variable declarations, 88
Variables
explanation of, 87, 101, 166
shadowing, 117
VDM, 216, 218
Virtual proxy, 618
Visibility of fields, 22
Visitor counter applet, 595–598

— W

Waterfall model, 5–6
Web pages, 67, 71
while loop, 96
White-box tests, 241–243
World Wide Web, 71–72. *See also*
Internet
Wrapper classes, 128–134

— X

Xerox PARC, 10

— Z

Z, 216, 218